NEW WINCHELSEA, SUSSEX
A Medieval Port Town

NEW WINCHELSEA, SUSSEX
A Medieval Port Town

David and Barbara Martin

with contributions by
Jill Eddison, David Rudling and David Sylvester

PUBLISHED BY HERITAGE MARKETING AND PUBLICATIONS LTD.
ON BEHALF OF UNIVERSITY COLLEGE LONDON FIELD ARCHAEOLOGY UNIT
IN ASSOCIATION WITH ENGLISH HERITAGE

2004

FIELD ARCHAEOLOGY UNIT MONOGRAPH NO.2,
INSTITUTE OF ARCHAEOLOGY, UNIVERSITY COLLEGE LONDON

First published 2004 by Heritage Marketing and Publications Ltd on behalf of University College London Field Archaeology Unit in association with English Heritage.

Heritage Marketing and Publications Ltd.
Hill Farm – Unit F, Castle Acre Road, Great Dunham, King's Lynn, Norfolk PE32 2LP

ISBN 0 9544456 51

University College London Field Archaeology Unit and English Heritage are greatly indebted to the National Trust, East Sussex County Council, and The Friends of the Ancient Monuments and Museum of Winchelsea for generous grants towards the costs of research.

CONTENTS

LIST OF ILLUSTRATIONS

PREFACE

INTRODUCTION

Amongst English towns Winchelsea is special. As a major planned royal port, the town flourished for half a century from the date of its refoundation in the 1280s following severe coastal erosion of its original site. During this period of wealth, Winchelsea can claim to have been one of the principal international ports of the realm - its ships ruled the Channel, challenging foreign and English vessels alike. Yet, for a variety of reasons, from the middle years of the 14th century it suffered decline, and during the 16th century all but failed. By the 17th century it had shrunk to the size of a village.

During the last quarter of the 20th century a considerable amount of research - including archaeological excavations, landscape surveys, geophysical investigations, standing-building interpretations and documentary analysis - was undertaken regarding the past fabric of this town with its exceptional planned grid-system. But, with one exception, because of the methods of past funding, none of this work was carried through to publication with the result that, even amongst academics, few people were aware of this research, let alone able to benefit from its results. Works of synthesis published during that time, academic and popular overviews alike, have included outdated and inaccurate statements concerning the town. These statements were derived principally from W. M. Homan's ground-breaking article 'The Founding of New Winchelsea', which appeared in 1949 in volume 88 of the *Sussex Archaeological Collections*. Using an exceptionally detailed rental of 1292, Homan reconstructed the entire town as first laid out. His article is the basis of virtually all historical plans of the town which have been published subsequently. Yet it represents only a tiny part of the research, both documentary and architectural, which he undertook on Winchelsea during the 1930s and 1940s, and some scholars have been able to benefit from his more extensive work which is deposited at the East Sussex Record Office.

The work carried out during the late 20th century has shown that rather than a catastrophic, 'single-event' failure of the town during the middle years of the 14th century, its decline occurred in stages. During the late 14th century and throughout the 15th century Winchelsea was still considered to be an urban centre of local importance. Houses within the town underwent complex sequences of expansion and reconstruction, and this continued into the early 16th century. The new research has considerably augmented that of Homan and earlier scholars. Whilst confirming many of their conclusions, however, newly available data have made it possible to correct some fundamental errors regarding the original layout of the town. It is, for instance, now known that Winchelsea's main market occupied a large, purposely designed square rather than a widening in the street. In addition, the layout suggested by Homan in the southern part of the town is now known to be erroneous, an error which arose from a 17th-century confusion regarding the location of properties in this abandoned part of the town. Similarly, although it has long been known that in the early 15th century the residents of Winchelsea planned a new town defence of lesser circuit, a detailed inquiry into its route and the properties likely to be affected by it was not known to Homan. As a result, his suggested route for this defence is wrong, as also is his suggested route for the earlier defences. Of all the recent discoveries, however, perhaps the most surprising was the realization in 1994 that a substantial section of the early-15th-century town defences, complete with bastions, still stands as a retaining wall up to one-and-a-half metres high skirting the cliff top on the eastern side of the town. Incredible as it may seem, these remains, located upon land owned by the National Trust, only came to light during the compilation of an Archaeological and Historic Landscape Survey for the Trust in 1994 (Martin *et al*

1994b). It had been missed by earlier archaeological surveys.

Although the non-publication of so much new data concerning the town had for some time been seen as an embarrassment to those who had undertaken the research, the discovery of this substantial section of previously unknown surviving town wall highlighted beyond doubt the need to put the new work into print. In particular, it was becoming increasingly clear that those responsible for managing the future of this important heritage site could not carry out their duties adequately without full up-to-date data. Equally, neither academics nor the wider public were able to benefit from the discoveries of the past quarter century. This latter point is well illustrated by a recent important and as yet largely unpublished PhD dissertation by David Sylvester, which studies the maritime economic history of Winchelsea during the period of its greatest prosperity. Despite an extensive programme of documentary research carried out in the relevant record offices, and despite discussions with several university archaeologists, Sylvester had been totally unaware of the archaeological work carried out within the town since 1974. As a result, all his topographical detail is based upon outdated information, to the detriment of his work.

Another problem, equally serious, was becoming apparent. Because of the delay in writing up the excavations, the data and finds had become dispersed and were in serious danger of being lost unless prompt action was taken. Of particular concern was arguably the most important of the excavations: that carried out adjacent to Blackfriars Barn in Quarter 15. This excavation had been undertaken for the National Trust as a Manpower Services project under the direction of John Bell. He, however, had subsequently severed his links with the archaeological world.

THE WINCHELSEA RE-ASSESSMENT PROJECT

In 1998 the Winchelsea Re-assessment Project was set up with the specific aim of addressing these concerns. In December of that year a project outline was submitted to English Heritage, who subsequently commissioned the University College London Field Archaeology Unit to submit a detailed project design for carrying out the work (Martin, Rudling and Barber 1999). The project was to be funded principally by English Heritage, but partnership funding was sought (and obtained) from the National Trust, both as a principal landowner within the town, and as the organization which had commissioned two of the principal unpublished excavations, and from East Sussex County Council. Additional funding was obtained from The Friends of the Ancient Monuments and Museum of Winchelsea. The full project was commissioned in August 1999 with an anticipated completion date of December 2000. This was subsequently extended to allow time to carry out additional documentary research, aimed principally at correcting errors discovered in work published previously and to catalogue and analyze the 16th-century Corporation records more fully.

Accordingly, the principal aims of the project were twofold:

- to make the data amassed since 1974 available in a form which would assist in the management of the resource
- to publish the results so as to make them accessible both to the academic establishment and to the general public.

To meet the above objectives four documents have been produced:

i) A detailed Quarter-by-Quarter analysis of the town, drawing together all the known data in a topographical format, in order to make this information easily available to the residents, to planners and to academics alike (Martin and Martin 2002a). In addition to the copies of this document which have been lodged with English Heritage, The National Trust, East Sussex County Council, and the Friends of the Ancient Monuments and Museum of Winchelsea, a copy has been lodged at the East Sussex Record Office in Lewes to make the information accessible to the public;

ii) An overview of the town in the form of an Extensive Urban Survey (Martin and Martin 2002b). This is intended to be used by those professionals charged with the care of our heritage, to enhance the East Sussex Sites and Monuments Record and to draft future planning policies for the town;

iii) A report on the excavations carried out within the town during the period 1974-2000 (Martin and Rudling 2004);

iv) An academic publication entitled *New Winchelsea, Sussex: A Medieval Port Town* (this volume). It is this volume which is intended to make the results of the research accessible to a wider audience.

THIS VOLUME

The objective of this monograph is to give an up-to-date overview of the town's development up to its collapse in the 16th century. Brief introductory chapters consider why it was necessary to refound the town upon a new site, what economic activities underpinned its wealth, and why the town faltered in the mid-14th century and collapsed in the early 16th century. The remainder of the volume considers the morphology of the town's fabric. Results of recent research, both archaeological, architectural and documentary, are integrated with earlier studies to examine the town's infrastructure (streets, markets, quays *etc.*), the form of its defences, municipal buildings, churches, friaries and hospitals, before attention is turned to the properties of the residents themselves.

RELEVANT PAST RESEARCH

Much has previously been written about the evolution of the marshlands upon the edge of which Winchelsea is built, about the founding of (New) Winchelsea, and the economic background of the town during its period of greatest prosperity. As these topics fall outside the main thrust of this monograph, only a summarized account is included within these pages. Those wishing to have further details are directed to the bibliography included at the end of this volume. In particular, although some of the topographical details are now known to be out of date, nevertheless, those readers who require a detailed account of the mechanics behind the town's refounding are directed to W. M. Homan's seminal work 'The Founding of New Winchelsea' in *Sussex Archaeological Collections* **88** (1949), augmented by the section entitled 'Edward I and Thomas Alard: New Winchelsea' in Chapter 2 of Maurice Beresford's book *New Towns of the Middle Ages* (1967). In considering the latter work, caution is needed regarding the calculations of the rents per plot paid to the king by the late 13th-century occupants of the town: something went seriously wrong when these figures were being analyzed by Beresford. This caution is additional to that relating to the now out-of-date topographical details. Notwithstanding these problems, Beresford's work is important in that it discusses the involvement of one of Winchelsea's principal residents in the planning of the town and, subsequently, in the planning of Berwick-upon-Tweed, and examines the possible influence of Edward I's French Bastides on English town-planning at this period. In this latter respect, G. Chamber's article 'The French Bastides and the Town Plan of Winchelsea', which appeared in *Archaeological Journal* **94 (2)** (1937), pp. 177-206, is also worthy of consideration.

Despite having been written more than 150 years ago, *The History of Winchelsea* by W. D. Cooper remains the best and most comprehensive general history of the town. Serious students who have access to the East Sussex Record Office are also recommended to consult the unpublished research undertaken by W. M. Homan. In reading both Homan’s and Cooper's work care should be taken to ensure that any topographical details given have not been superseded by more recent research. Cooper, for instance, erroneously refers to the remains of a castle upon the hill at Winchelsea and misidentifies the remains of a medieval house (at the time in use as a barn) as being those of the Dominican Friary. Although, alas, as yet unpublished, undoubtedly the best economic history of the town during its period of prosperity is the recent PhD dissertation by David Sylvester. Some of this research appears within Chapter 2 of this volume, but for the full account the reader is directed to the copy of his dissertation which is accessible at the East Sussex Record Office, again bearing in mind that care is needed when considering statements relating to topography. Those readers wishing to read a good, summarized, easily accessible general history of the town can do no better than to consult the relevant pages in Volume 9 of *The Victoria History of the Counties of England: Sussex* (*VCH Sussex*). The more recent history of the town is dealt with by Malcolm Pratt in his 1998 publication, *Winchelsea, A Port of Stranded Pride.*

ACKNOWLEDGEMENTS

It goes without saying that a project of the size and scope of this re-assessment has involved commitment by many more people than the principal authors of the present volume: without their imput the work would not have been possible. In particular, David Rudling, until recently the director of the University College London Field Archaeology Unit, has been involved with the archaeology of the town since 1976 and it is he who has been largely responsible for writing up the past excavations and coordinating the work on the finds.

Another essential aspect of the project has been the documentary work carried out by Christopher Whittick. His dogged determination to track down elusive documents and to answer particular questions posed by other members of the team generally bore fruit. It was he too who initially drew to our attention David Sylvester's 1999 PhD dissertation on the economic history of the town, and who finally traced Sylvester's present whereabouts, allowing him the opportunity to contribute to the project. We also wish to extend our thanks to Jill Eddison and David Sylvester for readily agreeing to contribute the opening chapters at very short notice, to Maryanne Kowaleski for her detailed comments regarding the economic history of the town, to Mark Gardiner and Sarah Pearson for helpful comments and advice regarding specific elements, and to Gwen Jones, who has had the unenviable task not just of copy-editing the work for consistency, but of making grammatical sense of our occasional ramblings!

Thanks must also go to our colleagues, in particular Simon Knight, who has been responsible for preparing most of the figures which illustrate this volume. The architectural drawings of the town gates and of the remains of the Grey Friars church are based upon survey work carried out by Peter Leach in the 1980s for East Sussex County Council during his employment with the University College London Field Archaeology

Unit (then the Sussex Archaeological Field Unit). It was he too who undertook the first of two earthwork surveys carried out within the town; the second was by the Royal Commission on the Historical Monuments of England (now part of English Heritage). The geophysical survey of the Black Friars site was undertaken by Dr. Andrew Woodcock, the County Archaeologist for East Sussex, aided by Winchelsea residents. We thank him for making the results available to us.

Peter Kendall (EH), Caroline Thackray (NT) and Dr Andrew Woodcock (ESCC) gave much needed support and encouragement during the formative stages of the project, and have shown continued interest since. During the progress of the project Peter Kendall's role as EH Inspector covering East Sussex was taken over by Paul Roberts, and both he and the EH project monitor, Helen Keeley, continued to give invaluable assistance in bringing the work to fruition. In particular, we thank Helen Keeley for her support during the more problematic periods of the work.

Throughout the quarter century during which fieldwork has taken place within Winchelsea, the residents have shown every courtesy and given extensive assistance in the furtherance of our aims, either by allowing access to their buildings and their land, or, in the case of some of the excavations, intrusion into their gardens. It is clear that they have great pride in their town. This must, we feel, in part be a legacy of the work undertaken by the late W. M. Homan during the 1930s and 1940s. A number of the residents have copies of his unpublished research, which they readily produce for inspection. To his memory this present volume is dedicated. Until recently, his daughter, Mrs Goldie, still resided in the town and gave much help and encouragement during the carrying out of our fieldwork in the 1970s and 1980s. It was she who first alerted us to the wealth of unpublished material produced by her father.

Acknowledgement must also be given to the late Mrs Crogan who farmed Wickham Manor Farm as a life-tenant, both for her keen cooperation whilst carrying out work on the land owned by the National Trust, and for constantly encouraging us to achieve our aims. Other residents too have given invaluable help during the undertaking of the re-assessment project. In particular, Dominic Leahey, past chairman of the Friends of the Ancient Monuments and Museum of Winchelsea, has served as a contact with the community at large, as too has Malcolm Pratt, both in his capacity as Town Clerk and as author of *Winchelsea: A Port of Stranded Pride* (*see* above). It is Malcolm's intention to produce a second book outlining the early history of the town, and it is our hope that our work will be of as much help to him as his has been to us.

To the many other people - too numerous to be mentioned individually - who contributed in numerous ways both to the early stages of research and to this re-assessment, we extend our thanks and our hope that they are not disappointed with the end result. Every effort has been made to eliminate any factual errors which had crept into early drafts of the text. For those errors which remain, the authors take full responsibility.

David and Barbara Martin
University College London Field Archaeology Unit
January 2004

SUMMARY

Winchelsea is mentioned in most books which discuss medieval England, but perhaps inevitably, given the nature of the published literature, the references mainly concentrate on the town as a member of the Cinque Ports and on its planned grid system of streets. Other comments, if there are any, are cursory. It rarely appears amongst the lists of significant medieval English towns and ports, unless the ranking is based upon participation in the maritime activities of the medieval realm. The implication is that Winchelsea was just another example of a small medieval port catering to local needs. Indeed, this is the impression gained when talking to many medieval archaeologists and historians active in the field. Most know that the town is a prime example of a planned settlement, that it was laid out on a grand scale by Edward I, and that it ultimately failed. Many assume that it failed before it was able to become established, others that it collapsed into insignificance after a very brief and mildly successful flowering. Today, Winchelsea is a small sleepy village with an insignificant, stream-like river passing below it on its northern side. Visitors can be forgiven for regarding as 'unfounded exaggeration' the claims made for the town by its modern residents and for assuming them to be the result of misplaced pride. To the casual visitor the only hints of a more important past are the grid of streets, three ruined town gates (one of which most tourists are unlikely to find) and the fragment of an imposing church. In the light of recent research our views of Winchelsea's role in history need to be reconsidered.

The objective of this monograph is to give an up-to-date overview of the town's development up to its collapse in the 16th century. Brief introductory chapters consider why it was necessary to refound the town upon a new site, what economic activities underpinned its wealth, and why the town faltered in the mid-14th century and collapsed in the early 16th century. The remainder of the volume considers the morphology of the town's fabric. Results of recent research, both archaeological, architectural and documentary, are integrated with earlier studies to examine the town's infrastructure (streets, markets, quays etc.), the form of its defences, municipal buildings, churches, friaries and hospitals, before attention is turned to the properties of the residents themselves.

A final chapter draws together the various strands of research which have fed into the volume. It concludes that Winchelsea may have been considerably larger and more influential during the 13th and early 14th centuries than is usually considered to have been the case. But by the second half of the 14th century the town was in serious trouble. However, in this respect too the evidence presented does not support the commonly held notion that Winchelsea's collapse was meteoric. It is not true that it descended from being a significant port to little more than a village over a short period during the middle decades of the 14th century. Rather the evidence points to a two-stage decline with a far more important late 14th- and 15th-century role in the southeast of England than is generally realized. Winchelsea may at this period have been small in comparison to many English towns, but, set against the generally small size of the towns in Kent and Sussex, until the early 16th century it was still a port that was not to be ignored.

It is to be hoped that the points discussed within the volume will help redress past misconceptions and encourage those who research English medieval urban settlements to give greater consideration to this potentially underrated town.

Summary text: *David Martin*

RÉSUMÉ

La plupart des livres qui ont pour sujet l'Angleterre médiévale font mention de Winchelsea, mais inévitablement peut-être, étant donné la nature de la littérature déjà publiée, leurs références portent surtout sur deux aspects: Winchelsea, membre de la Confédération des Cinque Ports et Winchelsea la ville quadrillée par un réseau de rues planifié dès sa fondation sur un nouveau site. Winchelsea ne figure que rarement dans les listes de villes et de ports anglais qui jouèrent un rôle important à l'époque médiévale sans que sa place là-dedans ne soit attribuée à sa participation dans les activités maritimes du pays en fournissant des bateaux pour le roi. Cela implique que Winchelsea n'était qu'un petit port qui répondait seulement aux besoins de sa région et n'avait aucune importance en dehors.

En fait, c'est là l'impression qu'on gagne en parlant avec beaucoup d'archéologues et d'historiens qui étudient cette époque. La plupart savent que Winchelsea offre un des meilleurs exemples d'une ville conçue et planifiée par le roi Edouard 1er sur une grande échelle mais qu'à la longue son importance décrut. Les uns assument que la déchéance se produisit même avant que la ville se fût établie, les autres pensent que la ville tomba en décadence après une floraison commerciale courte mais assez marquée.

Aujourd'hui Winchelsea n'est qu'un petit village endormi avec une petite rivière (jadis un fleuve) qui coule devant son côte nord. On peut pardonner un certain manque de foi aux visiteurs qui considèrent comme exagérées et sans fondation les histoires du passé glorieux racontées par les habitants, jugeant que leur fierté est mal placée. A vrai dire, pour le visiteur qui ne fait que passer quelques heures dans la ville, seuls le réseau quadrillé des rues, les trois portes (dont une restera probablement introuvable) et le fragment d'une église imposante indiquent le passé remarquable de Winchelsea.

Nous avons donc besoin de reformuler à la lumière de la recherche récente nos idées sur le rôle historique de Winchelsea. Cette monographie a comme but de présenter une vue d'ensemble sur le développement de la ville jusqu'à son déclin au seizième siècle. De courts chapitres d'introduction considèrent les thèmes suivants: pourquoi il fut nécessaire de rebâtir la ville sur un nouveau site; quelles activités économiques étayèrent sa prospérité ensuite; pourquoi ses finances déclinèrent au milieu du quatorzième siècle et puis s'effondrèrent tout à fait pendant les premières années du seizième. Le reste du volume considère la morphologie de la ville. Les résultats des recherches publiés plus tôt ont été intégrés avec ceux des études récentes sur l'archéologie, l'architecture et les archives pour examiner les rues, les marchés, les quais de la ville, la forme de ses défenses, ses bâtiments municipaux, ses églises, ses abbayes et ses hôpitaux avant de tourner l'attention finalement sur les maisons des habitants eux-mêmes.

Les fils de tous les arguments repris dans le chapitre final mènent à la conclusion que Winchelsea fut vraisemblablement bien plus grande et plus influente pendant le treizième siècle et au début du quatorzième qu'on n'eut cru jusqu'ici. Il est exact que pendant la seconde moitié du quatorzième siècle Winchelsea éprouvait de sérieuses difficultés, mais à cet égard aussi, l'évidence ne supporte pas la notion souvent exprimée que la ville subit vite un revers catastrophique. Ce n'est pas vrai que la ville de Winchelsea, considérée comme un port important au début du quatorzième siècle devint pendant les quelques décennies au milieu du siècle rien qu'un village insignifiant. L'évidence indique plutôt deux étapes dans son déclin. Pendant les dernières années du quatorzième siècle et pendant le quinzième Winchelsea jouait un rôle plus important dans le sud-est de l'Angleterre qu'on n'avait cru. Il est vrai que par rapport à d'autres villes à cette époque Winchelsea était plus petite, mais, parmi les petites villes typiques des comtés de Kent et de Sussex, la ville et son port restèrent importants jusqu'au début du seizième siècle.

Il est à espérer que les arguments proposés dans ce volume corrigeront les idées fausses et encourageront ceux qui étudient les villes médiévales anglaises à reconsidérer cette ville potentiellement mésestimée.

Traduction: *Gwen Jones*

ZUSAMMENFASSUNG

Winchelsea wird in den meisten Büchern über das mittelalterliche England erwähnt, doch ist es vielleicht unvermeidbar, daß sich die Referenzen in dieser Art von Veröffentlichungen hauptsächlich auf die Stadt als Mitglied der Cinque Ports und auf das geplante, schachbrettartige Straßensystem beschränken; weiterführende Bemerkungen bleiben, sofern existent, oberflächlich. Die Stadt wird selten zu den bedeutenden mittelalterlichen Städten und Häfen Englands gezählt, außer wenn die Rangfolge auf der Teilnahme an maritimen Aktivitäten im mittelalterlichen Königreich beruht. Dies führt zu der Schlußfolgerung, daß Winchelsea lediglich ein weiteres Beispiel für einen kleinen mittelalterlichen Hafen darstellt, der von örtlichem Nutzen war. In der Tat entsteht dieser Eindruck im Gespräch mit zahlreichen, auf das Mittelalter spezialisierten Archäologen und Historikern, die in diesem Feld arbeiten. Die meisten kennen die Stadt als Musterbeispiel einer geplanten Siedlung, die im großen Maßstab von Edward I. angelegt wurde und letztendlich scheiterte. Viele vermuten, daß sie scheiterte bevor sie sich etablieren konnte, andere, daß sie nach einer sehr kurzen und begrenzt erfolgreichen Blütezeit in Bedeutungslosigkeit verfiel. Heute ist Winchelsea ein kleines, verschlafenes Dorf mit einem unbedeutenden bachartigen Fluß, der unterhalb des nördlichen Stadtteils verläuft. Besuchern sei verziehen, wenn sie die von den heutigen Einwohnern gemachten Behauptungen zugunsten der Stadt als unbegründete Übertreibungen und als das Ergebnis eines falschen Stolzes ansehen. Für den gewöhnlichen Besucher zeigen sich die Spuren einer bedeutenderen Vergangenheit lediglich in dem schachbrettartig angelegten Straßennetz, drei zerfallenen Stadttoren (von denen eines für die meisten Touristen schwer zu finden ist) und den Fragmenten einer imposanten Kirche. Im Hinblick auf die neueste Forschung müssen unsere Ansichten hinsichtlich der historischen Rolle Winchelseas neu überdacht werden.

Das Ziel dieser Monographie ist es, einen zeitgemäßen Überblick zu der Entwicklung der Stadt bis zu ihrem Verfall im 16. Jahrhundert zu geben. Kurze einführende Kapitel erwägen, warum es notwendig war, die Stadt an einer neuen Stelle neu zu gründen, welche wirtschaftlichen Aktivitäten ihren Wohlstand untermauerten und warum die Stadt in der Mitte des 14. Jahrhunderts ins Schwanken geriet und dann im 16. Jahrhundert verfiel. Der restliche Band betrachtet die Morphologie des Stadtstruktur. Die Ergebnisse der neuesten Forschung auf archäologischem, architektonischem und dokumentarischem Gebiet sind in frühere Studien integriert, um die Infrastruktur der Stadt (Straßen, Märkte, Hafenufer etc.), die Art der Verteidigungsanlagen sowie die städtischen Gebäude, Kirchen, Klöster und Krankenhäuser zu untersuchen, um dann die Aufmerksamkeit auf die Besitztümer der eigentlichen Einwohner zu lenken.

Das Schlußkapitel vereint die verschiedenen Forschungszweige, die in diesen Band einflossen. Es folgert, daß Winchelsea während des 13. und frühen 14. Jahrhunderts möglicherweise wesentlich größer und einflußreicher gewesen ist, als bisher angenommen. Aber in der zweiten Hälfte des 14. Jahrhunderts war die Stadt in großen Nöten. Jedoch können die aufgeführten Befunde auch in dieser Hinsicht die gewöhnlich vertretene Auffassung von einem meteorischen Niedergang Winchelseas nicht unterstützen. Es ist nicht wahr, daß die Stadt von einem bedeutenden Hafen zu wenig mehr als einem Dorf innerhalb einer kurzen Zeitspanne während der mittleren Jahrzehnte des 14. Jahrhunderts absank. Die Befunde weisen eher auf einen zweiteiligen Niedergang mit einer wesentlich wichtigeren Rolle im späten 14. und 15. Jahrhundert für den Südosten Englands hin als gewöhnlich angenommen. Winchelsea mag zu diesem Zeitpunkt klein im Vergleich mit vielen englischen Städten gewesen sein, aber, im Hinblick auf die generell kleinen Städte in Kent und Sussex, konnte der Hafen bis ins frühe 16. Jahrhundert keineswegs ignoriert werden.

Es bleibt zu hoffen, daß die diskutierten Punkte des Bandes helfen, vergangene Missdeutungen wiedergutzumachen und daß diejenigen, die Forschung zu mitterlalterlichen englischen Siedlungen betreiben, dieser potentiell unterschätzten Stadt größere Aufmerksamkeit schenken.

Übersetzung: *Martina Johnson*

1. THE ORIGINS OF WINCHELSEA

Jill Eddison

Winchelsea, which was founded on its present site towards the end of the 13th century, lies near the eastern end of East Sussex on the south coast of England. It is perched high up on a peninsula which forms the eastern extremity of one of the Wealden ridges and is almost completely surrounded by reclaimed marshland, all of which has always been liable to flooding by fresh or salt water. The River Brede, now a minor stream, flows close under the northern cliffs where, then much enhanced by tidal flow, it provided the base for an important medieval harbour. A broad, flat-bottomed valley stretches away to the west, disproportionally large in relation to the present diminutive size of the river. Some two miles (3km.) away to the northeast, Rye stands on a comparable position on a peninsula at the extremity of another Wealden ridge. Beyond that lies the great expanse of Walland and Romney Marshes.

To the south and east Winchelsea is separated from the sea by the reclaimed marsh of Pett Level and a sea wall which was built in the 1940s. Northeast of the marsh and the wall the coastline consists of fans of shingle ridges which have accumulated since the 15th century.[1] Unfortunately for historians, however, the coastline there has undergone such radical changes since Winchelsea was established in the 13th century, that the coast of today provides no guidance as to that of the medieval period (*see* Figure 1.1).

Although now over a mile (nearly 2km.) from the sea, Winchelsea enjoyed very considerable prosperity as a seaport in the 13th and early 14th centuries, owing to its strategic position near the shortest crossing of the English Channel to Normandy and because it must have had a large, sheltered anchorage (*see* Figure 1.1). Not only, however, was its period of prosperity notably brief, but during that short time the town occupied two sites, one after the other. The site of the first town and its port is now somewhere out in Rye Bay, having been lost progressively to the sea during the 13th century. In 1280, when the first site was evidently doomed, Edward I sent three senior officers to negotiate the purchase of land in order to transfer the town to its present hilltop site, which is the subject of this volume. The history of this, the second Winchelsea, may be summed up in three phases. A time of prosperity lasted from the late 13th to the mid-14th century. This was followed by rapid decline and Winchelsea became a port of only regional importance, which continued to be the case for some two hundred years. Finally, decay set in during the early decades of the 16th century when the town found itself reduced to purely local significance.[2]

COASTAL CHANGES

Since coastal changes were critical to both sites of Winchelsea, it is essential to provide a brief description of the processes which brought those changes about. Firstly, the coastal marshes between Fairlight and Hythe had evolved over the past 5,000 to 6,000 years behind a massive offshore barrier of flint pebbles, described here as shingle. The barrier eventually allowed progressive occupation of the marshland. Pebbles are easily moved by the waves, whose activity and force increases in rough weather. Thus, while some pebbles are moved about even in calm weather, great quantities are moved in storms. In periods of storminess, therefore, rapid alterations could, and did, take place in the configuration of the barrier. Secondly, when breaches occurred in the shingle barrier, the tides flowed in over the marshes behind, where they deposited their load of silt and sand. While this had the advantage of building up the level of the marshes it also, much less conveniently and beneficially, blocked channels and harbours. Thirdly, although four wide, flat-bottomed valleys including that of the Brede lead into the marshland from the west, it is now the view of

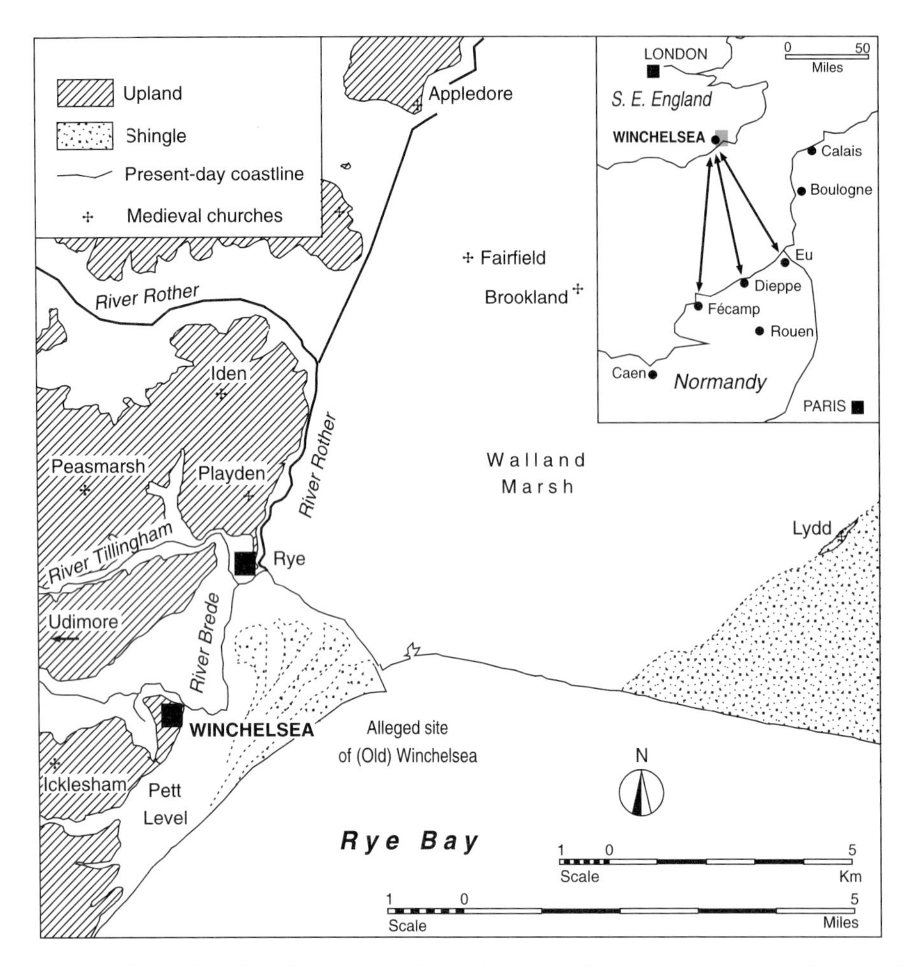

Fig. 1.1
The location of Winchelsea and its present surroundings. Note that the medieval coastline was very different.

geomorphologists that the power of the rivers has been unduly exaggerated. It is now recognized that the valleys were carved out during the Ice Age when sea level was much lower than it is today, and that in historic times the power and influx of the tides and their deposits of silt has been of far greater importance than the outflow of or deposition of sediment by the rivers.[3]

(OLD) WINCHELSEA: THE HISTORICAL AND GEOGRAPHICAL BACKGROUND

The history of the first town of Winchelsea is summarized here in order to provide a context for the later town. For some 5,000 years before the 13th century the major shingle barrier extending northeast from Fairlight to Lydd and beyond kept the open seas well to the south of the present Rye Bay.[4] It can be assumed that the first town of Winchelsea must have stood, like New Romney and Lydd, on the relatively high, well-drained foundation of the early shingle barrier, in preference to the lower-lying marshland. But, in view of the rapidity of removal of shingle barriers and the speed of coastal changes in general, it is very unlikely that the site or any of the materials of the old town survived in place for long after 1280, when the town was described as being 'for the most part submerged by the sea'.[5]

Since the site is totally lost, the history of the town and its changing surroundings have to be constructed from documentary sources, which initially are very sketchy. From the 11th century onwards, the English Channel was an important artery for shipping (Figure 1.1). A number of small ports grew up, based on fishing but equally importantly also serving cross-Channel shipping, and providing vital shelter at times of rough weather for ships passing up and down the Channel from Flanders to the Bay of Biscay and beyond. (Old) Winchelsea was most probably one of these, although nothing specific is known of its origins. It does, however, seem certain that it was the port where King William landed on his return to England from Dieppe in December 1067, having crossed the Channel in only one night. Close relations developed between (Old) Winchelsea and neighbouring English ports and those on the Normandy coast.[6]

The vast Saxon manor of *Rameslie* had already been granted by King Canute to the Abbey of Fécamp in Normandy in *c*.1017. This covered a large area of the east end of Sussex, and Domesday Book (1086) recorded that it included a *Novus Burgus*, although the debate as to the identity of this new town is inconclusive.[7] The manor also included the exceptionally high, if nominal, number

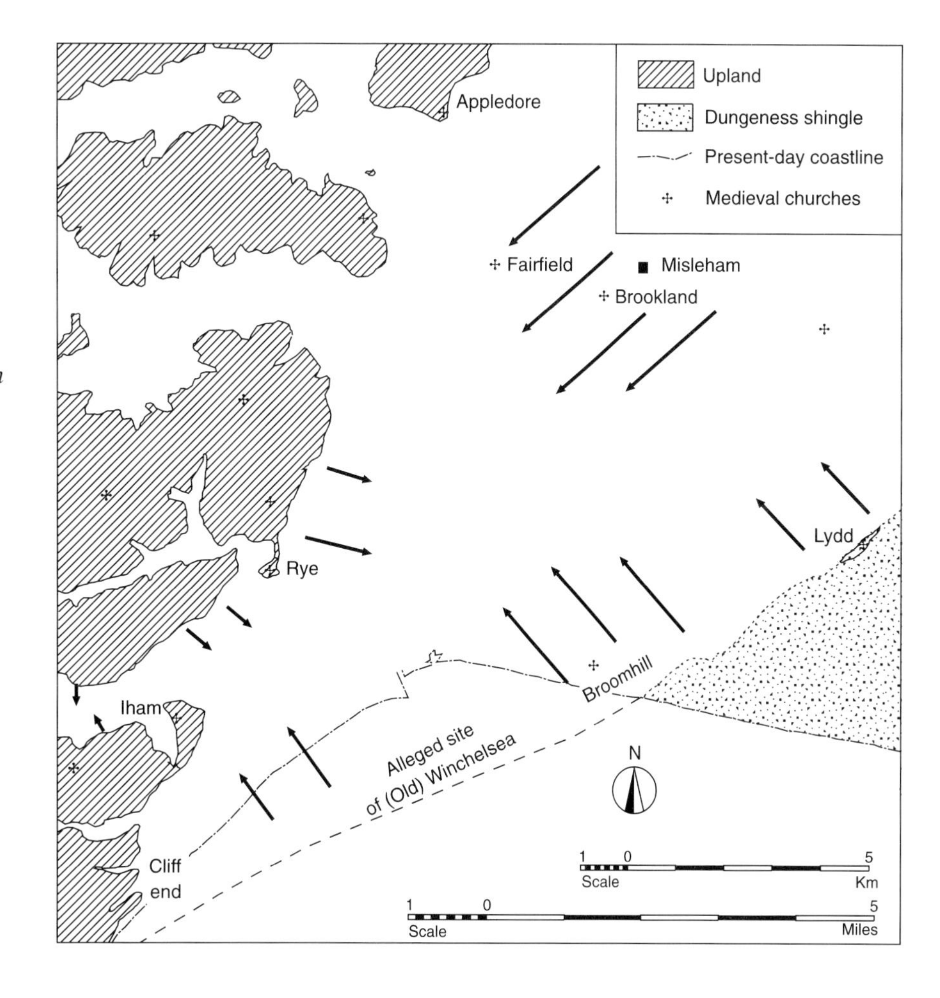

Fig. 1.2
A schematic sketch map illustrating 12th- and 13th-century colonization of the marshes surrounding (Old) Winchelsea and Rye, and on Walland Marsh. At that time the area must have been well sheltered from the sea.

The arrows indicate the direction of colonization into the salt marsh.

of 100 salt pans, and although these have not been located, they are a clear indication that extensive salt marshes existed in this area. The source of salt water for the salt-works is debatable. It may have been let in through a restricted and perhaps temporary gap in the local shingle. On the other hand, the works may well have been near the tidal limits - the usual situation - of a channel running southwest from an inlet which reached the sea near New Romney, some 10 miles (16km.) to the northeast, and known in later centuries as the Wainway (*see* Figures 1.3 and 1.4).[8]

Both (Old) Winchelsea and Rye are mentioned in the Pipe Rolls of 1131 and 1164-5, showing that they were significant ports at those dates. The earliest surviving charter to the two towns dates from 1191, but confirms liberties which had been granted to them earlier, in the reign of Henry II (1154-89). By 1190 they had joined the association of Cinque Ports as the *Two Ancient Towns*, but at that stage their shipping was still very inferior to that of their head port, Hastings.[9]

(Old) Winchelsea seems to have risen to prosperity around, or somewhat before, 1200. As far as can be ascertained from a financial document which is incomplete - Hythe and Hastings are omitted - the Pipe Roll of 1204, which records the taxation of one fifteenth on merchants at seaports, shows that (Old) Winchelsea was already clearly well-established. It featured at the head of the second rank of ports, behind only London and Southampton on the southeast coast. It was also considerably more important than its neighbour Rye, since the merchants of Winchelsea paid £62.2s.4d in tax compared to Rye's £10.13s.5d.[10] Up to the 1240s, the records speak of (Old) Winchelsea as a very prosperous centre with not only extensive fisheries, but also shipbuilding, royal dockyards and overseas trade.[11]

However, whereas the climate of the 11th, 12th and early 13th centuries seems to have been particularly tranquil, 1236 heralded a period of exceptional storms which continued until at least 1288.[12] The site of (Old) Winchelsea was especially vulnerable to potential changes in the shingle barrier on which it stood. Evidence from elsewhere strongly suggests that the barrier remained more or less intact until the 1240s, since reclamation of the salt marshes proceeded apace in Walland Marsh and Broomhill, and indeed near Rye and Winchelsea until then (Figure 1.2).[13] This reclamation could not have been achieved had the marshes been exposed to the open sea. On the other hand, whereas no records survive of marshland enclosure after 1243, from 1244 onwards (Old) Winchelsea was receiving grants to

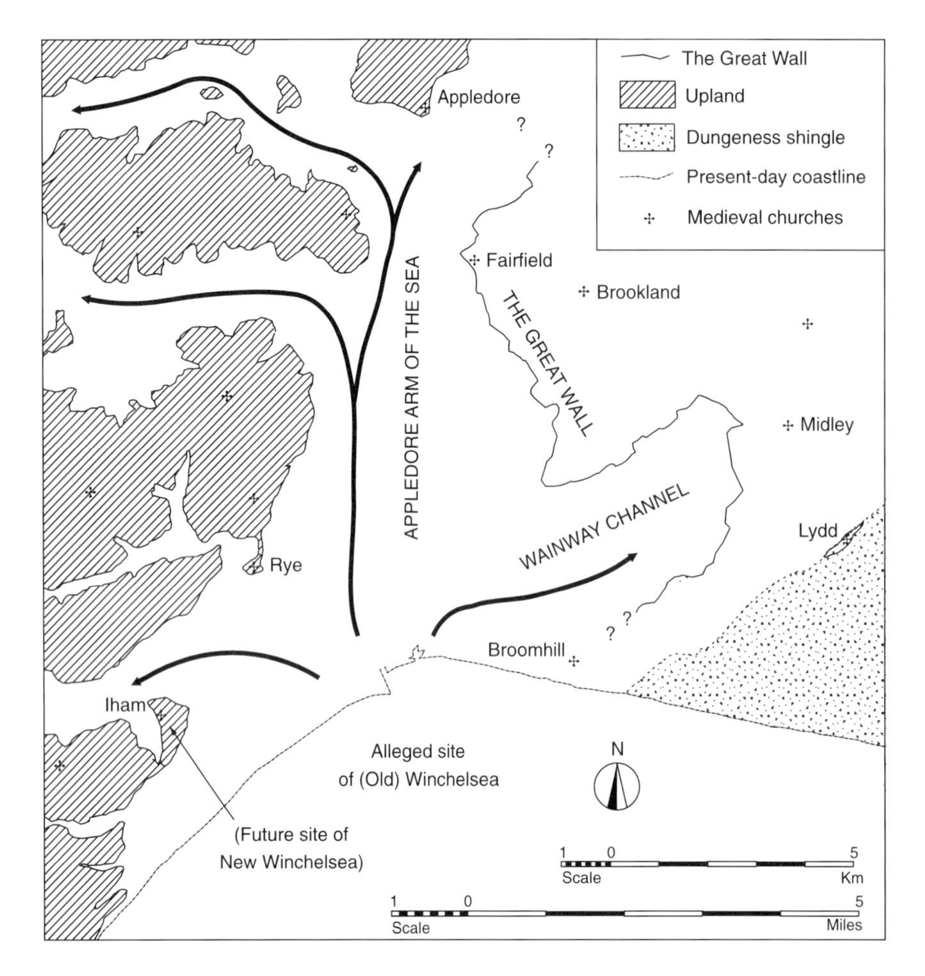

Fig. 1.3
The influx of the sea after 1250 which resulted from the breakdown of the shingle barrier on which (Old) Winchelsea stood. The arrows indicate the general position of the marsh channels up which the tides would have flowed. The names of those channels mostly date from the 15th century.

improve its sea defences on an almost annual basis. It seems that by the 1240s the barrier was already under stress, and this was greatly increased by severe storms.

The two great storms recorded by Matthew Paris in October 1250 and January 1252 (and probably others which went unrecorded) evidently not only caused immense damage to the town and its surroundings, but seem to have made a permanent breach in the barrier, possibly enlarging a relatively stable pre-existing one.[14] By 1258 the tides were running up to Appledore, some 8 miles (13km.) north of (Old) Winchelsea (Figure 1.3). Three years later, when the barons of Winchelsea, Rye, Hastings and Pevensey were summoned to pay homage to the king at Lydd, they had to cross an 'arm of the sea'.[15] The tides were also making advances across the marshes behind the barrier, for in the 1260s and 1270s the communities there were already contributing to the upkeep of the 'Great Wall', a major defensive rampart which extended across the width of the Marsh some 5 miles (8km.) north of the present-day coastline at Camber (Figure 1.3).[16] It can be assumed that simultaneously the tides were flowing increasingly far up the river valleys, including that of the Brede.

No description of the harbour of the first Winchelsea exists, but it should be envisaged as having been both spacious and sheltered, for it was used regularly as a port of assembly for naval craft. In 1247 Henry III claimed back the towns and ports of (Old) Winchelsea and Rye from the abbey of Fécamp.[17] This move was made for political reasons: because it was undesirable at that time to allow the French to have command of two English ports. But the strategic importance of those ports strongly indicates the existence of an extensive harbour, or haven, with several main tidal channels. Although no field evidence has been recognized of the anchorage(s) on which Old Winchelsea was based, ships probably would have been anchored stem-to-stern along channels and lain in the mud at low tide, as at Rye today. Such a situation is illustrated pictorially on the map of Rye Harbour made by Prowez in *c.*1572.[18]

In the meantime, in and after the 1250s the town received numerous grants for attempts to protect it from the sea, further indications that the shingle barrier was breaking down. Despite all efforts and expense, the course of erosion of the town was unrelenting. In 1271 the 'quay on the south side of the church of St Thomas [had been] carried away by the floods and the tempests of the sea, and a great part of the said church [had] fallen.'[19] And by 1280 the site was said to be for the most

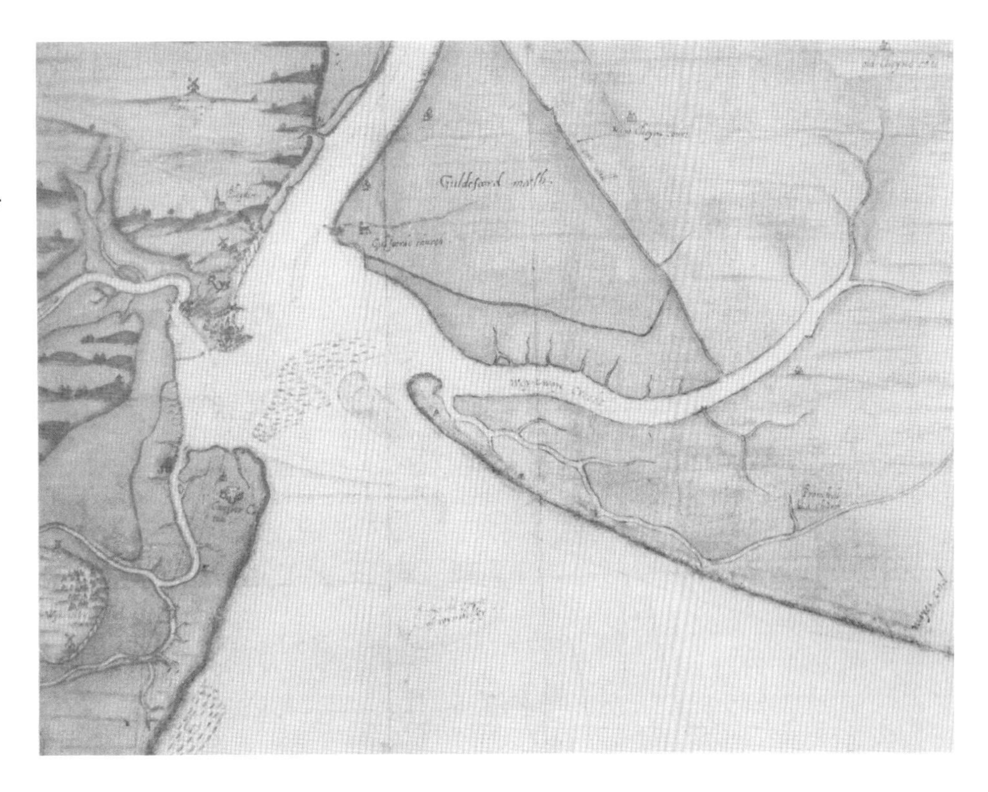

Fig. 1.4
Part of Philip Symondson's map of 1594 entitled 'The decayed harborough of Rye', with a general representation of the site of (Old) Winchelsea in very shadowy form, since it had been lost to the sea three centuries earlier. ESRO ACC 6364.

part submerged by the sea.[20] In November that year, therefore, under instructions from Edward I, preparations began to transfer the town to its present hilltop site.

THE NEW SITE OF WINCHELSEA

In the earliest documents the site of the planned new town was called New Iham (taking the name of a pre-existing settlement) but, not surprisingly, the name New Iham was very soon superseded by that of New Winchelsea. From surviving documents which relate to its foundation it is possible to reconstruct a picture of the hill in the 1280s, on the eve of its transformation into a major new town. Just under half the site was occupied by the manor house, buildings, gardens and courtyards of Iham Manor, together with 66½ acres of its demesne, which consisted of arable land, a quarry, a coppice, and the hill slopes. A further 28¾ acres were then the property of John Bone of Wickham in Icklesham, who in c.1285 granted 4 acres of this total to the Grey Friars for their new site. Another 35¼ acres were owned by the heirs of John Langhurst, whilst sundry persons, including the Abbots of Battle and Fécamp, held a further two houses and 22¼ acres between them. All these lands were needed for the new town and were acquired accordingly, either through exchange or purchase.

A further 18 holdings, including 16 houses, amounting in all to 16 acres were not required; nor was the church of St Leonard's of Iham, nor the Abbot of Fécamp's 'little town of Iham' within which the church was located. Almost certainly all these excluded lands were located around Little Iham on the northwestern corner of the hill. These lands did not form part of the manor of Iham and remained outside the newly extended boundaries of the Liberty of Winchelsea. They made up the parish of Iham. Retained by Fécamp Abbey, they became part of that abbey's Manor of Brede and still formed part of the Liberty of Hastings until the late 19th century. As such, they fell outside the jurisdiction of the new town and were administered separately throughout.[21]

Not only were the properties on the hill purchased as part of Edward I's scheme to refound Winchelsea, but also the entire manor of Iham, much of which to the southeast of the hill was marshland already occupied by (Old) Winchelsea residents. Other associated properties owned with Iham were also acquired, including the manor of Iden, to the north of Rye.

Having secured the new site, in October 1283 Edward instructed commissioners to plan streets, lanes and a market and to set out suitable places for the churches of St Thomas and St Giles, to lay out the tenements and to give directions regarding the harbour. In all the King took over about 150 acres of land on the hill, 12 acres of which he retained for his own use. In total the new town comprised 802 plots, 723 on the hill and 79 flanking the harbour on the Brede estuary. Perhaps the true foundation date for the new town can be given as July 1288, when the Bishop of Ely, acting as the king's representative, formally granted seisin of the site to its new residents.[22] However, for modern scholarship the most significant date occurred four years later in 1292, when the town's rent roll was drawn up, presumably in readiness for collecting the first rents, which had been respited for seven years. Further details of the layout of the new town are given in Chapter 4.

THE END OF THE OLD TOWN

In 1287-88, almost coincidentally with the rise of the new town, three great storms occurred within the space of 14 months.[23] Only the effects of the last of these, that of 4 February 1288, are recorded for the Winchelsea area. The continuator of the chronicle of Gervase of Canterbury wrote that 'the sea flooded so greatly . . . . in the marsh of *Romenal* and all adjacent places, that all the walls were broken down and almost all the lands covered from the great wall of Appledore towards the south and the west as far as Winchelsea'.[24] To judge from the almost complete silence about it in subsequent records, its final destruction seems to have been swift and total: the only known reference to it after 1292 is a quitclaim of 1294/5 relating to properties 'within the new and old towns of Winchelsea'.[25] The earliest maps, made more than three centuries later, show it simply as a shadowy *(i.e.* non-existent) feature somewhere off the present mouth of the Rother (Figure 1.4).

2. THE DEVELOPMENT OF WINCHELSEA AND ITS MARITIME ECONOMY

David Sylvester

Few urban communities in medieval England were as thoroughly oriented to the sea as the port town of Winchelsea. While never a town of first-rank economic importance, Winchelsea flourished after the arrival of the Normans and earned, in the 12th century, official inclusion in the Cinque Ports, medieval England's confederacy of Sussex and Kent port towns that enjoyed economic, judicial and political liberties in return for naval service to the crown. The port developed as an important import/export centre of timber, grain and Gascon wine, a home port to an active local and offshore fishing fleet, a strategic location for the assembly of royal maritime forces, and as a source of naval expertise, manpower, and ships. Winchelsea quickly surpassed the prosperity of its head port, Hastings, and achieved in the 13th century - along with its neighbour Rye - the title of 'Ancient Towne' of the alliance, a legal status equivalent to that of the original head ports.[1] In the century and a half before the Black Death, Winchelsea's strategic and naval importance and its economic vitality were reflected in its position as one of the largest contributors of ships to royal fleets and in its designation (by no less than

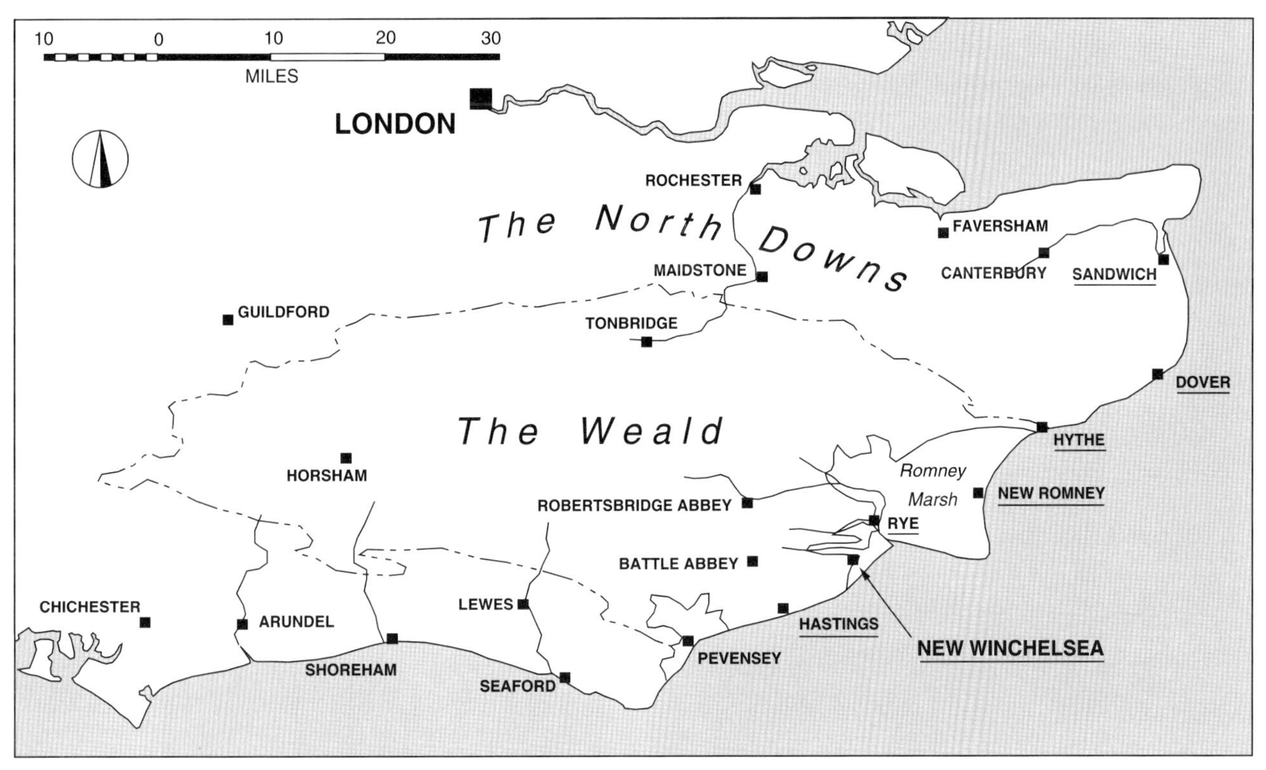

Fig. 2.1
The south-east of England showing the medieval coastal ports and selected other towns. The Cinque Ports and the 'Two Ancient Towns' are shown underlined.

King Henry III), as one of the 'more noble' members of the Cinque Ports.[2] As a result, Winchelsea enjoyed a remarkable degree of royal patronage and protection, especially during the reign of Edward I (1272-1307). It was the king who, when the town faced extinction caused by flooding during the second half of the 13th century, intervened and cooperated with local residents to ensure the port's survival.[3]

Although the focus of the current study is the site of the refounded borough of Winchelsea, any account of the historical importance of the community must look at the economic development of the town in its entirety. The community's translation to the hilltop site on the old Iham manor during the reign of Edward I brought new challenges and opportunities, but in many ways it was simply a confirmation of Winchelsea's established and ongoing prosperity and strategic importance. The progress of medieval Winchelsea, moreover, and its eventual decline beginning in the later 14th century, can only be understood if placed within the context of the development of the Cinque Ports overall.

MARITIME ORIENTATION

The common geography shared by the Cinque Ports dictated their similar economic interests and fostered a corporate identity which provided the basis for their relationship with the crown. The coastal region of Sussex and Kent constituted a unified geographic area bound by common access to the sea, and the region's natural orientation to the Channel was reinforced by the topography of the inland region called the Weald. This hilly, forested area stretching from western Sussex into central Kent functioned as a barrier to land transportation and promoted communication and cooperation between coastal and riverine communities. The Kentish North Downs, an escarpment that stretched through the west-central region until it turned south to reach the coast at Dover (*see* Figure 2.1), further restricted inland transportation in the region. While limited access into the relatively resource-poor and underpopulated hinterland of the southeastern towns forced the residents of Winchelsea and its allies to look to the sea, we should not conclude (as have Brandon and Short) that this led to a 'sense of [regional] isolation and remoteness . . . ', either economic or social.[4] The maritime orientation of the entire coastal region was, in fact, the key to its prosperity and one of the defining characteristics of Winchelsea and its urban neighbours. The story of Winchelsea is revealed, then, in the patterns of its communication with domestic and overseas settlements and in the principal activities of its residents, namely trading, fishing, and shipping, both commercial and naval.

One of medieval Winchelsea's principal maritime relationships was with the largest port town in northern Europe, London.[5] Matthew Paris claimed in 1252 that Winchelsea was a borough of great import, 'especially to Londoners', and the medieval record indicates that, economically at least, the chronicler was on the right track.[6] The barons of Winchelsea and of the other Cinque Ports regularly attended the capital's markets and participated in a well-established coastwise trade.[7] The coastal regions of Kent and eastern Sussex were within the catchment area of the metropolis for the supply of bulk foods such as grain, and the towns of the Cinque Ports served as collection centres for the regional commodities shipped to London and for the distribution of goods transferred from the capital.[8] Winchelsea was also a leading supplier of fish to the royal tables at Westminster in the 13th century.[9]

Regional maritime communication was not only directed towards the capital, however; the Brede, Tillingham, and Rother rivers in Sussex, and the Stour river in Kent provided limited, though valuable riverine access to inland resources, markets and monastic centres. Winchelsea and Rye were important markets for the hilltop Benedictine monastery at Battle (located approximately 15 kilometres west of the Camber along the Brede river) and, to a lesser extent, for the monks of Canterbury.[10] Winchelsea functioned as one of Battle's principal entrepôts for overseas wine, North Sea herring, and a variety of commodities transshipped from London.[11] During the 14th century, Winchelsea also functioned as an important regional centre for trade to other English coastal communities such as Portsmouth, located over 100 kilometres to the west.[12]

Winchelsea and the ports of the region served not only as a collection and distribution point for goods produced regionally - primarily fuel, timber, and fish - but also as an entrepôt for commodities originating from overseas. Winchelsea's economic connections to Flanders and eastern Normandy are clearly evident in the medieval documentary and archaeological record, which indicate that a vibrant trade existed from at least the middle of the 13th century.[13] The towns of the Cinque Ports even maintained an agreement with their Norman neighbours whereby mariners taken at sea were held for a standard fee known as 'head money'.[14] The predominance of Saintonge earthenware found in Winchelsea during this period attests to the strong link with Gascony, a pattern evident in other leading wine-importing ports such as Southampton, Hull and Plymouth.[15] Winchelsea was a stepping-stone for pilgrims travelling to and from the Continent, as far afield as Santiago de Compostella, and Spanish merchants were regular visitors to the port.[16] Far from isolated, the urban centres of the southeast communicated with each other and with their regional competitors and communities as far afield as Gascony, Spain and Scandinavia. Geography had a crucial role in determining the patterns of exchange, and the medium of their economic, social, and legal interaction was the sea.

SHIPPING AND TRADE

Some sense of the scale of Winchelsea's maritime prosperity can be determined in the decade following its official inclusion in the Cinque Ports. King John's 1204 levy on merchants indicates that (Old) Winchelsea flourished as a centre of overseas exchange by the early 13th century.[17] Although not a port of the first order such as London, Boston, Southampton, Lincoln, or King's Lynn, Winchelsea ranked tenth overall among English port towns with an assessment of approximately £62, and its merchants were assessed at more than double the amount of other members of the Cinque Ports. Only Dover came close to Winchelsea's ranking (paying £32), while the meagre tax paid at neighbouring Rye and Pevensey indicate that these port towns participated only moderately in the overseas trade of wool during this period. Even Sandwich, a town which emerged as a leading port in the wool, cloth and wine trades later in the century, paid only a third of what merchants did at Winchelsea.[18]

The vitality of (Old) Winchelsea's shipping during this period is more clearly evident in the local accounts of the town, which survive from the middle of the 13th century.[19] In a 32-week period between December 1266 and April 1267, the bailiff of Winchelsea collected anchorage fees from no fewer than 114 non-resident ships arriving in the harbour (Figures 2.2 and 2.3). The origin of these vessels varied greatly: they came from as far away as Spain and as nearby as Chichester and Shoreham in Sussex, and Teignmouth in Devon. The most frequent visitors, however (almost 50 per cent of identifiable shippers), came from the Norman port towns located along the eastern end of the Channel. Winchelsea was primarily an importer of bulk commodities, notably iron, salt, wine, fish, and foodstuffs. A decade later, at the close of the 13th century, Norman and Flemish shippers were still very active in the port, but the record also shows English ships, especially those from west-Channel port towns, visiting the port on a regular basis (Figure 2.2).[20]

During the early years of the 14th century, the refounded community continued to stand out as one of the principal shipping centres on the southeastern coast of England, not so much for the value of the commodities which passed through its harbour, but for the scale of its shipping traffic.[21] (New) Winchelsea specialized in the export of Wealden wood products.[22] The export trade of Sandwich and Dover, which comprised largely wheat, cheese, wool and cloth from Sandwich and horses from Dover, was worth far more per shipment than Winchelsea's shipments of wood, timber, and oak bark, yet a full 71 per cent of export traffic recorded in the Cinque Ports in 1307/08 originated in Winchelsea. The total value of these exports was worth more than that of Sandwich and Dover combined. Shipments into Sandwich and Dover, on the other hand, were worth much more per shipment than imports into Winchelsea (on average £21 compared to £3 per shipment). The 1307/08 accounts leave the impression that Winchelsea was not much of a centre of importation: it accounted for less than 5 per cent of ship arrivals and total value of goods. Winchelsea's smaller hinterland and the difficulties of overland transport through the Weald limited the demand for commodities imported through the port. The overall scale of Winchelsea's shipping, however, was remarkable. Even though the total value of trade passing through Sandwich was more than six times that of Winchelsea, the number of shipments in and out of the ports was, in real terms, equal: 163 ships called at Sandwich while 161 anchored at Winchelsea.[23]

A decade and a half later, just prior to the

	1266/67		1273/74	
Region	**Port of Origin**	**Shipments**	**Port of Origin**	**Shipments**
Flanders/Normandy	Boulogne	19	Boulogne	6
	Barfleur	2	Barfleur	8
	Dieppe	13	Dieppe	7
	Calais	2	Calais	8
	Gravelines	4	Etaples	1
	Damme	3	Dunkirk	1
	St. Valéry	3	Croil	1
	Le Tréport	14	Sluys	1
	Swyne	1		
Bay of Biscayne	Bayonne	3	Bayonne	11
Northern Spain	Fontarabia	6		
	St Sebastion	2		
England	Teignmouth	2	Teignmouth	4
	Chichester	1	Chichester	2
	Yarmouth	1	Yarmouth	5
	Poole	1	Poole	4
	Hull	1	Exmouth	4
			Sidmouth	3
			Lyme (Regis)	8
			Wareham	1
			Plymouth	1
Unidentified		36		60
Total Shipments		**114**		**129**

Source: PRO *SC6/1031/19*; PRO *SC6/1031/23* and PRO *E122/124/16*.

Fig. 2.2
Origin of Ships Importing into Winchelsea, 1266/67 and 1273/74

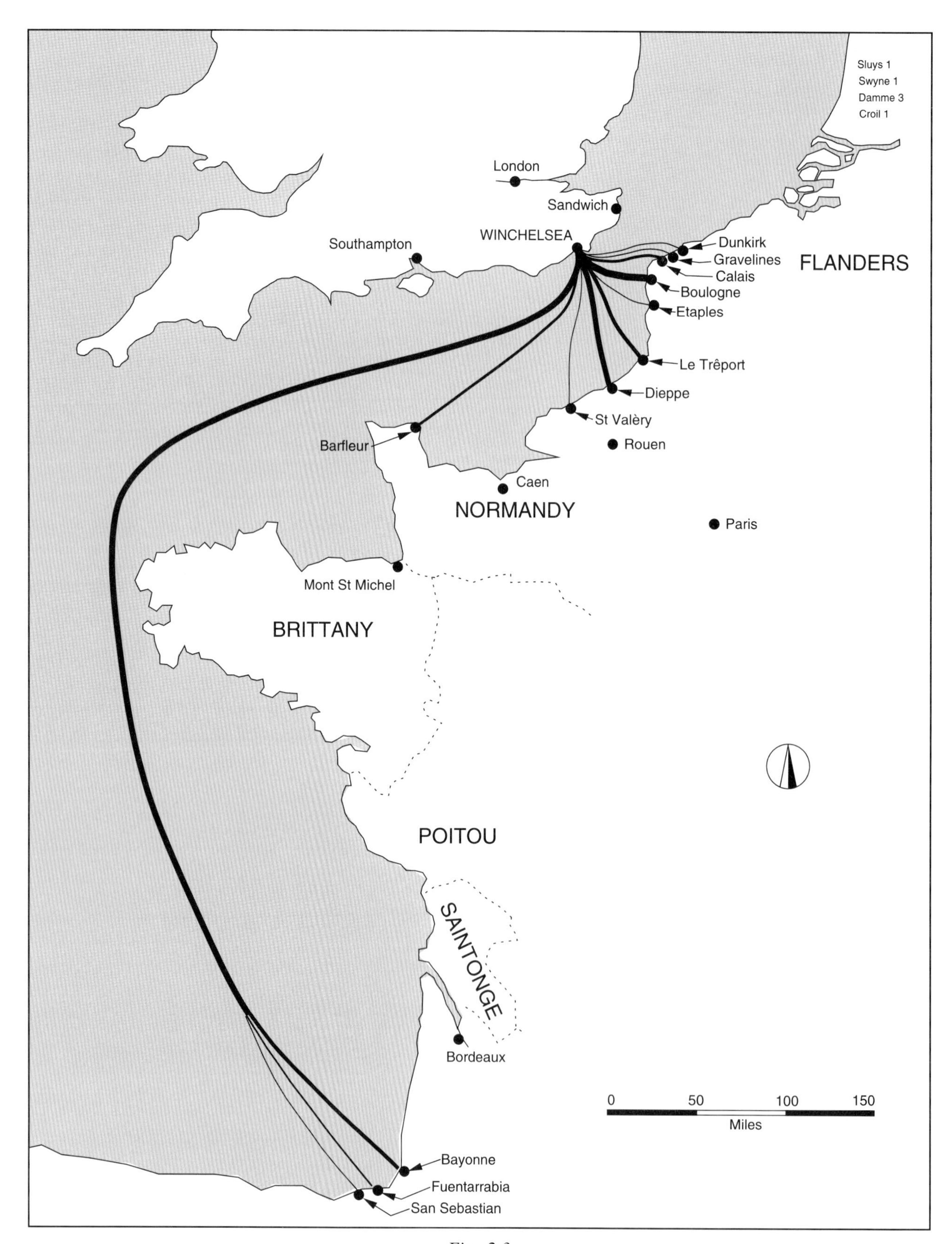

Fig. 2.3
Origin of ships (where known) importing goods into Winchelsea, 1266/7 and 1273/4 (See also Fig. 2.2). The line thicknesses reflect the relative number of vessels from each port.

Year	Imports		Exports	
	No. Shipments	(£ value)	No. Shipments	(£ value)
1322/23	59	(104)	118	(147)
1323/24	38	(153)	63	(111)
1324/25	13	(44)	86	(154)
1325/26	28	(190)	75	(359)
1326/27	23	(96)	31	(166)
1327/28	89	(435)	73	(491)
1328/29	84	(457)	83	(430)
Total	**334**	**(1,479**	**529**	**(1,574)**
Av. value per shipment		**5**		**4**

Source: PRO *E122/12/17-18; and* PRO *E122/32/6, 147/13, 147/14* discussed in Pelham 1929, 107-11.

Fig. 2.4
The Overseas Trade of Winchelsea, 1307, 1323-29

outbreak of the Hundred Years' War, Winchelsea's balance of trade appears markedly improved (Figure 2.4). Over a six-year period a total of 334 ships imported goods valued at roughly £1,479 into the port, while 529 ships exported goods worth approximately £1,574. Imported goods continued to be, on average, more valuable per shipment than the wood products exported from the port (for which *see* Figure 2.5), but the overall balance of trade was again favourable to Winchelsea. These ships brought in a wide variety of goods destined both for local consumption and for use in English manufacturing and fishing trades. Importations included finished goods such as mirrors, cloth, and copper cups; foodstuffs such as fruits, garlic and corn; and building materials such as Caen stone, bricks, plaster, and millstones. As was the case during the 13th century, salt and fish were imported into the town on a rather large scale.[24]

The trade and transport of wine also played a particularly important role in the prosperity of the Cinque Ports and shaped the topography and character of Winchelsea. The extensive network of cellars built at Winchelsea during the refounding attest to the town's ongoing investment in the importation of wine (*see* Chapter 9), and the community's involvement in the wine trade was apparent from its earliest days. A local vintner, Manasses de Winchelsea, was the first recorded farmer of the borough in 1204 and Daniel Pincerne of Winchelsea sold 50 tuns of wine for 125 marks (£83) to the king's agent in 1213.[25] Winchelsea wine traders were active in London, and merchants and shippers from the town and its confederate ports participated in the two-way trade with Gascony.[26]

In large part, Winchelsea's commitment to the

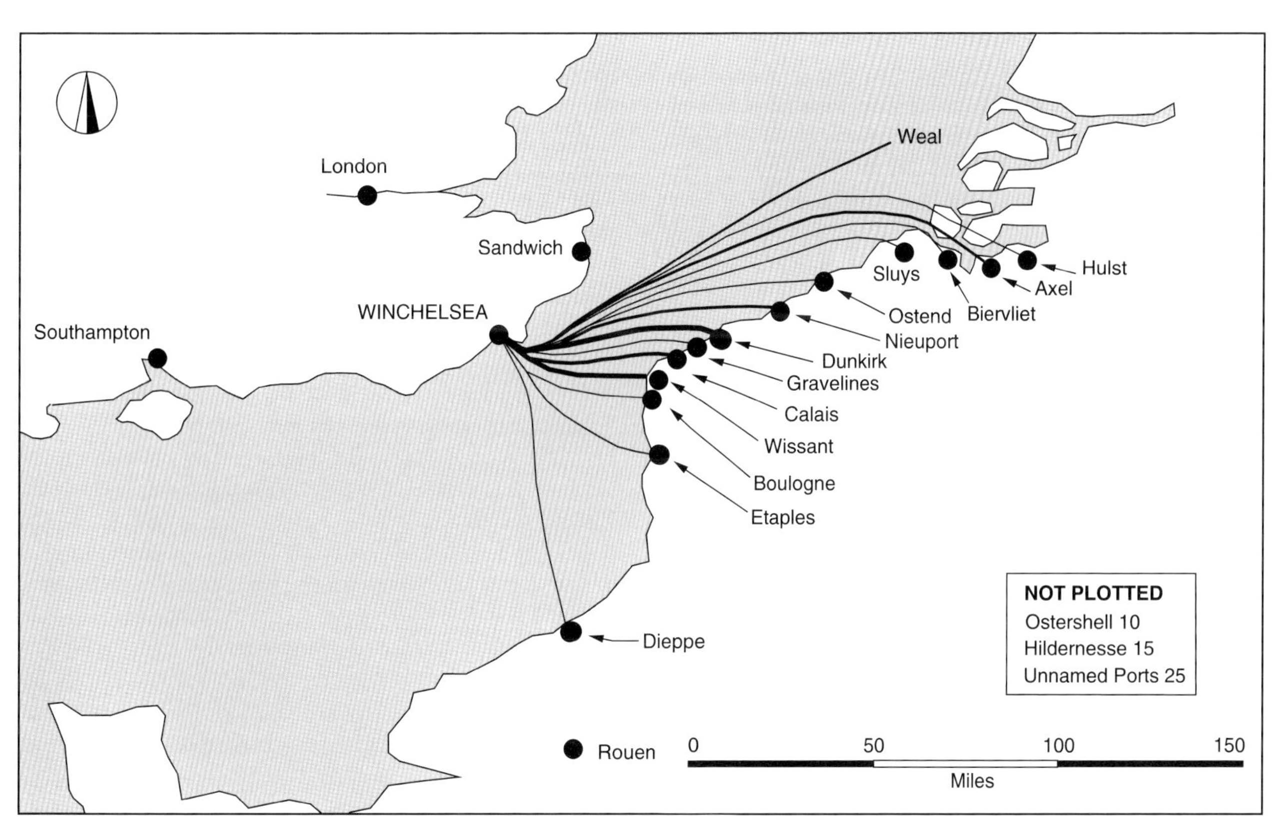

Fig. 2.5
Foreign merchants exporting wood from Winchelsea, 1323-29 (After Sylvester 1999, 199)
The line thicknesses reflect the number of vessels involved in the trade.

wine trade was a result of the Cinque Ports exemption from the royal prise on wine granted to its members in 1278 in consideration of their naval service.[27] The port's location at the eastern end of the Channel, easily accessible by sea to boats sailing both to and from London and Flanders, also served to promote these towns as ports of call for Gascon and Spanish ships importing wine and participating in the cloth trade.[28] Again, Battle Abbey relied upon Winchelsea, along with Hastings, as a principal source of its wine. Though the monks consumed considerable ale, Battle was above all a wine-drinking community. The monks were permitted a ration of one pint of wine per day and received one gallon each on special feasts.[29]

Winchelsea itself functioned as an important centre of the wine trade in a variety of ways. It was to some degree a port of destination for incoming wine shipments: in 1301, 13 ships imported some 1,300 tuns of wine into Winchelsea; in 1322/23 107 tuns; and in 1350/51 214 tuns.[30] In 1328, the port of Winchelsea was ranked ninth as a centre of English wine imports and second amongst southeastern ports.[31] Winchelsea naturally functioned as a market for wine and an administrative centre of the trade. In 1342, Winchelsea was designated as one of three ports responsible for the gauging of incoming wine.[32] The town's barons prominent in maritime trade also served as local representatives of the crown, both as wine gaugers and collectors of *prisage*. Along with Sandwich, Winchelsea figured prominently in the provisioning of wine for royal naval enterprises. In 1336, the two towns provided over 13 per cent of the wine bought in England in the preparations made for the invasion of Scotland.[33]

Winchelsea was also a home base for traders and shippers engaged in the wine trade, an entrepôt for the transshipment of wine, and as a stopover harbour for ships en route to other ports.[34] Between 1303 and 1308, 80 Winchelsea ships ranging in size from 30 to 201 tons imported wine into England.[35] Winchelsea ships regularly imported wine into London, Sandwich and Southampton.[36] Alien merchants were active in the English wine trade in the region throughout the 13th century; the merchants of Abbeville, St Omer, Bruges, Bayonne, Ypres, and Dieppe, were regularly recorded bringing wine in to Winchelsea.[37] They often contracted local vessels to carry the cargo. In 1212, Ypres and Ghent merchants brought 120 tuns of wine into Winchelsea aboard the ship of Geoffrey, son of Michael de Rye.[38] In 1236 Geoffrey and Simon de Winchelsea were hired to transport Erm de Peregoz's wine from Gascony to London and Boston.[39] Around the same time, Rouen merchants shipped wine to Sandwich aboard two Winchelsea ships, the *Gunnild* and the *St Anne*.[40] In the case of Bernard de Compre of *Prymerole*, who shipped 50 tuns of wine from Bordeaux to London in Peter de Logar's ship *le Fraunceys* of Bayonne, the Winchelsea stopover proved fortunate. The king's sergeant in London seized de Compre's wine upon his arrival since he came from a port town loyal to the French king. De Compre eventually kept his wine, however, because he showed that he had embarked while his home town was still loyal to Edward III and that his journey had taken some time because he stopped at Winchelsea.[41] Proximity to markets and a good harbour were not the only attraction for alien wine merchants. During the 14th century, Gascon vintners took up residence there and at Sandwich in order to enjoy the tax exemptions afforded to denizens of the Cinque Ports.[42]

While the participation of Winchelsea shippers and merchants in the medieval wine trade was significant both before and after the town's refounding, a dramatic decrease is evident by the middle of the 14th century.[43] In part, Winchelsea was subjected to the fluctuations in the wine trade caused by the on-again/off-again disruptions associated with the Hundred Years' War and the ultimate loss of Gascony in the mid-15th century. But the port town also fits into a broader decline in shipping affecting the eastern ports during the period, one marked by a shift in England's export trade from wool to cloth and the emerging economic dominance of London.[44] Against this backdrop, the ships of the western ports were better situated to capitalize on the wine and cloth trades, while the eastern ports, like Winchelsea, were further removed and more vulnerable to the travails of wartime and coastal inundations of the period.

What remains clear, however, is that Winchelsea shipping flourished following the relocation of the town. The port continued to welcome English and alien shippers; throughout most of the 1320s, an annual average of over 140 tax-paying, non-resident vessels passed through Winchelsea's harbour. It is important to remember that the extant records regularly excluded the numerous custom-exempt foreign and domestic ships, as well as the many vessels of the Cinque Ports. While Winchelsea shippers and merchants were clearly involved in overseas importing and exporting, they were also using the port as a centre of redistribution, loading goods onto coastal vessels for shipment elsewhere in Britain.[45] The port's role in domestic shipping, both commercial and in the service of the crown, was by no means insignificant.

The coastal trade of Winchelsea is not, unfortunately, recorded consistently in medieval documents and we can only get an impression of the patterns of such trade from isolated or indirect evidence. Winchelsea ships could be found transporting wine from Winchelsea to Portsmouth and shipping herring (largely a domestic product) to Exeter in 1317.[46] The 13th-century local accounts for Winchelsea are filled with ships from English port towns, and since many paid only anchorage tolls, it may be that they were exporting coastwise from

Home Port	Ships		Crewmembers		Crewmembers
	No.	%	No.	%	per Ship
Winchelsea	13	26	701	30	54
Sandwich	12	24	552	23	46
Rye	7	14	300	13	43
Romney	6	12	336	14	56
Dover	7	14	298	13	42.5
Hastings	3	6	112	5	37.5
Hythe	2	4	66	3	33
Total	**50**	**100**	**2365**	**100**	**47.5**

Source: *PRO E101/5/28*

Fig. 2.6
Ships of the Cinque Ports transporting Edmund Lancaster to Gascony, 1296

the port.[47] This component of the maritime economy should not be underestimated; it was crucial to the prosperity of medieval Exeter - accounting for as much as 70 per cent of the port's trade - and constituted 80 per cent of all incoming traffic into late-14th-century Hythe.[48] As Kowaleski has argued, coastal trade had a diversifying impact on the maritime economy. It was less subject to disruptions caused by international disputes, less risky than long-distance trade, and provided a more accessible investment option to a wider group of port town residents. In the case of Winchelsea, it certainly helped to constitute the port's tremendous shipping capacity. Like the port of Dartmouth, Winchelsea's ability to put men and ships to sea was remarkable given its relatively modest population and wealth.

NAVAL SERVICE

The Cinque Ports, and in particular Winchelsea, played an enormously important role in the naval policy of medieval England, contributing a substantial number of ships and mariners to the royal fleets both under the chartered arrangement with the crown as well as through the system of impressment. Though the quota of ships established in 1229 required Winchelsea to provide but 10 ships out of 57 (Dover was called to send 21, Hastings 6, and Rye, Sandwich, Romney, and Hythe 5 each), the town's actual contribution was far greater than its share of the confederacy's obligation.[49] Winchelsea was a middling borough by pre-plague standards; as a source of ships and mariners, however, the community was a first-rank provider of naval shipping not only within the Cinque Ports but among all English port towns. In the early 13th century, Winchelsea and Rye were specifically mentioned as home ports for the king's galleys and sites of royal dockyards and storehouses.[50] Winchelsea was oftentimes a centre of royal shipbuilding and royal galleys and barges were ordered to be built there in 1232, 1257 and 1336.[51] In 1235, Dover hosted a council for the discussion of naval affairs to which Winchelsea sent 18 representatives, more than any other member of the confederacy.[52] The ships and mariners of the Cinque Ports were a major component of the 1296 expedition to Gascony and Thomas Alard of Winchelsea was designated commissioner for the assembly of the fleet in Sussex (Figure 2.6).[53] Winchelsea provided roughly a third of all ships and mariners and, along with Romney, the largest vessels in the Cinque Ports' fleet.[54] In 1297, an enormous English fleet sailed from Winchelsea (a reported 1500 cavalry and 50,000 foot soldiers). After a disastrous landing at Sluys (a mêlée broke out between the barons and their Great Yarmouth counterparts) and an unsuccessful winter campaign, Edward returned to Sandwich aboard Cinque Port vessels in March, 1298.[55]

Winchelsea continued into the 14th century as one of England's premier naval ports. In the lead up to the Hundred Years' War, Winchelsea's naval contribution surpassed that of other regional shipping centres such as Southampton and Portsmouth and was comparable to that of Dartmouth and Great Yarmouth. In 1326, the king ordered all vessels from Channel port towns to assemble at Portsmouth for a proposed campaign against the French.[56] Winchelsea provided more ships and mariners than any other community (18 ships and 667 mariners), and only Southampton (13 ships and 458 mariners) and Dartmouth (10 ships and 282 mariners) could be considered first-rank contributors with Winchelsea. Though the Cinque Ports provided only 27 per cent of the ships, Winchelsea alone contributed over half of the confederacy's total (53 per cent); and the average crew onboard the ships of the Cinque Ports was significantly larger than that carried by other southern and west-Channel vessels.[57] Again in 1336, the Camber ports of Winchelsea and Rye did more than provide their share of the required naval forces. Their joint contribution constituted 43 per cent of all ships, 49 per cent of all mariners, and 51 per cent of the total ship tonnage. Moreover, these ports were home to the largest ships in the Cinque Port squadron, with Rye supplying the 240-ton *la Michel* and the 170-ton *la Edmund*, while all of Winchelsea's vessels were in excess of 100 tons, including the 160-ton *la Blith*.[58]

The assembly of the Western Fleet at the outbreak of the Hundred Years' War confirms Winchelsea's leading role on the south coast as supplier to the king's navy. Edward's III's summons of 1337 calling the ships to Sandwich was issued as a response to Philip VI's May invasion of the English-held duchy of Aquitaine, and subsequent occupation of the county of Ponthieu and the Channel Islands. In all, some 169 ships carrying almost 5,000 mariners and soldiers descended on the Kent harbour. Though the contribution of the Cinque Ports as a whole was less than remarkable (32 per cent of the entire effort), Winchelsea provided more ships

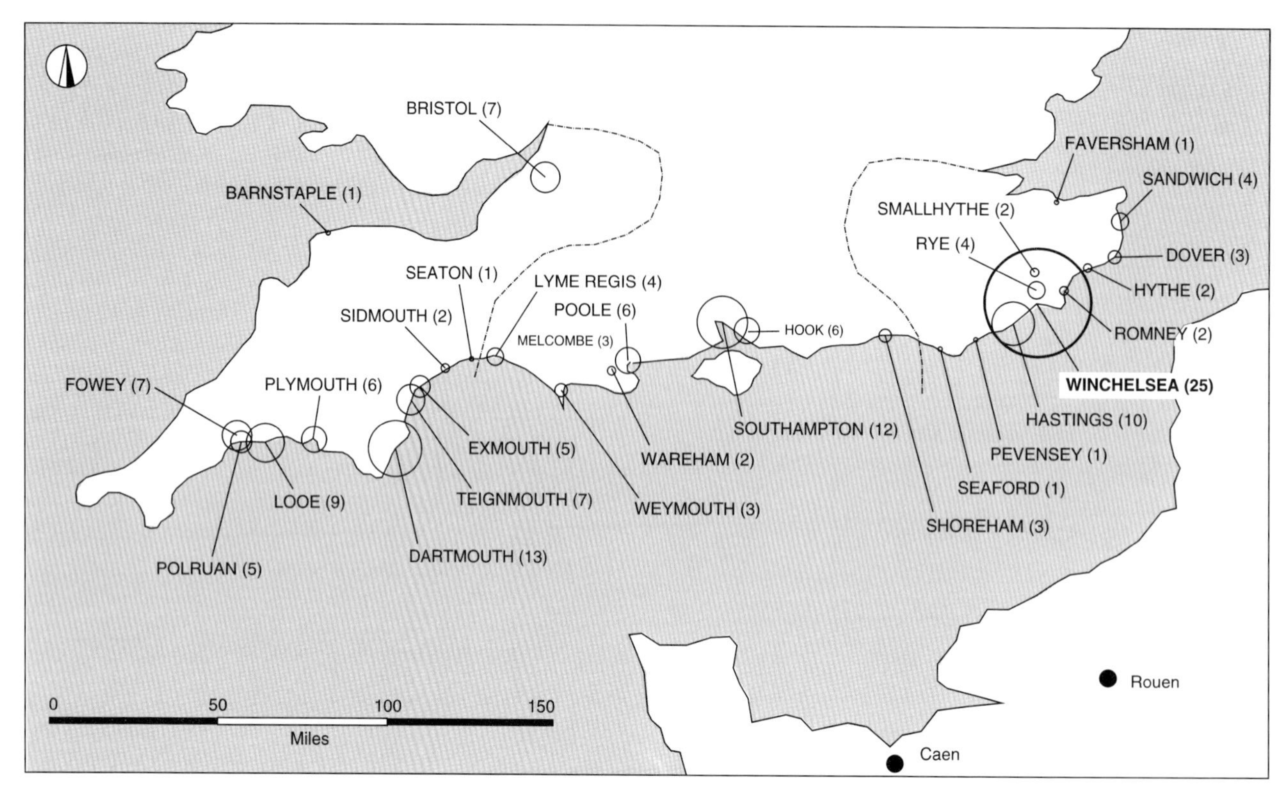

Fig. 2.7
Port of origin of ships assembled at Sandwich in 1337. The western group represent the Western Fleet; the central group the South-Western Fleet; the eastern group the Cinque Ports Fleet. Also present (but not shown in this map) were one ship from Lincoln; one ship from Gosford Haven; one ship from London; four ships from Tenby in Wales; three ships from Camarthen in Wales and two foreign mercenaries. (After Sylvester 1999, 147).

(25 vessels) and more mariners (658) than any other English port town taking part (Figure 2.7). As in the earlier 1326 fleet, only Dartmouth (with 13 ships) and Southampton (with 12 ships) came close to matching Winchelsea's contribution. Within the confederacy, Winchelsea provided almost half of all Cinque Port vessels and mariners, contributing 17 ships more than Rye and Sandwich combined. Moreover, when the following summer the entire English fleet gathered at the mouth of the River Orwell, near Ipswich in Suffolk, (361 ships representing some 73 port towns carrying almost 13,000 mariners and soldiers), Winchelsea provided a greater number of ships and more mariners than any other English port town, save for Great Yarmouth in Norfolk.[59] A comparison of these and other national ship surveys and summonses that took place between 1300 and 1347, which included over 1700 vessels from 180 different port towns, shows that Winchelsea provided 82 ships, second only to Great Yarmouth's significant contribution of 133 ships. Winchelsea's naval effort was comparable to Dartmouth's 81 ships and greater than that of any of the western port towns (Figure 2.8).[60]

Although these examples of naval service represent service during individual campaigns, they reflect the general trend of naval contribution over a 50-year period and are, therefore, representative of the naval activity of the period. In the naval pay lists that facilitate a comparison of the Cinque Ports, Winchelsea is clearly the dominant supplier of ships to the king's fleet from at least the 1280s until the middle of the 14th century. Winchelsea consistently supplied about 35 per cent of the confederacy's shipping in the five decades after its refounding, providing over 40 per cent more ships than the next member, Sandwich.

After the Battle of Sluys in 1340, the immediate naval demands upon Winchelsea and its neighbours lessened, but these communities remained at the centre of the conflict with France, suffering devastating raids from Norman mariners. Winchelsea continued to appear regularly in the naval pay lists of the crown, overshadowing the occasions of service of other members of the Cinque Ports.[61] The Cinque Ports and Winchelsea maintained a consistent, albeit modest, presence in the naval affairs of the crown through to the

Homeport	Shipping No.	% of Total
Great Yarmouth	133	8
Winchelsea	82	5
Dartmouth	81	5
Fowey	74	4
Southampton	59	3
Plymouth	47	3
Total	**1714**	**(100 %)**

Notes:
The author consulted original manuscripts and pr
1326, 1337, 1340, and 1343 and relied upon Rod
For comments on the reliability of the Calais
Kowaleski 2000; and Rodger 1996, 645, n. 11.

Fig. 2.8
Leading Naval Providers in National Fleets, 1301-1347

middle of the 15th century. An assessment of English and Welsh ships participating in the larger naval expeditions during three important stages of the Hundred Years' War indicates that Winchelsea, Rye and Sandwich together provided 6.6 per cent of all shipping in 1336-1346, 4.5 per cent in 1377-1395 and 9.4 per cent in 1439-1450.[62] These assessments also reveal a steady decrease in the overall contribution of eastern ports, and the crown's increasing reliance on western ports to meet its naval needs. This trend is supported by the view that the Cinque Ports became less important to the crown as, beginning in the mid-14th century, its interests shifted away from Flanders and Normandy and more toward Gascony and the Atlantic.[63] The ports of the region struggled to play a meaningful role in naval designs of the crown in the face of general economic decline and Tudor defence policy, which sought to introduce a network of castles for coastal defence and to centralize naval administration. What profit could be made from naval service during the 16th century - naval pay, the right to seized goods, and the right to ransom captured mariners - was revoked by Elizabeth I in 1563.[64] Although the crown invested enormous amounts in the defences of Rye during the mid-16th century, Winchelsea's responsibility to provide at least 150 tons of dressed stone from the ruins of St Giles's church for the project in 1545 indicated that the town was no longer flourishing (*see* Chapters 3 and 7 below).[65] The Cinque Ports provided only six ships to the English fleet that confronted the Armada.[66]

During the 13th century and through the first stages of the Hundred Years' War, Winchelsea was clearly a first-rank contributor to the king's fleets, in the number of ships it provided, the size of the vessels serving, and the total number of mariners participating in naval service. Consequently, we should not assume that a port town's population or overall corporate wealth determined its ability to provided naval service. The capacity of this relatively small port town to provide naval service on the scale it did suggests that a significant portion of the population participated directly in shipping and related maritime activity, in addition to the trading interests of its merchants. Winchelsea's involvement in the carrying trades and fishing provided the ships and experienced mariners required by the crown. Medieval naval enterprise - much like the carrying trades - was not as profitable as trading, but it was a great employer of sailors, shipbuilders, sail-makers, corders, and coopers, not to mention innkeepers, brewers, and prostitutes. Naval activity touched all members of the port town and had an important role in shaping its occupational and political structure, as well as its topography.

FISHING

Despite the disparaging commentary of Bede - that St Wilfred found the coastal inhabitants of seventh-century Sussex unable to use fishing nets - the eastern communities along the Channel coast were centres of a vibrant fishery throughout the Middle Ages.[67] More than any other activity, fishing dominated the interests of Winchelsea residents. The individual towns of the Cinque Ports played a central role in the medieval fisheries, and their mutual interest and investment in the North Sea herring fishery bound them together as much as any royal need for naval power. Winchelsea's prosperity, its maritime expertise and its ability to provide the king with a remarkably large number of ships, was directly tied to its role as a fishing community. The first mention of the fisheries in the immediate area of Winchelsea is in the 12th-century agreement between the Abbey of Fécamp and the community of Rye.[68] The Norman monastic house had a particularly strong connection with the sea on both sides of the Channel; its wealth on the continent was founded upon extensive coastal properties between Le Tréport and the Cotentin. According to Michel Mollat, the monks were masters at exploiting the coastal resources at their disposal, and "... Fécamp vit essentiellement de la mer": an assessment reflected in the medieval records on the English side of the Channel, which frequently referred to the monks from the Abbey of 'Fishcamp'.[69] The Abbey's lands in England centred on the Sussex manor of *Rameslie,* which had been granted by Cnut sometime between 1017 and 1030 and included the new port of Rye and the future site of (Old) Winchelsea.[70] The Fécamp accord required each Rye vessel engaged in fishing to render a percentage (a share) of its catch to the Abbot, based upon the size of the vessel.[71] The practice of disbursing the profits of a fishing enterprise according to shares, (*saræ* in the Fécamp cartulary) was common along the southeast coast of England throughout the Middle

Ages.[72] The share system operated at other English fisheries during the Middle Ages, notably at Great Yarmouth in Norfolk, where the rector of the Church of St Nicholas and the town each claimed half of one share known as 'Christ's dole'.[73] Mariners from Suffolk port towns engaged in the North Sea herring fishery also followed the custom of shares.[74] In 13th-century Winchelsea, the bailiff's accounts record the collection of *scar'* or *scharz* of the fisheries and provided the crown with a share equivalent to 'what one sailor would get'.[75]

The most important fishery for the community of Winchelsea was the North Sea herring fishery based at Great Yarmouth in East Anglia. The men of the Cinque Ports had been attending the fair since the 11th century and held special privileges, including the right to occupy the shore, dry their nets, and sell their catch without charge.[76] During the later 13th century, their right to collect 2d. from other ships for the maintenance of the fire beacons was confirmed, as was their participation in the administration of justice during the fair.[77] The fair took place each autumn, and the preparations and departure of the fishing fleet required a substantial effort. Winchelsea maintained a sizable fleet at the fair, sending an average of 15 vessels each year during the late 13th century; a number 50 per cent higher than the 10 vessels it was chartered to provide annually for naval service and double the number of Rye ships attending the fair during this period (Figure 2.9). Winchelsea sent close to 200 men every year to Norfolk to fish and oversee the administration of justice at the Great Yarmouth fair.[78] A sufficient number of townspeople were engaged in this fishery to require the suspension of local courts and markets and the collection of certain taxes throughout the Cinque Ports because, in the words of the barons of Rye, '*totes gentz du pais en la Mere pur pescher*'.[79] Attendance at the Cinque Ports' Brodhull court was eventually regularized to allow for the election of bailiffs going to Yarmouth and to resolve any unfinished business after the fair had taken place.[80] Fish were sufficiently important to Ralph Ivegod, a baron of Winchelsea, for him to include one in the middle of his personal seal.[81] Many of the Winchelsea ships that travelled to Yarmouth also took part in the 'Saltfare', which was probably the cod fishery off Yorkshire.[82]

The 13th-century borough accounts for Winchelsea record that the ships returning from the herring fair rendered shares (recorded as '*scar 'Gernemut'* ') worth an average of £6 annually.[83] An average of six vessels each year attended Saltfare, paying £2 annually ('*scar 'Saltfar'* '). Assuming the town's (*i.e.* the king's) share was worth a traditional half-share, the combined offshore fisheries were worth an estimated £450 annually (£366 and £80 respectively), excluding whatever was caught and sold at the fairs themselves.[84] The shares from the local inshore fisheries were rendered

Year	No. of vessels to Yarmouth	No. of vessels to Saltfare
1267	14	10
1268	18	8
1269	—	—
1270	—	—
1271	—	—
1272	20	6
1273	9	4
1274	11	3
1275	15	5
Av. no. vessels	**14.5**	**6**

Source: PRO *SC6 1031/19-24.*

Fig. 2.9
Winchelsea Fishing Fleets (1267-1275)

weekly from the owners of smaller boats ('*scar' vill collect' de minut' batell'* ') During this period, the local fisheries at Winchelsea were worth between £240 and £400 annually.[85]

These estimates, based upon the actual shares rendered at Winchelsea during the 13th century, are very conservative when compared to the conclusions of a Sussex jury representing the barons of the Cinque Ports in 1303. In that year, the fishers of Winchelsea, Rye, Hastings, and their members complained that losses resulting from their exclusion from the fair at Great Yarmouth amounted to £2,300 in lost trade for the previous year alone and over £11,300 for the five-year period leading up to the inquest.[86] Although the barons were undoubtedly exaggerating their losses to ensure a generous settlement, the suit emphasizes their financial and political commitment to the medieval fisheries, and in particular, the community's reliance upon the profits secured at Great Yarmouth. The town's involvement in the North Sea fisheries and the vitality of the local fisheries prove that Winchelsea was an active fishing centre during the Middle Ages. In 1267 alone, fishing shares made up 48 per cent of the town's entire revenues, and the total amount of the fish shares collected at Winchelsea were approximately six times greater than those collected for Rye.[87] Unfortunately, the Winchelsea accounts of the 14th century do not maintain the same level of detail as the earlier record, and overall the shares collected in the 14th century are much lower than those collected in the old town.[88] It is unclear whether the North Sea revenues were lumped in with the local fisheries by the bailiff's clerks, or whether they were negotiated away by the crown to some other interest. It is, therefore, difficult to determine whether the fisheries were in sharp decline after the re-founding. Certainly, the barons' claims before the king would indicate that their involvement at Great Yarmouth had not diminished.

With a fleet active in regional and long-distance

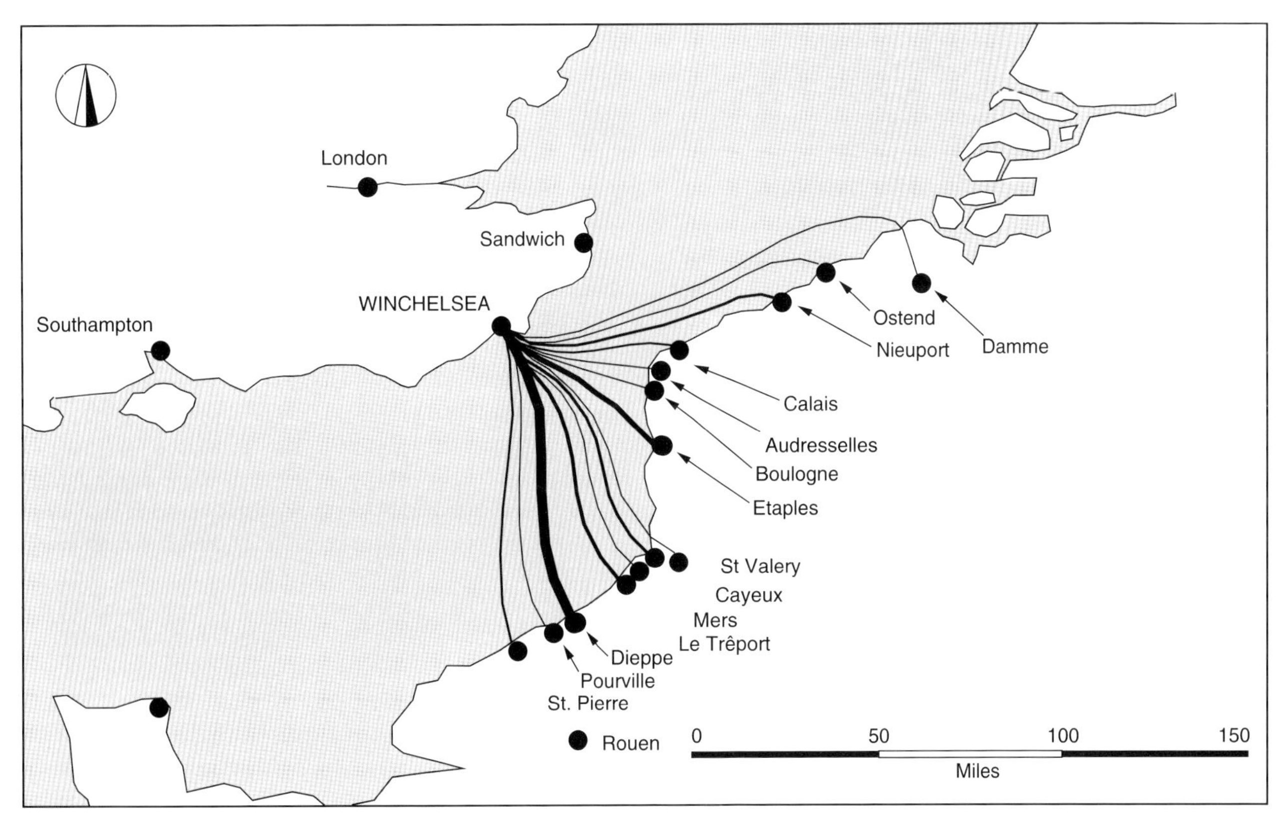

Fig. 2.10
Foreign merchants landing fish at Winchelsea in 1323/4 (After Pelham 1929, 112). The line thicknesses reflect the number of vessels making landings.

fisheries, it makes sense that Winchelsea functioned as a distribution centre of fish for local and regional consumers. The importation of herring, cod, mackerel, and other types of fish evident in both the national and local port customs accounts attests to the town's role as a point of fish consumption and exchange.[89] The regular importation of salt into Winchelsea, where it was sometimes referred to as fish salt, indicates that the port town was also a centre of fish-processing.[90] The vitality of Winchelsea as a regional fish market is evident in the Battle cellarer's accounts, which indicate the town and its neighbour, Hastings, were the Abbey's principal sources of fish and salt in the two centuries leading up to the Black Death.[91] The Abbot's cellarer employed a buyer (referred to as a 'fishman' or *Fyssher*) in both these ports to ensure a sufficient supply of the commodity.[92] The staple fish food of the monks of Battle Abbey was herring, though cod, mackerel, salmon, oysters, shrimp, and mussels were served too. The Battle *Fyssher* purchased smaller quantities of more exotic types of seafood at the Sussex markets, including dolphin, porpoise, and eel.[93] The Abbey also paid much of the customary work on its estate in herrings, and in *c*.1250, the cellarer anticipated that this would cost at least 26,000 herrings annually.[94] Over a period of 10 years in which the cellarer accounted for purchases of fish at Winchelsea and Hastings, a minimum of £781 was paid to fishmongers of those towns, excluding payments for transportation to the Abbey.[95] Robert Alard of Winchelsea sold salt herrings and 21 lasts of gutted herrings to the monks in 1320/21 for £5.6s.8d.[96] In the same year, Godwin Turk sold cod (*milewell*) and stockfish to the Abbey's representative at Winchelsea for £1.9s.6d and received an additional £1.15s.3d to cart it to Battle.[97]

The Abbey was certainly not the only market for Winchelsea fish; the local Winchelsea fair held each May from no later than the 1340s was also an important source of fish for the Archbishop of Canterbury, Robertsbridge Abbey, and the earl of Richmond (overlord of the Rape of Hastings) who employed fish haulers (*rippiers*) to secure sufficient supplies of fish for their post-Lenten needs.[98] The merchants of the town were also busy at London. Throughout the 13th century Winchelsea supplied substantial quantities of fish to the king's household. Plaice and whiting dominated the royal purchases at Winchelsea, but sole, conger, dories, and haddock were also required at Westminster.[99] Although the king would normally rely upon London fish-sellers for his supply of herring, Winchelsea provided the fish for the October Feast of St Edward in 1261.[100] Winchelsea and Rye shippers also traded in

London on behalf of Battle Abbey. Their familiarity with the markets in the capital and the overland transportation costs through the Weald made coastwise transport cost-effective.[101]

WINCHELSEA'S FALL FROM PROMINENCE

After the refounding of Winchelsea at the close of the 13th century, the general revenues of the town increased for several decades. New Winchelsea did flourish, and clearly the investment on the part of the crown and the residents of the town was justified. The crown's expectation that Winchelsea would remain a reliable naval source was also realized. Edward I wasted no time in expressing his confidence in the new town when he designated it as his port of assembly for the huge English fleet sailing to Flanders in 1297.[102] During the first half of the 14th century, Winchelsea and its outer harbour continued to function as a staging ground for royal naval campaigns. It was the leading Cinque Port contributor of ships and mariners through several of the campaigns leading up through the first decades of the Hundred Years' War.[103] During these assemblies, the town's cellars were used to store grain and wine for the king's forces on the continent.[104] Winchelsea served as a point of assembly in the spring of 1341, and a decade later Edward III and his son, the Black Prince, defeated a Castilian fleet of 47 ships in an engagement described by Froissart and subsequent historians as the 'Battle of Winchelsea'.[105]

The declaration of war with France in the 1330s at once elevated Winchelsea to international prominence, yet signalled the town's major decline. On the front line of England's defences, Winchelsea was weakened by trade embargoes and prolonged ship service, and was devastated by rampant privateering in the Channel. Winchelsea's ships and men were continually called to naval service during this ongoing conflict, which had the double effect of removing them from commercial enterprise while placing them directly in harm's way. The eastern Channel ports were especially vulnerable to French raiders and Winchelsea was the target of several attacks that traumatized its population, damaged its harbour and temporarily crippled its shipping capability.[106] While the south coast enjoyed something of a respite after the naval victory at Sluys in 1340, the French were back in 1359 and 1360 and ravaged the Cinque Ports and their residents. According to chroniclers, the especially brutal attack against Winchelsea in 1360 included looting, burning, gang rape, and mass executions, prompting King Edward III to mount a direct attack of reprisal against Paris itself.[107] It is worth noting that during a subsequent attack that resulted in the capture of Rye and the burning of Hastings, it was Hamo, the Abbot of Battle, who repelled the French at Winchelsea.[108] Winchelsea had had no problem recovering from similar raids in the past and had always found ways to profit from naval campaigns, but other forces were also at work during this period.

Around this time, the viability of Winchelsea's tidal harbour was increasingly compromised. Ballast-dumping and marsh enclosures, which reduced the flows needed to clear away silt build-up, were taking their toll.[109] Not only did costal deterioration limit established shipping at Winchelsea, but harbour deterioration made many of the Cinque Ports an unsuitable home for the increasingly larger ships required for overseas trade and naval service.[110]

The 14th century also witnessed a shift of commercial English shipping away from the eastern ports to the western Channel ports and Bristol, ports that were in a better position to exploit the growing trade with Spain, the Mediterranean, and eventually, the Atlantic fisheries.[111] The importance of the Cinque Ports in the 12th, 13th and early 14th centuries centred largely on their preferred commercial and strategic location; as the interests of the crown and English shippers shifted westward beginning in the later 14th century, the port towns of the confederacy found themselves increasingly marginal to the important business of the realm. Combined, these factors weakened the shipping capability of the southeastern ports, and of Winchelsea in particular.

But silting harbours and shifting markets were also manageable if the residents of a port perceived a viable future and were able to capitalize on new economic opportunities. Rye was able to recover from the 14th-century difficulties because the water flow changes that led to the choking off of the Winchelsea harbour actually improved its own.[112] Royal interest could also prolong the life of a town's harbour, as it had Winchlesea's during the reign of Edward I. Dover, for example, was no less susceptible to silting than many of the other Cinque Ports, but its strategic importance for passenger traffic and the presence of the very substantial Dover Castle ensured the crown's ongoing commitment to investment in the town and its harbour facilities.[113]

One variable that has been overlooked in the deterioration of the overall scale and quality of the confederacy's shipping capacity during the later Middle Ages is the mid-14th-century decline of the Great Yarmouth herring fishery. Saul has catalogued and analyzed the evidence detailing the crisis facing Great Yarmouth at the time. These symptoms included, but were not limited to a steady drop in overall attendance at the fair beginning in the mid-1360s; to a decline in herring and wool exports as recorded in the customs accounts (especially of the part of Gascon shippers); to a falling off in London investment in Yarmouth; and to an overall reduction in the size of Yarmouth merchant and naval fleets relative to other English port towns.[114] A variety of causes were at the root of Great Yarmouth's decline. Certainly, the Black Death put a temporary though noticeable dent in the demand for foodstuffs (including fish) throughout northern Europe, and Great Yarmouth and Scarborough were themselves directly affected by the plague.[115] The outbreak of the Hundred Years' War had the dual impact of interrupting English shipping and diverting commercial fleets to naval activity. Edward III's strategy to please competing English interests at the herring fair (especially London investors) failed, and resulted in an artificial rise in Yarmouth prices beginning in 1350.[116] Storms during the 1360s and 1370s devastated both Scarborough and Yarmouth, forcing larger vessels to transship cargoes through Kirkley Roads, to find alternative landing facilities, or to cure their catch at sea.[117] An expensive harbour restoration programme imposed a tax of 1s. on each last of herring coming into the port.[118]

As a result of Yarmouth's many problems, continental fishers increasingly showed a preference for Hull, Boston and Lynn.[119] The disruptions at Yarmouth and Scarborough also resulted in a temporary improvement in the fortunes of smaller villages with access to North Sea herring.[120] These adjustments and fluctuations in the North Sea fisheries had a direct impact on the Cinque Ports, for the the barons' rights applied only to the fair at Great Yarmouth. The decline in the barons' trade there had a direct impact on their fishing revenues, as recorded in the returns for Rye between 1342 and 1357.[121] The developments unfolding at Great Yarmouth merely complicated the chance for Winchelsea's revival. While geographic decline and technological advance weakened the Cinque Ports, the lost revenues associated with the herring fair may have provided the proverbial nail in the coffin of those Cinque Ports, such as Winchelsea, that were already struggling.

As a result of overall economic weakening, the naval contribution of Winchelsea, relative to the new scale of naval enterprise in the late 14th century, declined. As Winchelsea's importance to the crown faded, so too did its chances of another royal bail-out. The difficulties experienced by its confederate neighbours at the same time meant that Winchelsea found little help within the Cinque Ports. As the Hundred Years' War progressed, the crown looked increasingly to western ports to provide for its fleets, and Winchelsea faded to regional importance after it was sacked and burned by French privateers in 1380. In 1415, new walls were commissioned, partly on account of the old fortifications, but also, as the residents of the town pointed out, because the empty spaces within the enclosure made it too difficult to defend the town.[122] The difficulties encountered by Winchelsea and the confederacy during its decline resulted in a closer union characterized by an almost officious observance of ceremony. The continued regularization of the Brodhull Court in the later Middle Ages represented a cooperative effort to reduce the costs associated with sending bailiffs to Great Yarmouth and to lobby for tax relief; an effort described by Murray as the Ports' somewhat pathetic effort to develop 'an elaborate system of government, for the purpose of maintaining the obsolete privileges of an otherwise purposeless association'.[123]

Winchelsea's harbour was indeed a hub of maritime activity during the 13th and 14th centuries, but the scale of its shipping activity was probably even greater than is revealed in the local accounts and national records of trade. During the 13th and 14th centuries, the port town was able to produce huge numbers of ships and qualified mariners for the king's navies, and the number of Winchelsea 'commercial' vessels visiting Gascony in the early 14th century to collect wine surpassed the shipping of many larger English trading centres.[124] Like Dartmouth in Devon, Winchelsea (both Old and New) should be properly recognized for its role in the carrying trades rather than its standing as a trading port. The residents of Winchelsea looked to the sea for opportunities, and they successfully carved out a place for themselves in the maritime transport industry of the period.

3. A FIGHT FOR SURVIVAL: THE SIXTEENTH CENTURY AND BEYOND

David and Barbara Martin

Despite the increasingly silted state of Winchelsea's harbour, as late as 1433 it was still able to receive vessels of up to 200 tons and was in 1434 listed as a principal port of embarkation for pilgrims bound for St James of Compostella.[1] Four years later, in 1438, it was from Winchelsea that Richard Woodville and 1,000 troops crossed to Honfleur. Long-distance ships were still using the port in 1455, for in that year Italian merchants were barred from trading at Fowey, Falmouth, Plymouth, Dartmouth and Winchelsea. However, soon after this date Winchelsea ceased to be used by pilgrims bound for Compostella.[2] Up to at least 1491 the town was able to contribute its full quota of ten ships to the Cinque Ports fleet, but it is clear that by the close of the century silting within the creek was causing very serious concern. The port remained in use during the first part of the 16th century and as late as 1524 the town was called upon to provide ships for royal service. On this occasion, however, it was only able to provide four vessels, which totalled 96 tons and were manned by 15 mariners. By 1544 it could only provide six hoys.[3] If there remained any question of the economic viability of Winchelsea surviving beyond the medieval period, it was not evident in the 1548 Act, which renewed prohibitions against the destructive practice of ballast dumping at Winchelsea: the proposal itself described the measure as 'too little several centuries too late'.[4]

Having relied primarily upon its seaborne trade (*see* Chapter 2 above), the town now entered its final phase of decline. With the loss of its harbour, the merchants and fishermen moved away. It is no coincidence that the 16th century was neighbouring Rye's period of greatest prosperity, for, being located further down the estuary, it was at that time unaffected by the silting. This reversal of fortunes was graphically illustrated by Mayhew who used the Port of Chichester's customs returns for the period 1489-1560 and pointed out that:

> '. . . the customs revenues from [Winchelsea], which, during the early years of Henry VII's reign, was still the predominant trading centre among the Sussex ports, had declined to almost nothing by 1550. The same period saw Rye's rise to pre-eminence amongst the coastal towns included under the jurisdiction of the customs officials of the Port of Chichester (all ports between Folkestone and Chichester). The combined share of trade of the two towns situated on the Camber (77.2 per cent of the revenues of the Port of Chichester in 1489/90, 76.5 per cent in 1549/50 [*recte* 1548/49]) remained remarkably constant during this period of transformation.'.[5]

If, as seems likely, the customs returns are a true

Year	Winchelsea Value £ s d	Winchelsea %	Rye Value £ s d	Rye %	All Other Ports Value £ s d	All Other Ports %
1489/90	69 10 10¾	60	19 19 6	17	26 10 9¾	23
1490/91	88 16 7¾	65	12 8 1¾	9	34 19 11¼	26
1513/14	46 4 2¼	41	44 9 8¼	39	21 12 1½	20
1528/29	51 12 3¼	13	206 10 10¾	51	146 9 4¾	36
1531/32	18 15 2¾	5	243 2 1	64	120 18 10¼	31
1537/38	31 8 9½	13	130 14 5¾	54	78 10 9¾	33
1538/39	17 1 4¼	7	103 5 7½	41	128 16 0¾	52
1543/44	22 14 1	18	64 6 2½	51	37 13 9	31
1545/46	12 19 5½	7	113 19 3¼	65	48 10 1½	28
1548/49	10 16 3¾	9	80 19 0½	67	28 4 9¼	24
1549/50	1 4 9	1	96 14 6	59	66 11 11	40
1559/60	1 5 5	-	573 1 7	92	46 15 7¾	8

Based upon Mayhew 1987, Table 36.
Sources: *PRO E122/35/7-8; E122/36/1,7,10,13; E122/37/3-4; E122/38/11,13.*

Fig. 3.1
Changes in the amounts of customs revenues paid by Winchelsea, Rye and the other ports under the jurisdiction of the customs officials of the Port of Chichester, 1489-1560.

reflection of economic activity at the port, it was during the 40 years between 1490 and *c.*1530 that the rapid decline occurred. The town's percentage contribution to the Port of Chichester's revenues dropped from a healthy 65 per cent in 1490/91, to 41 per cent in 1513/14, 13 per cent in 1528/9, and just 5 per cent by 1531/2. In 1490/1 Winchelsea's customs revenues had been seven times those of Rye, but by 1513/14 the revenues from both ports were equal. By 1528/9 Winchelsea's figures had fallen to a quarter those of Rye, and by 1531/2 they were a meagre thirteenth of Rye's total (*see* Figure 3.1). A further indication of this shift in the balance of economic activity is to be seen in the lay subsidy returns of 1524, which record no fewer than 32 foreigners taxed within Rye, but only 18 in Winchelsea. Even Hastings, by then a minor port, had 21 resident foreigners.[6]

Given the picture depicted by the customs returns, it is hardly surprising that already during the first 30 years of the 16th century, decay was making itself felt within the town centre in the form of vacant plots and unoccupied and derelict houses. The attrition rate accelerated as the century passed (*see* Chapters 8 and 10). The town's much reduced circumstances are illustrated by a benevolence return made in 1545 for the eastern Sussex ports. Of the five ports included, only at Pevensey and Seaford did fewer people contribute. Both in terms of the number of people paying and the total sum given, Winchelsea's contribution was a fraction that of Rye's (Figure 3.2).[7] The major decline of the early/mid-16th century is reflected in other ways too. In 1541 the parishes of St Giles and St Thomas were amalgamated and in 1548 the Corporation was so impoverished that it was forced to sell both the 'great chalice' and the bells of the 'great cross' in order to defray debts.[8] In 1563, in an attempt to stem the tide of house demolitions, an order was issued forbidding materials from any buildings within the town from being removed from the Liberty. Yet already during the same year the Corporation had granted a licence for a house to be taken down and transported to Udimore and subsequently the granting of licences to remove building materials or to demolish buildings became common.[9]

By 1565 only 109 inhabited houses remained[10] and in 1570 the Corporation admitted the 'poor and most lamentable state' of the town. Even so, when the Queen was entertained there three years later, she referred to Winchelsea as a 'Little London'. Demolitions evidently continued apace during the late 1560s and early 1570s, for by 1575 the number of inhabited houses was reported to be not above 60 – 'and those, for the most part, poorly peopled: all which happened by reason of the sea having forsaken the town'.[11] The situation had become such that loans were sought to bring the decayed state before Parliament, and in a vain attempt to reverse the trend, in 1576 a decree was issued requiring all future freeman to

Port	Total contribution (£. s. d.)	No. of people contributing
Hastings	£67 7s. 8d.	48
Pevensey	£34 4s. 0d.	18
Seaford	£10 4s. 2d.	5
Winchelsea Castle	£12 16s. 4d.	13
Winchelsea	£54 5s. 8d.	25
Rye	£338 6s. 0d.	122

Source: PRO *E179/190/200.*
Winchelsea Castle = Henry VIII's artillery fort at Camber (Camber Castle).

Fig. 3.2
Return of a benevolence from ports in eastern Sussex, 1545.

invest in merchant shipping or in the fishery 'to prevent the complete decay of the maritime trade of Winchelsea'.[12] The following year only 120 able-bodied men were reported to be within the town.[13]

As with the 1548 Act prohibiting the dumping of ballast within the harbour, the Corporation's efforts to encourage maritime trade in 1576 appears to have been rather late, for in their returns made 15 years earlier in 1561, they had stated that there were then no ships, boats or crayers based at Winchelsea, and but four mariners resident within the town.[14] Neither did their initiative bear fruit, for by 1587 there were no ships, captains or mariners, and only one sailor.[15] Iron, however, was still being shipped through Winchelsea from the Wealden ironworks in 1581, and as late as 1595, 20 tons of iron were shipped from the town to London in the *Mayflower* of Hastings.[16]

During the 1570s and 1580s the church of St Thomas was recorded as becoming ruinous. The Corporation was forced to raise funds to help with its repair and in 1589, the jurats accepted that from then on, only two Hundred Courts would be held each year, owing to the 'decay of the town'.[17] A visitation made in 1603 reported 180 communicants, suggesting that the number of households had at that time dropped little, if at all, since 1575, but a tax raised on 'all the habitants of Winchelsea' in 1619 lists only 72 resident heads of households. They paid, according to ability, from £2.0s.0d. to as little as 2d.[18]

The mid- to late 17th century saw no improvement, perhaps even a further worsening of the town's plight. A description made in 1652 referred to it as 'all in rubbish and [only] a few despicable hovels and cottages standing'; another late-17th-century commentator described it as 'a pitiful spectacle of poverty and desertion'. Both may have been exaggerated for dramatic effect, but probably not by very much, for by 1676 there were just 91 communicants within the town, probably living within 30 or so houses.[19] Despite this, the late-16th- and 17th-century Corporation records show a high proportion of gentlemen living within the town, perhaps attracted there by its ancient privileges and tax exemptions.

Even though Winchelsea was nothing more than a village by the 17th century, it still retained its two parliamentary seats. Throughout that century at least one of the candidates were nominated by the Lord Warden of the Cinque Ports, and by 1700 the borough had fallen completely under Treasury patronage. During the middle years of the 18th century certain MPs encouraged would-be nominees to invest in property around the town. Two such nominees were William Belchier and Albert Nesbitt. Belchier, a London banker, acquired the Winchelsea estate of John Caryll which included the manor of Iham and some 939 acres of land, of which 68 acres were located within the town itself. Nesbitt, a London merchant, was a friend and relation of the Pelham family and, under their encouragement, he built up a small estate prior to his unexpected death in 1753. The following year the Prime Minister, Henry Pelham, insisted that Albert's nephew, Arnold Nesbitt, stand in opposition to Belchier. Nesbitt was the successful candidate, and over the years that followed he built up a sizable local estate.

The Belchier/Nesbitt rivalry brought about a small revival in Winchelsea's fortunes. Belchier built at least four new dwellings in order to house his principal voting tenants. Nesbitt's activities were more significant. In 1761 he, with other promoters, set up within the town a manufactory for cambric. Two years later this was incorporated under the title of 'The English Linen Company'. The industry was supervised by two Frenchmen.[20] Nesbitt and his partners converted some existing houses and built a number of new dwellings to accommodate the workmen. The Nesbitt survey of 1767 lists 22 'manufactory houses' at that date, including one new block of five and another new block of fifteen.[21] When in Winchelsea, Nesbitt himself occupied Periteau House, a former merchant's capital messuage located on the southwestern corner of Quarter 7. Cambric manufacture was later replaced by Italian crape. The industry survived the financial difficulties of various of its proprietors (including Nesbitt) and continued until 1810, when it moved to Norwich. For a long time it was the principal occupation of Winchelsea's residents.

The town was by this period once more growing. The number of houses shown in the maps of the town made in 1758 and 1763, prior to the construction of the new Manufactory houses, was between 49 and 52. By the 1801 census there were 105 inhabited dwellings occupied by 123 families, but it should be stressed that the percentage increase at Winchelsea was no greater than within most local parishes at this time. The number of houses continued to increase over the next 40 years. However, the effects of the loss of the linen industry, and of the Napoleonic barracks which succeeded them, is well illustrated by the 1841 return: it records only 106 inhabited houses. A further 22 were uninhabited and there were none under construction.[22]

St Thomas's is still an ecclesiastical parish, but in 1896 for all civil purposes the town became a ward within the newly constituted civil parish of Icklesham.[23] Despite further development during the second half of the 20th century, Winchelsea remains, in effect, a small village restricted to the northeastern corner of the original site. In deference to its past importance, it has been allowed to retain its mayor and jurats for ceremonial purposes.

4. THE TOWN'S HISTORIC INFRASTRUCTURE

David Martin

Having set the scene regarding the landscape within which the doomed town of (Old) Winchelsea stood, together with that of the hill of Iham on the eve of its transformation into a major port town, and having examined the economic fortunes of the town - both good and bad - it is time to consider the fabric of the town itself. Arguably, after the physical landscape of the site the most important feature in shaping the character of any town is its infrastructure: the access routes linking it to its surrounding hinterland, its streets, markets, open spaces and, in the case of a port like Winchelsea, the form of its waterfront and associated quays. The basic skeleton which Edward's commissioners set out in the 1280s has formed the framework for the town down to the present day, although inevitably there have been considerable modifications within the parts which were later abandoned. It is this infrastructure, and the ways in which it has been adapted which will be addressed here.

As Jill Eddison pointed out (Chapter 1), the site selected by Edward for the new town was in many ways an obvious choice: a relatively flat-topped hill formed by a spur which projects almost a mile (1.6km.) northwards into the marshlands from the end of the Icklesham ridge. Being on the edge of the navigable Brede estuary, approximately 3 miles (5km.) to the west of (Old) Winchelsea, the hill must have seemed almost perfect as a replacement site for the doomed town. The hill is roughly triangular in plan with its long axis aligned north-south and the somewhat blunted point of the triangle to the south. At just under 40 metres (130ft.) O.D., the highest ground is on the north, from which the land slopes down gently to approximately 10 metres (30ft.) O.D. at the extreme southern end where a narrow spur projects westwards to join the hill to the main upland ridge. On its northern, eastern and southern sides the hill is flanked by steep, partially degraded cliffs, but along the western side the slope is more gentle. The estuary of the River Brede - which served as the town's harbour, but which is now no more than a narrow river channel - flows eastwards, beneath the northern cliffs, before turning north towards Rye.

ACCESS FROM THE SURROUNDING HINTERLAND *(Figure 4.1)*

Even those ports which served principally as an entrepôt for goods intended for transshipment needed good road connections with their hinterland. Winchelsea's immediate hinterland was always small. To the east the river estuary effectively barred everyday trade with the extensive flatlands of Romney Marsh, which were in any case amply served by the port towns of New Romney and Hythe. To the north the River Brede formed an inconvenient barrier between the town and the upland ridges which connect to the heavily wooded High Weald, with the result that the settlements in that area tended to look to Rye, Winchelsea's near neighbour, for day-to-day trading. Winchelsea's primary hinterland was therefore to the southwest, where land routes linked to the villages of Icklesham, Guestling, Pett, Fairlight and beyond. Yet even in this direction, the port town of Hastings, only 8 miles (13km.) distant to the southwest must always have been a serious rival. It is true that because of Winchelsea's much greater size and importance in comparison to its neighbours, during the late 13th and 14th centuries it fulfilled the role of regional centre, despite its more difficult access routes. For instance, throughout this period the great Benedictine abbey at Battle regarded Winchelsea as its primary trading partner, and this was probably true of secular lords too. Certainly, the locally influential Etchingham family maintained close ties with the town during the late 13th and early 14th centuries and one younger son married the daughter of a Winchelsea merchant. Because of its large population, Winchelsea would have been the

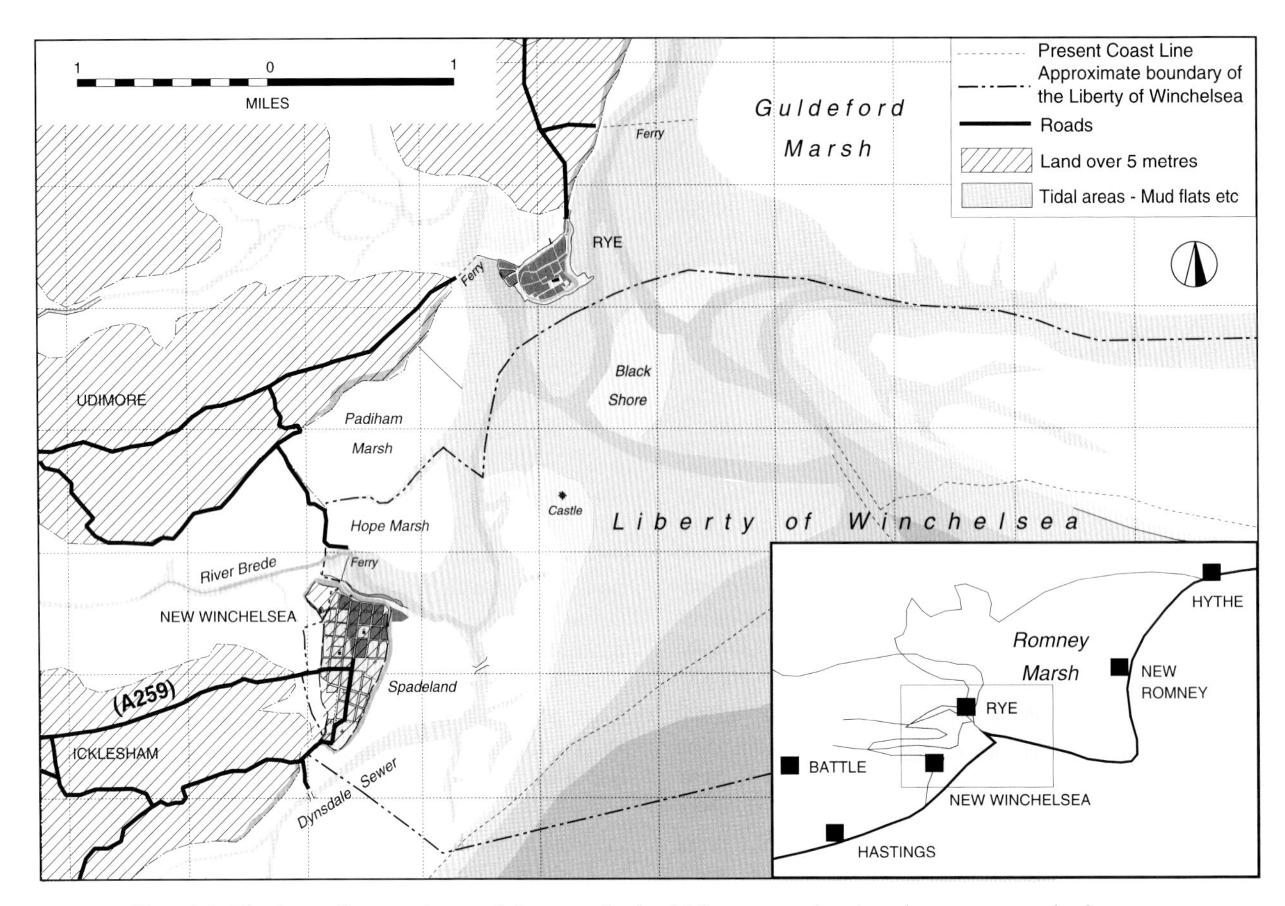

Fig. 4.1 The immediate environs of the town in the 16th century showing the access roads, ferry etc. (With an inset showing Hastings, Rye, New Romney and Hythe).

natural choice for the disposal of agricultural surpluses.

Given the natural barrier caused by the river estuary to the east and north, there were only two overland routes to the town. The principal route survives today as the A259. It drops gently down the end of a low ridge from Icklesham to the west before crossing a narrow inlet of marshland to reach the hill. Whether this route existed prior to the laying out of the town in the 1280s is unclear: if not, then it must have been constructed at that time, for the town's grid of streets was purposely designed to be entered from it. Its earliest specific mention is in an extent of the boundaries of the Liberty of Winchelsea compiled in 1330.[1] The present road crosses the marsh slightly to the south of a raised embankment visible in the field to the north, running parallel to the road. It has been suggested that this carried the highway, though it is equally possible that the embankment represents a sea defence constructed to prevent high tides from running up St Leonard's Creek to the north and overrunning the road (see Figure 4.2). Two service trenches cut through the embankment during the middle years of the 20th century failed to reveal signs of metalling, though a metalled surface was found buried 2.30 metres (7ft.6ins.) below the present road, some 750 millimetres (2ft.6ins.) below the surface of the adjacent marsh at this point.[2]

The second, less important overland route entered the town through New Gate in the extreme south. It linked Winchelsea by a narrow winding lane to the villages of Pett and Fairlight to the southwest. The lane crossed the town dyke by bridge immediately in front of New Gate. This bridge has now been replaced by an earth embankment, though its slight remains are still visible today.

A reference to the construction of a bridge and causeway beneath the town for the passage of the king and the carts of his army in 1292/3 probably relates to nothing more major than the formation of a way across salt marshes and across an inlet beside the Brede estuary. If not, then the bridge was short-lived, for until as late as the mid-17th century access to the town and quay from the Brede/Udimore ridge to the north, and from the neighbouring port town of Rye 2 miles (3km.) to the northeast was by ferry across the River Brede at the point where it met the estuary, approximately 100 metres (300ft.) north of the hill. This ferry was a perquisite of the Abbey of Fécamp's manor of Brede and was therefore probably of greater antiquity than the new town itself, having originally served the small Fécamp township of Iham.[3] The original access to the ferry was by a trackway which curved in an arc northwards around the edge of the estuary before turning eastwards along a spit of slightly higher ground (see Figure 4.2). The crossing point itself may have migrated eastwards over time as the spit of higher ground extended into the estuary, but the site became fixed following the construction of a straight causeway running northwards across the salt flats from the bottom of the hill leading down from Pipewell Gate. The stone-built Ferry House survives. The ferry itself was still in use in the 1640s, but appears to have been replaced by a bridge when a sluice was constructed there in 1658. Certainly, a toll bridge had replaced it by 1758, though confusingly this bridge continued to be called *The Ferry* as late as the mid-19th century. The present bridge is modern.[4]

Until at least the mid-17th century the ferry remained the only route from Winchelsea to Rye without taking a boat down the estuary, but by 1758, with the continued inning of the salts and mud flats, an alternative overland route had been established running eastwards from the Strand across the marshes.[5] Late-18th-century maps suggest that this cross-marsh track ran along the southern wall of the River Brede and crossed the river, either by bridge or ferry, some distance from the town. It was only when the Royal Military Canal was dug between 1804 and 1809 that the associated Royal Military Road gave a direct and well-maintained connection between the two towns. Construction of the canal and road included a new bridge near the Strand, taking the Royal Military Road over the river.

Throughout the medieval and post-medieval periods salts and fresh marshes extended south-eastwards from New Winchelsea, between the Brede estuary and the sea. It was upon the shingle barrier which formerly separated these marshes from the sea that (Old) Winchelsea had stood. Some of the marshland was inundated when the old town was destroyed and more was to follow during the ensuing century. Even so, throughout the 14th and 15th centuries marshland in this area continued to be owned and used by residents of Winchelsea, and thus regular access to it was required from the town. This meant not only crossing the town dyke, but also a more serious obstacle in the form of the Dynsdale Sewer, a tidal creek which joined the Brede estuary some 300 metres (1000ft.) to the east of the town. Those parts of the marsh which lay beyond the Dynsdale Sewer and had escaped inundation by the sea were probably concentrated to the southeast of the town, and thus the Dynsdale was probably crossed by a bridge sited well up the creek, to the south of New Gate. Certainly, a bridge had existed here before the town was founded, allowing the highway from Iham to the old town to cross, and there was still a bridge here in the post-medieval period.

During the 14th and 15th centuries a new shingle spit developed between the sea and the River Brede, to the east of the Dynsdale Sewer. On those occasions during the medieval period when access to this was required it is likely that the mouth of the creek was crossed by boat. However, around 1500 the Guldeford family, then the lords of Iham Manor, constructed a defensive tower (later incorporated into Camber Castle) on the headland at the end of this spit in order to protect the estuary and harbour better. As a result, access to the headland was required on a more regular basis (see Chapter 5). It is known that from 1528 a bridge crossed the mouth of the Dynsdale Sewer, for in that year a contractor was paid extra because the new bridge he had built measured 340 feet (103.65m.) long, 100 feet (30.50m.) longer than stated in the contract. The fact that the required length of the bridge was unknown until built perhaps implies that it did not replace a predecessor. It was reached from Fishers' Dock at the Strand via a footpath across the salts (*see* Figure 4.15). This bridge was itself rebuilt in 1577.[6]

GENERAL LAYOUT OF THE TOWN

As refounded upon its new site, Winchelsea is a textbook example of a town laid out on a grand scale using a grid system of north-south and east-west streets to form a net of roughly rectangular blocks or insulae (Figure 4.2). From the outset these were known as 'quarters' and were identified by numbers. The quarter numbers commence in the northeastern corner and progress across the town from east to west, returning at the end of each pass to the eastern end of the next strip south, finishing with Quarter 39 at the New Gate in the extreme south of the town, approximately 1 mile (1.6km.) in distance from the Quay to the north. At the other well-known new town based on a grid-system - Salisbury, founded *c.*1220 - the quarters were named, mostly after inns or hostelries. In Winchelsea, however, with the exception of Quarter 7 (known in the 18th century as Bear Square) the quarter numbers remained in general use into the 18th century, and, for some purposes, beyond. Numbers were never allocated to the quarters occupied by St Thomas' church, the precinct of the Grey Friars, and the Monday Market, nor to the small open spaces or greens on the periphery. These were instead identified by name.

The number of medieval towns recognized as laid out on a grid is increasing and some of these grids, such as that at the southern end of the nearby Old Town, Hastings, appear to predate Winchelsea by at least 200 years. Despite this, perhaps because of its grand scale, Winchelsea remains the most commonly illustrated example. Most of the illustrations - such as that reproduced by Beresford in his seminal work, *New Towns*

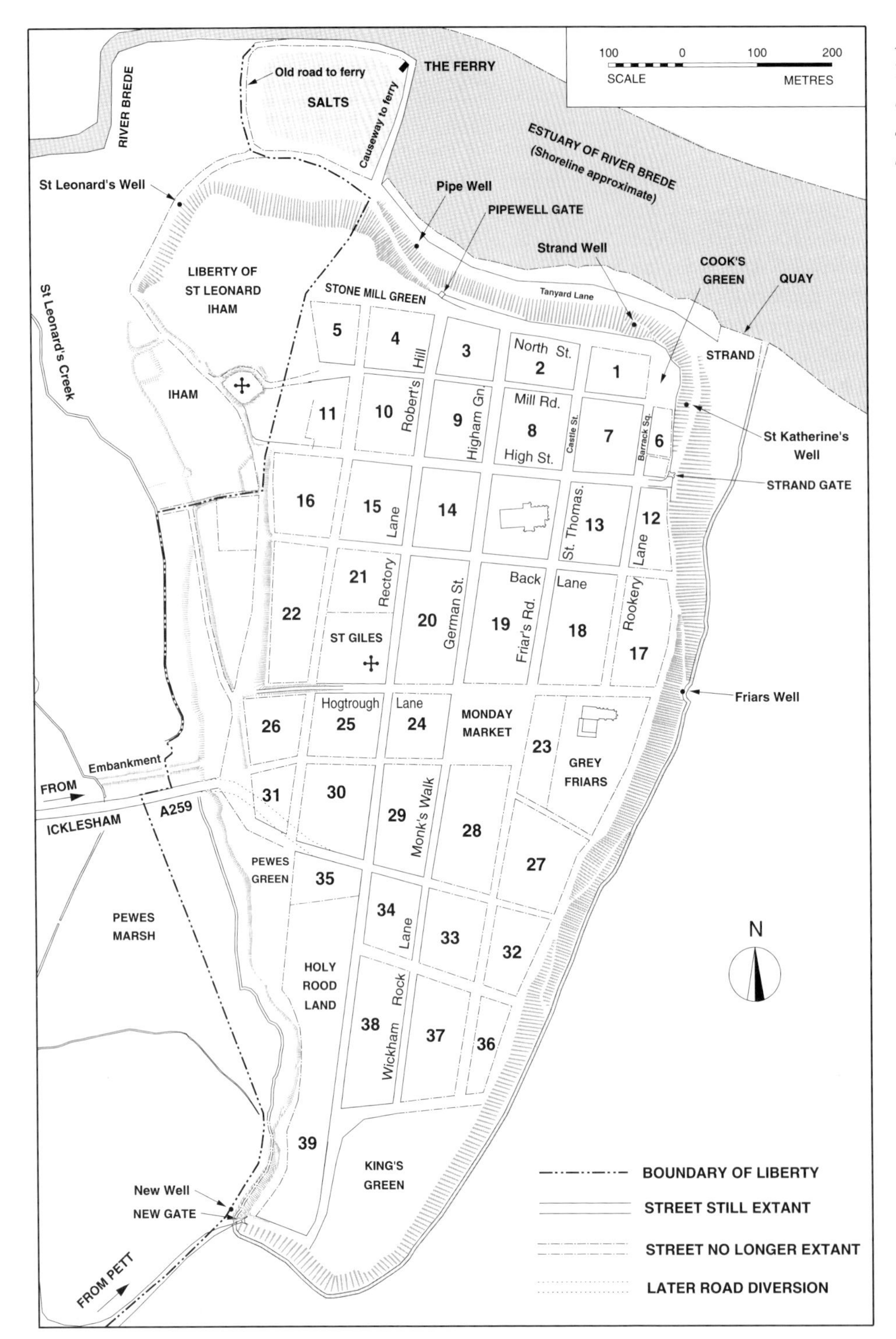

Fig. 4.2
The town as laid out in the late 13th century. The street names shown are the modern names.

of the Middle Ages, are simplified versions of the detailed reconstruction published by William MacLean Homan in 1949. This reconstruction, based upon an analysis of the 1292 foundation rental is a masterly piece of work and has stood the test of time well. However, some later documents of considerable significance were not available to Homan and these, together with the results of recent earthwork surveys, show that a few important details in his plan are incorrect, although his basic thesis remains sound. The plans of the town included within this present volume have been adjusted to correct the known errors.[7]

THE STREETS

One of the most impressive features of Winchelsea as initially laid out is its spaciousness,

Fig. 4.3 Barrack Square looking north. A typical Winchelsea street showing the spaciousness of the town. This street had a medium-width of 2½ virgae.

particularly with regard to the width of its streets (Figure 4.3). As Homan pointed out, the original width of the streets varied, depending upon their perceived importance. He noted that 'the streets running east-west appear to have been 2 *virgae* (33ft. or 10m.) or less wide except those on either side of St Thomas' churchyard [*recte* the street on the north side of the church only] which seem for part of their length to be 2½ *virgae* (41ft.3ins. or 12.6 m.) wide'. The north-south streets which passed immediately to the east and west of the churchyard and market square were evidently considered the most important and were each 3 *virgae* (49ft.6ins. or 15.1m.) wide, whereas the others running in this direction were 2½ *virgae* (41ft.3ins. or 12.6m.).[8]

As Figure 4.2 shows, the streets forming the grid are not laid out at right angles to one another, and, although all the north-south streets are parallel, there is some variation in the east-west alignments. The principal point of contact and exchange between the townsfolk and the rural hinterland was the market. It is therefore perhaps not surprising that the town's market square occupied a site in the central area of the hill, in line with the principal overland road from Icklesham. Whereas the two east-west streets flanking the market square are aligned almost true east-west, those to the north and south are swung slightly south-south-eastwards. This variation is more pronounced to the south of the market square than to the north. It is possible that the orientation of the two streets to the south of the market was purposely canted in order to ease access to this part of town from the main overland route from Icklesham to the west and it is surely no coincidence that the southern boundary of Quarter 31 is kinked to make a better link between the more northern of the two streets and the Icklesham road. It is perhaps even more significant that the section of street to the north, running between Quarters 26 and 31, is likewise deliberately kinked so as to guide incoming overland travellers up to the market square.

If, as seems likely, this was the objective, it failed. This particular section of street was exceptionally steep. The limited degree of erosion indicates that it was little used. Most people heading for the market during the town's greatest prosperity in the early 14th century evidently chose the slightly less direct, but more gradual climb onto the hill. That way they rose gently along the western side of Quarter 26 before turning abruptly into Fifth Street, skirting along the northern sides of Quarters 26 to 24 and entering the market square at its

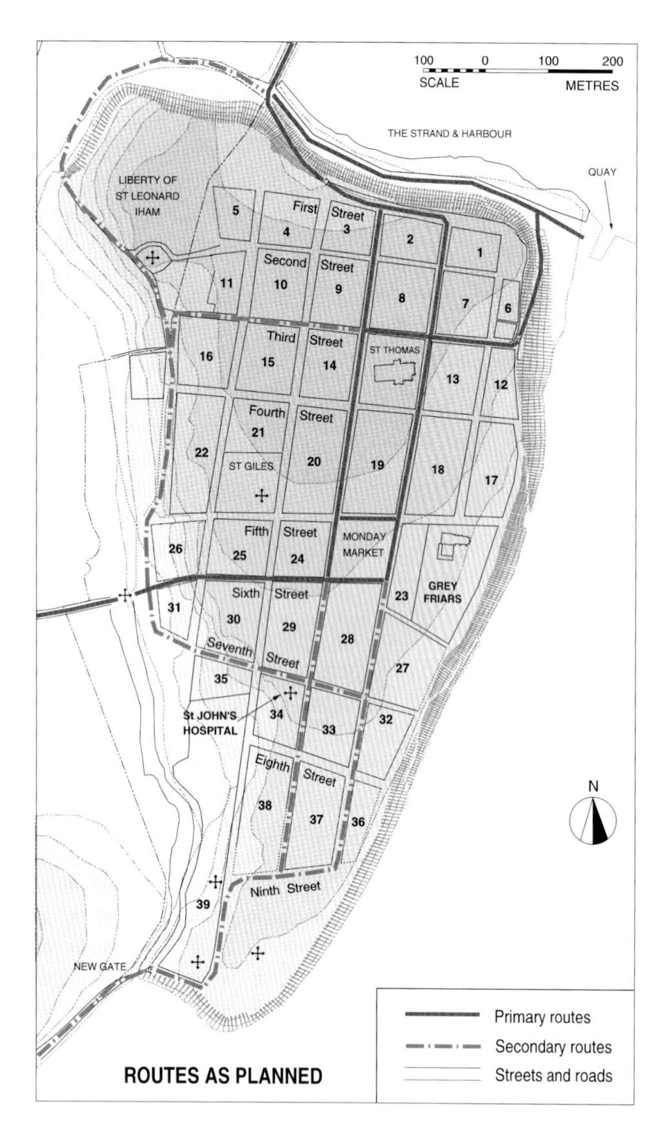

Fig. 4.4
Primary streets within the town as planned.

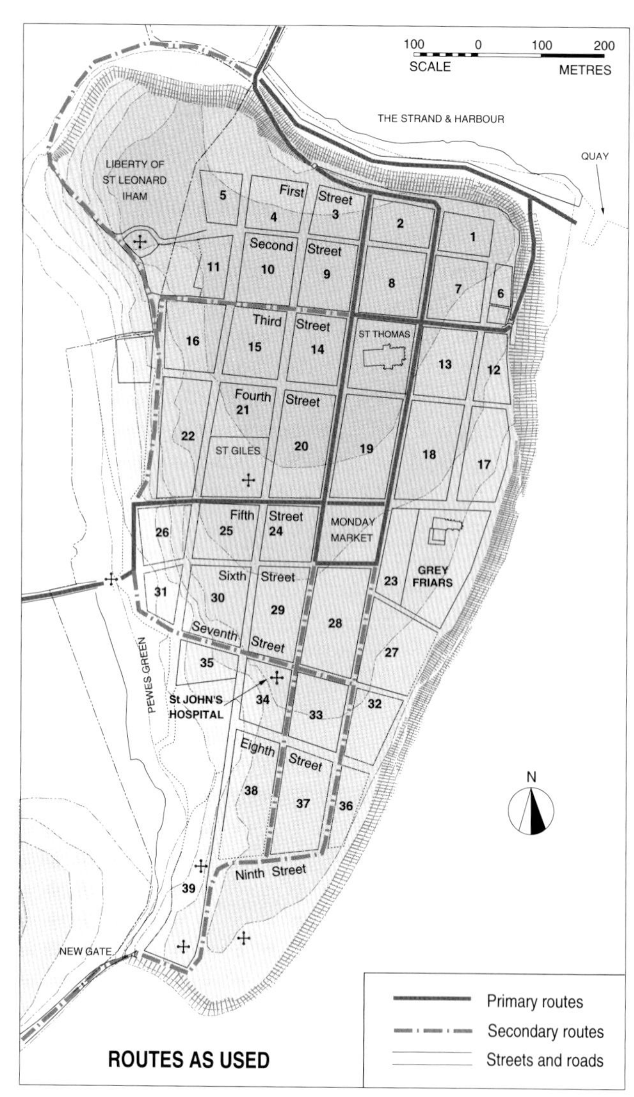

Fig. 4.5 Primary streets within the town at the height of its prosperity.

northwestern, rather than its southwestern corner (compare Figures 4.4 and 4.5). Even using this less direct route, the climb was only made tolerable by cutting the western part of the street deeply into natural rock, by over 2.5 metres (8ft.) in places, effectively interrupting north-south traffic passing along the western side of St Giles' churchyard and beyond. Where the street was deeply sunken into the cutting its width was reduced to just 2.5-3.0 metres (8ft.–9ft.9ins.), leaving ample room on either side for the north-south streets to turn and flank the cutting as an elevated lane. No doubt some incoming travellers heading for the market from Icklesham chose the even less direct, but much more gentle approach, turning southeastwards along Seventh Street to meet the north-south street from New Gate at St John's Hospital, one block south of the market square. By the early 15th century this had apparently become the preferred route for reaching the market (see below).

A very obvious break in the symmetry of the street layout is caused by the southern edge of the Grey Friars precinct, north of Quarter 27. The street which bounded this side of the precinct is not only offset, but is seriously misaligned when compared to the adjacent streets. The explanation for this is probably due to the fact that the Grey Friars were granted their 4-acre plot just prior to Edward I's formal compulsory purchase of the properties upon the hill. The boundaries are therefore probably historical ones which relate to a pre-foundation field or close. This explains why the Grey Friars site was not acquired by the king when he cleared the hill.[9] Indeed, it is probable that the friars had already started to build before the town was formally laid out. One possible explanation for their apparent impatience to move to their new site is that the friary buildings within the old town were by 1285 already in the process of being destroyed by the sea. If this suggested sequence of events is correct, then the northern and western boundaries of their plot probably influenced the entire grid of the town.

One road upon the hill which certainly predated the foundation of the town and survived in part into the 17th century was the gently curving north-south highway which skirted the western side of the hill. This originally ran northwards from New Gate at the extreme southern end of the site, crossed the Icklesham road at the foot of the hill and skirted the western fringe of the grid system, climbing gently all the time, before passing through the abbey of Fécamp's small township of Little Iham, as it descended once more to run around the base of the northern cliff. The road appears to be identifiable as 'the long street which leads from Iham bridge towards [Old] Winchelsea' mentioned in a deed of *c.*1240 granting to Battle Abbey 1¾ acres 'on the slopes of the hill of Iham'. Battle Abbey's plot was one of those acquired by the king for the new town.[10] Signs of the road's pitched-stone paving are still visible in areas of erosion within Little Iham (see below). Although the existing route of this highway had the effect of determining the western boundary of the town's quarters, it in fact had little influence upon the detailed layout of the grid. This is because, rather than running along the top of the hill slope, the road was positioned part way down it, and thus there is a sizeable bank or lynchet between it and the grid of the planned town. There must presumably have been a second street or lane running along the top of the bank in order to link the western ends of the east-west streets. The plots which abutted the lane are known to have been large and field-like, and thus the high-level lane was probably never of any importance. A similar narrow lane is known to have fringed the eastern edge of the grid, running along the cliff top behind the later town wall.

In addition to serving the ferry which crossed the River Brede to Rye and Udimore, the western highway's northern continuation took it around the foot of the northern cliff, servicing the harbour plots before finally reaching the Strand and the common quay nestling below the northeastern corner of the town. From the highway two terraced roads, known historically as *Pipewell Causeway* and *Strand Causeway* (otherwise *Watchbell Causeway*), climbed diagonally up the degraded cliff from the harbour to the planned town. Three other lesser terraced trackways climbed the eastern cliff, giving access between the town and the wells at the foot of the cliff and beyond to the fresh marshes.

From the late 14th century onwards the town declined and contracted. As a result, the relative importance of some streets changed (Figure 4.6). Thus, as the southern end of the site became less densely populated, and with the eventual abandonment in the 16th century of the main market square in favour of a new site near St Thomas' church, the north-south streets flanking

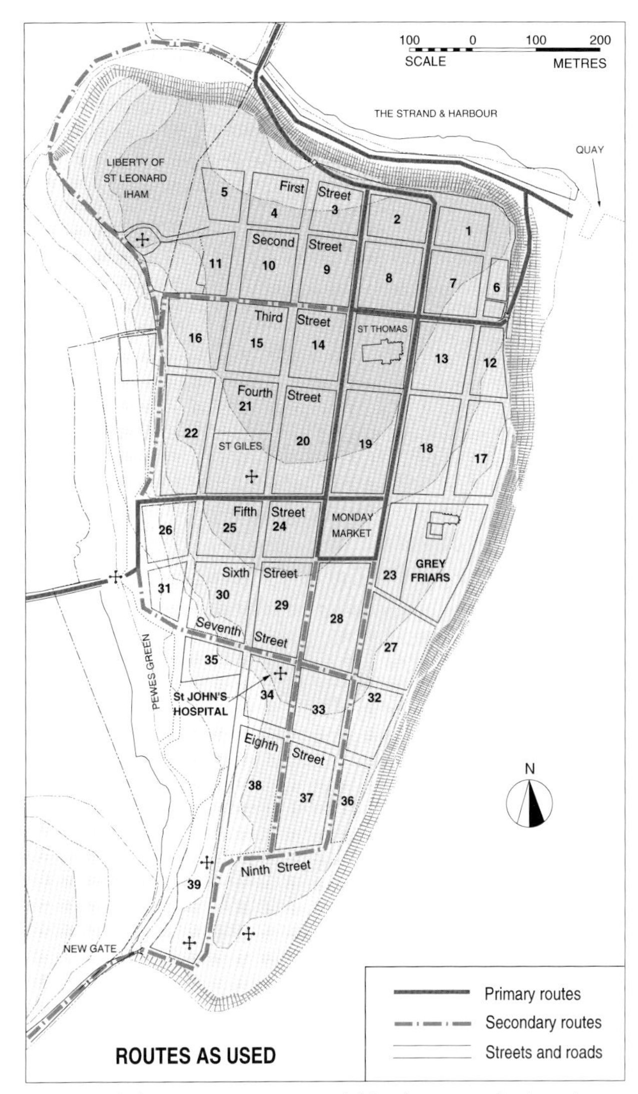

Fig. 4.6 Primary streets within the town during the 15th and 16th centuries.

the eastern and western sides of the church and market square became less important. The eastern half of Third Street (present-day High Street), entering the town from the harbour via Strand Gate, had always been one of the main streets within the town. By the 15th century this street had become the focal point of the contracted settlement. Already by 1415, when it was planned to reduce the circuit of the town wall dramatically, it was proposed that the western end of this street should be protected by a new town gate. At that time the market square still remained in use for both markets and fairs, even though it was then peripheral to the built-up area. Significantly, it was not proposed to build a new gate through the wall at the point where Fifth Street, leading up to the northwestern corner of the market from Icklesham and beyond crossed the wall. Instead, this street was to be blocked off.[11] Furthermore, Sixth Street, leading to the southwestern corner of the market square was to be totally destroyed by the ditch in front of the new wall. The implication of this must be that already by this date most traffic entering the town was either climbing to St John's Hospital and turning north up to the market, or continuing along the highway flanking the western side of the town and climbing gently onto the hill before turning eastwards into what is today the abandoned western end of High Street (*see* Figure 4.6). Once established as the principal route into town, the western approach into High Street remained dominant throughout the 15th and 16th centuries. However, not all traffic using the western approach bothered to enter the town centre. As in earlier times, it was possible to continue along the western street without turning, and to pass through Iham and down into the marsh to the ferry and harbour, thereby bypassing Winchelsea altogether. This route was still usable as late as 1583, in which year it was used by Lord Cobham to avoid riding through the town, much to the annoyance of the awaiting town dignitaries.[12]

It was only during the 17th or early 18th century that the western route into town finally went out of use in favour of the present more indirect approach from Icklesham, which climbs steeply onto the hill without turning northwards until reaching the remains of St John's Hospital. The establishing of this new overland route into Winchelsea was accompanied and perhaps influenced by improvements to the alignment of the road as it climbed Gallows Hill (compare Figures. 4.6 and 4.7). In the mid-20th century the line of the A259 was diverted along Rectory Lane and down the hill via Pipewell Causeway, effectively bypassing Winchelsea.

By the time the earliest detailed plans of the town were drawn in 1758 and 1763 the present much reduced street system was in place, the only street to have been lost since that date is that extending along the southern side of Quarter 18, to the north of the Grey Friars.[13] Surprisingly, despite the contraction of the town during the late 14th and 15th centuries, the entire late-13th-century street system still survived intact in the middle years of the 16th century.[14] It was only during the late 16th and 17th centuries that many of the redundant streets occupying the by then long-abandoned southern and western parts of the grid were sold off by the town and subsequently merged into adjacent fields.[15] The alignments of some are marked by field boundaries on the 1758 and 1763 town maps, whilst most of the lost streets are today still evidenced by earthworks (*see* Figures 4.7 and 4.8).

Most of the surviving documents identify the location of individual properties within the town by reference to the quarter number upon which they are located, and thus there are few references to street names. In the foundation rental the eight east-west streets are simply referred to as First Street, Second Street, Third

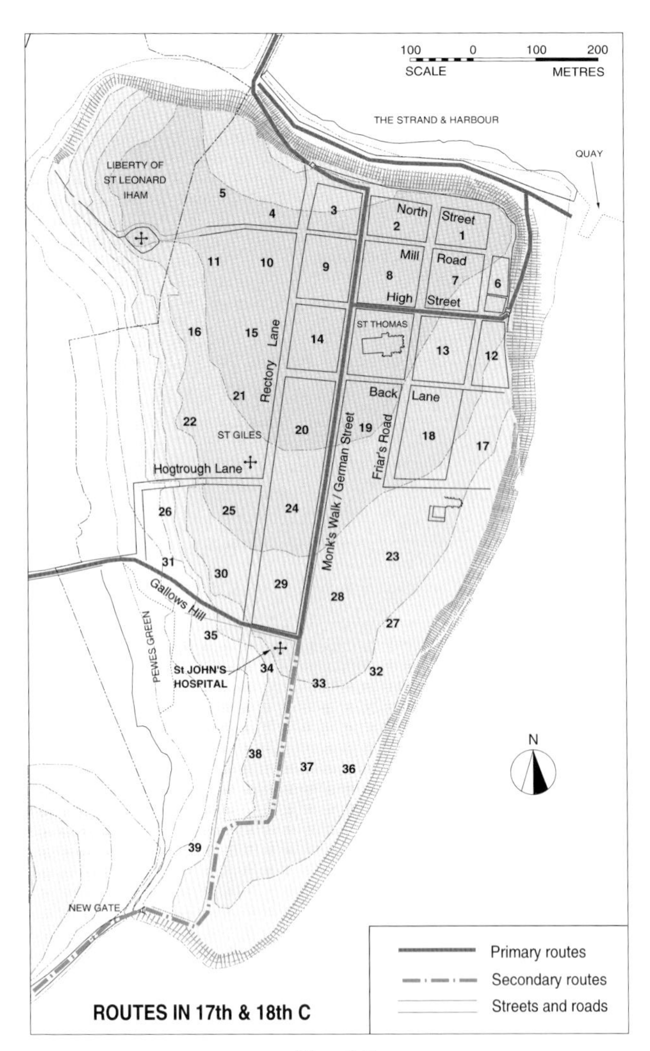

Fig. 4.7
The relative importance of the streets during the post-medieval period.

Street and so on, working from north to south. The five north-south streets are not specifically referred to. Even the town wall inquiry of 1415 merely identifies the streets by points between which they ran.[16] However, a few 16th-century documents confirm that by that date the streets were known by name. There are references to Fisher Street (present-day Mill Road), Middle Street otherwise High Street (still so called), Great Street otherwise Broad Street (probably the street flanking the western side of St Thomas' Church) and St John's Street (now Monk's Walk). From at least the 15th century present-day Friar's Road was known as Butchery Street otherwise *The Butcheries* and this had probably been the

RIGHT:- Fig. 4.8
Winchelsea in the late 20th century, including extant earthworks (Based upon a survey by RCHME and 25" OS plan - Crown Copyright Ordnance Survey 100021184. All rights reserved)

N
100
0
100
200
SCALE
METRES
RIVER BREDE

case since the town was founded.[17]

It is clear from archaeological excavations that the street levels have not, as Homan thought, risen since medieval times by 3 or 4 feet (0.90 - 1.20m.), but are in the main close to their original level[18]. As in most of our historic towns, what is less certain is the extent to which the streets were paved. A murage grant of 1321 authorized Winchelsea to levy a special custom for seven years for the purpose of enclosing and paving the town, indicating the Corporation's early intention to pave its streets. However, raising money for a cause and carrying it out are two different matters.[19] Assuming that street paving was undertaken during this early period, there remain important questions. Were all streets included or merely the principal thoroughfares? Were they paved for their full width, or merely the margins close into the buildings, leaving a wide, muddy central area where improvements were restricted to tipping rubble into potholes as and when they developed? Were all the paved streets surfaced to the same standard, or did the quality vary markedly according to the importance of the street? What is certain is that, given the town's extensive grid system and the exceptionally generous width of its streets, any paving scheme would have been a major and very expensive undertaking.

There are at present few clues as to the answers to the questions posed above. One obvious method of gleaning extra knowledge would be to carry out watching briefs whenever road works are undertaken within the town, especially those involving drainage or services even where these are sited within adjacent verges. Surprisingly, to date no such watching briefs have been commissioned.

Casual observation of two trenches excavated within High Street failed to detect any indications of earlier road surfaces below the modern tarmac - the surfacing and its subbase was laid directly onto what appeared to be undisturbed clay. Thus, any surfacing which may have existed in these areas had been removed. More informative was a pit excavated within the street at the junction of Back Lane with Rookery Lane where a buried road level was revealed. This was not paved, but instead comprised a relatively thick build-up of soil mixed with much debris. At one point stone rubble had been spread, but the area was quite discrete.[20] That paved surfaces do exist within the town has been demonstrated through archaeological fieldwork, both in the form of observation and excavation. To date three areas of street paving have been recovered through excavation: a small area adjacent to plot 21 on the eastern side of Quarter 15; an area extending down the western side of plot 11 on Quarter 18; and along the western side of the southwestern corner plot (11) on Quarter 19. In all cases the excavations extended only a little distance into the street, and thus the paving may have been restricted to a relatively narrow pavement-like margin. The latter two areas were on streets extending northwards from the market square, very close to the market itself. That adjacent to Quarter 19 mostly comprised relatively large slabs of local, hard-wearing Tilgate stone laid flat (Figure 4.9). At its southern end it incorporated a stone-on-edge kerb, apparently designed to deflect surface water away from the house. The paving adjacent to Quarter 18 likewise ran along a built-up frontage and was of Tilgate stone. In this instance slabs laid flat were mixed in with areas of pitched paving in which smaller stones were laid on edge, aligned across the street (Figure 4.10). The area investigated adjacent to Quarter 15 was too small to give a reliable indication of its nature. None of the areas could be dated.

Two areas of early street surfacing can be observed without the need for archaeological excavation.

Fig. 4.9
Area of street paving in German Street (Quarter 19, Plot 11) excavated in 1974.

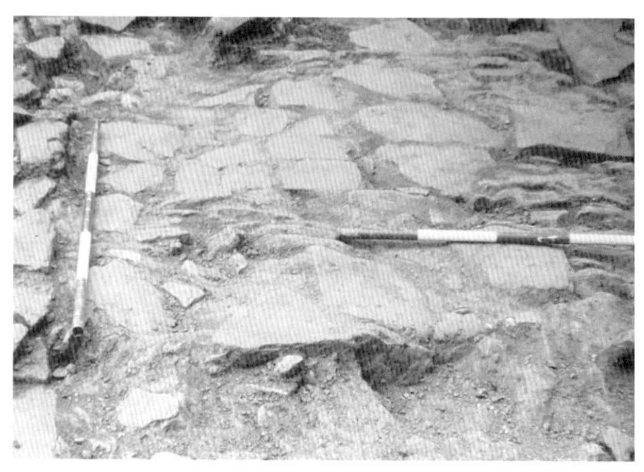

Fig. 4.10
Area of street paving in Friars Road (Quarter 18, Plot 11) excavated in 2003.

Fig. 4.11
An area of pitched paving similar to that which formed the road surface within Pipewell Gate and on the hill leading northwards down from St Leonard's Church, Iham, into the marshes. This example, excavated in 1976 at the rear of Blackfriars Barn, Rectory Lane, is considerably later in date, but very similar in character.

Within one of the town's gates - Pipewell Gate - a small area of paving still survives adjacent to the north wall (see Chapter 5). The second section, paving the street which descended the hill down into the marshes from St Leonard's church, Iham, is more extensive, but more difficult to see. It is visible in the side of a deeply sunken track at the point where it intersects the earlier road and is exposed intermittently over a considerable length. Both are almost exclusively of Tilgate stone pitched on edge so as to give a tightly packed, exceptionally hard-wearing surface (*see* Figure 4.11). It is tempting to suggest that these areas of pitched paving were more typical of the average Winchelsea streets.

Following the town's rapid decline during the first half of the 16th century, keeping its many streets in repair must have been an ever-increasing challenge, and it seems likely that even if the more peripheral streets had once been paved, they were now falling into rapid disrepair. There are indications in the Corporation records that attempts were made to keep the principal streets in the built-up area in some sort of repair. Thus, in 1582 it was ordered that the road leading up to the Watchbell (*i.e.* present-day Strand Gate) should be paved at the Corporation's expense, whilst the owners of property adjoining present-day High Street as far as Watchbell Gate (*i.e.* Strand Gate) were 'to pave the gutter or channel of the street at their own charge'. Seven years later, in 1587, the Corporation ordered that 'the town's drum used for calling out the people for the repairing of highways' should be recovered from a named townsman, perhaps indicating that repairs were then imminent.[21]

MARKETS

When the town was refounded it was agreed that the barons should be allowed to 'hold a fair to last 15 days at the feast of the Holy Cross (in May) and a Market three days a week, as it was in [Old] Winchelsea, and also a fair at St Andrew's Day to last seven days'. By at least 1415 the main market area of the town was known as Monday Market (or Mondays Market). In that year an inquiry into the line of the proposed new town wall found that the mayor and commonalty of the town had 'in their market called "Moondayesmarket" where they hold their market and fair as they have been used to do hitherto' almost 3 acres and that after construction of the new defence just over 2¼ acres would remain, which was considered enough for holding their market and fair.[22] Given the decayed state of the town by that date, and the name then given to the market-place, it is possible that by the early 15th century only one main market was held per week. However, it is possible that from the beginning not all the markets were held in the main market-square. Certainly, in 1565 a daily fish market was held at the Strand and it seems likely that from the outset not only fish, but many other imported bulk commodities were traded here rather than in the main market-square. That Winchelsea maintained a harbour market attended by its residents in the late 13th and 14th centuries is demonstrated by the town's customal (only known from a 16th-century version) which describes the rights of denizens in the sharing of cargoes arriving at the port. This regulation was intended to prevent forestalling and eliminate middlemen who would have raised the prices to the detriment of the residents.[23] The precise location of the quayside market is unknown, though it probably occupied much of the Strand.

In his reconstruction of the town plan Homan shows Monday Market as a street market located within what he considered to be a purposely wide street between Quarters 23-24 and 28-29, but it is now known that this is incorrect. The original market-place occupied an entire 'Quarter' of the town (see Figures 4.2 and 4.12) and, as the town wall inquiry shows, this was still the case in 1415. Subsequently it fell out of use (except perhaps for fairs) and from at least 1583 parts were being let out by the Corporation. In 1608 it was decreed that a bowling-place be made there. A field in the area was still called Monday Market in 1758, but the site was then in private hands and had long ceased to be used for its original purpose, even as a fair ground. Whether there was ever a market hall within Monday Market is not known, though the likelihood must be that there was: certainly there was a market cross, for in 1548 the Corporation sold the bells of the Great Cross in an attempt to defer its debts.[24]

By the late 16th century the market, by then

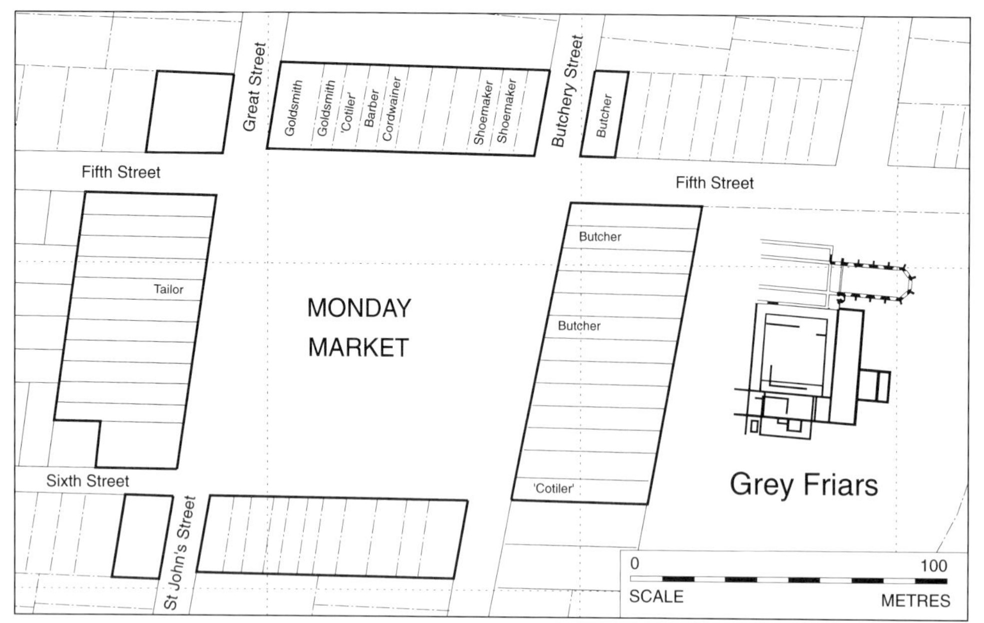

Fig. 4.12 Reconstruction of the market square and the commercial tenements fronting the square, 1292. Trades shown where known.

greatly diminished in size and importance, had evidently moved to the area around St Thomas' church, for in 1584 the town houses at the church gate were converted into a market house, whilst reference is found the following year to the market-place at the church gate. The origin of this move can probably be traced to 1572 when the Corporation decreed that in future a weekly market should be held near the pillory on Friday between the hours of 9 a.m. and 2 p.m. The commons were to be allowed to attend free from arrest, with free standings and no tolls.[25] Whether the decree was an attempt to resurrect a failed market formerly held at Monday Market is unclear, but, if so, it evidently succeeded. The move to the new location was certainly a logical one given that Monday Market was by this date well away from the centre of population and that the Court Hall had already moved near the church (see Chapter 6). A market was still held in the town as late as 1792, though it then took place on Saturdays. It ceased soon afterwards.[26]

THE WATERFRONT AND THE TOWN'S COMMON QUAY

Although sited close to the mouth of the River Brede, New Winchelsea is a river port rather than a coastal port. Its principal anchorage was the well-protected bay which formed the river estuary, between the town and the sea - this it shared with Rye on the opposite side of the estuary. The width of the river estuary under the northern cliffs of the town in the late 13th and 14th centuries is unclear. It was probably still quite wide at this point, but much of the expanse is likely to have been tidal mud flats and salt marsh, overflowed only at high tides. In comparison, the primary navigable channel was perhaps quite narrow. The existence until a late date of the ferry crossing the river at the western (upstream) end of the water frontage may indicate more the need to maintain passage upstream for river traffic than the unbridgeable width of the river, a point which is to some extent reinforced by the site of the ferry terminal some distance from the undercliff road, at the end of a causeway. It is likely that the present exceedingly narrow channel of the Brede still approximately follows the earlier line of the main navigable channel. If so, as figure 4.13 shows, the channel was close in beneath the town at its northeastern corner, but meandered further away towards the west. This would have meant that rather than having continual access to the sea, the private waterfront plots set out along the base of the town's northern cliff may only have been accessible to ships at high tide. The 1292 foundation rental preambles the list of waterfront plots with the introductory note: 'Here are the places delivered for building and rented, under the pendants of the hill on the north side, on the land next to the salt water and perilous at all flowings of the tide'.[27] The need to improve access to this tidal area may have been in the mind of the town's urban elite when, at the foundation, they included amongst their requests to the king that he give assistance in enlarging the harbour.[28] Such an interpretation may also at least partially explain why as early as 1344/5, when few, mostly peripheral, tenements within the town were deserted, 33 of the 79 waterfront plots - over 40% of the total - had been abandoned.[29] Those which remained were grouped in three clusters (Figure 4.13) perhaps reflecting where waterborne access was viable.

Although evidence from the 16th century indicates that some of the harbour plots laid out along the banks of the Brede estuary possessed private wharves and

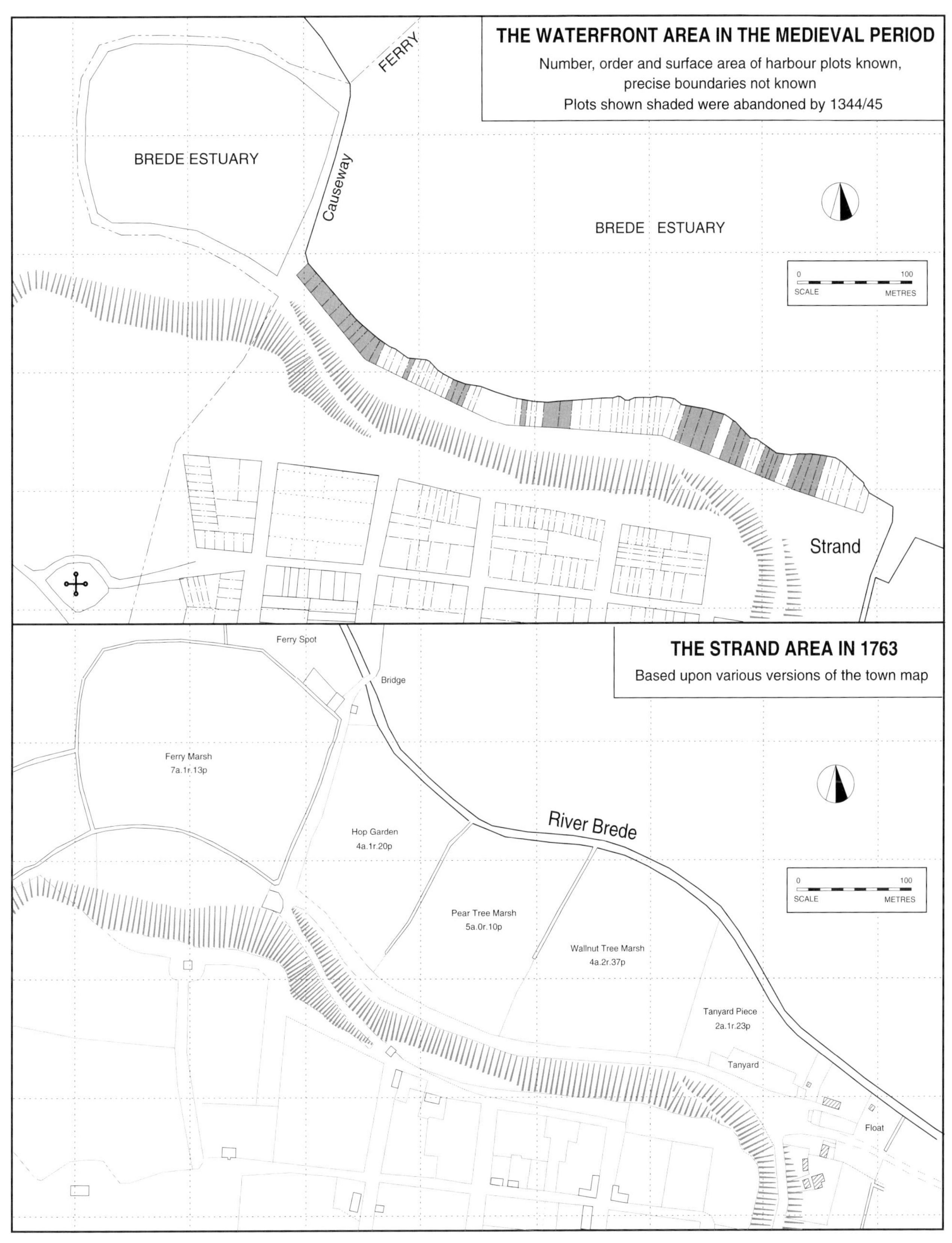

Fig. 4.13
Above: Schematic representation of the waterfront properties laid out in the late 13th century, indicating the degree and pattern of abandonment which had occurred by 1344/5. Below: The same area in 1763.

quays (*see* below) from the outset visiting ships, both English and foreign, would have principally used the town's common quay, and as the private waterfront plots decayed, this would undoubtedly also have been used by resident merchants. Sited near the present Bridge Inn, at the end of the terraced causeway leading down from Strand Gate, the common quay was bounded by the River Brede on the north and the public open space known as the Strand on the south, and was sited at the eastern end of the privately owned waterside plots at the point where the river remains closest to the town. References to the quayside are to be found in the late 13th and early 14th centuries and in 1325 Winchelsea was described as a port where 'on account of its size, several vessels can land at once'.[30] Much later, in 1440, when the town was in decline, an order made regarding shipping at Winchelsea mentions the payment of one penny for every mooring rope fastening a vessel to the common quay. It further states that vessels should lie at the quay only whilst loading or discharging, otherwise wharfage charge would be levied every time the ship was moved.[31] The implication is that, because of the diminished width of the navigable channel, boats moored at the Quay impeded the passage of vessels passing up the river.

It is disappointing that so little is known of the waterfront area prior to the commencement of extant Corporation court records in the mid-16th century. As a result, our best insight of the Strand area comes mainly from the period after a final rapid phase of silting had devastated Winchelsea's seaborne trade and reduced traffic to nothing more than the occasional small river boat. Properties near the quay had been confiscated from foreign beer-makers in 1442 and these were subsequently used by Maline (otherwise Maud) Farncombe to endow a chantry. After the dissolution of the chantries in 1547 these properties fell into the hands of the Corporation, increasing considerably the town-owned lands at the Strand. They included a number of 'shops' - in this context they were almost certainly workshops used for the preparation and storage of goods and the repair and storage of equipment relating to fishing and shipping. Such shops were a common waterfront feature and are mentioned in many 16th- and 17th-century documents relating to the neighbouring ports of Rye and Hastings.[32] Another building present on most waterfronts was a town storehouse in which those using the port stored their goods. Winchelsea was no exception. Its storehouse at the Strand is mentioned a number of times in the Corporation records between 1553 and 1587 and, despite the collapse of the port, was then still in use for its original purpose. For example, in 1578 the Corporation instructed that a valuation be made on a quantity of hops which had 'lain long in the storehouse', whilst in 1584 iron at the storehouse was distrained for the payment of duty. It would appear that soon after 1587 the building may either have been destroyed or, more likely, became derelict, for in 1594 John Vincent requested that a storehouse be built at the Strand, towards the cost of which he was willing to contribute. Evidently this was done, as eight years later the Corporation re-entered the property for non-payment of rent. It was then described as having once been granted to Vincent.[33]

Other documents of the period refer to wasteland at the Strand and to a network of small lanes. There are mid- to late-16th-century references to the Town Dock and to Fisher Quay or Fisher Dock. Indeed, despite the total decay of the harbour, in 1574 a contribution was offered towards a new quay or wharf at the Strand 'when the town sets about it'. Even in 1570 there was at least one house on the waterfront with its own private quay or wharf.[34] Subsequently, the river became so narrow that any boat mooring against its bank would have prevented other traffic from continuing upstream. As a result, the quay degenerated to nothing more than a tidal mooring inlet, known as *The Float*, probably formed within the northern end of the former town dyke. Although infilled, the site was still so called on the 1758 and 1763 town maps.[35]

OTHER OPEN SPACES

In order to form a regular grid upon the irregular hilltop, a number of open spaces were left around the edge of the hill, adjacent to the cliff (Figure 4.14). In addition, a larger area at the southern end of the town ('A' in Figure 4.14) was retained by the king. The southern part of this latter area was given to the Black Friars in 1318 for the foundation of their friary but the remainder became open space and by the 16th century was known as King's Green. By this date the original area of the green had been extended to the northeast to take over abandoned parts of Quarters 32, 36 and 37.[36] Two other open areas - a plot of sloping ground to the north of Holy Cross Hospital ('B' in Figure 4.14) and another area to the north of Quarter 4 ('C' in Figure 4.14) - were granted out during the medieval period to Holy Cross Hospital and Black Friars respectively and were enclosed, but the other areas were regarded as common ground, and were described in the 16th century as Pewes Green, Stonemill Green, King's Green, Cook's Green and Fishers' Green (location of the latter unknown). The uses to which the greens were put is not always clear, though in 1561 Cook's Green, in the northeastern corner of the town, was in use as a bowling green, whilst in 1564 archery butts were set up upon it and in 1583 it was described as a sporting place. During the late 16th and 17th centuries the Corporation sold off the greens and they became enclosed.[37]

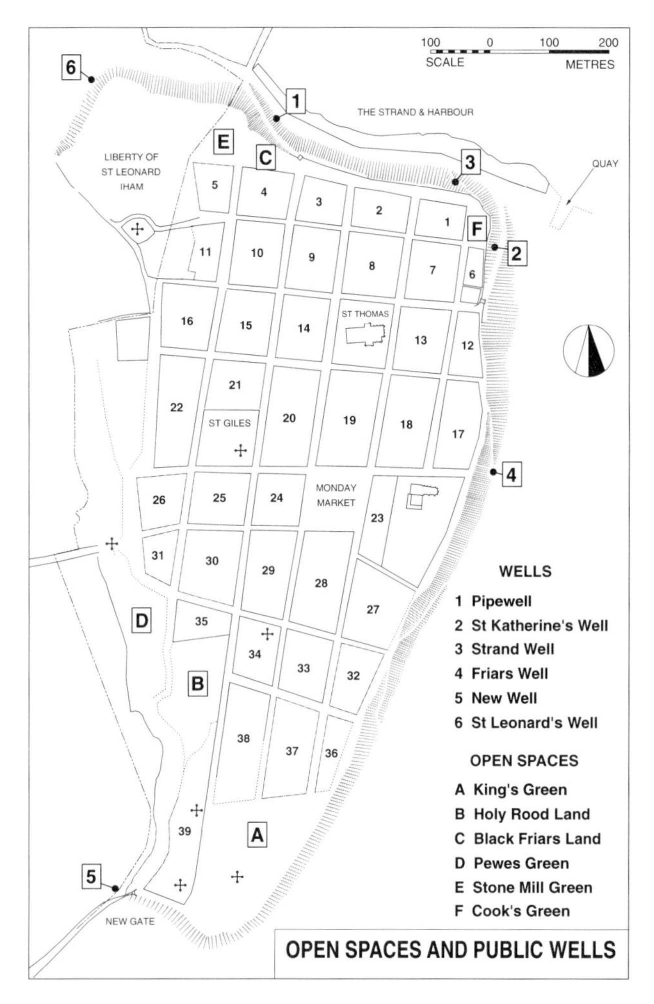

Fig. 4.14
The open spaces and public wells within the town.

THE WATER SUPPLY

There are two oblique references to wells in a document of 1330 (surviving only as a 16th-century copy) relating to the boundaries of the Liberty of New Winchelsea - one to Walewell (assuming this not to be a misreading of Walewall) and another to Gryndepepper Well.[38] Both were on the boundary with the Liberty of Iham. Walewell was evidently near the foot of the western hill, whilst Gryndepepper Well was beneath the northern hill. With these exceptions, there are no specific references to the town's water supply until the Corporation records start in the early 16th century. By that date it is clear that there were a series of public springheads (called wells) ringing the foot of the cliff upon which the town is built. That they were not solely located adjacent to the then occupied northeastern part of the hill, but to the abandoned southern and western areas too, suggests that they were of ancient origin, as too do the religious dedications given to two of the springs. Cooper, writing in 1850, states:

'Water, so scarce in Rye, was amply supplied to this town from six open wells;- Viz. Pipe Well, situated near the Ferry, close by the entrance of the town by the former Rye road: St Katherine's Well, situated half way up the hill leading from Rye, and below Cook's Green, the water of which is slightly chalybeate: the Strand Well, on the hanging of the hill (above the former tan yard) destroyed a few years since by the falling in of the cliff: the Friars' Well, now enclosed, situated in a field recently called the Peartree or Wellfield, to the east of the Gray Friars; the New Well on the outside of New Gate; and the Vale Well, now called St Leonard's Well, at the north-west of the town, under the old castle [*i.e.* below Castle Field].[39] (For the location of these wells see Figure 4.14).

The references in the Corporation records mostly relate to reserving rights of way to the wells, and to their maintenance. Thus in 1563, when a piece of the cliff near Watchbell Gate [Strand Gate] was granted out, a right of way was reserved to a common well there (presumably St Katherines Well). The following year a licence to dig stone refers to Friars Well. In 1589 a decree was issued regarding the pollution of the town wells, whilst in 1599 orders were given that both the Pipe Well and St Leonard's Well should be mended, as too should the way down to Friars Well. The wells were still being maintained in the mid-17th century, for in 1649 John Richardson promised to *new make* the Pipe Well and maintain it for seven years, whilst in 1653 it was agreed that the wells of the town were to be made good and a new horsepond made near the Friars Well. When part of the cliff to the south of Friars Well was granted out in 1655 three rights of way, including paths leading down to the well [Friars Well] were reserved, though just four years later the town sold Friars Well. Two other wells - Pipe Well and Strand Well - were still in use in 1660. Despite its isolated location, St Leonard's Well remained in use until the 18th century, for in 1768 it was reported that the pump and enclosure at St Leonard's Well had (to quote the complainant) been 'pinched'.[40]

Whether the common townsfolk initially relied solely upon these peripheral spring heads, or whether from the outset the Corporation supplied a common well (or wells) within the town, upon the hill itself, is unknown. The fact that in 1647 two townsfolk were fined 'for digging away the bottom of the well at King's Green' on the hill at the abandoned southern end of the town suggests that there may have been public wells upon the hill, though it is perhaps more likely that this was a private well which had fallen into the hands of the Corporation following the abandonment of this part of the town. As late as 1606 the Corporation agreed to built a pump beside the pillory within the town, but whether this was carried out is uncertain. If a public well - whether equipped with a pump or not - had existed upon

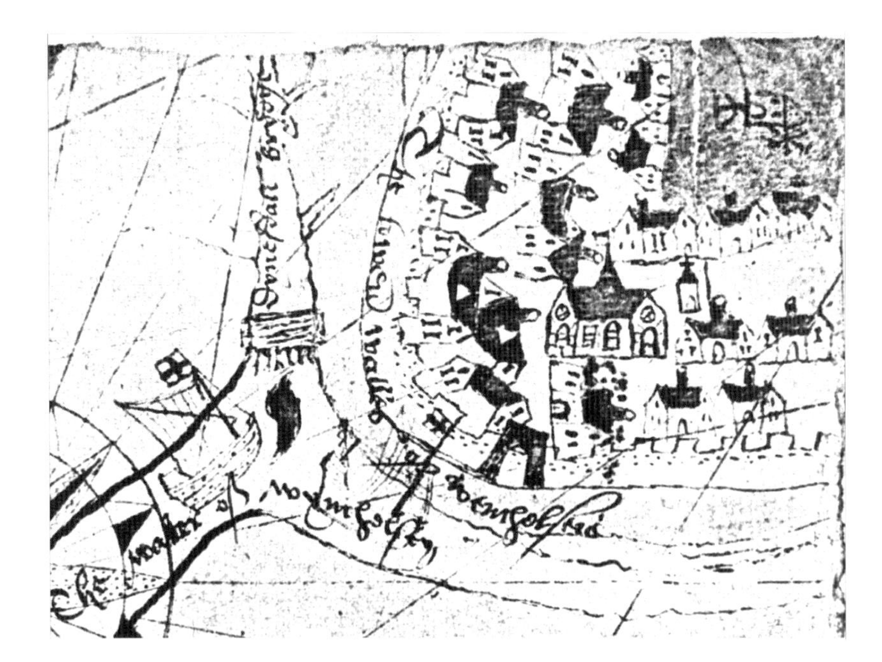

Fig. 4.15

Extract from a corner of John Prowze's map of Rye Harbour 1572, in the custody of the Public Record Office: document reference MPF 212 (ex SP12/254(751). North is to the bottom of the plan. The extract shows the town of Winchelsea complete with its town walls, and depicts St Thomas's Church with a central spire and a spire on its detached western tower. Also shown are 'The waters of Wynchelsey' complete with ship, and the 'Dynesdale brydge'.

the hill, it had evidently fallen out of use by the early 19th century, for at that time the hill lacked any form of public water supply. It was not until 1851 that a private benefactor, Mr Dawes, offered to build at his own expense the present public well and wellhouse in Castle Street.[41]

It is all but certain that from the outset the more wealthy of the town's inhabitants would not have relied upon the common wells, but would have dug their own private wells upon their properties. Such a well is mentioned in the will of Goddard White, gent. in 1589, whilst two probable examples and one possible example have been identified through excavation.[42] Isolated private wells are shown in a map of 1767 on the property of Arnold Nesbitt esq. on Quarters 4 (within the former precinct of the Black Friars) and on Quarter 24.[43] Wells for the personal use of individuals continued to be dug during the 16th and 17th centuries. Only those excavated on public property are mentioned in the documentary record. Thus in 1590 Mr Ashburnham was given permission to enclose with rails the new well he had made adjacent to the Watchbell Causeway, whilst in 1604 a licence was granted for a private well to be dug beside the footway to Icklesham, and in 1689 two neighbours living upon Quarter 13 were specifically granted a piece of waste on the eastern side of St Thomas' churchyard so that they could dig a well and erect a wellhouse for their use only.[4]

5. THE DEFENCES

David and Barbara Martin

INTRODUCTION

Winchelsea had at least two circuits of town defences: an initial ambitious outer ring which enclosed the entire hill upon which the town is built, and a much shorter route initiated as a consequence of a Royal inquiry carried out in 1415. The latter scheme was abandoned at a relatively early stage in its construction, and there are suggestions in the documentary record that the early scheme may likewise never have been fully implemented. Today, apart from the Strand Gate, Pipewell Gate and New Gate, the defences of Winchelsea are visible only in a stretch of retaining wall (with turrets) in Rookery Field to the south of Strand Gate, in a fragment of wall at the head of the cliff some distance to the west of Pipewell Gate, in an upstanding corner of wall to the north of Mill Farmhouse, in some traces of foundations, and in isolated sections of earthwork (some very impressive and others less so) associated with at least two phases of the former Town Dyke (Figure 5.1).

Both Cooper writing in the mid-19th century and Homan in the mid-20th century attempted to interpret the likely routes and form of the town defences, although in the absence of comprehensive catalogues to documentary sources and of detailed earthwork surveys of the physical remains, both relied heavily upon conjecture.[1] Homan's writings are far more extensive than Cooper's. In his reconstruction plan of the town reproduced in his article on the founding of New Winchelsea published in 1949, Homan marked what he considered to be the probable line of the early town wall, together with the probable route of that planned in 1415. Although he was thus aware that a new wall of shorter circuit had been planned in 1415, and knew that money had subsequently been expended upon this work, he did not have access to documents relating to the extensive inquiry held into the proposed route. This inquiry gives details of every street and property to be affected by the work and is an invaluable source of information.[2] It indicates that Homan's conjectured route was incorrect. His theory that the southern extent of the early town wall was indicated by a change of rent per acre paid to the King has also proven incorrect, as has his hypothetical alignment for the wall on the western side of the town (*see* below).

THE DEFENSIVE CIRCUIT PRIOR TO 1415

(Figure 5.2)

It seems likely that it had always been the intention to supply the new town with defences. Their construction became more urgent when, on 1 August 1295 Dover was sacked and destroyed. Given the circumstances, it is not surprising that in September of that year the King authorized the men of 'the new town of Winchelsea' to levy a special custom duty at the port for five years to assist the town to build its walls.[3] That these were already partly built by 1297 is shown by a contemporary account of an incident which befell Edward I during a visit to the town in that year.[4] The account, which contains much good topographical detail, reads as follows:

> 'The town of Winchelsea, where the port is, is sited on a hill of rugged height on that side from which it either overlooks the sea or hangs over the anchorage of the ships; from it a way leads down from a gate to the port. This way does not take the direct route, lest it should force people descending it to go headlong because of the great steepness, or people ascending it to creep up using their hands rather than to walk, but it often zigzags at an angle on the side, now to one side and now to the other with sinuous bends.
>
> 'Nevertheless, the town is girded not with a stone wall but with a bank made of earth on this steep side, *in modum meoniorum* [?in the manner of defensive

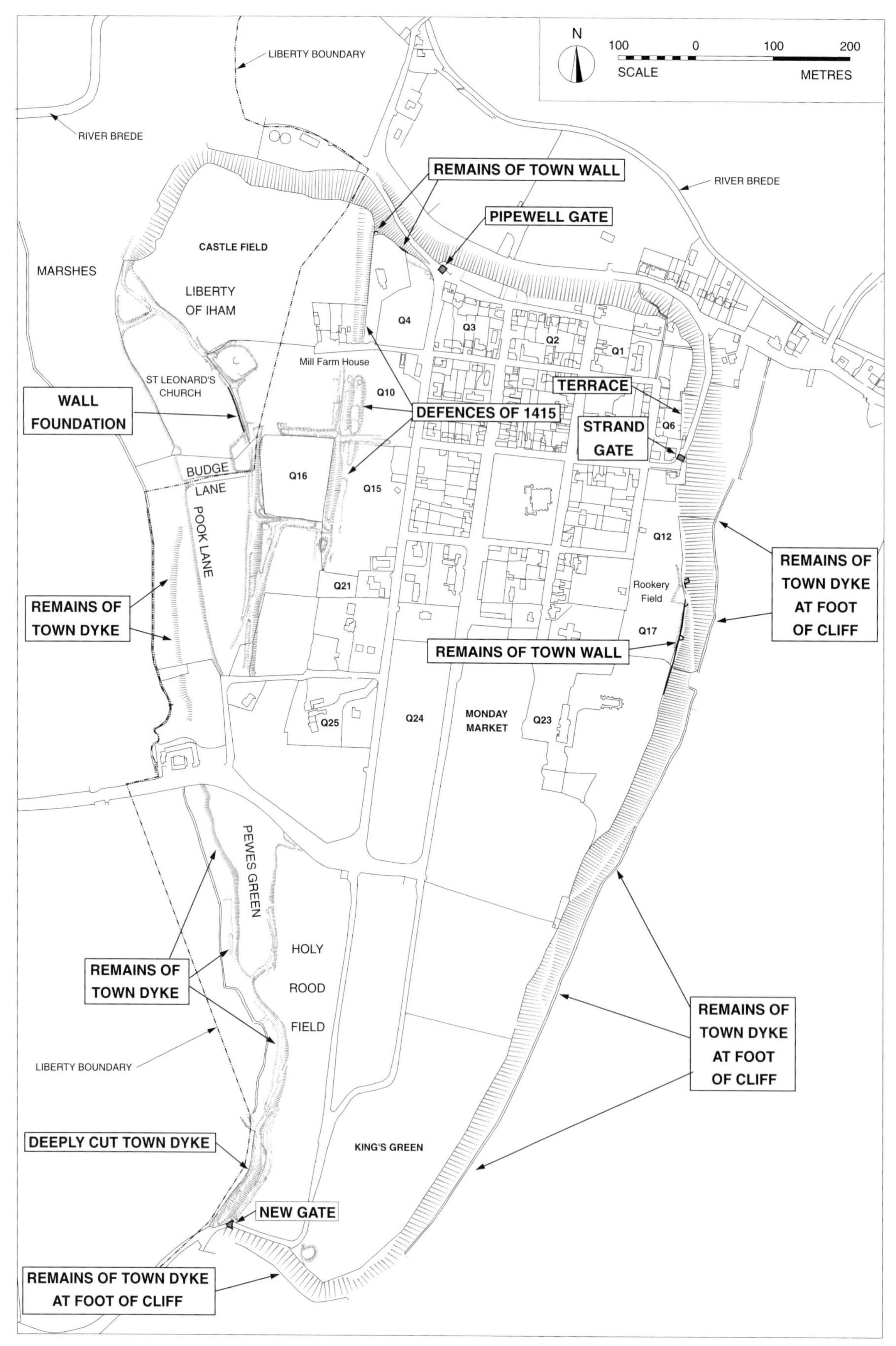

Fig. 5.1 Simplified plan of the town as existing, showing the extant remains of the town defences. (Base plan Crown Copyright Ordnance Survey 100021184. All rights reserved)

walls],[5] built to the height of a man; between its *propugnacula* [?crenellations, ?turrets] there opens up a view to the ships.

'And so the King, having entered the town, when he was riding up beside the *propugnacula* of the rampart, looking at the fleet at anchor below, happened to be approaching a mill, which was being driven by the wind - of which there are very many in the town.

'But the King's horse, frightened by the noise of the sails, which were being blown round very quickly by the wind, while it refused to advance and the King, to [make it] advance, was urging it on now with blows of the whip which he wielded in his hand and now with the spurs dug in, leapt across the *propugnacula* at the side of the rampart.

'Upon which, a crowd of people on horseback and on foot, which was following the King or had assembled to see him, stood completely thunderstruck, with no-one believing anything other than that the King, not appearing on the steep slope, had perished in this leap.

'But with divine virtue disposing the horse, from so great a height, landed on its feet on the path which we have described; on which path, somewhat dissolved into mud as a result of the recent rain, although slithering, slid for a space of twelve feet; it did not, however, fall, but, pulled round gradually by the King by one rein, climbed straight back to the gate. When the King entered, safe, through this gate, the people who stood around were filled with wonder and great joy, contemplating the divine miracle [performed] for the King's safety *super se solum* [?on him alone]'.

Tradition sets this incident at a place still known as 'King's Leap' near the northern side of Quarter 1. Certainly this location fits the description well in that it not only has a good view over the harbour and the sea, but at this point there is a zigzag path descending the cliff to Strand Well and the port below. It seems clear that the path in question was neither that which climbs to the Strand Gate nor to the Pipewell Gate, for not only do both run diagonally up the cliff without bends, but were intended to take wheeled traffic from the outset: the description refers specifically to use by pedestrians. In addition to telling us that parts of the defences existed by that early date, the quote is important for a number of reasons: it tells us that the walls incorporated gates to protect the lesser paths entering the town, they were not of stone, and on the townward side they rose to the height of a man only. In fact, they seem similar to the later walls illustrated in Figure 5.7, except that they were not of stone.

What the 1297 quote does not tell is how quickly work upon the defences proceeded: this is now impossible to judge. In view of the large size of the town, it stands to reason that the circuit of the defences would have progressed sequentially, with the more vulnerable parts of the town protected first. Most vulnerable of all must have been the principal entry points, especially the roads leading up from the harbour. The cliffs on the south, east and north sides provided a natural defence and would have needed nothing more than minimal protection at their head, explaining the slight height referred to in 1297. More difficult to protect was the western margin of the town where there is no cliff.

Evidently the town did not rely solely upon its built structures for its protection, for in 1304 '200 round stones fit for engines' were sent to Winchelsea from Pevensey, suggesting that New Winchelsea possessed at least one siege engine to aid its defence.[6]

The levy to assist in the construction of the defences ran until 1300. Whether the initial works continued up to or much beyond this date is unknown. Again in 1321 the town was authorized by the King to levy a duty for seven years for the purpose of enclosing and paving the town; in this instance the levy was to be on all goods entering Winchelsea. That work on the defences was actively in progress in 1321 is indicated by a complaint made to the King by the Abbot of Fécamp during the same year. This states that the Mayor and Barons of Winchelsea at the King's command had walled (note the use of the past tense) the King's town of Winchelsea together with the Abbot's town of Iham adjoining Winchelsea. In making the fosse around the town, they had interfered with the Abbot's tenements in Iham. He sought compensation or asked that the King take over the town which had been thus enclosed with Winchelsea and provide other land in exchange. An inquisition held the following year confirmed the Abbot's statement. It found that 200 perches by 12 perches, equivalent to 3,300 feet by 198 feet or 1,006 metres by 60.35 metres and amounting to 15 acres in area, had been enclosed.[7]

By 1330 at the latest the New Gate at the extreme southern end of the town had been built, as too had the impressive section of dyke which cuts off the hill from the ridge to the west. Both are mentioned in an extent of the boundaries of the Liberty of Winchelsea taken at that date.[8] The name 'New Gate', which had already been given to the structure by then, implies that this was the last of the principal gates to be constructed – which is not surprising, given its distance both from the harbour and from the commercial heart of the town (*see* Figure 5.2).

There are no indications, either documentary or physical, to suggest any serious attempt to defend the waterfront area at the foot of the hill. Although the Town Dyke did extend out to the river, at least on its eastern side, so far as is known the town walls were

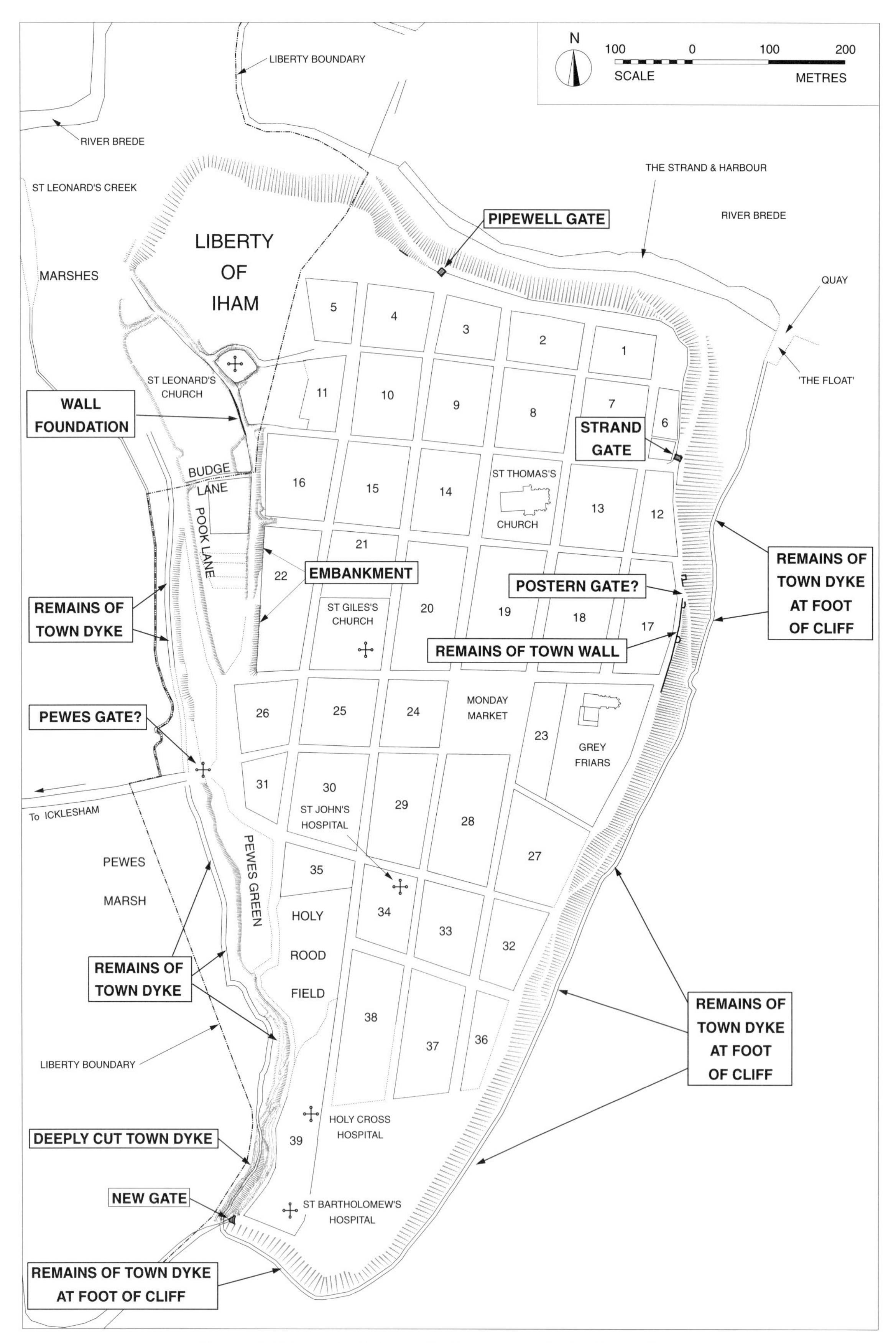

Fig. 5.2 The early defences in the context of the planned town.

restricted to the top of the hill (*see* below). It may, of course, have been possible to lay raisable chains across the estuary at a point immediately to the east of the town, and it is known that chains were employed within the estuary. In 1344, for example, the men of the Abbot of Fécamp's 'town of Iham near Winchelsea' (by this date effectively a separately administered suburb of Winchelsea occupying the northwest corner of the hill) complained to the King that their ships and boats were denied free access to 'the port of water leading from their town to the sea' because stakes had been put into the water and iron chains stretched across.[9] Whether this was a defensive measure on the part of Winchelsea, or the result of a dispute between the two neighbours is unclear. Given the location of Iham and the wording of the complaint, this barrier is likely to have been upstream from the town's harbour plots, cutting off the creek which skirted part way along the western side of the town, towards The Pewes and may therefore have been aimed at strengthening the defences on the town's vulnerable western flank.

Winchelsea's defences were put to the test on several occasions. There is evidence to suggest that in 1326 the French attacked and burnt about a quarter of the houses within the town.[10] It escaped unscathed when the French attacked and burnt Rye and Hastings in 1339, but on 15th March 1360 they attacked and captured the town and wrought havoc both upon it and its inhabitants.[11] Rye was captured in 1377, but on this occasion reinforcements led by the Abbot of Battle successfully defended Winchelsea. However, the Abbot's attempts at a similar defence when the Spanish attacked three years later, in 1380, were unsuccessful and as a result the town was sacked. Cooper specifically stated that during the 1380 raid the walls were seriously damaged, whilst the Land Gate or Pipewell Gate was destroyed.[12] Although no direct documentary evidence has as yet been found to substantiate this statement, such an interpretation is consistent with the King's appointment of the Abbot of Battle, Edward Dallingridge and William Batesford in that year reciting that the town was not sufficiently secured and was liable to further hostile attack. They were directed to survey the town and to enquire how it could best be secured and at whose expense. Parliament took up the cause as a national question and the Commons petitioned the King to remedy the defences of Rye and Winchelsea, which had so often been injured and almost destroyed by the burnings and invasions of the enemy 'because if those towns were taken, which God forbid, the whole country would be destroyed'.[13] Action was promised, and in 1386, when several French ships laden with the greater part of a prefabricated wooden palisade with 'towers and armaments' were taken, the King 'at once ordered it to be erected round Winchelsey'.[14]

Although the Corporation records do not commence until 1527, from references contained within them valuable detail regarding the form and, more importantly, the circuit of the early defences prior to 1415 can be gleaned. The most instructive relate to the defences on the western side of the town where the line of the original circuit is otherwise in doubt. The earliest reference regarding this area is for 1578, when a proclamation was made asking why the Town Dyke against Bartholomew Field and Holy Rood Field (at the southern end of the town) should not be laid open to the town commons.[15] The extreme southern end of this dyke cuts across the spur of the hill and is still very distinct, although further north the earthwork shows today as nothing more than a lynchet and, in its present form, would be regarded neither as a dyke nor a defensive feature. The documents indicate that in 1583 the Corporation took the decision either to let or to sell the entire western stretch of Town Dyke. In 1583, the southern section, stretching 'from New Gate all the length of Bartholomew Field' was let for 21 years, whilst the following year the same tenant took a lease of that section immediately to the north, against both Holy Rood Field and a small piece of land near 'the Horseshoe'. The next year that section to the north, described as being on both sides (*i.e.* to south and north) of the Icklesham to Winchelsea highway, was disposed of and later the same year the next section north, near Pook Lane, was likewise sold, but a right of way was reserved to 'those who have the dyke against the land of Edmund Weekes'. This final northern section, described as the 'dyke against a piece of land near Budge Lane occupied by Edmund Weekes' was the same year let by the Corporation, reserving a footway to the lands of the Manor of Icklesham.[16] Budge Lane and the footway which extended its alignment westwards (via a bridge) to the lands of Icklesham Manor formed the boundary between the Liberties of Winchelsea and Iham; the latter had by this date passed out of the hands of Fécamp Abbey and formed part of the Cinque Port of Hastings. Any extension of the Town Dyke northwards beyond the boundary would thus have passed through land which was not under the jurisdiction of Winchelsea Corporation and which would therefore not have been theirs to grant out.[17] It is known that the Dyke or Fosse did extend into the Liberty of Iham from the complaints made by the Abbot of Fécamp in 1321 (*see* above).

The fields and lanes mentioned in the 16th-century grants and leases referred to can be plotted from other documents with complete confidence, and thus the alignment of the Town Dyke can be identified. It was not sited at the most obvious defensive location, but at the foot of the hill, against the adjacent marshland (*see* Figure 5.2). Owing to deliberate backfilling since the 16th century, the physical remains are now slight. Higher up the hill, forming the western edge of the planned grid, is a far more impressive embankment with a sunken road on its downhill side. The road extends northwards into the Liberty of Iham as a terrace. Along its western (downhill) side the foundations of a wide, defensive-looking masonry wall are still visible. Whether this represents the alignment of a later, though pre-1415 defence, or whether from the outset the early defences on the western side of the town took the form of two separate alignments - a dyke at the foot of the hill with a defensive wall at the top - is at present unclear.

Whereas the alignment of the defences on the western side of the town still presents some problems, particularly within the Liberty of Iham, the line of those on the northern, eastern and southern sides is obvious: the degraded cliff forms a natural barrier. The Corporation documents make it clear, however, that on the eastern and southern sides a town ditch or dyke protected the base of the cliff. (Figures 5.2 and 5.3). In 1564, for example, permission was granted to dig (fallen?) stone in the Town Dyke between Watchbell (Strand) Gate and Friars Well, whilst in 1613, an action was begun against persons who had cut wood and reed in the Town Dyke against 'The Strake by Coney Field' at the southeast corner of the town. In 1646 the Corporation granted to Mr (George) Sampson (of the former Grey Friars) the hill slopes (cliff) next to his property, together with 'the long slip called the Town Dyke'.[18] Both are shown on a 1738 map of the Friary property: they extended from the New Gate in the south to the northern boundary of The Friary. The dyke is also shown in the town map of 1763, where it is depicted extending northwards as far as 'The Float' at the Strand. This northern end of the dyke is mentioned in 1617, when John Beeson (of the Tannery at The Strand) was given licence to lay his tan upon 'the end of the Town Dyke between his land, the pendants (*i.e.* cliff) and Mr Evernden's land'.[19]

THE PLANNED 15TH-CENTURY DEFENSIVE CIRCUIT *(Figure 5.3)*

Despite the town's much contracted size, the reconstruction or repair of the Pipewell Gate during the years around 1400 reflect a renewed interest in the long-term defence of the site. It was perhaps in association with this work that a section of stone-built town wall to the west of the gate was erected. Certainly by 1415 this section of the defences took the form of a wall: in the detailed inquiry taken that year regarding the intended new line of the town wall and ditch, the road which extended westwards from Pipewell Gate along the head of the cliff is described as 'the king's street stretching from the mill called the Stonemill between the close of the said friars (Black Friars) and the town wall on the north cliff as far as the north gate of the town'.

In contrast, where the opposite end of the proposed wall was to meet the eastern cliff, the road to be blocked by the proposed wall was described as 'the king's street stretching lengthways from north to south from the close of the Friars Minor of the town (*i.e.* the Grey Friars) on the west to the cliff on the east'. Since in this instance no reference was made to a town wall, the implication must be that at most a light palisade or fence existed adjacent to the Grey Friars.[20] The scar of a town wall attached to the southern side of Strand Gate, together with the surviving turreted lower courses of the wall as it runs along the eastern edge of Rookery Field, are physical proof that a stone wall was at some date built in this area, extending along the head of the cliff southwards from the gate. The scar at Strand Gate is not well bonded to the structure, which implies a difference in date. Confirming the physical evidence which remains, the town wall is given in boundary clauses relating to properties in Quarter 12 in 1529, and is depicted extant in maps drawn in 1572 and *c.*1597 (*see* Figure 5.4).[21]

Stubs of town wall visible in the eastern face of Pipewell Gate and the northern face of Strand Gate likewise indicate that these two gates were once linked by a stone town wall, and again this fact is confirmed by the 1572 and *c.*1597 plans and by 16th-century boundary clauses.[22] Not only is the wall stub at Pipewell Gate fully bonded to the gate's structure, the same appears to be true of that visible on the northern side of the Strand Gate. Despite this, the 1297 description quoted above suggests that the wall is more likely to date from the early-15th-century reconstruction works.

The principal innovation of the early-15th-century scheme for the redesign of the defences at Winchelsea was the proposed downsizing of the circuit. In the words of the inquiry held in 1415, the '. . site is now too large for the inhabitants and to enclose it would be unbearable'. The new plan was to protect 21 Quarters in the northeast corner of the original town, abandoning the near-unpopulated Quarters to the west and south. The proposed line placed the precinct of the Grey Friars in the southeast corner, the precinct of the Black Friars in the northwest corner, and the Church of St Giles near the southwest corner. The new circuit involved the construction of a 'wall with the ditch necessary therefore'. It was to run along the line of the existing streets, but these were too narrow to accommodate the width of the wall and ditch combined, and in consequence, the boundaries of the tenements on the townward side of the streets were to be moved back. At first sight it seems surprising that it was on the townward, rather than on the extramural side that the boundaries were to be moved, but the inquiry shows that the town had shrunk so seriously that only four houses would be destroyed by the work.

Those streets which were to be blocked by the

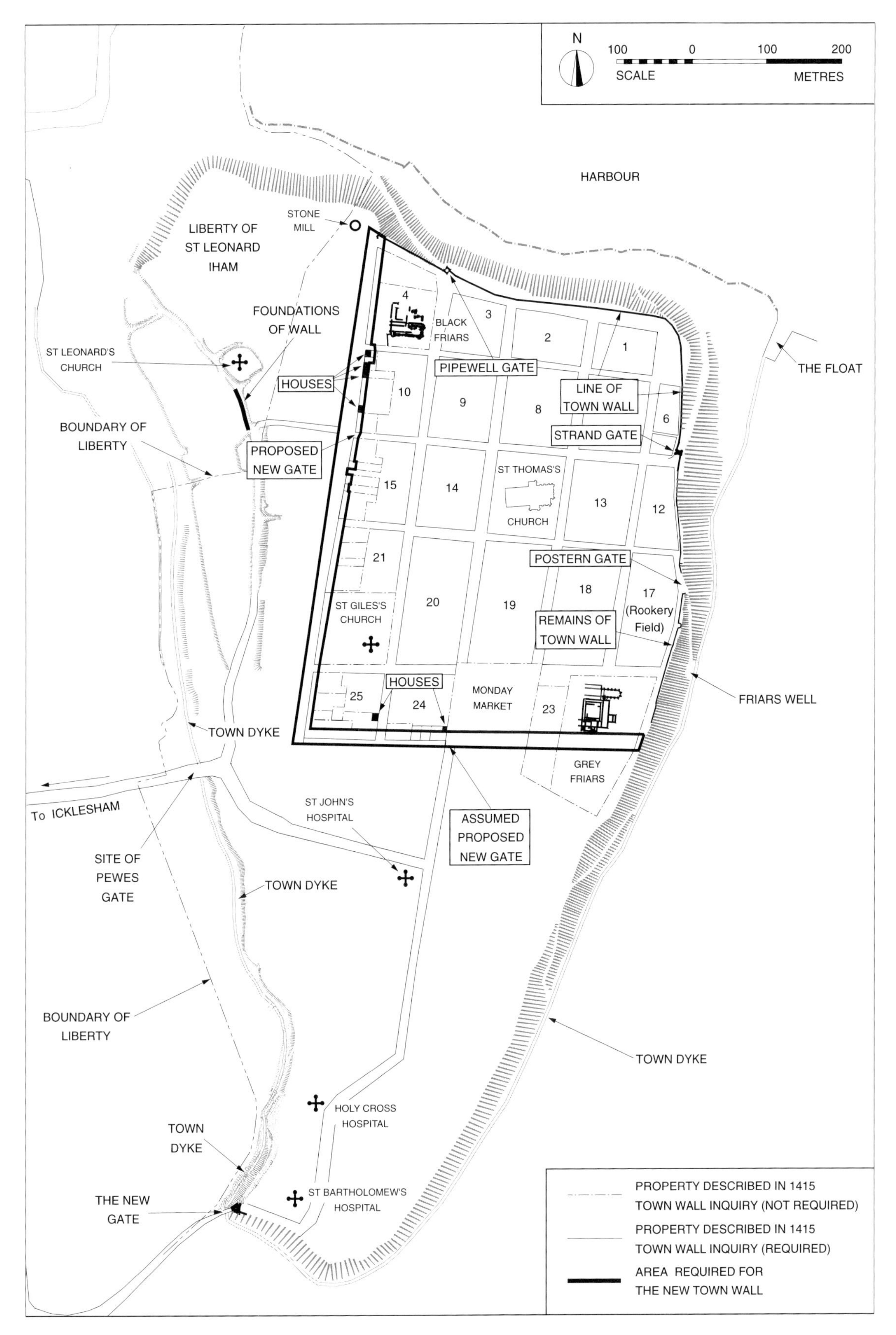

Fig. 5.3 The town wall inquiry of 1415 and the 15th-century defences.

proposed wall were thus noted, and, perhaps surprisingly, included the street 'stretching from the church of St Leonard in Iham'. Perhaps by then St Leonard's church was already all but redundant and the township of Iham depopulated! Likewise, the street 'stretching from the South [Gate] to the North Gate was to be blocked'. Running as it does between New Gate in the south and Pipewell Gate in the north, this might seem surprising, though in truth, because of the lie of the land, there was no easy access between this street and Pipewell Gate. Instead, the road through Pipewell Gate led eastwards and thus it was far easier to take the next street, which not only led to St Thomas's Church, but to the Monday Market. This street also gave an alternative route to the hospitals and New Gate to the south. Only two streets are not specifically mentioned as 'to be blocked'. Between Quarters 10 and 15, where the wall crossed 'the king's street stretching lengthways from Bartholomew Morye's plot to the East Gate of the town' (*i.e.* the Strand Gate) it was proposed 'to build a gate convenient for the commonalty'. This proposed new west gate would have protected the road leading into the town from Icklesham. Although no gate is specifically mentioned at the point where the street at Monday Market crossed the line of the new wall, it must be significant that the inquiry does not specify that this street was to be blocked. This was an important thoroughfare, not only because of the market, but also because it allowed direct access to the hospitals and New Gate to the south of the proposed wall.[23]

The King found in favour of the proposals, upon condition that the rent paid to him by the town was not to be reduced, and he offered 600 marks out of the Treasury towards the cost of the works.[24] Construction was commenced and some money was paid by the Treasury, but it would seem that a peace treaty with France gave the excuse for Treasury funds to be suspended and the work finally ceased far short of completion, leaving the town to rely upon its earlier outer defences. Even as late as 1562 the Crown made a grant to John Guldeford of 'as much land within the walls as assigned by former sovereigns', suggesting that the circuit of the old defensive walls was still recognizable as a boundary at that late date.[25]

Fig. 5.4
Enlarged detail from a map of c.1597 showing the extant town wall to the north and east of the town. Part of the wall is depicted with crenellations intact, but the remainder appears to be shown in ruins. Pipewell Gate is just visible at the left-hand margin, whilst Strand Gate is more obviously depicted with a further ?postern gate to its south. (Bodleian Library, KeS/15). [Reproduced with permission of The Warden and Fellows of All Souls College, Oxford]. (See also Figure 4.15).

THE EXTANT REMAINS OF THE TOWN WALL AND ITS ASSOCIATED DITCH

(Figures 5.1, 5.5-12)

The new defences as proposed in the 1415 inquiry were to comprise a stone wall protected along its external perimeter by a ditch. By calculation the north-south section, bounding the western edge of the shrunken town, would have measured approximately 680 metres (2,230ft.) long, and the east-west section, forming the southern boundary of the town, *c.*450 metres (1,476ft.).

A substantial length of the new ditch, extending *c.*430 metres (1,410ft.) southwards from the northern cliff, was commenced, (the southern end of the extant section terminates very abruptly at the point where the work stopped).

The central section of the earthwork, between Second Street and Third Street (adjacent to Quarter 10) has either been backfilled or was never completed - it shows today only as a gentle linear hollow. Even so, the western edge is clearly visible as a low, but very distinct bank. To the east of the depression is a wide but shallow 'mound', on average 500 millimetres (1ft.8ins.) high. The spoil forming the mound was spread to produce a gentle incline down to the ground within Quarter 10. The intended effect was to build up the ground behind the line of the proposed town wall so as to gain height over that outside the new defences. The mound was formed by

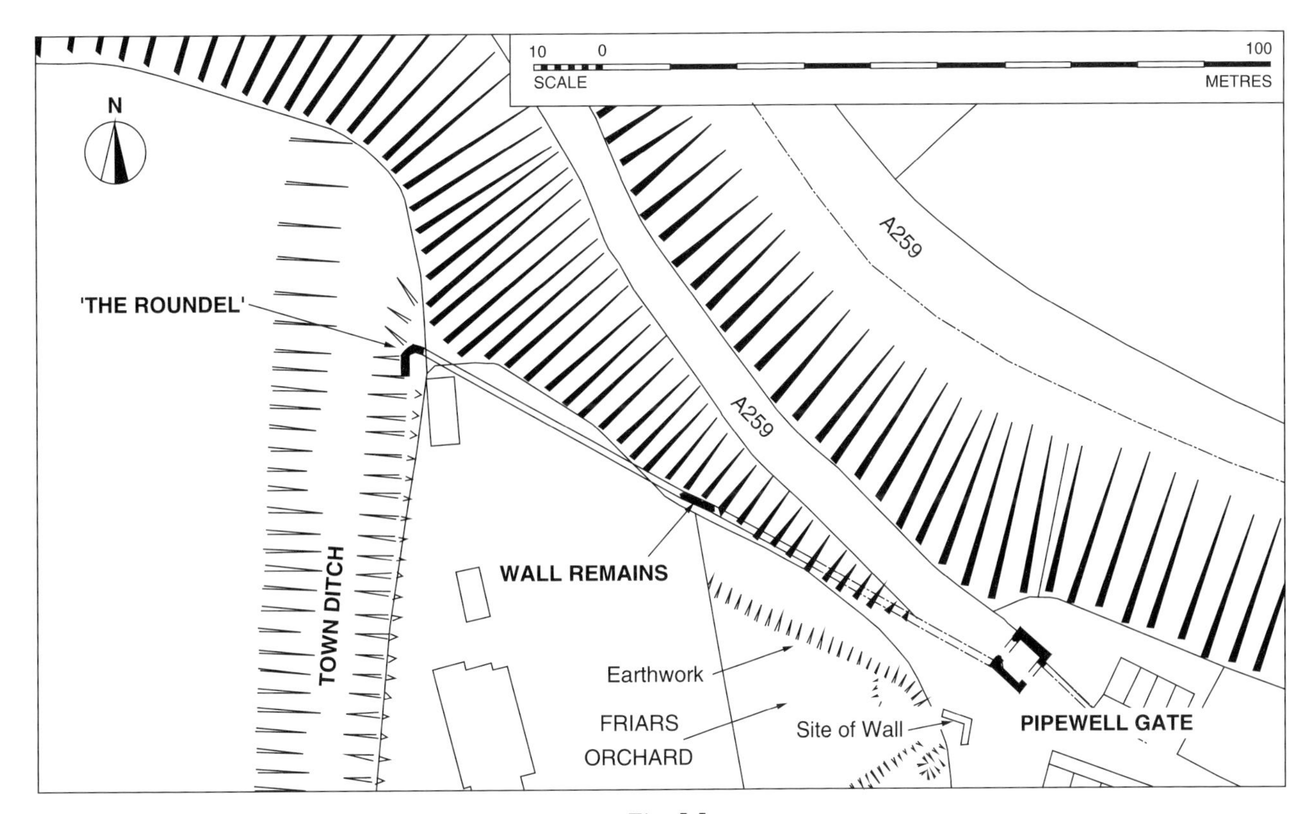

Fig. 5.5
Plan showing the section of town wall between the Pipewell Gate and 'The Roundel' and associated town ditch of c.1415. (Base plan Crown Copyright Ordnance Survey 100021184. All rights reserved)

spreading the spoil from the excavations. Whether the spoil originated from the adjacent section of ditch (since backfilled?), or from the extant section against Quarter 15 is unknown, for the natural lie of the ground at Quarter 15 gave the required height advantage without the need to spread spoil in this area.

This southern section of ditch, running along the western edge of Quarter 15 and as far as the northwest corner of Quarter 21, is the best preserved section of the early-15th-century earthworks. Measuring *c*.17 metres (*c*.56ft.) wide and having steep sides cut through the natural strata of soft sandstone, it still survives to a depth of 4.25 metres (14ft.) on its eastern side, reducing (owing to the natural ground slope) to *c*.2.30 metres (*c*.7ft.6ins.) on the west.

At the northern end, against Quarter 4, the profile of the ditch has been much softened by infilling, ploughing and gardening, although the earthwork is still easily recognizable, especially along its eastern edge where, as at Quarter 10, the spoil has been spread to form a low mound on the townward side. Extending along the side of the mound, near its top, is a scatter of stone suggesting the line of a buried foundation. That these stones relate to the line of the town wall is indicated by a surviving upstanding fragment of wall at the extreme northern end of the bank. Now known as *The Roundel* - probably a name transferred to it from the tower of the Stone Mill after the mill's demolition - this fragment represents the northwest corner of the early-15th-century defences (Figures 5.5 and 5.6). It measures only 650 millimetres (2ft.2ins.) thick and is faced in roughly coursed Tilgate rubble. Its lower section (*c*.1.0 metre or *c*.3ft.) acts as a retaining wall, the ground on the east being above that on the west. On the lower western side the fragment of wall still stands to a height of *c*.3.50 metres (11ft.6ins.), which must be near to its original height. To overcome the acute angle formed where the northern and western sections of wall meet, there is no corner quoin, but instead the corner is gently rounded. The northern external face, towards the cliff, is battered back, but there is no corresponding batter on the western external face.

The jagged eastern end of The Roundel, together with a scar at the northwest corner of Pipewell Gate, confirm the documentary reference in the 1415 inquiry to a length of Town Wall running along the top of the cliff to the north of Quarter 4. It has in the past been assumed that a distinct bank and associated lynchet running parallel to the northern edge of Friars Orchard, approximately 7 metres (23ft.) to the south of the cliff, indicates the line of the former town wall. The strip of ground between this feature and the cliff edge is set at a

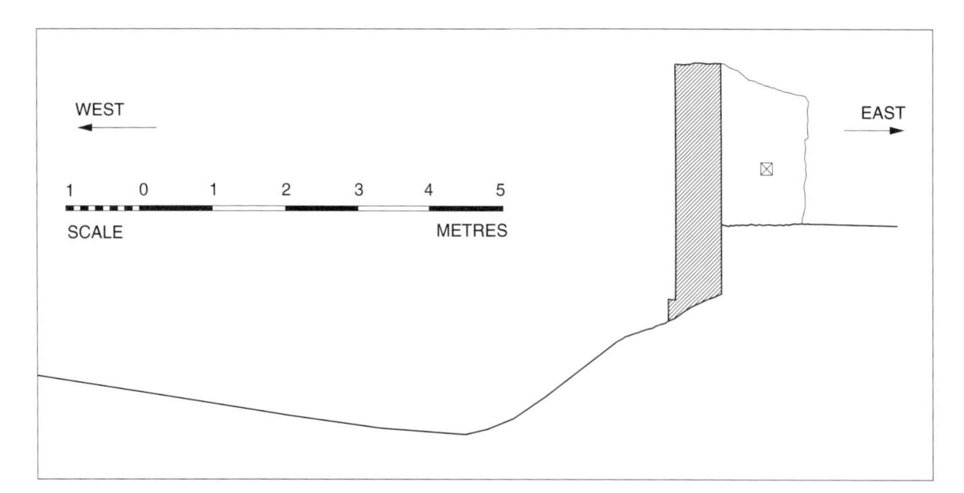

Fig. 5.6 (Left)

Section across 'The Roundel' and the town ditch.

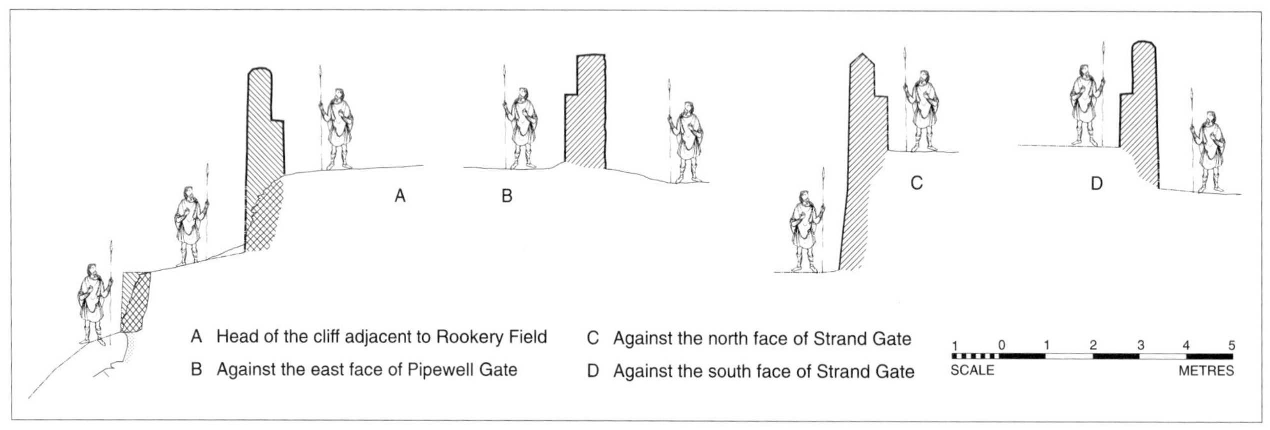

Fig. 5.7
Reconstructed sections through the town wall at known points (height of wall in detail 'A' based upon the internal height at sections 'B' to 'D').

slightly lower level to the remainder of the field and forms a terrace climbing westwards away from Pipewell Gate (Figure 5.5). Until the mid-1970s, the eastern end of the earthwork terminated at the highway (A259) in an upstanding section of wall. Early drawings show it with a quoin at its extreme eastern end, a feature which is unlikely, given that the wall once continued further eastwards to abut the Pipewell Gate. It is surely relevant that if the alignment of the earthwork is projected eastwards, it passes some distance to the south of the gate and could only be made to join the gate by incorporating a distinct change of direction. Any such change of direction would not be consistent with the alignment of the Town Wall indicated by the surviving wall stub attached to the gate.

That the bank, lynchet and former fragment of upstanding wall do not represent the line of the town wall is indicated both by a scatter of Tilgate stone further to the north, along the upper slopes of the degraded cliff, and by a short surviving section of wall *c.*900 millimetres (2ft.11ins.) thick located at a point approximately 50 metres (*c.*164ft.) to the west-north-west of Pipewell Gate (Figure 5.5). On either side of the fragment the top of the cliff has slipped, taking those sections of wall with it. The surviving fragment has a total length of approximately 5.60 metres (18ft.4ins.) and a total height at its greatest extent of 1.80 metres (*c.*6ft.), measured from the highest point of the core to the lowest visible point of the north face. The wall does not stand so high on its southern side, there being a marked difference in ground level on either side of the fragment. Most of the exposed work is core, but a section of the northern face 1.20 metres (4ft.) long by 650 millimetres (2ft.2ins.) high is visible. As with the facing to The Roundel, it is of roughly coursed slabs of Tilgate stone. The surviving fragment of wall makes it clear that the Town Wall extended along the cliff edge in a straight line from The Roundel to the northeast corner of Pipewell Gate, which it met at an angle to the quoin. The terrace and line of earthworks at the northern end of Friars Orchard represent the street mentioned in 1415, running along the townward side of the town wall, between it and the northern wall of the Black Friars precincts (*see* Chapter 7).

Extending eastwards from Pipewell Gate and northwards from Strand Gate are short stubs of stone wall

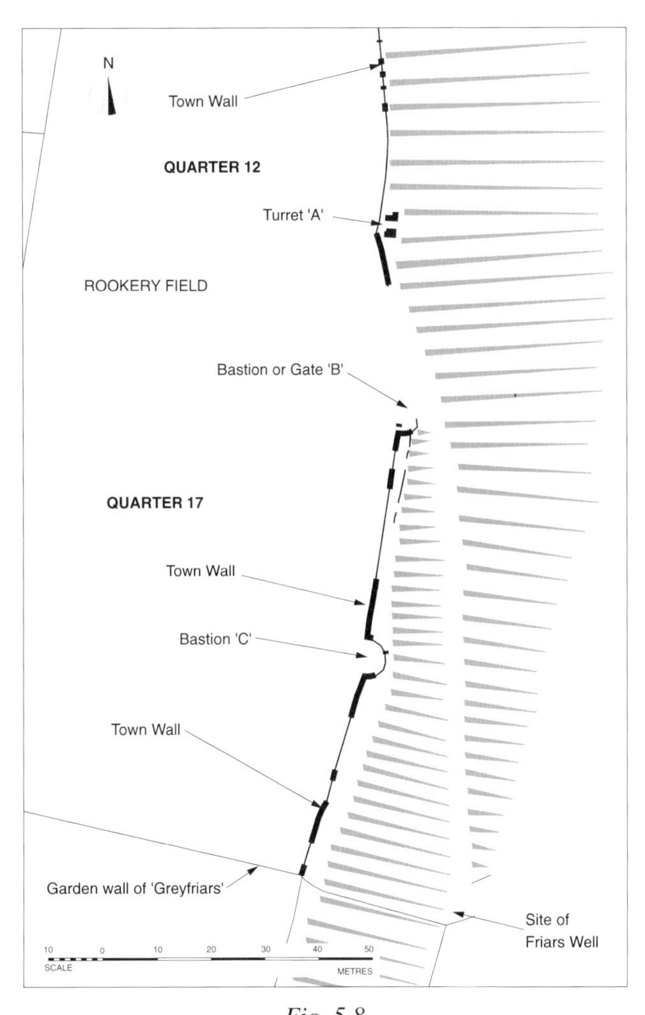

Fig. 5.8
Remains of the town wall flanking Rookery Field (Quarters 12 and 17). (For location see Figure 5.1).

Fig. 5.9
Turret 'A' viewed from the south following excavation in 2002.

810 millimetres (2ft.8ins.) thick, confirming that the depictions of a stone town wall extending along the cliff edge between the two gates in the maps of 1572 and *c.*1597 can be believed (*see* Figure 5.4).[26] Both stubs indicate a wall which on the townward side rose to no great height, the scar at Strand Gate suggesting a height of approximately 2.0 metres (6ft.6ins.) and at Pipewell Gate of approximately 2.40 metres (7ft.10ins.) (Figure 5.7). At Strand Gate the height on the side away from the town was greatly increased by the level of the terraced roadway climbing the cliff, the wall at its greatest extent being 4.50 metres (14ft.9ins.) high (Figure 5.7C). At Pipewell Gate there was only a slight difference in ground level on either side of the wall (Figure 5.7B). Only where the public footpath running north from Barrack Square crosses the line of the wall are any remains of the circuit between the two gates recognizable today, and even here the remains are limited to a short stretch of foundation. Nineteenth-century and modern development in the area of Quarter 1 has modified the ground levels along the northern side of this Quarter, whilst the ground adjacent to the road on the northern side of much of Quarter 2 was built up in 1999/2000 to give a gentle bank sloping away from the road. A steep bank previously ran along the northern side of the road in this area and this still survives further to the west.

Running along the eastern side of Quarter 6, extending southwards towards Strand Gate, the cliff and its adjacent area has been landscaped to form terraced gardens. One of these terraces stretches almost the full length of the Quarter and is flanked on its western side by walls of Tilgate stone forming the rear boundaries of the Barrack Square properties (*see* Figure 5.1). Most of these walls are of considerable age and incorporate straight joints where they meet the east-west boundaries between the properties. This upper terrace represents the lane mentioned in the 16th-century deeds as running along the inside of the town wall, between it and the tenements. Along the eastern edge of the terrace, on the line of the town wall, is what appears to be a modern retaining wall holding back a drop of up to two metres between the terrace/lane and the slopes of the cliff. Built off the wall is a row of high garden piers forming an edge to the

Fig. 5.10
Remains of the town wall adjacent to Rookery Field looking north. Photograph taken following the cleaning of the remains in 2002 and showing an extant turret in background.

terrace. Whether the present retaining wall replaces the town wall or merely represents a refacing is unknown.

The 16th-century maps and deeds indicate that the stone-built town wall extended southwards from Strand Gate, separated from the eastern boundaries of Quarters 12 and 17 by a lane. Here too, a scar on the southern face of Strand Gate's southeast turret marks where the 800-millimetre (2ft.8ins.) thick wall joined the gate. In this instance the two are not well bonded together and it would appear that the town wall postdated the gate. On the townward side it measured approximately 2.50 metres (8ft.3ins.) high, although because of the cliff, the height on the eastern side would have been greater (*see* Figure 5.7D). The line which extends southwards from the gate, along the eastern side of The Lookout and Lookout Cottage, is today marked by a stone path running along the downhill side of a modern retaining wall. Thus here too the wall would have been considerably higher on its external face than on the townward side. Further south still, along the eastern edge of Quarter 12 - now the northern part of Rookery Field - intermittent foundations visible through the grass on the line of a decayed fence indicate the route of the wall. At a point in line with former Fourth Street the alignment becomes more distinct and here the light foundations of some form of small tower or platform are visible eroding out of the cliff edge. The projection, marked 'A' in Figure 5.8, measures approximately 3.0 metres (*c.*10ft.) square and has mortar-bonded foundations only *c.*600 millimetres (2ft.) thick (*see* Figure 5.9). It is built at a point where the alignment of the wall changes. This change of alignment apparently accommodates the head of a path which descends down the cliff to Friars Well. It may be significant that the plan of *c.*1597 shows a town gate in approximately this location (*see* Figure 5.4) and it is possible that this was the postern gate referred to in 1539, when permission was granted to set up a warren along a short section of the cliff.[27]

Although unknown to scholars until 1994, the remains of the town wall to the south of this presumed postern gate, extend for a length of more than 84 metres (275ft.) along the eastern edge of Quarter 17. It is the most impressive extant section of the wall (Figure 5.10). As elsewhere along the circuit, it flanks a man-made terrace extending along the cliff edge, the ground on the townward side being approximately 1.60 metres (5ft.3ins.) higher than along the head of the cliff (*see* Figure 5.7A). The remains are those of the section which formed a retaining wall at the foot of the town wall. Much of it survives as corework only, although in some areas substantial patches of external facing are still in place. As elsewhere, the facing is mostly of roughly coursed Tilgate rubble. Archaeological work carried out in 2002 in advance of the remains being consolidated

Fig. 5.11
Remains of lime render adhering to the face of the clay-bedded wall.

Fig. 5.12
Bonded junction between the turret 'C' (right) and the town wall (left).

indicated that this section of the wall is clay-bedded rather than mortared and that the external (eastern) face of the masonry was intended to be masked by white, lime-mortar rendering (Figure 5.11). The same was true of the town gates (*see* below). At a distance of 38.50 metres (126ft.3ins.) north of the southern boundary of Rookery Field, a bank projects from the face of the wall ('C' in Figure 5.8). On the southern and northern sides the bank is stone-faced with the facing fully bonded into the town wall (Figure 5.12). The projection represents the remains of a small 'D'-shaped turret *c.*8.50 metres (*c.*27ft.10ins.) wide. The southern, stone-faced return of a second projection is just visible approximately 37 metres (121ft.) to the north of the turret (marked 'B' on Figure 5.8). Here too the surviving facework indicates some form of curved bastion projecting from the town wall. The projecting earthen platform associated with it is more substantial in size than that further south. Given that it is located hard against the path which descends to Friars Well, the projection may be related to the postern gate depicted in the *c.*1597 plan. Running parallel on the downhill side of the wall at this point a stone-revetted terrace can be seen, perhaps an addition aimed at arresting slippage of the cliff face (Figures 5.7A and 5.8). A 'turret of stone' is referred to in the Corporation records in 1584, but whether this was part of the town defences or a turret attached to a domestic building is unknown.[28]

To date it has not been possible to ascertain how far to the south of Rookery Field the remains of the town wall extend, although through the thick undergrowth some form of revetted terrace continuing southwards is visible. This as yet unexplored section would have bounded the precincts of the Grey Friars where, at the southern edge of the precinct, it would have joined the proposed new (1415) southern section of town wall. It is worth recalling the wording of the 1415 inquiry, which suggests that no town wall existed in the area of Grey Friars at that date. It may therefore be relevant that the *c.*1597 plan does not show the section of stone wall then extant extending as far south as the proposed new 1415 southern alignment.

OTHER DEFENCES (*Figure 5.1*).

It has been argued that in addition to the town walls and their associated gates and earthworks, Edward I intended to build a castle at Winchelsea and that for this purpose he reserved 12 acres at the northwest corner of the hill, immediately to the north of the church of St Leonard, Iham (Figure 5.1). Indeed, writing in the mid-19th century, Cooper was more specific. He stated that in addition to the town walls 'there was a stronghold or castle built by the king at the northwest corner of the town, on the ten acres reserved by him and called by Leland (*c.*1540) 'the King Mede without the Town': it immediately overlooked the parish church of St Leonard, and commanded completely the inner harbour. Some remains of the clustered columns of the entrance gate are yet to be seen on the side of the Pipewell or Ferry Gate, leading to Udimore'.[29] From their location within the town, beside Pipewell Gate, the 'clustered columns of the entrance gate' could not have related to a castle and were almost certainly the remains of the gate giving access to the precincts of the Black Friars, Quarter 4. Homan, picking up Cooper's theme, stated the point less forcibly, merely noting that of the 149½ acres on the hill taken over by the King, he retained 12 acres '. . for his own use; probably the latter were northwest of the town, where a field has for centuries been known as Castle Field'.[30] It is beyond dispute that a field in this area has been known as Castle Field for centuries: a rental of the land at Iham within the Manor of Brede taken in 1500/1 includes an entry which reads 'the same Harry (Fyshe) for Castell land, 12d', whilst the lands and rents of the late Black Friars included within the Queen's grant to the Corporation in 1586 referred to a 12-acre plot called 'Castle Field'.[31] However, it must be borne in mind that all this part of the hill was extramural to the town and Liberty of Winchelsea and formed part of the Liberty of Iham within the Cinque Port of Hastings. It was land which had not been taken over by the King when Winchelsea was founded but which remained with the Abbot of Fécamp, and subsequently with the Abbey of Syon. It therefore seems more likely that the 12 acres reserved by the King can be identified as King's Green, sited adjacent to the hospitals at the southern end of Winchelsea. Whether this is the case or not and even if Edward had reserved land within the town for a future castle, there is no evidence to suggest that any such fortification was commenced. Only Cooper has suggested otherwise, this based upon a misidentification of the remains of a gate adjacent to Pipewell Gate. How Castle Field obtained its name remains a mystery - perhaps it relates to a use predating the medieval period!

Evidently part of King's Green at the southern end of the town was subsequently put to defensive use, for in 1585 sentence was passed on four men who 'in the night did pull down the fort on the Kings grene whereby thexercyse of Martiall causes hath bene much hindered'.[32] No identifiable earthworks can be associated with this fort, the small earthworks which survive are probably mill sites.

Winchelsea did in effect finally achieve a castle, but only because Camber Castle, erected by Henry VIII to protect the mouth of Rye Harbour, was during the 16th and 17th centuries often known as 'Winchelsea Castle'. In 1486 Sir Richard Guldeford had been granted the lordship or manor of Iham at the service of maintaining a tower, to be built within the next two years, in the marsh near the port of Camber. Whether the tower was built is uncertain, but between 1512 and 1514 his son, Sir Edward Guldeford, received over £1300 from the Treasury towards making 'a new bridge and tower' for the defence of the Camber. This tower formed the core of Henry VIII's castle designed in 1538 and completed in 1543. Philip Chute was appointed as the first captain of the castle with 8 soldiers and 6 gunners under his command.[33] The only means of overland access to the castle was via Winchelsea, and thus it is not surprising to find Chute owning houses and property in the town.[34] As the estuary became silted the castle was rendered useless and in 1626 a commission was appointed to decide its future. Upon this occasion it survived and in 1632 the King granted its custody to Thomas Porter esq. and appointed him to the office of Constable. However, it was decommissioned in 1637 and on 26 August 1642, by order of the House of Commons, the ordnance, muskets, powder and other ammunition were removed to the town of Rye.[35]

The construction between 1804 and 1809 of the Royal Military Canal and its associated Royal Military Road, which skirted beneath the eastern and southern cliff of Winchelsea, is excluded from this account of Winchelsea's defences.

THE GATES

Introduction

Gates protecting the principal entry points to the town were an early priority. Three gates still survive: Strand Gate (also called Watchbell Gate, Bell Gate or East Gate), protecting the road up from the Quay; Pipewell Gate (also called Land Gate, Ferry Gate or North Gate), protecting the way up from the ferry to Udimore and Rye and the western end of the harbour, and New Gate (also called South Gate), protecting Wickham Rock Lane leading in from Pett and beyond. The Strand Gate and New Gate date from *c.*1300 and the early 14th century respectively; Pipewell Gate represents a reconstruction of *c.*1400, which perhaps incorporated some earlier work. New Gate has been subjected to a number of medieval modifications, including the widening of its main arch. All three gates are now in a ruined state and are described in greater detail below. Other gates also once existed. It would be surprising had gates not been built to protect the road leading through Iham from the harbour, and to protect the principal landward road leading in from Icklesham, on the line of the present A259. As Figure 5.2 shows, having crossed Pewes Marsh, the road from Icklesham entered the town at Pewes Green. In view of these place-names, an order for the removal of the 'Pewes Gate' issued by the Corporation in 1546 may relate to the destruction of what must have been one of the town's principal gates.[36]

In addition to the principal entry points, there were other tracks which ascended the cliffs, particularly those leading up from the wells. Presumably these tracks would have required the construction of postern gates through the defences. One such postern gate appears to

Fig. 5.13
Strand Gate viewed from the north, looking towards the town.

be mentioned in 1297, another is mentioned in the Corporation records in 1593. A plan of *c.*1597 shows such a gate to the south of Strand Gate, protecting the track climbing the cliff from Friars Well. As already noted above, what appear to be traces of this gate can still be seen.

When in 1415 it was planned to lessen the circuit of the town defences, a new town gate was proposed on the new line, between Quarters 10 and 15, at the point where the wall was to cross the street entering the contracted part of the town from the west. This would have protected the former western end of the present High Street, although the project was probably abandoned before construction work on the gate commenced. A further gate was presumably envisaged where the southern part of the new wall crossed the street running south from the town towards New Gate.[37]

The Strand Gate *(NGR TQ 9060 1740)*
(Figures 5.13-5.18)

The Strand Gate is built astride the eastern end of the High Street (formerly Third Street) with its principal (external) elevation facing north. Because by this point the road is already beginning its descent to The Strand and in consequence runs between elevated pavements, the western side of the gate is terraced into the hillside, its lower part serving as a retaining wall. In contrast, the east elevation towers above the steeply-banked cliff which skirts this side of the town. Protecting the terraced road which climbs diagonally up the cliff from the former quay below, the gate must always have been regarded as one of the principal entrances into the town, and this is reflected in its design. It is the only one of the three surviving gates to have incorporated portcullises and decorative architectural features.

The gate was probably built soon after the

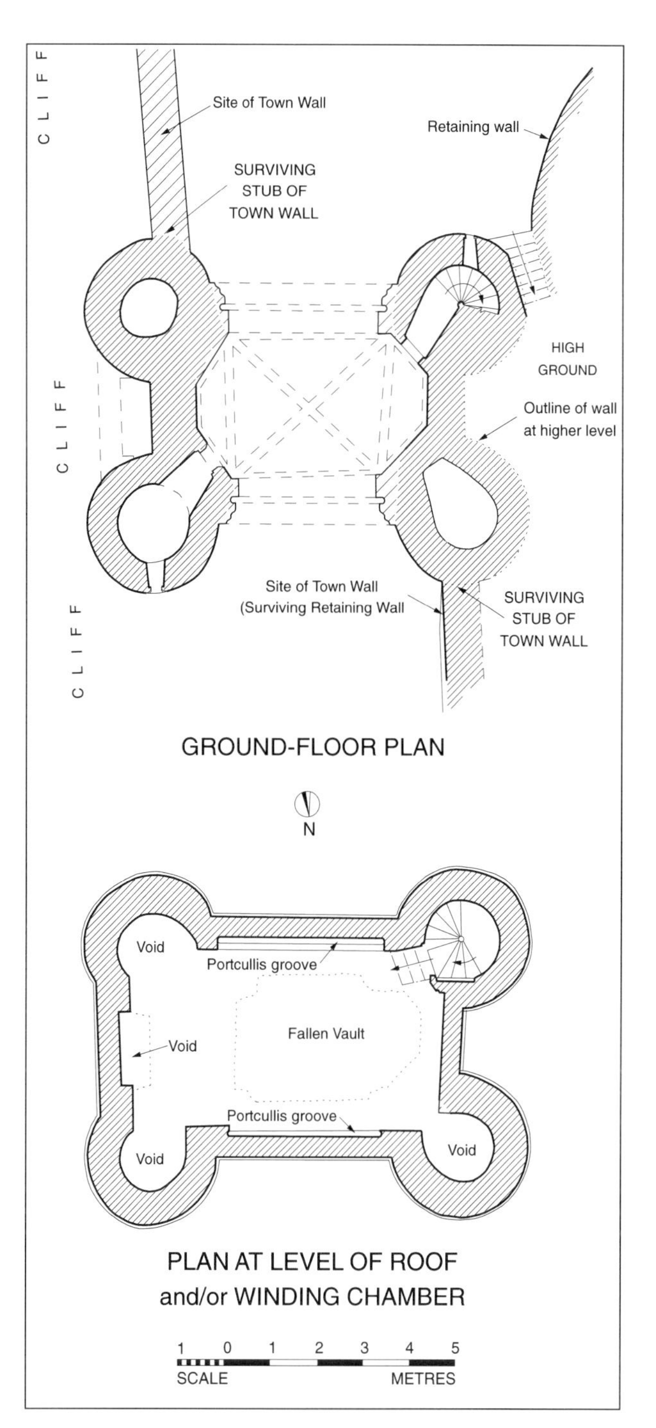

Fig. 5.14
Strand Gate: ground-floor plan and roof-level plan as existing.

foundation of the town and, on stylistic evidence, dates from *c.*1300. On the ground floor it comprises a rectangular entrance passage protected at each corner by a three-quarter-round turret. The plan is not quite square, the southern of the two main elevations is slightly the longer. Both the external (northern) and internal (southern) entrance arches were protected by a portcullis, and in addition, a surviving pintle indicates that the

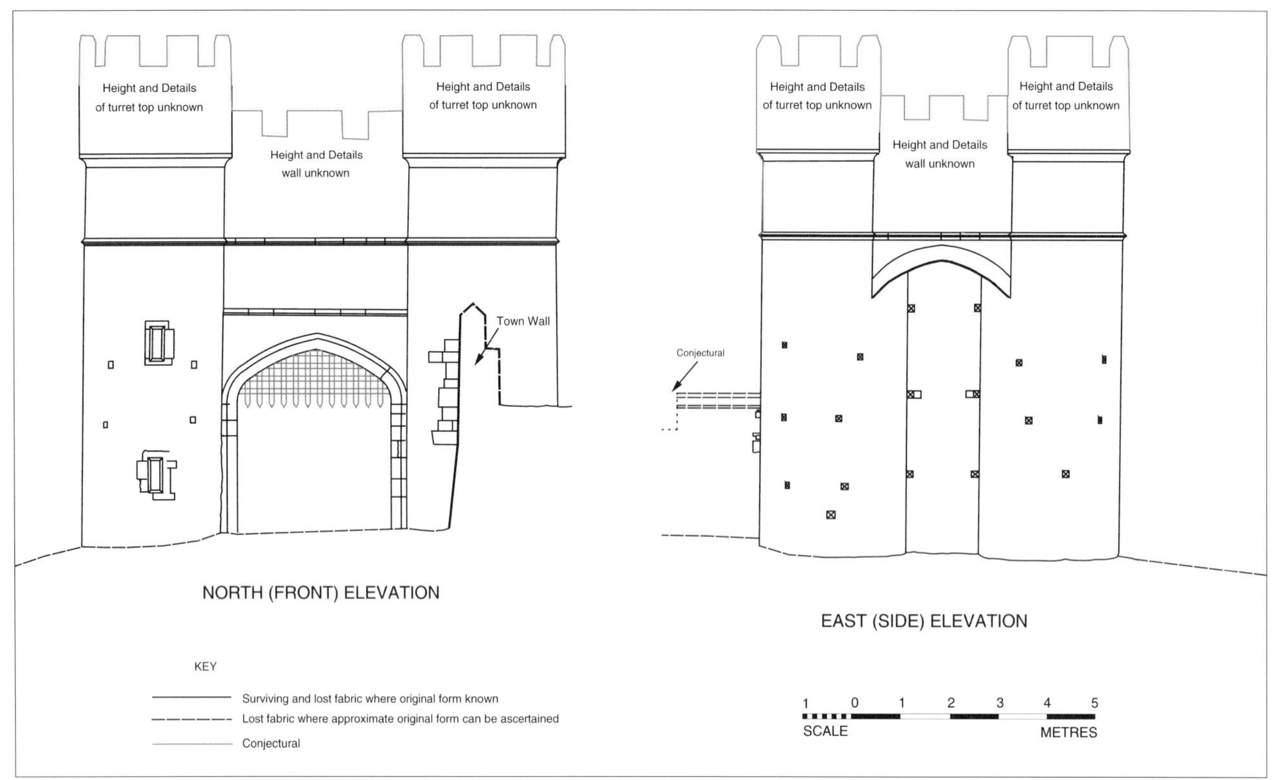

Fig. 5.15
Strand Gate: partly conjectural reconstructions of the north and east elevations. The height shown is the likely minimum height of the gate.

external arch could be barred by a pair of doors. Whether there was a similar pair of doors to the southern arch, facing into the town, is unclear. The entrance passage itself is an eight-sided space, the corners having been chamfered off to allow room for the corner turrets. The vault over the passage has now mostly fallen (Figure 5.14).

A ground-floor doorway in the northeast corner of the passage area allowed access to the interior of the northeast turret. This appears to have served as a porter's lodge, for a small window in the northern face looked over the road climbing to the gate. There is no evidence to suggest that the interiors of either the southeast or northwest turrets were intended to be accessible at this level, but, as with that at the northeast corner, a doorway gave entrance to the southwest turret. This turret housed a spiral staircase rising to the area above the vaulted entrance passage. In this upper area must have been the winding gear for raising the two portcullises. What is not clear is whether the gate was a single-storeyed structure with the winding gear housed on its flat roof, or whether there was a first-floor winding chamber. If it was flat-roofed, then the parapet walls must have been very tall in order to protect both the upper parts of the two portcullises, when they were raised, and the overhead pulleys necessary to raise them. On balance, it seems more likely that the gatehouse was originally two-storeyed, perhaps with a pitched roof. Whichever was the case, in its original form the gate was considerably taller than it now is and would have been far more imposing (Figure 5.15).

On the eastern side of the gate the upper levels of the east wall are carried on a wide arch of 'Flemish' brickwork, which springs from the walls of the adjacent turrets, and project well proud of the lower parts. The purpose of this projection was to allow the formation of murder holes in the upper floor, which gave additional protection to this side of the gate.

Although the spiral staircase within the southwest turret was separated by a doorway from the chamber or roof above the entrance passage, the interiors of the other three turrets were open to it. Indeed, because of the cantilevered eastern wall, at this level the two eastern turrets effectively formed nothing more than shallow semi-circular projections at the corners (Figure 5.14).

Because the gatehouse is built upon a terrace cut into the side of the cliff, the entire western wall of the structure serves as a retaining wall. As a result, the narrow back lane, which formerly ran beside both the gate and town wall, is elevated high above that section of road which passes through the gate. The principal means

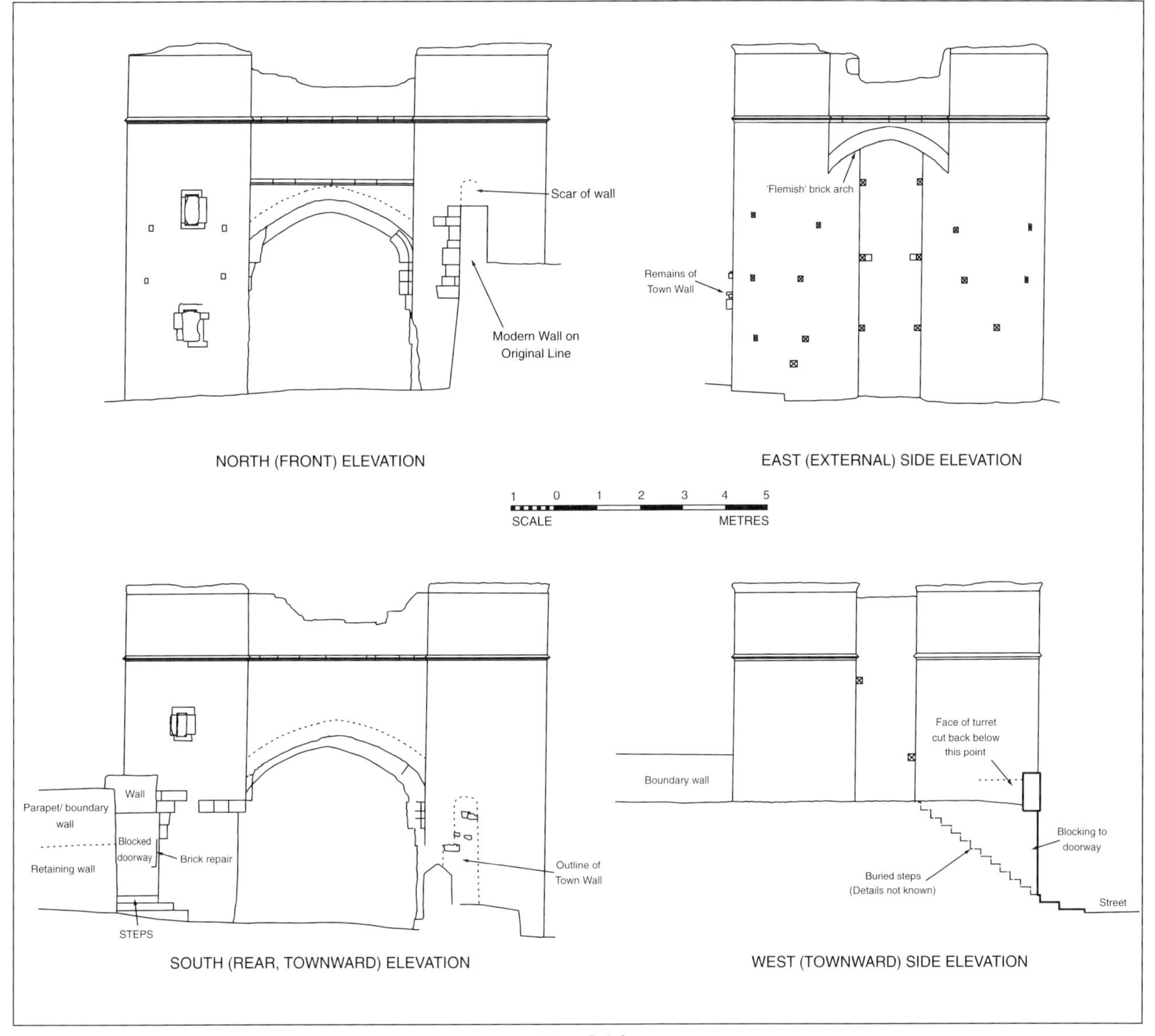

Fig. 5.16
Strand Gate: external elevations as existing.

of access to the back lane was via a high pavement located between the main road and the houses on the southern side of Quarter 6. However, a flight of steps against the southwest turret of the gate allowed secondary access to the lane from the main road. The lane still existed in the 16th century, when it was given as the eastern abutment to properties in Quarter 6, but it has now long ceased to exist and has been subsumed into private gardens.[38] Even so, as late as 1900 the steps remained in use and gave access to the garden of Tower Cottage. This gateway has now been blocked, though its site and the lower steps of the flight are still clearly visible.

In the northern face of the gate's northwest turret the dressed sandstone quoin and stub of the former Town Wall which extended northwards from the gate can be seen. Similarly, a scar in the southern face of the southeast turret show the outline of the southern section of Town Wall (*see* above).

Constructional Details

The walls of the gatehouse are not particularly thick; they measure approximately 1.0 metre (3ft.3ins.) on the ground floor, and reduce to only 400-650 millimetres (1ft.4ins-2ft.2ins.) at the upper level. They are faced with slabs of Tilgate stone rubble which, to judge from the surviving traces of white lime-mortar render, were originally masked from view both externally and internally. In contrast, all window and door openings were dressed in a soft sandstone, now very badly weathered. The hollow-chamfered ribs of the vault

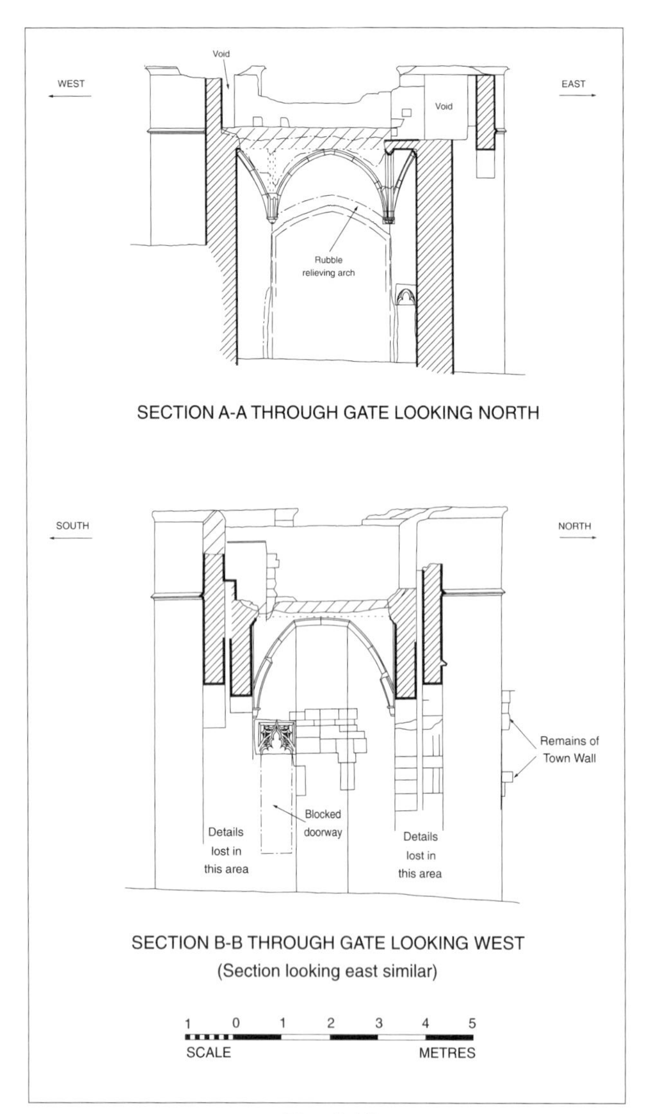

Fig. 5.17
Strand Gate: cross-sections through the gate as existing.

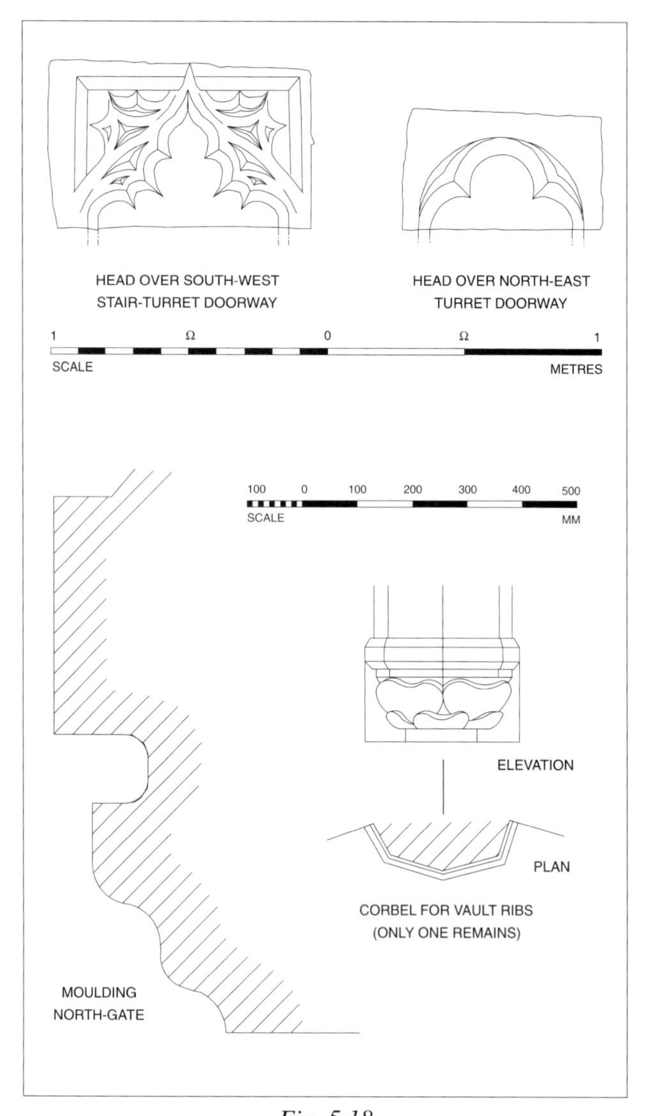

Fig. 5.18
Strand Gate: architectural details.

(now mostly fallen), the horizontal hood mouldings over the two main arches, the string course which runs around the entire gatehouse and the hollow-chamfered projecting cornices at the present-day heads of the corner turrets are all likewise of local sandstone (Figure 5.16).

Little dressed stone now survives in the northern and southern arches spanning the road and those blocks which do remain are too badly weathered to determine the profile of the mouldings. However, it is clear that the arches themselves were depressed. The two narrow, square-headed openings set into the chamfered corners of the entrance passage to allow access to the northeast and southwest turrets have both lost the dressed stones forming the jambs. The southwest doorway is now blocked, but that leading to the northeast turret remains open. The heads of both openings are formed by large, thin, rectangular slabs of stone laid on edge and carved on the surface facing into the passage (Figure 5.18), but in both instances the carvings are now badly weathered. That on the doorhead leading into the 'Porter's Lodge' is the less elaborate of the two, being carved to imitate a cusped semicircular arch. That over the doorway leading to the spiral staircase is larger and is carved to imitate an ogee arch with multiple cusping, all set beneath a chamfered square surround with cusping to the spandrels. The first-floor doorway at the head of the stair turret is severely damaged, but sufficient remains to show a closing rebate for a door hung to open westwards, across the spiral staircase. Owing to the level of the doorway's cill, located approximately 700 millimetres (2ft.4ins.) below the top surface of the vault spanning the entrance passage, a more conventional and convenient eastward-opening door was impossible. In order to reach the winding chamber or roof, a short flight of steps, rising over the web of the vault beyond the doorway, was necessary.

Both the northeast and southwest turrets are lit at the lower levels by small, square-headed windows with chamfered surrounds on the external face which are now very weathered. Internally they have splayed jambs and flat rear arches. In each case the rear arch is formed by one large, thin slab of undressed Tilgate stone.

Sufficient survives of the vault over the passage through the gate to indicate that the central rectangular area was capped by a single bay of quadripartite vaulting supported by dressed, hollow-chamfered ribs which sprang from corbels built into the angles of the passage. Only one corbel now survives. It has a moulded abacus supported by a carved bell. The bell is perhaps of stylized foliage (*see* Figure 5.18). The central boss, together with the central section of the vault, fell long ago. Flanking the central quadripartite bay are small areas of barrel vault which are purposely designed to take into account the canted sides of these areas. All three bays of the vault incorporate half ribs built into the side walls.

The Pipewell Gate *(NGR TQ 9038 1763)* *(Figures 5.19-5.22)*

Pipewell Gate is sited at the northwest corner of the present shrunken town, part way along the northern cliff. It originally stood astride a terraced road, which rose obliquely up the cliff from the estuary and harbour plots beneath and from the ferry crossing to Udimore parish on the opposite side of the estuary, and thence to Rye. Today the terrace carries the A259, but this road turns southwards, passing immediately to the west of the gate, through the line of the former town wall (now demolished). This diversion had already occurred by 1758, but the cutting which takes the road across the line of the wall was considerably widened in the second half of the 20th century (Figure 5.19).[39]

Although this was one of the original gates of the town, it is alleged to have been destroyed by the French in 1380 and rebuilt around 1400 by John Helde, mayor of the town in 1399 and 1404.[40] The above 'facts' should be taken with caution: the term 'destroyed' can be interpreted in a number of ways, as too can 'rebuilt'. It is unlikely that the French would have completely razed the gate to the ground or so badly damaged it that no part could be reused. Nor is it likely, bearing in mind the town's diminished economic base, that the Corporation would have demolished reusable fabric. Therefore the possibility that the original gate was merely heavily repaired and partially rebuilt in *c.*1400 should not be ruled out. The gate now contains few features which would be out of keeping either in *c.*1400 or a century earlier, although the three-centred head to the western entrance arch, immediately beneath a commemorative plaque, is more consistent with a date of *c.*1400, as is the character of the slightly projecting parapet wall. Both features are located at high level within the structure. Inconsistencies in the vault over the entrance passage may also suggest repair (*see* below).

Fig. 5.19
Pipewell Gate viewed from the east in the early 20th century prior to the widening of the A259 (on the left). Note the remains of the precinct wall of the Black Friars on the extreme left. The remains have since been removed. [J E Ray Collection, Hastings Public Library]

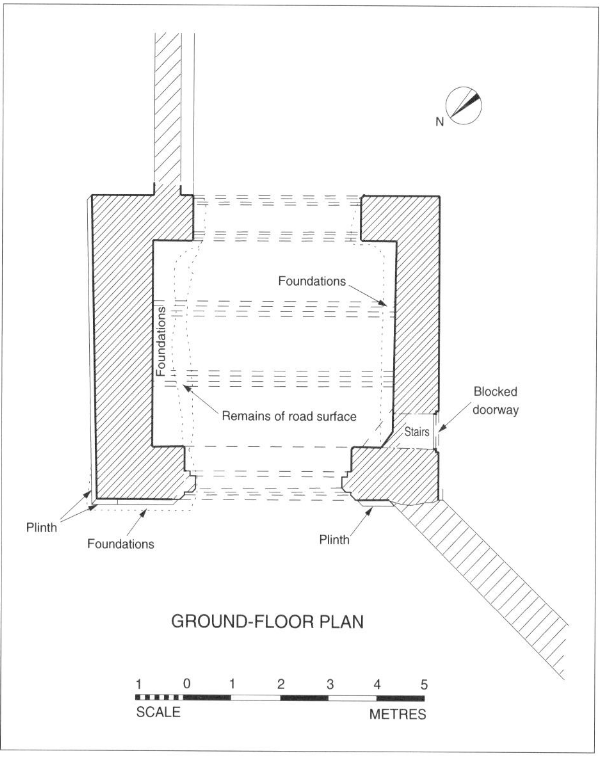

Fig. 5.20
Pipewell Gate: ground-floor plan as existing.

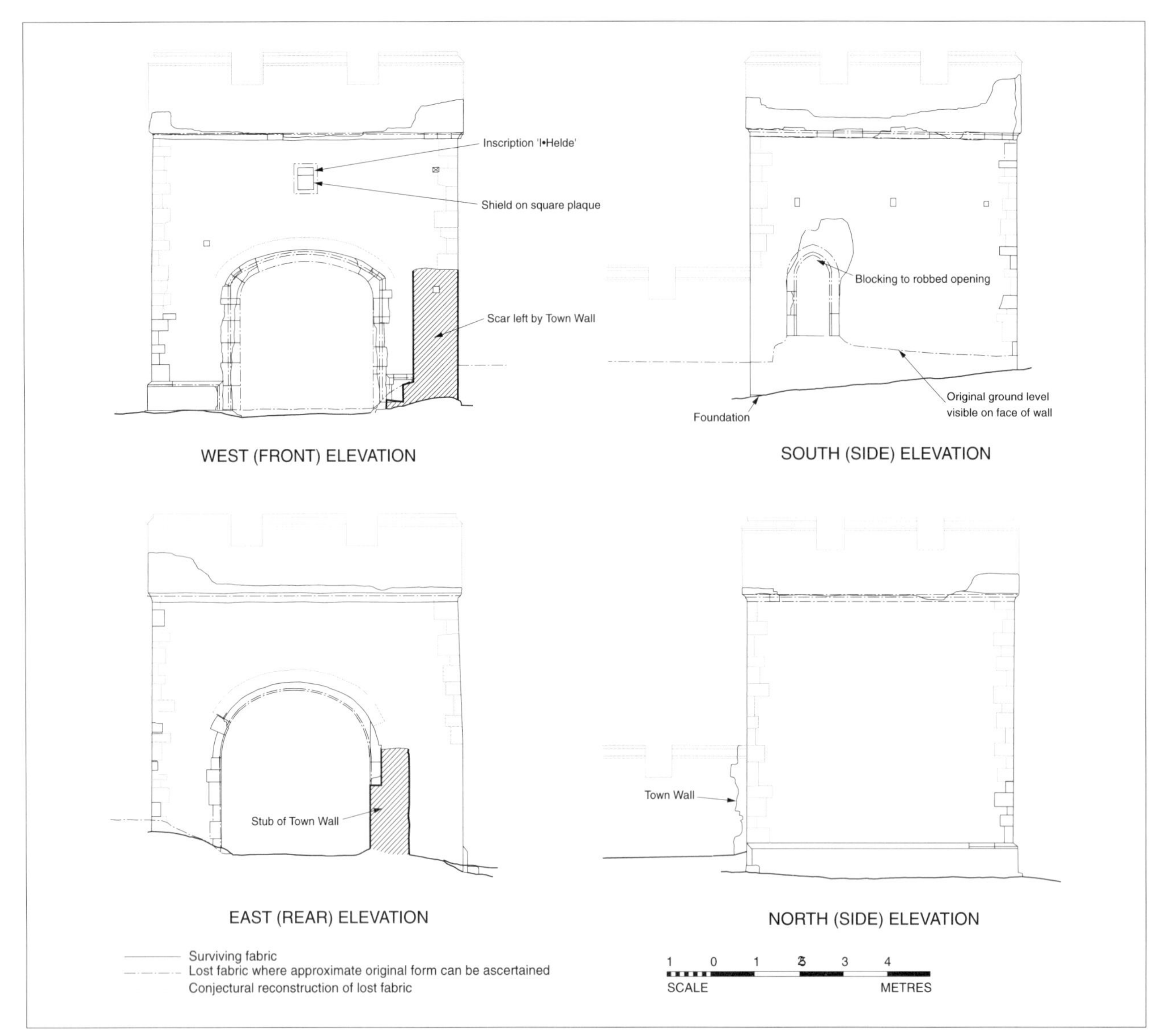

Fig. 5.21
Pipewell Gate: elevations as existing. Lost parapet walls and town wall are shown (partly conjecturally).

The gate is a simple, single-storeyed, rectangular stone structure. It measures 7.10 metres by 6.00 metres (23ft.3ins. by 19ft.8ins.) overall and was originally capped by a flat roof protected by a parapet which was probably crenellated (Figure 5.21). Built astride the highway, which at this point is aligned southeast-northwest, the gate's principal elevation faces northwest (hereafter assumed to be west). Although the gradient of the road rising from the harbour has slackened by the time it reaches the gate, it is still rising eastwards as it passes under it towards the town. This gradient, together with a slight crossfall towards the north, is taken into account in the design of the structure. Thus, the plinth steps down between the southern and northern jamb of the main entrance, whilst the crown of the eastern entrance arch (facing the town) is set higher than that in the western facade (Figure 5.22). The scars where the town wall butted against the gate are still clearly visible: indeed, a short stub of the wall still survives where it abuts the east elevation against the northern jamb of the entrance arch. On the external (western) face of the gate, the town wall projected at an angle from the southern end of the elevation (*see* Figure 5.20).

Internally, the gate incorporates nothing more than a single 'room' which served as an entrance passage. It was entered from the western (external) side under an arch 3.15 metres (10ft.4ins.) wide which, allowing for the slightly higher level of the medieval road, measured approximately 3.45 metres (11ft.4ins.)

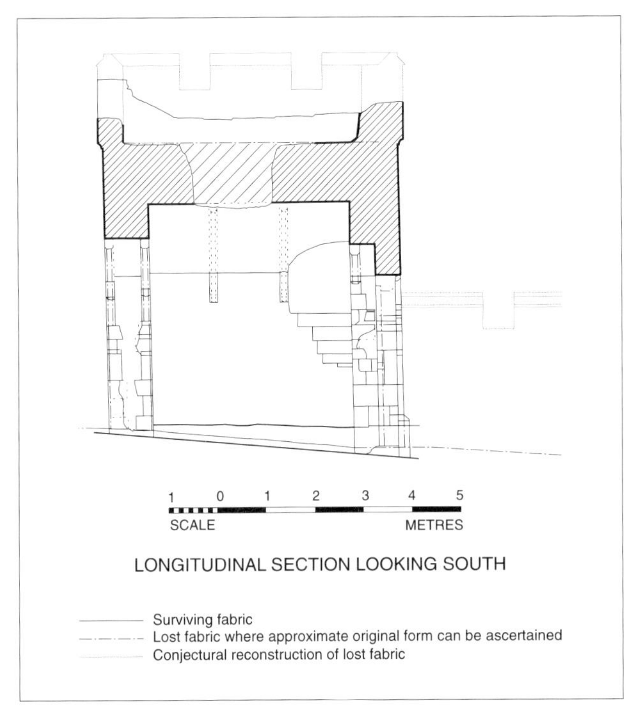

Fig. 5.22
Pipewell Gate: section through the gatehouse as existing. Lost parapet walls and town wall are shown (partly conjecturally).

high to its crown. This entrance was never elaborately moulded and was only lightly defended: it was protected neither by drawbridge, ditch nor portcullis, and was closed only by an inward-opening, two-leaf door. The passage, which is capped by a barrel vault, is wider than the entrance arch and its side walls are built off foundations which rise above the medieval road surface and thus project into the 'room'. The top surfaces of these foundations are now badly damaged, but the projections may have served as low wall benches. Apart from the chamfered ribs, which supported the arched head, the western entrance facing the town is entirely plain and was never closed by a door. Thus the interior of the gate was always accessible to the townsfolk.

The parapeted flat roof of the gate was doubtless used as a lookout and fighting platform and was reached via a flight of steps rising within the southwest corner. The steps were reached via an external doorway (now blocked) situated towards the western end of the south elevation, immediately behind the former town wall. The level of the ground in this area was reduced when the town wall was demolished and in consequence, the cill of the doorway is now well above the ground.

Constructional Details

The gate is constructed of thin slabs of Tilgate stone, typical of work found throughout Winchelsea. All quoins and openings were originally dressed in a soft, grey/buff sandstone, but many of the stones have disintegrated and have mostly been replaced at the quoins using rough Tilgate rubble slabs. Within the western and northern facades, facing away from the town, a chamfered plinth of dressed sandstone is included a little above the ground surface, and the level of this reduces in height either side of the entrance, taking into account the ground slope. There is no plinth on the eastern and southern elevations facing into the town. Set at roof level within all four external walls are the remains of a projecting, hollow-chamfered cornice of dressed sandstone, marking the base of the parapet. Only fragments of the parapet survive and nowhere can either its original height or direct evidence of its crenellations be ascertained. The segmental barrel vault above the entrance passage is constructed of thin Tilgate slabs laid on edge. Where the central section has fallen, it shows the vault to be thick and to be capped by a course of horizontally-laid slabs, forming the paved surface of the roof. The now badly damaged hollow-chamfered springers of two sets of vaulting ribs indicate that the vault was once divided into three bays in similar fashion to many of the Winchelsea cellars. Within the cellars, a mortar scar can usually be detected running across the soffit of the barrel where the ribs have fallen. No such scars are visible within the vault of the gate, despite patches of original rendering on the vault. The extant render appears to extend continuously across the line of the ribs. It is therefore possible that the springers for the ribs represent work of *c.*1300 and that the vault was reconstructed in *c.*1400 without ribs. If so, the springers for the earlier ribs were hacked back flush with the wall surface (Figure 5.22). Unfortunately, it is now impossible to tell whether the springers were deliberately cut away, or whether the projecting faces have merely fallen.

Sufficient render survives about the gate to indicate that all internal and external surfaces were originally rendered, hiding from view the Tilgate rubble walling, including that in the relieving arches over the main entrances. The render is of white lime mortar and was always thin and finished with a rippled, undulating surface. Only the sandstone dressings at the quoins and around the openings were left exposed. Within the south elevation the base of the rendering still indicates the original level of the external ground surface. The wall face beneath the base of the render is more roughly finished and some of the stones project well proud of the face. Other areas of the substructure wall show large patches of projecting mortar still adhering to the stones. Both features indicate that the lower courses of the wall were built hard against the face of a foundation trench. Similar evidence indicates the level of the medieval ground surface at the southern end of the west elevation.

From these data it is possible to show that at the gate there was a difference of *c*.900 millimetres (3ft.) in ground level on either side of the town wall, and thus its lower part acted as a retaining wall.

Despite the dressed stones being badly worn and broken, sufficient survive to indicate that the outer face of the arch was of two simply-chamfered orders. The outer order was the narrower and rose to a chamfered segmental arch. In contrast, the inner order incorporated a three-centred arch and sprang from the jambs fully 400 millimetres (1ft.4ins.) below the springing of the segmental arch. The lowest voussoir on the southern side of the arch still retains the door rebate in its eastern face. Above the dressed arch is a relieving arch of Tilgate slabs laid on edge, and set at a higher level there is a similar relieving arch carrying the eastern face of the wall. Incorporated into the wall above are two dressed Caen-stone blocks. The lower block incorporates an incised border surrounding a heart-shaped shield carrying a beast - said to be a squirrel. The upper block is rectangular and has the incised description 'I · HELDE' - presumably referring to John Helde, mayor in 1399 and 1404.[41] But could the townsfolk have used the name of their mayor on this inscription as a conceit or pun, announcing to all that the gate held against the French assaults, even if badly damaged? If so, it illustrates the symbolic value of the gate to the town - its repair was perhaps an assertion of the town's survival, and even regeneration.

The dressed jamb stones of the entrance rise from a rough projecting foundation, the base of the jamb being set above the present road surface. This indicates that the road level has been reduced by approximately 200 millimetres (8ins.) as the result of erosion. This is confirmed by a strip of pitched-stone road surface which still survives adjacent to the foundation supporting the northern wall of the gate. As in the walls, the stones are Tilgate: their upper edges are worn.

In contrast to the gate's main entrance, the eastern entrance has plain jambs of dressed sandstone, supporting the remains of two fully-chamfered ribs, one set against the eastern face of the relieving arch, the other against the western face. Both formed a nearly semicircular arch. Between them, the recessed soffit of the Tilgate slab relieving arch was rendered. It should be noted that the northern jamb of the opening incorporates only two dressed stones, the lower section of the reveal being extended eastwards to form the southern face of the town wall. The face of the town wall steps in at the point where the jamb stones commence, although additional stonework has been added to the offset subsequently, apparently to form a weathering.

Incorporated into the south elevation, towards its western end, the lower jamb stones of the doorway which opened onto the stairs leading to the gate's roof survive. It still retains its worn cill formed by a long, thin slab of Tilgate stone. Both the upper stones and the arch have either fallen or been robbed, and the opening has been blocked. Those jamb stones which survive incorporate a closing rebate in their external leading edges, it being necessary for the door to open outwards to avoid its being fouled by the staircase. The broken-off shaft of a pintle incorporated into the eastern jamb indicates that the door was hung on its eastern side. Within the gate, in the southwest corner, the underside of the steps to the staircase, cutting across the corner of the passage are visible. They are of undressed Tilgate stone.

The New Gate *(NGR TQ 9010 1644)*
(Figures 5.23-5.27)

At about a mile from the town's quay, a narrow saddle of raised ground flanked by marshland to both

Fig. 5.23
New Gate viewed from the west showing its isolated rural location.

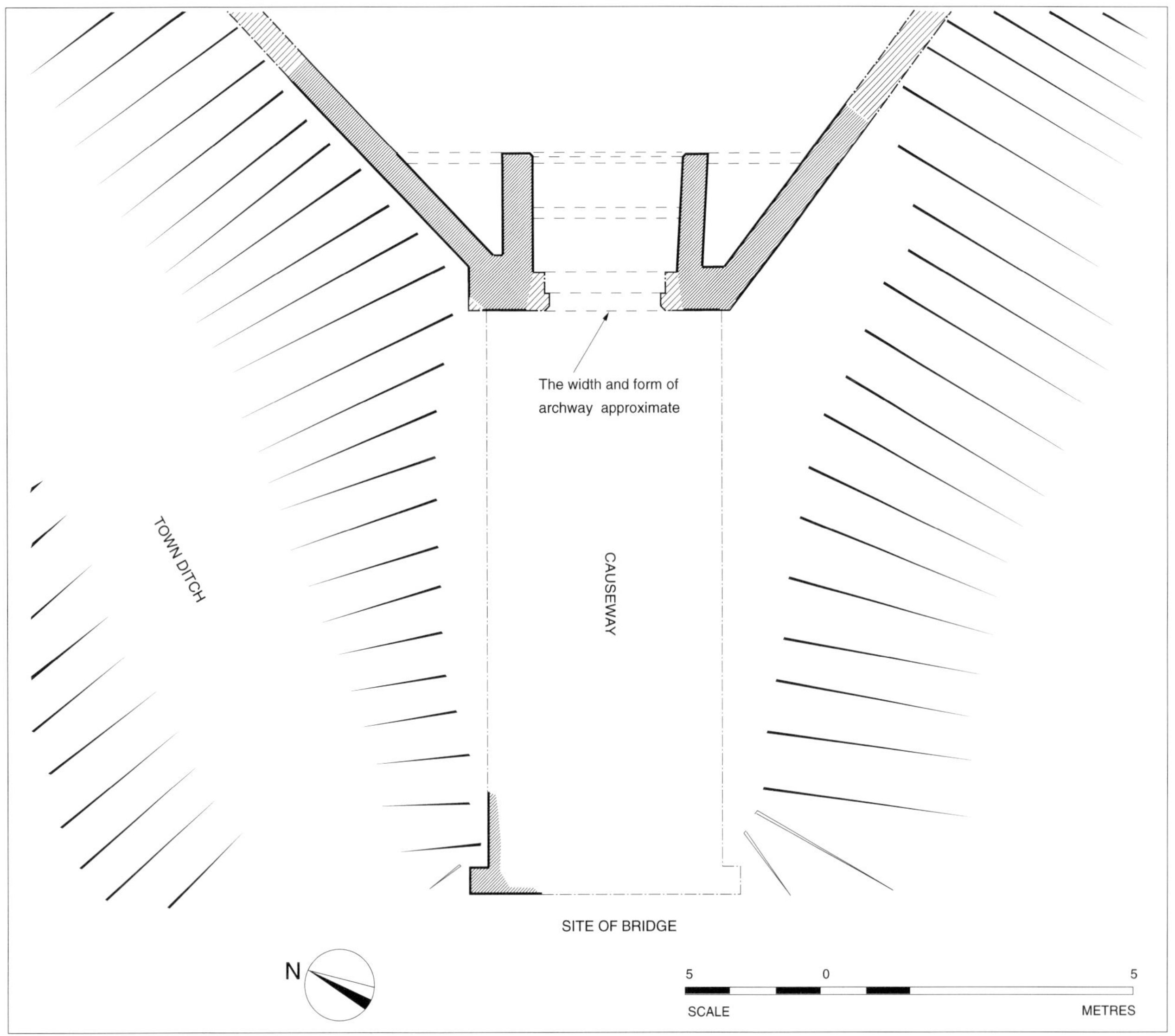

Fig. 5.24
New Gate: plan of gatehouse as first built.

south and north connects the southern end of Winchelsea Hill to the eastern tip of the Icklesham ridge. Either when the town was laid out, or very soon afterwards, the saddle was cut by a very deep section of Town Dyke, linking the two marshes and isolating Winchelsea from the adjacent upland. The New Gate was constructed at the point where the lane from Pett and Fairlight crossed the Town Dyke. Here the southern and western sections of town wall met approximately at right angles to each other, although the angle was eased by canting a short section of wall at the intersection. It was within this that the gate was sited (Figure 5.24). Its name implies that it was built after the other principal gates, but it was already known as the 'New Gate' by 1330, by which date the adjacent section of Town Dyke had been excavated.[42]

Although an impressive structure, it is the simplest of the three surviving gates and comprises an archway which leads into a passage 3.20 metres (10ft.6ins.) wide. The passage stretches back 2.55 metres (8ft.4ins.) from the internal face of the wall (Figures 5.24-5.27) and its sides are formed by two buttress-like spur walls which in turn support a very high, two-centred barrel vault divided by ribs into two bays. Two further barrel vaults set at the same high level flank the passageway, linking it to the elevated ends of the town wall. The areas roofed by these flanking vaults are triangular in plan. Thus as initially built, the gatehouse was trapezoidal in plan and comprised a central passage with flanking areas, all of which rose high above the adjacent sections of town wall. It is not now known whether the trapezoidal area above the three vaults rose to form a high chamber, or whether it acted as the gate's roof, protected by battlements. Given the extreme height of the platform and the lack of any built-in stairway, the latter arrangement seems the more likely.

Extending in front of the gate an earthen causeway carries the road across the Town Dyke. Twelve and a half metres (41ft.) from the gate, the buttressed wall of a bridge abutment is visible in the northern bank together with a stone revetment wall running back towards the gate. This implies that the revetted causeway projected only part way across the Town Dyke and had some form of removable bridge at its western end.

Constructional Details:

As with the other gates, the walls are not thick: they vary from 600 millimetres (2ft.) at the southern flanking wall, to 950 millimetres (3ft.2ins.) at the front wall. They are faced with slabs of Tilgate stone rubble, whilst all dressings to the quoins, openings and vaulting ribs are of neatly-tooled sandstone blocks. Cleaning and repointing has removed any traces of external render that there may have been, so that it is not clear whether the rubble facing was originally left exposed or masked from view. The main opening through the wall was later rebuilt to a greater width and thus its original details have been lost. However, straight joints in the masonry indicate that the opening incorporated projecting jambs, whilst the original segmental relieving arch of Tilgate stone laid on edge survives and suggests an original width for the opening of only *c.*2.40 metres (*c.*7ft.10ins.). At the opposite end of the passage the quoins of the flanking walls are plain, save for inward-facing chamfers. The gatehouse incorporated no windows, the areas flanking the passage were entirely open on their townward side. The three 'compartments' of the gatehouse are capped by segmental barrel vaults of undressed Tilgate slabs laid on edge. All three vaults are terminated along their townward edge by a chamfered rib of dressed sandstone. The vaults of both flanking areas

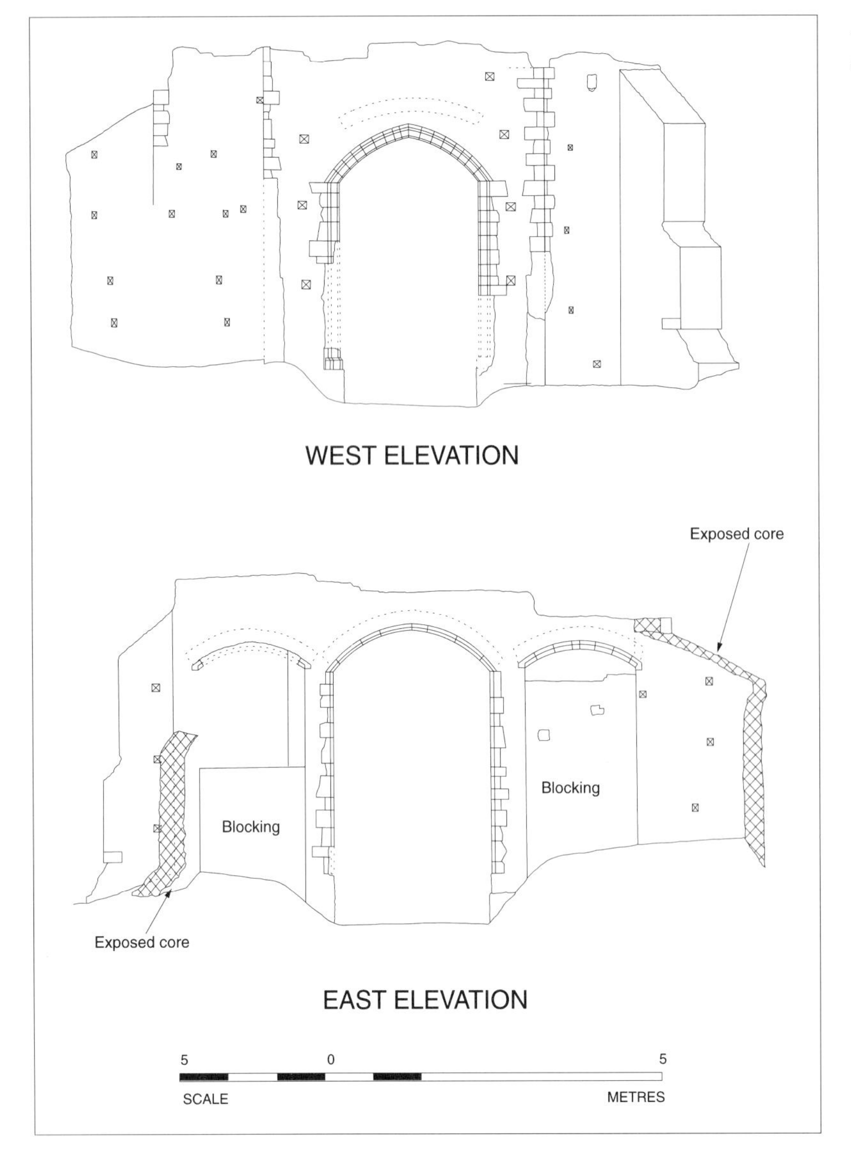

Fig. 5.25 (Left)
New Gate: elevations as existing.

are of one bay only, but that over the passage is of two bays divided by a chamfered rib.

Subsequent Alterations (Figures 5.26 and 5.27)

Four ancient modifications to the design of the gatehouse are identifiable. The most dramatic of these was the widening of the main entrance, increasing the archway to the same width as the passage. Straight joints in the masonry, marking the point where the wall of the passage originally turned to form the reveals to the original narrower opening, can be seen at a point 800 millimetres (2ft.8ins.) from the external face of the gate within both jambs of the main entrance. Further evidence of the alteration is indicated by the vault over the entrance passage, which is now of two unequal bays. With the reveals intact, both bays would have been equal. A further point to note is that the relieving arch over the present opening is narrower than the opening itself. The new archway has a depressed two-centred head of dressed sandstone with double-chamfered jambs and voussoirs. The base of the southern jamb has been lost, but that of the northern jamb survives. It incorporates a chamfered offset and is of Caen stone, rather than sandstone. It could represent a later repair. Its level indicates that the road surface has dropped considerably since the archway was rebuilt. Internally the opening is rebated for a pair of doorways, but there is no groove for a portcullis.

Built against the external southern face of the wall, adjacent to the southeast quoin, is a heavy Tilgate stone buttress incorporating three offsets. Where they survive the quoins are of dressed sandstone, as the canted offsets (now lost) would also have been. The buttress is

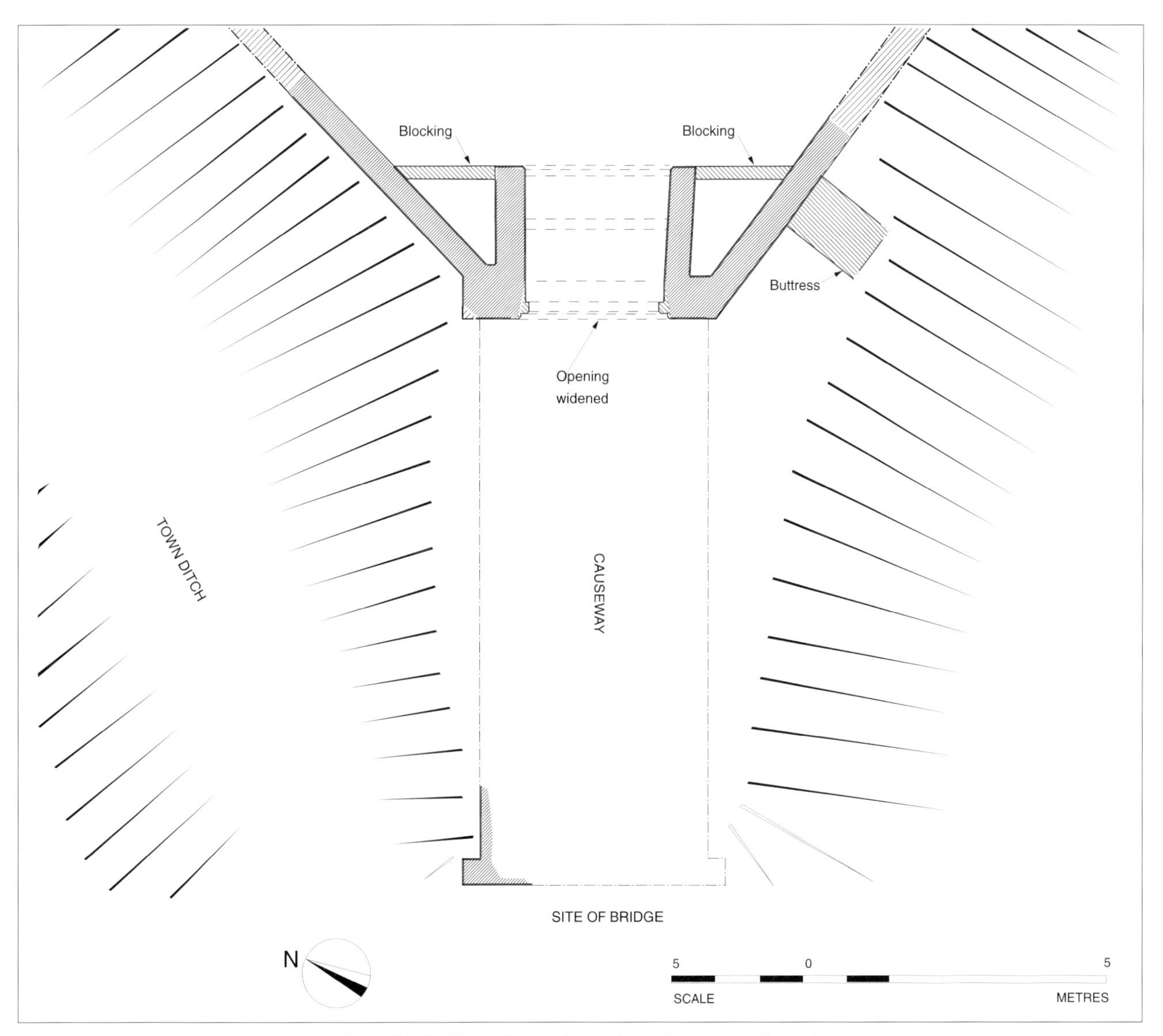

Fig. 5.26 New Gate: plan of gatehouse as altered.

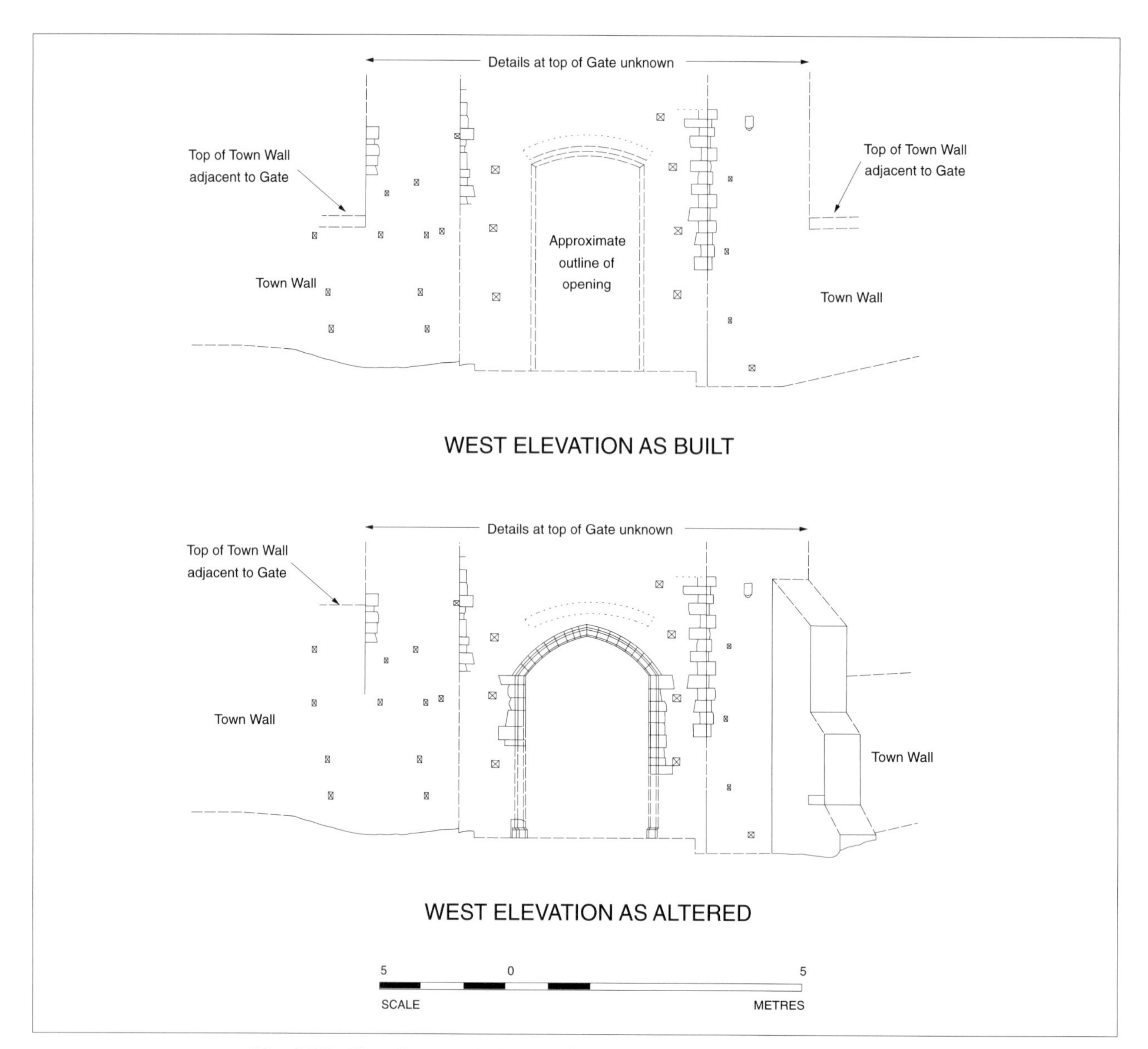

Fig. 5.27 New Gate: main (west) elevation before and after alterations.

straight jointed to the wall and therefore was an addition.

A further alteration was the heightening of the western section of town wall where it met the gate. The quoin forming the northern corner of the gate is visible in the west elevation and for some considerable distance extends down past the head of the town wall. A similar straight joint is visible between the upper part of the town wall and the gatehouse in the townward elevation, and here a lift line or levelling course is visible in the face of the town wall, coinciding with the base of the straight joint. The bottom extent of the straight joint is set at an identical level and indicates the original height of the town wall. It was of similar height to the southern section of town wall, as indicated by its scar on the gatehouse. How far northwards the increase in height extended is unknown.

The final modification involved alterations to the areas flanking the entrance passage. Although initially these were small vaulted open recesses of triangular plan, they were subsequently blocked by walls of Tilgate rubble 300 millimetres (1ft.) thick constructed across their eastern faces, thus converting them into inaccessible voids. The upper parts of the blocking have now fallen.

There is no way of ascertaining whether the four modifications described above were carried out simultaneously or as a series of sequential alterations. Given that by 1414 the New Gate was located well beyond the populated part of the town, it seems likely that any road widening undertaken after that date would have resulted in the demolition of the gate. The alterations are, therefore, probably of early date.

6. GOVERNMENT AND THE MUNICIPAL BUILDINGS

David and Barbara Martin

GOVERNMENT OF THE TOWN

As a full member of the Cinque Ports confederation, Winchelsea enjoyed extensive liberties in return for ship service to the Crown. These privileges included exemption from the secular jurisdictions to which the surrounding area was subject – *i.e.* the Sheriff's County Court, the Lathe Court of the Lord of the Rape of Hastings, and Guestling Hundred Court. The town held its own courts instead. In an administrative context, not only were the residents of the town exempt from most royal taxation, but the freemen also enjoyed the same exemption within external hundreds in which they held property. None of these privileges applied to resident aliens, nor to non-resident merchants trading with the port town.

From the time that Winchelsea was acquired by the Crown from Fécamp Abbey in 1249, it was governed by a royal bailiff appointed by the king. Although the bailiff represented the king's interests within the royal borough, from the middle of the 13th century he was usually a Winchelsea resident. Already by 1252 there are indications that the town was achieving a degree of self-government, for in that year a royal mandate was directed to the barons (principal residents) of Winchelsea to elect from among themselves twelve of the more discreet and faithful men of the town to advise what aid should be levied for the defence against the encroachment of the sea.[1] When the town was refounded upon its present site, the barons attempted to formalize their interests by including, amongst nine requests to Edward I, the desire that their courts and other privileges should be as before and that the town should have a mayor elected from among themselves and twelve jurats (leading residents - similar to aldermen - chosen to serve as a council). To the first request the king agreed, but to the second he replied, 'Let them have bailiffs as they have been accustomed'.[2] Nevertheless, despite this reply, he appears to have partly relented, for when in July 1288 the Bishop of Ely delivered seisin of the land to the town's commonalty (inhabitants) on behalf of the king, a temporary administration composed of a mayor and 24 jurats was appointed to allocate plots to the residents and to set the 'king's rent' due from each. In total, the rents allocated to the plots were to equate to the £14.11s.5¾d. which had been due from the land prior to the foundation of the town. For the first seven years no rent was to be paid to the Crown, but thereafter it was the responsibility of the mayor and commonalty to pay to the bailiff, as king's representative, the fee farm rent comprising the total rents allocated to the building plots.

The foundation rental was drawn up in 1292 - presumably in readiness for the payment of the first rents - and it would have been around this date too that the temporary administration was replaced by the first elected mayor and twelve jurats. The rental included a one-acre plot on Quarter 27 allocated to the 'Mayor of Winchelsea whosoever he may be' at a king's rent of 40d.[3] This was probably a plot reserved for the holding of the open-air hundred courts.

The result of these (assumed) concessions by Edward I was the creation of what was in effect a dual administration: one headed by the bailiff, representing the Crown, the other by the mayor, representing the commonalty. In 1294/5 the elected mayor was Gervase Alard, junior, whilst two years later his (assumed) relation, Thomas Alard, presented accounts in his capacity as king's bailiff. Not surprisingly, both are identifiable in the 1292 rental amongst the 13 principal members of the town's urban elite (*see* Chapter 8).

Within the town's dual administration the bailiff continued to be the head officer of Winchelsea throughout the medieval period. As the late-13th- and early-14th-century bailiffs' accounts show, the bailiff was responsible for the fee farm rent, for the letting of all vacant lands both within and without the town, for tolls of markets and fairs, for the custom due on merchandise (arriving both by sea and by land) for the custom (called shares) of fishing ships and boats, for collecting other port dues such as lastage, stallage, terrage, anchorage, wharfage, bulkage, tronage, and passage, and for the perquisites of courts and leets. He also accounted for the forfeited chattels of felons. The latest extant bailiff's account, dated 1372, illustrates his activity in holding courts: in that year he called 19 courts for residents and an unspecified number for strangers. In his duties as coroner, the bailiff acted jointly with the mayor. To assist him, the bailiff had his own officials, including sergeants. Throughout the first half of the 14th century the bailiffs tended to be Winchelsea residents, as during the last years of (Old) Winchelsea, but as the town's importance diminished, it became increasingly the practice to lease out the bailiwick as a reward to royal servants. Even so, it remained in the hands of the Crown until 1506 when it was granted, together with the office of bailiff and the manor of Iham, to Sir Richard Guldeford of Hempstead Place, Benenden, Kent.[5] It was probably during the late 14th century, as the bailiwick increasingly became a mere perquisite, that the duties (but not the profits) of the bailiff were taken over by the town's elected mayor. Even so, as late as 1612, the Guldeford family continued to have part of the court hall allocated to them for use as a prison.[6]

According to a copy of the town's customal made in 1557, the mayor was chosen annually by the commonalty of Winchelsea on the Monday after Easter at an assembly held in the Hundred Place. Upon his election he chose 12 jurats from the freemen of the town to serve as his council. At the same time a common clerk, a sergeant and other officials were chosen. In 1850 Cooper listed the town officials as a town clerk, a chamberlain, a sergeant-at-mace, a town sergeant, a water bailiff (not to be confused with the bailiff), a gaoler, six constables and a pound driver. The two sergeants no doubt reflect the merging by this date of the duties of those officials answerable to the bailiff and those answerable to the mayor. Despite the many duties listed above, the customal indicates that the bailiff's court duties were not all-embracing and that some lesser courts, principally those concerning the internal affairs of the residents, were in the sole charge of the mayor and jurats, whilst in others the bailiff sat jointly with the mayor and jurats. In this way, as with the office of coroner, the duties were shared. Despite the internal administrative and legal duties cited above, in the 14th century the mayor and jurats were principally concerned with representing the town at the various courts of the Cinque Ports confederation and in Parliament. For performing their duties the mayor and his officials (but not the jurats) received a fee. In 1388 the mayor's quarterly fee was 20s., that of his town clerk 10d. quarterly, whilst a wage of 12d. each per quarter was paid to a collector of *malitot* and a collector of *malitot carnificum*. The existence of these last two officers indicates that in addition to land rents, profits were received by the Corporation from taxes on fishermen and butchers.[7]

The main organ of administration within the town was the court. From 1527, when the surviving court books commence, the principal courts were the Hundred Court and the Common Court (later called the Court of Record). Some of the sessions at the Common Court are called Piepowder Courts or Courts of Strangers. The immunity of the Cinque Ports from attendance at the County Courts meant that each town held its own Quarter Sessions for dealing with criminal justice, but the Sessions rolls relating to these are largely missing.[8] Generally, court pleas were to be held in the town's court hall, but pleas 'for member or for life' were to be held before the assembled hundred. All those condemned to death were to be 'hanged in the salt marsh, on the northern side of the town of Winchelsea, in the salt water of the same town'. [9]

THE MUNICIPAL BUILDINGS *(Figures 6.1-6.5)*

In addition to the 'Hundred Place' - a large open space for the holding of the hundred, at which the entire commonalty was required to attend - the seat of the town's administration was its Court Hall with its associated adjuncts. Homan concluded that the original municipal buildings had been situated upon the one-acre tenement held in perpetuity by the serving mayor on Quarter 27 and known in the 16th century as the 'mayor's acre'. In his opinion, this plot was located immediately adjacent to where he thought the Hundred Place had been: to the west of Grey Friars, in the heart of the town's commercial centre and close to the Monday Market.[10] However, in the light of new and conclusive documentary evidence, the reconstructed layout of this part of town has been revised, and has placed Quarter 23 upon the site Homan had postulated for the Hundred Place, and located the 'mayor's acre' on a much more isolated, cliff-edge location - an unlikely position for the centre of town government. It now seems more likely that the plot allocated to the mayor was for the open-air assembly of the hundred.

It is not at present known where any early municipal buildings stood, but they were probably in the market square. The first extant 14th-century town accounts are dated 1356 and already by then, three years before the disastrous French raid, the bailiff was hiring a court hall and prison from William Batesford.[11] Indeed, it is possible that the town had never owned its own court hall, for during the years immediately after the refounding, at least as late as 1295, the bailiff was paying rent for 'a building to hold courts and pleas'.[12]

The ruin now known as Blackfriars Barn on Quarter 15 must be a likely candidate either for the early hired court hall or for a guildhall. It is built at right angles to the street with a massive three-bay hall 11.10 metres (36ft.5ins.) long by, on average, 8.90 metres (29ft.2ins.) wide. The hall must originally have been lit by a large window in its street gable, where the main entrance must also have been. It had a fireplace from the outset. Except for the three-chamber vaulted cellar, which had its own separate entrance, there were two smaller rooms. There was, however, a sizable garderobe outshut served by a large cesspit, and some form of building - probably a kitchen - attached by a pentice at the rear. This general arrangement is reminiscent of a number of guildhalls, for example Trinity Guildhall and St George's Guildhall, both in King's Lynn.[13]

By 1499 'Blackfriars Barn' was in ruins. Regardless of whether that building served as the medieval municipal centre or not, by at least 1538 the court hall had moved into a late-13th-century house at the southwest corner of Quarter 8, opposite St Thomas's church. It remains upon this site to this day. In the late 13th and early 14th centuries, this high-status house had been owned first by Gervase Alard, junior (by coincidence, an early mayor) and later by his son, James Alard.[14] Alterations made to the structure during the 15th century - including the construction of the present crownpost roof (Figure 6.1) - suggest that the building was already in use as a municipal complex by that date. Today the building is a simple two-storeyed range with a single room open to the roof on its first floor. However, its 15th-century form was more complex. It not only incorporated two first-floor rooms, but also extended further eastwards in the form of an open hall (*see* Figure 6.4). Any original northern range may have been demolished when the building was converted from domestic use, for the northern part of the site was already being let out by the Corporation in 1538 and by 1562 this part was described as 'a piece of ground belonging to the Court House'.[15] When they finally sold the piece of ground in 1575, the Corporation reserved for their use a small area 'lying to the north door of the Freemans House'.[16] Thus, the present first-floor northern external doorway already existed by the late 16th century

Fig. 6.1
The Court Hall. 15th-century crownpost roof.

Fig. 6.2 (Left)
The Court Hall.
Exterior from the northwest showing the former internal northern wall with a blocked medieval first-floor doorway visible on the left and an intruded 16th-century first-floor doorway leading to rebuilt steps in the centre. Note how the quoins at the corner of the building terminate part way down the wall.

Fig. 6.3 (Left)
The Court Hall. Intruded (probably 16th-century) external doorway in the south wall. Note the blocked window immediately to the right (evidence for it is one surviving voussoir and jamb stones shared with the doorway, and a scar in the masonry immediately above the removed voussoirs). Above the shared jamb of the doorway and window is a recessed plaque bearing a coat of arms.

(Figure 6.2). The part of the building which survives today was then known either as the Freemans House or Freemans Halls. Incorporated into the south elevation was a doorway probably of the 16th century and adjacent to it, a window (now blocked). Over the shared central pillar between the doorway and the window is a plaque containing an unidentified coat of arms (Figure 6.3) and to either side of it a refixed niche? (Figure 6.4).

The Court Hall proper appears to have been the hall-like room (later made into the town pound and now a yard) immediately to the east of the present building.[17] There was a prison beneath the Freemans Hall. The

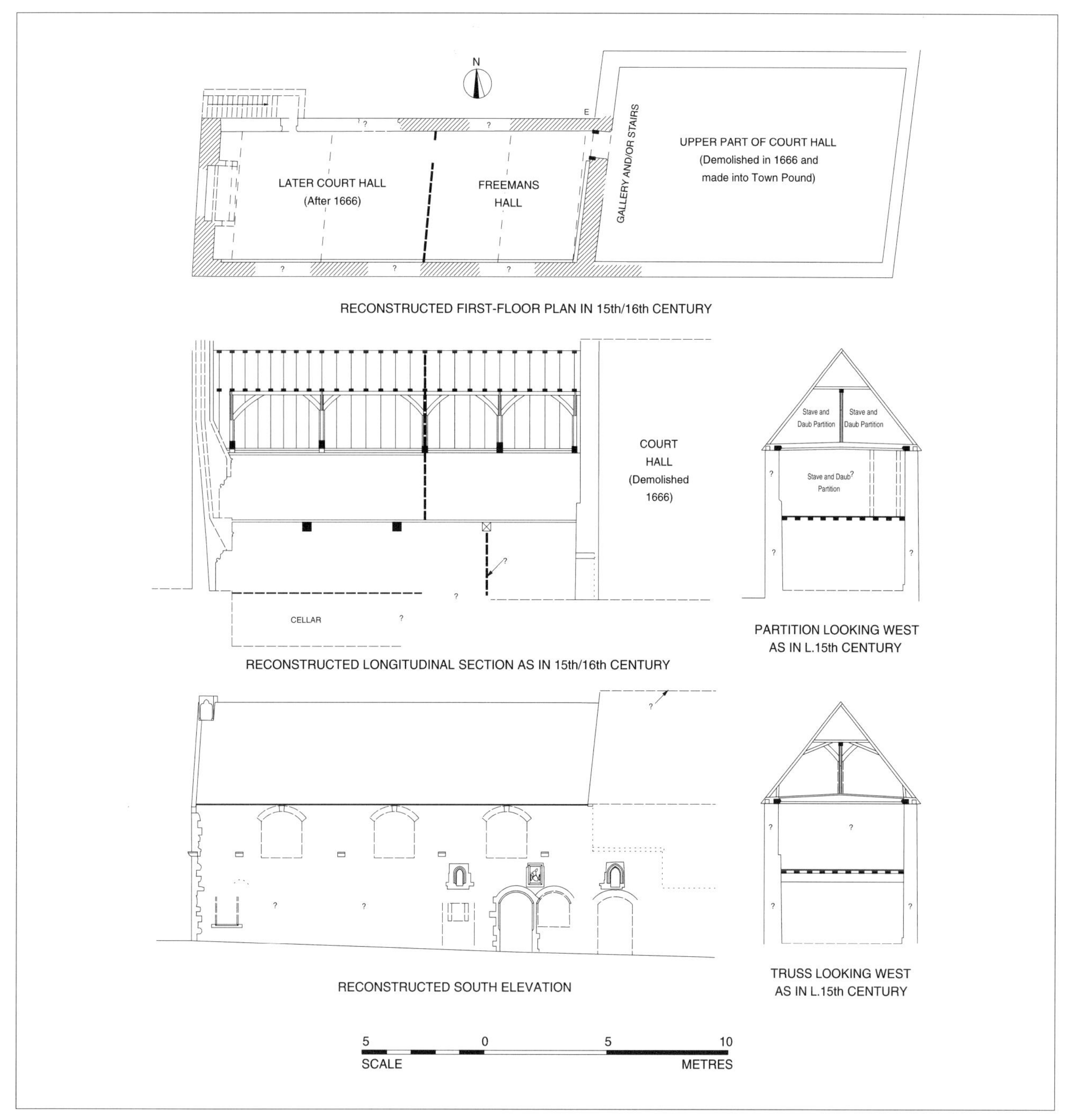

Fig. 6.4

Court Hall. Reconstruction drawings showing the likely form of the building in the 16th century.

Court Hall itself was demolished in 1666, at which date one of the two upper halls or chambers within the Freemans Hall was apparently made into a new court hall.[18] The upper floor was still divided into two rooms (then called The Court Hall and The Freemans Hall) in 1689, when they were let as a place of religious worship, the courts being held downstairs.[19] Part of the ground floor continued to be used as a prison and this remained the case until 1879, when it was closed. Thereafter prisoners were sent to Rye.[20] In addition to the Corporation's prison, there was evidently a second prison relating to the waterfront, for in 1641 the water bailiff, doubting the strength of his prison, was allowed to use the mayor's. The water bailiff's prison was evidently still out of repair in 1665 and is likely to have been left to decay and fall.[21]

The court hall and prison were not Winchelsea's only municipal buildings. Mention has already been made of the market house formed at the church gate in the 16th century, perhaps replacing an earlier market

Fig. 6.5 (Left).
The Corporation seal (c.1300).

Obverse: a ship with sail furled. On the forecastle is a plain banner, on the stern-castle are two men with trumpets, and below them is a man holding the steering oar. A sailor is climbing the rigging and four others haul on ropes. In the field is a shield of the leopards of England.

Reverse: a slender watch tower in the lower tier of which are two persons standing before a seated figure, all under a canopy. On the next tier is a figure within a niche, and on the battlements is a banner with three chevrons (possibly the arms of Lewknor - Sir Roger held a property in Quarter 17 in 1292) and a watchman holding a lantern. To the left is a representation of St Giles's church with spire-capped tower, nave/chancel and one aisle. Both nave/chancel and aisle have niches containing the figure of St Giles with his hind; on the aisle gable is a large bird. To the right is St Thomas's church, shown taller than that of St Giles. It is depicted with its spire-capped tower, nave/chancel and flanking aisles/chapels. Within the three niches the murder of St Thomas of Canterbury is depicted; above the left-hand aisle is a shield of England, whilst below both churches cross-winged houses on a base of waves are shown. The location of the watch tower within the town is unknown, but this tower may conceivably be identifiable as the tower which stood adjacent to the west end of St Thomas's church.
[VCH Sussex, ***9****, 69].*

house within the Monday Market (*see* Chapter 4). There appears also to have been some form of municipal tower, if the town's 14th-century seal is to be believed. On its reverse this shows representations of St Giles's and St Thomas's churches with, between them, a tall and slender tower (Figure 6.5). Depicted in its lower tier are two figures standing before a seated figure, all under a canopy. On the next tier is a figure within a niche, and on the battlements a banner with three chevrons and a watchman holding a lantern. Clearly the tower served as a lookout, but given the figures at the lower stages, did it also fulfil another function? Was it more akin to some of the continental examples, serving also as a belfry and a treasury for the Corporation manuscripts, regalia and other valuables? And, if so, where was the tower located? If the continental model was followed, the tower need not have been upon the same site as the court-hall complex - those at Bruges in Belgium and Beaune in France were quite separate. One possibility is that the tower shown on the seal depicts the tower known to have stood either attached to or adjacent to the west end of St Thomas's church. Perhaps it was in this tower that the town clock and its bells were installed at some date between 1389 and 1399. A prestigious item for any English town to own at this early period, the installation of the clock evidently changed some of the procedures followed in the everyday regulation of the town. Whereas in 1389 payments were made for the daily sounding of the curfew, by 1399 the accounts show the payment of five shillings a quarter for the care of the clock, and foreigners were required by then not to be in the streets after a certain hour 'of the clock'.[22]

7. ECCLESIASTICAL BUILDINGS AND HOSPITALS

David and Barbara Martin

INTRODUCTION (*Figure 7.1*)

The religious and charitable needs of (Old) Winchelsea had been served by two parish churches, (St Thomas and St Giles), by two hospitals (St John and Holy Cross), and by a house of Grey Friars which had been established in 1253. All these were transferred to the new town, where they were augmented by the existing parish church of St Leonard, Iham, and by what appears to have been a new hospital dedicated to St Bartholomew, to which no references are known prior to the move. Whether any of these institutions had owned property in the old town over and above their churchyards / precincts is not known.

Given the large size of (Old) Winchelsea, it is perhaps at first sight surprising that the town was not home to one of the major enclosed monastic orders. The reason for this is undoubtedly due to the early overlordship of the town by Fécamp, the great French Benedictine monastery. The monks of Fécamp would have resisted any attempt to set up a rival house within their town; only the foundation of a daughter house would have been accepted. In 1247 the town was freed from monastic control when Henry III reclaimed both (Old) Winchelsea and the neighbouring town of Rye, and placed both under his direct control. When Edward I was planning the town's move to its new site, the Barons of Winchelsea specifically requested that they should have no monastic houses within the town apart from that of the Grey Friars which already existed (but *see* below). Whether this apparent hostility towards the monastic orders was based upon earlier experiences whilst under the control of Fécamp, or upon knowledge of the influence exacted upon the adjacent town by abbeys such as nearby Battle, is impossible to tell. Indeed, the request may have been nothing more than an attempt to protect the interests of the friary, for which the townsfolk already had high regard. However, it may be no coincidence that none of the town's hospitals were under religious control; they were instead under the direct governance of the Mayor and Corporation.

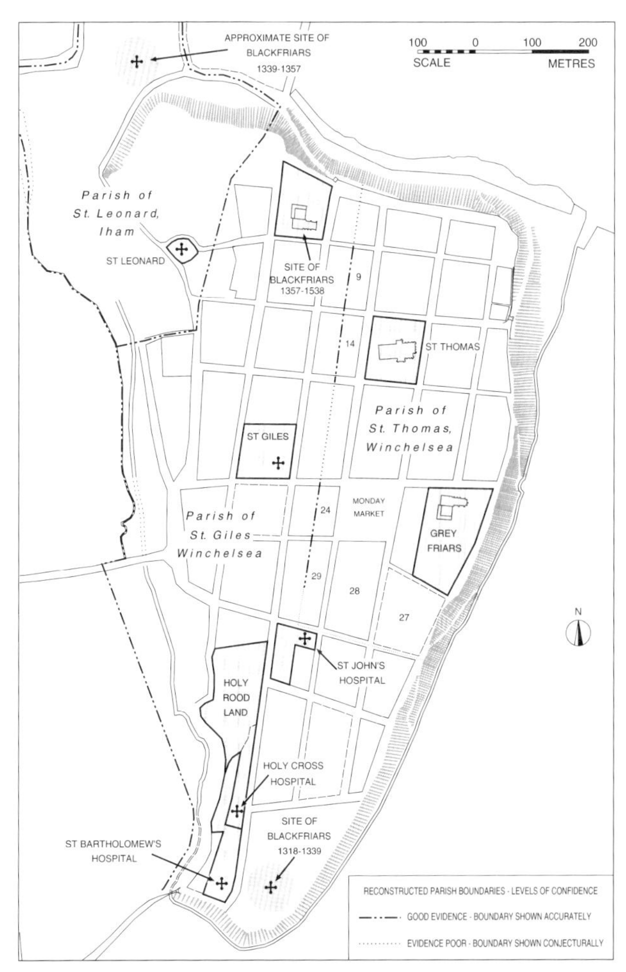

Fig. 7.1
The location of the churches, friaries and hospitals within the town.

The 14th century saw some involvement of other monasteries within the town. For instance, in 1312 and *c*.1320 respectively, chantries founded within St Thomas's Church by the wealthy Alard family were placed under the respective control of Langdon Abbey in Kent and Battle Abbey in East Sussex. In 1318, despite the earlier objections by the residents, the Black Friars were able to gain a foothold in the southern outskirts of the town. After an unsuccessful move to a marshland site to the north of the town, in 1357 they established themselves within permanent claustral buildings upon a more central site on Quarter 4.

Throughout the 14th and 15th centuries, the townsfolk appear to have been willing to grant the church and the charitable institutions either a rent interest in property, or full ownership. As a result, by the Dissolution of the friaries and chantries in the mid-16th century, the various institutions had built up considerable estates.[1]

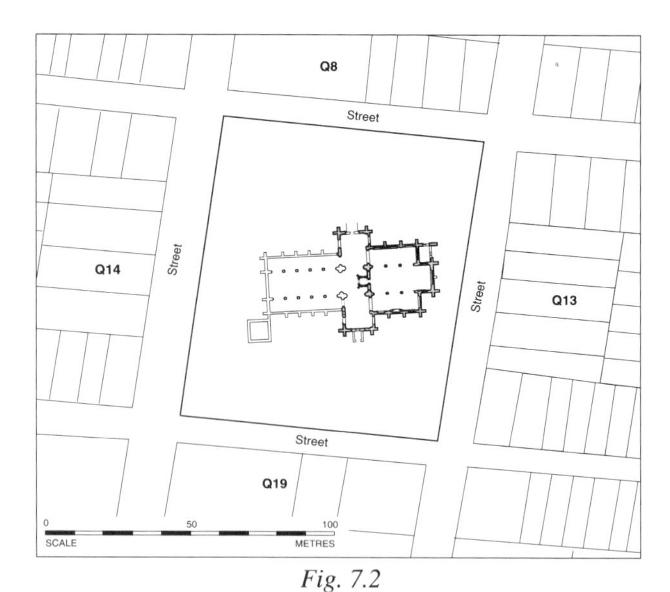

Fig. 7.2
St Thomas's Church. Location of the church within its churchyard.

CHURCHES

St Thomas's Church *(Figures 7.1-7.12)*

St Thomas's Church was foremost among the town's three churches (including St Leonard's, Iham) a point well illustrated by its valuation at £10.13s.4d. in 1291, compared to £6.13s.4d. for the church of St Giles and £4.13s.4d. for the church of St Leonard.[2] It is today the only church to survive. It stands on its own 2½-acre site occupying an entire Quarter of the town. Only the eastern end and the ruins of the transepts remain. Originally it would have dominated the block, stretching at a slight angle across almost the entire width, and measuring 58.5 metres (192ft.) long excluding its buttresses (Figures 7.2-4). As Pevsner has commented, the style of the extant part is consistently that of the (late 13th or) early 14th century and was intended to be on the proudest scale. Sufficient of the transepts stands to show that their east windows were each set in very deep recesses with strong jamb shafts (Figure 7.5), whilst the end and the west windows had narrow blank arches flanking them. The northern and southern end walls incorporate central doorways, both once protected by projecting porches. The crossing piers once supported a central tower, probably with a spire as indicated in the Corporation seal and in sketches of the town shown in 16th-century maps (*see* Figures 4.15 and 6.5).[3] In addition to the tower arches (of which the one surviving arch has been rebuilt much lower), further arches linked the transepts to the nave's relatively narrow side aisles and to the much wider chapels which flank the chancel. The interior of the church would thus have had a very open feel. When the transepts were reduced to a ruinous state, the eastern arches were blocked and a late-15th- or early-16th-century western porch with associated entrance was built.

Although it lacks a triforium, a clerestory and vaults, internally the surviving east end is architecturally rich, decoratively grand and, again quoting from Pevsner, 'in scale almost that of a cathedral'. The three-bay arcades which divided the chancel from the side chapels are supported by tall piers with shafts of 'Purbeck' marble which incorporate contrasting shaft rings of ordinary stone (Figure 7.6). The windows are all marble-shafted and, as in the transept, are flanked by narrow blank arches, the whole set beneath single, somewhat depressed overarches (Figure 7.7). The sedilia and piscina serving the chancel are of one composition with crocketted gables, buttress shafts, cinque-cusped arches, a ribbed vaulted roof and a back wall of small squared blocks, each ornamented with a stylized flower (Figure 7.8). The sedilia and piscina to the south chapel are similar, but with ogees and no ornamentation to the rear wall.[4]

All three steeply pitched roofs are medieval in date. The two roofs over the chancel and south chapel are each of four bays, although, because the south chapel is shorter than the chancel, the tiebeams here do not correspond to the arcade and windows. Both roofs are of paired-rafter-and-collar type, with ashlar pieces and soulaces, all morticed and tenoned into position. That to the south chapel has curved packing-pieces smoothing the outline of the roof at the joints between the ashlar pieces and rafters, rafters and soulaces, and between the soulaces and collars. These formerly carried an underplastered barrel-vaulted ceiling, but whether the packing pieces and ceiling represent an alteration or an original feature is unclear. Both roofs spring from

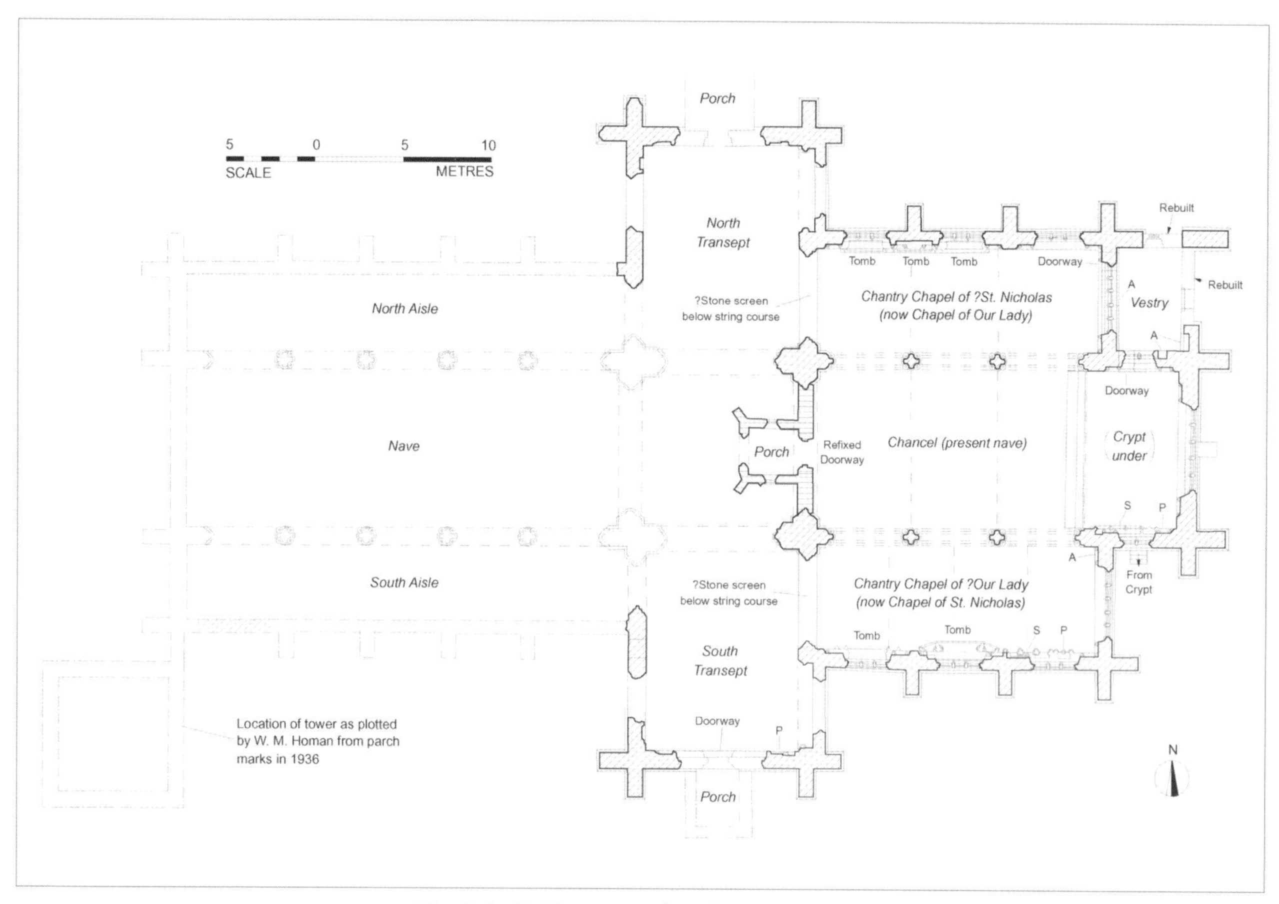

Fig. 7.3 St Thomas's Church. Ground plan.

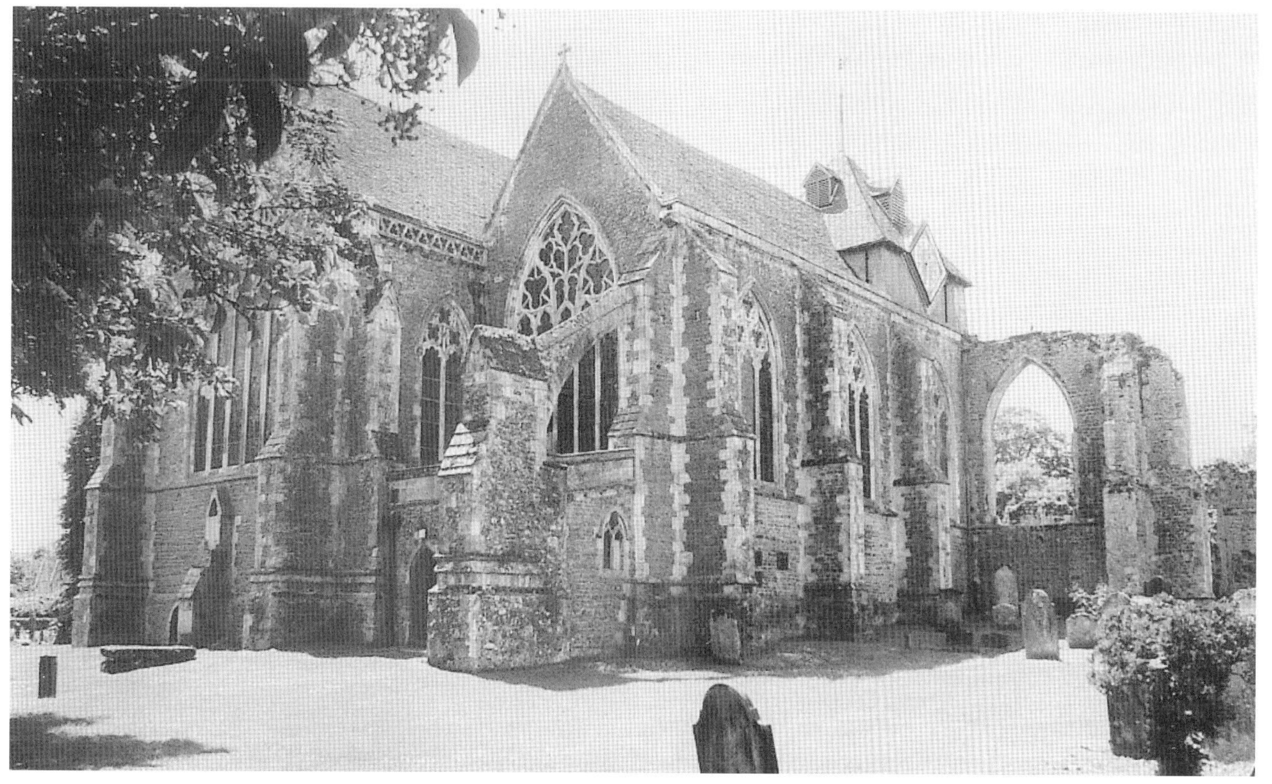

Fig. 7.4 St Thomas's Church. Exterior viewed from the northeast.

Fig. 7.5 (Above)

St Thomas's Church.
Remains of the church viewed from the west showing the full breadth of the building across its transepts. The central arch into the chancel together with the wall above was reconstructed at a lower level prior to the arch being blocked.

Fig. 7.6 (Left)
St Thomas's Church.
Detail of the shafting on the arcade between the south chapel and the chancel.

Fig. 7.7 (Right)

St Thomas's Church. A typical window.

wallplates moulded with a pair of quarter rolls separated by a quirk. The mouldings are stopped at the tiebeams, the stops within the chancel being of simple run-out form; those within the chapel are slightly more elaborate and are repeated on the tiebeams. The mouldings ought to be of 14th-century date and are very similar to those on the masonry detailing within the building. The roof over the northern chapel is certainly later and dates from either the 15th or very early 16th century. It is of three bays and is of crownpost construction. One crownpost is cruciform in section, the other has an octagonal shaft and moulded cap. The braces are very thin and blade-like. Within this roof too there are soulaces. The western bay is occupied by the bell-turret, which is probably of 17th-century date. It was perhaps within this turret that the little watch-bell was placed in 1676 after it had been taken down from the Strand Gate and hung up in the church for 'the more convenient calling of the congregation together'.[5]

Beneath the chancel's raised high altar is a barrel-vaulted crypt entered from the exterior via a doorway in the south wall. Aligned upon a north-south axis, the pointed vault is divided into four bays by chamfered ribs and in general follows the design of

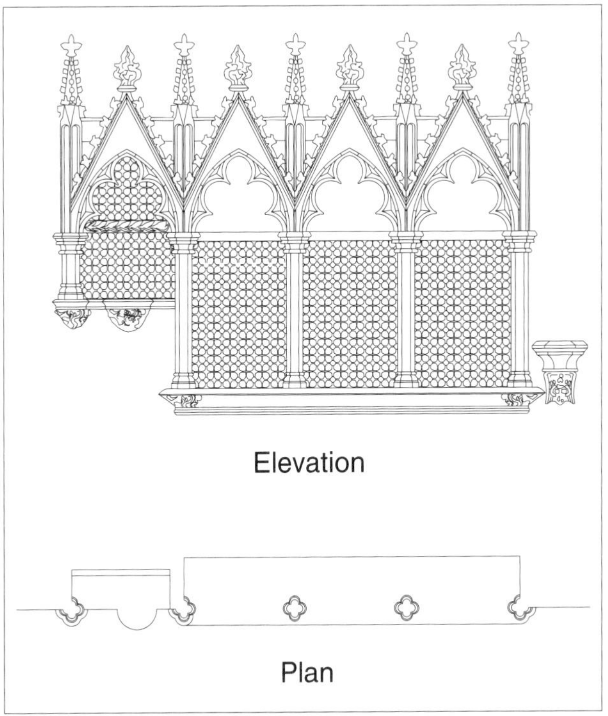

Fig. 7.8 St Thomas's Church. Sedilia on the south side of the chancel.

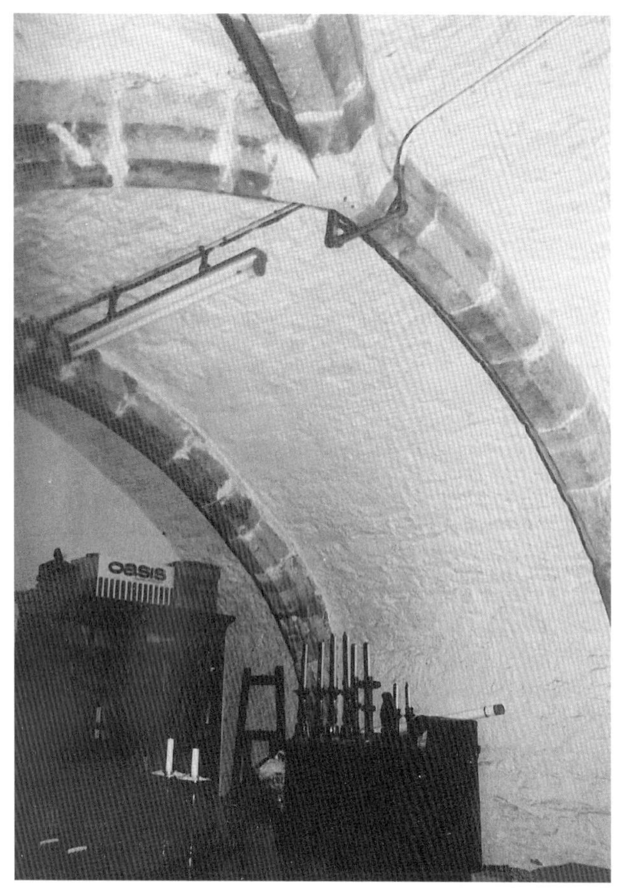

Fig. 7.9
St Thomas's Church. Crypt beneath the altar looking west and showing tripartite vaulting.

Fig. 7.10
St Thomas's Church. Crypt beneath the altar looking east and showing 'forked' ribbing to avoid the eastern window.

Winchelsea's vaulted cellars. However, because of the location of the two eastern windows lighting the crypt, two of the three ribs divide centrally to give a 'Y'-plan tripartite configuration (Figures 7.9-7.10).

Plans of the church published in 1850 and 1937 both show the demolished nave in outline, although there are variations in the details. Both plans appear to have been based upon very little evidence, for Cooper specifically stated that 'no trace of the foundations, after a recent and very diligent search could be found, except for the central great piers and a small portion of the wall at the SW angle, of what was the south aisle'. Cooper's plan shows in hachure the foundations which were discovered.[6] Elsewhere Cooper stated that stone from the nave foundations was removed in 1790 for use at Rye Harbour. What may be an upstanding section of the nave and south aisle's western wall is shown in a view of the church made by G. Rowe in *c.*1825.[7]

The 1758 and 1763 town plans and a number of other 18th-century illustrations show a detached tower standing immediately to the south of the church's former western end, near the southwest corner of the churchyard. It is depicted as being of two stages separated from one another by a corbel table (Figure 7.11). This, together with the tall height of the lower stage suggests that, at least on its southern and western sides, it was once surrounded by lean-to roofed outshuts. The 18th-century illustrations depict it roofless, although a thumbnail sketch of the town made in *c.*1597 shows it capped by a tall spire.[8] However, this spire may only have been added when the central tower of the church was removed. Although perhaps constructed as a campanile, it is possible that it was built as a watchtower and may conceivably be that depicted on the Corporation seal (*see* Figure 6.5). In 1936/7 Homan was able to record the tower's precise location and size from parch marks visible in the grass.[9] Curiously, his dimensions, when plotted, place it attached to the western end of the south aisle rather than detached, as is usually assumed (*see* Figures 7.2 and 7.3). It may be that the ruins of this tower were shown by Rowe in his illustration of *c.*1825, but the location of the ruin depicted by him is more consistent with the western wall of the church (*see* above). Any such ruin which had

Fig. 7.11 (Right)

St Thomas's Church. Churchyard from the southwest showing the remains of the detached tower (reproduced from an engraving by Page. Published by Act of Parliament by Alexander Hogg, No.16, Paternoster Row).

survived until that date would have been hidden behind the remains of the tower in earlier views.

There are various theories as to the fate of the nave. Some argue that it was never built, though this seems highly unlikely given the known success of the town during its first 75 years or so, and the fact that the two large side chapels were given over to chantries (*see* below). Others suggest that it was destroyed during one of the French raids. Given the amount of demolition undertaken within the town for stone and other building materials, the most likely explanation is that following the major decline in population the church was simply downsized and the redundant part sold for its materials. The thumbnail sketch of the town contained within the plan of *c.*1597 confirms that the nave had been demolished by that date, although, as already noted, the bell-tower then possessed a tall spire. There are indications that the transepts may still have been roofed at that time, but no central tower is shown.[10] Documentary sources suggest that the timber from the transept roofs may have been removed in the 1640s.[11] In the first half of the 19th century the remaining part of the church was carefully repaired and restored to near its former state. Cooper, writing in 1850, gave extensive details of the works.[12]

The Chantries within St Thomas's Church (Figure 7.12)

Despite the high quality of the church's architecture in general, the features which stand out above all else are the canopied monuments built into the side walls of the two chapels which flank the chancel: there are two monuments in the south chapel and three in the north chapel. All are of the first quarter of the 14th century. Whereas the north group is of one composition, the south group is of two, of which the one on the east projects forward under a bold canopy, its rear wall decorated in identical fashion to that of the sedilia serving the chancel (*see* Figure 7.8). The whole ensemble of monuments is of excellent quality, with good effigies supported on the tomb chests and elaborate decoration to the recesses. The effigies were formerly thought to have been salvaged and moved to their present site from (Old) Winchelsea, but recently they have convincingly been shown to be early-14th century in date.[13] Both sets of tombs are believed to commemorate the Alard family, as different members of that family founded chanties in the side chapels.

The first of the chantries was founded in 1312 by Stephen Alard of Winchelsea, son of Nicholas and Isabel. It was administered by Langdon Abbey, Kent, who provided two chaplains to hold daily services in perpetuity in 'the chapel of Stephen Alard and his successors built [note the past tense] in the honour of the Blessed Mary in the church of Winchelsea St Thomas'. A house in the town, formerly Robert Jolivet's, and probably identifiable as Quarter 18, plot 34, was granted to the abbey as a dwelling for the chaplains.[14] The second chantry was founded between 1319 and 1323 by Robert, son of John Alard, and was administered by Battle Abbey. Four priests were provided to hold daily services in the chapel of St Nicholas to say masses for the souls of Henry, Robert's late brother, for his late wife Isabel, and for himself. At the Dissolution this latter

Fig. 7.12
St Thomas's Church.
Alard tomb monument against the south wall of the south chapel (reproduced from Cooper 1850).

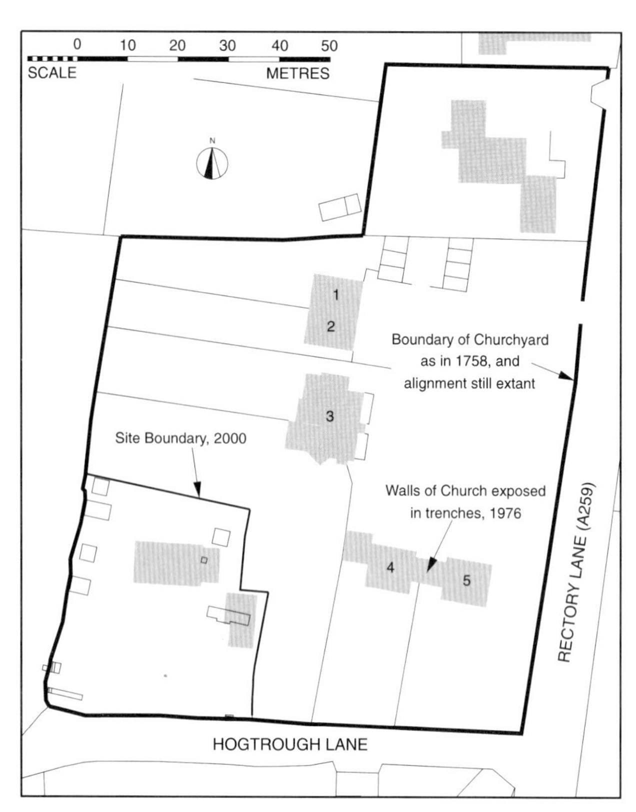

Fig. 7.13
St Giles's Church.
Plan as in 2000 showing the boundaries of the churchyard as existing in 1758.

chantry was still in operation, then served by a single priest. The other Alard chantry, within the chapel of St Mary, had ceased, although in 1477 Maline Farncombe was granted licence to found a chantry in that chapel. One priest was to say divine service daily for, amongst others, Maline Farncombe after her death, for her husband, Simon, for John Godfrey and his wife Alice, and for Simon Godfrey and his wife Joan. It was still operating at the Dissolution of the chantries in 1547.[15] Writing in 1850, Cooper guessed that St Nicholas's Chapel was located within the south aisle and the chapel of the Blessed Mary in the north and this is the arrangement used today. The tomb monuments themselves, however, suggest that the locations had been the other way round.[16]

St Giles's Church *(Figures 7.13-7.15)*

St Giles's Church and churchyard formerly occupied a 2½-acre plot at the southern half of Quarter 21, on the western side of Rectory Lane (present-day A259). The church served the less important of the two Winchelsea parishes and was valued in 1291 at £6.13s.4d., compared to £10.13s.4d. for St Thomas's.[17] Deeds indicate that the parish was 'L'-shaped and extended down the western side of the town (following the centre line of Quarters 9, 14, 24 and at least part of Quarter 29) before turning east, either through Quarters 29, 28 and 27 or along the street on their southern side, to take in the entire southern outlying area (*see* Figure 7.1).[18] These were generally the poorer parts of the town, and the first to be abandoned.

Following the French raid in 1360, a patent was issued for the enlargement of the churchyard owing to the numbers of burials of those slain in the conflict.[19] The issue of this patent supports the theory that it was within St Giles's church that, whilst at mass, the congregation was so villainously butchered by the French.[20] However, whether the patent was acted upon and the churchyard increased in size is doubtful. The inquiry of 1415 gives the area of the churchyard at that date as 2½ acres and all the holdings laid out in the late 13th century against the western street can be accounted for in the evidence presented at the inquiry.[21] Any extension which was made, therefore, must have been against the eastern street, perhaps taking over plots 1 and 15, both of which are shown in the 1758 town map as by

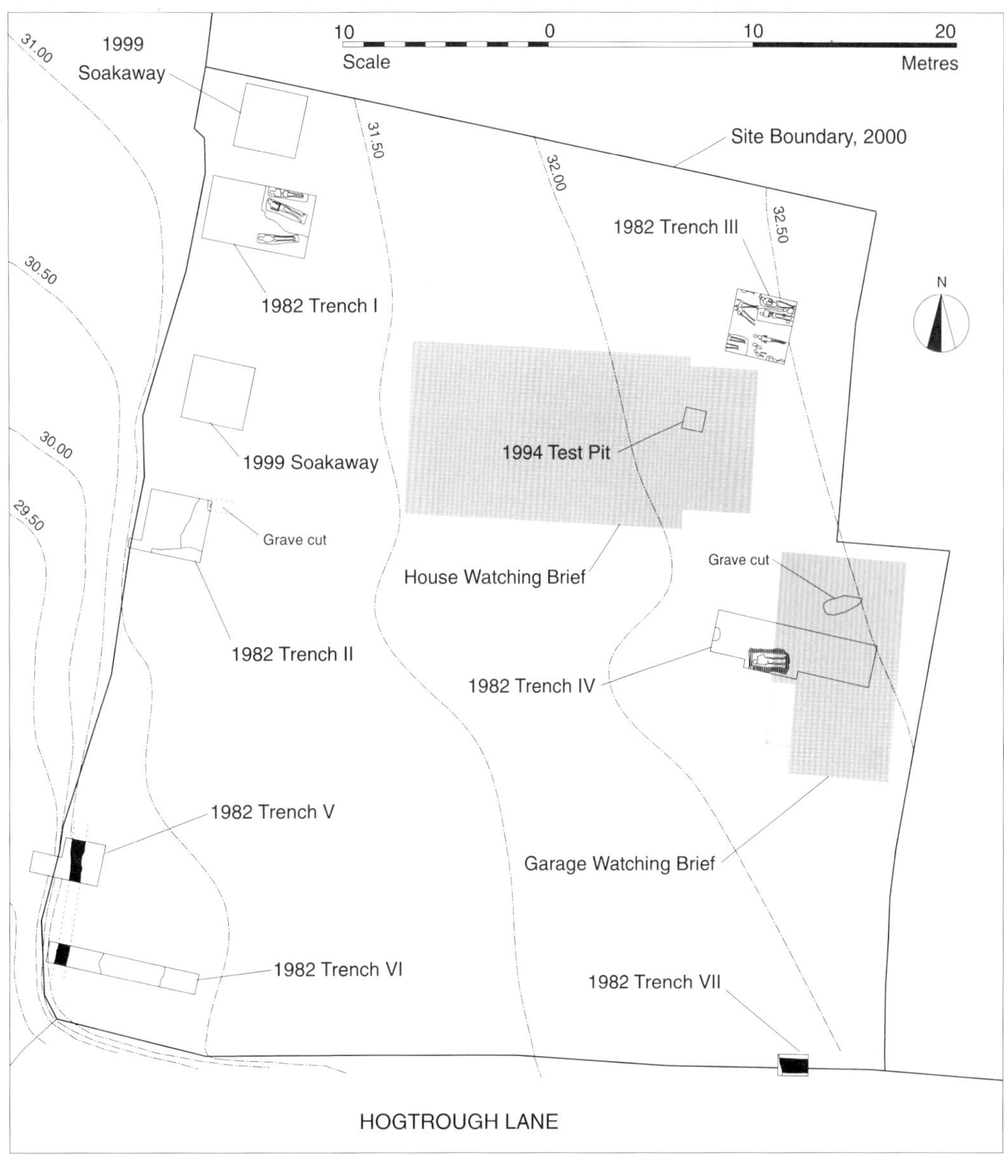

Fig. 7.14 (Right)

St Giles's Church. Plan showing the areas of excavation. The ground-level contours are as existing in 1982, prior to landscaping.

that date forming part of the churchyard (Figure 7.13).[22] However, a house granted for the use of the parson in 1359 is described as a messuage next to the churchyard of St Giles.[23] Therefore, plots 1 and 15 may represent the former site of this parsonage, which was held in 1543 at a king's rent of 15d.[24]

Very little is known regarding the church itself. No archaeological work was undertaken in 1976 when numbers 1 to 5, St Giles Close were built, this despite the fact that the foundations of numbers 4 and 5 cut through the masonry foundations of the church. In 1982 a subsequent application to build a house upon the southwest corner of the graveyard resulted in an evaluation excavation undertaken by the UCL Field Archaeology Unit and in limited follow-up work in 1994, 1999 and 2000.[25]

The area investigated was very small and did not include the site of the church, but it showed that the graveyard was bounded on its west and south by a masonry wall. Not surprisingly, there was a high concentration of burials within the parts of the graveyard investigated. This was particularly the case within Trench III, an area of nine square metres, where more than 13 burials were discovered. In contrast, the area against the boundary walls appears to have been kept free; perhaps it served as a pathway (Figure 7.14). In those instances where *in situ* burials were found, human remains occurred from approximately one metre deep. However, disarticulated human bones were found from higher levels. In some instances well-defined grave cuts and the presence of coffin nails indicate that wooden coffins were used, but other burials showed no evidence for coffins. Only one of the 17 graves investigated in 1982 was stone-lined and vaulted. This appears to have been sited close to the southwest corner of the church. Its occupant, a man of 25 to 35 years and 5 feet 7 inches

Fig. 7.15
St Giles's Church.
Stone-built tomb showing the skeleton of a male, aged 25-35 years, who had suffered from advanced vertebral tuberculosis.

Fig. 7.16
St Leonard's Church.
Fragmentary remains of the south wall of the nave as sketched in 1794 (By permission of the British Library, Ref. BL King's Library K. Top - XLII-26-D.) Note St Leonard's Mill shown on its original location prior to its move to the site of the church.

in height, had suffered from advanced vertebral tuberculosis, which had deformed his spine (Figure 7.15). Where their stature could be determined, the adult males ranged from 5 feet 6 inches to 5 feet 10 inches in height and with the exception of one woman of 5 feet 7 inches, the females ranged between 5 feet 1 inch and 5 feet 3 inches. Only two adults were obviously over 35 years of age. None of the burials could be closely dated.

It is suggested in volume 9 of the *Victoria History of the County of Sussex,* that the church may have been abandoned as early as 1413: it had been struck by lightning and burned on December 28 of that year, although the town wall inquiry of 1415 gives no hint that this was the case. Even if this were so, rectors continued to be presented until at least 1500.[26] By 1535, the clear value of St Giles's church had fallen to just £1.6s.8d. (small when compared with an assessment of £6.13s.4d. for St Thomas's church) and on 18 September 1541 the Bishop of Chichester issued a memorandum acknowledging that the patron of St Thomas and St Giles had confirmed his agreement that the two parishes should be amalgamated.[27] According to Homan, it was in 1543 that the parishes were formally united, although well into the 1560s many deeds continued to use both parish names to identify where the property was located. Nevertheless, in the early 1540s St Giles's church was decommissioned and in 1545 stone from its fabric was used to repair the town walls of Rye.[28] Some of its walls were allegedly still standing in 1570 and in 1608-9, when the church was described by Thomas Godfrey as ruinous. In 1587 a licence was granted to the parson of St Thomas and St Giles to sell the stones which had fallen down in the churchyard of St Giles, but he was to allow that part of the church then still standing to remain. An entry in the parish register for 1780 refers to the levelling of the ruins of the church.[29] Apparently in Cooper's time the foundations could be traced in dry summer weather. It was presumably from his observation of these that he was able to say that the church had comprised a nave, chancel, one aisle and a small tower. Until 1849, when the rectory was built upon the site, the former churchyard had become merely a field.[30]

St Leonard's Church, Iham *(Figure 7.16)*

Situated within the original settlement of Iham, the church of St Leonard was excluded when King Edward acquired the hill of Iham for the foundation of his new town, and so remained outside the confines of the town throughout. In 1291 it had been valued at £4.13s.4d., a respectable sum for such a small parish, but in 1404 it was one of the benefices so impoverished as to be excused taxation.[31] The inquiry held in 1415 into the line of Winchelsea's proposed new town wall saw no problems in blocking up the road leading into town from the church, implying that it was then little used.[32] The advowson followed the descent of Fécamp Abbey's manor of Brede, the last known presentment was made by Syon Abbey, Fécamp's successor, in 1484.[33]

A deposition made in 1565 records that the church was by that date 'already thrown down, except that some parts remain defaced and despoiled'. In 1610 the town decreed that the churchyard was to be laid open to the commons of the town.[34] A sketch of the site made in 1794 shows a short length of the south wall then still standing virtually to full height (Figure 7.16).[35] It was removed soon after and early in the 19th century St Leonard's windmill was moved to the site, where it continued to stand until blown down in the great storm of October 1987. The earthworks of St Leonard's church and of the relocated mill placed over it remain clearly visible. Protruding through the surface of the churchyard mound, towards the western side, are the foundations of the western end of the church, which appears to have had an internal width of *c*.5.90 metres (*c*.19ft.4ins.). Where visible, the external facing is of roughly-coursed and faced sandstone blocks. Lying on lower ground to the west of the churchyard is a piece of tumbled walling.

FRIARIES

The Grey Friars *(Figures 7.17-7.26)*

The Friars Minor (or Grey Friars) were established in (Old) Winchelsea by 1253 and when that town was washed away, the Barons of Winchelsea stipulated to Edward I that the New Town should have only one religious house, that of the Friars Minor.[36] About 1285, John Bone of Wickham in neighbouring Icklesham granted four of his 28 acres upon the hill of Iham to the friars for their new friary. They were already given as owners when Bone's other lands were compulsorily purchased by Edward I.[37] Bone's grant to the friars, therefore, definitely predated the formal foundation of the new town. The irregular sides of the precinct probably reflect the original boundaries of the close granted to them and must have had an effect upon the planned grid of the new town (*see* Figure 7.18). Resulting from the loss of a legal action, in 1291 it was resolved that the monks of Westminster should make a payment of 60 marks to the friaries at Lichfield in Staffordshire and Winchelsea, both establishments being

Fig. 7.17

Grey Friars. Remains of the Friary in 1737 showing the remains of the claustral buildings in the foreground, the west range on the left and the chancel of the church in the background. View by Samuel and Nathaniel Buck, March 25th 1737.

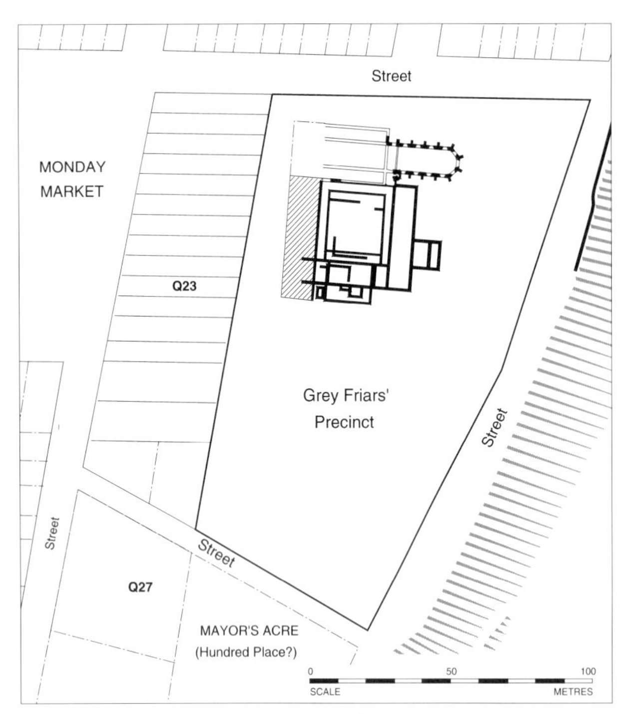

Fig. 7.18
Grey Friars.
The precinct (reconstructed from documentary and earthwork evidence) and the claustral buildings (surviving and revealed by parch marks). The west range (shown shaded) was demolished in the early 19th century, but is known from drawings.

then poverty stricken as a result of disasters recently suffered.[38]

Little documentation has been found relating to the history of the friary prior to the Dissolution. In 1413 the grant of an obit was made for a mass to be said on behalf of Vincent Finch and his wife Isabella at their death and for their names to be written amongst the chief benefactors in the gilt book of the friary, and inserted in the margin of the Missal at the Canon or next to the Remembrance of the Living.[39] The surviving wills of medieval townsfolk indicate that bequests continued to be made to the house up to the Dissolution, whilst as late as 1526 Gregory Wylgate noted that he wished to be buried in the Grey Friars' ground. Wardens of the friary are mentioned in 16th-century wills.[40] The establishment was dissolved in July 1538 and the buildings were placed under the custody of Philip Chute, (later made captain of Camber Castle). They were mostly demolished to provide additional material for the construction of that castle.[41] The property was sold into lay hands in 1545.[42]

As is often the case with monastic establishments, at the Dissolution the western range of the friary was left standing and converted into a gentry residence. This stood largely unaltered until demolished

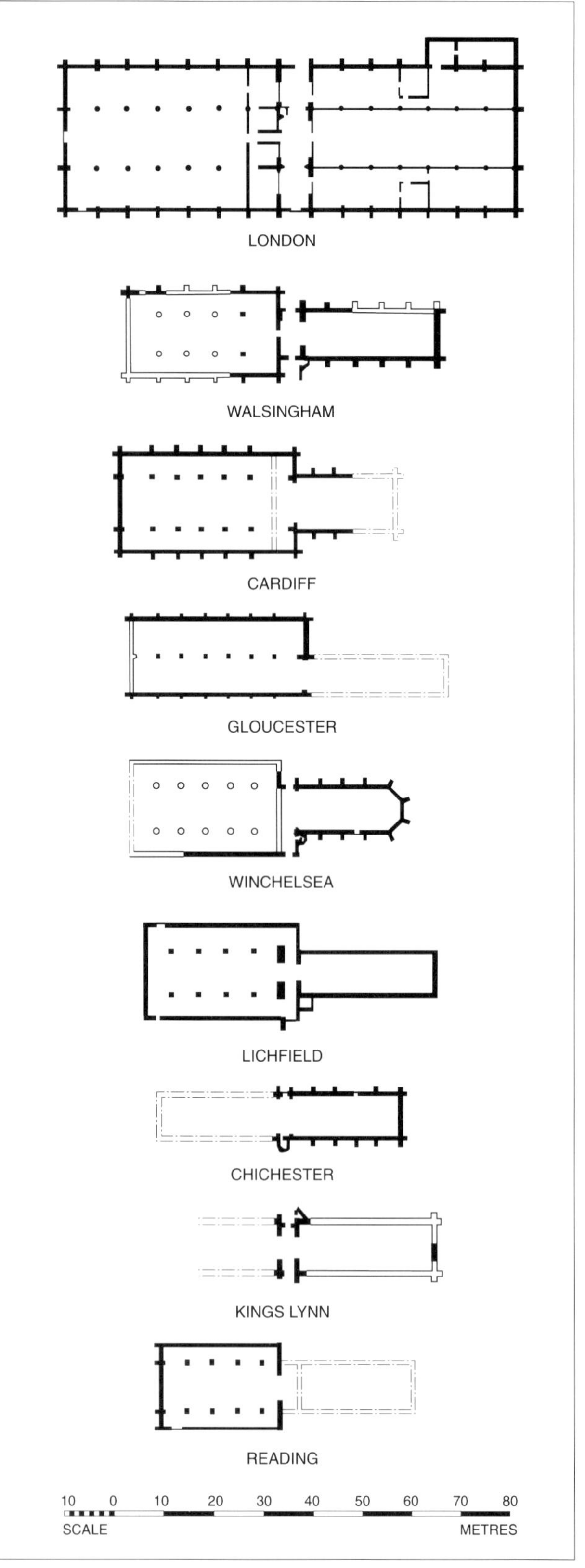

Fig. 7.19
Grey Friars.
Outline plans of the churches of a selection of English and Welsh Franciscan monasteries.

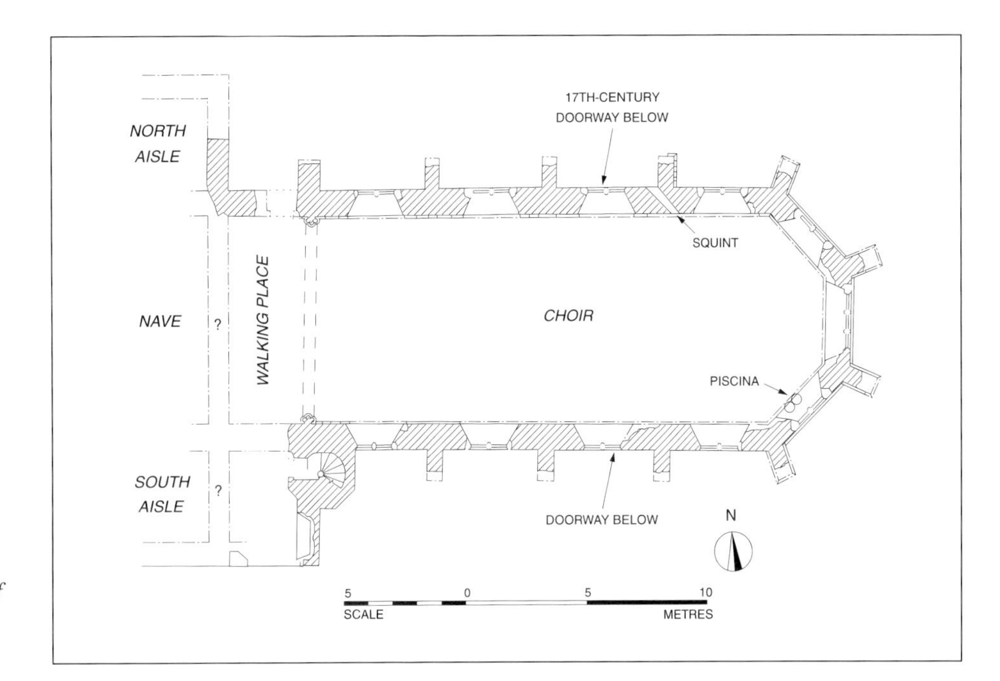

Fig. 7.20 (Right)

Grey Friars. Plan of the church as existing.

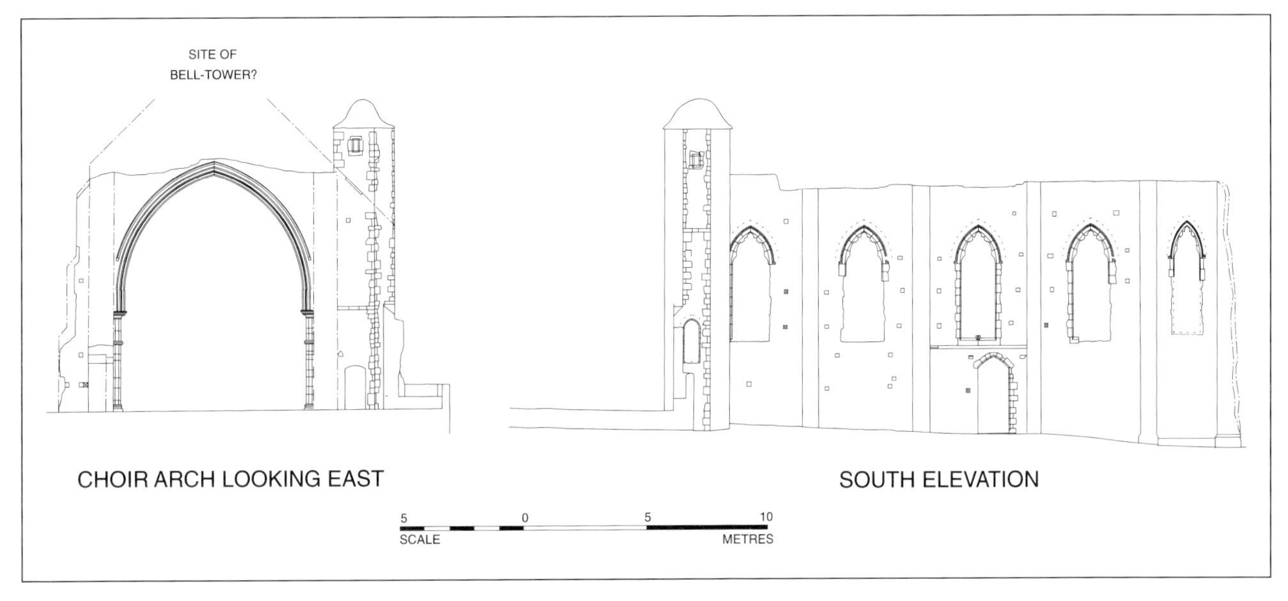

Fig. 7.21 (Below)

Grey Friars. Elevations of the church as existing.

by Stileman in 1819 and is shown in a lithograph by Samuel and Nathaniel Buck made in 1737 (*see* Figure 7.17). Their view also shows the east end of the church still extant, together with remains of the nave's south wall, the cloisters, and an associated small tower in the south range. A similar drawing made by Grimm in the 1780s likewise shows the mansion, the east end of the church, and the nave's south wall, complete with a corbel table associated with the roof of the cloisters, but by this date most of the ruined walls to the south appear to have been demolished. Even so, a further drawing gives a detail of what is alleged to be a window in the ruined south wall of the refectory. Both the view from the south and a view looking east within the church show the east end surviving very much as it does today.[43]

The Friary Church (Figures 7.20-7.26)

Pevsner noted that, 'Considering the dearth of Franciscan remains in England, this is one of the most impressive there are'.[44] As the plans of a group of English and Welsh Grey Friars' churches shown in Figure 7.19 makes clear, Winchelsea is unusual for its adoption of an apsidal east end. Including the three-sided apse the choir measures 21.0 metres (68ft.10ins.) long and had a clear span of 8.2 metres (26ft.10ins.). Although now roofless and devoid of many of its dressings, the walls still stand to their full height (Figures 7.20-7.22). The internal space of the choir was well lit: there were four lofty, two-light windows in each of its side walls and a further three in the sides of its

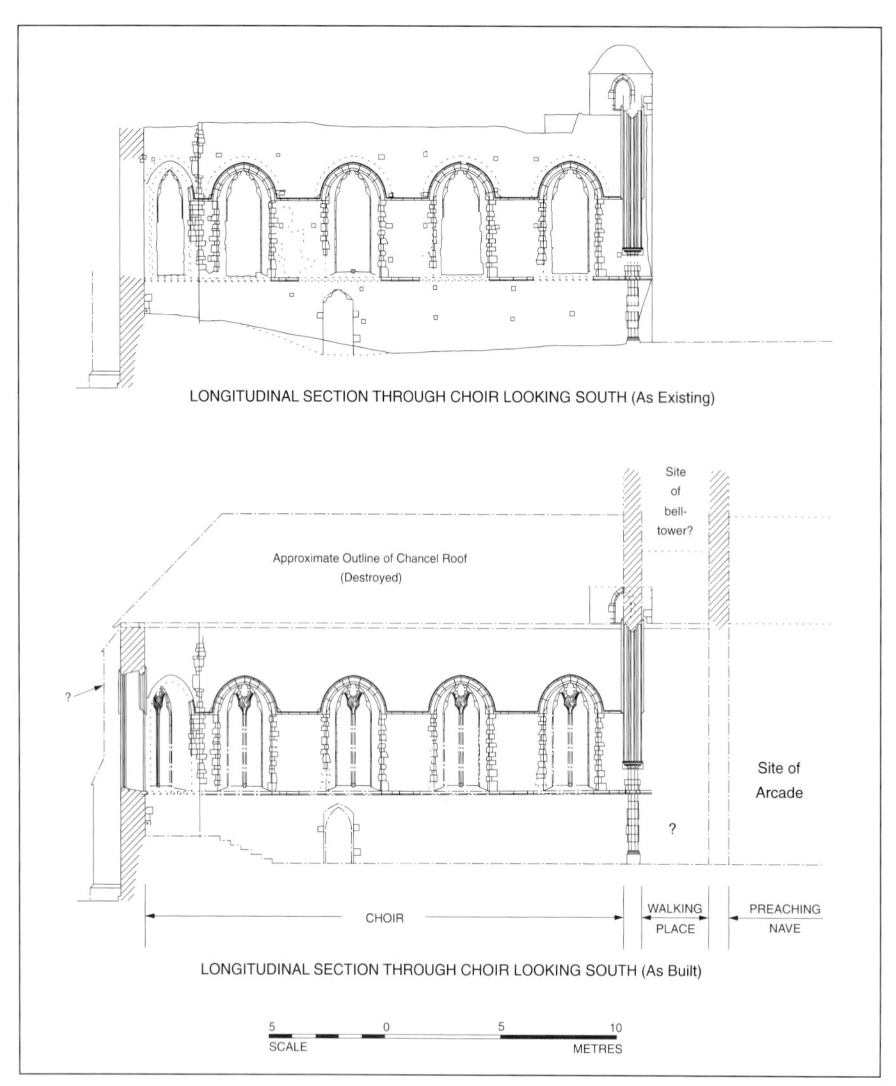

Fig. 7.22 (Left)

Grey Friars.
Section through the church both as existing and partly as a conjectural reconstruction.

polygonal apse. The east window appears to have been of three rather than two lights. All stand upon a continuous moulded internal string course. Although most of the window tracery has fallen, sufficient remains to show that the lights had trefoiled heads and quatrefoiled spandrels, all set beneath two-centred arches capped externally by simple hood-moulds which were stopped (Figures 7.23-7.24). Internally, the two-centred rear arches are hollow-chamfered and these too are capped by hood-mouldings, but in this instance they are returned to form a second, high-level string course. Between each of the windows are the remains of external buttresses with chamfered plinths.

In the south wall, beneath the 'central' window is a 14th-century doorway of which the external head is missing. Over the doorway, at window-cill level, is a string course extending between the buttresses. This served as a weathering to the lean-to roof of an outshut - presumably a porch. The wallplate of the outshut was carried upon corbels; two of these remain *in situ*. In the wall opposite is a further doorway, but this probably represents a 17th-century insertion.

The choir's western end is taken up by an exceptionally wide and elegant two-centred arch. The voussoirs are of two moulded orders springing from moulded caps supported by grouped, attached shafts which rise from moulded bases. The lower string course to the choir extends around both responds of the arch, serving as collars. Both faces of the arch are capped by moulded hoods, which terminate with stops, each carved with a human head. To the south of the choir arch is a projecting stair turret entered via a partially rebuilt doorway on the west side. Above it a small cross with trefoiled arms and a stepped base is carved in low relief (Figure 7.25). At about 2.4 metres (8ft.) up the stair is a south-facing doorway with a two-centred head. This formerly led to the first-floor room (presumably the dormitory) in the east range of the cloisters, and thus the stair turret appears to have doubled as a night stair. The east wall of the turret is lit part way up by a square, quatrefoiled window, and there is a further opening in the south wall at the top, lighting a doorway in the turret's

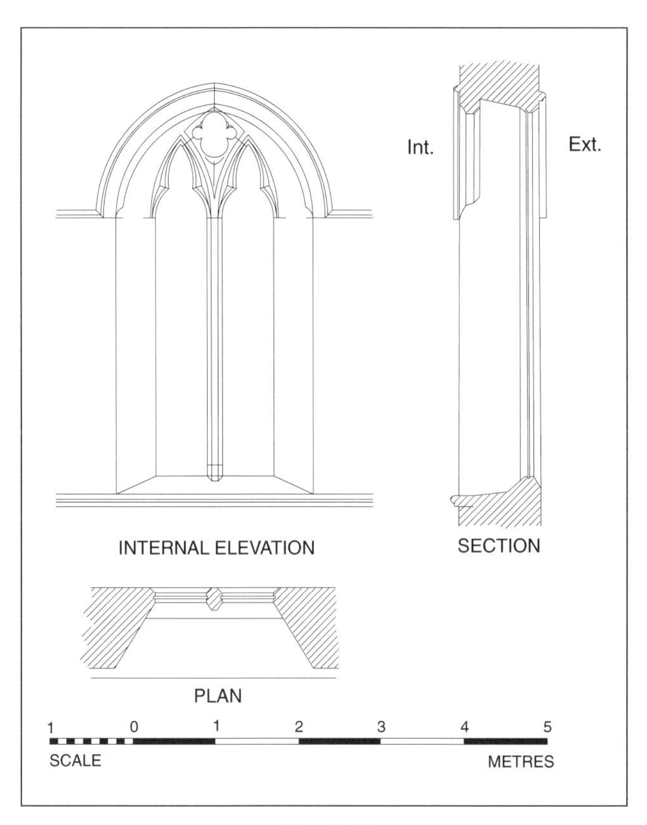

Fig. 7.23
Grey Friars.
Reconstructed details of a typical window within the choir.

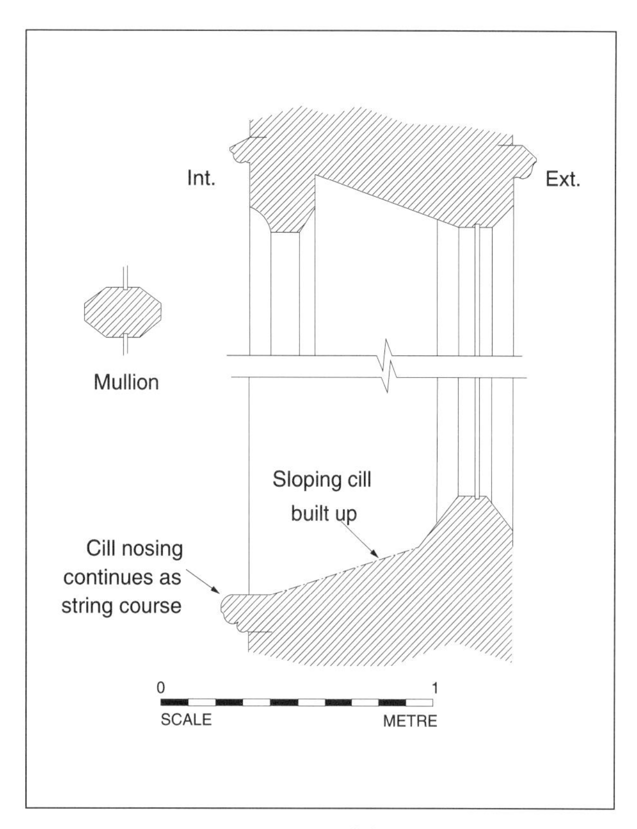

Fig. 7.24
Grey Friars.
Architectural details of a typical window within the choir.

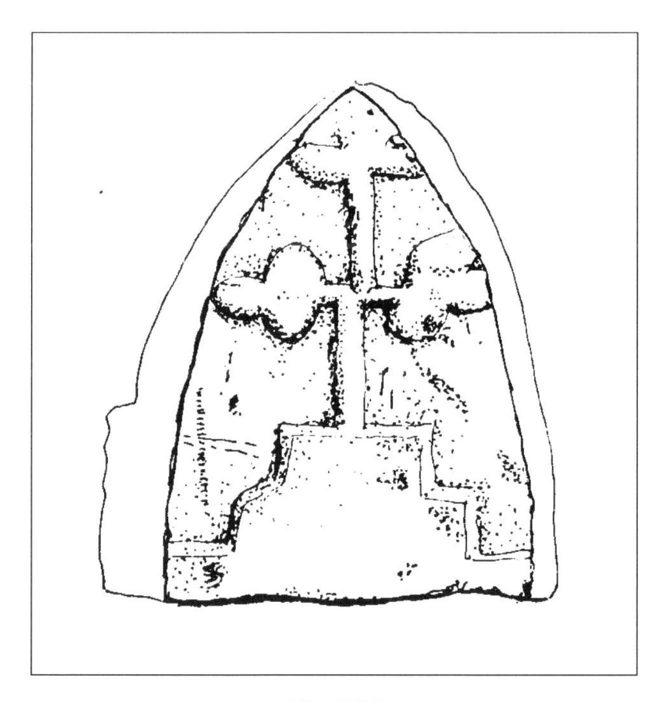

Fig. 7.25
Grey Friars.
Detail of a carving in the west wall of the stair turret.

north wall. This doorway probably led to a steeple-capped bell-tower supported by the upper parts of the nave's eastern wall and the choir arch, above the central walking place - a typical arrangement. A fragment of weathering course high on the western side of the stair turret indicates that the central bell-tower was flanked to north and south by a continuation of the nave roof, which, on the southern side, extended down over an adjunct to abut against the cloister. There was no such adjunct on the northern side - here the northern wall of the walking space was aligned with that of the choir.

The preaching nave has gone, but a fragment of wall standing at the northeast corner, and another towards the southwest corner show that it incorporated both a north and south aisle, giving an overall internal span of *c*.17.4 metres (57ft.). The upstanding fragment of the south aisle's south wall stands sufficiently high to retain part of the corbel table and weathering course associated with the lean-to timber roof of the cloister's northern alley (*see* Figure 7.26). Incorporated into the wall fragment's western end is the respond of a doorway linking the cloister to the church. As the floor of the cloister was set some distance below that of the church, the doorway incorporated a flight of steps.

Fig. 7.26
Grey Friars. Remains of the church from the southwest showing a fragment of the wall (left) between the cloister and the south aisle. Note the parch marks in the grass on the site of the cloister (foreground). Photograph - Andrew Woodcock, September 1995.

In dry weather the foundations of the claustral buildings are easily visible in the form of parch marks and from these it has been possible on two occasions to plot the outline of the complex. As Figure 7.18 shows, they were arranged around a cloister garth which measured approximately 25.3 metres (83ft.) by 26.4 metres (86ft.7ins.) including the walkways.[45]

The Black Friars *(Figures 7.27-7.29)*

In 1318 the Dominican Friars obtained a site at the extreme southern end of the town, just inside New Gate. Being far from habitation and little visited, however, in 1339 they moved to a new six-acre site within the Liberty of Iham, on the edge of the marsh just below the town. In 1342 the friars complained to the Pope that their site was in danger of being inundated. The Pope ordered the Bishop of Chichester to transfer them to a location within the town and in 1357 the friars took steps to acquire and occupy Quarter 4.[46]

Additional details of the friary can be gleaned from the inquiry taken in 1415 into the proposed line of

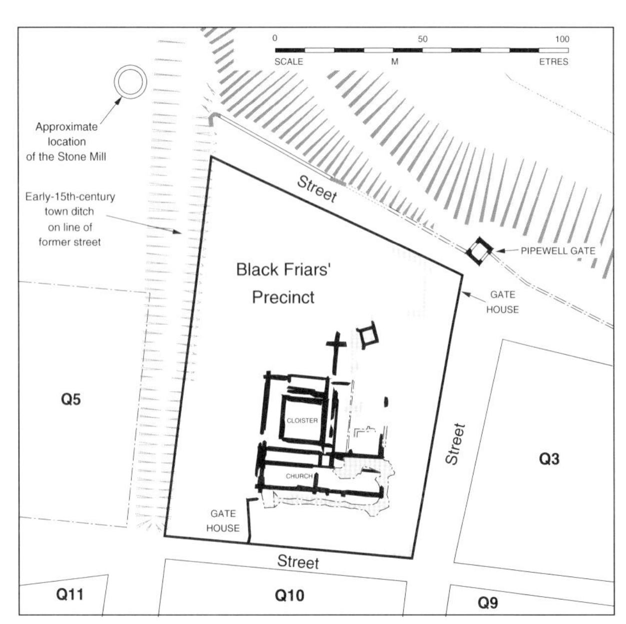

Fig. 7.27
Black Friars. Plan of the precinct and claustral buildings based upon documentary evidence, aerial photographs, parch marks and geophysical survey.

Fig. 7.28 (Right)

Black Friars. View by J.M.W. Turner showing the Pipewell Gate (right) viewed from the southwest. To the left of the gate the buttress corner of the Black Friars' precinct wall (probably incorporating the remains of a gatehouse) is clearly visible. In the background, on the hill above Pipewell Gate is shown the tower of the Old Stone Mill (reproduced from the Liber Studiorum, cxviii M).

Fig. 7.29 (Right)

Extract from an aerial photograph showing the precincts of the Black Friars viewed from the northwest. The foundations of the church (centre) and cloisters (left) are clearly visible. (© Copyright reserved Cambridge University Collection of Aerial Photographs. Ref. AAM 42 taken on 21 July 1959).

the new town wall. The inquiry makes clear that Quarter 4 was then 'largely built upon'. The area required for the new town wall included ' . . . a house of theirs . . . worth to them 10/- yearly', but 'their church, buildings and gardens' would be unaffected.[47] A reference in the inquiry to the southern gate of the friary implies that there was also a second gate. Of this second gate some remains still stood until the mid-20th century, when they were swept away during road widening. This was a section of wall to the southwest of the Pipewell Gate.

Photographs taken around 1900 show that it stood then to above the height of a man and incorporated some form of corner buttress. The wall is clearly shown in a drawing of *c.*1800 by Turner. At that date it stood almost as tall as the Pipewell Gate itself - clearly more than the mere remains of a precinct wall (Figure 7.28).[48] Cooper confirmed that it was the remains of the friary's northeast gate when, in 1850, he wrote that 'some remains of the clustered columns of the entrance gate (of the King's Castle) are yet to be seen on the side of Pipewell or Ferry Gate . . . '.[49] Cooper's reference to the remains as a castle gatehouse is erroneous - he thought that the site of the Black Friars stood to the south, on Quarter 15. The line of the friary's northern precinct wall is still clearly visible: it extends westwards from the former remains, crossing the field as a distinctive linear earthwork, at a distance of approximately 10 metres (33ft.) to the south of the town wall. The gap between the two represents a road referred to in the 1415 inquiry and shown on the 1758 town map.

The history of the Black Friars from its establishment on Quarter 4 until its dissolution was relatively uneventful. The friary was dedicated to the Blessed Virgin and in 1398 included, a 'lector' or teacher of philosophy and theology. A report made at its dissolution in July 1538 noted that the house had no lead, but slate and tile and was falling down. The buildings were pillaged for material to help build Camber Castle as were those of the Grey Friars.[50]

Despite the lack of upstanding remains and of any clear pattern discernible from the earthworks, the combined information given by parch marks and resistivity survey give a good impression of the size and form of the new monastery founded upon Quarter 4 (*see* Figures 7.27 and 7.29). The church measured approximately 43 metres (141ft.) long and appears to have been aisled: it had an overall width of approximately 18 metres (59ft.). As is to be expected of a friary church, there are no signs of transepts, though there are clear indications of the walking place which separated the preaching nave from the choir. There would probably have been a bell-turret (perhaps capped by a spire) over the walking place. Because the site slopes down from south to north, the claustral buildings were placed on the northern side of the church. The cloister garth (excluding the walks) measured approximately 14 metres (46ft.) square. Indications of the complex of buildings which surrounded the garth can be seen, but no clear detail is discernible. A wall extended southwards from the western end of the church to Mill Road, probably separating the public entrance (via the western end of the church) from the friars' cemetery to the church's south and east. The resistivity survey carried out appeared to indicate traces of buildings towards the northeast corner of the precinct.

HOSPITALS

When it was refounded, Winchelsea was endowed with three hospitals - St John, Holy Cross and St Bartholomew - all sited in the peripheral quarters towards the south of the hill. In addition, there was a hermitage or hospital dedicated to St Anthony on the marshes at the entrance to the harbour, some two or three miles to the east of the town.

St John's Hospital *(Figures 7.30-7.32)*

When laid out in the late 13th century, Quarter 34 included a large plot of over an acre held by the House of St John.[51] Contrary to the arrangement shown in Homan's reconstruction of the town, their plot was 'L'-shaped in plan (Figure 7.30). As with the hospital of St Bartholomew (*see* below), this was probably divided into a precinct and a field, the field occupying the sloping ground on the western side of the quarter. Whether the precinct extended across the entire northern frontage of the quarter or was restricted to the northeast corner can, at present, only be judged by guesswork.[52]

St John's Hospital was probably the oldest and the most important of the three hospitals at Winchelsea. From time immemorial rents had been assigned to it out of the issues of Great Yarmouth. It was not in the hands of a monastic order, but was under the control of the mayor. He was required to visit it once a year, had power to remove any objectionable inmate and, with the consent of the jurats, might admit any poor man or woman who had been 'in good love and fame all their time'.[53] Although modern descriptions usually state that

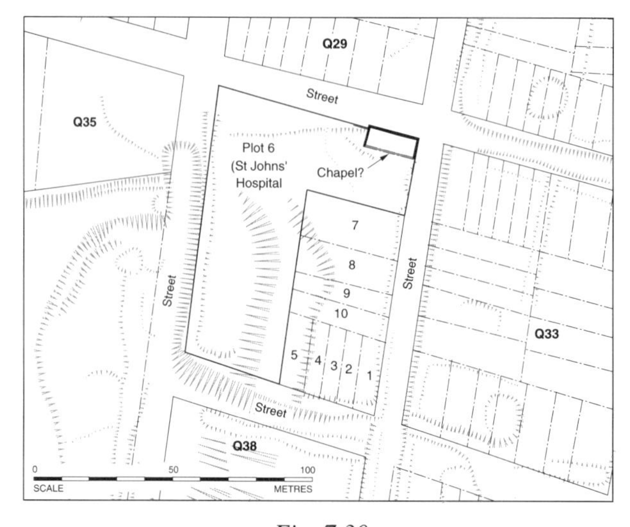

Fig. 7.30
St John's Hospital. Context of the hospital within the late-13th-century layout of Winchelsea.

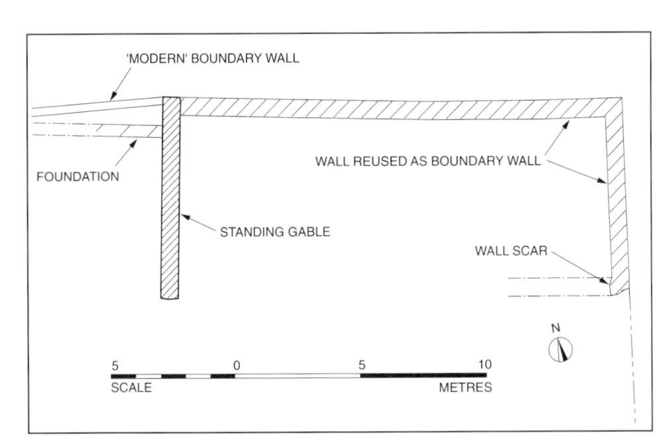

Fig. 7.31
St John's Hospital. Plan of the remains.

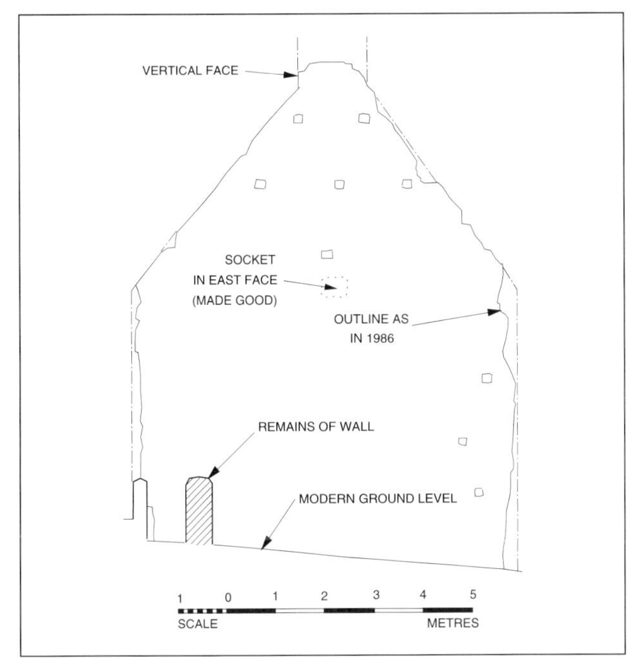

Fig. 7.32
St John's Hospital. West elevation of the standing gable.

the hospital had already been dissolved by 1557, records show that it continued in use until the late 1560s. The last reference to the appointment of a master is dated 1565. The wording of subsequent documents, dated 1568, 1569 and 1570, suggests that the hospital was then no longer in use and that its property was being granted out to private individuals. The site had certainly been abandoned by 1584, when an inquiry into concealed lands reported that 'the chapel or hospital of St John in Winchelsea [is] now demolished . . '.[54]

Medieval hospitals usually took one of two forms. They comprised either a communal infirmary hall with a chapel attached at the eastern end (as at St Mary's, Chichester, West Sussex), or a complex of adjacent or adjoining buildings. The complex would include individual houses for the inmates together with a chapel and a communal hall for meals (as at Holy Cross, Winchester, Hampshire). There are no indications regarding the early form of St John's, but by the 16th century it was a complex of buildings and was usually referred to as St John's Almshouse. The houses and chapel are mentioned in 1559.[55] The eastern end of the chapel evidently stood close to present-day Wickham Rock Lane, for a deed of 1587 refers to a small piece of land on the eastern side of that street as being 'at the east head of the chapel of St John's hospital'.[56]

All that now survives of the hospital buildings above ground are two low foundations and a tall gable wall standing beside the present road leading into Winchelsea. Although it contains no datable architectural features, the gable is certainly medieval (Figures 7.31-7.32). It formed the western gable of a structure 7.95 metres (*c.*26ft.) wide and *c.*18.50 metres (*c.*60ft.8ins.) long on an east-west alignment. The lower courses of the northern and eastern walls are built into the present field boundary, although part of the northern wall has recently been reconstructed. The scar of a further wall can be seen extending westwards from the gable. One of the most significant features of the gable is the short section of vertical quoin at the head of the northern roof slope. The most likely explanation for this feature is that the gable was capped by a small turret, which perhaps carried a bell. This may suggest that the building represents the hospital's chapel which, from the references commonly made to it in 16th-century documents, was clearly a dominant feature in the landscape. It survives because it was subsequently converted into a barn to which the earliest reference was made in 1618, when it was described as the 'barn called the Almshouse barn'.[57]

Hospital of Holy Cross

Like St John's hospital, Holy Cross was originally founded in Old Winchelsea. It was already in existence by 1252 and it is possible that this was the 'church of the lepers of Winchelsea' mentioned in 1287, although this could equally have been St Bartholomew's hospital. When Holy Cross was refounded upon the new site in the late 13th century, a one-acre plot was allocated to it, but this was subsequently increased to six and a half acres by the addition of open land to the north. This land became known as 'Holy Rood Land' or 'Holy Rood Field'. Protection was granted to the master and brethren of the hospital in 1314, and in 1427 Henry VI ratified the estate of Simon Moreley in the 'hospital or free chapel of Holy Cross'.[58]

The hospital's early-13th-century seal is circular and bears a cross with enlarged ends. The names of four

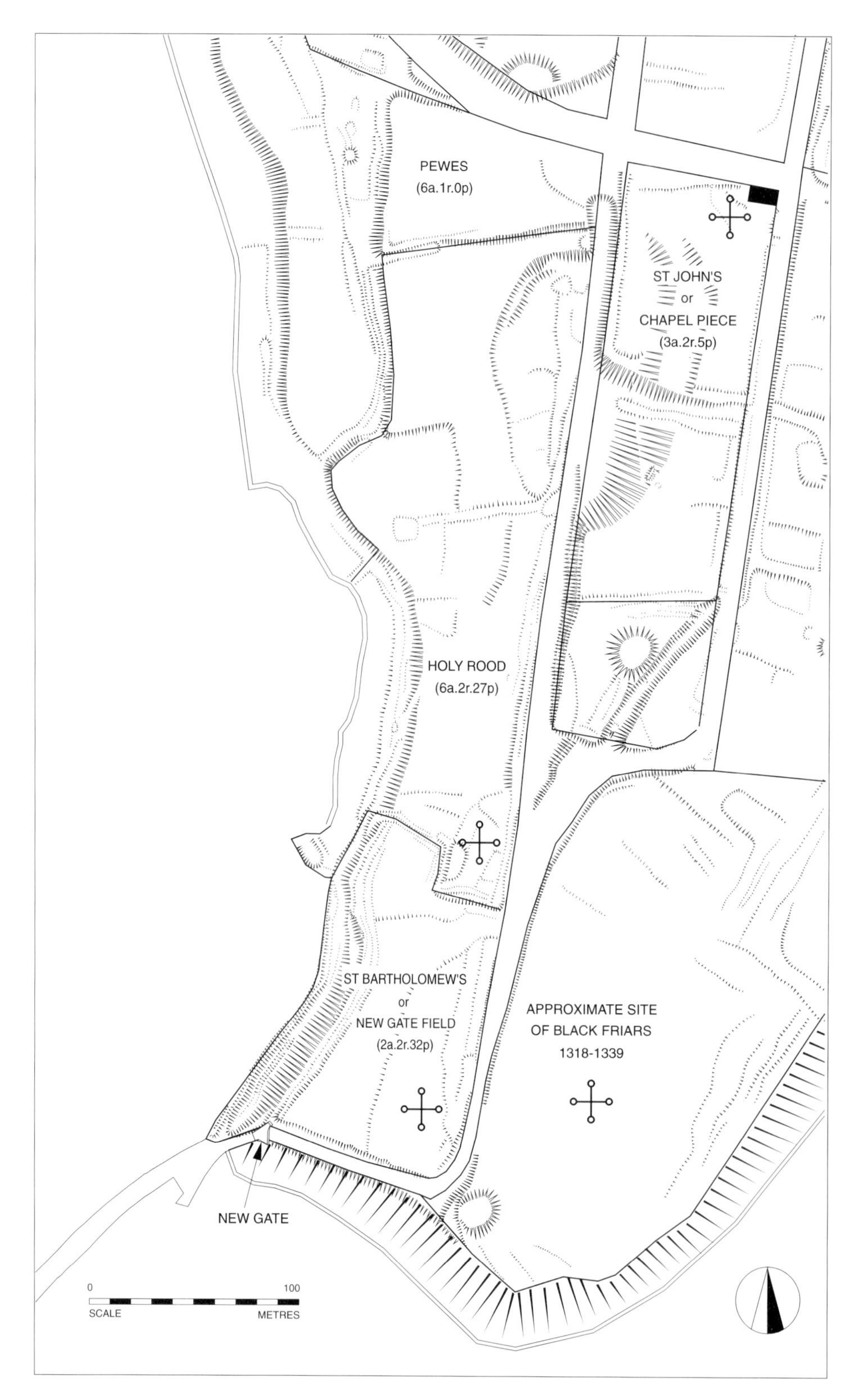

Fig. 7.33 (Left)

Southern end of Winchelsea showing the sites of the three hospitals and the early site of the Black Friars (each signified by a cross).

The outline map is based upon the town surveys of 1758 and 1763. The earthworks shown are as existing, based upon a survey by RCHME.

masters are known, the earliest from the year 1411, whilst the latest - Robert Wrothe - was appointed upon the death of his predecessor in 1501.[59] The hospital must have been dissolved very soon after that date, for in 1570 the mayor, jurats and commonalty of New Winchelsea issued a sealed testimonial declaring that to their knowledge there was no house, chapel or hospital of the Holy Cross or Holy Rood other than that now occupied by Thomas Guldeford of Hempstead, co. Kent or his farmers, and before him by Sir Edward and Sir John Guldeford, and that they had been in possession of it for 50 years or more. They also declared that they had seen in records more than 100 years old the words 'Domus scilicet Crucis in Winchelsea' but beyond this they had no knowledge of a hospital or free chapel of Holy Cross or Holy Rood.[60]

Earthworks at the extreme southern end of Holy Rood Land, adjacent to the street, probably indicate the site of the hospital, but otherwise little obvious archaeological field evidence is visible.

St Bartholomew's Hospital

No reference has been found to this hospital prior to the end of the 13th century. It may thus represent a new foundation contemporary with the town's move to its new site. It was a hospital for brethren and sisters and was endowed with two acres of land. Like St John's Hospital, it was under the control of the mayor and commonalty, who had the power of admitting suitable inmates.[61]

In name at least, it appears to have survived the Reformation, for in 1559 the Corporation appointed a master and mistress to the hospitals of St John and St Bartholomew and again in 1564 a master was appointed to the Hospitals (plural).[62] However, by this date both hospitals were probably combined upon the site of St John's, for the master and mistress were to live in the chapel and build up its houses and chapel within three years. No reference to buildings at St Bartholomew's was made in the declaration. St Bartholomew's land was already let to Thomas Holden by 1543 and he remained the occupier until 1573. It was then described as a messuage, barn and two acres of land called 'Bartholomew Field', but the reference to a 'messuage' may then have been outdated as it is questionable whether the house survived at that date.[63] All buildings appear to have been destroyed by 1586, when the property was described as a 'toft and 2 acres of arable . . . part of the late hospital of St Bartholomew's'.[64]

Lynchets in the south-eastern corner of the quarter could relate to boundaries associated with the hospital precinct, for deeds of the 1360s indicate that this is where the hospital stood. The remainder of their land formed a close abutting their precinct's northern boundary.[65]

The Hermitage or hospital of St Anthony

In 1593 the Recorder of Rye stated that he had seen written record that on Camber Beach in the parish of St Thomas of Winchelsea there had been a hermitage dedicated to St Anthony for the maintaining of a light for the harbour. Since the decay of that hermitage - which one witness said lay then half a mile out to sea - a house had been built for the same purpose. On a map of *c.*1597 two lights are shown standing on the northeast end of the Camber shingle spit, with two houses immediately to the northeast of Winchelsea Castle (*i.e.* Camber Castle). The hermitage already existed by 1267 when the king granted protection to 'the brethren of the Hospital of St Anthony upon the port of Winchelsea'. It may have been refounded upon a new, less vulnerable site following the inundations of the late 13th century. It was mentioned in 1330 and was still standing in December 1536, when the men of the Admiral of Sluys, in the Low Countries, 'burnt the hermitage of the Camber in despite and hewed an image of St Anthony with their swords, bidding it to call upon St George for help'.[66]

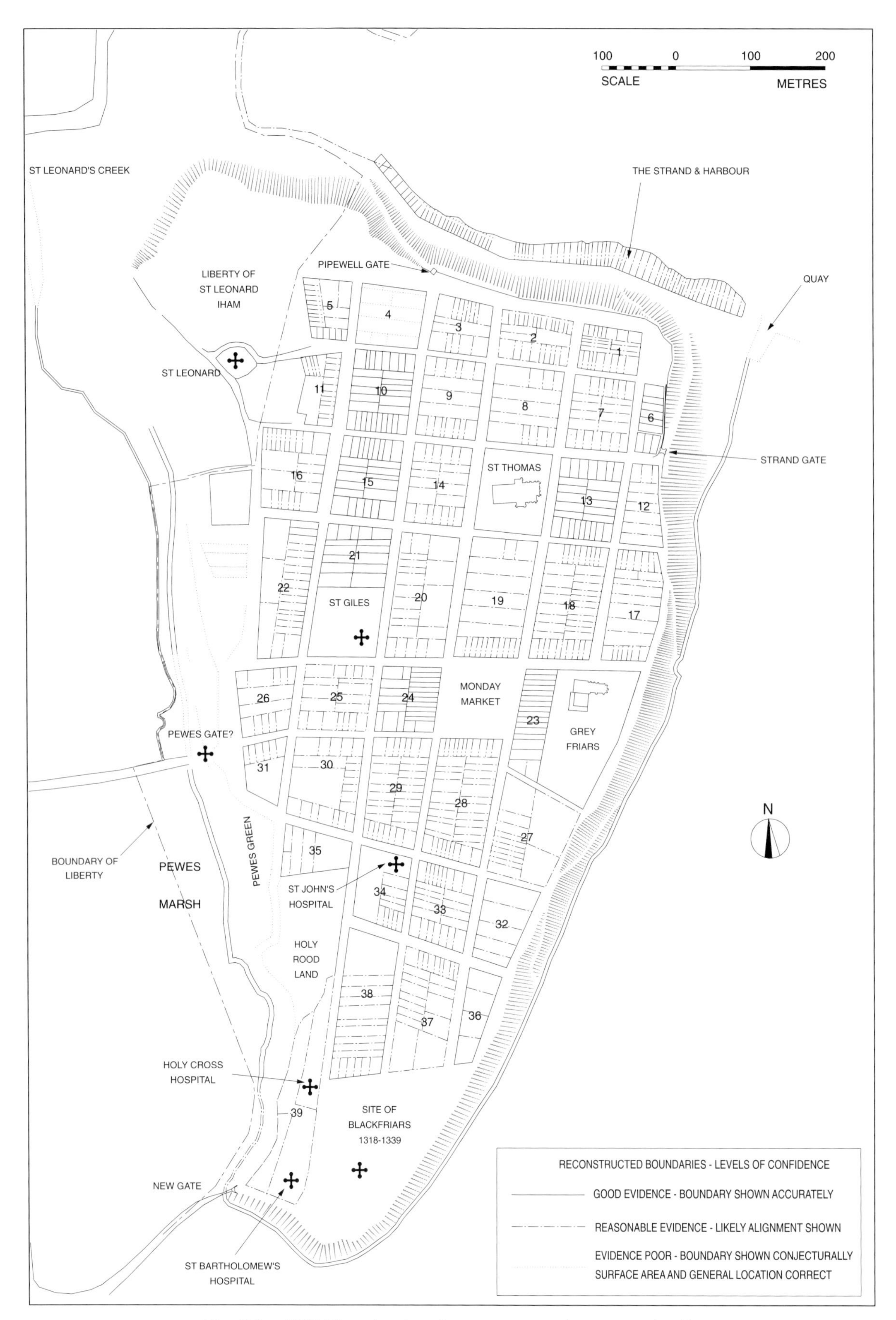

Fig. 8.1 1292 Plan showing the reconstructed tenement details.

8. THE BURGAGE PLOTS

David and Barbara Martin

THE PLOTS AS ORIGINALLY LAID OUT

New Winchelsea is unique amongst English medieval towns in as much as its foundation rental of 1292 allows its original layout to be reconstructed.[1] This detail extends not only to the number of building plots laid out, but to their location, size and rent. Furthermore, for many quarters the individual property boundaries are reconstructable, so that the street frontages of the plots as well as their depth can be ascertained. In total the new town comprised 802 plots - 723 on the hill and 79 harbour or quayside plots flanking the Brede estuary (Figure 8.1).[2]

The most common arrangement adopted in the setting out of the individual plots was to divide the quarters into four zones, one each along the southern and northern sides with the intervening central area occupied by plots fronting onto the east and west streets respectively. In the two principal quarters (Quarters 8 and 19) to the north and south of St Thomas's church, as well as within Quarter 9 to the northwest of the church, the central plots were extended across the full width, stretching from the eastern to the western streets. This arrangement allowed the principal inhabitants larger plots with dual frontages. Because of the narrow width of three of the cliff-edge quarters (6, 12, and 17), here too the central plots extended across from the western to the eastern street, though the eastern street was very narrow and was, in effect, nothing more than a cliff-top lane. In the case of Quarter 17 some of these larger plots were allocated to the local gentry - Sir Roger de Lewknor, Sir William de Etchingham, and his kinsman, Sir Simon - for their town houses. For such men these plots were worth having, for in addition to the town's royal connections and the legal advantages enjoyed by any property owner in the town, Winchelsea was also an important centre for the disposal of demesne produce from local manors such as Udimore.[3]

The layout within Quarter 20, to the southwest of St Thomas's church, also differs from the standard pattern in order to provide a further supply of larger plots for the use of the urban elite. These plots each had a frontage facing one of the principal streets leading between the church and market square. Other modifications to the standard pattern are to be found within the more peripheral quarters along the western, southern and eastern flanks of the town. The corner plots upon all of the quarters were much sought after, as they offered two adjoining street frontages for development. Indeed, it is noticeable that upon one of the principal quarters (Quarter 8) two particularly large corner plots were included at the southwest and northwest corners for the use of members of the Alard family.

The rent due to the king for all tenements was based upon a fixed rate per acre. However, this rate varied according to the potential commercial value of the quarter in relation to its location within the town. The properties fall into four groups (*see* Figure 8.2). At the commercial heart of the town, the 50 plots which flanked the four sides of Monday Market were by far the most expensive; the rent for each of these plots was calculated at 60d. per acre. Next in rank, calculated at 48d. per acre, were the 79 harbour or quayside plots flanking the estuary of the River Brede, beneath the northern cliff. Except for the eight southernmost quarters, the tenements within the remainder of the town (583 plots) were valued at 40d. per acre. Reflecting their lesser importance and more peripheral location, the rate per acre for the 90 plots occupying the eight southern quarters was reduced slightly to 36d.[4]

The 1292 foundation rental lists 690 persons holding property within the town. Most of the owners -

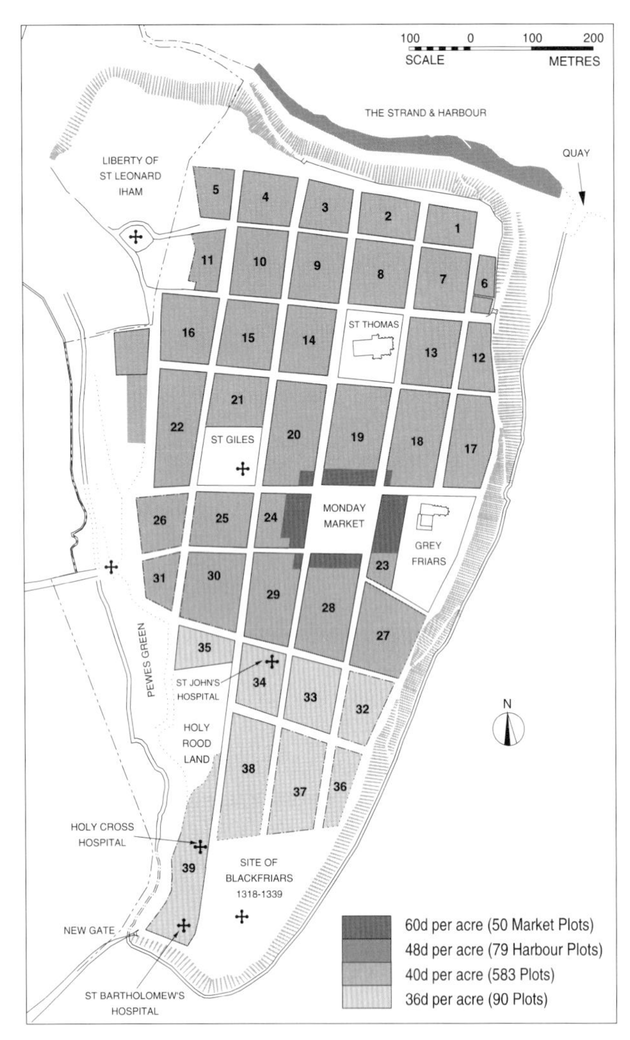

Fig. 8.2
The rents per acre, as in 1292.

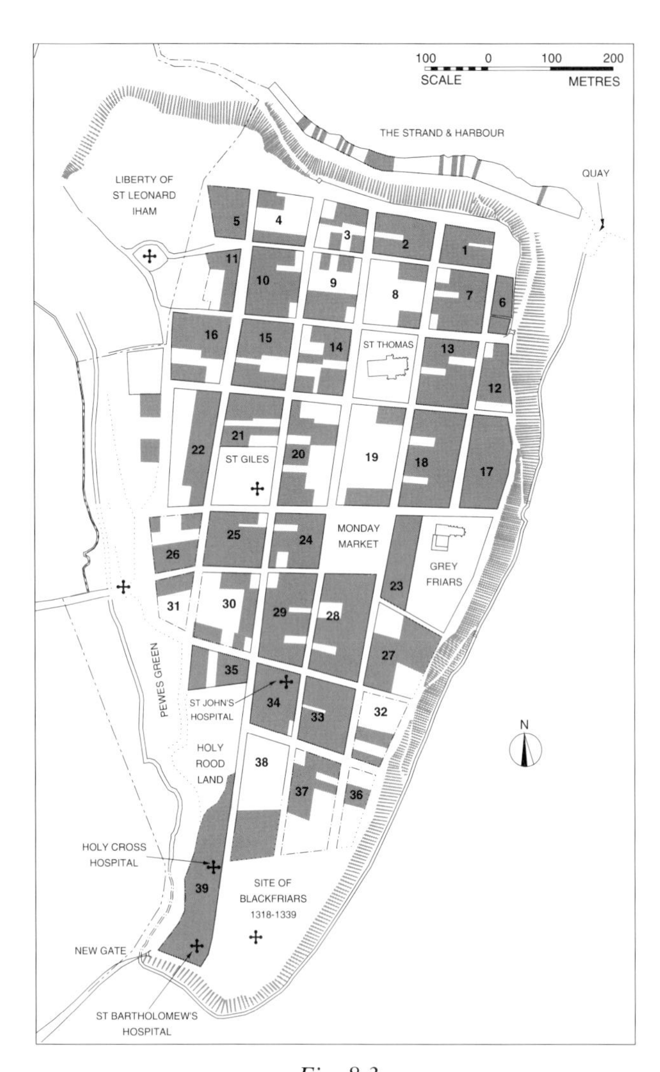

Fig. 8.3
Landowners holding a single plot in 1292.

virtually 90% of the total - held just one plot (Figure 8.3). Of these, 484 held a plot in the central part of town, 70 within the low-rent southern quarters, a further 15 possessed a harbour plot only, and 45 owned a high-rental plot facing the market square. Indeed, of the 50 owners of plots facing the market, only five held other property within the town: two had a harbour plot, two owned a property elsewhere in the main part of town (although one of these was a ¼-acre plot on the western periphery) and another had a plot within one of the low-rent southern quarters. The pattern of ownership regarding the high-rental plots fronting the market square suggests little link between these commercial plots and the harbour, perhaps reinforcing the notion that at least one of the town's markets may always have been held on the quayside (*see* Chapter 4). Of the owners holding more than one property within the town, 53 owned two plots; 17 held three, and 6 held four. In all but 15 instances one of the properties was a quayside plot (Figure 8.4). In one instance a father and son each owned a plot in the main part of town, but shared a harbour side plot. In another, two brothers jointly owned a small plot in the main part of town, but one brother also held two main plots and a harbour plot and the other brother held one main plot and a harbour plot.

Most of the properties within the town were tiny, though not so small as in some English towns of the period. The smallest individual tenements were two properties which amounted to only 3 *virgae* (perches) each, the equivalent of a plot 5 metres by 15 metres (16ft.6ins. by 49ft.6ins.). One of these was in the harbour area and the other within Quarter 2. A further ten plots - three in Quarter 1, six in Quarter 2 and one in Quarter 17 - measured 3½ *virgae* each. In all, 334 plots (37% of those on the hill and 85% of those in the harbour area) were of 10 *virgae* (*i.e.* one-sixteenth of an acre) or less. There was a general spread of all plot sizes throughout the town, though some quarters - such as Quarters 1 and 2 - had an above average number of small plots, whilst others, particularly the principal quarters (8, 9, 17, 19 and

Fig. 8.4
Landowners holding two or more plots in 1292.

Fig. 8.5
The properties of the principal 15 members of the urban elite in 1292.

20), incorporated an above average number of large plots.

Most landholders in Winchelsea - 642 out of the 690 - owed a total annual king's rent for their property of 12d. or less (where their property did not extend beyond a quarter of an acre) and only 19 held half an acre or more. The latter included the three hospitals and a plot held by the serving mayor. The remaining 15 were all leading residents of the town and are perhaps best collectively referred to as Winchelsea's 'urban elite' (Figure 8.6). All owned either two, three or four properties. They held a quayside plot and, with one exception (who lived in Quarter 12), they resided within one of the four principal quarters of the town - five within Quarter 8, two in Quarter 9, five in Quarter 19 and two in Quarter 20

Owner	Area (in Virgae)	Location of Principal Property	Location of other Property	
			Harbour Plot	Other Plots
James Paulyn	266v	Q20	●	Q38
Gervase Alard, jnr.	226v	Q8	●	Q4; Q16
Gervase Alard, snr.	200¾v	Q8	●	Q27; Q36
Henry Jacob	190¾v	Q9	●	Q27; Q30
John Alard	189¼v*	Q20	●	Q22; Q30
Vincent Herbard	188½v	Q9	●	Q36; Q37
Reynold Alard, snr.	178v	Q8	●	Q31
Thomas Godfrey	171¼v	Q19	●	Q32
Paul de Horne	163¼v	Q19	●	Q22
Walter Scappe	161¾v	Q19	●	Q22
Nicholas Alard	153v	Q8	●	Q8; Q32
Thomas Alard	130½v	Q8	●	Q4; Q11
Reynold Alard	98¼v	Q19	●	Q1
William Burgeys	86¾v	Q12	●	Q32
Henry Broun	83¾v	Q19	●	-

* Includes 50% of a jointly-owned 80v plot in Q22

Fig. 8.6 (Left)
Persons holding over half an acre of land in Winchelsea, 1292 (The hospitals and a plot held by the serving mayor are excluded).

(Figure 8.5). Almost half - no fewer than seven of the fifteen - were members of the Alard family. The other eight men were Thomas Godfrey, Vincent Herberd (ancestor of the Finch family, who eventually rose to become the Earls of Winchelsea), Paul de Horne, Henry Jacob, James Paulyn, Walter Scappe, William Burgeys and Henry Broun. At this time no single man held property within the town which totalled in excess of 1¾ acres.

What is clear from combining details contained within the 1292 rental with other data from the extant earthworks and surviving boundaries is that the individual plots were not laid out using frontages of standard width. Instead, although some sequences of equal-width plots existed, in many instances the frontages varied even along the sides of individual quarters. They ranged from as little as 4 metres (*c.*13ft.) upwards. Only 5% had frontages of less than 5.6 metres (*c.*18ft.6ins.) whilst half the properties within the town had street frontages of more than 10 metres (32ft.9ins.). Some of the most highly prized plots were those which boasted two adjoining street facades, being located upon the corners of the quarters: in all, these accounted for almost 20% of the total. Those within the heart of the town would obviously have been considerably more valuable than those in peripheral quarters.

In many instances very precise frontages can be calculated for entire lengths of street. For instance, the frontages of the seven plots along the northern side of Quarter 13 (now the south side of High Street, immediately to the east of the church) were generous. From west to east there were five plots of 12.5 metres (41ft.) one of 10 metres (32ft.9ins.) followed by a further plot of 12.5 metres (41ft.). The frontages to the plots along the eastern side of Quarter 15 were more variable. Here, working from north to south, was a frontage of 28.1 metres (92ft.2ins.) for the corner plot, followed by two of 9.2 metres (30ft.), one narrow plot of 5.8 metres (19ft.), two relatively wide plots of 13.75 metres (45ft.2ins.) and a corner plot with an eastern frontage of 24.1 metres (79ft.).

The properties within both of these sequences had street frontages which, with one exception, were of above average length. A group where the frontages were consistently relatively short were the high-rental plots around the market square. Here, along the northern side of the square (forming the southern side of Quarter 19) the 11 plots had consistent street facades of 7.25 metres (23ft.9ins.), excepting only the western corner plot, which was twice that size. This larger plot was partially excavated in 1974.[5] A similar larger plot was to be found at the western end of the square's southern side, although along this side of the square, the other frontages varied between 4.8 metres (15ft.9ins.) and 9.6 metres (31ft.6ins.). On the eastern side of the square, with two exceptions (one slightly smaller and one slightly larger) the plots were a consistent 7.0 metres (23ft.) in width, and likewise, except for a smaller corner plot, all those on the western side had frontages consistently 6.1 metres (20ft.) wide.

Some of the smallest plots with the shortest frontages were to be found along the northern side of Quarter 2. Working from west to east, the first two plots (including the corner plot) were the largest: each had a frontage of 9.7 metres (31ft.9ins.). The remainder was a mix of six plots with frontages of 4.8 metres (15ft.9ins.) and six plots with frontages of 7.3 metres (24ft.), with one further plot of just 4.2 metres (13ft.9ins.).

THE SUBSEQUENT EVOLUTION OF THE PLOTS

The topographical details recorded for Winchelsea at the moment of its inception must be the best for any English medieval town, and there is much more analysis which could be undertaken than that presented above. Even so, it should always be remembered that Winchelsea in 1292 was a town deliberately planned and, although the more influential men of (Old) Winchelsea would have had a say in the location and form of the plots they were allocated, the majority of residents within the old town would have had little or no control over which plots they were given. From the moment the residents took possession of their plots all this would have changed: the town then commenced its organic growth, with individual plots being sold, merged or divided in order to suit the aspirations and personal needs of the residents better.

Unfortunately, until 1543 (long after the settlement had shrunk to nothing more than a small town) there are no known detailed rentals to give a clear picture of the adjustments being made during the crucial first decades of the settlement's life. There are, however, a few documentary references and some evidence (both structural and excavated) which allow glimpses of the processes in action. For instance, in 1292, a single small 9-*virgae* property on the eastern side of Quarter 30 was allocated to Roger Pote. He subsequently acquired a larger holding on the southern side of another quarter (location unknown) and later he granted the western part of his new acquisition to his sister or sister-in-law. Upon Roger's death the residue of the property descended to his daughter, who, in 1329, sold off a strip of 6.1 metres (20ft.) together with the buildings standing upon it.[6] Thus, within 37 years of the town's foundation rental being drawn up, this single tenement had been subdivided into three separate holdings.

Nicholas Alard, a member of Winchelsea's urban elite, had been granted four properties within the town in 1292 (*see* Figure 8.5). However, by the death of his son and heir, Henry, in 1336, a considerable estate had been amassed within the town. In the intervening 44 years he and his father had acquired a number of additional properties, including four shops in The Butchery, probably built upon an area partitioned off from a larger property.[7] Whilst Nicholas and Henry were compiling an urban estate, other members of the Alard clan were disposing of building plots. For instance, in 1342, James, son of Gervase Alard junior, (another member of the urban elite) divided off and disposed of the unwanted eastern part of his tenement on the southwest corner of Quarter 8.[8]

There is both structural and excavated evidence to indicate that from an early date some plots were occupied by more than one dwelling, though whether the additional structures were built for letting at an annual rent, or sold in order to liquidate capital is now impossible to tell. The northwest corners of Quarters 2 and 8 each have two vaulted cellars of *c.*1300 with separate entrances, strongly suggesting two separate houses above (*see* Figure 9.2, Cellars 6 and 7; 21 and 22). Likewise, excavation has shown that although the southwest corner plot on Quarter 19, on the northern side of the market square, initially had a narrow stone range stretching along its western street, this was later replaced by a single-aisled hall which, from its location upon the plot, appears to have been occupied as a separate independent dwelling.[9] If the siting of an open hall discovered by archaeological excavation in 1981 is a guide, plot 2 on the southern side of Quarter 3 may also have been subdivided. The hall was set back from the street hard against the eastern boundary of a plot which, in 1292, had been laid out with a long street frontage (*see* Chapter 10). Although the evidence is from a much later date, the early-15th-century town wall inquiry indicates that the small (15-*virgae*), northwestern corner plot upon Quarter 10 had by 1415 been divided into three separate tiny plots of 8½, 4 and 4½ *virgae* each. By that period this part of town was in severe decline and thus the division is likely to have occurred much earlier. At the date of the inquiry the central plot of the three was empty, but the other two still had dwellings upon them.[10] Another small corner plot which became subdivided was that which occupied the southwest tenement on Quarter 13. This was divided so as to accommodate two dwellings, both of which were subsequently given to endow chantries.[11]

Adjustments to tenement boundaries were by no means restricted to the subdivision of properties. There is evidence, even at an early date, for the reverse procedure: plots were merged in order to increase their size. Thus the vaulted cellar beneath The Five Chimneys, which occupies the southwest corner of Quarter 1, was constructed upon what in 1292 had been two tenements. The same is true of the cellar at the northeast corner of Quarter 2, as well as that beneath Salutation Cottages on the southeast corner of the same quarter (*see* Figure 9.2, Cellars 1, 2 and 3). Firebrand, a stone-built house of *c.*1300 occupying the northwest corner of Quarter 13, likewise amalgamated two original plots, though in this instance its undercroft extends under only a small part of the house and is located entirely upon one of the two original plots. Thus, had the house above the cellar not survived, the fact that two plots had been combined would not have been apparent without resorting to archaeological excavation. Given that the main house never took up the entire northern frontage of the enlarged property, it is possible that from the outset the space to the east, (7.3m. or 24ft.) was occupied by a second structure. Thus it might be more accurate to see this example as an adjustment of boundary alignments rather than as an amalgamation of two plots. How long the small eastern plot continued to be owned with Firebrand is uncertain. It may already have been sold off by 1423, in which year it was given to the church of St Thomas. The site is now occupied by Wren Cottage, which is of 15th-century date, but whether built before or after the site was given to the church is not clear. Whatever the precise facts, it is interesting to note that even after the grant, Wren Cottage was exempted from payment of a king's rent. Instead, the entire king's rent for the two plots was paid by the owners of Firebrand.[12]

There are several known instances of similar adjustments to tenement boundaries. For example, in 1478 Robert Lucas sold to his neighbour a piece of land with a frontage of '13 feet 8 inches' (4.15m.) and a depth of '26 feet 6 inches' (8.1m.), together with the "*domus*" (dwelling) and workshop built upon it. The effect of this transaction was to move the property boundary 4.15 metres southwards.[13] In 1980 an archaeological excavation carried out in North Street, on the northern side of Quarter 2, recovered further evidence of tenement amalgamations and boundary adjustments. The fragmentary remains of three separate but adjoining buildings were recovered, one of which may have incorporated two dwellings. The excavated plots occupied a site between a pair of vaulted cellars and an upstanding stone gable wall. The upstanding wall coincides with a 1292 tenement boundary, as too does the wall between the two cellars and the boundary between the two western excavated houses. However, the two eastern houses were constructed upon three 1292 tenements and the party wall between them did not coincide with either of the two earlier tenement boundaries.[14] Perhaps all three plots had at some date been merged into one only later to be once more subdivided, this time into two rather than three with the boundary sited along a new alignment. Alternatively, as in the 1478 example quoted above, the adjustments may have been achieved by exchange between neighbours. Indeed, it is conceivable that, having fallen vacant, the central plot of the three was divided between the two neighbouring tenants, as appears to have happened with the central tenement of the three on the south side of Quarter 6.[15] Whether these adjustments occurred early in the life of the town, or during the later medieval period is not known. It may be significant that two of the three original plots upon Quarter 2 were recorded as decayed rents in 1363/4, and therefore the adjustments may have occurred when the plots were reoccupied subsequently. However, there is a complication in that too high a rent for the easternmost plot is quoted, perhaps suggesting that it and the next plot eastwards had already been combined by this date.[16] If this was the case, some adjustment to the original boundaries may have occurred early, perhaps even before any construction upon the site had started!

Although it is known that the town was founded with a total of 802 plots, the evidence presented above makes clear that with so many plots being subjected to subdivision and merger, it would be very dangerous to estimate, even very approximately, how many properties there may have been within the town at the height of its prosperity. An even more impossible task would be to estimate how many individual dwellings the town may have contained, for some plots, despite being in single ownership would have included a number of dwellings, warehouses and shops/workshops for rent. With a decline in the town's size and wealth in the mid-14th century, and the virtual abandonment of the southern and western quarters by 1415, the task becomes even more impossible. Even so, some useful observations can be made. By combining data derived from the 1543 town rental and from 16th-century enrolled deeds, it is certain that even at this late date the density of occupation on some of the quarters within the northeast corner of the settlement was greater than when the town was first laid out in the late 13th century. For instance, in the early/mid-16th century the eastern and southern sides of Quarter 7 incorporated at least 15 separate dwellings where only 12 plots had been laid out in the late 13th century. All three of the plots, which had originally stretched across Quarter 8 from street to street, had likewise been subdivided, as had the five plots which originally stretched across the width of Quarter 19. Here the western ends had been separated to form eight extra holdings, most of which still had buildings upon them in the early/mid-16th century. Some of this increase may have been the result of pressure resulting from the redistribution of settlement during the late 14th and 15th centuries, as the western and southern peripheral areas of the town were abandoned. Even so, it is perhaps more realistic to suggest that most of the increase occurred early, during the town's boom years. It is likely that the picture conveyed by the early-16th-century documents simply reflects the fact that this part of the town had still largely escaped the effects of the town's decline. It seems inconceivable, for instance, that the urban elite who occupied the long plots which stretched across Quarters 8 and 19 in the late 13th century would not have maximized revenue from the street frontages at both ends of their plots. It is, for instance, almost certain that Henry Alard's four shops, which he had within The Butchery in 1336, were built upon the eastern end of a plot upon Quarter 19, with probably a principal house occupying the western end of the same plot.

DENSITY OF OCCUPATION WITHIN THE TOWN

Although it would be naive to suggest that all of the plots laid out within the town were at some date built upon, it should be remembered that the circumstances at Winchelsea were very different from that experienced by most new towns of the period. New Winchelsea was not a speculative venture where plots were laid out in the hope that they would attract tenants: they were allotted to people who were already living within a thriving urban centre - a centre they were well aware would be destroyed within a very short time. For the residents of (Old) Winchelsea staying where they were was not an option. They had two choices – to move to the new site along with the rest of their fellow townsfolk, or to make an entirely new start somewhere else. Undoubtedly, the vast majority chose the former option. As has been demonstrated, some of the wealthiest residents were allotted more than one plot within the new town, and thus it could be argued that these people may have chosen to develop only one of their plots. Even so, it should be remembered that the vast majority of the residents - virtually 90% of the total - were granted only one plot. Unless they chose to rent within the town, their only hope of finding shelter was to build it. No doubt few of the population would have had sufficient wealth to carry out the necessary construction work without experiencing financial difficulty, and for many the initial structures they erected were probably very humble. It seems likely that many of these poorly built dwellings would have had a short lifespan and would have needed replacing after a relatively short time.

Despite the undoubted problems experienced by the poorer members of the community, all the available indications suggest that for the first 50 years following its foundation the town flourished. Only within parts of the quayside area, within Quarter 17 and on the extreme southern and western fringes of the town does the 1344/5 schedule of decayed rents suggest any contraction (Figure 8.7).[17] The existance of abandoned plots within the southern part of the town should be considered in conjunction with the observations made by the Black Friars in 1339 when they sought permission to move their house. It was, they said, so far removed from the

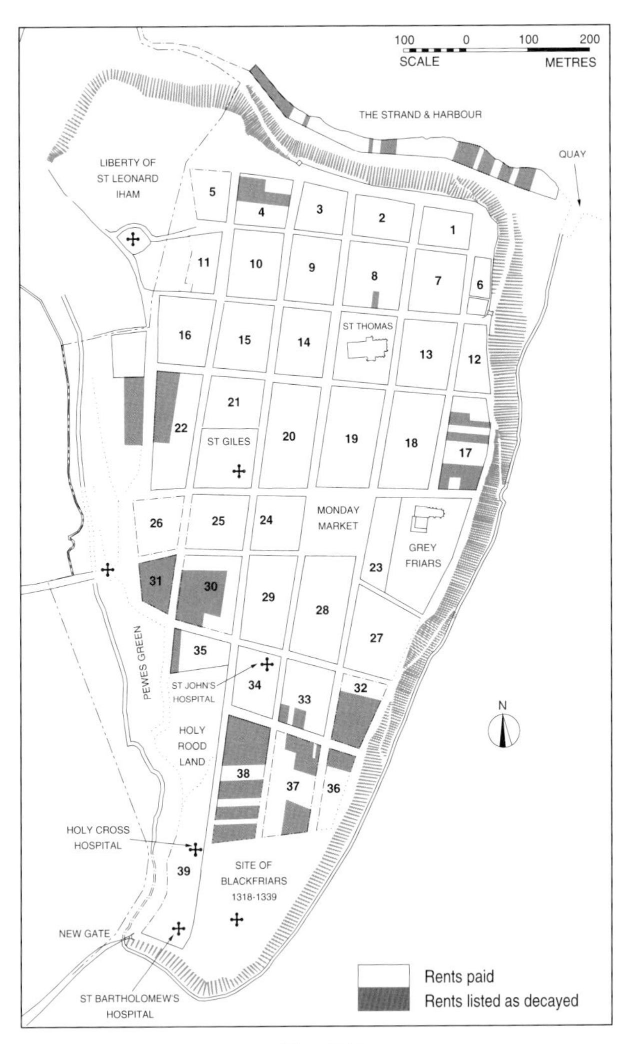

Fig. 8.7
Decayed rents, 1344/45.

Fig. 8.8
Decayed rents, 1363-9.

business quarters of the town that but few persons came to worship in the church, and as a result the alms bestowed were small.[18] By the late 1350s the situation appears to have changed markedly, with evidence of increasing desertion and houses standing unoccupied. For instance, by 1357 there were only five properties in Quarter 4, just inside the Pipewell Gate, half the 1292 total. One tenant, Robert Sely, had by that date acquired 63% of the entire quarter. All five plots are described as messuages, but only two had any monetary value, the remainder were described as worth nothing 'because they lie uncultivated and uninhabited on account of their debility'.[19] Two years later, in 1359, just prior to the fateful French raid, Robert de Brembre, clerk, sought permission to give the parson of St Giles a messuage adjoining the churchyard. An inquiry into the proposed gift found that the property was worth nothing beyond outgoings and that there were then within the town many inhabitable houses which were unlet and uninhabited.[20]

This situation, perhaps brought about by the combined effects of the Black Death, reduced overseas trading opportunities, especially with Gascony, and an increasing reluctance of the Crown to use Winchelsea as a muster port for its forces, was further exacerbated by the devastating French raid of 1360. As a result, the schedules of decayed rents of 1363-69 indicate widespread desertion across the entire town, the plots being described as 'waste, burnt and uninhabited' (*see* Figure 8.8).[21] Tenants, if not actually killed in the attack, had fled and were reluctant to return. A Letter Patent dated 3 March 1384, records that Winchelsea was:

> 'once well inhabited, but by being burnt by the King's enemies and much more by the withdrawal of its burgesses is now so desolate and almost destroyed that the proprietorship of vacant plots and tenements can scarce be known'.[22]

In response, the king ordered that the unoccupied properties be confiscated and regranted unless the houses were repaired and occupied either by their owners or by others. As a result of this, most of the

Fig. 8.9 (Left) Reconstructed plan of Winchelsea in c.1543 (Some details are approximate).

tenements were reoccupied, but as the 1415 town wall inquiry so graphically shows, except within the northeast corner of the town, they were not taken up for building, but as small closes (fields). Leaving aside the sites of the two friaries and of St Giles's churchyard, in 1292 there had been 38 plots along the intended line of the new wall. These same plots are listed in 1415, but by then groups of two, three and even four *tofts* (former house sites) had been merged with one another, reducing the actual number of properties to 23, this despite the early subdivision of one 1292 tenement into three (*see* above). Of these 23 properties, only six had houses upon them.[23] As a legacy of the once buoyant days, in addition to owing a king's rent, almost one third of the individual plots and tofts listed in the 1415 inquiry also owed an annual rent either to a rentier, to St Giles's church or to St John's hospital. It would appear that during the 14th century a considerable number of the principal town residents, as well as the church, had built up their own rent rolls. Other evidence regarding the parish of St

Fig. 8.10 (Right)
The town in 1758
(Based upon ESRO AMS 5806/3).

Thomas suggests that during the 15th century that church too amassed a sizeable rent roll.[24]

A 1529 survey of property owing rent to St Thomas's church describes properties to the north and east of St Thomas's as 'pulled down', 'fallen down', 'fell in to decay' and 'fell down' as well as 'standing void', indicating that by the late 1520s decay was affecting even the commercial core of the town.[25] Although there is no extant early plan of the town, the rental of 1543, combined with detail from deeds enrolled in the Corporation records and information obtained from other sources, allows a tolerably accurate plan of the town at that period to be reconstructed.[26] As Figure 8.9 illustrates, not surprisingly by then many of the outlying holdings had been amalgamated, although there were still a large number of properties on most of the peripheral quarters, suggesting that some may then have been only quite recently deserted as places of occupation. The 1543 rental excludes details of the Strand, down by the River Brede, but otherwise indicates that at that date there were approximately 103 property owners within the town, excluding the Corporation, but including the chantries and St John's hospital. Half the town's total king's rent was paid by just 13 owners. Much of their land was made up of outlying unoccupied plots (some, or perhaps many with the walls of abandoned buildings standing upon them), but at this date none of the holdings was by any means large enough to be called a farm. The largest estate was that of St John's hospital, which amounted to approximately 5¾ acres spread across eight separate quarters and held at a total king's rent of 18s.5d, whilst the second largest holding was that of Thomas Holden, who owned three houses on Quarter 19 and approximately 5 acres of land spread across Quarters 27, 28, 33, 38 and 39, held in all at a king's rent of 15s.4¾d. Sir Thomas Edwards, who lived in a house on Quarter 15 (excavated in 1977 - *see* Chapter 10) and was the chaplain to Godfrey's Chantry in St Thomas's church, was the eighth largest land holder with at least four houses and land in Quarters 2, 9, 11, 14, 15, 18, 21, and 30 held at a total king's rent of 7s.8½d. Another priest, Sir Mathew Brown, held the fifth largest estate in the town. Although by no means all of the standing houses are specifically mentioned within the rental, it is clear that even amongst the smaller property owners a number had more than one house, though how many of these were occupied and how many were standing empty is impossible to tell. As an example, John Bell, who occupied Firebrand, one of the surviving early stone houses (*see* Chapter 10), owned at least six houses; one on Quarter 2, three on Quarter 3, one on Quarter 14 and his main house on Quarter 13.[27]

The picture in 1758 and 1763, when the first reliable plans of the town were made, is very different.[28] By this date many of the outlying quarters were occupied by a single field and some had been merged with adjacent quarters (Figure 8.10). Some amalgamations had become sufficiently large to be viable farms - Thorn Farm, Mill Farm and the home farm attached to The Friary all existed by the 18th century.[29] As a comparison between Figures 8.9 and 8.10 shows, even within the core of the town many properties had been merged. Some quarters, which had clearly been occupied in 1543, were by 1758 almost deserted. A particularly graphic example of this is Quarter 7 where just two houses remained, both in the same ownership. However, already by this date the town had passed its lowest ebb (*see* Chapter 3).

9. THE WINCHELSEA CELLARS

David and Barbara Martin

INTRODUCTION

Of the physical medieval remains within the town, arguably the most remarkable and certainly the most important are the vaulted undercrofts or cellars. Many English towns have at least one or two medieval cellars beneath their buildings and in some places, such as at Winchester, there are known to have been greater numbers of them in specific areas. However, as Patrick Faulkner pointed out in his seminal paper on such structures first published in 1966: 'The principal concentrations of surviving medieval undercrofts [in England] are in Winchelsea, Chester and Southampton . . . '.[1] Almost all the examples from these three towns date from the 13th or early 14th centuries, and this appears also to be the case with the majority in other English towns too. All but nine of those in Chester are un-vaulted and, because for historical reasons the houses were built into steeply-rising ground, in this instance the cellars are largely above ground along their street frontage and only truly subterranean at the rear. In contrast, those at Southampton and Winchelsea are mostly vaulted and are largely below ground. Both towns boast a very similar number of known vaults. Within Winchelsea 33 are still accessible whilst at least 18 others are known (Figure 9.1). Others have been backfilled or destroyed.[2] A smaller number of vaulted cellars survive within Winchelsea's near neighbour, Rye.

Although none of the concentrations of cellars found in English towns compare to the wealth of similar structures existing in some French settlements, such as in the town of Provins in the Champagne region, a standard feature of both the English and Continental examples is that they were originally entered principally - and often solely - directly from the street via a wide flight of steps.

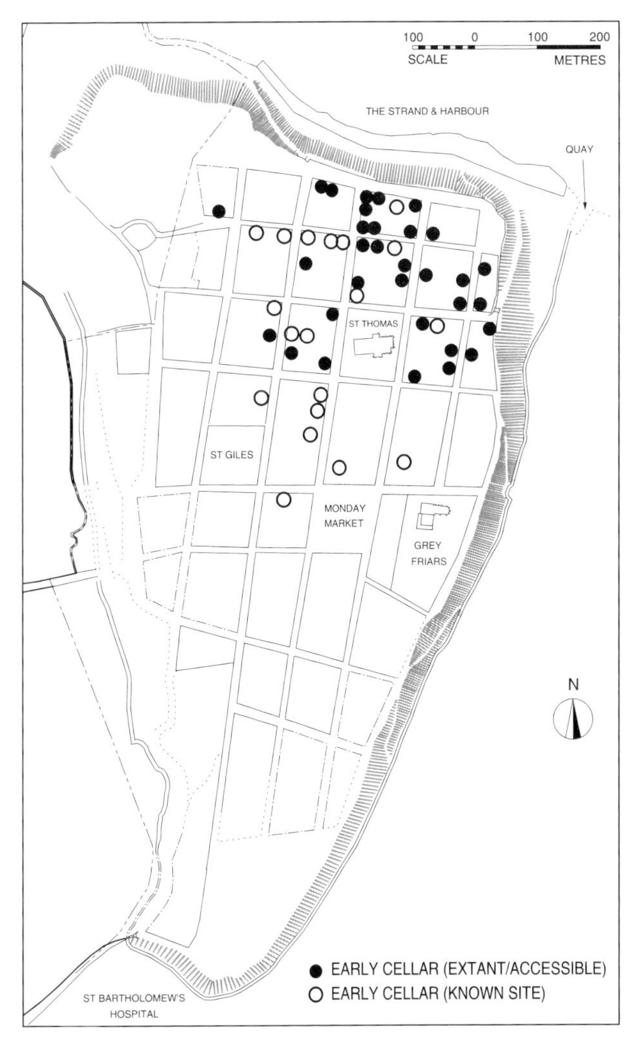

Fig. 9.1
The location of early cellars within the town

This, taken with their generally spacious size and their quality of construction, must indicate that they were not intended to serve as domestic storage for the houses above, but to fulfil a commercial function. Furthermore, this intended purpose was evidently sufficiently profitable to justify considerable investment in costly building work.[3]

In considering the Winchelsea cellars attention will first be given to their physical location, both within the town in general and in relation to the individual plots, and then to their physical form. Both the vaulted and unvaulted examples will be considered. These details are intended to serve as a comprehensive background against which to discuss why and for what purpose the cellars were built.

THE DISTRIBUTION OF CELLARS WITHIN THE TOWN

As Figure 9.1 illustrates, all the known cellars within Winchelsea are located upon the northern quarters of the town. This may in part be influenced by the later settlement pattern, for it is possible that the low level of human activity upon the more peripheral southern and western quarters during the last few centuries has resulted in a number of cellars having been forgotten. Equally, the low level of below-ground intervention in these areas has reduced the likelihood of any lost cellars being discovered by accident. However, it should always be remembered that settlement survives on the northeast corner of the town only because this was always the more wealthy, commercially active part of the town, being nearest to the port. It was here that the very people most likely to invest in cellars had been concentrated. Furthermore, in the mid-19th century, when the level of development even within this part of town was far less than it is today, Cooper was able to record the positions of ten 'crypts' which did not have buildings above them. Of these no fewer than seven were then in fields, yet he knew of none upon the similarly rural southern and western areas, where quarters had also been merged into fields.[4]

It is worth noting that the high-rental plots which surround Monday Market and which, in theory, represent the commercial heart of the town during its early years, fall outside the concentration of known cellars. At first sight this seems to run contrary to the argument that the distribution of cellars presently known reflects the approximate original coverage, for is not the area around the market square precisely where cellars are likely to have been most common? But this may be false reasoning. Much depends upon the use for which the cellars were intended. Perhaps the absence of known cellars in this area reflects the nature of the commercial activities which took place around the market square rather than the possibility that large numbers of cellars still await discovery in this area. The merchandise sold from the shops surrounding the square may not have required numerous subterranean cellars with easy, direct access from the street (*see* below). Indeed, it is perhaps significant that of the three cellars known in this area, in their location upon the plot those on the western side of Quarters 18 and on the southern side of Quarter 19 appear to differ from the cellars elsewhere in the town. Both seem to be set towards the rear of their plots and were probably not accessible from the street - at least not directly. It is perhaps also relevant that the known cellar on the northern side of Quarter 24, bounding the western edge of the market square, was not positioned fronting the market and likewise could not have been directly accessible from the square. Further evidence pointing towards a genuine rather than fortuitous dearth of cellars surrounding the market and in the area immediately to its south was provided by the results of a programme of geophysical investigation (including ground-penetrating radar) carried out by The Clark Laboratory, Museum of London Archaeology Service, in 1997: the work failed to produce any readings which might suggest the presence of unknown cellars.[5]

Whilst these observations do not prove that cellars were not built in the more peripheral western and southern quarters or in the area surrounding the market square, it suggests that the pattern shown in Figure 9.1 reflects, at least approximately, the probable distribution of the cellars within the late 13th- and 14th-century town even though further lost cellars almost certainly await discovery.

THE VAULTED CELLARS

Location upon the plots (*Figure 9.2*)

Of the 33 accessible cellars just under one third (10 examples) occupied corner plots and of these all but two are aligned east-west and were entered through the end wall from a north-south street. The almost square cellar beneath New Inn, Quarter 14 (Cellar 27), is one of the two exceptions in that access to it was from the northern street. The second is that beneath Lookout Cottage, Quarter 12 (Cellar 24), which is sited upon a somewhat unusual property in that although it was technically a corner plot, the street on the east was nothing more than a narrow lane backing onto the town wall. Access in this case was from the north, from the main street entering the town via the Strand Gate.

With the 23 examples where the cellar does not occupy a corner plot, it might seem logical to conclude that the length of the plot's street frontage would have been instrumental in dictating whether the vault was built

Fig. 9.2
The location of known and suspected medieval cellars in relation to their plots. Probable, but now inaccessible cellars are marked by a cross. Not all of these inaccessible cellars were vaulted. Un-vaulted cellars of uncertain date are indicated by a triangle. Those beneath 11/12 High Street and The Glebe, both on Quarter 13, are almost certainly post-medieval in date and are not shown.

end-on to the street or parallel with it. However, in most instances it can be shown that this was not so. All but seven of these 23 vaults were turned at right angles to the street, and of these only one occupied the entire frontage. This was Cellar 30, the large three-roomed cellar which occupies the entire area beneath the stone-built hall now known as Blackfriars Barn on Quarter 15. Even here the northern wall is inset slightly from the tenement boundary. In the other fifteen the space to the side of the cellar varied from as little as 2.60 metres (8ft.6ins.) upwards.

In only two of the seven instances in which the cellar was built parallel to the street does the cellar occupy the entire street frontage, although in another, the space left was only about 1.25 metres (4ft.). It could be argued that, regardless of whether built at right angles to the street or parallel with it, the space to one side was left in order to allow access to the rear of the plot. In some cases this may have been so, although at Cellar 12, beneath Mount Edge, Quarter 6 - one of the cellars with a small area to one side - a secondary stair projects in this direction. Thus in this instance the area was probably built over and, even if it was not, it is unlikely to have been used to gain wagon access to the rear of the plot. This impression is reinforced by two cellars which were built at right angles to the street and still have a contemporary stone-built house above them: Cellar 17 beneath The Armory, Quarter 7, and Cellar 26 beneath Firebrand, Quarter 13 (*see* Chapter 10, Figures 10.4 and 10.27). In both the cellar is restricted to the area beneath the services and cross-passage of a house built parallel to the street.

At least two cellars - numbers 18 and 19 beneath Old Castle House and St Anthonys, both on the eastern side of Quarter 8 - are located centrally within the street frontage of their broad plots, yet are still constructed at right angles to the street. In both instances parts of the stone walls relating to the contemporary buildings above survive and in the case of Old Castle House, these remains are sufficient to suggest that the building above was constructed parallel to the street, probably with a rear hall (*see* Chapter 10).

In most cases, however, either the house over the vault is later or has been destroyed. In a few examples the location of windows or ventilation shafts implies the position of external walls above, whilst at Rookery Cottage, Quarter 13, (Cellar 31) the position of a masonry internal wall is indicated by a double-width vaulting rib (Figure 9.3), but in most the relationship of the cellar to the original house remains a matter of total conjecture. The Five Chimneys, Quarter 1; Salutation Cottages, Quarter 2; and The Retreat, Quarter 6, over Cellars 1, 3 and 13 respectively are timber-framed structures of 15th-century date and almost certainly replace buildings of similar construction. These show

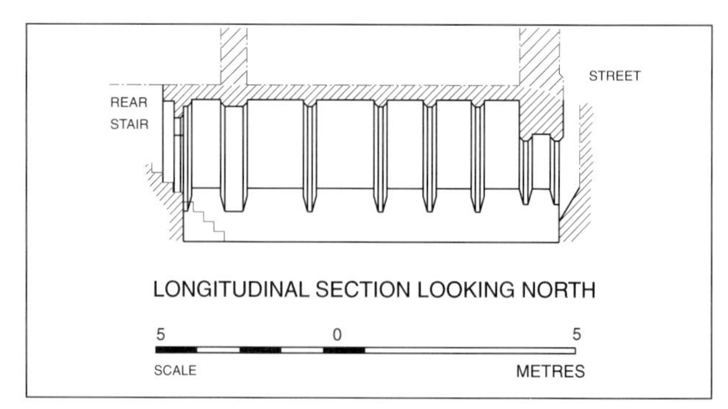

Fig. 9.3
Cellar 31. Reconstruction details.

that the presence of a vaulted cellar does not necessarily indicate the former presence of a stone-built house; even at Old Castle House the part fronting the street was timber-framed, although the rear hall range had been built with masonry walls.

All the vaulted cellars which have been surveyed abut the street and were accessible directly from it. It is tempting to suggest that this was the only arrangement adopted in Winchelsea. There is, however, evidence which shows that there were a few smaller cellars set well back from the street towards the rear of their plots and without direct access to the street. This was the case with a very small vaulted cellar recently discovered during archaeological excavations on Quarter 18, Plot 11, within the grounds of Winchelsea C. of E. School, Friars Road.[6] This cellar, which was apparently built hard against the southern boundary of the plot, was set back almost 19 metres (62ft.) from Friars Road and was entered via a flight of steps leading down from the garden or yard to the north. Similarly, excavation carried out on Quarter 2 (North Street) in 1980 revealed what appeared to be a small cellar located beneath the rear wing of a stone-built house, whilst the corner of what appeared to be yet another cellar was discovered against the rear boundary of Quarter 19, Plot 10 in 1974, some 28 metres (91ft.6ins.) back from the street.[7] Finally, in his book published in 1850, Cooper recorded yet another 'crypt' set hard against the rear boundary of Quarter 14, Plot 9, almost centrally within the quarter.[8] These examples serve as a reminder that not all the cellars within the town followed a standard pattern regarding either their location upon the plots, or, indeed, their means of access and, by implication, their intended function.

Size and layout of the cellars

In floor area the surviving accessible cellars vary from as little as 25 square metres (270 sq.ft.) (Cellar 28 at Yew Tree Platt, Quarter 14) to 125 square metres (1345 sq.ft.) (Cellar 30 at Blackfriars Barn, Quarter 15)

Cellar No.	Plot No.	Address	Orientation to road			Main access from street			Width of main stair	Gradient of main stair	Secondary stair		Size of Cellar		Floor area (M²) Excluding stair	Type of Vault			Bay ribs		Windows		
			Parallel	90°	Corner plot	Enclosed corner stair	Central stair	Others			Yes	No	Length	Width		Barrel	Quadri-partite	Mixed	Yes	No	Yes	No	Borrowed light only
1	1•8/9	Five Chimneys			●		●		1.35m	39°		●	6.40m	5.00m	32.0	●			●			●	
2	2•25/26	N.E. Corner Q.2			●	●			?	?		●	7.40m	4.60m	34.0	●			●			●	
3	2•1/2	The Salutation			●		●		1.50m	40°	?	?	17.20m	5.25m	90.3		●		●		○		
4	2•8	Lines End		●		●			1.40m	36°	●		7.95m	4.90m	32.9	●			●		○		
5	2•9	Manna Platt			●		●		1.35m	30°		●	8.35m	5.25m	43.8	●			●		●		
6	2•12	4/5 Five Houses		●		?	?	?	?	?		●	8.4m	5.30m	44.5	●			●		○		
7	2•12	2/3 Five Houses			●		●		?	?		●	8.00m	4.65m	37.2	●			●		?	?	?
8	2•13	1/2 Five Houses	●			●			1.50m	29°	○		7.00m	5.95m	41.8	●			●			●	
9	3•8	Moneysellers	●			?	?	?	?	?		●	12.35m	5.55m	68.4	●			●		●		
10	3•9	Adj. Moneysellers	●			●			1.35m	32°		●	5.55m	5.15m	28.6	●			●			●	
11	5•3	Mill Farm Ho.	●			●			1.35m	?	●		7.40m	4.80m	35.5			●	●				●
12	6•8	Mount Edge		●			●		1.25m	36°	●		4.95m	4.50m	32.1	●				●	●		
13	6•3	The Retreat			●		●		1.20m	43°		●	7.50m	4.75m	35.6	●			●		●		
14	7•21	Gdn. of The Armory		●		●			1.55m	34°		●	8.30m	4.10m	30.0	●			●		●		
15	7•21	Gdn. of The Armory		●				●	-	-		●	6.10m	5.20m	31.6	●				●	●		
16	7•1	The Stone House			●	?	?	?	?	?		●	>9.40m	5.00m	?	●			●		?	?	?
17	7•9	The Armory		●		●			1.35m	38°	●		8.20m	5.35m	43.9	●			●		●		
18	8•8	Old Castle Inn		●			●		1.50m	39°	●		10.40m	6.00m	62.4	●			●		●		
19	8•7	St Anthonys		●			●		?	?	?	?	8.75m	4.75m	41.5	●			●			○	
20	8•6	Bay Tree Ho.	●			●			1.45m	38°		●	8.50m	5.00m	37.8	●			●				●
21	8•9	NW corner Q8			●		●		1.40m	38°		●	6.80m	4.85m	33.0	●			●			●	
22	8•9	N. side Q8		●			●		0.88m	37°		●	8.80m	5.50m	48.1	●			●			●	
23	9•9	Higham Mews	●			●			1.20m	41°	?	?	11.3m	5.40m	55.5	●			●		●		
24	12•9	Lookout			●		●		?	?		●	10.70m	4.35m	46.5	●				●	●		
25	13•23	East side Q13		●		?	?	?	c.1.20m	?	●		c.7.0m	3.80m	26.4	●			●		?	?	?
26	13•16	Firebrand		●			●		1.35m	39°	●		9.20m	5.10m	47.0	●			●		●		
27	14•17	New Inn			●	●			?	?		●	7.40m	6.60m	48.8		●		●		?	?	?
28	14•1	Yew Tree Plat	●			●			1.25m	32°	○		5.50m	4.60m	25.3		●		●		?	?	?
29	14•8	Blackfriars Platt		●			●		1.30m	36°		●	7.80m	5.20m	40.8	●			●			●	
30	15•22	Blackfriars Barn		●		●			1.25m	34°		●	16.50m	7.90m	125.7			●	●		●		
31	13•26	Rookery Cottage		●		●			1.55m	38°	●		8.60m	4.10m	35.3	●			●		●		
32	13•8	Gdn. of Glebe		●		●			1.50m	?	○		c.9.0m	c.4.5m	c.34.0	●			●		●		
33	12•4	Rookery Field		●			○		?	?		○	7.30m	5.00m	34.0	●			●		?	?	?
● = Proven ○ = Probable			7	16	10	14	13/14	1			8/11	18/19				28	3	2	30	3	14/17	7/8	2

Fig. 9.4
General details of accessible cellars.

although the vast majority (about three-quarters of the total - three are smaller and five larger) fall within the range of 30 - 50 square metres (325-540 sq.ft.) (Figure 9.4). The floor areas quoted above exclude the space occupied by the entrance staircases.

Most of the variation is in the length: the shortest (Cellar 12 at Mount Edge, Quarter 6) is 4.95 metres (16ft.3ins.) and the longest (Cellar 3 at Salutation Cottages, Quarter 2) 17.2 metres (56ft.5ins.). The widest cellar is that beneath Blackfriars Barn (Cellar 30, Quarter 15), which measures 7.90 metres (25ft.11ins.). This, however, is a combination of three narrower compartments: the clear span of the two identical-sized principal rooms is 6.10 metres (20ft.) whilst the central room has a span of only 4.30 metres (14ft.2ins.) (*see* Figure 9.5). At 6.60 metres (21ft.8ins.) the widest single-cell example is the now collapsed double-span, quadripartite-vaulted room under New Inn (Cellar 27, Quarter 14). With a width of only 3.80 metres (12ft.6ins.) the narrowest extant span is Cellar 25, Quarter 13, although a destroyed, backfilled example discovered in 2003 during archaeological excavations in the grounds of Winchelsea C. of E. School on Quarter 18, measured just 2.4 metres (7ft.10ins.) internally.[9] The majority of cellars are between 4.6 metres and 5.5 metres (15ft.-18ft.) wide. There is no obvious variation in width, length or floor area between cellars occupying a corner plot and those partway along a street frontage, nor between those built at right angles to the street and those constructed with their long wall against the highway.

Most of the cellars comprise a single chamber, but, as already noted, Cellar 30 beneath Blackfriars Barn has three interlinked rooms. In four others, (Cellars 14/15, 16, 19 and 23 on Quarters 7, 8 and 9) there are two interlinked rooms (Figure 9.5). The rear compartment at Cellar 14/15 represents a 15th-century addition, linked to the earlier cellar by an intruded 15th-century, four-centred moulded doorway, but all other accessible examples date in their entirety from *c.*1300.

All of these were entered directly from the street via a straight flight of steps which, with one narrow exception, varied between 1.20 metres and 1.55 metres (4ft.-5ft.2ins.) wide and were pitched at between 29 and 43 degrees. In at least 19 instances this was the only means of access, and thus in these examples the

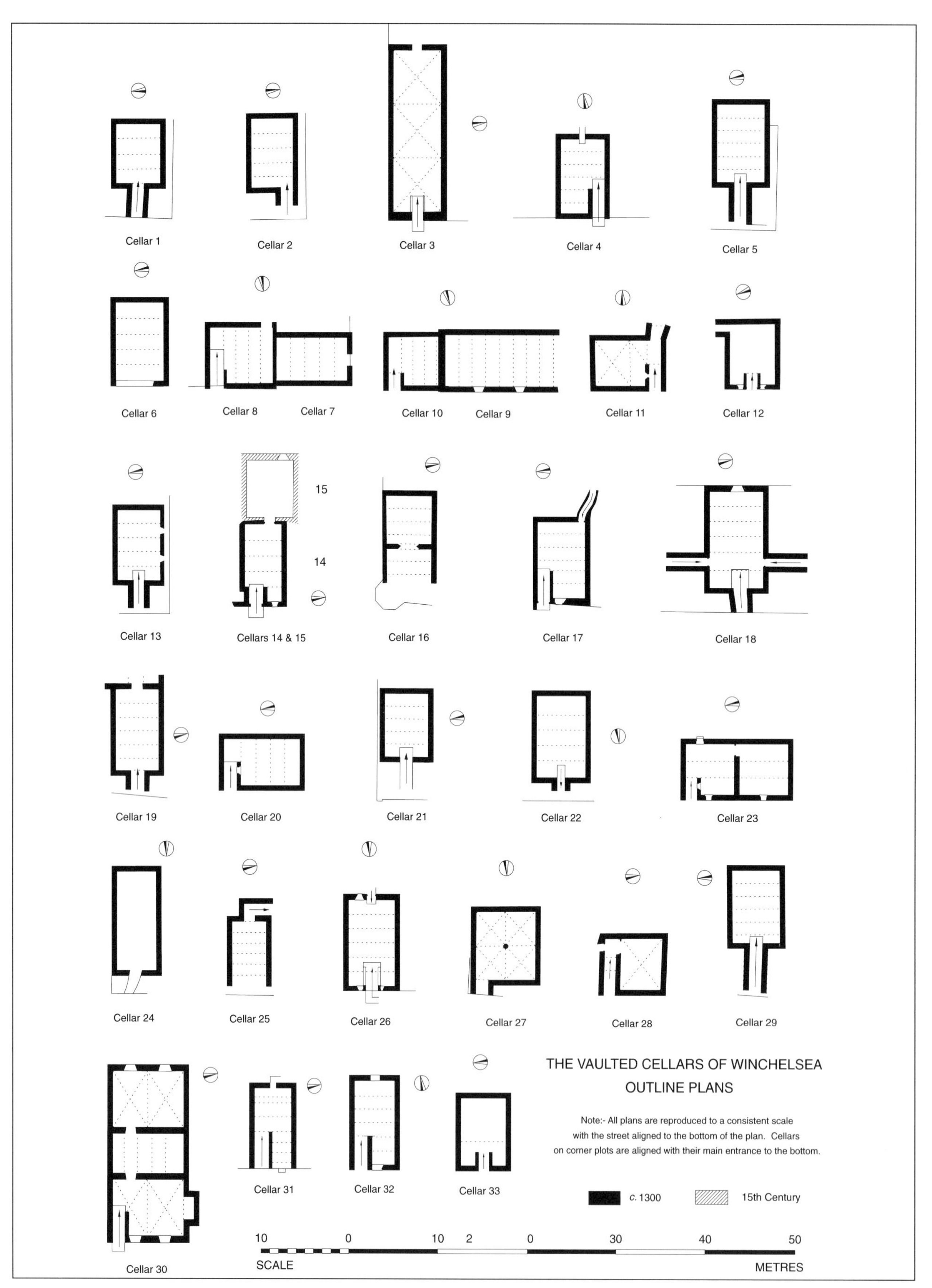
Cellar 1
Cellar 2
Cellar 3
Cellar 4
Cellar 5
Cellar 6
Cellar 8
Cellar 7
Cellar 10
Cellar 9
Cellar 11
Cellar 12
15
14
Cellar 13
Cellars 14 & 15
Cellar 16
Cellar 17
Cellar 18
Cellar 19
Cellar 20
Cellar 21
Cellar 22
Cellar 23
Cellar 24
Cellar 25
Cellar 26
Cellar 27
Cellar 28
Cellar 29
THE VAULTED CELLARS OF WINCHELSEA
OUTLINE PLANS
Note:- All plans are reproduced to a consistent scale with the street aligned to the bottom of the plan. Cellars on corner plots are aligned with their main entrance to the bottom.
c. 1300
15th Century
Cellar 30
Cellar 31
Cellar 32
Cellar 33
10 0 10 2 0 30 40 50
SCALE
METRES

Fig. 9.5

cellar was separate from the house above and could easily have been independently leased out from it. However, at least eight have a contemporary narrow, relatively steep secondary stair (or in one case two) which allowed internal access from the house above (*see* Figure 9.28). In Cellar 26 beneath Firebrand, Quarter 13 a doorway led to an external stair rising into the rear yard (*see* Figure 9.32). Unlike the openings associated with secondary internal stairways, the rear arch of this doorway faces inwards, towards the cellar, in like manner to the normal arrangement at an external doorway. Similar normal width, two-centred doorways in the rear walls of Cellar 8 beneath The Five Houses on Quarter 2 and Cellar 23 beneath Higham Mews on Quarter 9 suggest the same arrangement here too, although the possibility that these openings led to now-inaccessible rear cellars (as was the case with Cellar 19 on Quarter 8) cannot be ruled out.

DESIGN AND FORM

Types of vaulting

The majority of the accessible Winchelsea cellars (28 examples) are barrel-vaulted, and in all but three of these the vaults are divided into short bays by chamfered ribs, some plain, others hollow-chamfered (Figure 9.6). The ribs rise directly from the side walls without corbels (Figure 9.7). In some examples they are noticeably cut to the wrong curvature, perhaps indicating that they had been salvaged from buildings within (Old) Winchelsea. The barrel vaults of the remaining three cellars lack ribs and are entirely plain (Figure 9.8). The vaulting varies from semi-circular to a fairly pointed two-centred arch (for example, compare Figures 9.6, 9.9, 9.16).

Where the structural detailing at the end walls is visible, it is noticeable that in a number of cellars - perhaps the majority - either one or both of the end walls are straight-jointed to the sides of the cellar and to the

Fig. 9.6
Cellar 14. A steeply-pointed barrel vault with a typical staircase enclosure and an adjacent window in the street (end) facade.

Left: Fig. 9.7
Cellar 21.
A typical detail of a vaulting rib springing directly from a cellar side wall.

Fig. 9.8
Cellar 12. A plain, unribbed cellar with a central entrance doorway and steps flanked by wing walls projecting into the room. Note the original window to the right of the wing wall. There is a similar window to the left of the entrance.

Fig. 9.9
Cellar 17. View looking towards the rear wall of a relatively shallow-pointed, barrel-vaulted cellar incorporating a narrow doorway leading to a rear staircase. Note the plain square-headed cupboard recess in the centre of the rear wall.

Fig. 9.10
The west wall of cellar on site of C. of E. School during excavation, 2003. Note the absence of a joint at the right-hand end of the wall for the former end wall built against clay. This end wall was straight-jointed and has been robbed out. The left-hand section of the cellar was not investigated.

Fig. 9.11
Cellar at C. of E. School during excavation, 2003 showing the impression of robbed steps against the eastern side wall.

Fig. 9.12
Cellar 11. A typical quadripartite vault.

barrel vault itself, giving the impression that the vault has been shortened subsequent to construction.[10] This impression is incorrect. Archaeological excavations carried out at Blackfriars Barn, Quarter 15 in 1976-7 showed that the straight joints resulted from the sequence of construction, in that the side walls and barrel were built first. The end walls were not constructed until the barrel vault itself had been completed. The same sequence was recognized in two other examples: firstly in relation to a small cellar beneath the rear range of a stone house on Quarter 2, North Street, when its end wall was briefly investigated during archaeological excavations undertaken in 1980, and secondly, in the small cellar partially investigated during excavations carried out in 2003 at Winchelsea C of E School on Quarter 18. In the latter example the northern end wall was totally robbed when the cellar was abandoned. Because the end of the cellar had been butt-jointed to the western side wall, the face showed no scar to indicate the former existence of the end wall. A flight of external steps descended through the eastern end of the north wall, against the face of the eastern side wall (Figures 9.10 and 9.11).[11]

Of the five non-standard vaults, three are of quadripartite design (Figure 9.12) and two are composite, combining barrel vaulting and quadripartite vaulting (*see* Figure 9.4). The former vault beneath the New Inn, Quarter 14, is the only example within the town to have incorporated a central pillar, comprising as it did two rows of two bays each. The ribs of the quadripartite

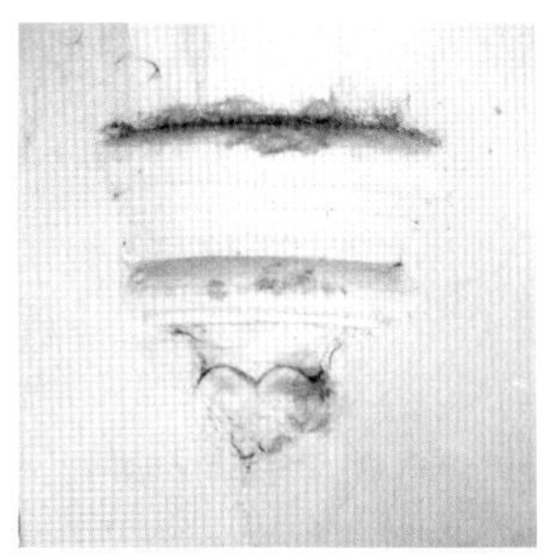
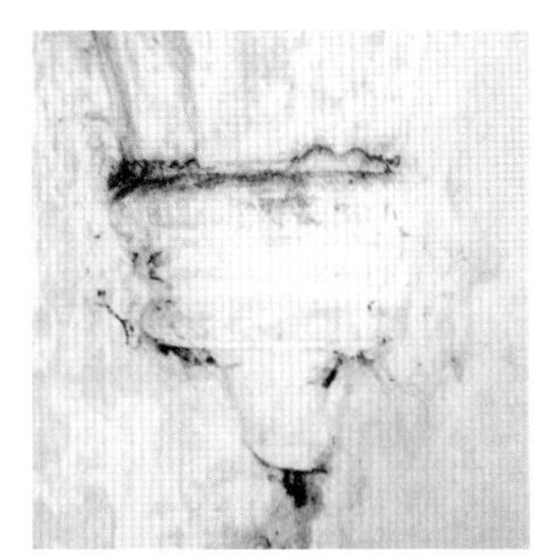

Figs. 9.13 and 9.14
Cellar 28. Decorative corbels supporting the ribs of a quadripartite vault.

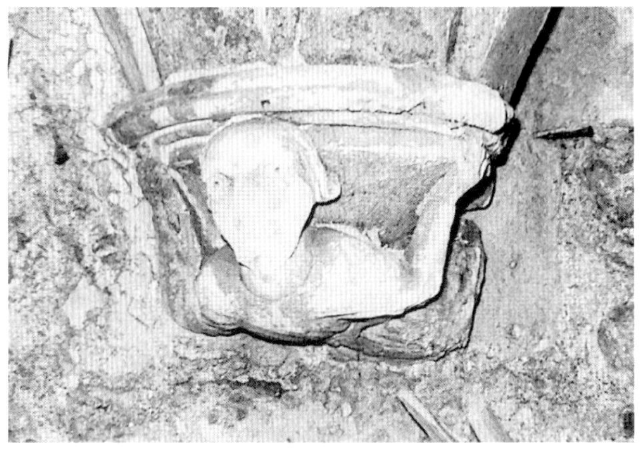

Fig. 9.15
Cellar 3. The decorative corbel supporting the rib of a quadripartite vault.

Fig. 9.16
Cellar 20. The entrance area showing a doorway in the stair enclosure and a borrowed light in the side wall of the enclosure.

Fig. 9.17
Cellar 23. The remains of a stair enclosure with borrowed light. Note the remains of a window in the front wall (left) with steeply-sloping cill.

vaults beneath Salutation Cottages (Cellar 3, Quarter 2), Yew Tree Platt (Cellar 28, Quarter 14), and Blackfriars Barn (Cellar 30, Quarter 15) spring from moulded wall corbels; some of those at Salutation Cottages were further elaborated with carvings of figures (*see* Figures 9.13, 9.14 and 9.15).

Windows

Contrary to hypothetical comments made by Homan in the 1940s in the absence of archaeologically excavated remains, it is now known that all the extant cellars were effectively sited wholly below ground level, with the ground floors of the houses set either level with, or, in the case of sloping sites, partly level with the street or rear yard.[12] Surprisingly, at least 27% and perhaps as many as half of the cellars lacked external windows; the sole means of natural light was through the main doorway, aided in two instances (Cellars 11 and 20) by a borrowed light in the side wall of the staircase (Figure 9.16). Borrowed lights also occur in the stair walls of cellars which had external windows, examples being Cellars 23 on Quarter 9 and 32 on Quarter 13 (Figures 9.17 and 9.18, No.6). In three cellars the external windows are of uncertain date, but in 14 examples windows are known to have been present originally. Of these 14 examples, only at Old Castle House, Quarter 8, where the cellar is set back from the street, is there no window within the street facade, although of necessity, rear lighting was used within Cellar 15 on Quarter 7 - a 15th-century example added at the rear of an earlier cellar with street fenestration.

Windows were incorporated within the rear wall at Blackfriars Barn, Quarter 15 in order to light the rear compartment of this three-roomed cellar. In this instance the central barrel-vaulted compartment was unlit. Otherwise, only Cellar 26 beneath Firebrand on Quarter 13 had windows within both its front and rear walls, although some others incorporated rear vent-like features (*see* below). In three examples located on

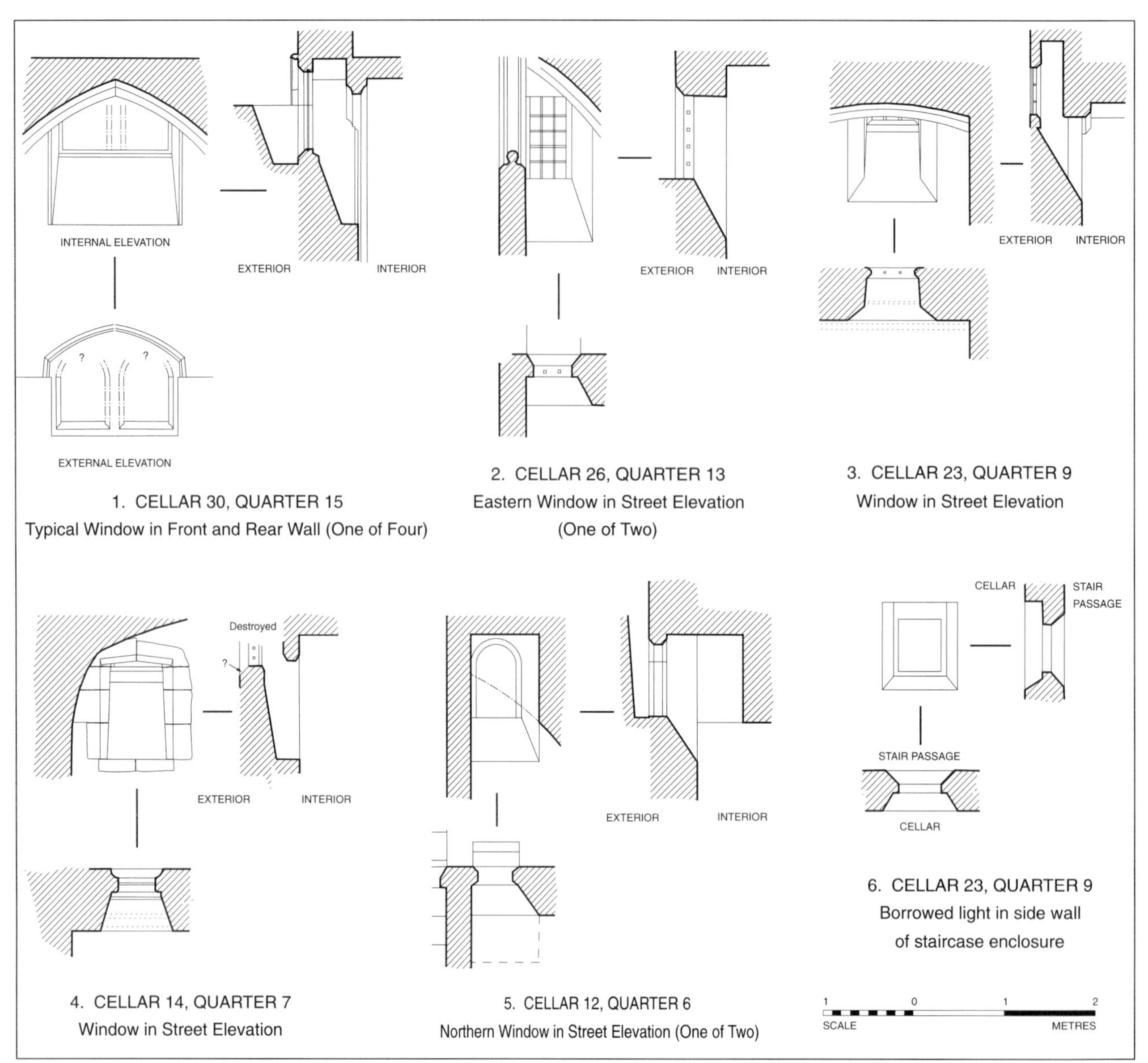

Fig. 9.18
Details of the windows and borrowed lights.

corner plots and thus possessing two facades, the windows were sited within the side wall, whereas the main entrance was through the end wall (Cellar 3 beneath Salutation Cottages, Quarter 2, Cellar 5 at Manna Platt, also on Quarter 2, and Cellar 13 beneath The Retreat, Quarter 6). With the exception of the windows lighting Cellar 3 beneath Salutation Cottages, and those lighting the front and rear vaults of Cellar 30 beneath Blackfriars Barn, the windows tended to be very small. Because of the level of the external ground, the windows were set high in the walls above steeply-sloping internal cills (Figure 9.18, Nos. 1-5; *see* also Figure 9.17 and 9.19). Even then, the external window surrounds were largely below the ground. In only six cellars do the external openings themselves now survive.

Light was also allowed in by means of 'open areas', best described as stone-lined 'boxes' set into the ground immediately in front of the windows. The fronts of the examples excavated at Blackfriars Barn were built sloping, allowing a greater amount of light to penetrate into the depths of the cellar (Figures 9.18, No. 1 and 9.20), and the same is true of the extant examples in Cellar 12 beneath Mount Edge, Quarter 6. The remains of the windows at Blackfriars Barn incorporated glazing grooves, otherwise, however, the surviving windows were unglazed, but were barred by metal grilles (*see* the example in Figure 9.21). None of the surviving windows are elaborate: some have arched heads, others plain square heads.

An unusual lighting arrangement exists within

Fig. 9.19
Cellar 12. Detail of the window beside the entrance doorway.

Fig. 9.21
Cellar 26. The parapeted handrail flanking the main entrance stairway projecting into the cellar. Note the original grilled window to the right.

Fig. 9.20
Cellar 30. The open area beyond the rear window as revealed by archaeological excavation.

Fig. 9.22
Cellar 31. Arch supporting front wall of house.

the front of cellar 31 beneath Rookery Cottage, Quarter 13. Here, within the cellar, the masonry front of the house was supported upon a low arch, which allowed the cellar to extend beneath it. This meant that there was no need for a normal window. Instead, the end wall of the cellar incorporated an open area with a very steep sloping cill (*see* Figures 9.3 and 9.22). Whether technically this arrangement should be classified as a window or a light well is debatable, but its effect was the same: it allowed natural light into the cellar.

Entrance Areas

The upper steps of virtually all the main entrance stairs projected into the street as did the open areas in front of the cellar windows. As a result, the heads of the main entrance doorways in the facades of the houses were set partially below street level (*see* reconstructed detail from Cellar 30, Figure 9.23). Preventing rainwater from entering the cellars must always have been a problem, a point illustrated in 1583, when permission was granted for the erection of a penthouse on posts 'all the length of his [Philip Durrant's] house near the stonemill to save the stairs of the vault from the rain'[13] Very few of the external doorways survive, even in fragmentary form. The most easily visible example is that of Cellar 3 beneath Salutation Cottages on Quarter 2. In this instance the two-centred arched doorway is richly moulded (Figure 9.24, No.1), but this is an exceptionally elaborate cellar. Most of the entrances were probably more plainly decorated. For example, the external doorways to Cellar 12 at Mount Edge on Quarter 6 and Cellar 14 on the eastern side of Quarter 7 are continuously chamfered (Figures 9.24, No.2 and 9.25), whilst that to Cellar 30 beneath Blackfriars Barn, Quarter 15 is also quite simple:

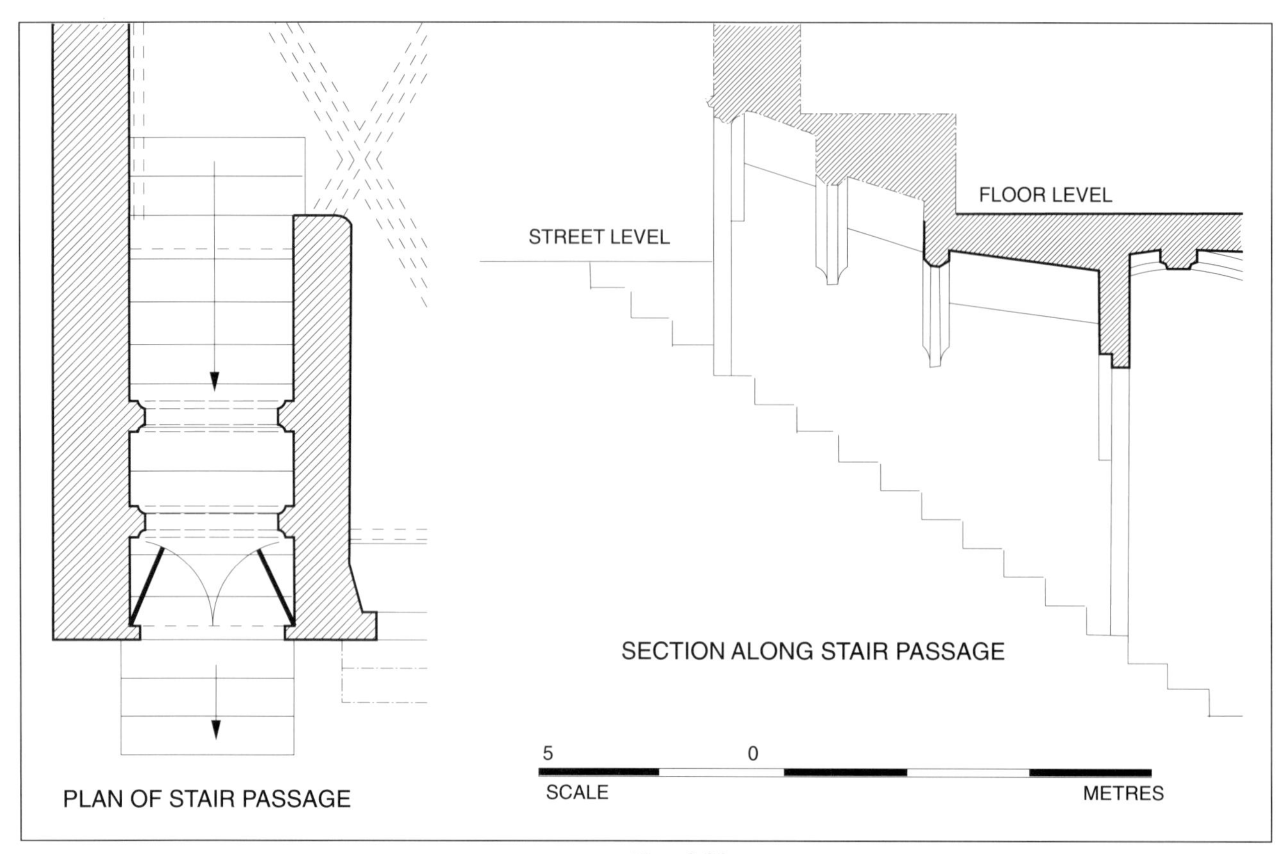

Fig. 9.23
Cellar 30. Detail of the entrance and staircase enclosure. Although this cellar has a quadripartite vault, the details of the staircase enclosure are typical of the arrangements found in many other cellars within the town.

it has a quarter roll with associated hollow chamfer (Figure 9.24, No.3). Even so, the adjacent hollow-chamfered window at Blackfriars Barn was capped by a simple hood-mould (as shown in Figures 9.18 No.1 and 9.26), and the same seems likely for the doorway. Where the evidence survives, the closing rebates and the location of hinge rides indicate that the street doors opened inwards and were divided vertically into two leaves, one hung on each jamb. In order to allow the doors to open inwards, the ceiling of the stairway was level for fully 600 millimetres (2ft.) from the entrance before the barrel-vaulted ceiling commenced its downward slope. This upper part would have projected above the floor of the house within a bulkhead, forming a raised shelf-like area within the ground-floor of the house above. Most stair vaults incorporate interval ribs, and in some, but not all instances the level of the vault steps down at these (Figures 9.23). A similar arrangement is to be found over the narrow passages which accommodate the steep secondary staircases (Figures 9.27 and 9.28).

Reference to Figures 9.4 and 9.5 will show that the entrance stairs themselves were either sited against one side wall of the vault (14 known examples) or

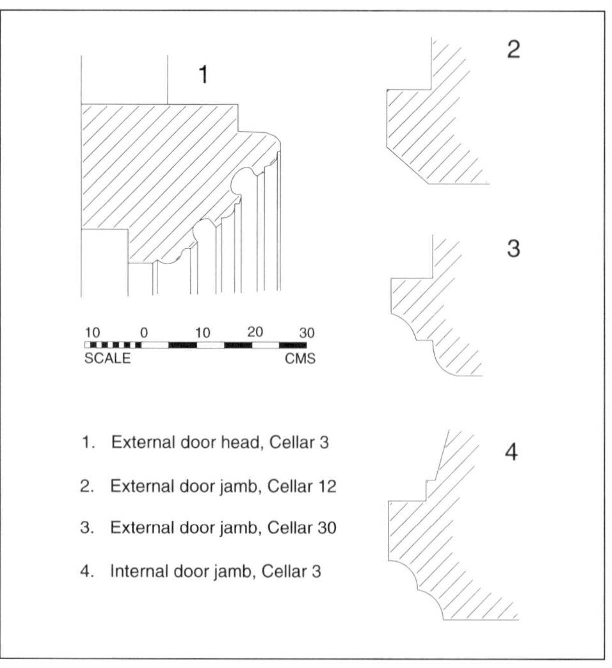

Fig. 9.24
Details of the mouldings on the main entrance doorways.

Fig. 9.25
Cellar 12. Detail of the main entrance doorway.

Fig. 9.26
Cellar 30. Return stop to the hood mould on the cellar window adjacent to the main entrance steps.

centrally, entering through the end wall (13 known examples). In the former arrangement the stair was contained within its own enclosed vaulted passage, which usually projected into the corner of the cellar in the manner shown in Figures 9.23, 9.29 and 9.30 - *see* also Figures 9.6, 9.16 and 9.17. In the case of Cellar 28 beneath Yew Tree Platt, Quarter 14, the passage was to

Fig. 9.27
Cellar 18. The steep internal stair passage with a vaulted roof.

one side of the cellar itself, being sited beyond its side wall. Of the 13 examples where a centrally-placed entrance was used, in nine instances the end wall of the cellar was itself inset some distance back from the street facade of the house. This was done so that most of the staircase was housed within its own stair passage beyond the cellar, with only the upper steps projecting into the street and the lower few steps into the cellar (*see* Figure 9.31). However, in four examples the cellar wall was located immediately below that of the house above and thus, as with the entrances set against the side walls, the stair projects by some distance into the cellar. At Cellar 12 beneath Mount Edge, Quarter 6 (*see* Figure 9.8) and Cellar 33 in Rookery Field, Quarter 12, most of the staircase is sited between its own full-height side walls, forming an enclosure which projects boldly into the room. However, at Cellar 3 beneath Salutation Cottages on Quarter 2 and Cellar 26 beneath Firebrand, Quarter 13, the detailing is more expertly dealt with: the side walls rise only part height so as to form solid stone parapet walls capped by moulded sloping handrails (Figures 9.32 and 9.33. *See* also Figure 9.21).

Left: Fig. 9.28
Cellar 4. The narrow doorway leading to a rear staircase.

Below: Fig. 9.29
Cellar 4. A typical stair enclosure incorporated within the corner of the cellar. Note the cupboard recess in the right-hand side wall of the enclosure and the high-level window in the street facade (end wall) of the cellar.

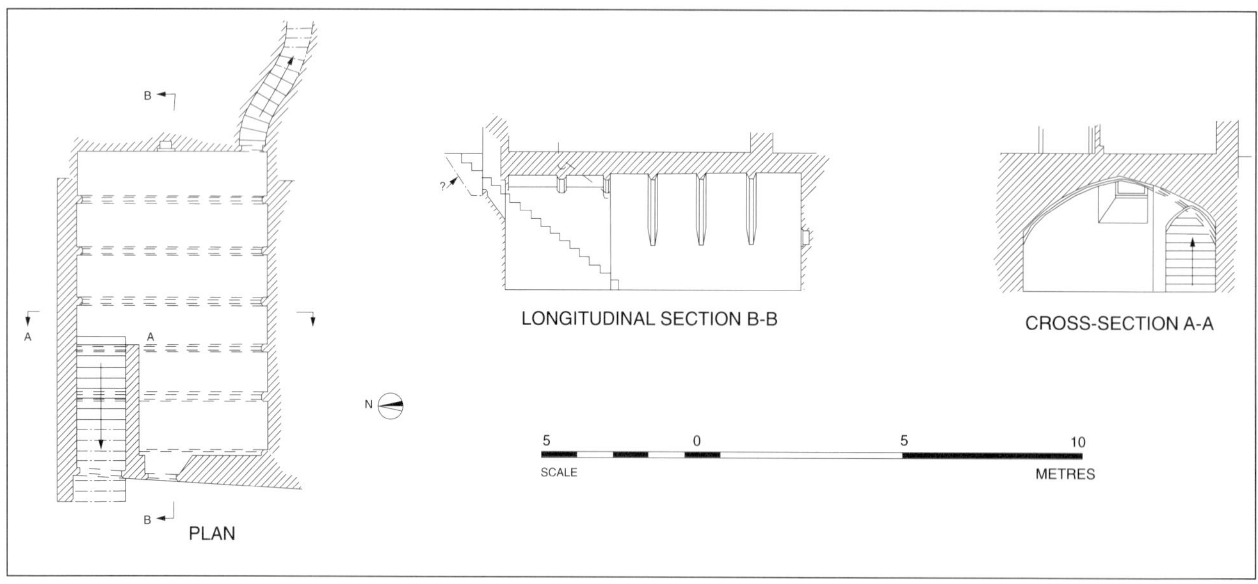

Fig. 9.30
Cellar 17. The typical barrel-vaulted cellar with a staircase enclosure.

Internal finishings, fixtures and fittings

The upper geological strata of the hill upon which Winchelsea is built are clay overlying sandstone and Tilgate stone, the depth of the clay overburden being variable. Particularly near the junction of Mill Road with School Hill/Higham Green, at the corners of Quarters 2, 3, 8 and 9 the sandrock rises relatively close to the surface. This may have been the location of the quarry mentioned in the late 13th century. In places the cellars

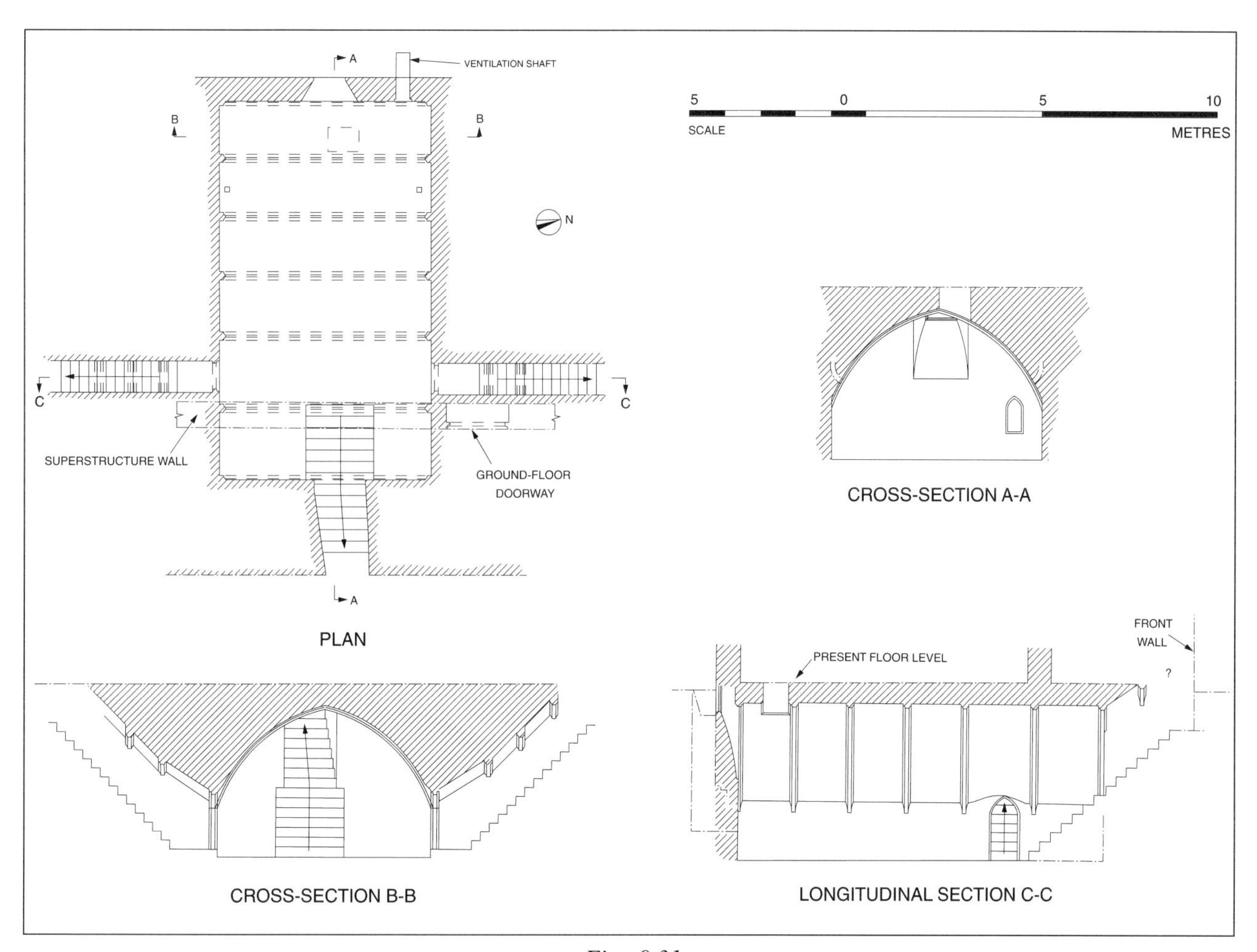

Fig. 9.31
Cellar 18. An example of a large barrel-vaulted cellar set back slightly from the street and incorporating a central entrance in its end wall. Note the two secondary staircases rising against the thick internal masonry wall.

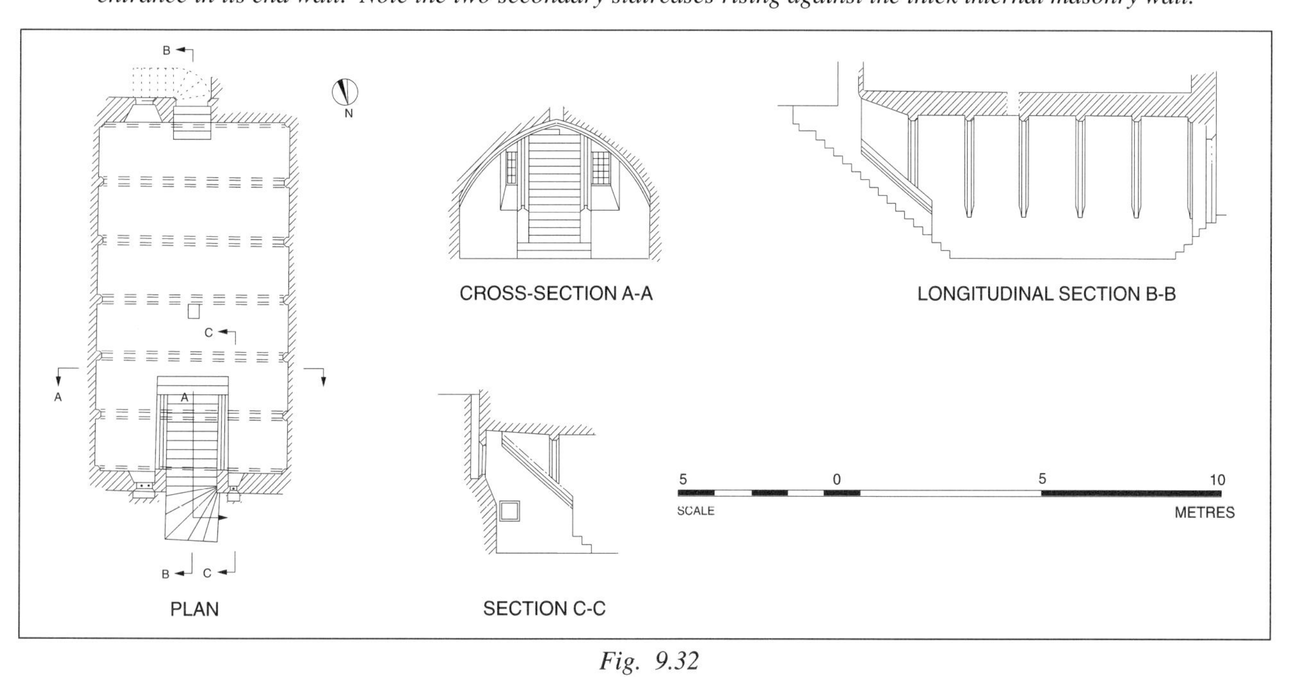

Fig. 9.32
Cellar 26. A typical barrel-vaulted cellar, in this instance entered via a staircase set centrally within the end wall, projecting into the room.

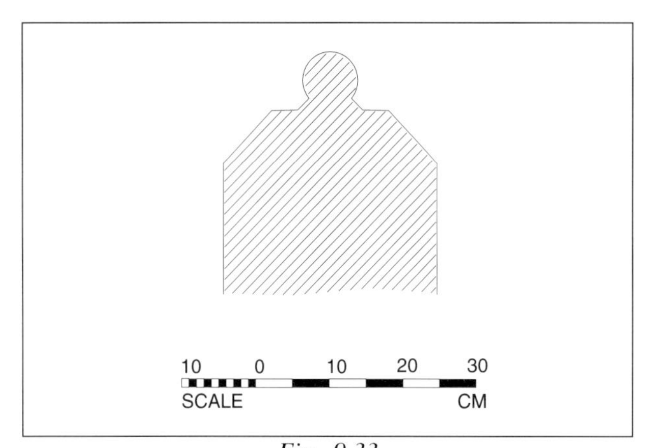

Fig. 9.33
Cellar 3. The handrail to the main entrance staircase. The detail within cellar 26 is similar.

Fig. 9.34
Cellar 21. The Impression of timber shuttering visible in the ceiling of the vault.

Fig. 9.35
Cellar 14. A cupboard recess with trefoil head.

in this area use small sections of the cut-back natural sandrock as un-faced cellar wall, this being particularly noticeable within Cellars 5 and 21, occupying opposite sides of Mill Road, on the corners on Quarters 2 and 8. Homan reported that other cellars use the soft natural sandrock as the floor.[14] Within the cellar under Rookery Cottage, Quarter 13, the present floor is a mixture of natural sandrock and Tilgate stone slabs, and here a small drain has been cut into the rock, passing diagonally under the north wall. A low arch at floor level within cellar 13, under The Retreat, Quarter 6, may be the opening to yet another drain.

A considerable number of cellars show evidence of plaster finishings, but some others, particularly those lacking windows, appear never to have been plastered. For example, this appears to have been the case with Cellar 21 on the northwest corner of Quarter 8, where the marks of the timber shuttering are still clearly visible in the rough mortar adhering to the underside of the vaulting (Figure 9.34). The shuttering had been held in place by the vaulting ribs and appears to have been left *in situ*, having only rotted out after the building above was destroyed. Other unlit cellars bear traces of the same feature.

Apart from the design of the entrance areas, windows and vaulting ribs, many of the interiors of the cellars are entirely devoid of architectural features. However, 15 cellars (about half the total) incorporate small cupboard-like recesses within the thickness of the walls, usually quite close to either the front or rear staircases. Almost all are rebated as if to take an outward-opening door, although in some instances no hinge points or locking points are visible. The recesses fall into two groups: simple niches with square heads (9 cellars) and those having arched heads (6 cellars).[15] Examples of the square-headed type are visible in Figures 9.9 and 9.21. Typically they extend about 350 millimetres (14ins.) into the wall, are about 600 millimetres (2ft.) wide and 450-600 millimetres (18-24ins.) high. The arch-headed example within Cellar 14, Quarter 7, has trefoiled cusping beneath a chamfered two-centred arch (Figures 9.35 and 9.36), but otherwise

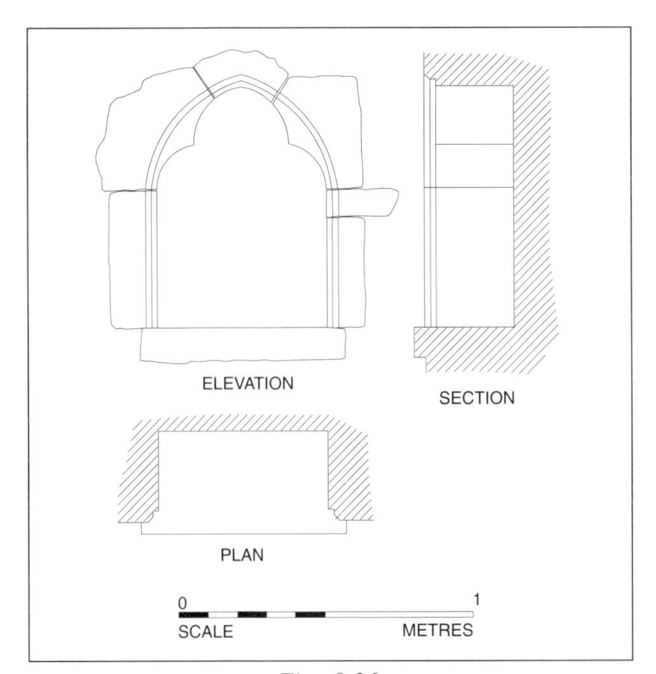

Fig. 9.36
Cellar 14. Detail of a cupboard recess.

Fig. 9.37
Cellar 3. A pair of cupboard recesses with two-centred arched heads adjacent to the doorway in the west wall.

Fig. 9.38
Cellar 4. A typical cupboard recess with two-centred head. Note the impression of a former timber shelf.

the heads are of simple, rebated, two-centred type (Figures 9.37 and 9.38). These recesses are of about the same depth and width as the square-headed examples, but are taller and some contain accurate grooves cut in the side and rear faces of the recess, which is clear evidence of a former shelf (*see* Figure 9.38).

A small number of the cellars incorporate purpose-built shafts within their vaults. The rear part of what at first appears to be a two-centred arched recess in the rear wall of Old Castle House, Quarter 8, rises in the form of a ventilation shaft set against the external face of the building (*see* Figure 9.31). This cellar also contains two exceptionally small, socket-like shafts built in yellow 'Flemish' bricks. The shafts are contemporary with the vault through which they rise, but their purpose is unknown. To the west a further, purposely-formed rectangular opening is set within the crown of the vault and apparently rises to form an opening within the ground floor of the room above. Similar internal, off-centre access shafts exist within Cellar 11 on Quarter 5 and within Cellar 26 beneath Firebrand, Quarter 13. In the latter instance the shaft rises within one of the service rooms (*see* Figure 9.32). Two other cellars incorporate external ventilation shafts within their rear walls, similar in form (though not in detail) to that within the rear wall at Old Castle House.

Perhaps the most surprising feature incorporated within any Winchelsea cellar is within the front room of the triple cellar beneath Blackfriars Barn on Quarter 15. Here, incorporated within the northern wall, is an original fireplace whose flue rises within the thickness of the wall above (Figure 9.39). Although this is the only known fireplace within a Winchelsea cellar, 13th- or 14th-century fireplaces serve the vaulted cellars at The Undercroft, Simnel Street, and The Woollen Hall, St Michael's Passage, both in Southampton.[16]

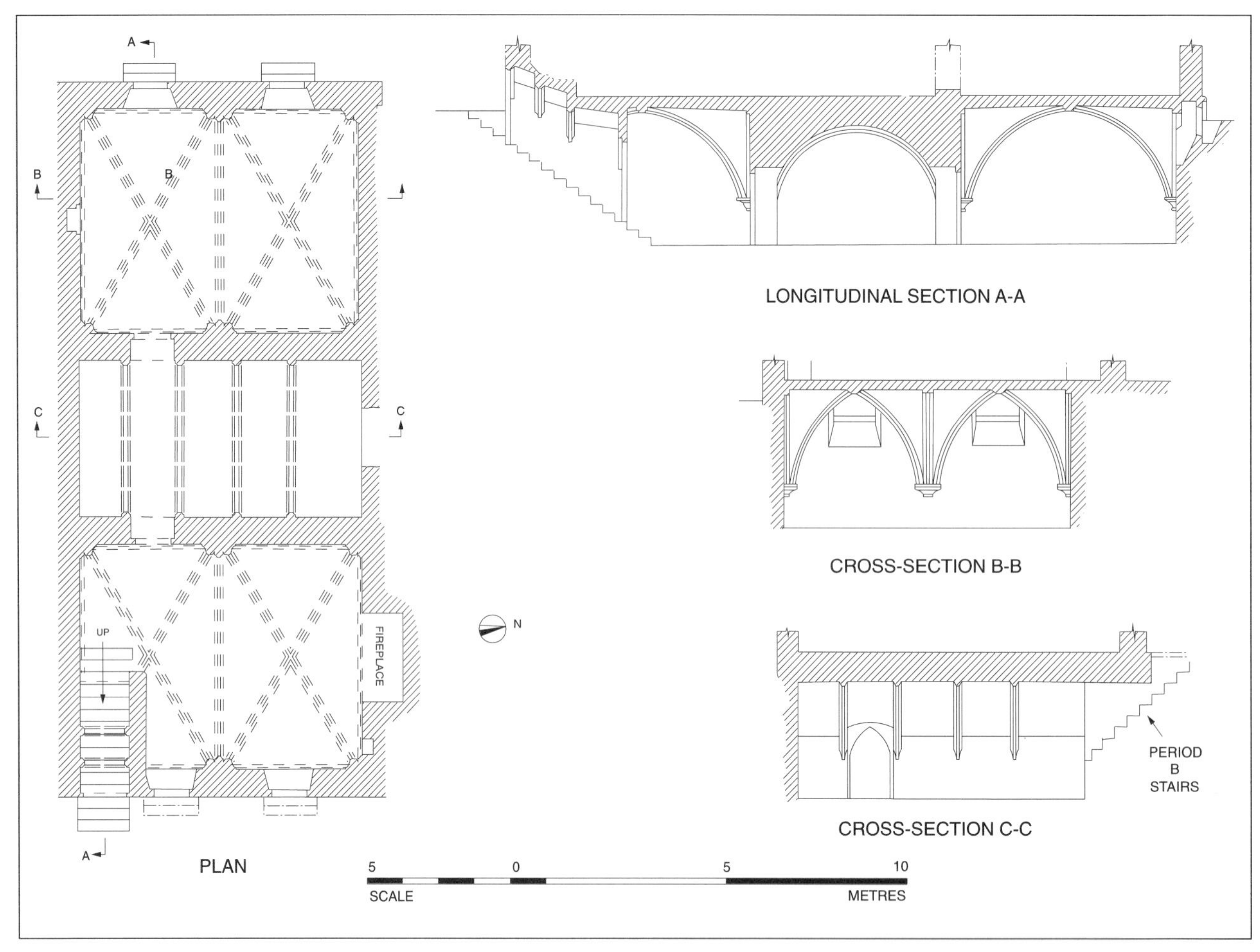

Fig. 9.39
Cellar 30. Details of the composite cellar beneath 'Blackfriars Barn'.

UN-VAULTED CELLARS

As Faulkner points out, although most of the early cellars known within our towns are vaulted, 'it by no means follows that this was the rule or that it had any significance relating to use. It may be a matter of selective survival or, more probably, selective recognition. An un-vaulted cellar, without any architectural features in its side walls, is almost undatable'.[17]

As recent research carried out in Chester and in Faversham, Kent, has shown, his warning is a good one. Keene notes that although at least three of the cellars in Winchester are vaulted, in most cases the ceilings were of timber.[18] At Winchelsea, a now inaccessible un-vaulted cellar beneath The Court Hall - built in *c*.1300 as part of the house of Gervase Alard, junior - must be contemporary with the building above, though the only vaguely datable feature is the arch-headed, continuously-chamfered external doorway.[19] Insufficient of the cellar on Quarter 19, Plot 10, discovered during the digging of a service trench has yet been seen to be certain that it was ever vaulted, whilst if that found during trial trenching on Quarter 20, Plot 19, was once vaulted, the vault has since been destroyed.[20] At least some of the un-vaulted cellars beneath Periteau House, High Street (Quarter 7); The Little Shop, High Street (Quarter 8); Nesbit, High Street (Quarter 13) and Platt Cottage, Back Lane (Quarter 19) are likely to be of medieval date, but none contain datable features. All are relatively small. However, from their contexts in relation to the houses above, the un-vaulted cellars under 11/12 High Street and The Glebe, both on Quarter 13, are almost certain to be post-medieval in date.[21]

USE OF THE CELLARS

Opinions have in the past varied as to why Winchelsea's cellars were built. Homan had no doubt that they were intended for the bulk storage of wine imported from Gascony. He pointed out that during the 1306-7 wine season alone 15 Winchelsea ships were involved in the trade with Bordeaux and during that period they carried 2,923½ tuns (almost three-quarters of a million gallons) of Gascon Red in 21 shipments. How many of these shipments were destined for Winchelsea, or how many 'non-Winchelsea' ships transported wine into the town during the same season is not known. Having calculated the storage capacity of the known cellars, Homan argued that this level of importation would easily explain the existence of the many cellars in the town. As further evidence he pointed out that in 1296/7 the king was not only hiring cellarage for the storage of wine at the quay, but also from Gilbert Cross and from two members of the Alard family within the town. As part of their expenditure Edward's officials purchased locks for the cellar doors and paid to have the cellars cleaned.[22] However, compelling as this documentary evidence appears to be, the use of Winchelsea as an entrepôt for Gascon wine does not in itself prove that the cellars were built with that trade in mind. Nor does the fact that Edward I hired cellars within the town for the storage of wine intended for his household and troops during their assembly at Winchelsea in 1296/7 necessarily mean that this was their normal purpose.

Contrary to Homan's view, Faulkner tended to dismiss the widespread use of the many Winchelsea and Southampton cellars for the bulk storage of wine, pointing out that such cellars also occur at inland towns and that, in his opinion, they were in any case not suited to bulk storage. He suggested that barn-like warehouses on the quays were more likely to have been used for this purpose because this would have avoided unnecessary transportation and the difficult task of manhandling the cumbersome casks into and out of the cellars. He quite rightly pointed out that some of the cellars incorporate very good architectural detailing, which would not have been necessary had they simply been intended as warehouses. He argued that rather than being regarded as bulk-storage warehouses, the cellars should be considered as combined selling areas and stockrooms and, as such, could have been used in connection with almost any commodity, including such luxury goods as silks. Given that many cellars had no direct connection with the building above, he further argued that they could have been independently let (as indeed were those hired to Edward I) and that the houses probably quite commonly included an upper tier of shops set above the cellars. Surviving examples of this arrangement are quoted from Southampton and other towns.[23] Homan and Faulkner were writing in the middle years of the 20th century, but the debate regarding the use of 13th- and 14th-century vaulted urban cellars continues. A consensus appears to be emerging which suggests that both of the above views have been overstated and that the truth lies in a blend of the two.

To anybody who knows them, one of the most notable and significant features of the Winchelsea and Southampton subterranean cellars is their consistent temperature - cool in summer, but never approaching freezing, even in the depths of winter. A record of temperatures taken at specific times within the cellar beneath Five Chimneys (Cellar 1, Quarter 1) and within the garden of the same property over a seven-month period between September 2002 and April 2003 gave a minimum cellar temperature of 11° C (52° F) and a maximum of 16° C (62° F), compared to -3° C (28° F) and 25° C (77° F) externally. As with sea temperatures, the lowest cellar reading lagged behind the lowest external air temperature by some two months.[24]

A further feature to bear in mind in considering their original use is that, although not wet, the cellars are never perfectly dry either - the air is always slightly damp. In this respect, regardless of any rich architectural detailing they might possess, they were not suited to the storage of costly, delicate goods such as silks, even for short periods. Extending the argument regarding temperature to above-ground storage, it seems reasonable to suggest that, contrary to Faulkner's views, bulk quantities of wine would not have been stored for anything other than short periods in above-ground warehouses where temperature could not be controlled. There is, however, one major obstacle to this view which is that although cellars are known to have been present in reasonable concentrations at Winchelsea, Southampton, and indeed in London, there are no known major concentrations of subterranean storage facilities at other major 13th- and 14th-century wine importing centres such as Sandwich, yet these towns must have stored their wines satisfactorily.

It is possible that the method of storage used within individual ports was influenced by the mode and timescale of the intended redistribution of the wine following its initial importation. For example, wine which was to be moved on to other destinations with little delay was presumably more likely to be stored close to the quayside, perhaps in warehouses, whilst that intended for storage, prior to its use or onward sale, would perhaps more probably have been placed within cellars. However, it must be admitted that at present this question remains unsolved.

Nevertheless, the fact remains that the cellars were eminently suited to the storage of perishable goods such as wine, which needed to be kept at an even, cool temperature. Furthermore, there is ample evidence from the late 13th and 14th centuries to indicate the normal use of cellars within ports for the storage of wine being brought into the country. For example, in the early 1290s when Edward I ordered that the goods of Gascon and other wine merchants be held until financial security had been found, it was directed that upon landing, the merchants must immediately discharge their cargo into cellars.[25]

As Margery James, the leading authority on the medieval wine trade, pointed out, the first concern of any seasonal Gascon trader, once he had chosen a port wherein to land his goods, was to hire a cellar or warehouse in which to store the wine for display or sale. The cellars available for hire within the ports were often allocated by a local official which could put the visiting Gascons at a disadvantage vis-à-vis the English importers and those of their countrymen who had permanent dwellings in England. This point is well illustrated in 1285 when the Gascons visiting Southampton complained that the bailiffs of that town had directed them to cellars which were not well-placed for buying and selling.[26] In London too, the wine was unloaded and transported directly to cellars, which were not uncommonly away from the wharfs.[27]

The visiting vintners hired cellars either for periods of up to three months or perhaps more, or, for as little as a week. In the main, despite being allowed a generous period of leave to stay in England, the preoccupation of most Gascon merchant vintners was to sell their wines as quickly as possible, and thus the hire periods were commonly short. They often used the cellars as more than simple business premises - some Gascons also ate, slept and entertained in them. Often a carpenter would be hired for a few days, and not until he had repaired the lock and prepared stands could the wine be safely deposited. Once it had been landed, porters carried the casks in carts or rolled them to the cellars, where the services of a cooper would be engaged for the repair of any damaged wine casks. Sometimes the wine was left on the quay until it was sold, or until arrangements were made for its carriage to some further destination overland.[28]

Work by James and others has confirmed Winchelsea's not inconsiderable involvement in the wine trade. Although New Winchelsea's immediate market was limited, the quantity of wine being brought in during the early years of its life on the new site suggest that, even taking into account peaks during the quite frequent times of naval assembly in the late 13th and early 14th century, the imports were intended for a somewhat wider distribution than the town's immediate hinterland. The high level of import may in part have been in response to the interest in the port shown by the Gascon vintners: the royal butlers deplored the widespread enfranchisement of Gascons both at Winchelsea and Sandwich, as well as at London and elsewhere.[29] Winchelsea was well located for ships to put in en route to London or to elsewhere up the east coast, and it is known that Winchelsea merchants were active in London, as they appear frequently in the city's record books.[30] All this opens the possibility that one class of shippers and ships handled the long-distance carriage (it is known that the turnaround time was often very tight) while another group handled the coastal transhipment to London and other consumer markets. This was certainly the case at Southampton.[31] An echo of this arrangement, though admittedly not involving a Winchelsea ship and much later in date, is to be found in the third quarter of the 15th century when a triangular voyage was planned from Kings Lynn to Zealand and Bordeaux. After being laded with wheat in Zealand, the master was to bring the ship to Winchelsea in order that another master could take over responsibility for the voyage to Bordeaux.[32]

It is difficult to gain an accurate impression of the precise level of wine being imported through Winchelsea based upon the available records. As a guide, of those ports where the Royal Prise was taken during the 1300-1 season the number of wine ships entering Winchelsea was, with Hull, the joint fifth highest of any English port and exceeded only by London, Sandwich, Boston and Bristol. In comparison, Southampton was eighth highest. Throughout the 1320s and 1330s Winchelsea was amongst the top ten English ports for the number of its wine ships laded by denizens, though the numbers mostly fall within the lower half of that range.[33] At Winchelsea in 1326 a total of 30 ships of between 55 and 250 tons 'which would have crossed to Gascony and Peyto in quest of wine . . . ' were arrested for ship service. Of these 'two thirds were wont to discharge their wines in England and one-third in Ireland'. One of the ships arrested was from Folkestone rather than Winchelsea, but two other Winchelsea wine ships were arrested whilst at port in North Wales.[34] In 1328 the town was ranked ninth in England as a centre of wine imports, behind London, Southampton, Boston, Bristol, Sandwich, Exeter, Ipswich and Yarmouth.[35] The 300 tons of 'good wine' bought in England in 1336 in preparation for the invasion of Scotland were supplied by Hull (120 tons), London (100 tons), Bristol (30 tons), Winchelsea and Sandwich (20 tons each) and Boston (10 tons).[36] In 1342 Winchelsea, Sandwich and Bristol were established as ports for the gauging of incoming wine.[37] During the period 28/2/1350 to 24/9/1351 Winchelsea was still one of the top ten wine ports, though by then the tonnage being brought in (214 tons) was insignificant when compared to that entering the five principal wine ports of London (4036 tons), Bristol (1686 tons), Sandwich (1674 tons), Hull (1134 tons) and Southampton (821 tons).[38] Quantities of wine continued to be imported into Winchelsea throughout the remainder of the 14th century, and indeed throughout the 15th century, but the port was no longer amongst the lead players. Even so, in 1429-30 there is record of a single purchase of 52½ tons of Gascon red from the town.[39]

Sylvester points out that it is noticeable that the owners of the cellars are often identifiable amongst the town's leading shippers and vintners. Bearing this in mind, although some cellars would doubtless have been hired out to Gascon importers, others would presumably have served to store the wine of their owners until they had secured shipment to London and elsewhere, or secured a buyer to take the cargo on.[40] Calculations by Roland Harris suggest that the storage of wine imported into Southampton and Winchelsea during the 1300-1 season would have required the use of approximately 63 and 65-70 cellars respectively. Although this was during a period of conflict when national imports were generally low, the quantities brought into both towns may have been artificially boosted in order to supply any assembly of the fleet.[41]

Bearing all the above points in mind, there seems little doubt that the primary intended purpose of the Winchelsea cellars was indeed the storage of wine. However, even at the height of the wine trade some cellars would no doubt - at least on occasions - have been utilized for the storage of other perishable foodstuffs such as, for example, preserved fish, a commodity which was perhaps even more important to Winchelsea's trade than wine. With this in mind, it should be emphasized that Gascon Red was not suitable for long-term storage, but was consumed within the year, and therefore the cellars would not have been used for the long-term laying down of wine. Furthermore, the period of trade in wine each year was quite short: a brief brisk spate of activity heralded by the arrival of the vintage wines usually in late September, followed by up to three months of slower, more cautious bargaining. Usually by Christmas all the vintage wines were sold. A second spate of activity accompanied shipment of the reek wines, which were themselves usually disposed of by the end of April. The remainder of the year was partly, if not largely spend in preparation for the next season, and this included buying up goods to be shipped back to Gascony and exchanged for the next cargo of wine. To this end, cereal products and fish were important, but many other commodities were involved too.[42] At least some of these accumulated products may well have found their way into storage within the empty cellars.

Faulkner's views regarding the probable use of the cellars may prove to have been overstated, but his opinion as to the quantity of goods which would have been stored in individual cellars is valid, as too is the need to explain the important differences noted between the features of individual cellars, despite their superficial similarities. The most significant of these differences is between those cellars which were served by windows and those which were not. Those cellars lacking natural light would surely have been used primarily - if not exclusively - for bulk storage. With this in mind, it is surely no coincidence that if the ribs are discounted (for these were partially used to support the centering during construction) the unlit cellars consistently lack any trace of decorative finish. On the other hand, to judge from their architectural embellishments, some of the Winchelsea cellars must have had a more prestigious use. Does this evidence support Faulkner's notion that these examples should be considered as combined selling areas and stockrooms - in effect subterranean shops used in connection with the retail of almost any type of commodity? Does this explain why cellars accessed directly from the street are not only found in the ports, but also within inland towns such as Winchester and Canterbury, albeit in lesser concentrations?

In considering these points it is important to bear in mind the way in which the medieval wine trade operated. Although there were a few major wine magnates, in the main, the trade was in the hands of many relatively small importers. Furthermore, there was no clear division into wholesale, retail for consumption off premises, and sales for consumption within the tavern itself. Instead, many operators traded at all levels. Once the wine reached the port there were two types of buyers. The large, rich households and monastic centres usually bought a bulk quantity sufficient for 6-12 months and then transported it home to be stored in their own cellars. In contrast, the poorer members of the 'gentry' and the ordinary people bought more regularly in small quantities, or consumed the wine in taverns. What this latter group lacked in wealth, they made up for in numbers, and probably in overall terms accounted for the bulk of sales. Not only the vintners, but the taverners at the ports were often importers of wine in their own right and engaged directly in the overseas trade. Other taverners bought stock either from Gascon merchants or from native importers. In addition to selling small quantities to customers for consumption both on and off the premises, both groups put wine on sale in their taverns for purchase by the tun. Many inland traders from both town and village came to the ports to buy very considerable quantities of wine for retail, and the port taverners were amongst those from whom they purchased.[43]

Some inland towns and cities not only purchased for their own needs, but their taverners and vintners served as local redistributors. Cities such as Canterbury and Winchester - both of which have a number of medieval cellars - would no doubt have operated in this manner, as well as servicing their own resident population and the hordes of visiting pilgrims. Set against this background, Keene suggests that in the late middle ages cellars were used principally for the storage and sale of wine, regardless of whether or not they were located within a port. In Winchester the greatest concentrations of medieval cellars were in the heart of the commercial centre, a point which, he argues, strongly suggests that they were intended for the sale of goods, as well as for simple storage. He points out that there is a clear association between these town-centre cellars and the wine trade. In the early 15th century there were usually 9-10 vintners or wine taverners in the city and a large proportion of these are known to have had cellars: four had two cellars each. All six properties which are identifiable as taverns had cellars. Furthermore, he points out that the terms cellar and tavern seem sometimes to have been interchangeable.[44]

In Cheapside, London, away from the commercial waterfront, 14 of the 31 cellars listed in documents were within buildings identified as taverns or occupied by taverners. Five of the taverns are identifiable as being at cellar level and others may have been. Of the remaining 17 cellars, five were in tenements owned by vintners and another was held by a corn-monger and described as a brewhouse: no common type of occupancy or ownership is discernible in the others.[45] It is probable that most of the taverns lined the main thoroughfare. Keene considers that the cellars in the side streets off the main thoroughfare were mostly intended for 'purely residential and storage functions', but those in Bow Lane were, he suggests, used as 'storage and distribution centres' in the wine trade.[46] The four back-of-plot cellars identified in Winchelsea (*see* above) were likewise presumably intended purely for the use of those living in the building.

As has already been pointed out, those Winchelsea cellars which were unlit and utilitarian in design would surely have served purely as bulk-storage warehouses. But, in the words of Roland Harris, 'The consistent evidence of scale of construction, fenestration, principal access to the street, fireproofing, and a high build quality which, on occasion, extended to decorative work, means that there can be little doubt that the undercroft . . . . . was [in these instances] intended for commercial use of a type that combined stocking of valuable, if bulky goods and the servicing of customers'.[47] In the light of the documentary evidence, it seems likely that in most, if not all instances these were the taverners' cellars in which relatively small quantities of wine were tasted and purchased throughout the year and/or where wine was consumed upon the premises. As an ideal model, Harris follows Faulkner in suggesting a two-roomed layout comprising shop/tavern at the front with storage to the rear. To support this, he gives examples from a number of towns.[48] By regulation, transactions in taverns had to be open and public and 'no cloth might be hung before the cellar door to prevent the purchaser seeing the wine drawn'.[49] Some of Harris' examples are very convincing in that despite two specific areas - one for serving and one for storage, the two are largely open to one another in order to maintain visibility as required by the regulations.

Although not as conclusive as the best examples produced by Harris, some of the Winchelsea cellars, it could be argued, conform to this pattern, with the main room either used as a cellar-level tavern, or for occasional tastings. In particular, the large triple cellar under Blackfriars Barn on Quarter 15 has a spacious, well-lit front room with a fireplace, whilst the central barrel-vaulted room, which separates the two quadripartite-vaulted areas, is totally unlit and would have served well for bulk storage. Two-roomed examples from Winchelsea are Cellar 16, Quarter 7, Cellar 19, Quarter 8, Cellar 23, Quarter 9, and (after enlargement in the 15th century) Cellar 14/15, Quarter 7. Cellar 16 is of particular interest in that the opening which divides the two areas is wide and was never closed by a door, giving clear visibility between the two parts. In this instance the front section of the front room has been destroyed and thus it is not known whether it was lit; nor whether it was served by a good-quality entrance arrangement. Cellar 19 was unlit, but Cellars 14/15 and 23 were. The spacious and particularly elaborate, well lit quadripartite vaulted cellar under Salutation Cottages (Cellar 3, Quarter 2) has a doorway in its western end which may have led to a now inaccessible storage vault beyond. With its carved corbels and entrance steps flanked by low walls capped by handrails, this is the most obvious candidate for a cellar-level tavern. Indeed, it may be no coincidence that the building was already a tavern called The Salutation before the late 17th century, but how far that use extended back in time is not known.[50] At the same period the principal inn within the town, known as The Bear, was located within the building above Cellar 17, Quarter 7, and although this cellar would not in itself have been suitable for use as anything more than a very small tavern, it is lit by a window and is one of the examples linked to the building above by a secondary flight of steps. Thus it could have served as a storage facility for a ground-level tavern and was sufficiently well lit to have been used for a tasting when a customer required a larger consignment of wine. Another former tavern of unknown age, The Three Kings on Quarter 8, also has cellars upon its plot.[51]

As appears to be the case regarding the use to which the cellars were put, Faulkner's model of two-tier commercial premises - one tier within the cellar, the other in the building above - should not be overstated. Though isolated examples of two-tier shops are known in a number of towns, both in England and on the Continent, the high concentrations within the 'Rows of Chester' are now seen as being exceptional - the product of a peculiar set of circumstances rather than a rare survival of a once common, even normal arrangement.[52] Away from Chester, only where cellars with access directly from the street exist within areas which incorporate short street frontages to the individual properties, and where commercial pressures were extreme, are two-tier commercial premises likely to have been adopted. Despite Roland Harris' recent suggestion that a wide area of Winchelsea's business district possessed a high concentration of split-level town houses operating commercially on two levels, the available evidence does not support this suggestion.[53] On the contrary, there are substantial remains of contemporary buildings above only three of the Winchelsea cellars (Cellars 17, 26 and 30) and all three lack shops on their ground floor. Shops within the street frontage over Cellar 18 at Old Castle House on Quarter 8 are a greater possibility, although the above ground remains are very fragmentary and the layout inconclusive. The same may have been the case above Cellar 19 immediately to the south of Old Castle House on the same quarter (*see* Chapter 10). There is a medieval shop over the entrance area of Cellar 13, within The Retreat, Quarter 6, but not only is the building 15th-century in date, but the shop and cellar are interconnected and cannot have operated independently of one another (*see* Chapter 10). Furthermore, the topography of Winchelsea as currently understood does not support the notion of two-tier commercial premises. As discussed in Chapter 8, Winchelsea was laid out on a grand scale with good-sized frontages to many of its plots. Although frontages were more restricted around the market square, all the evidence to date suggests that this was not an area in which cellars were concentrated. Elsewhere within the town there is unlikely to have been sufficient pressure along the streets to warrant the use of inconvenient split-level arrangements. If, following the town's foundation, the population had increased markedly and the town had developed into a major commercial and retailing centre, resulting in tenements being split into short-frontage plots, then numbers of shops may have developed above existing cellared areas. But in the event, the reverse happened and on most quarters the pressure relaxed rather than intensified. It cannot be proved that examples of split-level commercial premises did not exist in the town - indeed, the likelihood must be that some did - but the available evidence suggests that in the majority of instances the cellars did not have separately occupied retail premises immediately above them.

In summary, although some wine-importing centres appear to have, at least in part, utilized facilities other than cellars for their operations, both Winchelsea and Southampton relied heavily upon cellars. In this respect it should be remembered that Winchelsea was founded upon its new site at a time when the wine trade was at its most prosperous, a factor which may in itself have influenced the type of facilities provided. Although broadly similar in their design, the individual Winchelsea cellars do incorporate important differences which suggest that whereas some were built for bulk storage, others were stocked less fully and probably incorporated tasting areas, and in some instances served as taverns in their own right. In this respect the better finished, better lit examples perhaps functioned throughout the year, serving to supply the town's hinterland, whilst others are likely to have been utilized at the height of the wine season only, either lying unused or put to other purposes for the rest of the year. There is little or no evidence to suggest that the cellars represented the lower tier of a widespread two-tier commercial arrangement.

A final point worth consideration is that for much of the medieval period the town was almost certainly over-provided with cellars. The cellars were built at a time when the importation of wine was at its height and the Barons of Winchelsea were at their most optimistic. With a major downturn in the tonnage of wine imported into England after the 1330s, and a known serious reduction of imports into Winchelsea, many of the cellars must have fallen into disuse, or alternatively been put to alternative, less suitable purposes. This is, of course, a factor which was not just peculiar to Winchelsea. The downturn was national and permanent, and may in itself explain, at least in part, the references to cellars used in other towns during the late 14th and 15th centuries for purposes other than the sale of drink.[54] Even so, it is interesting to note that even when they were no longer in widespread use the townsfolk of Winchelsea remained proud of their cellars and promoted them as an important asset. They make specific reference to them in a report sent to the Privy Council in 1570, in which the cellars are described as '. . . great many costly vaults, arched and set forth with pillars of Caone (Caen) stone, such monuments as merit to have houses built over them meet for famous merchants'.[55] During the mid 16th century the Corporation presented people for casting soil and dung into cellars, though on at least one occasion - in 1589 - permission was granted for stone to be dug from a cellar and carried away.[56]

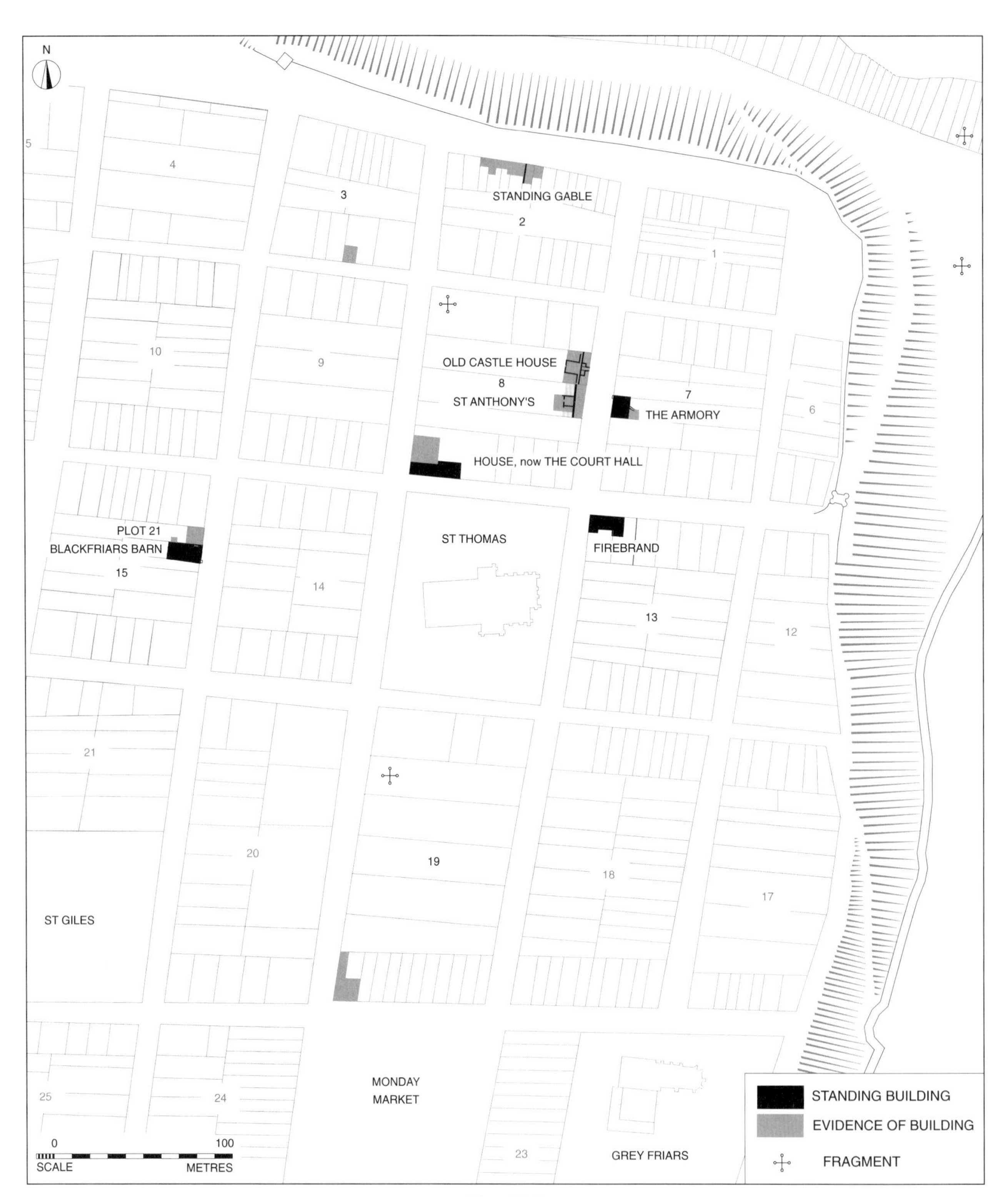

Fig. 10.1
The locations of the surviving and excavated early buildings.

10. DOMESTIC BUILDINGS: LAYOUT AND DESIGN

David and Barbara Martin

EARLY HOUSES (pre c.1350)

The remains of either six or seven houses are known to survive from the years immediately following Winchelsea's refoundation (Figure 10.1). Of these, only four - The Armory, Quarter 7; a house, now The Court Hall, Quarter 8; Firebrand, Quarter 13; and Blackfriars Barn, Quarter 15 - are relatively complete. The other three: Old Castle House and St Anthony's, both on Quarter 8, and a surviving stone gable of possibly early date on Quarter 2 - are very fragmentary. All were part of substantial stone structures built above cellars, although in one instance the cellar was apparently restricted to the rear of the building and in another the cellar was not vaulted. Almost certainly these remains represent the homes of leading merchants and/or ship owners. In their size and quality they are comparable to the homes of the local rural gentry.[1]

In addition to these seven buildings, there are a number of other minor upstanding stone remains within the town, which appear, at least in part, to date from *c.*1300. For example, at the northwest corner of Quarter 8 is a boundary wall, which incorporates a low clasping buttress with chamfered plinth and a sloping offset, and thus indicates that at least part of this wall is early. The buttress is important in that it fixes the corner of the former Alard house upon this site and positions that house in relation to the cellar beneath, but otherwise it reveals nothing of the building itself. Similarly, there is some evidence of a former thick stone wall which formed the boundary between Wren Cottage and 11/12 High Street on the northern side of Quarter 13, and this extends back to join what appear to be early stone garden walls, of which others exist further east. These are useful in confirming the alignment of early tenement boundaries. An elaborately moulded doorway incorporated within the walls of what was Little Trojans, on the western side of Quarter 19, suggests that at least part of the stone walls upon this large and important plot were of early date. Unfortunately, these walls were demolished without record in the mid-20th century in order to make way for a housing estate, but the doorway was saved and is now re-fixed in a modern wall in Back Lane. Finally, short sections of stone wall incorporated into both Strand House and The Old Malthouse on the Strand below the town may be the reused remains of earlier structures, indicating the former existence of substantial buildings down by the quay.

Details of a further six early houses, together with glimpses of others, are known from archaeological excavations, for the locations of which *see* Figure 10.1. Even by combining all these sources, the number of examples falls far short of that necessary to give anything more than the slightest impression of the town's original housing stock. This is true even for the class of building which survives the best: the houses of the urban elite.[2]

W. A. Pantin in his seminal article on medieval English town-house plans divided the basic plan forms into two broad categories: those with their hall ranges built parallel to the street and those set at right angles to the street.[3] He then further subdivided these two groups. Within the type built with their main hall range parallel to the road he identified four basic variations which he called the 'extended', 'contracted', 'double-range' and 'courtyard' plans (Figure 10.2, Nos.1a-1d).

Within the 'extended' category he grouped all those houses in which the hall is set towards the centre of a long range, with rooms and chambers beyond it at both ends. As the name implies, the 'contracted' form is found on plots with a narrower frontage, and in these the hall was at one end of the range and the private accommodation either on the first floor, over the services and/or commercial space at one end, or sited within a wing extending back from the main range. In both the 'extended' and 'contracted' forms the hall was sited hard

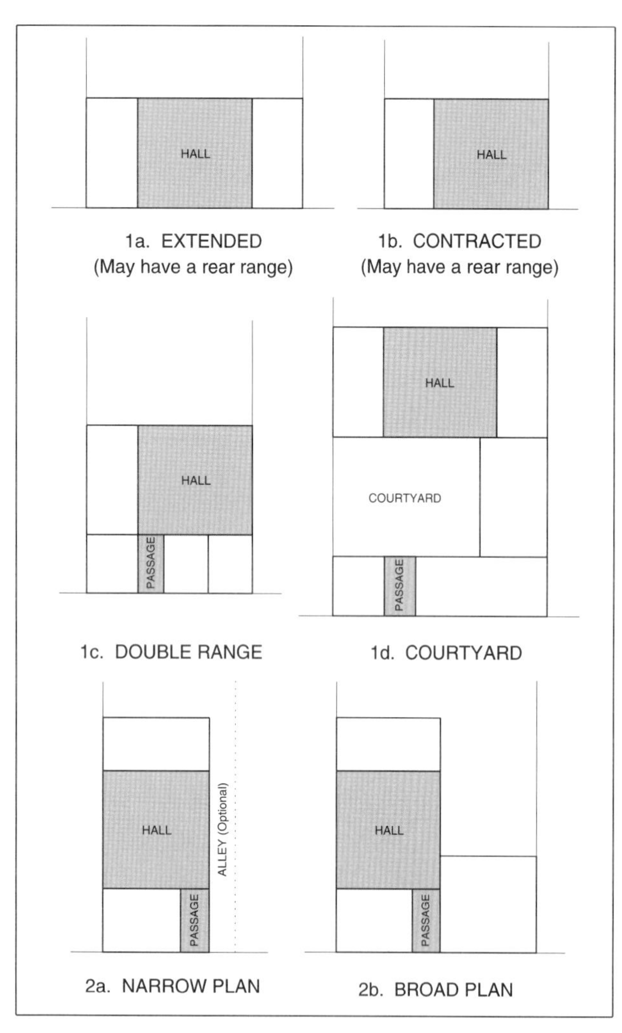

against the street.

In contrast, in the 'double-range' and 'courtyard' types, the hall was sited in a more private location, away from the street, but still aligned parallel with it. As the name implies, the 'double-range' building was two rooms deep, with the hall located hard against the rear wall of the street range. In the 'courtyard' form the hall range lay to the rear of a courtyard entered through the street range. The courtyard house was usually the most spacious and normally reflected the highest status. This is the only type currently unknown amongst the standing and excavated buildings within Winchelsea, though, given the high status of the leading urban elite and the spaciousness of their plots, it would be surprising had buildings of this type not originally been present within the town.

Only two subdivisions are found in the category of houses in which the hall range was built at right angles to the street: the 'narrow' plan and the 'broad' plan (Figure 10.2, Nos. 2a-2b). The 'narrow plan' house consisted of a single range only and either filled the entire width of the plot or had a narrow alley to one side, whereas the 'broad plan' house was 'L'-shaped, with a short range running parallel to the street, and the main hall range built at right-angles to it.

Of the types built parallel to the street, the only known example of the 'extended' form is Firebrand, a

Fig. 10.2 (Left)
A schematic representation of the basic plan forms of medieval urban houses (after Pantin).

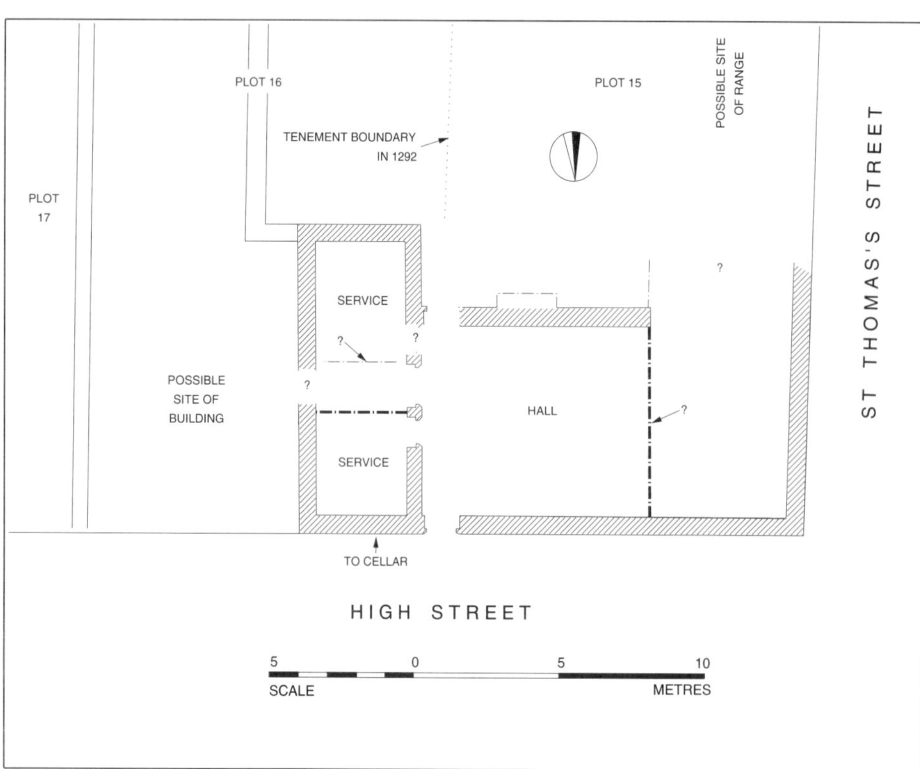

Fig. 10.3 (Left)
An interpretation of the ground-floor plan of Firebrand, Quarter 13 as built in c.1300.

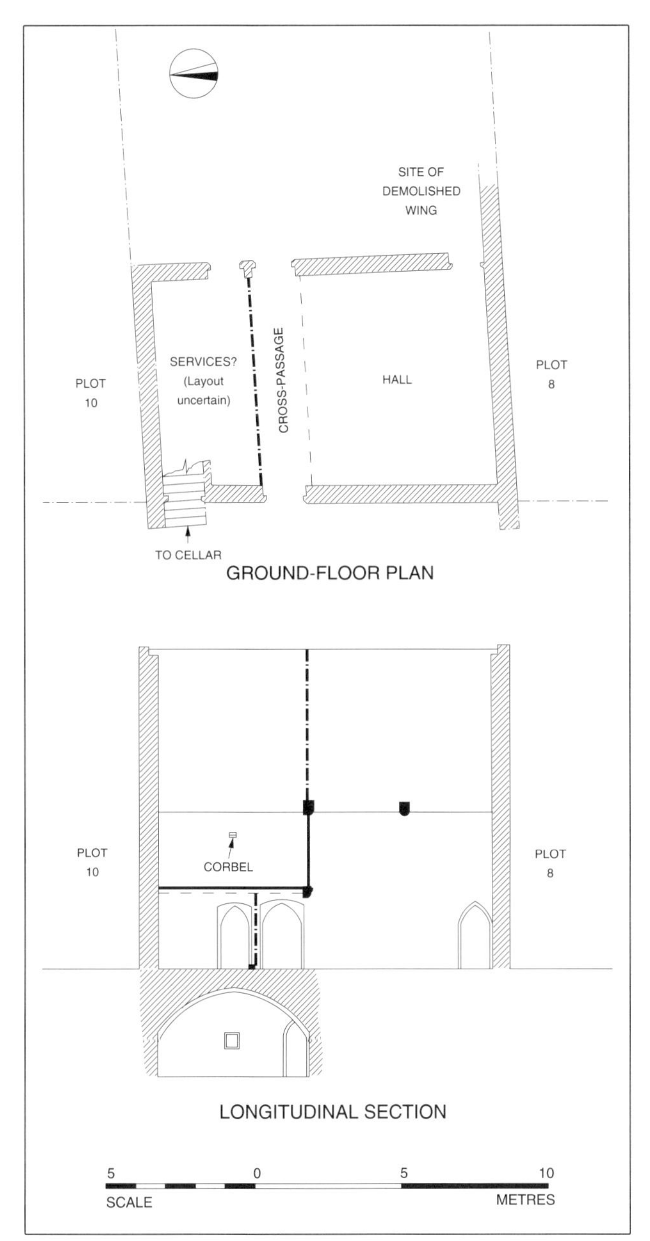

Fig. 10.4
An interpretation of the ground-floor plan and longitudinal section of The Armory, Quarter 7 as built in c.1300.

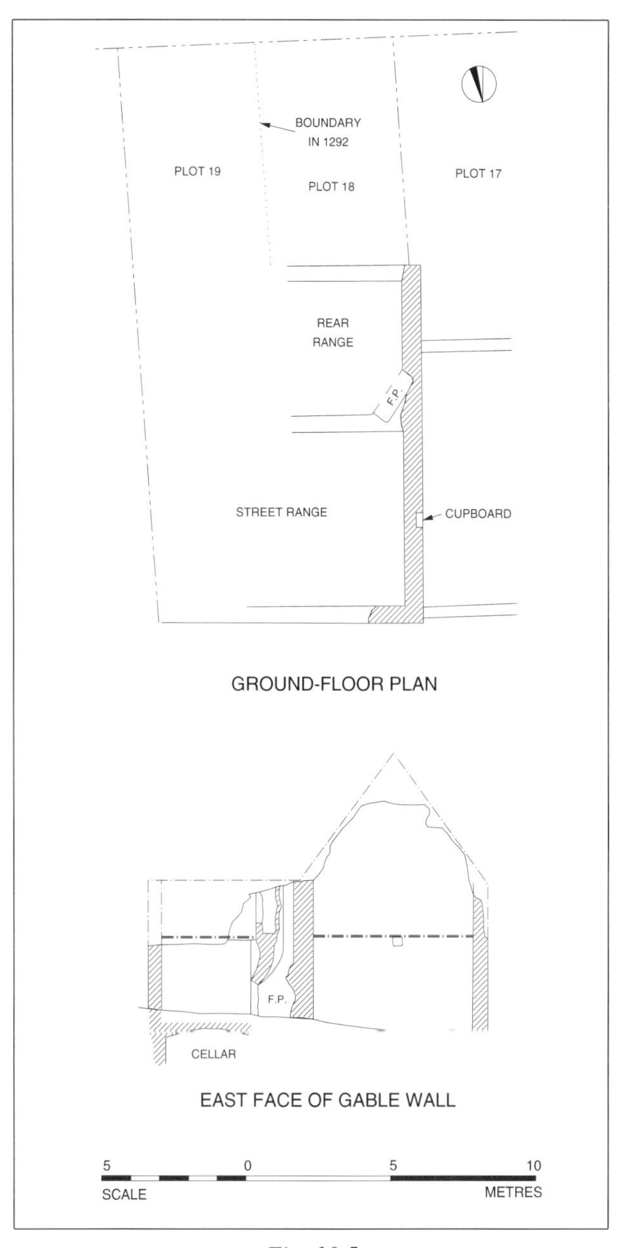

Fig. 10.5
Medieval stone gable in North Street, Quarter 2. Plan and elevation.

house 17.30 metres (56ft.9ins.) long which occupies an important corner plot on Quarter 13, near St Thomas's Church and was built across two of the town's original plots (Figure 10.3). There are some indications to suggest that there might originally have been a structure connected to the service end of the house, and perhaps either a narrow attached or detached range stretching down the adjacent western street. The best example of the contracted form is The Armory on Quarter 7 in Castle Street (Figure 10.4). Although it now stands alone, this and neighbouring houses originally formed a continuous street frontage. Despite having a generous façade (12.65 metres or 41ft.6ins.), the building's large proportions meant that with the 'services' at one end, the hall took up much of this length. Here additional accommodation appears to have been sited within a now-demolished range which stretched down the plot against the southern boundary, behind the high end of the hall, creating an 'L'-plan. Evidence of another similar house with its main range built parallel to the street and a second range built at right angles behind it, is provided by a stone gable of uncertain medieval date in North Street, part way along the northern side of Quarter 2 (Figure 10.5). In 1292 this property had a street frontage

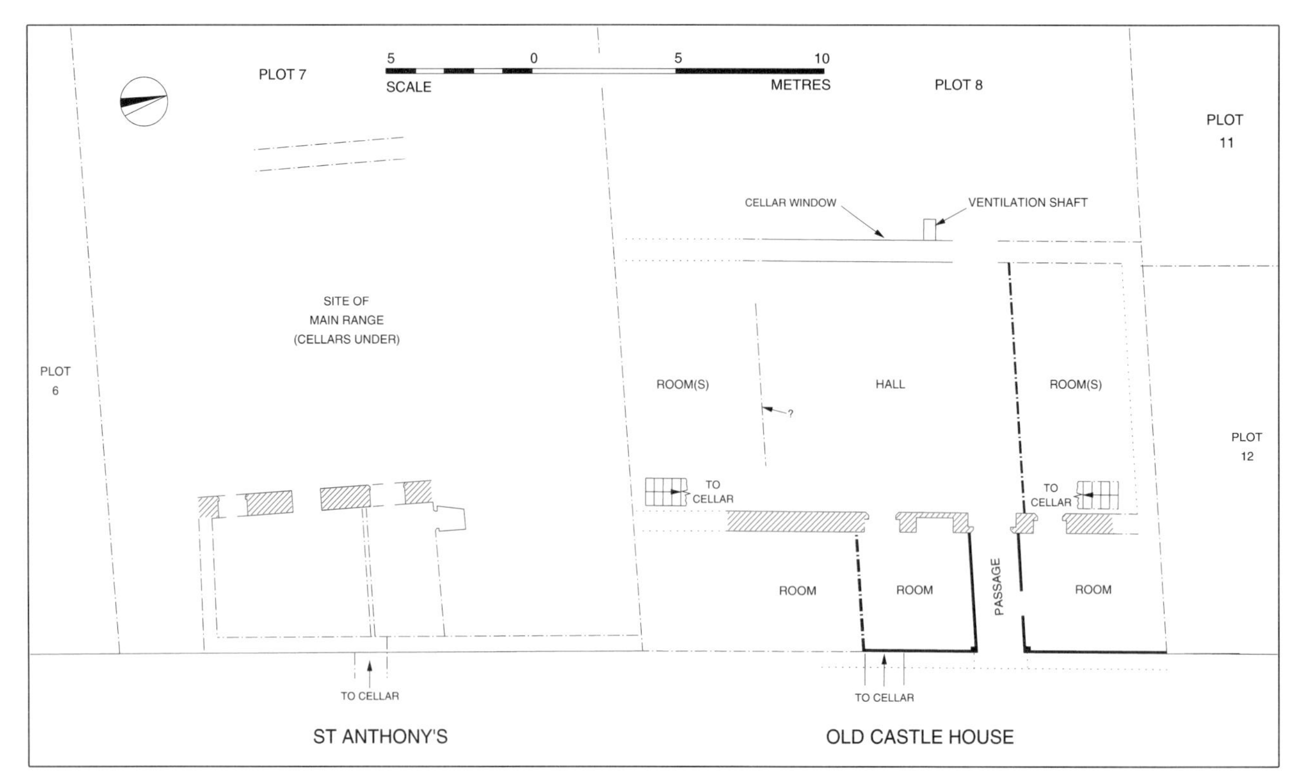

Fig. 10.6
Ground-floor plans of St Anthony's and Old Castle House, Quarter 8, showing known details. The walls to the east of the main stone wall at Old Castle House represent a c.1500 reconstruction.

of only *c.*4.75 metres (*c.*15ft.7ins.), at first glance suggesting that it must have been of contracted type. However, given the building's chosen design, it is possible, perhaps even probable that as with Firebrand, this house occupied two of the town's original plots. If so, it was of 'L'-plan layout. Since both adjacent plots were of identical size, if this was indeed the case, it would have increased length of the frontage to 9.50 metres (31ft.2ins.).

The fragmentary remains embedded within Old Castle House and the adjacent St Anthony's appear to represent two examples of Pantin's 'double-range' type (Figure 10.6). Both houses were built upon exceptionally large plots which extended fully across Quarter 8 - one of the principal quarters of the town with street frontages at both ends. In 1292 these plots were owned by Gervase Alard senior and Reynold Alard senior, both principal members of the urban elite (*see* Figure 8.6). Towards Castle Street both houses had generous frontages of *c.*17.7 metres (*c.*58ft.) and *c.*18.1 metres (*c.*59ft.4ins.) respectively. In both buildings only one stone wall now survives above ground: a wall aligned parallel to, but set back from, the street. That at Old Castle House is set back 3.90 metres (12ft.9ins.), whilst that at St Anthony's runs at a slight angle and is set back on average 4.70 metres (15ft.5ins.). There are large vaulted cellars beneath both houses.

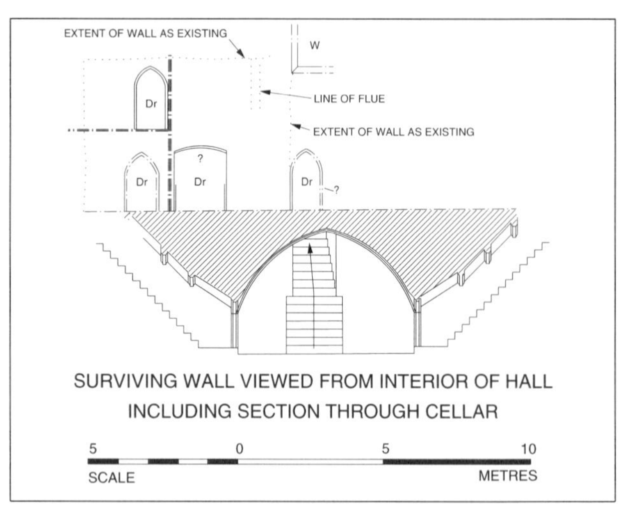

Fig. 10.7
Old Castle House, Quarter 8 showing architectural features contained within the upstanding masonry wall of c.1300, together with its relationship to the vaulted cellar beneath it.

By combining all the available information, including the architectural features contained within the cellars and the upstanding walls, it is possible to show that in each case some form of structure stood on the street side of the upstanding wall with a further, much

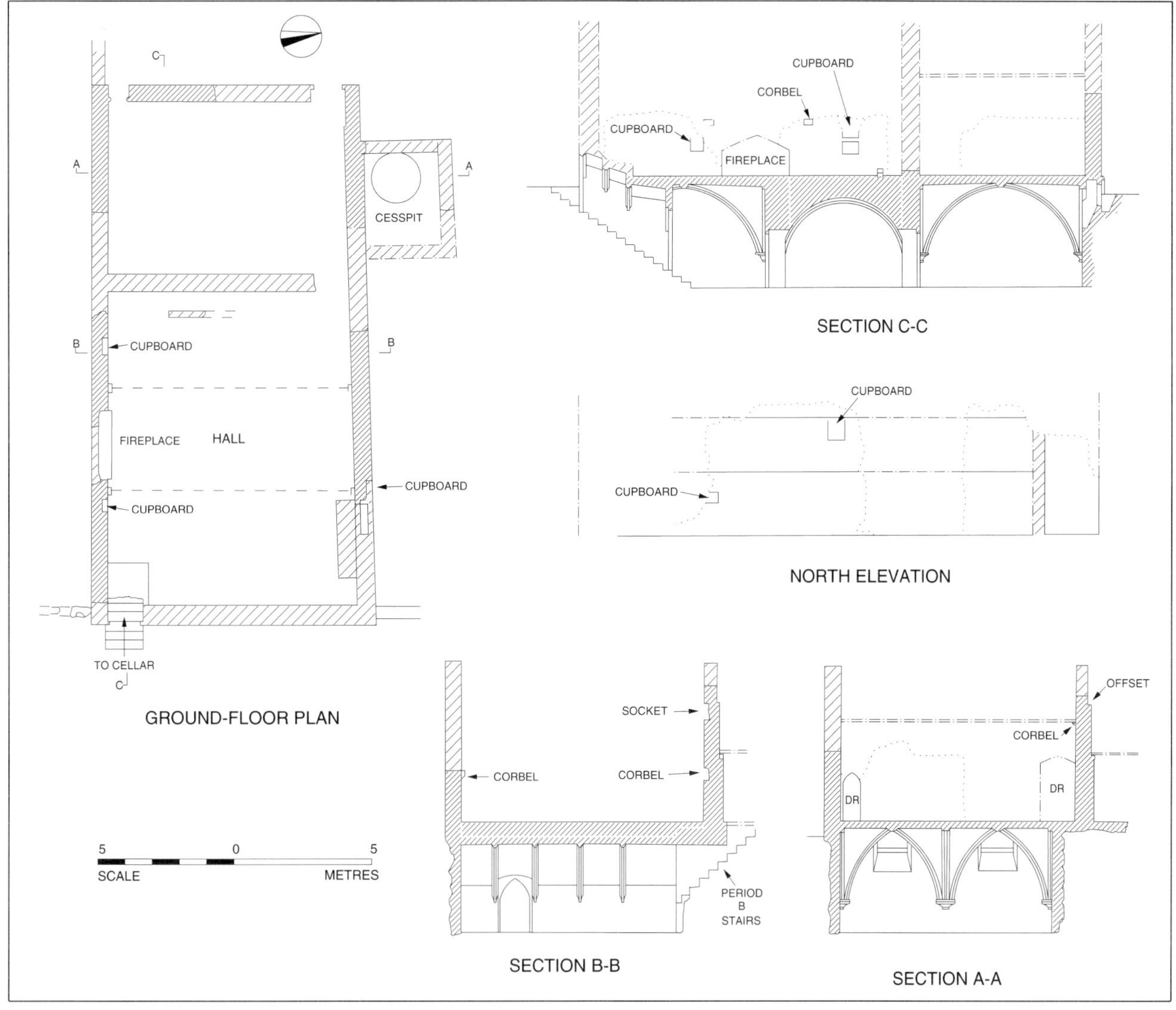

Fig. 10.8
Details of the ruined 'house' (now known as 'Blackfriars Barn') as built in c.1300.

more substantial range immediately behind it. In both instances the main range to the rear of the wall was very wide. At Old Castle House historic fabric still survives on the street side of the upstanding wall, but this dates from the 15th century, or perhaps even the opening years of the 16th century and, unlike the rear range, it is timber-framed. There was a jettied upper storey towards the street. If the original street range had been of stone it is unlikely to have been rebuilt. This implies that the later work replaces earlier timber framing upon the same site.

In Pantin's model for this plan form he argued that, except for a wide passage leading through to the house beyond, the ground floor of the front range was likely to have been occupied by a row of shops, with letting chambers above. The impression he gave is that the shops and chambers would have been occupied separately from the main house. However, the wall at Old Castle House incorporates three ground-floor doorways, only one of which linked directly to the street via a wide passage. The other two have their main arches facing west and lead forwards from the main range into two of the front units, one of which was served by a fireplace from the outset and is therefore unlikely to have been a shop (Figure 10.7). Less survives at St Anthony's, but here too, two doorways lead forward from the main rear range into the front rooms. A similar feature has been recognized in examples of this plan type in Chester.[4]

In most towns which incorporate houses which have their main range turned through 90 degrees to the street, the 'narrow' type in which the range occupies the entire width of the plot is usually only found in plots of restricted width. Given that about 190 of Winchelsea's plots measured 7.6 metres (25ft.) or less in width, and that approximately 90 were less than 6.5 metres

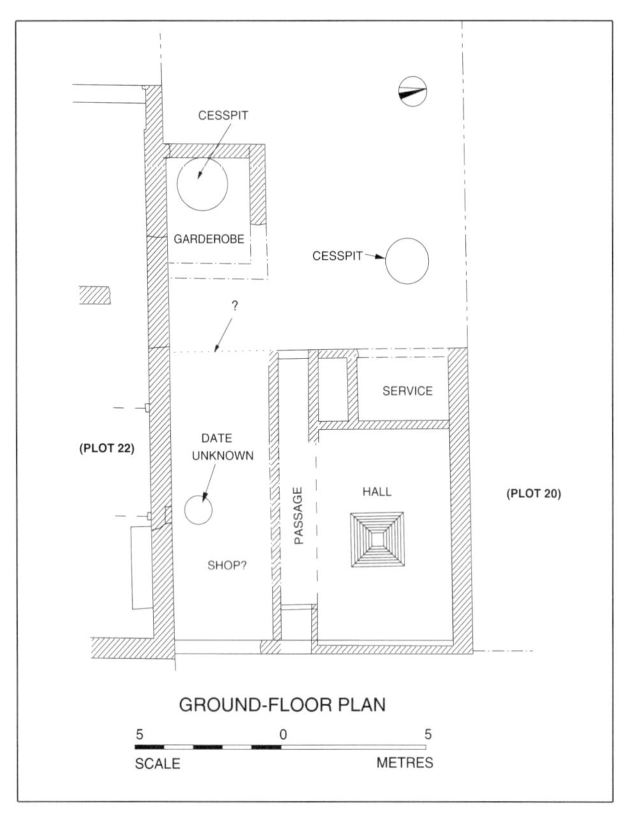

Fig. 10.9
Ground-floor plan of the house upon Plot 21 of Quarter 15 as built in c.1300.

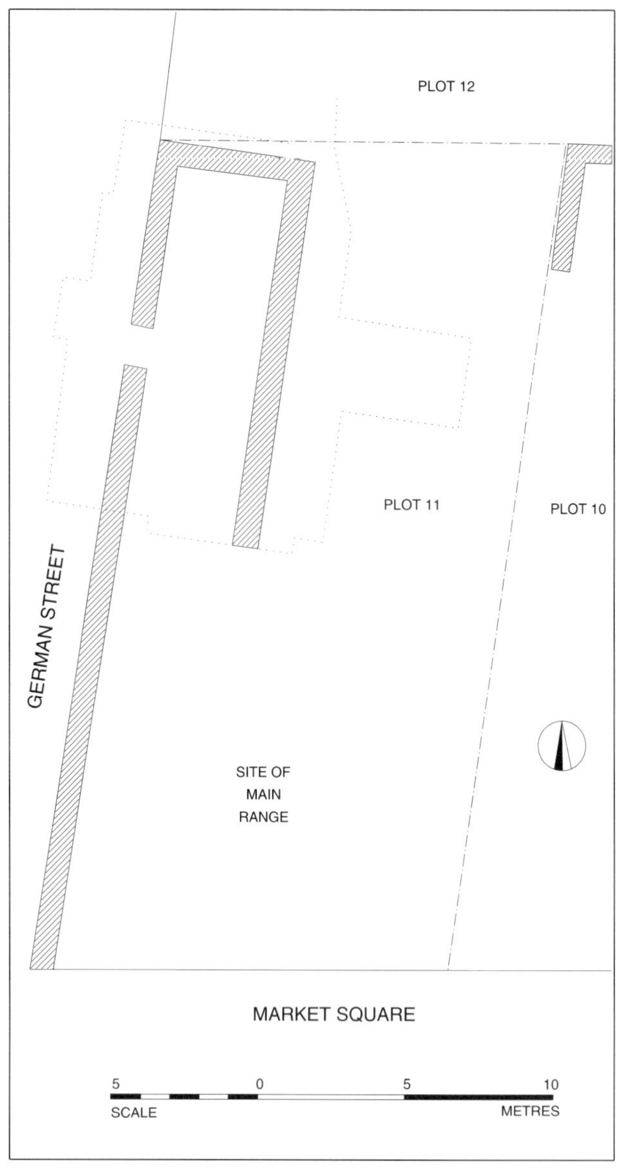

Fig. 10.10
Outline plan showing the known details of a house of c.1300 which occupied the southwest corner of Quarter 19.

(21ft.4ins.) wide, it is likely that this design was at one time popular here too. However, the only early example to survive in a recognizable form is the exceptionally large ruined building now known as Blackfriars Barn on Quarter 15 (Figure 10.8). This had a very generous overall street frontage of 10.3 metres (33ft.9ins.). Never owned by the Black Friars and only converted into a barn late in its life, its original function is to some extent uncertain. It may have been the home of a wealthy merchant, but its exceptionally large open hall, its dearth of domestic rooms and its spacious attached toilet block perhaps indicate a more public function. The three-bayed open hall was located hard against the street, flanked on either side by other houses and must therefore have been lit primarily, if not solely, by a large window within its monumental street gable.

The only probable example of the 'broad' type so far known was revealed by the excavation of the plot immediately to the north of Blackfriars Barn (Figure 10.9). Despite having a frontage of identical length to that of Blackfriars Barn, in its initial form the hall of this building was located hard against the street within the northeast corner. The building was probably roofed in two spans turned through 90º to the street. The services were to the rear of the hall and there was a further room (possibly a shop) against the street to the south of the hall. A passage giving access to the rear yard ran through the centre of the building, along the southern edge of the hall. The walls on the tenement boundaries were stone-built, no doubt to act as firebreaks, although otherwise the house was timber-framed.

The subsequent development of the plot adjacent to Blackfriars Barn (for which *see* Figure 10.30) demonstrates vividly the complex evolution of these urban houses. In 1974 similar complexity was demonstrated by excavations carried out on a high-rental, market-frontage plot upon Quarter 19, one of the four principal quarters of the town. The area excavated was

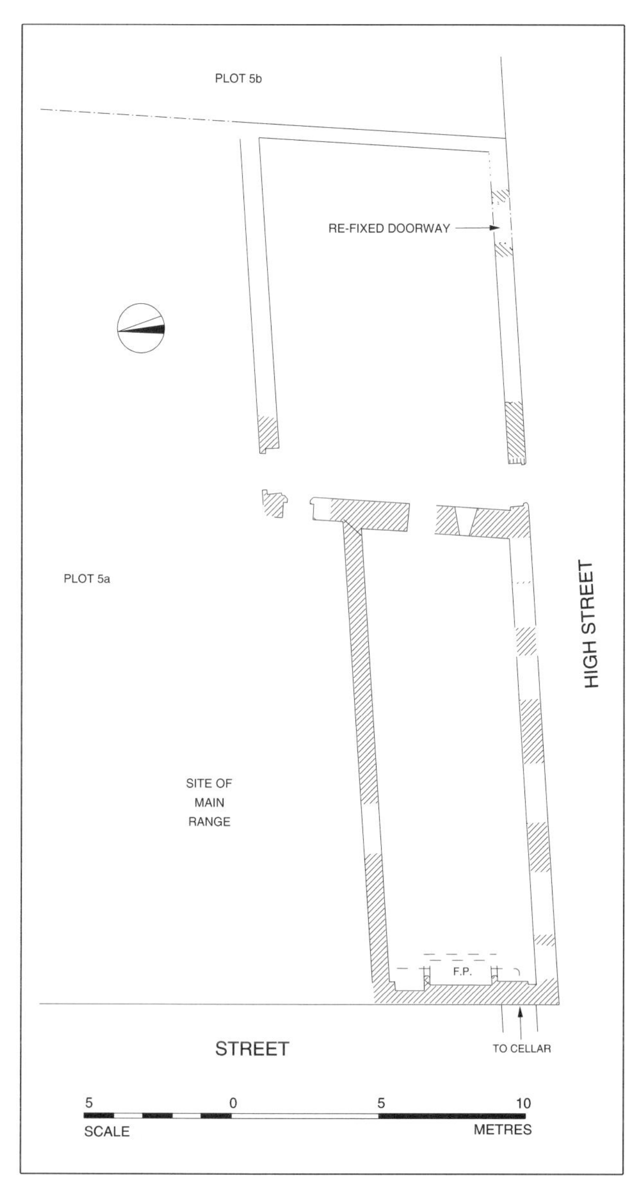

Fig. 10.11
Outline plan showing the known details of a house of c.1300 (later The Court Hall) occupying the southwest corner of Quarter 8.

limited to the northern part of the plot, away from the market frontage. This was not only a prime corner plot, but also the largest of the holdings fronting the market and held in 1292 by Stephen Aurifaber (*i.e.* Goldsmith). These three factors suggest that the building is likely to have been one of the high-status houses of the town. Later an open hall was built in this area (*see* below), but initially this part of the property was occupied by a long and relatively narrow stone-built range which, including its walls, measured only 5.5 metres (18ft.) wide (Figure 10.10). A blocked doorway shows that this narrow range had direct access from the street.

An equally complex evolution is indicated by the surviving remains incorporated into the Court Hall and its adjacent yard, both originally part of an early domestic building sited on another prime corner plot, in this instance occupying the southwest corner of Quarter 8. In 1292 this was the home of Gervase Alard junior, another of the leading members of the urban elite (*see* Chapter 8, Figure 8.6). As with the range excavated on Quarter 19, the principal surviving part is a relatively narrow, stone-built structure, but here too the range can be shown to be only part of a once much larger complex, in this instance stretching both northwards, fronting onto the western street, and eastwards along High Street (Figure 10.11). Only the outer walls of the first-phase building survived its conversion into a court hall complex, but what remains is not without interest. At roughly first-floor level both of the street facades incorporate a corbel table which presumably indicates some form of pentice roof jutting out into the street, protecting the lower storey. The constructional details of the present north wall, the existence of a blocked first-floor doorway and the remains of a doorway in the adjacent east wall indicate that the structure which formerly stood to the north was substantial. Otherwise nothing is known about it. To the east are the remains of another medieval stone-built range, which appears to have incorporated a hall. Alard's plot formerly extended further east than this (plot 5b in figure 10.11) but this eastern part was sold off to form a separate property in 1342.[5]

Pantin's article dealt only with houses which incorporate an open hall, and even regarding these, he did not discuss some of the more unusual combinations. For instance, structures such as the row erected against the precinct of Tewkesbury Abbey, Gloucestershire indicate that houses built parallel to the street under a single roof span could incorporate an open hall which was restricted to the rear part of the building only, with a shop, a room and a chamber within the front part.[6] Another example of this arrangement, although in this instance incorporating a hall which was never open to the roof, survives in Winchelsea at 2 Friars Road, Quarter 19 (*see* Figure 10.25 below). Both of these buildings are of late-medieval date, but excavations on a site in Mill Road, on Quarter 3, revealed a possibly early example with an open hearth set well back from the street, towards the rear of a building. The rear wall of this building was *c.*6.8 metres (*c.*22ft.4ins.) from the frontage (Figure 10.12).[7] The position of the hearth makes it all but certain that the open hall did not extend through to the street, yet the overall depth of the building seems insufficient for an 'L'-plan house, suggesting that, as in the examples cited above, the hall may have been located within the rear part of a standard street range.

Mill Road illustrates well the problems of interpreting scant excavated remains. Similar problems

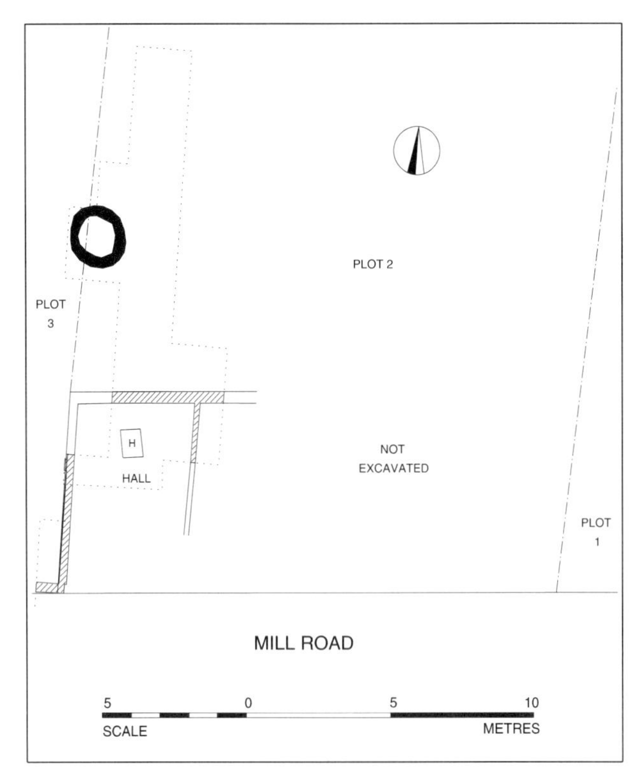

Fig. 10.12
Outline plan showing the known details of a house on Quarter 3, facing onto Mill Road.

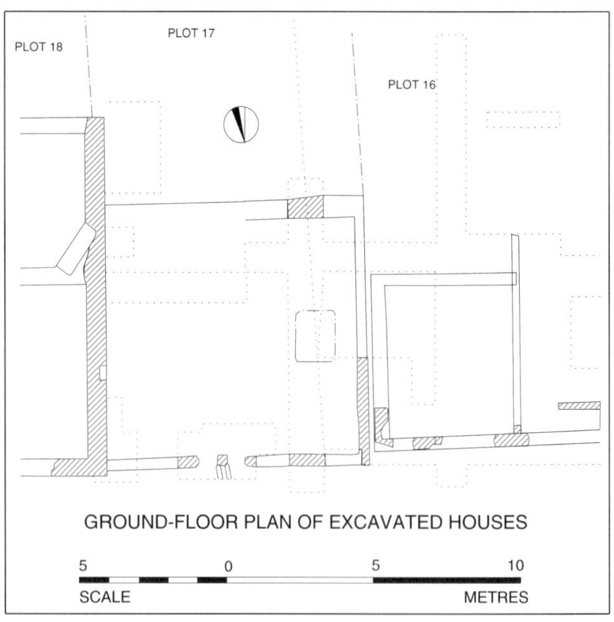

Fig. 10.13
Outline plan showing the known details of houses built on Quarter 2, facing onto North Street.

occur regarding the excavated remains at North Street, on Quarter 2 (Figure 10.13). Here, on a plot with a street frontage of 8.8 metres (28ft.10ins.), an open hearth was found in a central location between the front and rear walls of the building, but very close to the western side wall. The excavated remains are very fragmentary and as a result it was not possible to ascertain whether the building had comprised a pair of adjoining ranges built at right angles to the street, or a house of 'contracted' form located within a single, exceptionally wide street range.[8]

Work carried out subsequently to that of Pantin has shown that not all medieval urban houses incorporated an open hall, especially within the more congested, densely occupied urban centres where plot sizes were tiny and residents were forced to build upwards. These houses Roger Leach calls 'shophouses'.[9] Although examples of this form existed in Winchelsea at a later date (*see* below), no early examples are currently known.

Apart from the cellars (*see* Chapter 9) neither the surviving upstanding nor the excavated remains tell much about the commercial activities carried on within the early houses. Alterations made during later phases to the house shown in Figure 10.9, adjacent to Blackfriars Barn, suggest that the southern room, adjacent to the hall, may always have been a shop, and likewise some of the rooms within the narrow street ranges shown in Figure 10.6 in front of the hall blocks at Old Castle House and St Anthony's on Quarter 8 may have fulfilled commercial functions. The corbel table running along the street facades of the narrow range at the Court Hall (Figure 10.11) on the same quarter suggest pentice roofs, which perhaps protected a commercial facade, an interpretation partially supported by hints of large openings in the wall beneath the corbels. The fact that the similar narrow range excavated on Quarter 19 was entered straight from the street may indicate a commercial/workshop use for this range too (*see* Figure 10.10). It is possible that at Firebrand, Quarter 13, which was sited upon a corner plot, a narrow attached or detached range once extended along the frontage of the western street (*see* Figure 10.3). If so, this could have fulfilled a commercial/workshop function. In this sense these narrow ranges are comparable to the arrangement which existed in the early 16th century at The Flushing Inn in neighbouring Rye.[10] Flushing Inn (which as far as is known was not built as an inn) occupies an important corner-plot site similar to the Winchelsea examples. But all this is hypothetical: in reality the only positive proof of a shop in Winchelsea at street level comes from a 15th-century context at The Retreat, Quarter 6 (*see* below and Figure 10.16).

LATE-MEDIEVAL HOUSES (*c.*1350-1525)

More late 14th-, 15th- and early 16th-century houses survive within the town, than do examples from before *c.*1350 and the later houses tend to be better

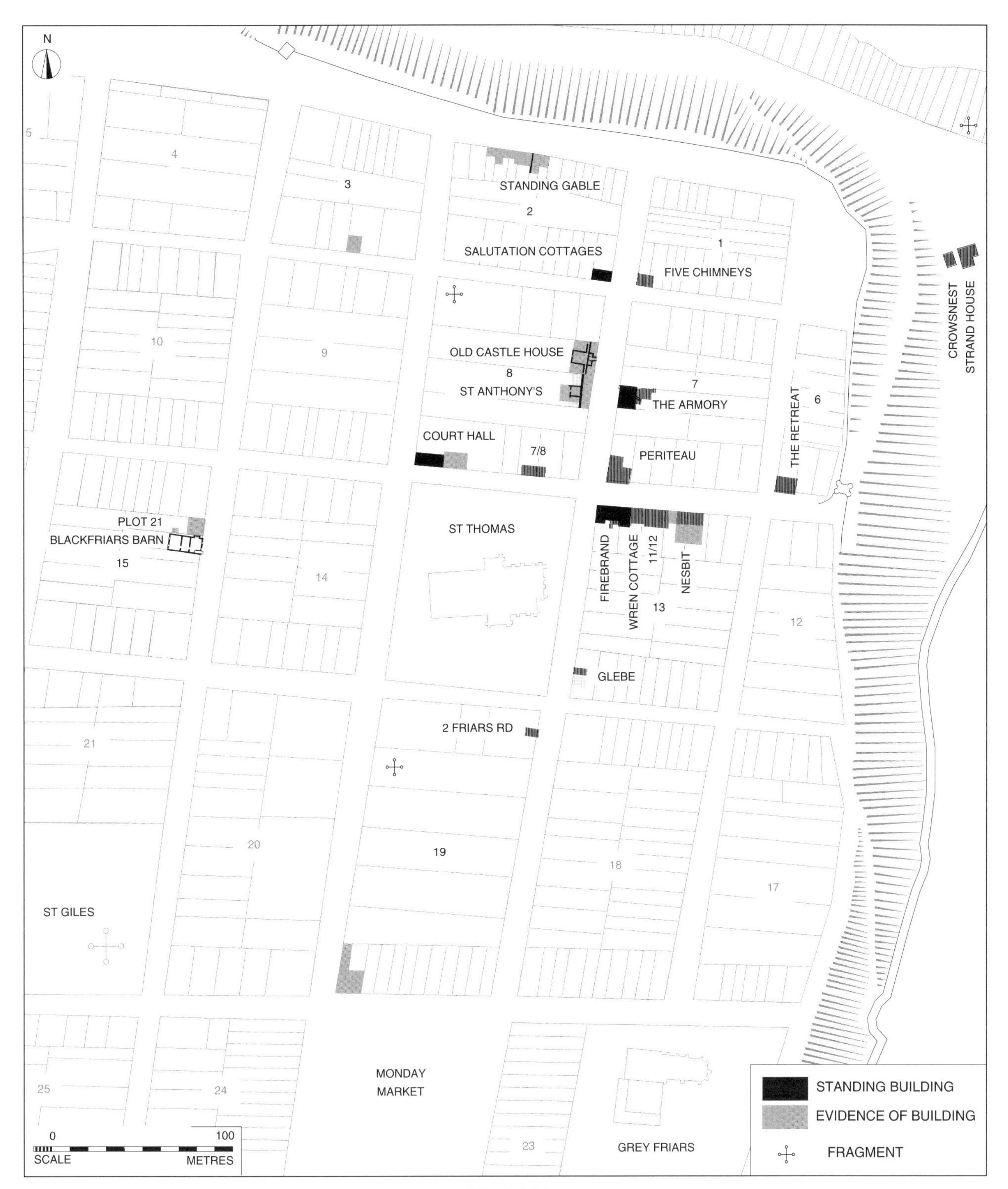

Fig. 10.14
The locations of the surviving and excavated medieval buildings.

preserved. For their locations *see* Figure 10.14. Despite their better survival, they are of considerably lesser academic importance in that houses of these periods are common in many English towns and the Winchelsea examples, built after the height of the town's prosperity, largely conform to the pattern found in other urban centres in south-east England. Substantial parts of 13 buildings survive from this time.[11] In marked contrast to those from the earlier period, all are timber-framed. Substantial alterations were made to the early houses

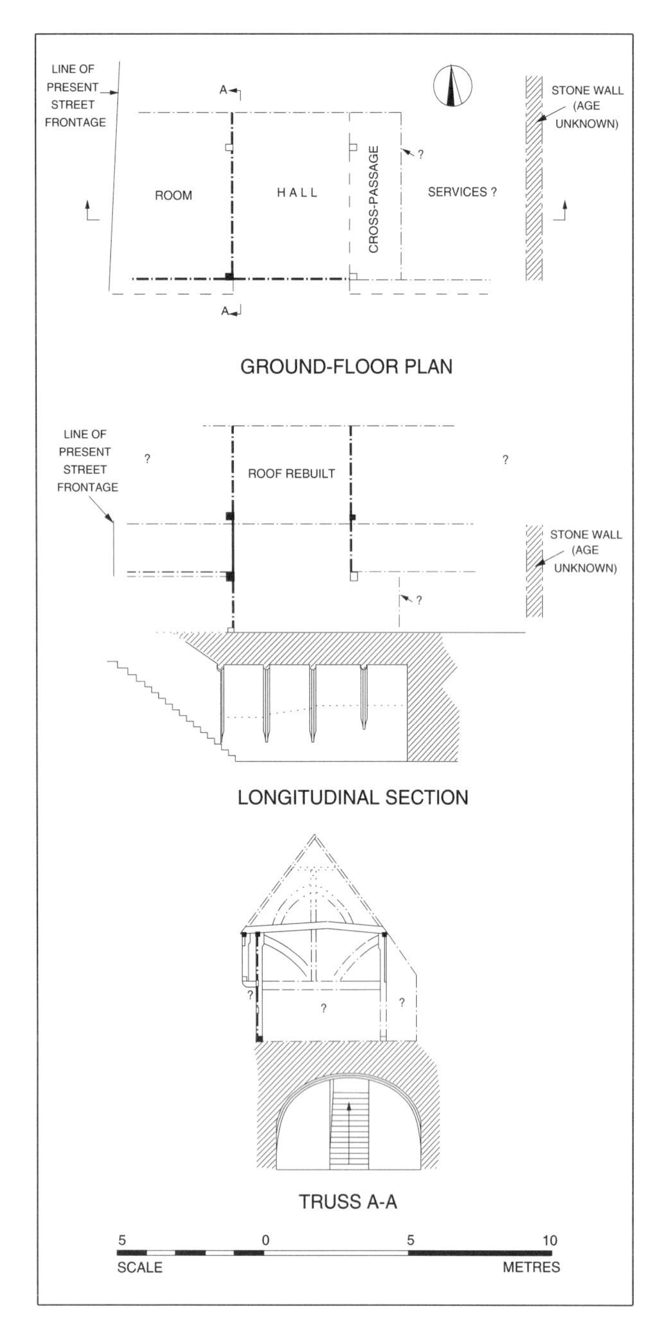

Fig. 10.15
The Five Chimneys, Quarter 1. Reconstruction drawings of the house as rebuilt in the 15th century above the earlier cellar.

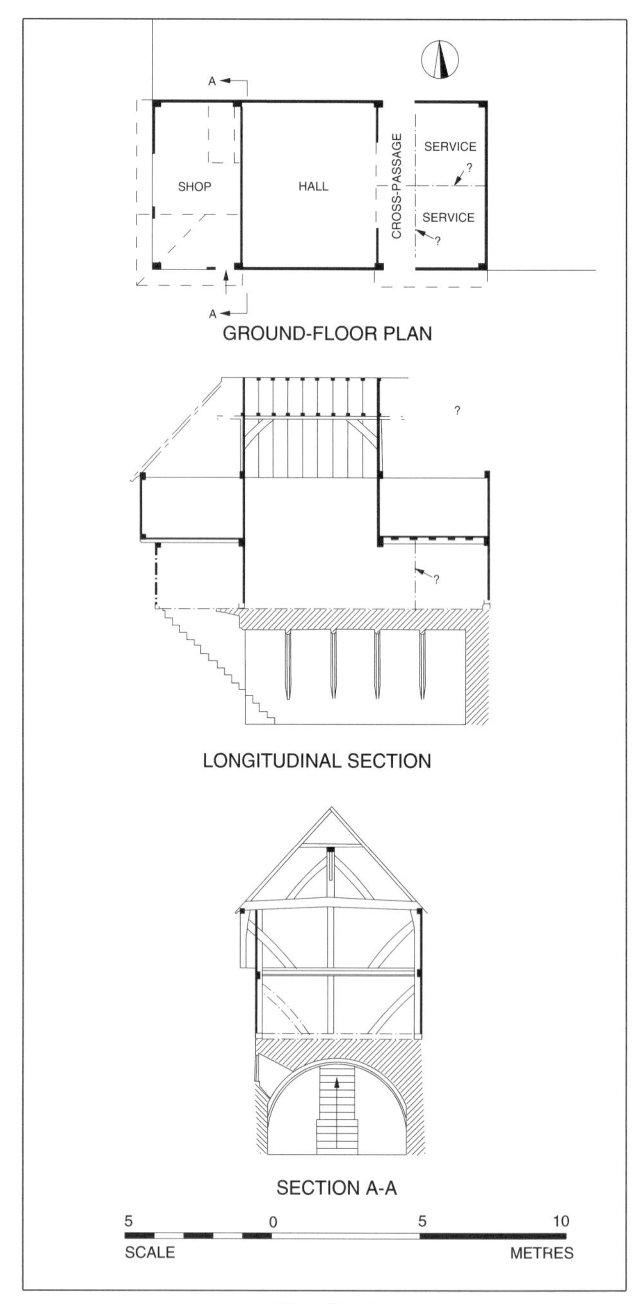

Fig. 10.16
The Retreat, Quarter 6. Reconstruction drawings of the house as rebuilt in the 15th century above the earlier cellar.

during this same period.

Houses incorporating open halls

Five of the 13 late-medieval houses can be shown to have incorporated open halls, and it is likely that this was also the case in four others. Three of the five known examples occupy corner plots and four of the five are built with their long axis parallel to the street: only at Nesbit on Quarter 13 is the building turned through 90 degrees. Five Chimneys on the southwest corner of Quarter 1 (Figure 10.15) and The Retreat on the southwest corner of Quarter 6 (Figure 10.16) are of 'Wealden' design. That is, the front wall of their open hall abuts hard against the street, whilst the upper chambers beyond the ends of the hall projected out over the street to give an overhang or jetty. The whole building was in each case set under a single roof, and thus the upper part of the hall's front wall was recessed back from that of the flanking chambers and from the

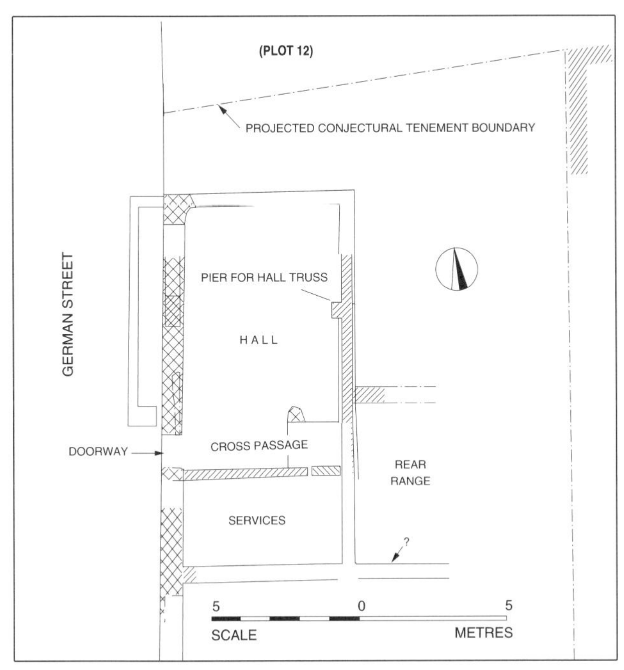

Fig. 10.17
Ground plan of the house upon Plot 11, Quarter 19, formed within the rear range of an earlier house during the mid/late 14th or early 15th century.

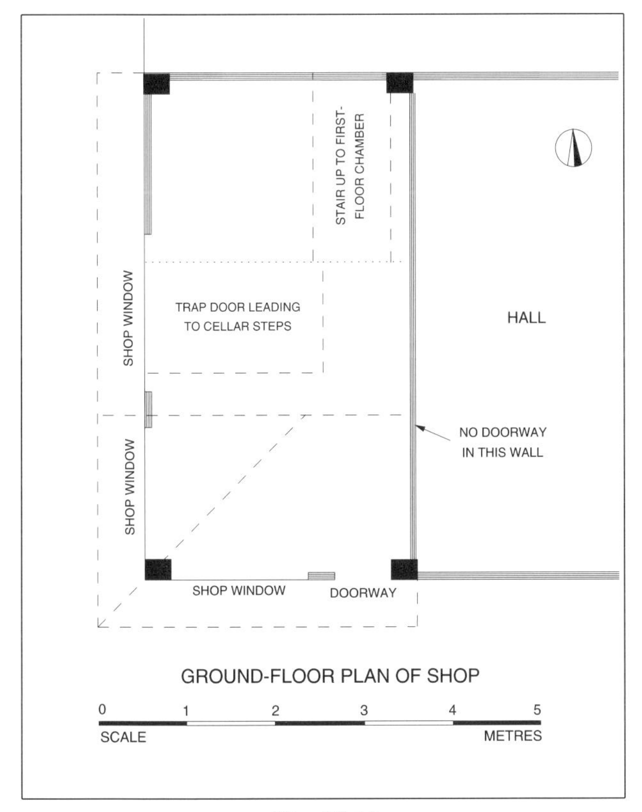

Fig. 10.18
Detail plan of the shop area within the western bay of The Retreat, Quarter 6, showing the relationship of doors and windows to the internal staircases.

roof's eaves. The only reason for building a house with a Wealden front was for visual effect; the design added considerably to construction costs without giving any practical advantages to the owner.

In addition to its Wealden front, Five Chimneys, shown in Figure 10.15, had an aisle extending along the rear of the property. A second single-aisled building within the town is known from archaeological excavations. This was the hall built to replace the *c.*1300 range facing onto German Street at the southwest corner of Quarter 19 (Figure 10.17). As the longitudinal sections in Figures 10.15 and 10.16 illustrate, the halls in both Five Chimneys and The Retreat had only one bay open to the roof, though beyond this, at the 'low end', was a cross-passage 'overshot' by the first-floor chamber over the services. In contrast, the excavated example from Quarter 19 had a large, two-bayed open hall and here the arcade between the main body of the hall and its rear aisle appears not to have incorporated an arcade post at the open truss dividing the two bays. This suggests that the open truss incorporated a base cruck, sling brace or hammer beam in order to keep the floor of the hall free from posts.[12]

In all of the houses mentioned above, the area beyond one end of the open hall could have contained a shop/workshop area within it, but only at The Retreat can the existence of such a feature be proven. Here, what would normally be regarded as the inner private room beyond the high end of the hall formed a shop with shop windows in its two street-facing walls. As Figure 10.18 shows, the shop was entered directly from the street via a narrow 'squeeze door' at the eastern end of the southern shop window. A trap door in the floor of the shop was the only means of access to a vaulted cellar beneath the house, whilst a staircase in the northeast corner led to the first-floor chamber. There was no internal doorway giving access between the shop and the hall, and therefore both the shop and the first-floor chamber above it, as well as the cellar beneath, could have been rented out separately from the remainder of the house.

It is worth stressing that all the late-medieval houses considered so far are not at all 'urban' in their design in that all appear to have been of standard plan, with layouts which would not have been out of place in any local small town, village or rural situation. The same is true of Salutation Cottages on the southeast corner of Quarter 2 (Figure 10.19) and the small two-bayed house called 'Crowsnest' on the Strand below the town (Figure 10.20). Crowsnest is tiny - only 7.90 metres by 4.80 metres (25ft.11ins. by 15ft.9ins.) overall – and, not surprisingly, is of contracted form, incorporating a single-bayed hall at one end with an overshot cross-passage and what appears to have been a standard service area at the other. Salutation Cottages is a more substantial house with a storeyed, high-end 'parlour' bay

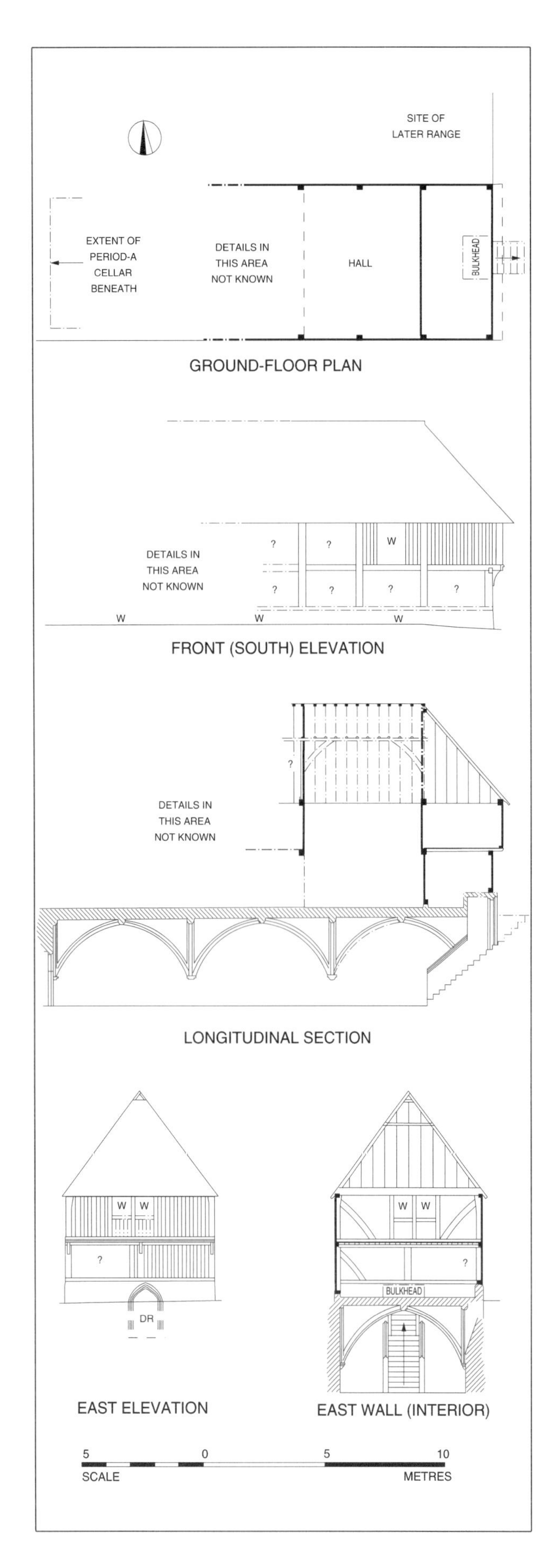

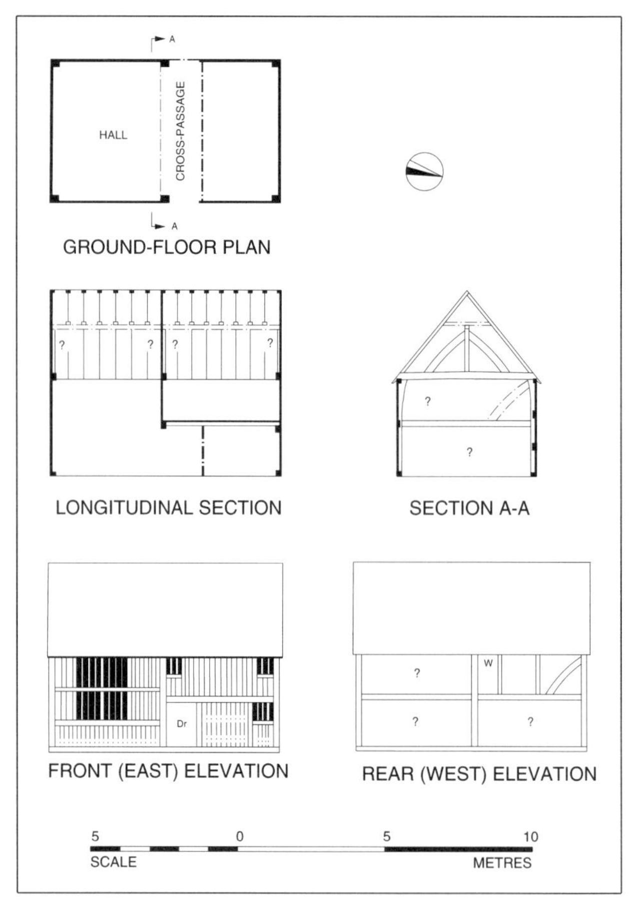

Fig. 10.20 (Above)
Crowsnest, The Strand. Reconstruction drawings of a small late-15th-century, two-cell hall house.

Fig. 10.19 (Left)
Salutation Cottages, Quarter 2. Reconstruction drawings of the house as rebuilt in the 15th century above the earlier cellar.

and an open hall, which appears to have been of two open bays rather than one. The arrangement beyond the low end of the hall has been lost owing to later modifications and partial reconstruction.

In contrast to the examples above, the medieval house incorporated within the eastern end of present day 'Nesbit' on Quarter 13, fronting the High Street, is wholly urban in its design. Probably dating from the late 14th or early 15th century, it is a relatively wide and lofty house built gable towards the street, with its open hall set back one room from the road (Figure 10.21, left in plan). It shows evidence of having incorporated a first-floor internal gallery running along the side of its open hall (now demolished) and linking the first-floor chambers at each end of the hall. This is a classic design found in densely built-up urban centres, a particularly fine and very complete example being 58 French Street, Southampton.[13] Adjoining Nesbit, and

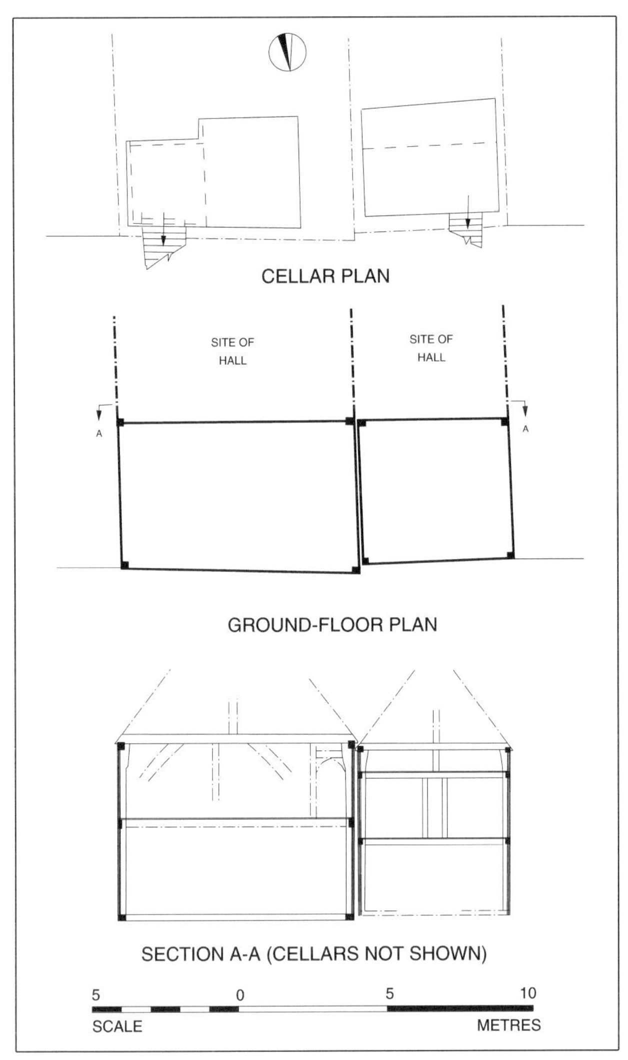

Fig. 10.21
Nesbit, High Street, Quarter 13. Reconstruction drawings showing the remains of two timber-framed houses built end-on to the street.

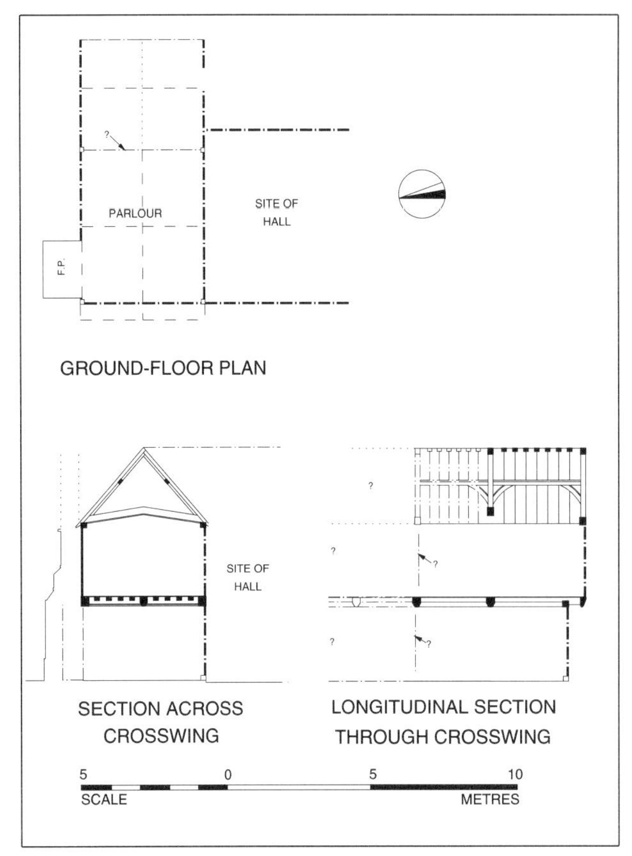

Fig. 10.22
Glebe, Quarter 13. Reconstruction drawings showing the remains of the crosswing.

now incorporated into it, is the front bay of a much narrower house, likewise turned end on to the street and of similar height, though in this instance having two-and-a-half storeys (Figure 10.21, right in plan). Whether the hall behind this bay was open or floored-over is not known: the former is the more likely.

Three other late-medieval houses which could have incorporated open halls survive within the town. On the western side of Quarter 13 is a house now known as 'Glebe' (Figure 10.22). It incorporates a high-quality, two-cell northern crosswing, formerly jettied towards the street and with moulded ceiling beams which indicate the high status of the crosswing's ground-floor front room, which is assumed to have been used as a parlour. Heated by a chimney built against its northern wall, this crosswing was almost certainly built in 1477 by Marline Farncombe. In that year she acquired from her neighbour a plot measuring 7ft.4ins. by 3ft.3ins. (2.35 metres by 1 metre), presumably in order to build this chimney upon it.[14] The main range to the south of the crosswing was rebuilt in 1583, but from the few details which remain, this is presumed to have incorporated an open hall. Strand House on the Strand, and number 7/8 High Street on the southern side of Quarter 8 may also have incorporated open halls, but are now too altered to be certain. Strand House is a particularly wide and low-walled building which presents many problems of interpretation. Number 7/8 High Street has either been truncated at its western end or was built against a neighbouring house now demolished. From the information available, it seems less likely to have had an open hall (Figure 10.23). Half of the present structure was occupied by a large ground-floor two-bayed room, whilst above it was a two-bayed chamber incorporating an open truss.

Houses without open halls

Four 15th-century domestic buildings within the town can be shown to have been built without open halls, and as a group these are far more urban in their

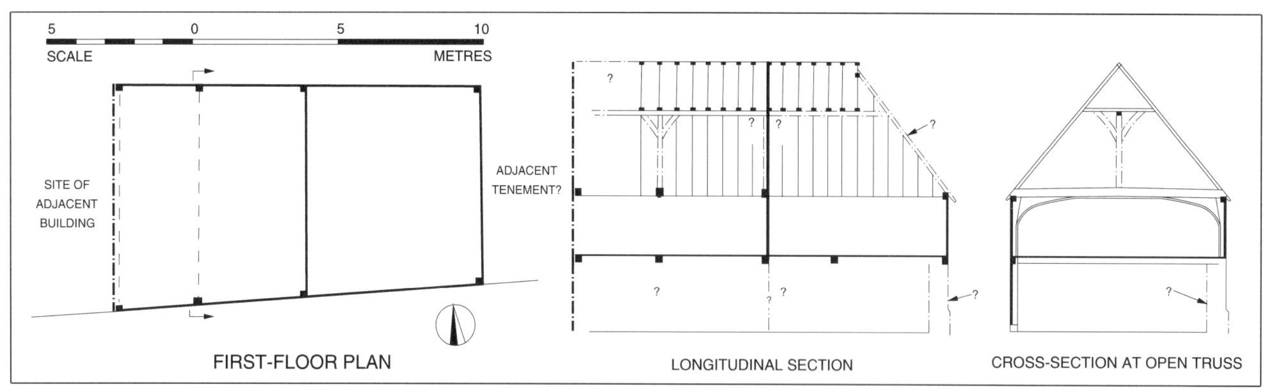

Fig. 10.23. 7/8 High Street, Quarter 8.
Reconstruction drawings showing the building as it existed in the late 15th century.

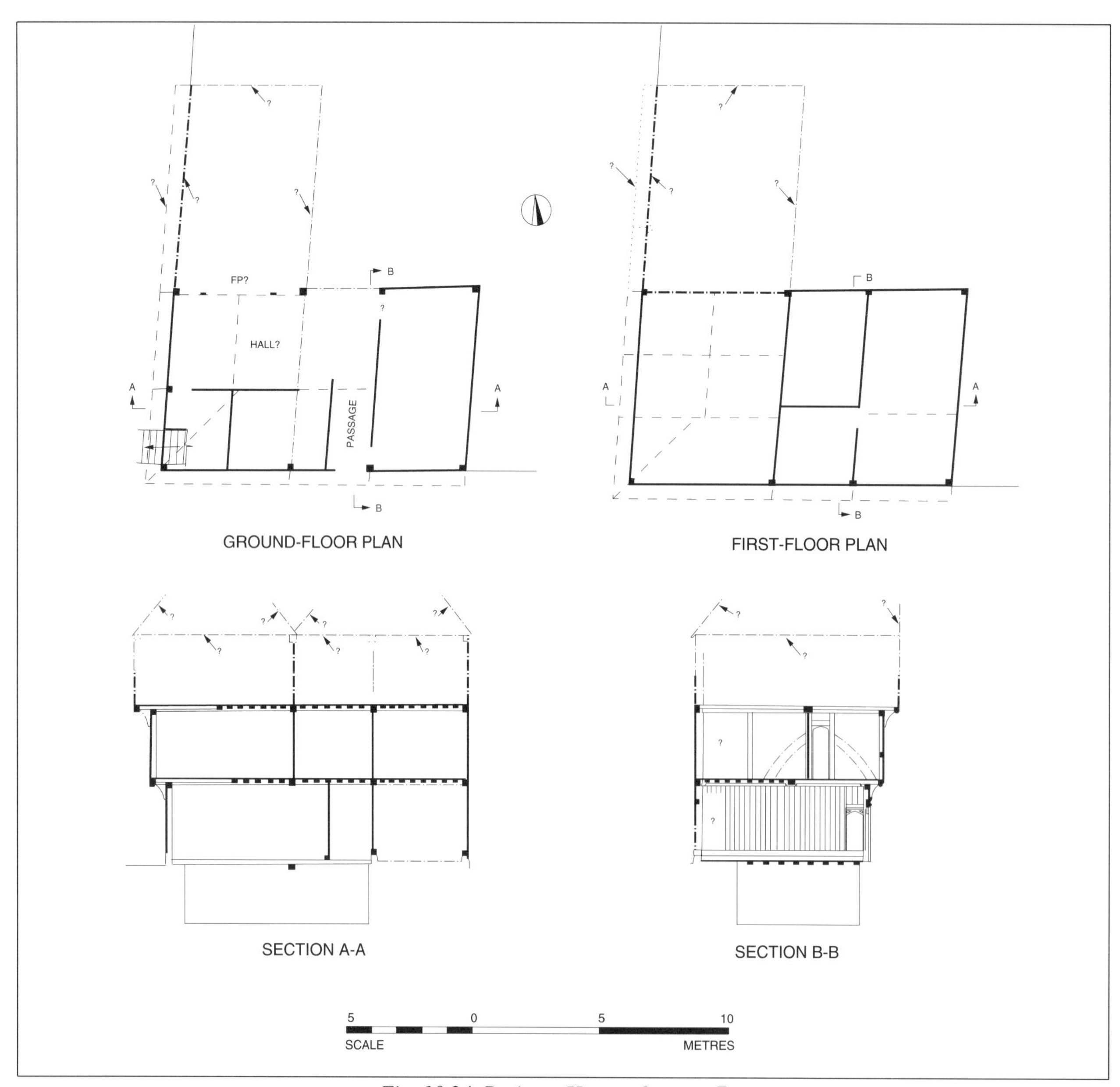

Fig. 10.24 Periteau House, Quarter 7.
Reconstruction drawings of a former jettied three-storeyed merchant's house occupying a corner plot.

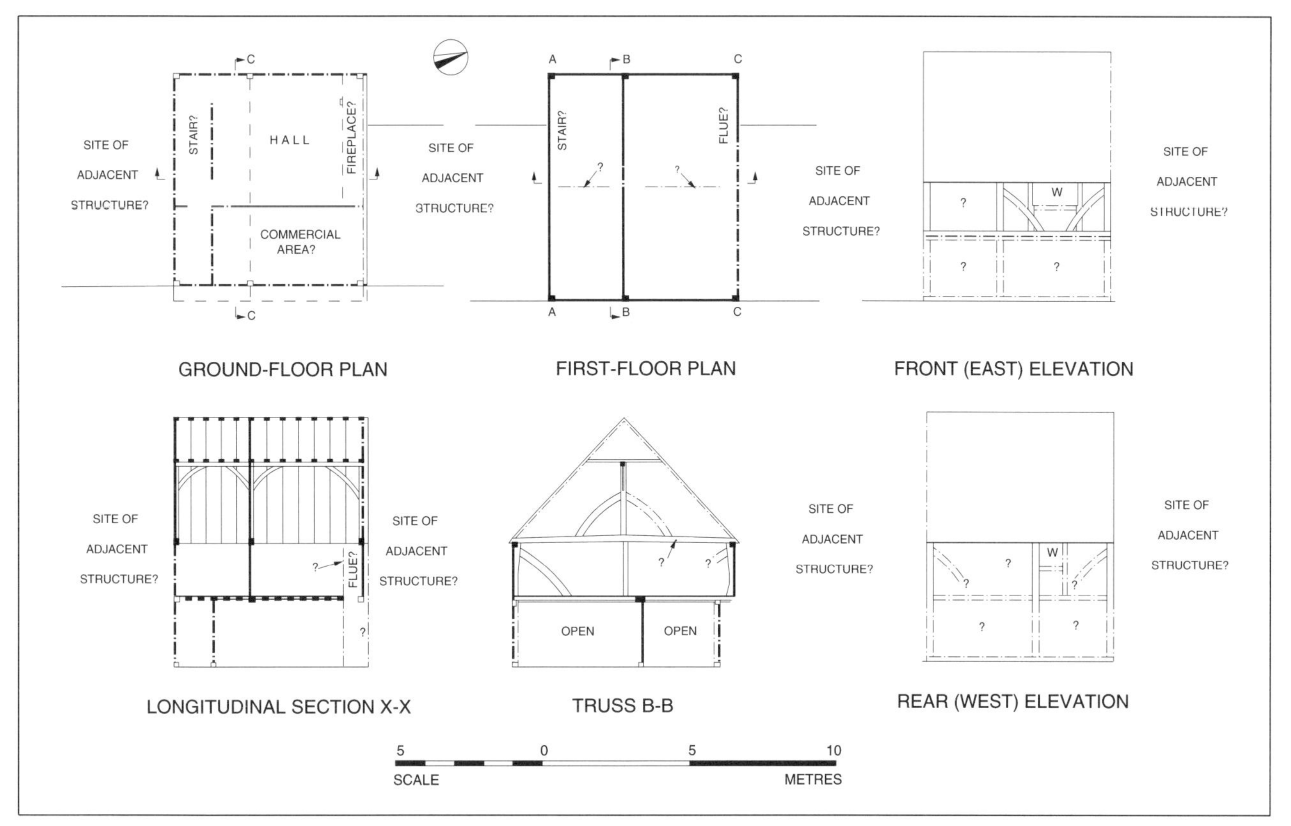

Fig. 10.25. 2 Friars Road, Quarter 19.
Reconstruction drawings of a short and exceptionally wide house of specialized plan.

character than the hall houses. For the location of these buildings *see* Figure 10.14. Wren Cottage on the southern side of the High Street (on Quarter 13) is probably the earliest and may date from the first half of the 15th century. Its eastern neighbour, 11/12 High Street, tree-ring dated to 1477-1501, is a single structure which incorporates two properties under the same roof. Likewise, tree-ring analysis indicates a date of 1482-1499 for number 2 Friars Road on the eastern side of Quarter 19.[15] The constructional details of Periteau House, which occupies the southwest corner of Quarter 7, suggests a very similar date for that building too.

Without doubt, Periteau House was the most costly and visually spectacular of this group. Despite its present early/mid-18th-century two-storeyed appearance, it was built as an 'L'-plan, three-storeyed house with two tiers of continuous jetties extending along its two street facades (Figure 10.24). The ceilings incorporate heavy, neatly-finished joists, moulded crossbeams and board-panels set within grooves cut into the sides of the joists, all wholly consistent with the building's high status (*see* below). Nothing is known regarding the layout of the second floor, this storey having been removed in the 18th century, but the other two floors were divided into a number of areas of which the largest was the first-floor chamber at the corner of the property. On the ground floor is a hall-like room heated by a large late-16th- or 17th-century fireplace which may have been built upon the site of a predecessor. One or more of the three ground-floor rooms fronting onto the High Street could have had a commercial function. Beneath the southwestern corner is a probably pre-existing, un-vaulted cellar, which was itself directly accessible from the western street. This building was the capital messuage (principal house) of Richard Barkeley, and it was probably he who had it rebuilt. His heirs held it in 1529. It was sold in 1541 to Thomas Hinxstead of Winchelsea, 'merchant'.[16]

A boarded ceiling similar to that at Periteau House appears to exist at Glebe, on Quarter 13, within the crosswing of 1477 (*see* above) and another example is to be seen at 2 Friars Road, Quarter 19, located in the area known in the 15th and 16th centuries as The Butchery (Figure 10.25). Constructed 1482-1499, 2 Friars Road is a very short building with a continuously-jettied street frontage of only 6.45 metres (21ft.1ins.), but it is wide, measuring 7.55 metres (24ft.9ins.) from front to back. Even so, it is roofed parallel to the street under a single span. On the ground floor the plan is two-rooms deep - a relatively small front commercial area with a heated main room (or floored-over hall) to the rear. The latter was accessed from the street via an internal passage

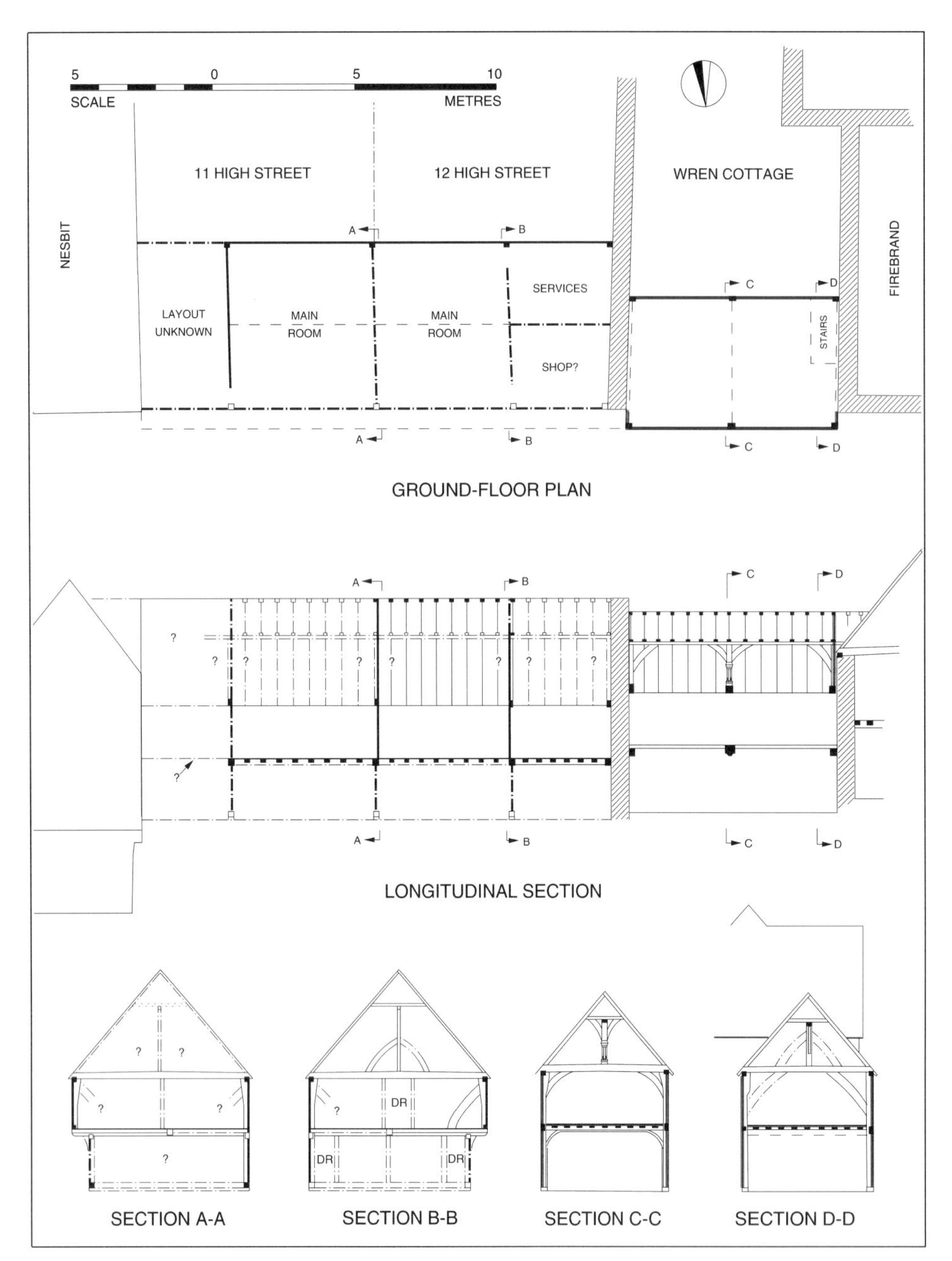

Fig. 10.26 (Left) 11-12 High Street and Wren Cottage, Quarter 13. Reconstruction drawings of three medieval houses without open halls.

against the south wall. On the first floor two unequal bays divide the building along its length into two chambers, but whether these were also sub-divided by an axial partition (as is the case now) is unclear. Despite the relatively small size of the building, the finish is good and a reasonable suite of rooms is included.

Wren Cottage in High Street, immediately to the east of the large stone house of *c.*1300 called Firebrand, is probably the earliest in the group (Figure 10.26, right). The site upon which it is constructed was granted to the church of St Thomas in 1423/4, but whether the present building already existed at that date or was built subsequently is impossible to tell from the surviving details.[17] Not including the stone boundary walls between which it is built, at 7.30 metres (24ft.) it has a similar length frontage to 2 Friars Road, but at only 4.50 metres (14ft.10ins.) wide, it is nonetheless much smaller. Constructed in two bays, this building consisted of just a single ground-floor room with one chamber above. Despite its small size, it is well-built and incorporates a moulded crossbeam within its ceiling and a finely moulded, free-standing crown-post within its upper chamber (*see* Figure 11.18). Surprisingly, given the evident quality of this building, there are no obvious signs of an original heating system.

Although each is of similar length to Wren Cottage, the pair of houses (11/12 High Street) to its east both comprise two bays and have an apparently unheated main room (?a single-bay, floored-over hall) with a smaller bay to one side (Figure 10.26, left). The smaller

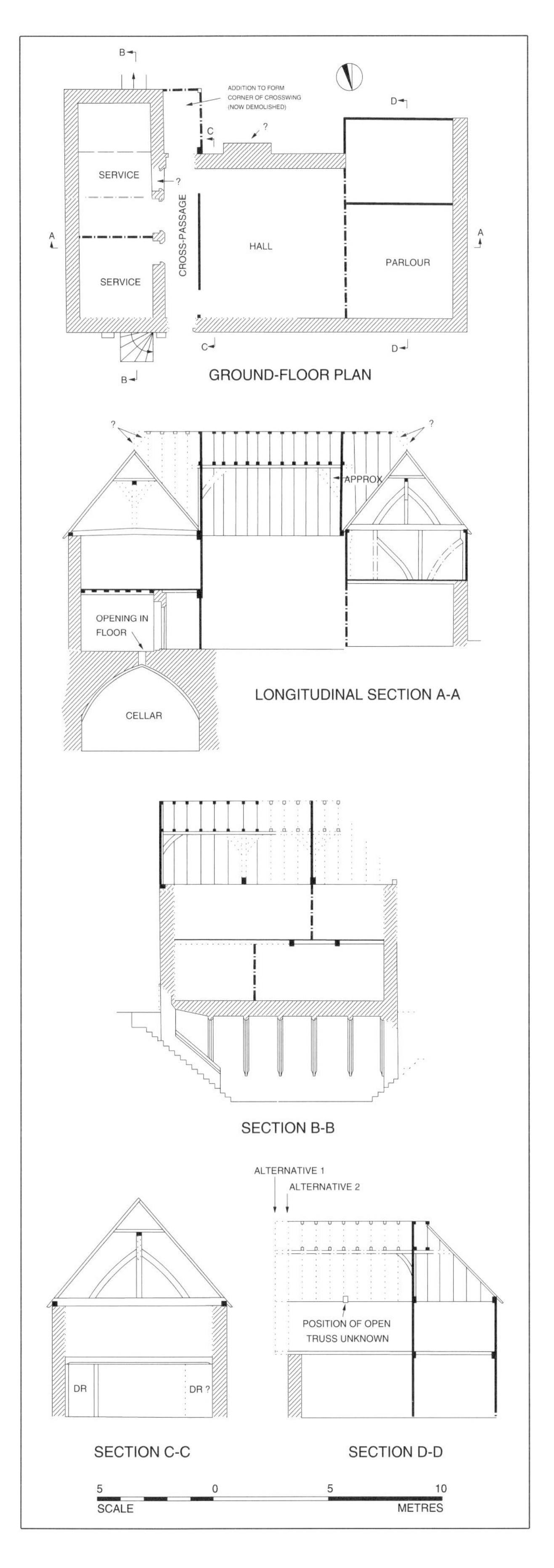

bay within the western house was originally divided into two rooms by an axial partition and, given the non-standard location of the doorways leading into these from the hall, it is quite possible that the front room served as a shop. The same arrangement may have existed in the eastern house too, though here the evidence is lost. Each house had two first-floor chambers. Of near identical size to each other, both houses are sited within the same continuously-jettied building and should be regarded as a handed semi-detached pair. As already noted, dendro-chronological analysis indicates that the building was constructed from timbers felled between 1477 and 1501.

Alterations to earlier buildings

It was during the 15th century that the *c.*1300 house at the southwest corner of Quarter 8 was modified to form the present Court Hall (for which *see* Chapter 6) and at least three of the other surviving early houses were likewise much altered at this same period. The timber-framed street range at Old Castle House was entirely rebuilt with close-studded internal partitions and a front jetty (*see* Figure 10.6). All timberwork within Firebrand was replaced during two phases of modification (Figure 10.27). The first phase, carried out *c.*1400, involved either reconstructing or remodelling the high-end crosswing. The second phase, in the 15th century, modified the service end by rebuilding the upper storey as a crosswing, thereby increasing the size of the low-end, first-floor accommodation by extending it into the hall, and converting the cross-entry at the low end of the hall into an overshot cross-passage. At The Armory a new, substantial, northern rear range was added. This possibly replaced the southern rear range, although - depending upon its width - the southern range may not have been demolished until later. The new range has a continuous southern jetty facing towards the rear yard and a northern wall of stone running along the boundary of the property (*see* Figure 10.28).

The alterations of this period were not restricted to those early houses which still survive today: the two most extensively excavated houses within the town show similar modifications. Probably during the mid/late 14th century, but perhaps in the early 15th century, the narrow *c.*1300 range abutting German Street, on the southwest corner of Quarter 19 was reconstructed as a single-aisled hall house, which was probably occupied independently of the attached structure to the south, facing the market square (*see* above). This new

Fig. 10.27 (Left) Firebrand, Quarter 13. Reconstruction drawings of the house as it existed late in the 15th century, after the end chambers had been reconstructed as crosswings.

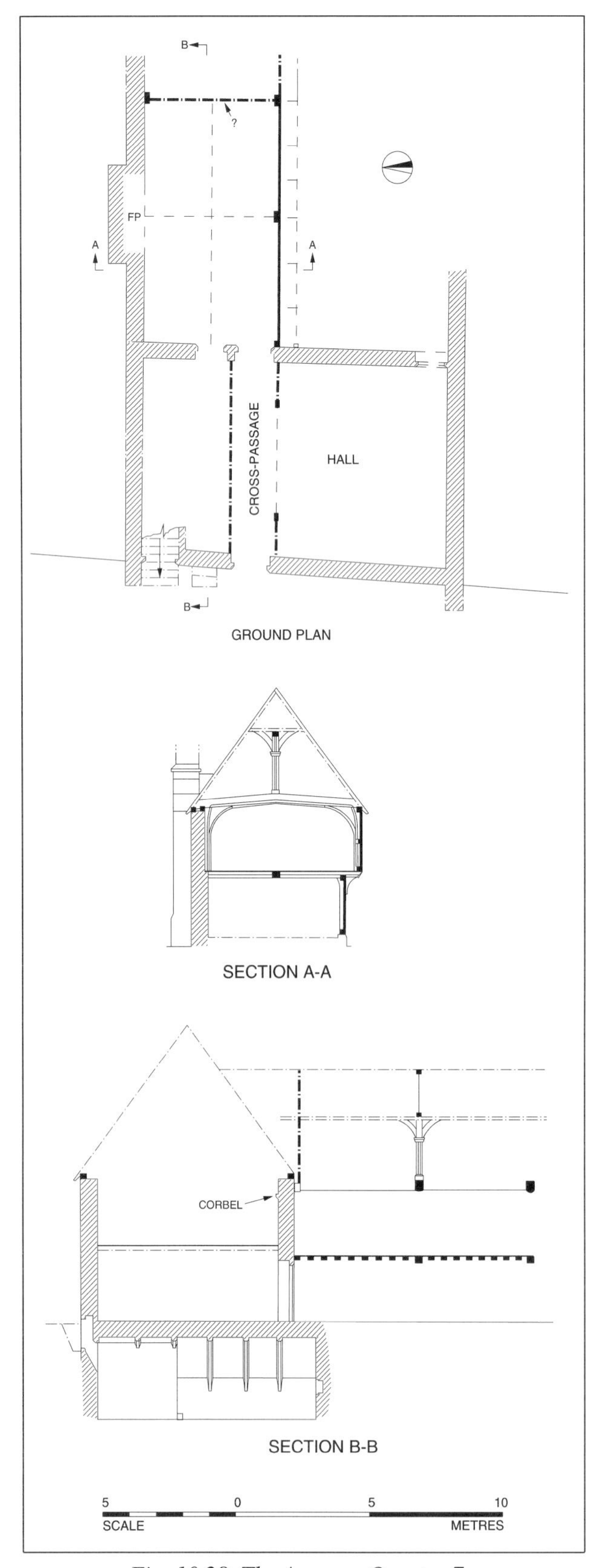

Fig. 10.28 The Armory, Quarter 7. Reconstruction drawings showing the house as it existed in c.1500. The northern rear range represents a late-medieval addition.

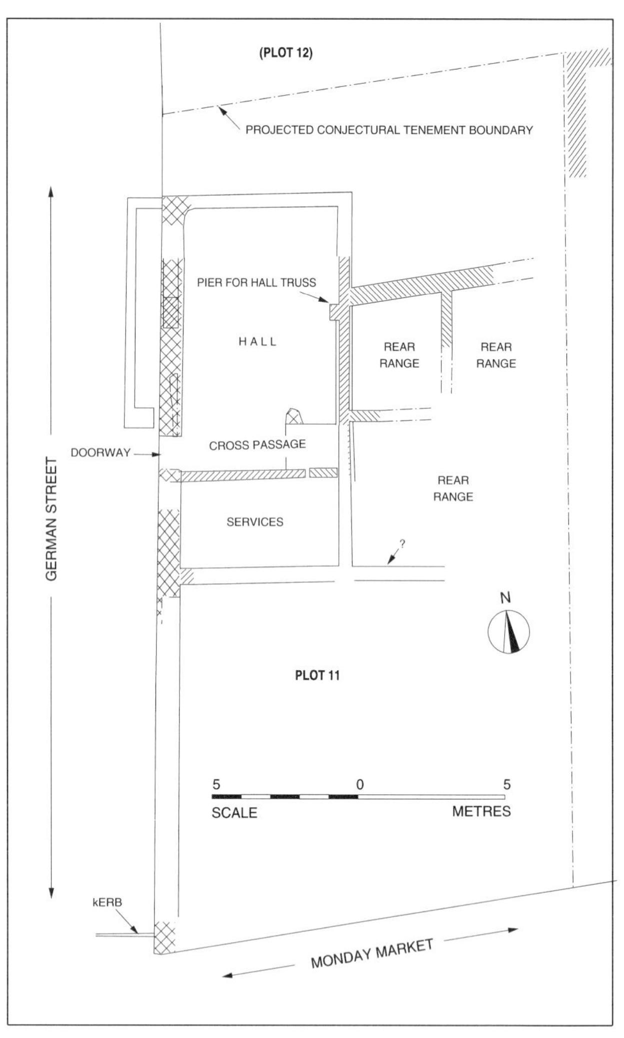

Fig. 10.29
Ground plan of the house upon Plot 11, Quarter 19 showing the alterations and additions made to the rear late in the medieval period.

northern house incorporated a contemporary, or near contemporary rear range extending back from the ?services and cross-passage at the low end of the hall. The rear range was itself rebuilt subsequently on a larger scale. Thus, as Figure 10.29 shows, by the end of the medieval period the corner plot had not only been divided to give two separate occupancies, but most of the plot had been built upon leaving very little open space.[18]

An even more complex evolution can be recognized on the plot immediately to the north of the building now known as 'Blackfriars Barn', on the eastern side of Quarter 15. As has already been noted in the discussion of early houses, the initial building upon this site was either of 'L'-plan or, more likely, consisted of a rectangular block set beneath two roofs aligned at right angles to the street. It incorporated an open hall within its northeast corner, facing onto the street (*see* above and Figure 10.9). The subsequent modifications are

Fig. 10.30 The house upon plot 21, Quarter 15.
The complex sequence of alterations carried out during the 14th and 15th centuries.

illustrated in Figure 10.30. Probably during the middle years of the 14th century the southern range was extended back as far as a garderobe block serving the adjacent building. At the same time modifications were made to the internal layout, and these included the construction of a flight of steps allowing internal access to the extensive vaulted cellar beneath the adjacent building. Subsequently, the cross-passage at the southern end of the hall was extended back in the form of a covered way in order to give sheltered access from the house to the garderobe, which was by then either shared or, more probably, used solely by the occupants of this house.

Prior to the close of the 14th century the size of the house was again markedly increased by the construction of a second rear range, which filled in the space between the covered way and the northern boundary. Incorporated within the thickness of its masonry northern wall was a fireplace, probably served by a projecting canopy. During the 15th century the garderobe fell out of use and the cesspit which served it was filled in. The area was then converted to use as a kitchen served by a large hearth built over the cesspit. The masonry walls forming the eastern half of the garderobe block were removed in order to increase the size of the kitchen, which was laid open to the covered way. Other internal alterations included the insertion of two new hearths, one in the added south range and the other within the added north range, replacing the earlier hearth incorporated within the northern boundary wall. In addition, the southern end of the timber-framed street facade of the house was removed at ground-floor level (and perhaps on the first floor too) and the building was extended out into the street for an unknown distance. Encroachments of this type are usually associated with commercial activity, suggesting that this part of the house was by this date (and perhaps from the outset) in use as a shop. Immediately to the north of the street encroachment was the main entrance to the house. Beyond it a wall was found and was interpreted as the base of a bench or stall running along the front wall of the open hall. Whether intended for sitting, or for the display of goods, is not clear.[19] A similar feature was found running along the front of the hall within the house excavated upon Quarter 19.

THE CONTEXT OF THE EARLY- AND LATE-MEDIEVAL HOUSES

When considering the relevance of Winchelsea's surviving and excavated houses the dearth of available information should always be borne in mind. The best estimates suggest that the early medieval houses, which either survive or have been revealed by excavation, represent no more than 1 in 60 of the houses which existed in *c.*1300. By *c.*1500 this figure increases to perhaps 1 in 10, but only because of the dramatic reduction in the number of households within the town. For the same reason, about a quarter of the houses which existed in the mid-16th century still remain today. Where the houses survive, in many instances the data are very incomplete.

Given these numbers, it would be foolish to draw anything more than the most general conclusions concerning the town's medieval housing stock. Nevertheless, it is useful to consider a number of general matters. For example, the unusual circumstances of New Winchelsea's founding must have had an effect on the form of the town's earliest houses. Because (Old) Winchelsea was at that time under imminent threat of being washed away, the residents had no choice but to move. In this important respect (New) Winchelsea differs from most other towns, even the other new towns of the period. For the residents of (Old) Winchelsea the upheaval must have been both an emotional strain and a financial disaster. For most the financial burden would have been particularly severe, for although there can be no doubt that at this period (Old) Winchelsea was a thriving and prosperous port, the vast bulk of the wealth would almost certainly have been concentrated in the hands of a tiny minority, most notably the leading ship owners and merchants. These privileged citizens would, no doubt, have weathered the financial strain of building anew without too much difficulty, and may even have seen it as an exciting new challenge.

For the majority of the population, however, one imagines that it would have been a struggle for them to organize a temporary roof over their heads, whilst at the same time continuing to earn a living. This situation would have been aggravated by the sheer scale of the disaster: re-housing so many families, whilst at the same time building from scratch the infrastructure of a major new town, would have resulted in a scarcity both of materials and of skilled builders. It is doubtless true that some materials would have been salvaged from the old town and some of the prefabricated timber-framed houses may have been carefully taken apart, transported, and re-erected. Even so, it seems a fair guess that for a large proportion of the town's population, the best they would have achieved was a temporary home designed to survive for a short time as a stopgap until circumstances permitted the construction of a more suitable replacement. Entire areas of the new town must have resembled a shantytown, and even in the commercial heart, there would have been second- and third-rate houses intermixed with the premises of the wealthier merchant classes. These poorer buildings would probably have lasted for one, or, at most, two generations. Under favourable economic conditions most would no doubt have been replaced by better, more permanent structures long before they reached the point of collapse. However, the economic downturn experienced by the town during the 1340s and 1350s, coupled with the major decrease in population which followed and the subsequent abandonment of the peripheral quarters late in the century, raises questions as to how many owners would have managed to rebuild their 'temporary' structures before the town shrank to its 15th-century size.

Another preconception which perhaps needs to be reconsidered is the tendency to think of all major medieval urban centres as being dominated by buildings designed for manufacture and trade, with areas set aside for use as retail shops, workshops, warehouses, taverns and the like. There is plenty of evidence that shops (sometimes used solely for retail, sometimes doubling as workshops) as well as warehouses were widespread in medieval towns by the early 14th century. Indeed, in the more important urban centres, shops, workshops and warehouses dominated the frontages of some streets. Some of these buildings were lock-ups, in others the domestic quarters of the occupier were relegated to the rear of the building or to the upper floor(s), away from the street. Yet this view should not be overstated. It might have been true of the commercial heart of a major town, around the market, along the principal streets, and perhaps concentrated at other focal points such as the main gate of a castle or monastery, but it is important to remember that away from these areas the streets were often much more residential with a less dense concentration of shops or, perhaps, no shops at all.

Although true of any inland town or city, the number of purely residential properties increased markedly within the ports, where a high proportion of the townsfolk were either seafarers (including fishermen) or served as labourers servicing the quayside and harbour. Others were involved in related occupations such as shipbuilding and repair, rope-making and other occupations which needed specialist premises next to the waterfront, away from the housing. With any port the proportion of the population employed as seafarers would have depended upon a number of factors, the most obvious being the size of the fleet and the size of the individual ships within that fleet. But it would also have been influenced by the degree to which the port town was dependent upon its ships. Some towns would have all but collapsed economically if robbed of their harbour: others were sufficiently important as centres of trade and manufacture to survive regardless. In a port town of the latter sort, the ratio of seafarers and others working in associated service occupations to townsfolk employed in trade and manufacture would have been far lower than in a port which relied heavily upon its harbour. All the available documentary details suggest that both Winchelsea and its near neighbour, Rye, were very heavily reliant upon their port. In 1565 Rye had 66 ships and boats of all sorts and of very variable size. Seafaring families accounted for 54% of the town's 530 households.[20] At the height of its prosperity during the early years of the 14th century, the proportion of seafaring households in Winchelsea must have been at least equal to that of Rye in the mid-16th century, and probably higher.

As an indication of the number of men needed to sail the larger ships engaged in long-distance trade and deep-sea fishing, the 13 Winchelsea ships engaged in the King's service in 1295 were manned by a total of 589 men, each ship having a master, a constable, and between 33 and 48 mariners, depending upon its size.[21] These 13 ships accounted for only part of town's sea-going fleet. In 1326 a total of 31 Winchelsea ships of between 55 and 250 tons, which would otherwise have been engaged in crossing to Gascony and Peyto in quest of wine, was arrested for King's service. Based upon the crew sizes of ships of comparable size, they would have required around 900 men to sail them.[22] Although unlikely, it is possible that this complement included Winchelsea's entire fleet of sea-going merchant ships, but it certainly excluded the smaller vessels engaged in daily fishing and coastal trade, the class of vessel which in Rye in 1565 employed by far the largest number of men. In 1347, when Winchelsea's vessels were perhaps of smaller average size, the town supplied to the king 21 ships sailed by 596 mariners.[23] In 1335/6, at the beginning of the Hundred Years' War, the crew aboard Winchelsea's ships of 100-160 tons had been increased to a master, constable, 3 or 4 boys and between 55 and 75 mariners and archers, the additional men being necessary in case of engagement with the enemy.[24] By 1565, when Winchelsea's harbour had silted and the town had reduced to only 109 households, the town had just 12 small boats (*i.e.* one hoy, six cockboats and five lighters) and there were only ten mariners and two fishermen resident. By contrast, the Corporation archives from the same period record at least seven tailors and seven innkeepers, not to mention butchers and an assortment of other trades.[25]

It is in this context that the houses described in the first part of this chapter should be considered. The seven early buildings which survive are of stone, and to these can be added a number of others known either from excavations, from structural details contained within cellars, or through casual documentary references. Until 1563 stone, timber, brick and other building materials could be taken out of the town without licence, and there is therefore no way of judging how many stone houses had been demolished prior to that date.[26] That stone houses were amongst those being destroyed thereafter is well illustrated by the 23 separate licences granted for the removal of stone between 1563 and 1624 and this was in addition to a general decree made in 1608 allowing any man to convey ragstone (*i.e.* Tilgate stone) out of the town for one year without penalty. The figure quoted above excludes one licence to dig stone from a cellar. A licence granted in 1596 was for the removal

Fig. 10.31
Exterior of The Armory (Quarter 7) as it existed in c.1900. [Hastings Museum and Art Gallery]

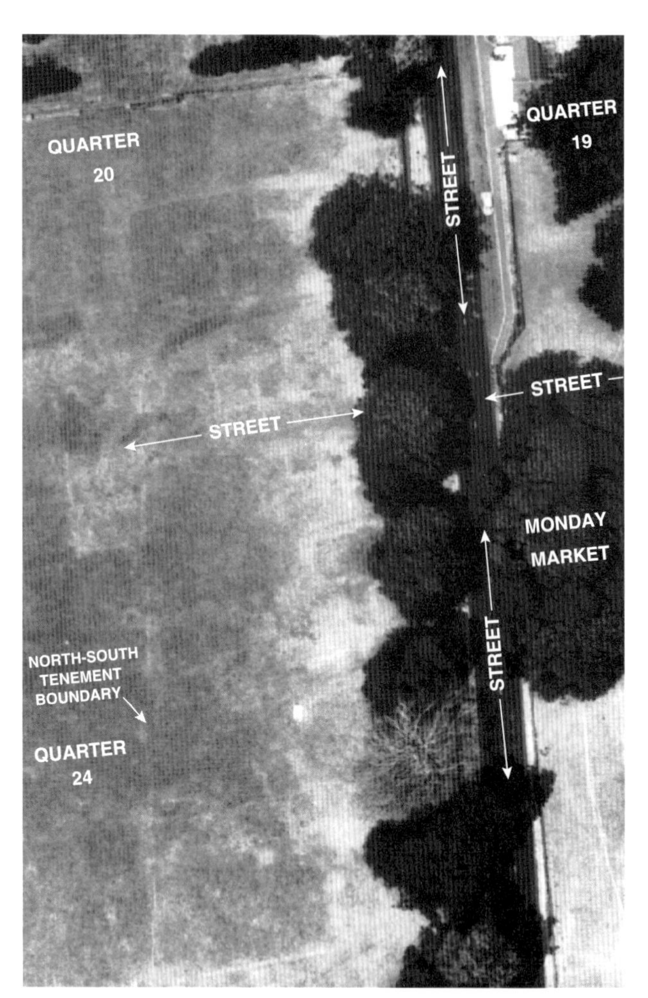

Fig. 10.32
Extract from an aerial photograph showing the eastern parts of Quarters 20 and 24. Note parch marks indicating the complex layout of the substantial houses which once fronted onto 'Great Street' and Monday Market (now German Street and Monk's Walk). (© Copyright reserved Cambridge University Collection of Aerial Photographs. Ref BZQ 58 taken on 12 July 1976).

from the town of a 'transom window of Caen stone'.[27] Although south-east England was an area of timber framing, stone houses can therefore be shown to have existed within the town in some numbers. Even so, they must always have represented a small minority of the total housing stock and were almost certainly the homes of the urban elite.

As the surviving and excavated remains show, even these houses sometimes mixed external walls of masonry and timber framing (*see* Old Castle House and the building adjacent to Blackfriars Barn described above). The ground-plan of two of the early houses (Firebrand on Quarter 13 and The Armory (formerly The Bear) on Quarter 7) are not what one would expect in the core area of a major urban centre (*see* Figure 10.31). Both are set longitudinally to the street in the manner of those found in small towns, or in the peripheral, under-developed suburban areas of larger towns. And there are other examples. Known from excavations, the 14th- or early-15th-century hall facing onto German Street, on the western side of Quarter 19 appears to have been very similar in size and layout to The Armory, whilst houses built in the late medieval period with their long axis against the street survive at Five Chimneys on Quarter 1, Salutation Cottages on Quarter 2, The Retreat on Quarter 6, and Crowsnest on the Strand. In addition, a lease granted by Battle Abbey in 1412 of a house on the western side of Quarter 18, states that the new tenant should 'repair and thereafter maintain the hall, the solars at its north and south ends, and a kitchen' indicating that here too the main part of the house was aligned along the street with rooms/chambers at both ends of the hall.[28]

The relatively generous street frontages allocated to many of the plots at the foundation of the town, however, must not allow these buildings to dominate our impression of medieval Winchelsea. Even amongst those plots which did incorporate generous frontages, a number of the early houses were built with wholly urban plan forms. For example, the ruin now called Blackfriars Barn and the excavated house which adjoined it are entirely urban in their form, as too were the two houses - Old Castle House and St Anthony's, on the eastern side of Quarter 8. Nor can the early houses which occupied the southwestern corners of Quarters 8 and 19 be described as non-urban in form. Despite the subsequent construction of a more standard hall house within the remains of the latter's rear range during the 14th or early 15th century, extensions in standard urban pattern increasingly encroached upon the rear yard of that plot. Both of these corner plots were subdivided to give additional building space, leaving very little of the plot undeveloped. On the opposite side of German Street to Quarter 19, on Quarters 20 and 24, parch marks in the field are evidence of a similar complex of substantially-built houses extending back from the street and occupying a large part of the plots (Figure 10.32). As with the house on the southwest corner of Quarter 19, these buildings on the eastern side of Quarter 24 fronted onto the market square.

As already discussed in Chapter 8, there is ample evidence to indicate that the back parts of the high-status plots, which extended across the full width of Quarters 8 and 19, were divided off for building, and those on the eastern side of Quarter 19 were themselves further subdivided along the street façade. This also happened elsewhere within the town. Of necessity, the houses on these subdivided plots, and on the other smaller plots too had a squashed 'urban' plan form. On Quarter 13, on the south side of High Street, there survives a group of five short-frontage plots whose street facades measure approximately 8.1 metres (26ft.7ins.), 5.1 metres (16ft.9ins.), 8.2 metres (26ft.10ins.), 8.2 metres (26ft.10ins.) and 7.8 metres (25ft.7ins) respectively. In two instances - both now incorporated into the house called Nesbit - the buildings were turned through 90 degrees to the street, whereas in each of the others, the accommodation was crammed into a single range roofed parallel to the street. This was also the case at 2 Friars Road. As already described, other compacted plan forms are known from excavations on Quarter 2, fronting onto North Street, and on Quarter 3 fronting onto Mill Road. Opposite the High Street group is Periteau House, again an entirely urban structure whose three jettied storeys occupied the corner of Quarter 7.

The observations above demonstrate that, at least within the northeast part of the town, houses were densely packed along the streets, despite the sometimes generous frontages of the plots. However, this does not indicate whether the principal streets were heavily commercialized. Given the small percentage of houses for which details are known, it is impossible to give a precise answer. The situation is complicated by the fact that the medieval town had two distinct phases to its life - the early prosperous period (up to *c.*1350) and the second phase during which the town was of much lesser importance (*c.*1350-1525). As has been shown, during the first phase the market - with its square doubtless surrounded by commercial properties - was located two blocks to the south of the main church in an area now occupied by fields. This is the area where, because of the narrow street frontages, the front parts of the buildings are most likely to have been dominated by trade premises, with residential occupation relegated to the rear of the plots. But, since only one plot has been partially excavated and parch marks are visible in only one small area, this view has yet to be fully substantiated.

During the second phase the market and commercial centre shifted to the area immediately to the north and east of the main church. For this period more evidence survives. Within the surviving houses of this period it is often impossible to tell whether the ground-floor rooms against the streets were put to commercial or residential use. However, the hall can usually be identified, and to certain extent its position in relation to the street indicates the degree of commercialization. The important factor is whether the hall, regardless of whether it was open to the roof or floored over, was located against the street or set back from it. In considering this point the large ruined building on Quarter 15 now known as Blackfriars Barn should be

Fig. 10.33
Reconstructed section of High Street in the early 16th century showing the surviving buildings and the location of their principal room (or hall) in relation to the street.

discounted because, although its hall is built hard against the street, the size of this room points to a specialized, probably public use. In any case there is a distinct possibility that it lay in ruins from the 1360s onwards.

Of the other surviving or excavated examples, in 19 instances sufficient detail remains to indicate the location of the hall. Of these, 12 were constructed with their halls against the street, and in only 7 were they set back to the rear, potentially leaving the whole frontage available for shops, warehouses, workshops or for study/office-like uses. Admittedly, even in those houses in which the hall was sited against the street, in no instance did it occupy the entire length of the frontage and thus part could have been put to commercial use. This was certainly the case at The Retreat on Quarter 6, and perhaps within the excavated house next to Blackfriars Barn on Quarter 15.

Assuming that these few surviving buildings are representative of the whole, they do not support the notion that Winchelsea incorporated streets wholly dedicated to trade and commerce. Out of the 19 houses, 14 are located within just two streets, both of which served as principal thoroughfares throughout the medieval period (*see* Chapter 4, Figures 4.4-4.6). In particular, the houses in High Street (Figure 10.33) are sited between the Strand Gate (leading up from the quay) and the site of the late-medieval market and court hall beside the main church.

In considering the implications of this, three caveats need to be taken into account. Firstly, the vaulted cellars accessed directly from the street: these must be considered as potential commercial space, even during this late period. Eight of the 14 buildings in the two streets mentioned above have such a cellar. Secondly, both Salutation Cottages (formerly The Salutation) and The Armory (formerly The Bear) may have served as taverns/inns during this period, as too may other houses in the sample. Their open halls therefore would probably have fulfilled a public, commercial function. Thirdly, in three 'houses' in High Street: Wren Cottage and numbers 11/12, there are no structural indications that they were heated. Although both 11 and 12 High Street each incorporated three ground-floor rooms and two upper chambers, Wren Cottage had but one room on each floor. Does the lack of a chimney indicate an alternative source of heat, such as a charcoal brazier?[29] With so little secure evidence it is difficult to take the debate any further.

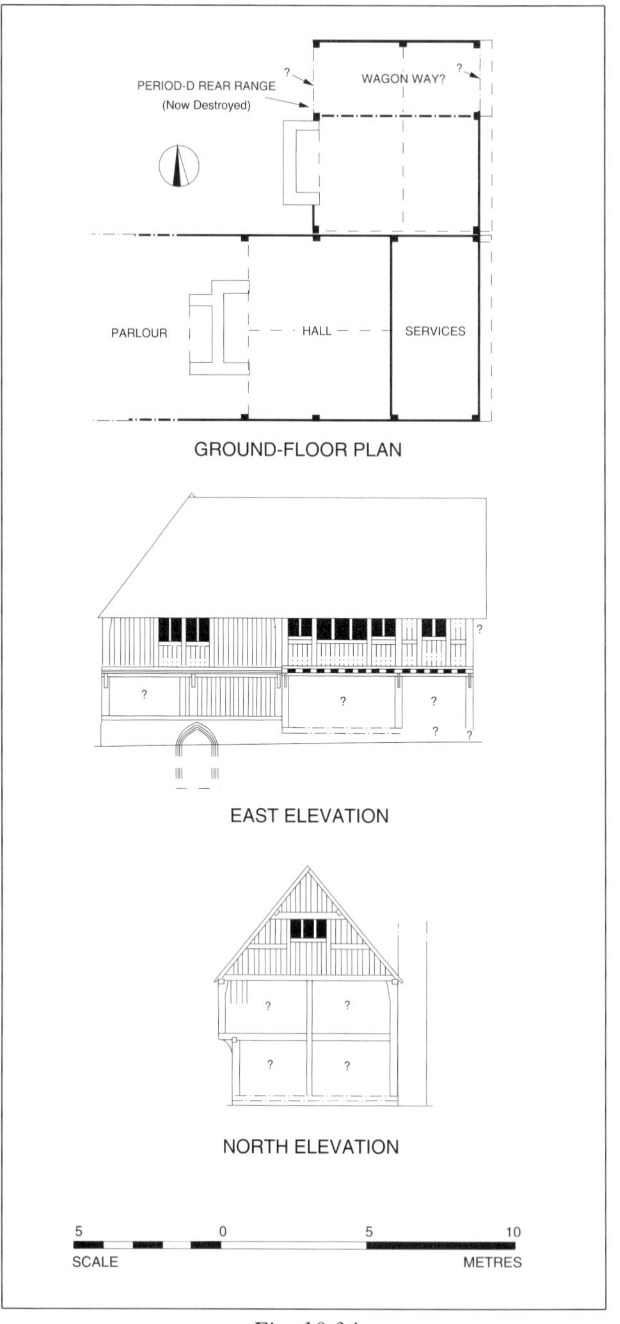

Fig. 10.34
Salutation Cottages, Quarter 2.
Reconstruction drawings showing details of the former rear range, added in c.1600.

THE POST-MEDIEVAL HOUSES (LATE 16TH CENTURY AND AFTER)

Given the number of houses which were either standing unoccupied or being demolished, it is perhaps not surprising that new houses were not being built within the town after the opening years of the 16th century. Indeed, in general new houses do not appear to have been constructed in Winchelsea until the middle years of the 18th century. One exception to this is the site adjacent to Blackfriars Barn on Quarter 15. The archaeological excavations upon this site indicate that it was during the mid/late 16th century that the complex medieval house described earlier was all but demolished

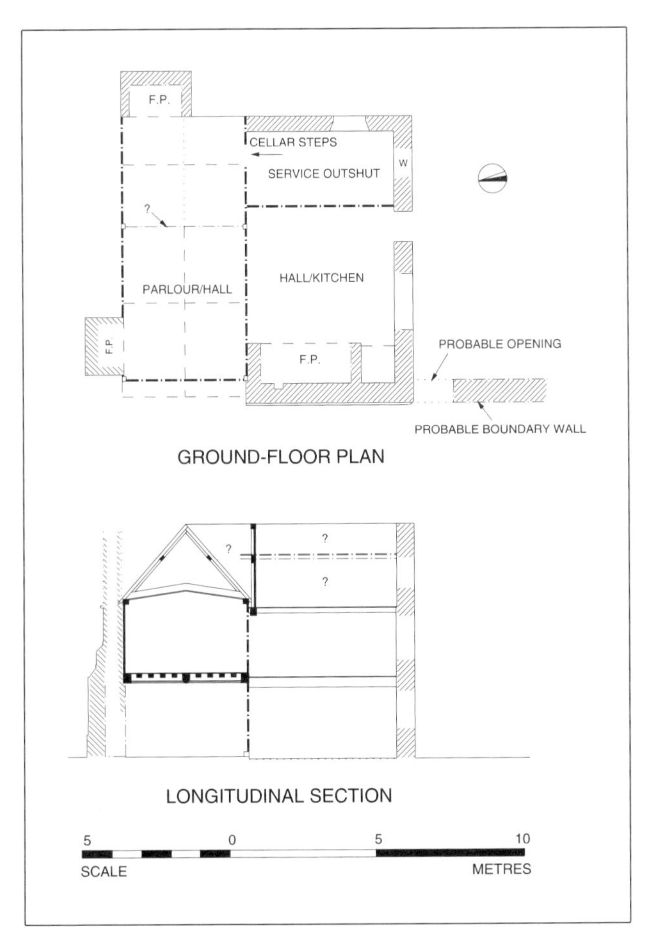

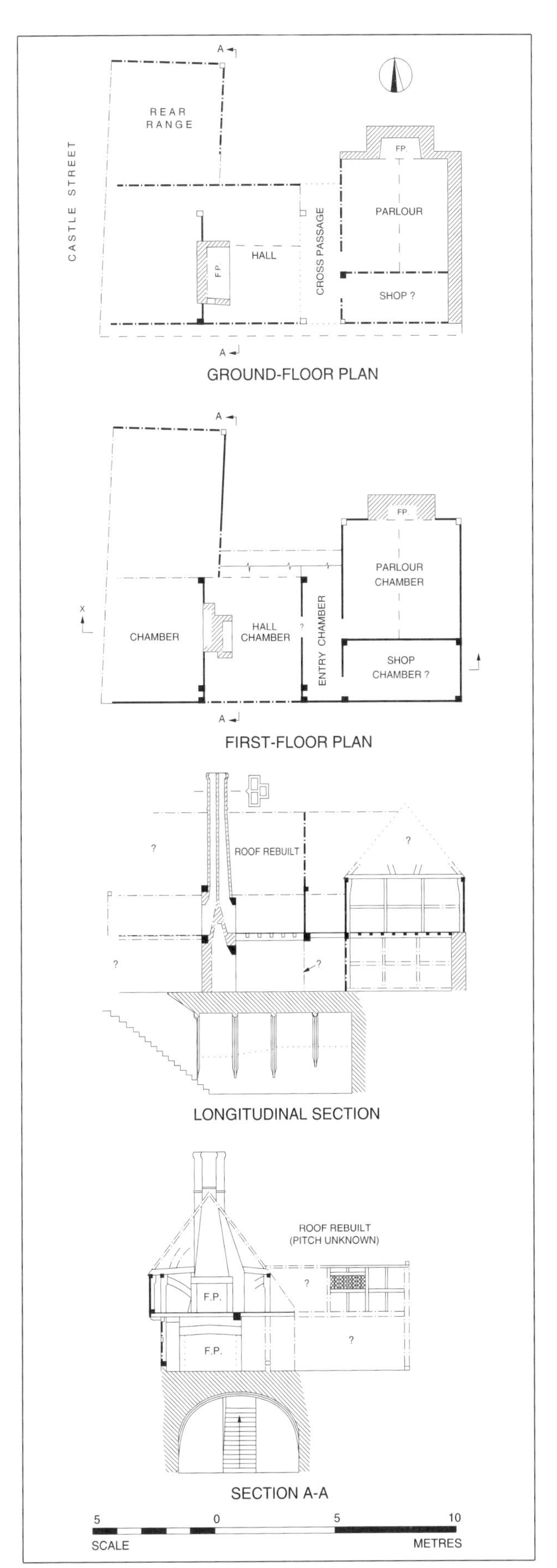

Fig. 10.35 (Above)
Glebe, Quarter 13, showing the rebuilt main range of 1583.

Fig. 10.36 (Right)
Five Chimneys, Quarter 1 showing the early 17th-century crosswing and rear range, together with the floor and chimney added into the open hall.

and rebuilt to a smaller size, though even this new house survived but a short period before itself being destroyed.

Although there was evidently no demand at this time for new houses, those earlier structures which remained in use continued to be upgraded. To put this into context, it should be borne in mind that although documents indicate the poor and lamentable state of the town as a whole during this period, a surprisingly high number of the inhabitants who remained were of relatively high status. In fact, the proportion of gentlemen and esquires living within the Borough was far higher than in other communities of similar size. It should not, therefore, be surprising to find that although surrounded by derelict and ruined tenements, most of those houses which remained in occupation were well maintained, and in some instances even partially rebuilt.[30]

A good example of this was the rear range (destroyed by enemy action during the Second World War) at Salutation Cottages (formerly The Salutation Inn) on the corner of Mill Road and Castle Street on Quarter 2. The detailed drawings of this range made by Homan indicate that it cannot have predated the second half of the 16th century.[31] Whether it replaced an earlier wing upon the same site is not known. As Figure 10.34 shows, it was built to a high specification and incorporated a continuously jettied upper storey towards the street, up-to-date small-panel framing (probably enriched with close studding), a large rear chimney, and a wagon entrance leading to the rear yard. And this is not the only example of improvements carried out to an earlier building during this period. In 1583 the main range of 'Glebe' on Quarter 13 was entirely rebuilt by William Morley esq., the then mayor, using salvaged stone. The new range is distinctive in that it incorporates a curious front chimney flanked on one side by a closet, both of which project out into the street upon an encroachment granted to him by the Corporation (Figure 10.35).[32] Around 1600 the northern range of Periteau House on the southwest corner of Quarter 7 was likewise all but rebuilt, whilst in the early 17th century a new crosswing and rear range were added to Five Chimneys on the southwest corner of Quarter 1 (Figure 10.36). Other buildings too underwent some change, though of a much less extensive nature.

From the 1730s onwards the construction of new houses recommenced within the town, albeit in small numbers. In consequence, there are a few good mid/late-18th century buildings, including the terraces of manufactory houses at Five Houses on Quarter 2, Barrack Square on Quarter 7, and at the rear of 7/8 High Street on Quarter 8 built during the 1760s to house the calico workers employed by the English Linen Company. The grandiose Mariteau House on Quarter 20 was built by one of the partners of the company in *c.*1765.[33] It was during this general period too, most likely in the 1740s, that the formerly three-storeyed, late-medieval Periteau House on the southwest corner of Quarter 7 took on its present external appearance: the upper storey was removed and its timber framed external walls replaced by good-quality brickwork.

11. MEDIEVAL AND 'TRANSITIONAL' DOMESTIC BUILDINGS: MATERIALS AND CONSTRUCTION

David and Barbara Martin

STONE WALLING

Extensive use of stone in early Winchelsea is indicated by both upstanding and excavated early remains and is confirmed by the 16th- and 17th-century licences granted for the demolition and removal of stone from the town (*see* Chapter 10). Usually only rough stone could be carted away. 'Caen stone' or 'hewn stone' was often specifically excluded.[1]

In common with the other masonry buildings which survive within the town, the walls of the domestic stone buildings were mostly constructed using distinctive thin slabs of local Tilgate stone (Figure 11.1). Tilgate, a very hard and durable calcareous sandstone, occurs in the Wadhurst Clay within the Hastings Beds. These beds were once extensively quarried in the area around Fairlight and Hastings, immediately to the southwest of Winchelsea, where the stone was known locally as 'Hastings Granite'.[2] Only in a very few buildings was other stone used, and even in these its use was very localized.[3] For instance, the front wall of a house in North Street, Quarter 2, of which only a standing gable remains, was faced in hewn, roughly-squared blocks of hard sandstone (Figure 11.2). But even this facing was returned only a short distance around the end wall, before the builder reverted to using standard Tilgate slabs where the wall became internalized within the formerly adjacent timber-framed house. Otherwise, occasional slabs and blocks of other stones are incorporated into walls built predominantly of Tilgate. Not surprisingly, most common amongst these are the local fine-grained, silty Wealden sandstones, but slabs of shelly limestone, also from the Wealden beds, and, in addition, Oolitic Limestone, Carstone and Greensand are occasionally encountered. Likewise, there are a few instances of

Fig. 11.1
Typical Tilgate stone wall at Blackfriars Barn.

Fig. 11.2
Roughly squared facing blocks at the Standing Gable, Quarter 2.

Kentish Ragstone, but this is not as common within the town as was once suggested, for some early commentators mistook Tilgate for Kentish Rag. Perhaps the most surprising absence, given the closeness of the town to the shore line, is the almost complete lack of water-worn flints (or cobble stones) either in knapped or un-knapped form. There is the very occasional inclusion of a flint nodule, but no walls are known where extensive use of this material was made. Similarly, clunch (a hard chalk), so readily available just along the coast at Beachy Head, is conspicuously absent. Its only known use within the town is in two isolated areas of the cellar vault beneath Rookery Cottage, Quarter 13.

The hewn or 'dressed' stone mentioned in the documents was mostly used in the construction of openings and for the quoins forming the corners of the buildings. The rear corners of the house now known as Blackfriars Barn, Quarter 15, do not make use of dressed stones. Instead they are formed of Tilgate slabs similar to those used for the main walls, and the same is true of the rear corner at the ruined gable on Quarter 2. Indeed, undressed quoins within the rear elevations of the houses may have been more common than is now realized. But in general, the dressings and architectural features make use either of local fine-grained silty sandstone or of Caen stone, the latter either reused from (Old) Winchelsea or directly imported from France. However, the use of Caen stone within the town tends to be overstated.

As is usual locally, the majority of the masonry walls range in width from 620 to 710 millimetres (2ft.1in. to 2ft.4ins.), although in the case of the standing gable on Quarter 2, the 620-millimetre walls (2ft.1in.) reduce to only 550 millimetres (1ft.10ins.) along the neatly-faced front elevation. Excavations have shown that at 500 millimetres (1ft.9ins.), the street facade of the narrow range facing German Street on Quarter 19 was even thinner. That this was the stub of a masonry wall rather than the foundation for a timber frame is indicated not only by the remains of a chamfered plinth, but also by the lower jamb stones of a doorway. Similarly, the internal masonry wall between hall and services at Firebrand (Quarter 13) measures only 510 millimetres (1ft.8ins.) thick. The latter wall - at least in its present form - rises to the level of the first floor only, and the same could have been true of that excavated upon Quarter 19.

On plot 21, Quarter 15, the house's southern party wall was shared with the adjacent stone-built house now known as Blackfriars Barn, whilst the northern party wall, which divided the house from its neighbour, was likewise of masonry and measured 650 millimetres (2ft.2ins.) thick. Elsewhere upon the site the foundations varied from 310 to 430 millimetres (1ft. to 1ft.5ins.) and were clearly designed to carry the soleplates of timber framing. Presumably in this instance the masonry walls were intended as firebreaks, and a similar masonry wall, assumed also to have been a firebreak wall, once existed between 11-12 High Street and Wren Cottage on Quarter 13. Likewise, at Old Castle House on Quarter 8, the end walls of the timber-framed street range are of stone, although in this instance the antiquity of the walls cannot be verified.

The surviving service wall at Firebrand and the excavated wall on Quarter 19 prove that medieval masonry walls in Winchelsea could, on occasions, be built as thin as 500-510 millimetres (*c.*1ft.8ins.), but no proven examples of lesser thickness are known. Rural sites excavated locally suggest that the foundations for timber-framed walls usually varied from 250-350 millimetres (10ins.-1ft.2ins.) thick. Given such ranges of thickness, it is sometimes hard to be certain whether an excavated foundation supported a slender masonry superstructure wall or was intended to carry timber framing. As an example, the excavated 380-millimetre (1ft.3ins.) rear wall at Mill Road (Quarter 3) was probably constructed to support timber framing, but the width is nevertheless generous for this purpose and it may just possibly represent the remains of an inferior masonry wall. If the wall did rise in masonry to any height it would not have been very strong: not only was it relatively thin, but it had only very shallow foundations and rather than being bedded in lime mortar, the individual stones were laid in clay. This use of clay to bed the stones does not preclude a masonry superstructure, however. Although the superstructure work within the front wall at German Street, Quarter 19, was bedded in lime mortar, the foundations were clay-bedded, as also are the surviving remains of the town wall where they skirt the eastern side of Rookery Field. As late as the early 17th century, clay was still occasionally chosen to bed the brick and stone used to construct local rural chimneys. However, it is true to say that in most masonry walls so far discovered within the town, lime mortar was used as the bedding material, and this is also true of many of the ground walls which supported timber frames. This lime mortar tends to be distinctive in that it includes a heavy admixture of very small, water-worn pebbles or grit.

THE USE OF BRICK IN STONE BUILDINGS

Most of the early stone buildings incorporate at least some small yellow brick, although it was not used in large quantities. However, a considerable proportion of the brick is so integrated into the structures that it is clear that it relates to the primary build of around 1300. For instance, yellow brick is used widely, but not extensively, throughout the construction of the house and cellar now known as Blackfriars Barn (Quarter 15). Besides being utilized in the rear walls of the hall's

Fig. 11.3
Old Castle House, Quarter 8. First-floor doorway.

cupboard recesses and fireplace, for the construction of the hearth, and in the threshold of one of the western doorways, yellow bricks are to be found lining the sides of most of the putlog holes and used as voussoirs to the interior relieving arches over the western windows lighting the cellar. This variety in its use at Blackfriars Barn is typical of that in other structures. Indeed, although it has not been found in large quantities, some yellow brick has been recovered from most of the excavations carried out within the town.[4] Early yellow brick (sometimes with pink/red tinged external surfaces and occasionally fawn in colour) is not exclusive to Winchelsea, but was used locally at Glottenham, an early-14th-century fortified manor house in Mountfield and at Bodiam Castle, Bodiam, built *c.*1385, whilst bricks of similar size and texture, but red in colour, were in use at Brede Place in the early 16th century.[5] Very similar red bricks of probable 16th-century date were used to reconstruct a clay-bedded wall excavated at Mill Road on Quarter 3.

The small size - typically 180-200 x 75-95 x 35-45 millimetres (7-8 x 3-3¾ x 1½-1¾inches) - and the

Fig. 11.4
Firebrand, Quarter 13. Service doorways viewed from the hall.

distinctive rebated press marks which often extend down the main edges are the most distinctive characteristics of the bricks. The fabric is soft, producing a lightweight, often crumbly brick. Bricks of this type are usually termed 'Flemish' and it is indeed known that quantities of bricks were being imported into Winchelsea from the Low Countries during the early 14th century. They were still being brought into neighbouring Rye from ports such as Middelburg and Ter Gouw at the end of the 16th century and they are to be seen in Winchelsea occasionally used in the construction of post-medieval chimneys, such as the chimney cap of *c.*1600 date on Quarter 1 at Attewall, Barrack Square.[6] Whether all these distinctive bricks do actually represent Low Country imports, or whether some were of local estuarine-silt manufacture is at present uncertain.[7]

ARCHITECTURAL FEATURES INCORPORATED WITHIN STONE WALLS

Apart from the windows, doorways and cupboard recesses associated with the cellars (for which *see* Chapter 9), little architectural detailing survives within the stone houses. In all, the remains of either 23 or 24 late-13th- and 14th-century masonry doorways have been recognized, of which either 20 or 21 are within the standing buildings, two are re-fixed, but from known contexts, and one further example was recovered by excavation. Of these, 18 are sufficiently complete for the shape of their arched heads to be ascertained. With the exception of one semicircular example at St Anthony's, Quarter 8, all are two-centred. The most elaborate is the heavily restored (if not rebuilt) front entrance at The Armory, Quarter 7, which in its present form has shafted jambs with moulded caps and bases,

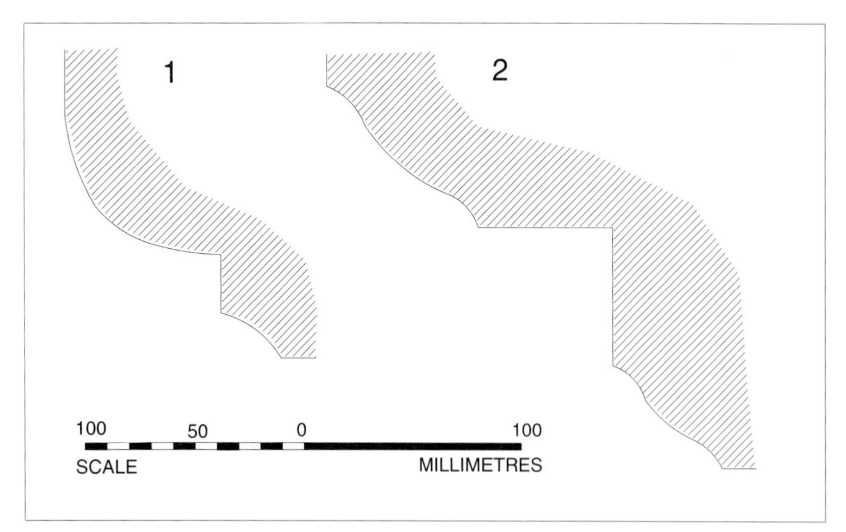

Fig. 11.5
Firebrand, Quarter 13.
Detail of the mouldings on the service doorways.
1. Moulding on the jamb of the northern doorway.
2. Moulding on the jamb of the southern doorway.

moulded voussoirs and a moulded hood. The details of the hood and voussoirs can be trusted; whether the same can be said for the jambs is uncertain, but given the high quality of an internal wall recess within the building, they probably can. Although not as elaborate, the re-fixed external doorways at the house which became the Court Hall, Quarter 8, and Little Trojans, Quarter 19, (now rebuilt within a wall at 1 Trojan's Platt) are comparable in quality to the doorway to the cellar beneath Salutation Cottages, Quarter 2, (*see* Figure 9.24). In comparison, the other openings are plain (Figure 11.3). The two service doorways at Firebrand, Quarter 13, have simple continuous mouldings (Figures 11.4 and 11.5), but otherwise all either have continuous plain chamfers or continuous hollow chamfers. Where the arched heads remain, all the internal doorways lack hood-moulds, whilst amongst the external doorways *in situ*, only the front entrance to the hall at The Armory, Quarter 7, and the rear entrance to the hall at Firebrand, Quarter 13, had hoods. The latter has a distinctive twirl stop with a decorative central element. More typical are the twirl stops which can be seen on the hood over the re-fixed doorway from Little Trojans, and another recovered from the excavations on Quarter 19 (Figure 11.6).[8] The hood over the re-fixed doorway leading into the yard (former hall) at what later became the Court Hall on Quarter 8 has simple square returns.

Evidence as to the form of the early windows is exceedingly sparse. Parts of the internal splayed jambs and the cill of a high-level hall window survive at Old Castle House, Quarter 8, as do those of another within the yard (former hall) at the house, later converted into the Court Hall, also on Quarter 8. No architectural details of these openings are recoverable. Within the roofed section of the Court Hall the window sill and part of a jamb at the western end of the front elevation can be seen, and in this instance, a shallow recess in the adjacent wall (intended to house the hinged shutter when open) indicates that the window was fitted with a two-centred, arched head (*see* Figure 11.23). Otherwise, the only evidence is a group of cusped voussoirs with ball terminals re-fixed into the rear wall of St Anthony's, Quarter 8.

The standing gable on Quarter 2, The Armory, Quarter 7, and both Blackfriars Barn and plot 21 on Quarter 15 all incorporate the remains of either cupboard recesses or open niches. Further examples are re-fixed into the south elevation of the present-day Court Hall, Quarter 8, and beneath the stairs in The Armory, Quarter 7. Of the examples *in situ*, by far the best is that in the north wall of the 'service chamber' at The Armory (Figures 11.7 and 11.8). One of the two recesses which flanked the fireplace at Blackfriars Barn incorporated a Caen-stone shelf and had an arched head, but otherwise the other *in-situ* examples are plain and resemble those found in the cellars.

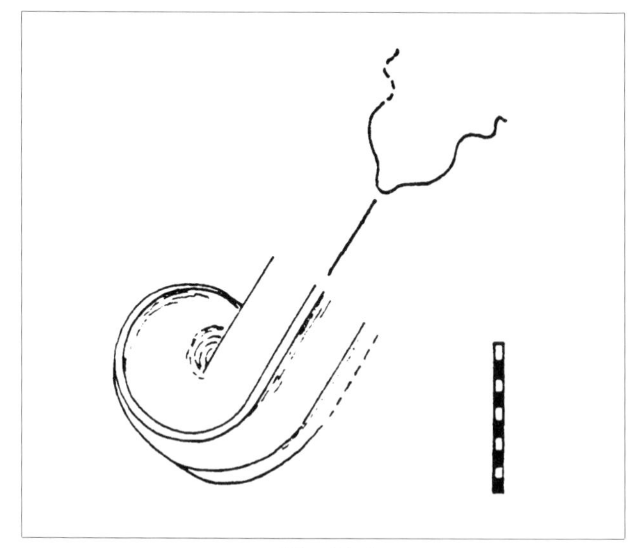

Fig. 11.6
Twirl stop to the hood-mould discovered during excavations in German Street, Quarter 19.

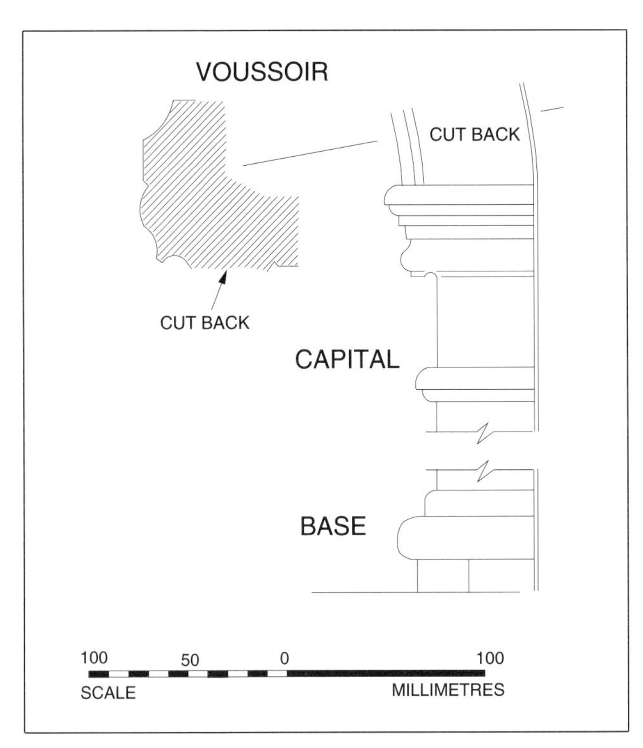

Fig. 11.7
The Armory, Quarter 7. Details of the capital, base and voussoir mouldings to the arch-headed recess in the north wall, first-floor level.

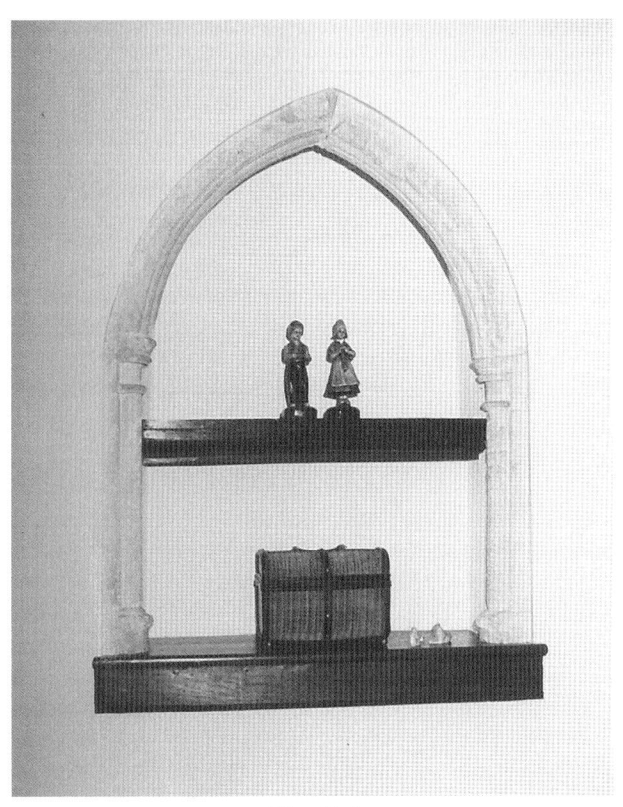

Fig. 11.8
The Armory, Quarter 7. Arch-headed recess in the north wall at first-floor level.

Corbels remain at The Armory, Quarter 7, Old Castle House, St Anthony's, the house later converted into the Court Hall (all Quarter 8) and at Blackfriars Barn, Quarter 15. All are simple in form, having half-rounded soffits, mostly with chamfered edges. The corbels at Court Hall are the only external domestic examples: they supported the timber plates of a roof, presumably associated with a pentice. Similar corbels are shown in an engraving of the 'bell-tower', which stood to the southwest of St Thomas's Church (*see* Figure 7.11). The corbels at Old Castle House, St Anthony's and Blackfriars Barn supported timber plates which carried the first-floor joists, whilst other corbels at Blackfriars Barn, together with one at The Armory, were intended to support wall posts associated with open trusses.

TIMBER FRAMING

It is disappointing that almost no early timber work survives within the town, despite the fact that most

Fig. 11.9
The Retreat, Quarter 6. Inset post for Wealden front with a footbrace halved across the face of the post.

Fig. 11.10 (Left)
Crowsnest, The Strand.
Close-studding
within the front elevation.

of the buildings would have used this form of construction. Even most stone houses used timber framing for most, and in many cases, all of their internal partitions. The only house which retains recognizable early work is The Armory, Quarter 7, where a moulded crossbeam at the low end of the hall and a pair of mutilated hall tiebeams remain *in situ*. The mouldings on all three are typical of those commonly in use during the late 13th century and the first two-thirds of the 14th century (Figure 11.11).

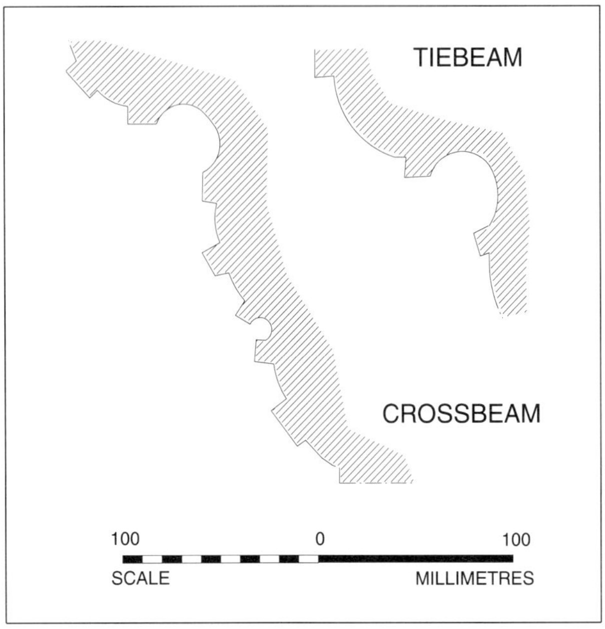

TIEBEAM
CROSSBEAM
100 0 100
SCALE MILLIMETRES

Fig. 11.11
The Armory, Quarter 7. Profile of the 14th-century moulded tiebeam and crossbeam.

In contrast to the early surviving buildings, timber framing predominates within the later medieval structures. Where the wall design is known, the details are typical of the region: either footbraced, large-panel framing (Figure 11.9) or close-studding (Figure 11.10). Headbracing, rather than footbracing, was used at Nesbit, Quarter 13 (*see* Figure 10.21). The braces and close-studs are thin, plank-like timbers which were exposed

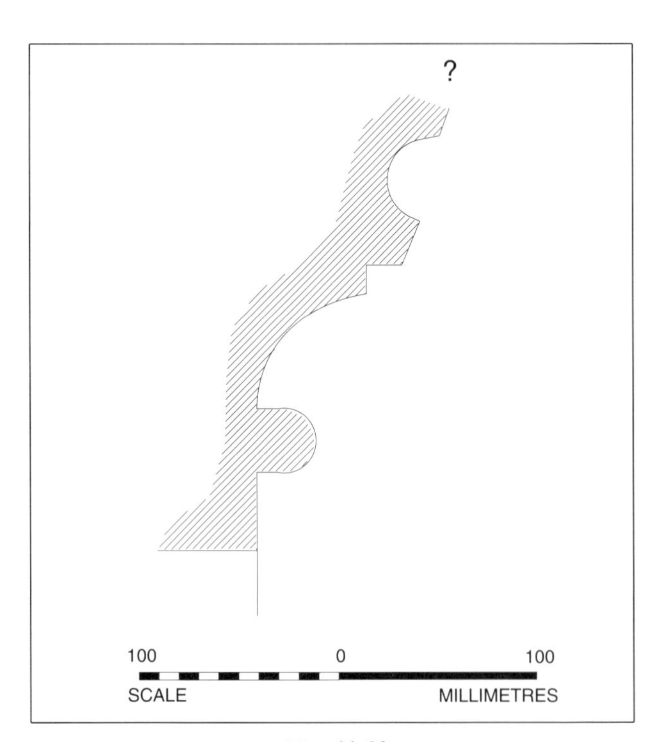

Fig. 11.12
The Retreat, Quarter 6. Detail of the moulding on the dais beam.

Fig. 11.13
Periteau House, Quarter 7. First-floor doorway showing a simple four-centred arched head.

within the principal face of the wall, but masked from view by lath and daub on the reverse face. This is entirely in keeping with the region. Except in the earliest examples, those walls visible from the streets were in most cases close-studded, whereas those which were not visible to the public used cheaper, large-panel framing. A good example of this is Crowsnest at The Strand (*see* Figure 10.20). Close-studding appears to have been introduced into this part of Sussex around 1430 and only became common during the second half of the 15th century.[9] Usually it was reserved for external elevations only, but in Winchelsea it was used within the partitions of the principal rooms at Periteau House, Quarter 7 (*see* Figure 10.24) and flanking the main entrance passage at Old Castle House.

In those houses where there were rooms beyond the high end of the open hall, it was usual in this part of England to incorporate a moulded dais beam crossing the end wall of the hall, and occasionally, a similarly moulded, though less elaborate, crossbeam was used at the hall's low end. An example of a crossbeam in early 'decorated' style exists at The Armory (Figure 11.11). Fifteenth-century moulded dais beams, all of typical 'perpendicular' style, exist at The Retreat (Figure 11.12), Salutation Cottages and Five Chimneys. Details at Firebrand are currently masked from view and thus it is not known whether the dais beam here is moulded, although the crossbeam at the low end of the hall adjacent to the cross-passage is merely chamfered.

Although the positions of a number of doorways and windows are recognizable within the timber-framed walls, virtually nothing is known regarding their detail. Only Periteau House, Quarter 7, retains extant doorways: they have hollow-chamfered surrounds incorporating four-centred, arched heads with sunken spandrels (Figure 11.13). There are hints that the ground-floor front window beneath the jetty at Glebe took the form of a projecting oriel.

Open first-floor trusses exist at Glebe (*see* Figure 10.22), 7/8 High Street (*see* Figure 10.23), Wren Cottage (*see* Figure 10.26 - section C-C), The Armory (*see* Figure 10.28), and Firebrand. Those within the added rear range at The Armory and within 7/8 High Street have, or had, solid-spandrel arch-braces with integral nibs to the tiebeam and principal posts - also the case with the ground-floor open truss at Wren Cottage. At The Armory the braces and nibs are chamfered, whereas in the other two instances they are cyma-moulded. Reflecting the lesser quality of the first-floor chamber at Wren Cottage, here the tiebeam is chamfered, but the braces are plain. Even so, the tiebeam supports a decorative crownpost (*see* below). The truss at Glebe has an acutely cranked tiebeam which is chamfered, but otherwise undecorated. It never incorporated braces and this is also the case with the open truss which crossed the two-bay, 15th-century service chamber at Firebrand.

FLOOR CONSTRUCTION AND JETTIES

So far as is known, no 14th-century first floors survive. Generally, the construction of the first floors within the 15th-century buildings followed the usual pattern for the area: large, plain joists, rectangular in section and laid flat were used. Depending upon the bay lengths and the presence or absence of a jettied upper storey, most joists were aligned across the building and were jointed at central span into a large-scantling spine beam. This was usually chamfered, although in the more important rooms of the principal houses they were moulded. This is the case at Periteau House

Fig. 11.14
Periteau House, Quarter 7. Ceiling joists to the ground-floor room showing the boarded ceiling and dovetails on every joist to accommodate the former jetty plate.

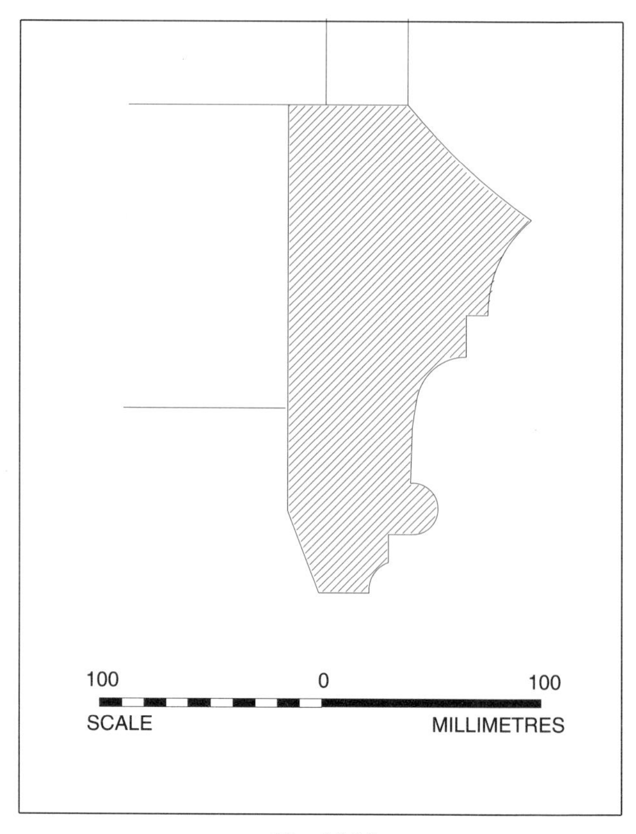

Fig. 11.15
Salutation Cottages, Quarter 2. Detail of the moulding on the jetty fascia.

(Figures 11.14 and 11.16A; Wren Cottage (Figure 11.16B) and Glebe (Figure 11.16C). At Glebe the joists are stop-chamfered. Those at Periteau House (Figure 11.16A) and 2 Friars Road are hollow-chamfered and in these instances they support timber ceiling panels formed by fixing boards into side grooves. Boards may also be present within the crosswing at Glebe. Ceilings of this type are very rare, the only other known examples in East Sussex are at St Anthony's, Church Square, Rye, and the now-destroyed Portland Cottages, Burwash.[10] Jetties were incorporated within at least eight of the surviving 15th-century structures, but in most the details are masked by later alterations. At Salutation Cottages (Figure 11.15), Glebe, and Periteau House the ends of the joists were masked from view by heavy, moulded fascia beams. It was more normal locally to leave the joist ends exposed, and this was certainly the case at The Retreat.

ROOF CONSTRUCTION

No early roofs survive within the town, nor are there any hints within the early stone walls as to their likely form. The original roof construction of two of the late-medieval houses is unknown. Otherwise, with the exception of the crosswing at Glebe (*see* below), all the 15th-century roofs are of paired-rafter-and-collar design, mostly with crownposts. Because the majority of the rooms and chambers were of one bay only, most of the crownposts are of partition type and consist of a plain post with footbraces rising from the tiebeams. However, there was a free-standing crownpost (destroyed) over the two-bay chamber at 7/8 High Street, Quarter 8, and another (surviving but re-fixed) within the added rear range at The Armory on Quarter 7 (Figure 11.17). The latter crownpost has an octagonal shaft and moulded cap and base. The short crownpost at Wren Cottage likewise has an octagonal shaft with moulded cap and base, although in this instance the shaft is very stubby and incorporates broach stops at the junction between the square moulded base and the shaft (Figure 11.18). Other crownposts, of simple cruciform section, exist within the 15th-century roof added over the newly converted Court Hall (*see* Figure 6.1).

The roof at Glebe (Figure 11.19) is of a type which is not local and has in-line interrupted side purlins, which supported continuous common rafters. Its open truss has principal rafters without either collar or struts. There is full wind-bracing.

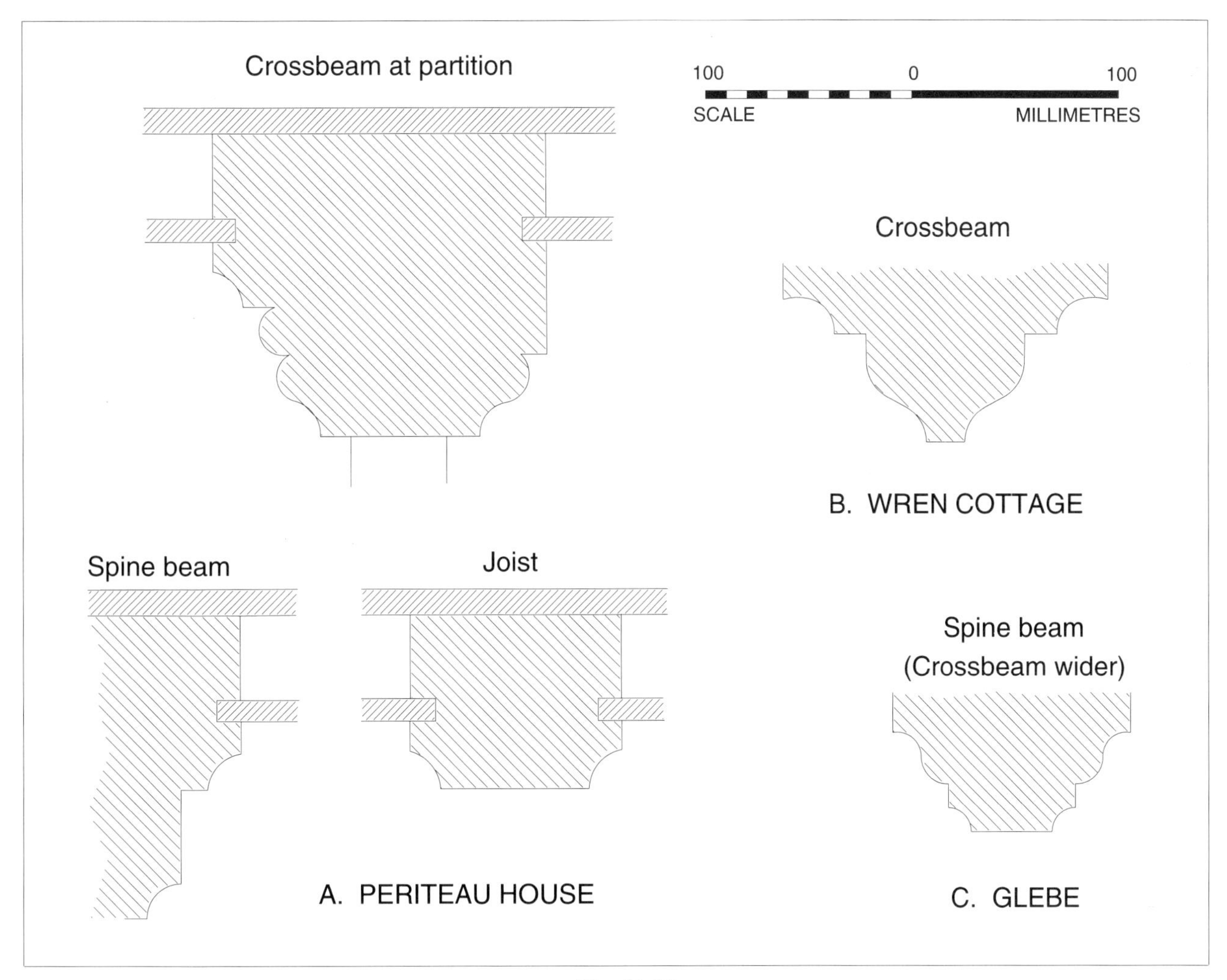

Fig. 11.16
Details of moulded ceiling beams and boarded ceiling panels.

ROOF COVERINGS AND ROOF FURNITURE

No *in situ* roof coverings survive, and thus excavation is the only source of information regarding the types of materials used during the medieval period. Neither thatch nor timber shingles have left any record, but clay tile was recovered, especially from the Mill Road and Truncheons excavations. Generally, however, the quantities of tile found were slight in comparison to the large quantities of blue/silver-grey West-Country slate recovered. With the exception of Mill Road, all the sites produced significant quantities of this material. It was certainly the predominant roof covering used upon at least one of the houses facing North Street, Quarter 2, as well as on the roofs of the house adjacent to Blackfriars Barn on Quarter 15, and on the house facing German Street on Quarter 19.

The most interesting of the roof fixtures recovered from the excavations within the town must be the remains of six probably 14th-century glazed ceramic louvres - three from the cesspit fill from Blackfriars Barn, one from the North Street excavations, and two from the excavations at Mill Road.[11] Placed astride the ridges of the roof above a room which incorporated an open hearth, the purpose of these elaborate fixtures was to allow smoke from the open fire to escape. Based upon evidence from other sites, they appear not to have been used individually, but to have been arranged in groups of two, three, or perhaps more. The fact that two nearly identical louvres were amongst the three found within the backfilled cesspit on Quarter 15 is evidence consistent with this thinking. Two types were manufactured:

- 'Separate Louvres', so called because when manufactured, they were not made integral with their supporting structure: they were made either with a flat base so as to be fitted onto some form of 'platform' (as in Figure 11.20, No. 1 from Mill Road), or alternatively the base was trimmed to sit over a specially manufactured ridge tile (as in

*Fig. 11.17 (Left)
The Armory,
Quarter 7.
Re-fixed free-
standing
crownpost within
the
rear range.*

*Fig. 11.18
Wren Cottage, Quarter 13.
Formerly free-standing crownpost
to the first-floor chamber.*

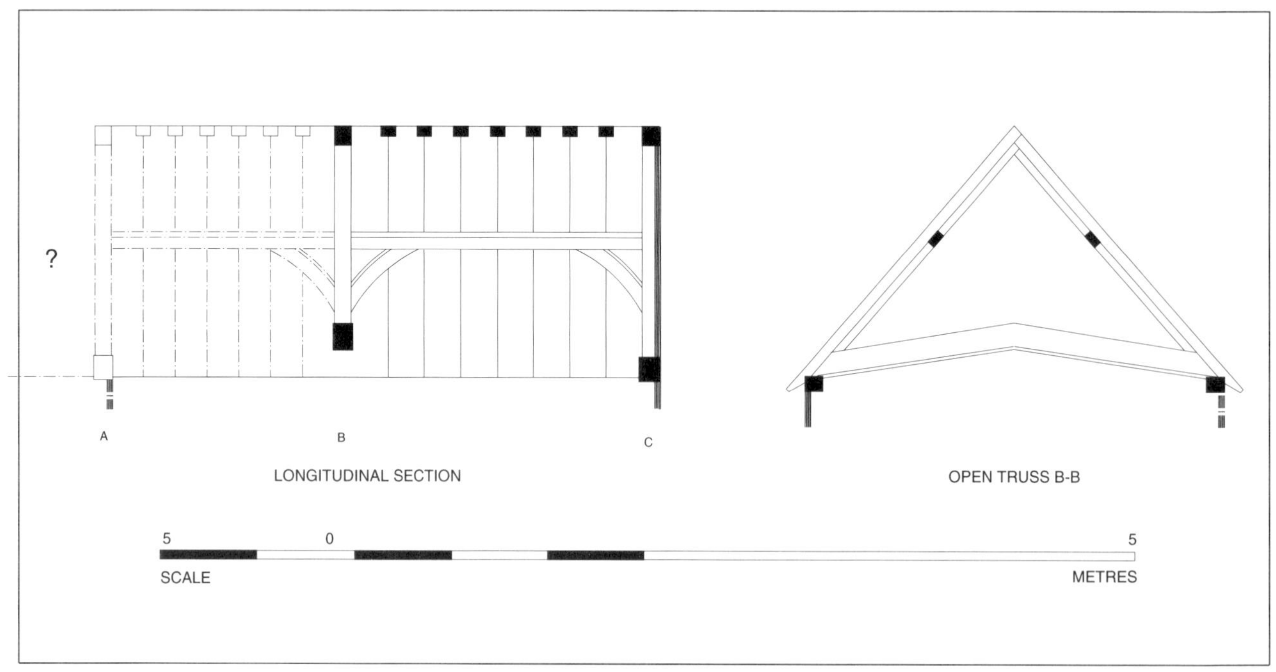

*Fig. 11.19
Glebe, Quarter 13. Details of roof.*

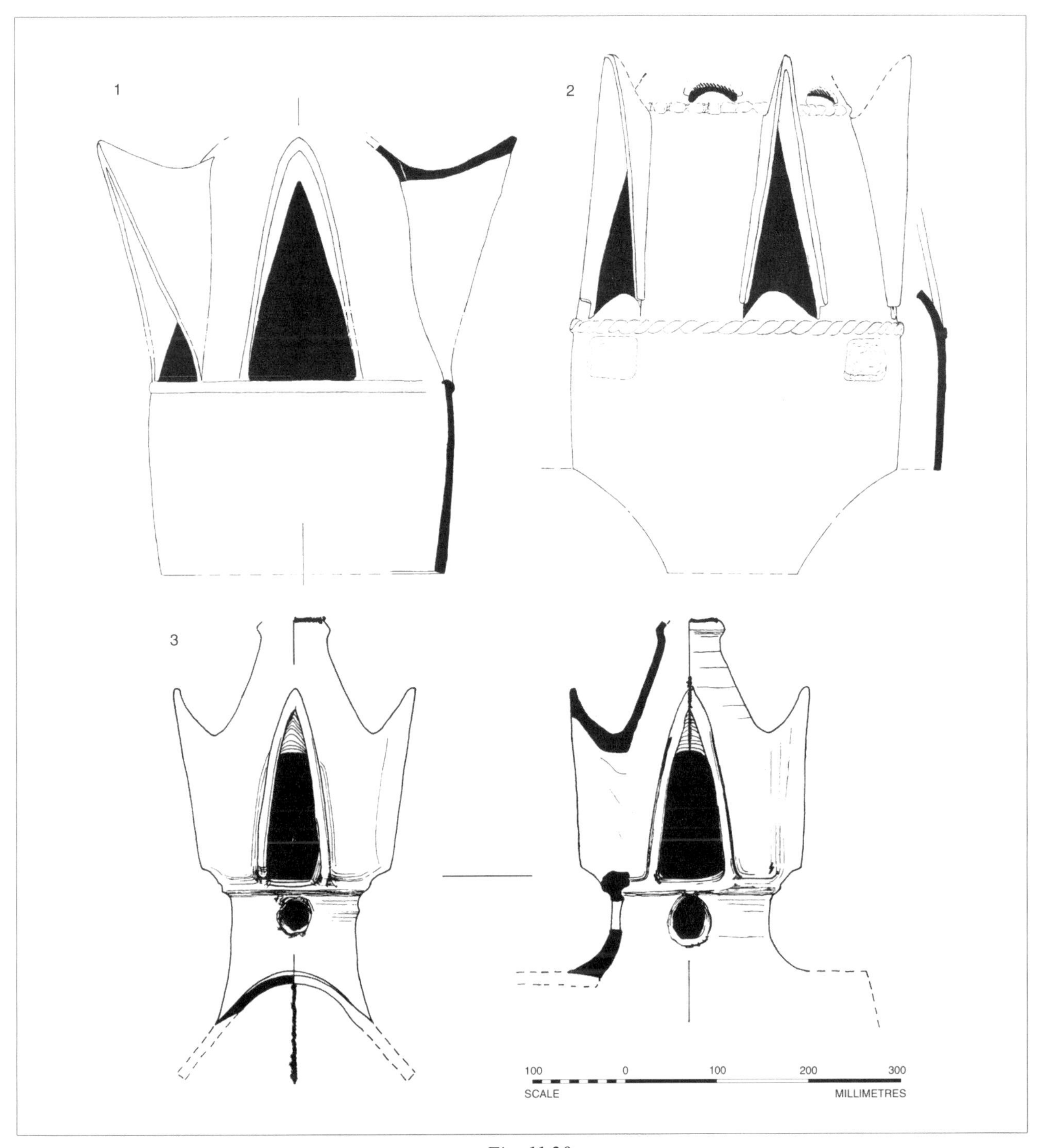

Fig. 11.20
Ceramic roof louvres recovered from Mill Road, Quarter 3 (No. 1) and from a backfilled stone-lined cesspit adjacent to Blackfriars Barn, Quarter 15 (Nos. 2-3).

Figure 11.20, No. 2, from the cesspit adjacent to Blackfriars Barn).

- 'Attached Louvres', which were moulded onto a ridge tile before firing so that both the ridge tile and louvre formed an integral fitting: for an example *see* Figure 11.20. No. 3.

Both types have apertures which are protected from the rain by means of projecting hoods. All the Winchelsea examples are green-glazed.

HEARTHS, FIREPLACES AND CHIMNEYS

The excavations in Winchelsea have revealed good details of three open hearths, one each from North

Fig. 11.21
Detail of the open hearth within the hall of the house formerly adjacent to Blackfriars Barn, Quarter 15.

Street, Quarter 2; Mill Road, Quarter 3; and plot 21, adjacent to Blackfriars Barn on Quarter 15. It is assumed that all three served open halls. All were sited at mid-span between the side walls, but were located relatively close to what is assumed to have been the 'high-end' wall - at a distance of 750 millimetres (2ft.6ins.) in the case of North Street, 800 millimetres (2ft.8ins.) at Mill Road, and 1.60 metres (5ft.3ins.) in the house adjacent to Blackfriars Barn. The locations of the hearths at North Street and Mill Road are too close to the end wall to have allowed room for the high-end bench and table which is normally assumed to have been present, and even within the hall on Quarter 15, where evidence of a bench appears to survive, there would only just have been room for a table.

All three hearths were constructed of brick. In plan they measured respectively *c.*1.35 metres by *c.*1.30 metres (4ft.5ins. by 4ft.3ins.), *c.*0.70 metres by *c.*1.00 metre (2ft.3ins. by 3ft.3ins.) and 1.75 metres square (5ft.8ins. square). That at Mill Road is both the smallest and most crudely constructed: its bricks were laid flat in roughly straight courses. Its small size may indicate that it was intended as the base for a brazier rather than as an open fire. In the other two examples the bricks were laid on edge and were set to a pattern, arranged around a central square stone block (Figures 11.21 and 11.22).[12]

Winchelsea's former wealth is well reflected in the number of medieval fireplaces discovered within the town, usually a fireplace was a rare feature before the 16th century.[13] Most fireplaces built in England during the 13th and 14th centuries consisted of a shallow recess built into the wall. Projecting above the recess was a hood of either stone or daub-infilled timber framing carried on corbels.

Although now very fragmentary, two examples of this type survive at the southwest corner of Quarter 8, within the western end wall at the house later converted into the Court Hall. One fireplace serves the ground-floor room and the other the first-floor chamber (Figure 11.23). The feature is of sufficient importance to warrant description in some detail. Despite the now much mutilated and inaccurately-restored state of the fireplaces, good details can still be recovered from what remains. It should be stressed that a pair of relieving arches incorporated within the external face of the west wall, behind the ground-floor fireplace, appear not to relate to the fireplace and most probably survive from an earlier period. If so, then the fireplaces are not primary to the first build. This point is further suggested by the level of early floor offsets incorporated within the east and south walls, for these do not correspond to the level of the first-floor fireplace. Even so, the fireplaces appear early and probably date from before the close of the 14th century. Both are very robust and chunky in their appearance. The canopies were carried by large dressed

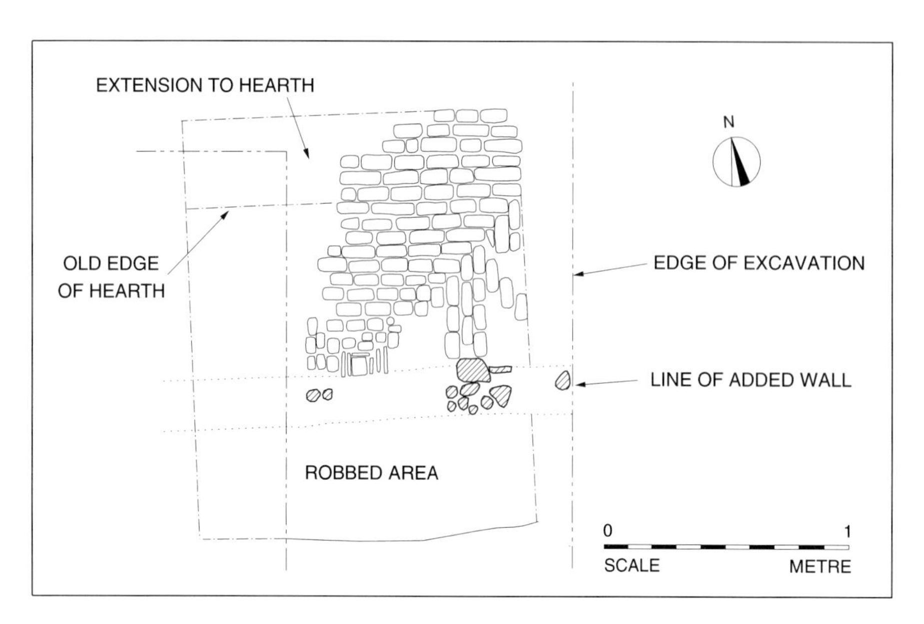

Fig. 11.22 (Left)
Detail of a hearth within a hall on Quarter 2, adjacent to the Standing Gable, North Street.

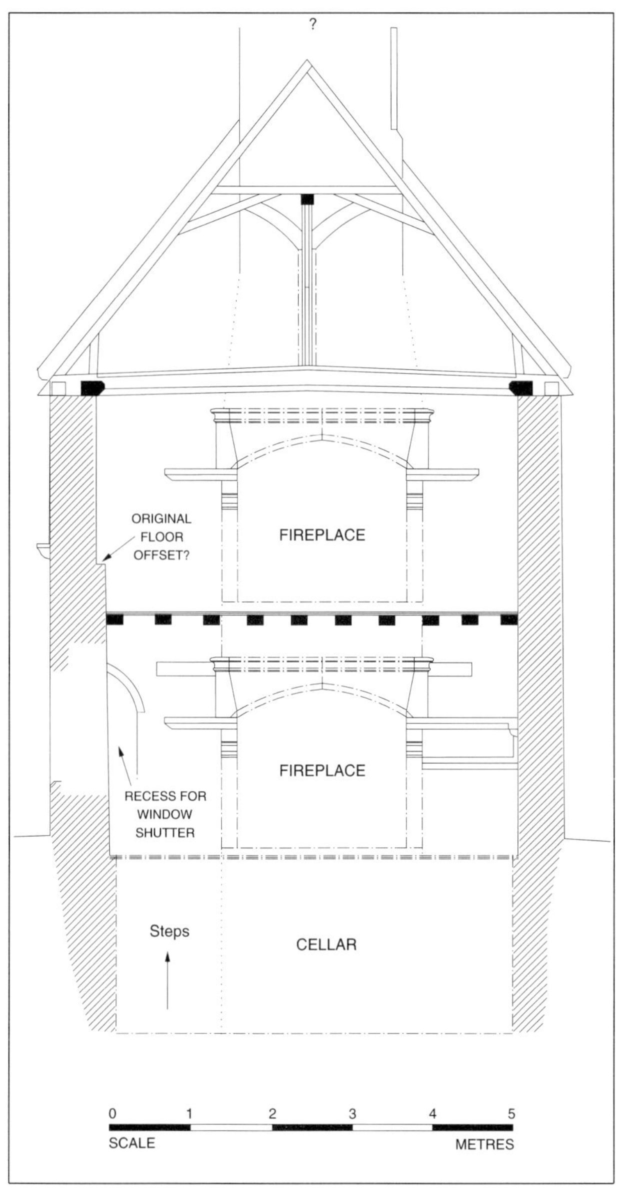

Fig. 11.23
The Court Hall, Quarter 8.
Details of the early chimney incorporated within the western gable.

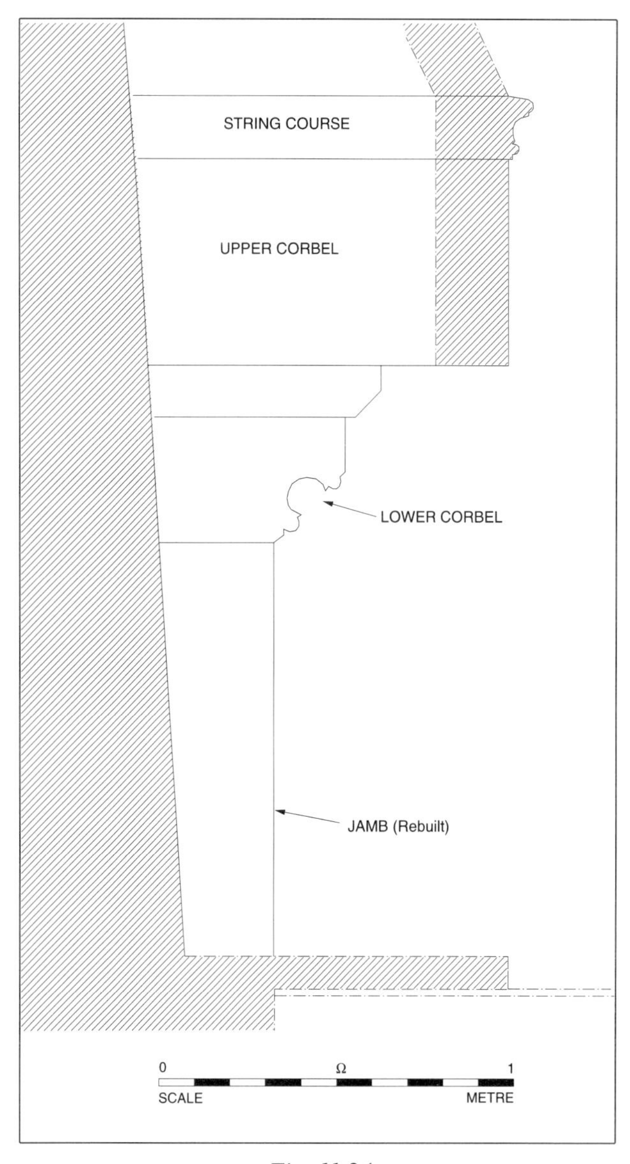

Fig. 11.24
The Court Hall, Quarter 8.
Section through the ground-floor fireplace showing the moulded corbel and hood support.

blocks of sandstone which are laid on edge and extend through the full thickness of the west wall. The exposed ends of these blocks have led several commentators to mistake them for the voussoirs of arches which, they argue, once sprang westwards from the building, into the road.

The better preserved of the two fireplaces is that on the ground floor. The present slightly projecting jambs are modern and replace either lost or damaged originals. Above these are corbels of dressed sandstone blocks laid on edge. The face of each corbel is moulded with a three-quarter hollow and a roll which, in profile, are of late-13th- or 14th-century design (Figures 11.24). As figures 11.25 and 11.26 show, primarily these support heavily chamfered, but otherwise plain shelves of dressed sandstone flanking the hood. Above this level are the massive, plain corbels of sandstone which extend through the wall and serve as the principal supports to the hood. They project into the room by 960 millimetres (3ft.2ins.) and measure 270 millimetres (11ins.) wide and 560 millimetres (1ft.10ins.) high. The internal side faces of both were formerly cut to a cant in order to support either a timber or stone lintel which carried the front face of the hood above. These canted cuts have been made good with modern stone, but the joint in each block is still clearly visible. Extending along the top of the lintel,

Fig. 11.25
The Court Hall, Quarter 8.
South side of the fireplace showing the moulded corbels supporting the remains of the former ground-floor fireplace hood.
Note the adjacent 'candle' shelves.

between it and the hood, are the remains of a roll-moulded, stone string-course. The roll moulding on the front edge is returned back to the wall at each end. Built into the external angles at string-course level, between the hood and the adjacent wall, is a further tier of very distinctive, but plain shelves. Unlike those of the lower tier, both are triangular in plan. The sloping brick back to the fireplace is of later date, but (unless it is built using old bricks) it is nonetheless of considerable age.

The first-floor fireplace has been all but destroyed. A rather poor and inaccurate replica was inserted upon the site as part of alterations carried out in 1890/91, which further confused the evidence. The existence of the original fireplace is indicated by two features: the built-in ends of the main corbels (visible in the external west elevation) and the hacked-back remains of a pair of projecting chamfered shelves flanking the former corbels and matching those on the ground floor.

Visible in the gable, above the fireplaces, and now supported internally upon a modern arch, is the slightly projecting two-flue chimney cap. Externally, the lower part of this cap survives and incorporates attached three-quarter roll moulded corner columns rising from moulded bases. The columns support un-moulded cinquefoil heads, and frame a sunken panel in both the

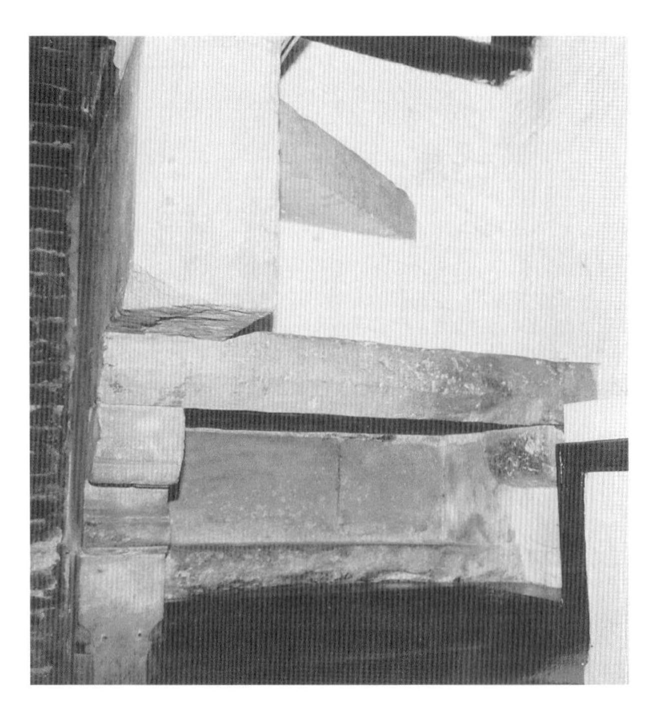

Fig. 11.26
The Court Hall, Quarter 8.
North side of the fireplace showing the moulded corbels supporting the remains of the former ground-floor fireplace hood.
Note the adjacent 'candle' shelves.

front and rear faces of the cap (Figure 11.27). The effect is both distinctive and very unusual. What form the top of the chimney took is unknown - the present top is relatively modern and includes a coping of mullions reused from a glazed stone window.

The fragmentary remains of what appears to have been another canopied fireplace, this time within a timber-framed building constructed between masonry 'firebreak' walls, were discovered during excavation of the plot immediately to the north of Blackfriars Barn on Quarter 15. The fireplace was included as part of the phase-III alterations undertaken during the 14th century. In this instance the corbels supporting the hood were evidently carried by Caen-stone pilasters, whilst the 'reredos screen' against which the fire was built consisted of 'Flemish' brickwork laid in stretcher bond, built against the infill of the timber frame and extending partly over the frame's soleplate (Figure 11.28). The reredos had become so hot that the soleplate had charred.[14] It is interesting to note that the fireplace was built against the existing timber-framed northern wall of the room it was intended to serve, rather than against the room's non-combustible masonry southern wall.

A shallow fireplace, possibly also of canopied type, was built into the thickness (*c*.750 millimetres or 2ft.6ins.) of the masonry party wall which was part of a phase-IV rear addition made to the same building

Fig. 11.27
The Court Hall, Quarter 8. Medieval chimney cap showing the cusped head to the recess and the attached corner shafts in the south face.

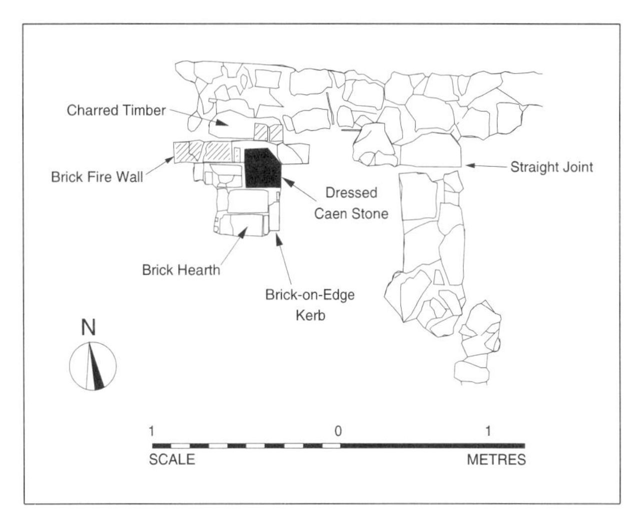

Fig. 11.28
Simplified plan of the excavated remains of the fireplace excavated within the house formerly adjacent to Blackfriars Barn, Quarter 15.

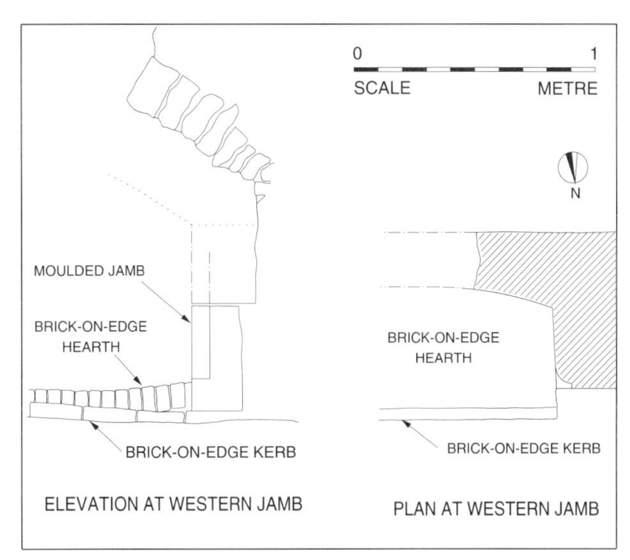

Fig. 11.29
Blackfriars Barn, Quarter 15. Details of the western jamb of the fireplace serving the hall.

probably late in the 14th century. Its 'Flemish'-brick hearth projected 300 millimetres (1ft.) into the room and did not incorporate projecting side jambs. Likewise, the fireplace built into the 700-millimetre (2ft.3ins.) masonry wall at Old Castle House, Quarter 8, may have incorporated a hood.[15] In both instances the remains are now too fragmentary to tell. Under normal circumstances one would expect fireplace recesses as shallow as these to have been fitted with canopies in order to collect the smoke. However, the hearth and remains of another exceptionally shallow fireplace built into the south wall of the hall at Blackfriars Barn, Quarter 15, was almost certainly never fitted with a hood and this must cast doubt on the design of those on the adjacent plot and at Old Castle House.

The hall fireplace at Blackfriars Barn can be shown to have been contemporary with the *c.*1300 build. It measured 2.44 metres (8 ft.) wide, but was only 320 millimetres (1ft.1in.) deep at the jambs. The rear wall curved a little to give a slightly increased depth of *c.*400 mm (1ft.4ins.) at the centre. The sandstone jambs were embellished with a quarter-roll moulding and formerly supported a surprisingly low, dressed-stone arch (now destroyed). Above the fireplace was a relieving arch of which only a short section now remains (Fig. 11.29). From what survives it would appear that the arch was of a depressed, two-centred type. The remains of the fireplace's rear wall, together with the rear parts of the jambs are of yellow 'Flemish'-type brickwork, rendered over. Yellow brick was also used to form the shallow (*c.*520 millimetres or 1ft.9ins.) hearth,

Fig. 11.30
Blackfriars Barn, Quarter 15. Remains of the blocked fireplace serving the hall. Note the hearth of 'Flemish' style bricks laid on edge.

which projects by *c.*120 millimetres (5ins.) into the room. It consisted of bricks placed on edge and set at 90° to the wall. As is usual in Winchelsea, there was never a stone kerb at the front; instead, the hearth was edged with similar bricks set lengthwise (Figures 11.29 and 11.30). In cross-section the flue itself was tiny and measured only c.220 millimetres (9ins.) deep. Very unusually, neither the fireplace enclosure nor its flue projected beyond the 600-millimetre (2ft.) thickness of the wall, there being no internal or external projection to the chimney.

In England, the late 14th century is usually regarded as a period of transition during which canopied fireplaces were abandoned in favour of the 'modern' type. In this type the hearth was set within a deep, flush-fronted enclosure whose side jambs projected forward to the front of the hearth in order to carry a lintel to support the front wall of the flue. Good local examples of canopied fireplaces exist within Tonbridge Castle Gatehouse, Kent (mid/late 13th century), the Priors Lodgings at Michelham Priory, Sussex (early 14th century), and the kitchens at Bodiam Castle (*c.*1385). The earliest known local rural example of a 'modern'-type fireplace is in the manor house of Battle Abbey at Great Maxfield, Guestling, Sussex (1372/3), where a massive projecting stone side stack serves the (later rebuilt) parlour crosswing.[16] Other examples occur at Bodiam Castle (*c.*1385) where they are located within the thickness of the massive external walls. Given the dates of these, and bearing in mind the apparent 'transitional' design of the hall fireplace at Blackfriars Barn, under normal circumstances it would be regarded as a key example illustrating the transition between the two forms. However, Blackfriars Barn also possesses a

Fig. 11.31
Standing Gable, Quarter 2, North Street. Corner chimney showing the remains of the flue rising within the wall.

Fig. 11.32
Standing Gable, Quarter 2, North Street. Remains of the ground-floor fireplace showing the canted front wall.

Fig. 11.33
Standing Gable, Quarter 2, North Street. Remains of the ground-floor fireplace showing the remains of the side jamb.

fully developed 'modern-style' fireplace - measuring 2.40 metres (7ft.10ins.) wide and 1.10 metres (3ft.7ins.) deep - within its front cellar. Its location precludes the possibility of its having been added at a later date. But as Margaret Wood has pointed out, the later fireplaces have much in common with those in use during the 12th century, and thus the canopied form should perhaps be regarded more as a fashion statement than as a precursor to the later forms.[17]

Whilst taking these factors into account, the shallow ground-floor fireplace at Blackfriars Barn is nonetheless exceptional in that it serves an open hall. Even in great houses such as Bodiam Castle (*c.*1385) and Herstmonceux Castle (1440), the halls are served by open hearths, and this despite the use of standard fireplaces elsewhere within both buildings. No other medieval open hall in Winchelsea has been proved to have been heated by a fireplace, rather than an open hearth. What is assumed to be a projecting chimney built into the rear wall of the hall at Firebrand, Quarter 13, could conceivably be of early date, although, to judge from soot-blackening on the timbers of the 15th-century roof, it almost certainly represents a post-medieval insertion, added when the hall was floored over.

The town does have houses served by conventional chimney stacks of late-medieval date, but these heat rooms and chambers rather than halls. A late-15th-century stone-built projecting chimney, probably constructed in 1477, survives at Glebe, Quarter 13, where it heats the parlour crosswing (*see* Chapter 10). Another late-15th- or early-16th-century stone chimney is that which serves the added northern rear range at The Armory, Quarter 7, (*see* Figure 10.28). Similar projecting external stacks at Five Chimneys, Quarter 1, and Salutation Cottages, Quarter 2, are almost certainly of post-medieval date.

In addition to those mentioned above, excavations have revealed four further examples of medieval hearths. Two of these, at New Inn, Quarter 14, and Truncheons, Quarter 20, were only partly excavated and thus neither their context within the buildings nor their dates could be ascertained.[18] The other two formed part of alterations made to the rear of the house adjacent to Blackfriars Barn. A probably late-14th-century hearth built to heat the small room behind the open hall was not enclosed by side jambs and thus could have incorporated a hood, though it is perhaps more likely to have been served by a timber-framed flue supported by the timbers of the first floor. The same is true of the hearth built in the ?15th century to serve the back kitchen. In this instance the hearth extended across the full 2.65-metre (8ft.8ins.) width of the room.

In only one instance have modifications to a hearth been recognized. At North Street, Quarter 2, the southern half of the 'Flemish' brick open hearth had been robbed-out, the robbing line being straight, cutting some of the bricks. Running across the impression of the robbed portion, against the retained part, was a shallow robber 'trench', and to the south of the 'trench', the floor had been made good over the discarded section of the hearth (*see* Figure 11.22).[19] These features may indicate that the hearth had been cut by a newly-inserted cross-partition and that the northern part of the hearth had been retained and extended northwards, perhaps to form the hearth of a smoke bay or canopied fireplace, with a fire set against the partition. This modification could have been made in response to either the total or partial flooring-over of the open hall. The adjusted flue arrangement may have been similar to that which appears to have existed at 2 Friars Road on Quarter 19, which has been tree-ring dated to between 1482 and 1499. At Friars Road there is evidence in the floor joisting of a very shallow, probably timber-framed flue or shallow smoke-bay rising hard against the end wall of the hall chamber and serving the hall below. This flue was later superseded by a larger chimney of brick and stone built upon the same site, though this may reuse its predecessor's carved timber lintel.

One further Winchelsea heating system deserves a mention. The remains of a very unusual pair of fireplaces can be seen incorporated within what is assumed to be an early standing gable on Quarter 2 - one heating the rear room on the ground floor, the other the rear chamber on the first floor. As with the fireplaces at Old Castle House and within the hall at Blackfriars Barn, the fireplaces are constructed within the thickness of the wall, but in this instance they are canted across the angle in the corner of the room and chamber (Figures 11.31-33. *See also* Figure 10.5). Usually corner fireplaces of this type were not used until late in the post-medieval period, these examples, however, are fully integrated into what is certainly a medieval gable. They incorporate 'Flemish'-type bricks identical to those used in many of the town's early buildings.

12. WASTE DISPOSAL

David and Barbara Martin

How a settlement - whether an individual cottage, isolated farm, or an entire town - disposed of its waste material can say much about that community's attitudes towards itself. It is therefore surprising that, although archaeologists make much of the contents of rubbish pits, middens and the like, very little has been written about the disposal methods used. Waste can be divided into three basic types: human excreta, domestic debris, and industrial waste. Regarding the latter, the Winchelsea evidence is silent, and even in respect of the first two groups the information is far from being as detailed as might be hoped. Nonetheless, the data which are available are worthy of consideration, albeit briefly.

SEWAGE DISPOSAL

The cesspits form one of the most impressive classes of structure encountered during the archaeological work undertaken within the town. The first one was discovered in the mid-20th century. Located approximately 2½ metres (8ft.) to the rear of Cellar 15 fronting Barrack Square, Quarter 7, adjacent to a tenement boundary, it was emptied by the owner of the property without any archaeological supervision. It is circular in plan, 2 metres (6ft.6ins.) in diameter and just over 2½ metres (8ft.) deep, apparently built upon the natural slope of the bedrock so as to aid drainage. It is lined with a masonry wall of Tilgate stone and is assumed to have originally been sited beneath a projecting garderobe turret attached to the rear of a structure which once stood over the cellar.[1]

Fig. 12.1
Cesspit at Mill Road

Since the discovery of this pit, four other examples have been archaeologically excavated: one at Mill Road, Quarter 3, another at Richmond House, Quarter 6, and two adjacent to Blackfriars Barn on Quarter 15 (*see* Figure 12.2).[2] Like that on Quarter 7, all are circular in plan and of very similar depth, ranging from 2.70 metres (8ft.10ins.) to 2.90 metres (9ft.6ins.) measured from medieval ground level.[3] There is more variation in their diameters. The largest of the examples excavated archaeologically was attached to the side of the ruined building now known as Blackfriars Barn on Quarter 15 and, with a diameter of 1.95 metres (6ft.4ins.), is of similar size to that on Quarter 7. The two smallest are the one at the rear of Richmond House, which has an average diameter of just 1.30 metres (4ft.3ins.) and that on the plot adjacent to Blackfriars Barn on Quarter 15 (*see* below). The cesspit from Mill Road, Quarter 3, likewise measures only 1.30 metres (4ft.3ins.) at floor level, but widens out to a diameter of 1.70 metres (5ft.7ins.) across the base. Like the cesspit on Quarter 7, the pits at Mill Road, Richmond House, and at Blackfriars Barn are stone-lined (Figure 12.1). In contrast, the second of the pits on Quarter 15, shown in Figure 12.3, was either entirely unlined or partially lined in timber.[4] It is of relatively slight diameter, and tapers from 1.45 metres (4ft.9ins.) at the top to a diameter of only 820 millimetres (2ft.8ins.) across its base.

It is probably no coincidence that the cesspits are located well back from the street and in all but one

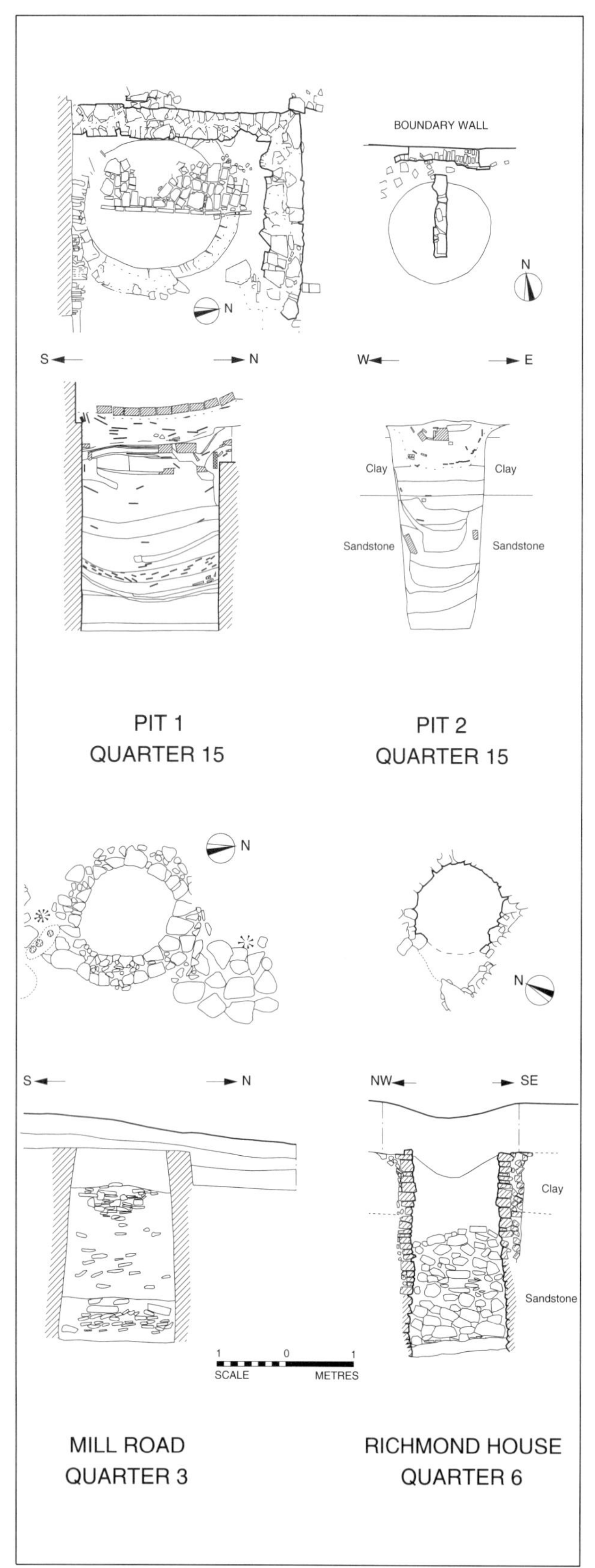

Fig. 12.2
Plans and sections through the archaeologically excavated cesspits.

Fig. 12.3
Cesspit 2, Quarter 15

example, are sited against a tenement boundary. Even the exception at Richmond House is not that far removed from the edge of the tenement. Similar locations have been noted within a number of other medieval towns.[5] The cesspit at Mill Road could have been shared by two properties. The large stone-lined pit attached to Blackfriars Barn initially served that building, although it was constructed upon the neighbouring plot. Indeed, it is possible that here too, both properties initially shared the use of the structure. This pit is sited beneath the remains of a generously proportioned stone garderobe block, which projected northwards from the side wall of the building. Incorporated into the west wall of the pit are the slight remains of the canted base to a garderobe chute, which originally extended down within the thickness of the wall from the toilet above. After the main structure fell out of use in the 14th century, both the garderobe and its pit were taken over by the adjacent house. The pit was backfilled in the 15th century, when the garderobe block was converted to use as a kitchen.

As with that at Blackfriars Barn, all the cesspits would have been capped either by a substantial garderobe block or by a lightly-constructed, detached privy building. Areas of paving adjacent to the pits at Mill Road and Richmond House were probably associated with these structures, although otherwise no remains of the buildings were found. Despite the lack of direct evidence, the second of the two cesspits on Quarter 15 was almost certainly located immediately beneath an outhouse which incorporated a latrine. This pit was made redundant in the 14th century when a large rear extension was built over it. Those at Mill Road and Richmond House appear to have been abandoned in the 16th century.

Bulk storage pits of the type described above were common, particularly in towns, and were considered by L. F. Salzman to have been 'the normal form of latrine'. As he pointed out, those employed in the occasional emptying of such pits, who sometimes had to remove literally tons of human waste, tended to be well paid for their services.[6] It is worth noting that in terms of faeces the Winchelsea pits contained residual deposits only, and therefore had been cleaned immediately prior to their abandonment.

Whether cesspits were the principal means of disposal, as Salzman suggested, is open to question, for there are many sites in England where no cesspits have been found. In addition, there are considerable numbers of examples, in southern England and elsewhere, of medieval and 16th-century houses which incorporated a garderobe turret fitted with a mucking-out hole at its base.[7] Unlike cesspits, such arrangements would have required regular cleansing. Together with the use of 'closed stools' (*i.e.* commodes), they probably represent the most common arrangements. These methods of disposal could be incorporated equally well into either an integrated garderobe or a detached privy. A third arrangement, particularly popular on monastic sites and in larger houses, involved diverting a stream or ditch under the latrine in order to flush away the excreta. In a hilltop town, however, this option was not available to the residents of Winchelsea.

THE DISPOSAL OF DOMESTIC RUBBISH

Although not in the same league as a modern 21st-century household, all medieval houses would have generated large quantities of rubbish, year in and year out. Admittedly much of this would have been biodegradable, but by no means all of it. Upon those plots which possessed a small garden, the biodegradable debris would doubtless have been recycled in the form of compost, placed either in heaps or in shallow, purposely dug pits. Regardless of the method adopted, the compost would have been removed annually, and thus the archaeological evidence left by this activity would consist of a series of re-cut pits or shallow scoops. Similar evidence would be left by heaps of rubbish not intended for compost, which was accumulated for periodic disposal.

Within Winchelsea, the most extensively investigated back-of-plot area is that at Mill Road, relating to Plot 2 on Quarter 3. Here, a number of shallow scoops containing residual rubbish were examined within the area immediately to the rear of the house.[8] Of particular interest was a complex group of 13 shallow inter-cut scoops clustered in an area two to four metres back from the house, and between it and the stone-lined cesspit, close to the tenement boundary (Figure 12.4). In addition to containing reasonable assemblages of pottery fragments, the residual fills to these scoops yielded a wide range of dietary data, including food bones and the shells of marine molluscs. Also present was charcoal from a number of tree and shrub species. Whilst the uppermost fills in this complex of scoops belong to the late 15th and 16th centuries, the lowest fills are much earlier and possibly date from the years following the refoundation of the town. The evidence is therefore consistent with long-term use of this area for the temporary storage of rubbish prior to its permanent disposal.

The excavations carried out elsewhere within the town up to 1998 have revealed a few other shallow scoops or pit-like features up to 300 millimetres (1ft.) in depth, but nothing which can definitively be described as a purposely dug rubbish pit.[9] This is not to say that pits and troughs containing rubbish do not exist within Winchelsea. On the contrary, as Schofield and Vince pointed out regarding other towns, the pits or troughs are usually features which, although dug for other purposes, have 'ended up as convenient places to dump rubbish'.[10] At the end of their lives the cesspits within the town were used for this purpose, as indeed were the well on Plot 21, Quarter 15, and some of the cellars. The cellar discovered in 2003 in the grounds of the primary school on Quarter 18 had been backfilled in this way, although during the medieval and Tudor periods the Corporation appears to have discouraged the destruction of the town's cellars by such actions. Thus, in 1561 offences brought

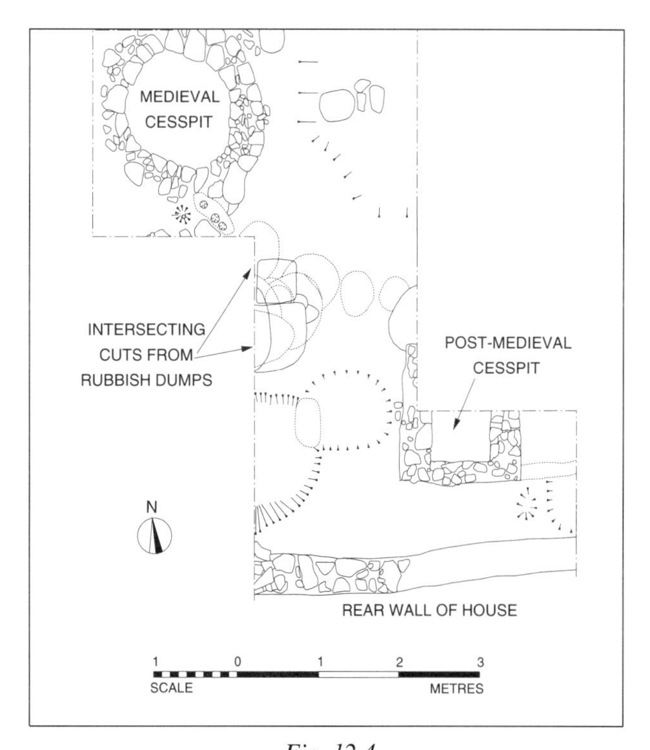

Fig. 12.4
Intersecting scoops left after removal of rubbish accumulated in an area at the rear of a house excavated in Mill Road, 1981

before the Corporation included casting 'soil' into cellars, whilst the following year a further presentment was made relating to the 'casting of dung' into a cellar in The Butchery.[11] Fieldwalking carried out for the National Trust in 1993 in the area of Stonemill Green, immediately to the north of Quarter 5, recovered finds which suggest that in the 16th century, the former town ditch of 1415 was being used as a town rubbish dump. The same is probably true of other sections of the town dyke during the late medieval and early modern periods. But in common with other port towns, the bulk of the town's rubbish probably found its way down to the waterfront - to the area described in the 1292 rental as the 'land next to the salt water which was dangerous at all flowings of the tide'. Here it was doubtless used during the town's period of greatest prosperity to make up ground levels behind new wharf and quayside revetments.[12] This is an area of the town which has not as yet been subjected to archaeological investigation. What the excavations to date do suggest is that, at least within the principal Quarters, during the medieval period the town was for the most part kept clean. The occupation layers encountered have been devoid of debris. Only within the construction and destruction layers have build-ups of discarded material been noted.

13. TRADE AND STATUS: AN ARCHAEOLOGICAL PERSPECTIVE

David Rudling

New Winchelsea, the prestigious and mercantile late medieval town, and the much smaller Tudor settlement which succeeded it, provide archaeologists with important opportunities for the recovery of artefactual evidence which can help to document changes in both economic and social aspects of this urban settlement and port.

Archaeological fieldwork undertaken at Winchelsea since 1974 has yielded a wide range of finds: pottery, glass, coins, other metalwork, building materials, artefacts made of stone, and human, animal and plant remains. Of particular importance in this instance are the large quantities of pottery finds, not only for local ceramic studies, but also for research into regional and international trade.[1] With the exception of the building materials, which are included elsewhere in this book, this chapter provides summaries of the main Winchelsea finds' reports and highlights how these finds provide information with regard to three main themes: local and long distance trade, craft and industrial activities and living standards and status.

THE POTTERY: SOURCES AND CONSUMER CHOICES

A study of all the pottery finds recovered at Winchelsea between 1976 and 1982 was undertaken by Clive Orton.[2] Most of what follows is summarized from Orton's report which is divided into two parts: presentation of the pottery as a type-series; and the presentation and discussion of the major assemblages of pottery from the various sites. Orton divided the pottery into three broad chronological groups: late medieval (*c.*1300-1450/1500); transitional or Tudor (*c.*1450/1500-1600); and post-medieval (1600-present day). Only the first two groups are considered here.

The Late Medieval Pottery

Three main pottery types were recognized by Orton: Saintonge ware, Rye ware and black ware. Collectively these wares account for 95% of all the medieval pottery assemblage. There were also some minor imports and two minor local fabrics. Since the transition from late medieval to Tudor traditions of manufacture and vessel forms did not take place at a single date, some examples of 'Tudor' wares (especially Tudor green ware and Dutch red ware) may be of late medieval date as defined by Orton.

Saintonge wares

About one quarter of all the medieval pottery from Winchelsea that Orton examined was from Saintonge in southwest France. This includes both fine wares and coarse ware. The fine wares, which form 22% of the total medieval pottery assemblage, can be divided into four main types: polychrome (about 3%), green-glazed (20%); mottled green-glazed (50%) and unglazed (27%). The first type, which consists entirely of jugs of form Chapelot (1983) 123 or 125, has very attractive painted decoration in three styles: birds and shields (Figure 13.1), foliar scroll, and filled zone. There are also examples of face-masks applied to the rim, as with the example illustrated in Figure 13.1. Although Saintonge green-glazed ware is also represented by jugs similar in form to those in polychrome ware, this pottery type also includes small jugs or mugs. The mottled green-glazed fine ware was also used for jugs mostly of Chapelot (1983) form 126, but also for small bowls and a large three-handled pitcher. The fourth type of fine ware, which is unglazed and may include the unglazed parts of vessels in other fine-ware categories, is represented by jugs and by a single lid.

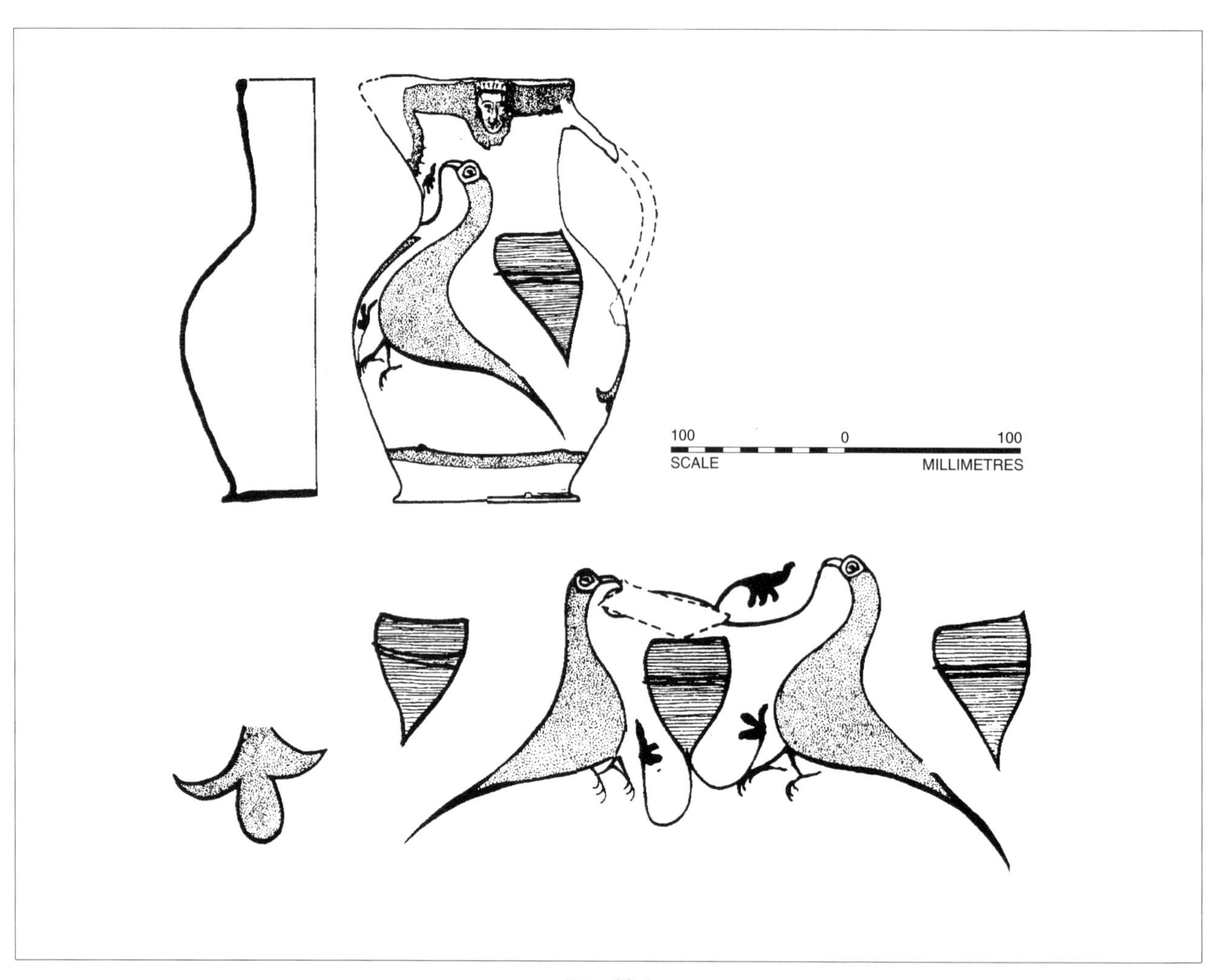

Fig. 13.1
Polychrome Saintonge ware jug decorated with birds and shields

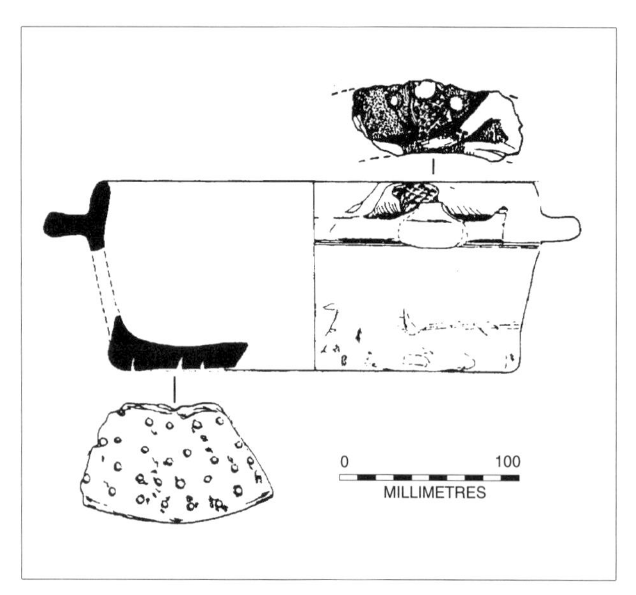

Fig. 13.2
Mortar in Saintonge coarse ware

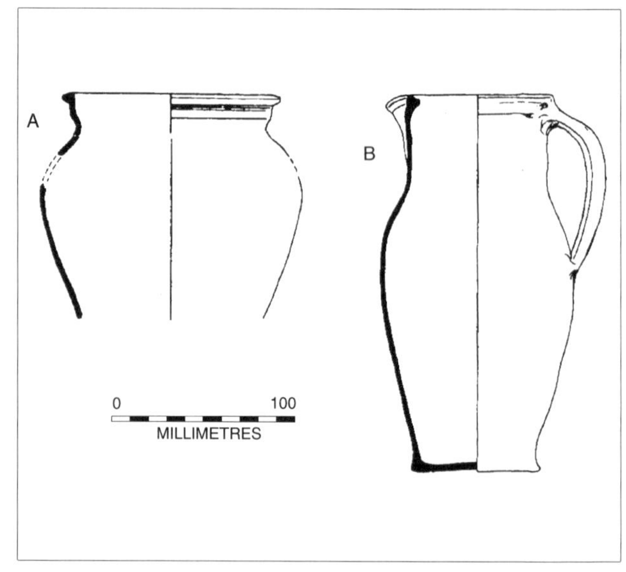

Fig. 13.3.
Examples of imported wares, other than Saintonge

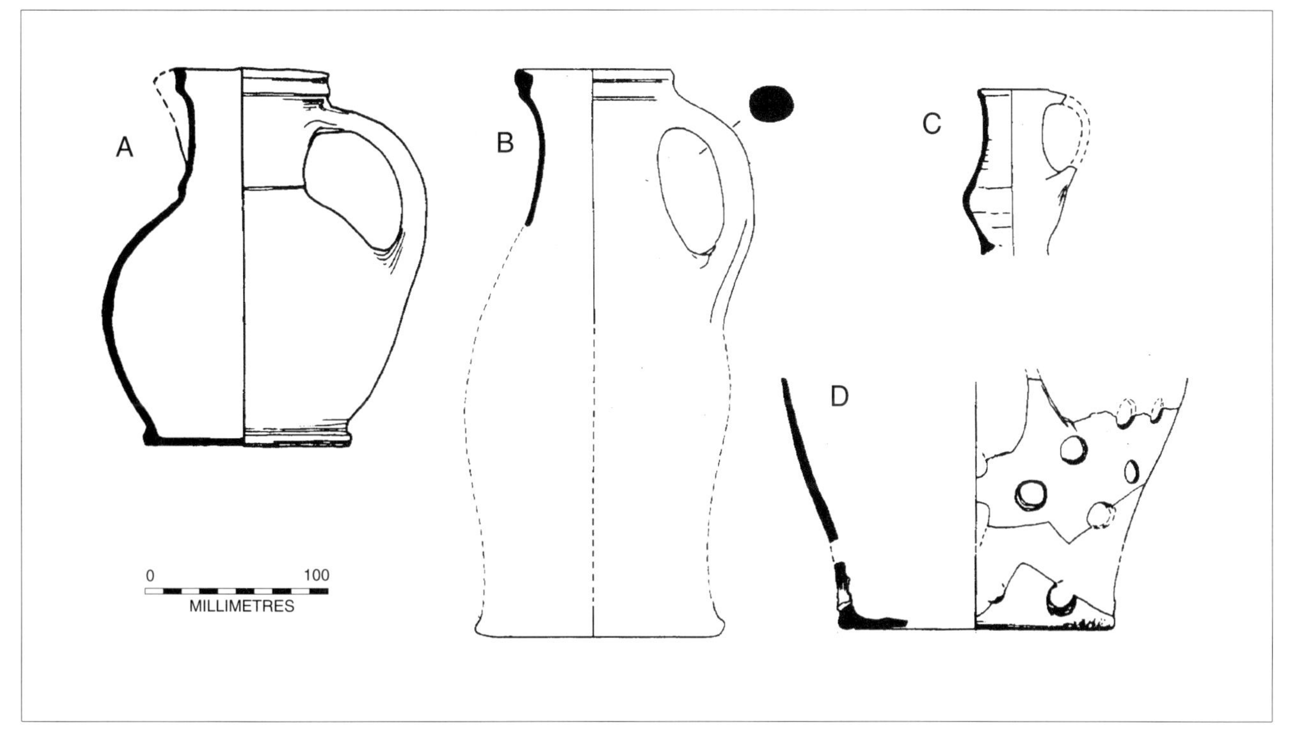

Fig. 13.4. Vessels of Rye A and B wares

Whilst the Saintonge fine wares found at Winchelsea were mainly used as high quality tableware or drinking vessels, Saintonge coarse ware (3.5% of the medieval assemblage) was used for a range of more utilitarian forms and did not include jugs. The most distinctive vessel in this group is the mortar illustrated in Figure 13.2. There are also two dripping-pans, a possible chafing-dish, and a bowl, all with mottled green glaze. A possible cooking-pot and a pitcher have no glaze but do have red-painted decoration.

Other medieval imported pottery

One cooking-pot (Figure 13.3, A), in a pale brown fabric with moderate inclusions of schist, is thought to have been made on the Continent, with the Central and Armorican massifs in France or Southern Spain being possible manufacture sites. Four body sherds in a soft, light-red fabric are similar to two sherds of *céramique onctueuse* (oily ware) in the British Museum, and thus are probably from the same general area of southern Brittany. The imports of *céramique onctueuse* which have been found are thinly distributed along the south coast, examples come from Dover, Seaford and Southampton.[3] Another probable French import is a jug with a mottled green glaze (Fig. 13.3, B). This vessel is thought to have been made in northern France.

Other medieval imports include a stoneware mug from Siegburg in Germany, two possible sherds of Andenne ware and two sherds of Aardburg ware from the Low Countries.

Rye Wares

Almost half (47%) of all the Winchelsea medieval pottery was assigned to the local Rye kilns. The pottery can be subdivided into three main fabric groupings: A, B and C.

Rye A and B wares, which both have lead glaze on the exterior but differ in terms of fineness, hardness and colour, were mainly used to produce wheel-thrown jugs, examples of which are shown in Figure 13.4, A and B. Decorative techniques include 'raspberry' and six-pointed star prunts, applied annuli, pellets and six-pointed stars, combing, horizontal grooving and painted lines.[4] One unusual vessel in Rye A ware is a miniature jug of apparently standard form, but about one third of the usual size (Figure 13.4, C). Two other unusual vessels in what appears to be Rye B ware are also present: the base of a pot of unknown function whose walls are pierced by a large number of circular holes about 15 millimetres in diameter (Figure 13.4, D), and three legs from a free-standing figure, perhaps an aquamanile.

Rye C ware is similar to Rye A ware except in colour and the location of the glaze, which is only consistently found on the interior of bases. The larger forms may be decorated with thumbed clay strips, usually applied diagonally. The most common form (50%) is the cooking-pot, an example of which is illustrated in

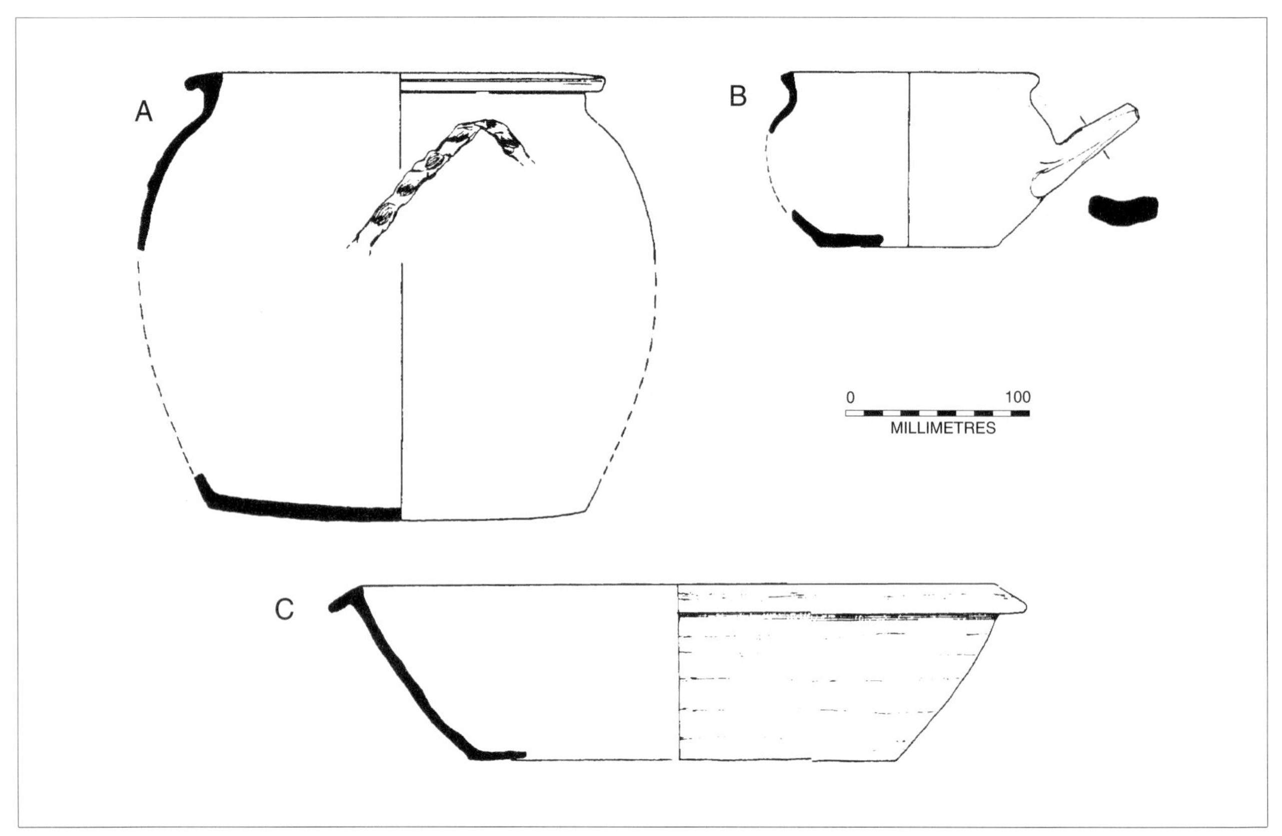

Fig. 13.5.
Vessels of Rye C ware

Figure 13.5, A. Next most common (about 12% each) are pitchers and small skillets (Figure 13.5, B). Bowls (Figure 13.5, C) and 'frying-pan' forms are minor elements in the assemblage (7 and 5% respectively). There are also single examples of a lid and a small cylindrical vessel with a hole of unknown function in its base.

Overall, the most common Rye ware products are jugs (40%), cooking-pots (30%), skillets (9%) and pitchers (7%), with no other form exceeding 5% of the total.

Black ware

Examples of this ware in Winchelsea and Hastings Museums have been called 'Winchelsea black ware', but since there is no firm evidence that this ware was produced at Winchelsea, a less specific name seems preferable at present .[5] The fabric is hard, with variable quantities of shell and/or iron-ore inclusions, and the surfaces are dark grey or black. Vessels are wheel-thrown but unglazed. This ware, which forms about 22.5% of the medieval assemblage at Winchelsea, comprises: cooking-pots (52%; Figure 13.6, A); jugs and pitchers (26%); and bowls (17%; Figure 13.6, B). Other vessel forms include skillets, a strainer, a lid and a curfew.

The quantities of black ware found at Winchelsea indicate to Orton that 'the source of these vessels is no further from Winchelsea than Rye, and that since there are no other suitable sites in the area, Winchelsea itself is the most likely source'. This conclusion, 'quantitatively supported', thus concurs with the source originally suggested by Barton. Other possible evidence for medieval pottery- and tile-production at Winchelsea includes some wasters recovered in 1993 from a field near Holy Rood. Whilst the pottery wasters are not of black ware, they can be assigned to the 14th century. They are oxidized throughout and include both cooking-pots and glazed jugs.[6]

Other English sources of medieval pottery

Other medieval pottery fabrics present at Winchelsea include flint-tempered ware and shelly ware. Cooking-pots, bowls and a large jug all made of flint-tempered ware may have been produced at Abbot's Wood, near Hailsham, in East Sussex.[7] Such pottery, however, represents less than 1% of the medieval assemblage at Winchelsea. The source of a single cooking-pot in shelly ware is unknown.

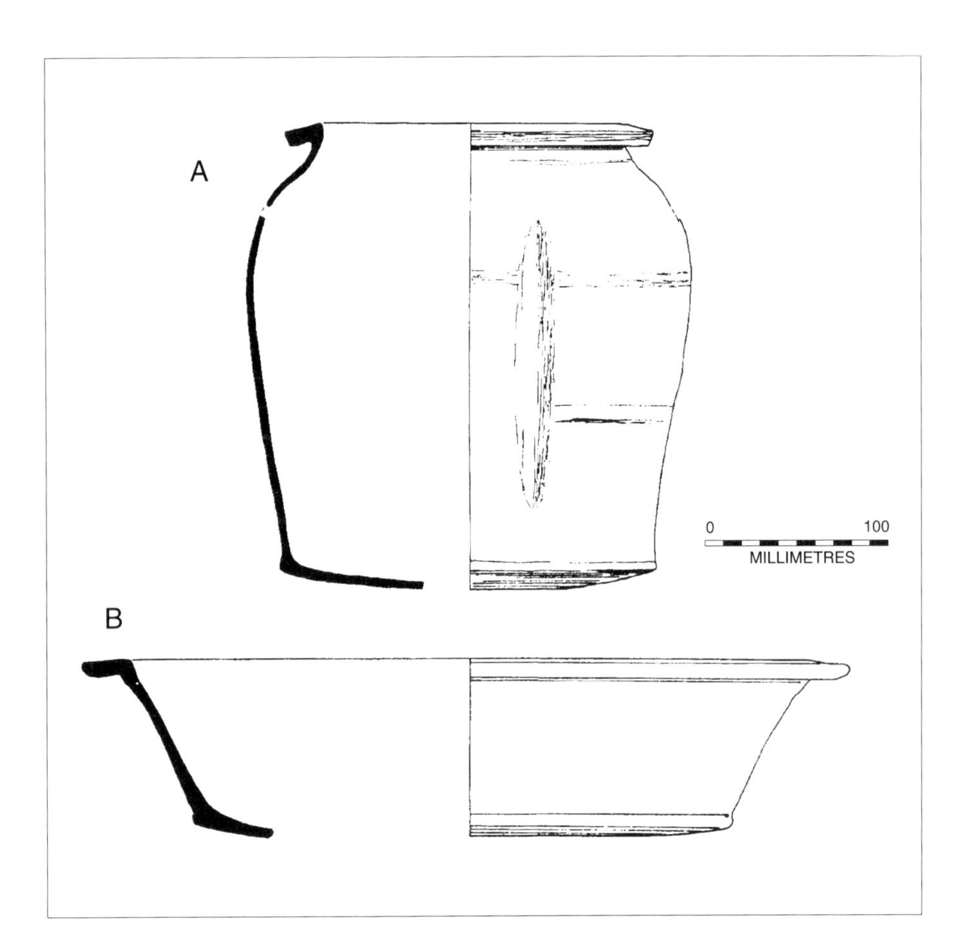

Fig. 13.6. (Right)
Vessels of local black ware

Discussion

The most striking feature of the medieval pottery assemblage at Winchelsea is the very high proportion of Saintonge wares, especially as there are very few other imports. Orton notes that accurate comparative figures from other towns are still not common, although a survey by Allan indicates comparable figures from selected groups at Southampton and Plymouth, in contrast to a generally much lower figure along the south coast, and a scarcity of imports inland.[8] A more local survey highlights the relatively small quantities of medieval imports in Sussex, but Hurst suggests that this may reflect patterns of archaeological excavation rather than patterns of trade.[9] From elsewhere in England the Winchelsea data can be compared with a total of 10 to 15% imports in 14th-century groups at Trig Lane, London, and 20 to 30% of Saintonge ware in groups from Hull.[10] Orton notes that since the figures from Winchelsea relate to a generally undifferentiated date range of *c*.1300-1450/1500 as opposed to selected groups of an appropriate date, and given that Saintonge imports may generally belong to the period before 1350, the percentage of imports in the date range 1300-1350 may be even higher than the overall late medieval figure of 25%.[11] Alternatively, as advocated by Watkins, Saintonge imports belonging to the period 1350-1450 may be more common than has previously been supposed.[12] Whatever the case, the Winchelsea Saintonge figures are comparable with those from the major contemporary ports of Plymouth, Southampton and Hull. Considered against the small number of other pottery imports, this is consistent with direct contact between Winchelsea and the pottery markets of southwest France, rather than redistribution from other ports along the English coast. Such trading presumably developed, and may finally have declined, alongside the much more important shipment of wine from Gascony. The importation of the Saintonge pots (most of which are jugs), should be considered against the local availability of high quality, but presumably cheaper, jugs from the kilns at Rye, about three miles away. It is thus possible that the well-made and attractively decorated jugs from Saintonge may have had a status value.

Whilst other non-local sources of medieval pottery are rare at Winchelsea (*see* above and Figure 13.7), local potters at Rye, and probably also at or near Winchelsea, produced the bulk of the town's pottery requirements other than jugs. In the case of the Rye kilns, they also supplied a substantial proportion of the jugs. It is thus possible that pottery manufacture was an important medieval industry at Winchelsea. Given the

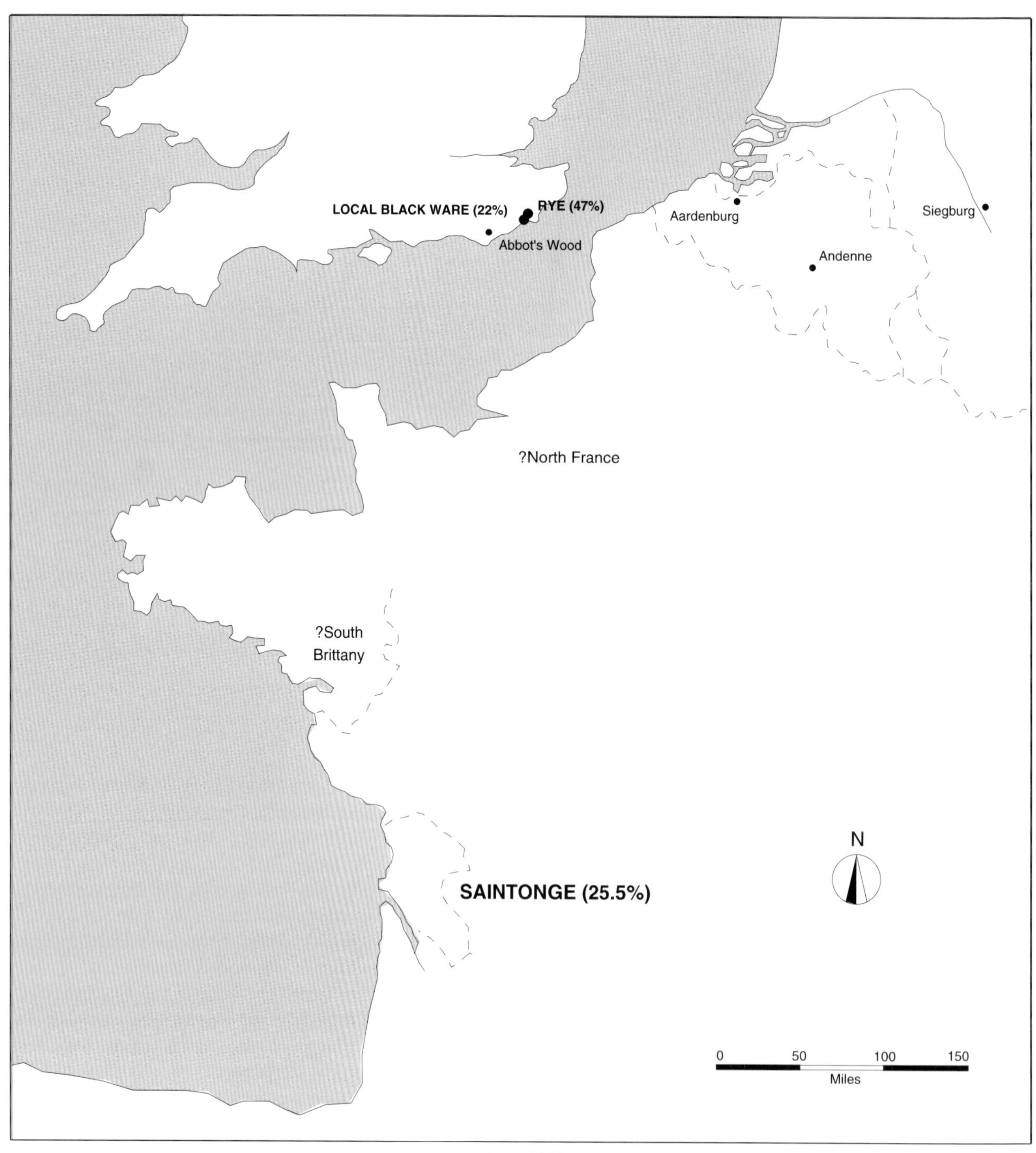

Fig. 13.7
Sources of medieval pottery discovered in Winchelsea. Vessel-equivalent quantities for the principal sources are given in brackets. ?South Brittany = un-proven provenance. Central and Armorican massifs not shown.

lack of known kiln sites for the production of black ware, it is important to continue the study of this type of ceramic by the recording and quantification of such pottery at sites other than Winchelsea, such as at Rye and on the Romney Marsh.

With regard to variations in the sources of medieval pottery found at different sites in Winchelsea, Orton notes that these variations are small and possibly reflect a relatively homogeneous social structure.

The Transitional (or Tudor) Pottery

The pattern of sources of pottery used at Winchelsea during the Tudor period is completely

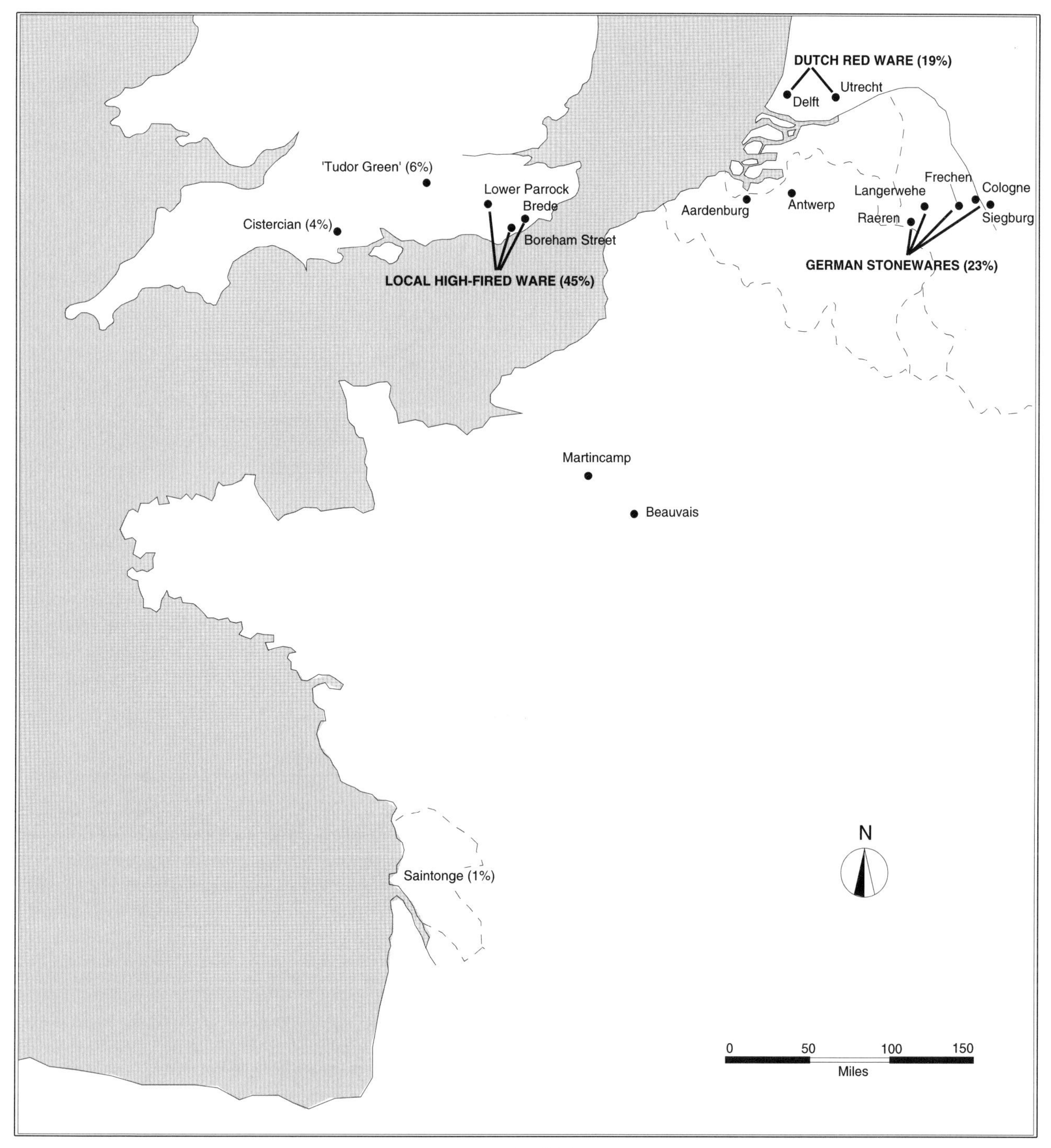

Fig. 13.8
Sources of post-medieval pottery discovered in Winchelsea.
Vessel-equivalent quantities for the principal sources are given in brackets.

different. Local sources contract to less than half the pottery, whilst stonewares (mostly Raeren) and Dutch red earthenwares contribute about 20% each. Non-local English sources (Tudor green and Cistercian wares) together make up another 10%. Although comparative data are less readily available for this period than for the medieval period, Orton is of the opinion that the high proportion of imported stoneware is not out of line with other port sites. The high proportion of Dutch red earthenware can be matched at Hull and Newcastle,[13] but is higher than Orton would expect from London, and larger than is usual on the south coast.[14] By this period there were very few French imports, including products from Saintonge. Orton concludes that 'there seems to be

Fig. 13.9 (Above)
German stoneware mugs

Fig. 13.10 (Right).
Dutch red ware cooking-pot

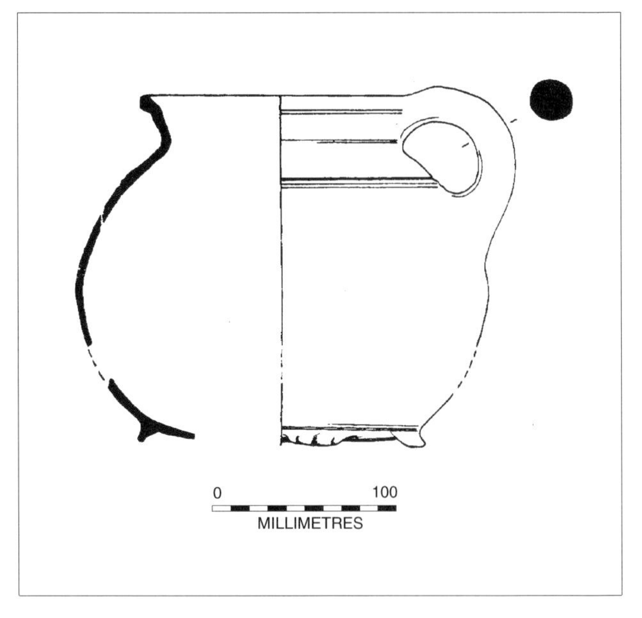

a distinct change from an English Channel and generally westward orientation to a North Sea and eastward orientation at this date' (*see* Figure 13.8).

German stonewares

Three sources of imported stoneware mugs were identified: Raeren (including possibly Langerwehe) (Figure 13.9), Siegburg, and Cologne/Frechen.

Dutch red ware

The most common Dutch red ware vessel form at Winchelsea is the cauldron-type cooking-pot (Figure 13.10). Other forms include chafing-dishes, bowls, strainers, pans, dripping-pans and a plate or dish.

Other imported pottery

The Saintonge kilns are represented by a number of sherds, of which the majority appears to be from chafing-dishes. One cylindrical fragment is interpreted by Orton as a leg from a free-standing figurine, probably animal rather than human. From Beauvais there are two examples of plates with sgraffito decoration and an undecorated bowl. Martincamp is represented by a few sherds from a flask. The few Dutch tin-glazed, Delft-ware sherds are from two altar vases and a mug. Representing links with Spain is a single sherd from a costrel.

Perhaps the most interesting of the Tudor imports is a small jar from the site of St Giles's churchyard (Figure 13.11). Anthony Streeten has identified it as a type of vessel thought to have been imported from the east Mediterranean, probably as a container for mercury. Other such finds from the abbey sites at Battle and Bayham indicate that mercury jars were among imports which reached Sussex during the early 16th century.[15] Additional examples of these jars are known from London, Canterbury and Southampton. The association of such jars at both Battle and Bayham with distilling apparatus has led to the suggestion that the contents of the jars probably had an association with alchemy.

English non-local wares

Tudor green ware from Hampshire/Surrey is represented at Winchelsea by various mugs (for example, Figure 13.12), and probably also by an albarello. A single cooking-pot is the sole example of Hampshire/ Dorset ware. Cistercian ware is also present and includes at least one mug.

High-fired local earthenwares

This category of pottery is a collective name given to a group of at least three very hard, usually light-red fabrics which share characteristics and forms. The most common form is the jug or pitcher (Figure 13.13, A), some of which have bungholes. The only other common form is the cooking-pot (Figure 13.13, B). Other vessels include a deep bowl or jar and a plate. Sources of such hard-fired earthenwares in East Sussex have been discussed by Streeten.[16] Comparative analysis of both fabric texture and inclusion sizes undertaken by Streeten and Orton suggests that the majority of the type 'A' hard-fired earthenwares at Winchelsea were manufactured either at Lower Parrock in Hartfield[17] or at Boreham Street in Wartling, although Brede could be another, and more convenient possibility. The other fabrics present at Winchelsea appear to Orton to be very

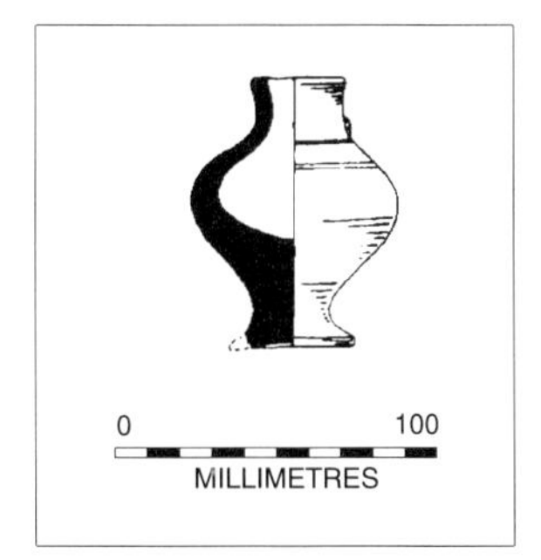

Fig. 13.11.
16th-century mercury jar

Fig. 13.12.
Two-handled Tudor green ware mug

similar to the medieval Rye A and B fabrics, and he concludes that it is possible that there were Tudor kilns at Rye. Comparisons of the Winchelsea data with those from Camber Castle indicate that during the 16th century these sites may have shared a trend away from Low Countries red wares towards local, hard-fired red wares.[18]

Discussion

In addition to the major changes outlined above in the supply of Tudor pottery to Winchelsea, the pattern of vessel forms used also appears superficially different from that of the late-medieval period: mugs (35%) were the most common, followed by pitchers (32%), cooking-pots (23%) and bowls/pans (4%). Orton points out, however, that any contrasts with the past may be misleading as there is probably little difference in function between the large medieval jugs and the Tudor pitchers, while smaller jugs may well have functioned as mugs (*i.e.* as drinking vessels). If this is indeed so, there is almost no change in the proportions of pottery forms. He concludes that the pattern thus shows an increasing functional differentiation: small jugs becoming mugs and large jugs becoming pitchers. Orton also notes changes in the form of cooking-pots: the Tudor examples were of 'cauldron' type, with two looped handles and three short feet, and usually a rounded base. He suggests that these differences may reflect changes in cooking techniques.

THE GLASS: DRINKING VESSELS AND WINDOW PANES

The excavations of 1976 to 1982 yielded some pieces of late medieval/early post-medieval glass, both from vessels and windows. John Shepherd has reported on all such finds, which mainly date to the 15th and 16th centuries.[19] Other glass of similar date was found during the excavation of a stone-lined cesspit in the garden of

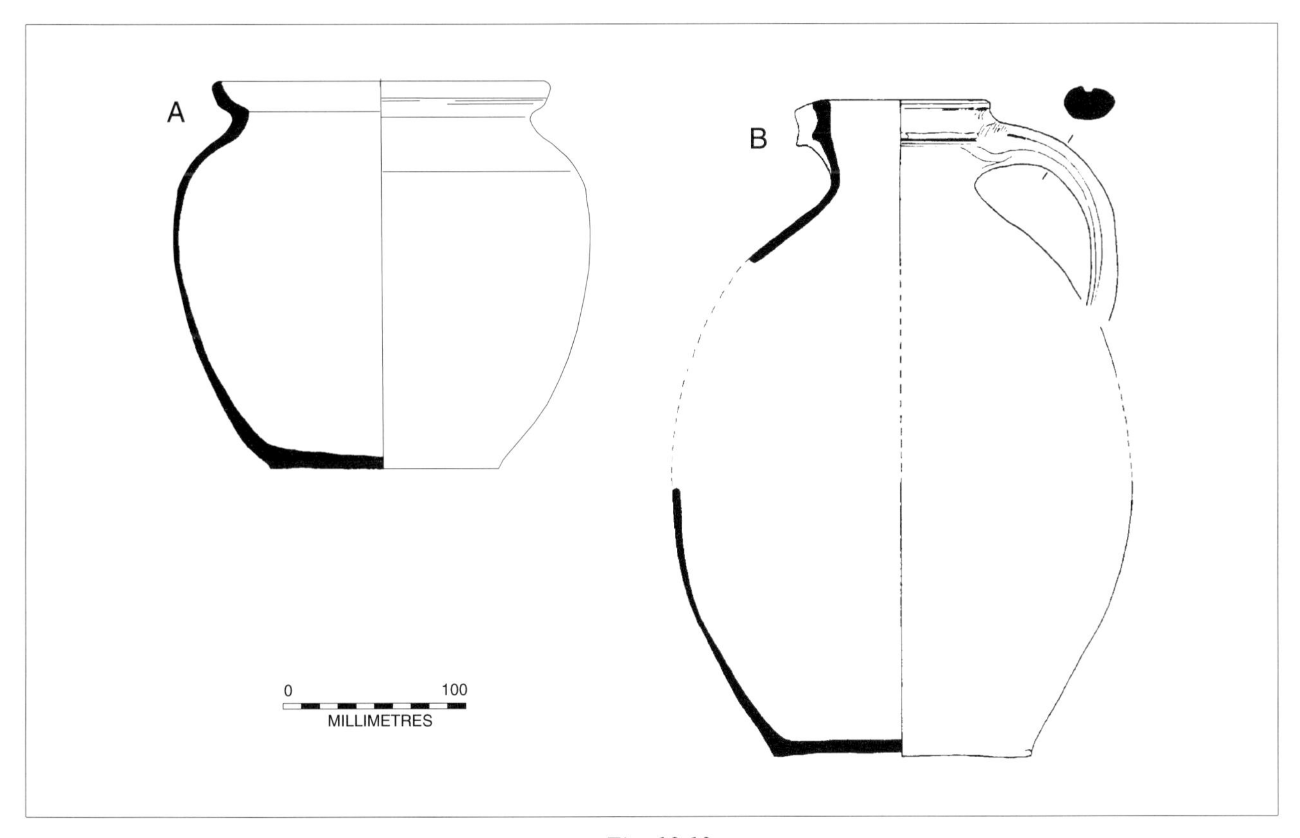

Fig. 13.13.
Vessels of hard-fired local earthenware

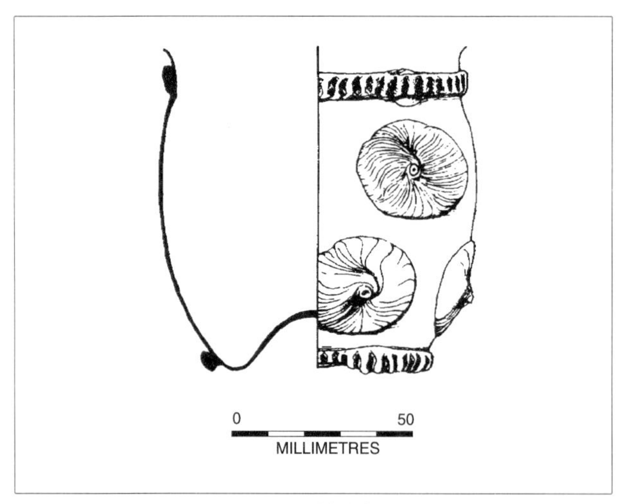

Fig. 13.14.
Glass beaker

Richmond House.[20] In both cases the finds comprised both imported glass and forest (potash) glass, the latter having probably been made in the Surrey-Sussex Weald, although sources on the Continent, such as the Netherlands, are also possible.[21]

Some of the most significant finds were recovered at Quarter 15, plot 21. Here parts of at least three, and possibly more, beakers from a well-known series of vessels decorated with applied 'prunts' were recovered. An example is shown in Figure 13.14. Known as *Krautstrunk* (cabbage-stalk) or, simply, *Nuppenbecher* (prunted beakers), during the late 15th and early 16th centuries this type of vessel was most popular in Germany, and slightly less so in the Netherlands.[22] It is probable that the Winchelsea examples originated from a continental, probably Rhineland German source. The discovery of 'prunted' beakers in England is not common, and their presence at Winchelsea and also at Southampton might indicate that they were not traded far inland. Other possible continental imports from the same site include a base from a flask or beaker, and a piece from a beaker or the bowl of a goblet; a 16th- or 17th-century date was assigned to the latter.

From the same site, but probably the products of Wealden glasshouses, are fragments of vessels which include either a goblet or beaker, a bottle or conical beaker, part of a spherical urinal or flask, as well as other beakers and flasks. Their periods of manufacture are unknown. Part of a Wealden goblet found at Mill Road is dated to the late 16th to early 17th century.

The cesspit at Richmond House also yielded fragments from glass vessels which may be of Wealden manufacture.[23] Two of these fragments are from cylindrical beakers dated to the late 16th or early 17th century. The cesspit also yielded fragments from various drinking glasses, including a two-piece goblet with the remains of a gilded frieze. Another goblet, but of one-piece type, has mould-blown ribbing on the interior. Another vessel is part of a cylindrical beaker with gadrooned ribs. Maxwell-Stewart dates this glass assemblage to the mid to late 16th century and is of the opinion that:

> 'much of this glass has strong Venetian features. It is, however, not sophisticated enough to come from Murano, but more likely to be Façon de Venise from the Netherlands'.

It would thus appear that at least during Tudor times, the inhabitants of various sites in Winchelsea, and also the garrison at nearby Camber Castle, were able to obtain high-quality, imported drinking vessels.[24] They, and others, also had access to inferior forest glass. At both Winchelsea and Camber Castle the preponderance of drinking vessels (beakers, goblets, *etc.*) is a status indicator, as on the whole glass was preferred to other materials by those who could afford it, whilst for the gentry, wine was the respected drink: it indicated the wealth needed to obtain such imports.[25]

Window glass has also been found at various sites in Winchelsea. The most important assemblage of such material was recovered from the cesspit at Richmond House and includes a number of pieces of patterned, stained glass.[26] Elsewhere plain window glass has been found at various sites. In most cases the triangular, diamond or rectangular window quarries were fairly small. Whilst the discovery of window glass in the vicinity of St Giles's Church is to be expected, the finding of similar material at domestic sites may be a status indicator. However, much depends upon the date of this material, as during the second half of the 16th century domestic window glass became widely available. The limited contextual dating evidence for the discoveries of window glass on domestic sites at Winchelsea indicates that it was available for such sites by at least the 16th century, but the dating cannot be more specific.

MONEY MATTERS

The archaeological fieldwork undertaken at Winchelsea prior to 2003 yielded very few coins or jetons, and no lead tokens or coin weights; the latter were needed by various individuals, such as merchants, to check the weights of both English and Continental coins. However, a few more discoveries have been recovered as chance finds.[27]

Representing medieval times, when Winchelsea was at its peak, are just three coins. One, from the Mill Road excavations, is a silver halfpenny of Edward I or II (*c.*1302-1310). Another, a surface find, is a silver penny of Edward IV (1461-1482). A further surface find is a copper *gigot* of Marie de Bourgogne (Mary of Burgundy), Countess of Flanders (1477-1482), and

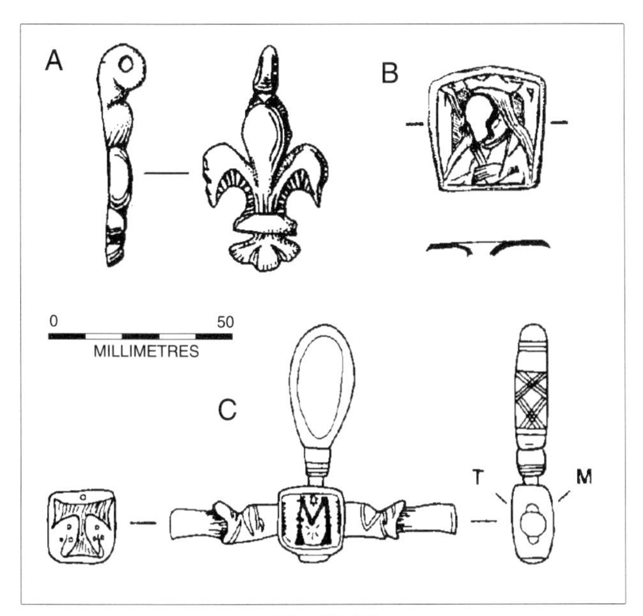

Fig. 13.15.
Copper-alloy objects

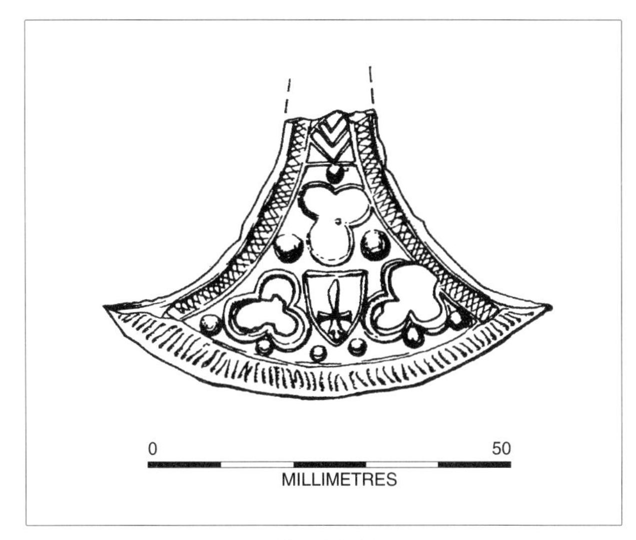

Fig. 13.16.
Lead pilgrim souvenir

presumably represents a trade contact with the Low Countries. Dating to the early 17th century is a copper 'Harrington' farthing (*c.*1613-14) of James I, which was recovered from one of the upper fills of the cesspit at Richmond House.[28] Of earlier manufacture, but retrieved from the same cesspit is a German brass jeton (casting counter) of Hans Schultes I (1553-1584) of Nuremburg. In England and on the Continent from late medieval times, jetons were used on a counting board for calculation purposes. At nearby Camber Castle a total of 16 Nuremberg jetons were recovered, but that site too has yielded very little actual coinage: just two examples dated to the final 17th-century stages of occupation at the site.[29]

The very small number of recorded coins and jetons from Winchelsea is surprising, especially since the medieval town was such an important mercantile centre. The shortage of coinage recovered from the 1974-1982 excavations can perhaps partly be explained by the non-use of metal detectors and a lack of large-scale wet sieving. It is worth noting that in the summer of 2003, 11 medieval coins and/or jetons were found during hand-dug excavation in advance of development at the Church of England primary school, but at the time of writing these coins had not been cleaned or identified. Why this site has yielded a relatively large assemblage of coins in contrast to the earlier excavations is unclear, but its location near the Monday Market may indicate a commercial importance, and thus a greater usage, and loss, of coinage.

Despite the shortage of coin finds at Winchelsea, there have been two discoveries of late medieval purse-frames (*see* below).

METAL OBJECTS AND METALLURGY

Although no medieval or early post-medieval items made either of gold or silver (other than coins) have been found at Winchelsea, a wide range of objects made of copper alloy, lead, lead alloy or iron has been recovered. In addition, samples of both bronze-working and iron-forging slags have also been found.

Objects made of copper alloy, lead or lead alloy

The various finds made of copper alloy or lead from the 1976-1982 excavations were catalogued by Alison Goodall. She reports that they form a diverse group of items of mainly medieval and early post-medieval date and of a largely domestic nature, such as would have been in use on a habitation site.[30] While none of the dress accessories are highly ornamental, some of the other finds are indicative of high status. A copper-alloy fleur-de-lis pendant is the most decorative of the finds (Figure 13.15, A). A decorated copper-alloy knife-handle plate of the Tudor period comes from what must have been a very fine object for use at the meal table. The incised decoration on this object shows a crowned female figure (Figure 13.15, B). A 16th-century copper-alloy purse-bar in Winchelsea Museum has niello-ornament and the initials M and T (Figure 13.15, C). There is also a second, but much less ornate, 16th-century purse-bar. A lead badge or pilgrim souvenir with heraldic or pseudo-heraldic decoration may also be an indicator of high status (Figure 13.16). Similarly, the discovery at Mill Road of pieces of window lead may be further evidence of glazing to domestic properties.

Indicators of either craft activity or trade are scarce, but include a copper-alloy needle with triangular-

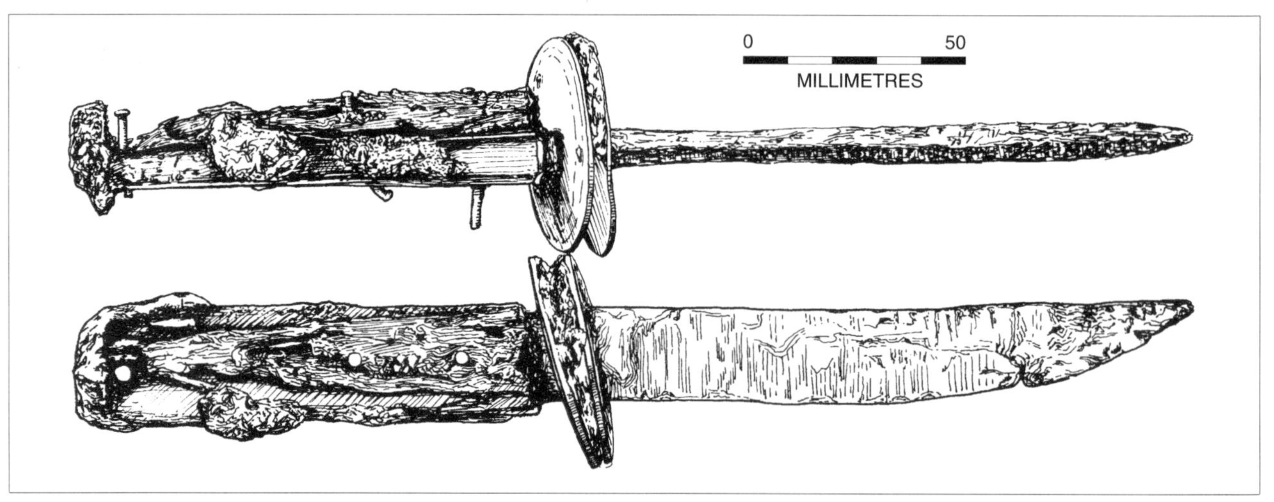

Fig. 13.17
Rondel-dagger from North Street

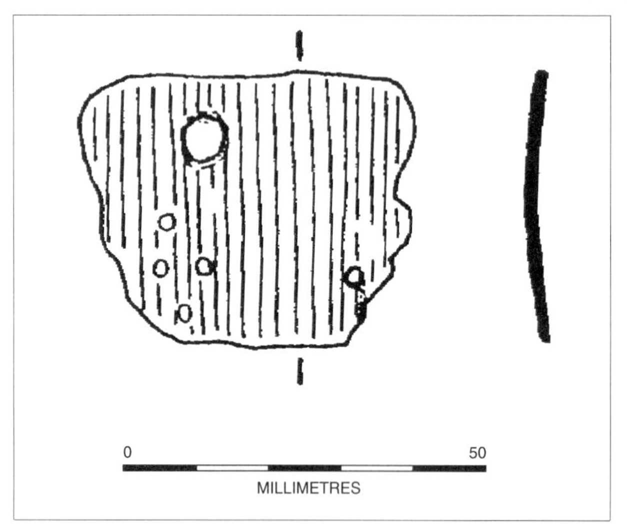

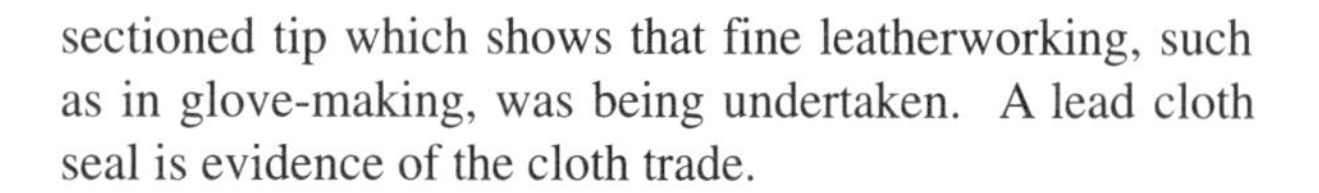

Fig. 13.18
Piece of iron plate-armour

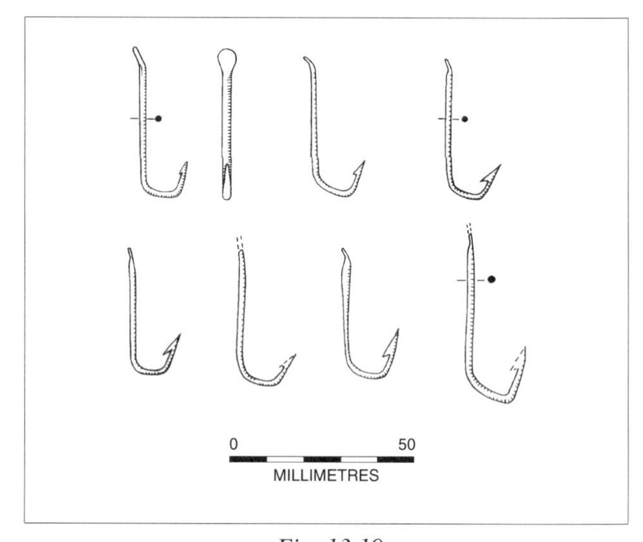

Fig. 13.19
A selection of iron fish-hooks

sectioned tip which shows that fine leatherworking, such as in glove-making, was being undertaken. A lead cloth seal is evidence of the cloth trade.

Iron Objects

The various iron objects were catalogued by Ian Goodall, who notes that they cover a wide range of artefact types.[31] Whilst a dagger and a piece of armour are the most significant finds, the remainder, including a spade-iron, fish-hooks, knives, nails, items of structural ironwork and some keys, are more routine discoveries. Most of the iron objects are medieval in date, although some later material was also found. The reader's attention is also drawn to an armour-piercing arrowhead recovered during the 1974 excavations in German Street.[32]

The most important iron object to have been recovered by excavation in Winchelsea is the rondel-dagger illustrated in Figure 13.17. This weapon, which was found in North Street, has been studied in detail by Nicky Moyle. Dating perhaps to the third quarter of the 15th century, the dagger is a composite item, which also includes wood and copper-alloy parts.

Another important iron object, from Mill Road, is a piece of iron plate-armour from a brigandine (or possibly a jack) (Figure 13.18). Brigandines were sleeveless jackets lined with plates or scales of iron riveted together beneath a covering of cloth. From the 14th to the 17th century they were worn for protection, in Europe mainly by royalty and nobility, but also by some burgesses.[33] The Winchelsea example is dated to *c.*1435-1490.

The more routine ironwork includes a number of fish-hooks (Figure 13.19) which provide physical evidence of what was an important maritime industry for

Fig. 13.20
Decorative floor tiles

medieval Winchelsea. Those fish-hooks which are sufficiently complete all have barbed hooks and flattened, expanded heads for attachment to the line. Other finds which could also have been associated with maritime activities include some of the clench bolts which might have been used to join double thicknesses of timber in boat construction. Alternatively, these could have been used in the construction of domestic doors, either to fix boards to ledges or to clench together the boards of double-skinned doors.

Metallurgical remains

Samples of slag were recovered during two of the excavations and are evidence of craft activity within the medieval town. The samples were examined by Rod Clough. He identified those from North Street as pieces of iron-forging slag, and those from Mill Road as pieces of bronze-working slag.[34]

FLOOR TILES

Various sites in Winchelsea have yielded medieval floor tiles, and those discovered between 1976 and 1982 have been examined by Elizabeth Eames.[35] All these tiles provide important information with regard to both trade and the distribution and dating of the so-called 'Lewes' group of decorated tiles.

The French Tiles

These tiles include both decorated, two-colour tiles and plain, glazed tiles. The decorated tiles are of particular interest as they belong to a group which has been recognized for many years, but whose place of manufacture has been uncertain. However, it now seems clear to Eames that the tiles were made in Normandy, probably in the hinterland of Dieppe, and were distributed as part of a coastwise trade (they are recorded from sites in Sussex, Kent, London, York and Ireland). The presence of such tiles in Winchelsea provides a date for the period during which they were being manufactured as their use for paving in the church of St Thomas is likely to have occurred in the early 14th century. The decorative designs on the Winchelsea tiles are of various types (*e.g.* Figure 13.20), and one of the tiles, which is larger than the others, may be a local copy. Most of the recent finds of French tiles at Winchelsea have come from the churchyards of St Giles and St Thomas, and it is supposed that they originally paved the churches.

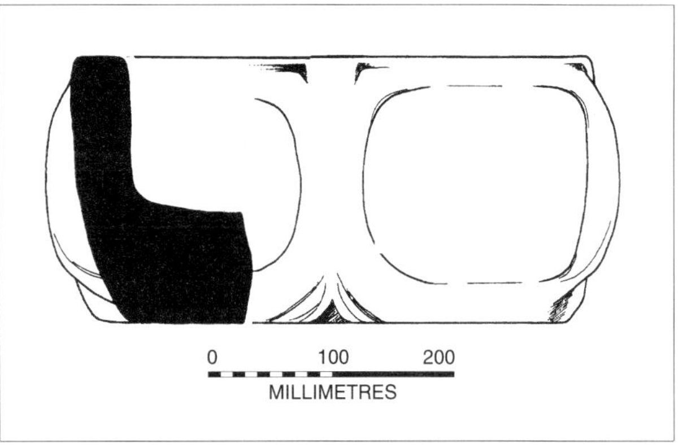

Fig. 13.21
Sandstone mortar from Blackfriars Barn

Other glazed tiles: probably Netherlandish

The other plain glazed tiles found at Winchelsea are probably Netherlandish. Whilst some of these tiles were found in the vicinities of the churches of St Thomas and St Giles, others have been recovered from domestic sites.

USE OF STONE

The various site finds from Winchelsea of geological materials, used both in artefacts and for building purposes, were recorded by Caroline Cartwright who notes that, not surprisingly, much of this material was obtained from Cretaceous (and perhaps to a lesser extent, Upper Jurassic) deposits in the Wealden area.[36] Examples of such exploitation of Wealden deposits for artefacts at Winchelsea are four medieval mortars from Blackfriars Barn, one of which is illustrated in Figure 13.21.

Other finds, such as West Country roofing slates, French Caen stone for building purposes, German Mayen lava quern stones, and mica-schist whetstones or rubbers or hones, for which possible sources include south-western England, France, or Norway, were obtained from much greater distances, presumably by coastwise trade.

THE HUMAN REMAINS

Excavations on the site of St Giles's churchyard in 1982 provided an opportunity for the recovery of some of the actual remains of inhabitants of medieval and Tudor Winchelsea. All the recovered human bones were studied by Sue Browne, whose report considers various aspects such as age, sex, stature, dentition and pathology/ incidence of disease.[37] Browne records that the bone assemblage represents a minimum of 26 individuals (21 adults and 5 children) of which 11 are males or probably males, 9 are females or probably females, and 6 are of indeterminate sex. The oldest male was at least 45 years old, whilst the oldest female was at least 35 years old. Estimations of stature for males range from approximately 1.67 metres to 1.77 metres (5ft.6ins. to 5ft.10ins.) and for females from approximately 1.55 metres to 1.70 metres (5ft.1in. to 5ft.7ins.).

Information could be gleaned about the general health of this small sample of former inhabitants of Winchelsea. The presence of some caries cavities in teeth, ante-mortem tooth loss, at least ten Harris's lines in the tibia of one individual, and several cases of tooth enamel hypoplasia indicates that these individuals had experienced phases of malnutrition or infection in early life. One case of tuberculosis was noted, as was one case of spinal hyperstosis, one case of moderate arthropathy in the hip, and early stage tibial inflamation and/or mild arthropathy in several individuals. Six fractures were noted, and with one exception, had healed well without any displacement. The individual with vertebral tuberculosis is of particular interest as this male aged 25 to 35 years at death was the only burial to have had a tomb built of stone, which presumably indicates that the deceased was of relatively high status (*see* Figure 7.15).

DIET AND ANIMAL HUSBANDRY: THE ANIMAL AND PLANT REMAINS

Unfortunately, the excavations undertaken at Winchelsea between 1976 and 1982 did not include a systematic policy (as is now standard practice) for wet-sieving for the recovery of faunal and charred plant remains. There is thus a major bias in the recovered bone assemblages towards the larger bone fragments, and only small quantities of fish-bones and charred plant remains. All of the recovered finds were recorded however, the animal, bird and fish-bones by Myrtle Kyllo, the marine molluscs and charcoal by Caroline Cartwright and the charred seeds/grain by Pat Hinton.[38] A few general observations follow with regard mainly to aspects of diet in medieval and Tudor Winchelsea.

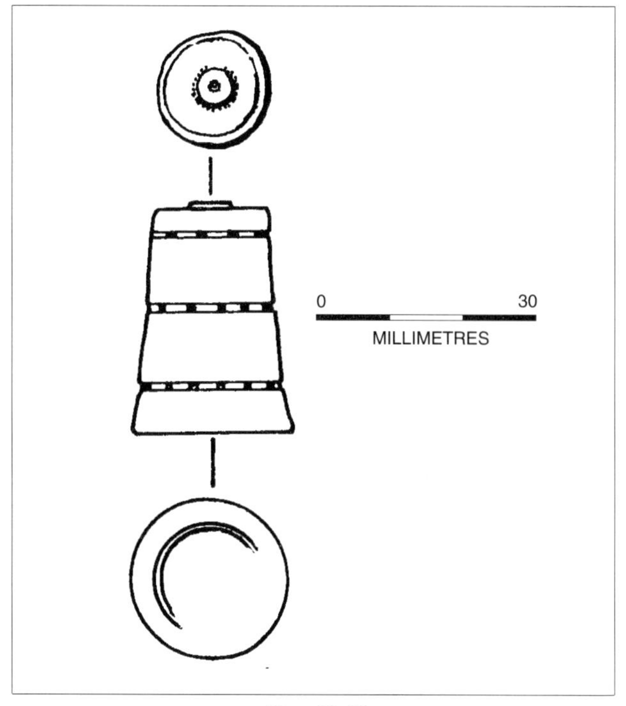

Fig. 13.22
Bone or ivory gaming piece from Mill Road

Kyllo reports that the bone assemblages from Winchelsea consist almost entirely of domestic refuse. Of the animal bones, cattle are the most frequently represented, followed by sheep. The reverse situation occurs at nearby Camber Castle which was occupied from 1539-1637.[39] Few pig bones were found. Domestic fowl were found in many layers, and some sieved deposits yielded fish-bones. Some of the bones of food animals showed clear evidence of butchery. Only a few bones could not be attributed to food animals, and on all sites many bones had been gnawed by dogs. Of the main meat-providing animals, few of the bones were from very young animals. An exception, however, was noted at Blackfriars Barn, where just over half of the sheep remains in a Tudor deposit were under 3½ years of age. They may thus have been reared as a source of food, and not just eaten when their useful life as providers of wool and milk had ended. The rewards of hunting may have included deer, hare, rabbit and fox. Domestic fowl included chicken, duck and goose, whilst gannet, and possibly pigeon, were also a source of food. Animals other than those slaughtered for food included dog and cat, and perhaps horse (one bone only).

Some animal bones may have been used to manufacture artefacts, the most impressive such find from Winchelsea being the bone or ivory gaming-piece (for chess?) from Mill Road shown in Figure 13.22. Dating to the 16th century, this item offers a rare insight into the recreational activities of the inhabitants of the town.

All of the identified fish-bones are from marine species, namely: cod, whiting, haddock, conger eel, tub gurnard, grey gurnard, herring, mackeral, plaice, flounder, roker, sea bream, and ling. All of these species are recorded as being present off the south coast of England, and indicate that fish was often included in the diet at Winchelsea. Obviously, this conclusion should be no surprise as documentary sources (Chapter 2) record the importance of fishing as an industry at Winchelsea, and other archaeological evidence for such an activity includes the iron fish-hooks noted above.

Another important maritime source of food at Winchelsea was shellfish. Caroline Cartwright's study of the remains of the marine molluscs indicates an obvious preference for oysters, whose shells form *c*.75% of the total assemblage. The other edible species include cockle, limpet, periwinkle, whelk, mussel and scallop. All would have been available from appropriate local stretches of the coastline.

The meagre information available regarding the use of plant foods at Winchelsea consists of a few charred grains of wheat, one grain of oats and one blackberry seed!

14. CONCLUSIONS

David Martin [1] *(incorporating comments by David Sylvester).*

Winchelsea is mentioned in most books which discuss medieval England, but perhaps inevitably, given the nature of the published literature, the references mainly concentrate on the town as a member of the Cinque Ports and on its planned grid system of streets. Other comments, if there are any, are cursory. It rarely appears amongst the lists of significant medieval English towns and ports, unless the ranking is based upon participation in the maritime activities of the medieval realm. The implication is that Winchelsea was just another example of a small medieval port catering to local needs. Indeed, this is the impression gained when talking to many medieval archaeologists and historians active in the field. Most know that the town is a prime example of a planned settlement, that it was laid out on a grand scale by Edward I, and that it ultimately failed. Many assume that it failed before it was able to become established, others that it collapsed into insignificance after a very brief and mildly successful flowering. Today, Winchelsea is a small sleepy village with an insignificant, stream-like river passing below it on its northern side. Visitors can be forgiven for regarding as 'unfounded exaggeration' the claims made for the town by its modern residents and for assuming them to be the result of misplaced pride. To the casual visitor the only hints of a more important past are the grid of streets, three ruined town gates (one of which most tourists are unlikely to find) and the fragment of an imposing church.

In the light of the present study our views of Winchelsea's role in history need to be reconsidered. Divided into two parts, this chapter will discuss Winchelsea up to and during the mid-14th century and Winchelsea from the mid-14th century up to the mid-16th century. The status of the town during its years of final decline (mid-16th century and beyond) is not in question.

THE MID-14th CENTURY AND BEFORE

In drawing together the various strands of research which have fed into this present volume it has become apparent how often Winchelsea stands out as being more significant than had been anticipated when the project was initiated. By the early 13th century the town had emerged as an important centre of export of wool and hides.[2] By the mid-13th century it had become, along with Sandwich, one of the most visible members of the Cinque-Ports Confederation. It was home to a sizeable fishing fleet operating both locally and in the North Sea, was a centre for the importation of Gascon wine, and, perhaps most significant of all, it was a principal supplier of ships and men to the royal fleet. The port's strategic and economic importance was recognized by the crown when, in 1247, Henry II took back both Winchelsea and its near neighbour, Rye from its Norman overlord, the abbot of Fécamp.

(Old) Winchelsea's significance was confirmed when it was threatened and eventually destroyed by inundations caused by an endless assault of violent storms in the latter part of the 13th century. In spite of valiant efforts to protect the town, it became increasingly clear by the third quarter of the 13th century that these measures were doomed to failure. It was to the king, their seigniorial lord, that the residents of Winchelsea turned for salvation. For this reason, it is important to recognize that the relocation of Winchelsea to its neighbouring hilltop location does not fit the pattern of Edward I's 'plantations' of this period, although town migration and resettlement were not unique during the period.[3] The founding of New Winchelsea was above all a rescue package aimed at averting the sea's total destruction of a very successful port town which, in the words of the chronicler, Mathew Paris, was a borough of great import, especially to Londoners. New Winchelsea has been seen by some as one of a number of new plantations made during this period by both the crown and seigniorial lords, who were taking advantage of the economic and demographic growth experienced during the 13th century. As Beresford has shown, speculative ventures of this kind were popular at this period and could be very profitable.[4] Against this background, the foundation of New Winchelsea is sometimes treated by historians as nothing more than

Edward's exploitation of the economic advantage of his newly acquired harbour: he founded an entirely new town upon a site which he considered economically more favourable than the sites of the existing port towns at Rye and (Old) Winchelsea. However, it is wrong to see New Winchelsea in this light. One major difference between the circumstances here and those of other new plantations - and this should be stressed - is that New Winchelsea was founded on land not already owned by Edward. Effectively, he acquired the land on which the town was to be built by compulsory purchase.

Some idea of the importance he placed upon saving the town - and therefore of its importance to him - is perhaps suggested by the status of the commissioners he appointed to oversee the move. Henry le Waleys had been successively major of Bordeaux and London, Gregory de Rokesle was another London major, and Stephen de Pencester was Warden of the Cinque Ports. It is arguable that the appointment of these men denotes the importance of the endangered town as a significant port with international connections. The port's economic role at the time may have been influential in Edward's decision to refound the town, but it was perhaps the town's importance to the crown as a major contributor of ships and of naval expertise which persuaded him to take the course of action he did. If this was so, it is perhaps significant that Edward did not see his new town as a fortified centre facing France - no castle appears to have been planned and certainly none was built. He appears to have considered the residents to be more than capable of looking after their own defences without the help of a royal garrison.

The town of New Winchelsea should therefore always be regarded as the transplantation of an existing, thriving town rather than as a new town *per se*. There is good evidence to indicate that despite the later collapse, the transplantation was successful. It is possible that some decline occurred in the fishery, but the indications are that wine importation remained buoyant through the first part of the 14th century. Until the middle years of the 14th century Winchelsea was consistently amongst the top ten wine-importing towns in the country. The numerous vaulted cellars are confirmation of success in this respect. Although it could be argued that these cellars were built speculatively and were little used, the wealth for their construction had to be available in the first instance.

The town's involvement both in fishing and in the wine trade, impressive as it was, was eclipsed by its contribution to ship service. Extending from the time the residents re-established themselves upon their new site through to the late 1340s, Winchelsea was a leading supplier of ships and men to the royal fleet. Amongst English ports during this period only Yarmouth contributed more. Winchelsea's and Dartmouth's contributions were each very similar, ahead of Fowey, Southampton and Plymouth (*see* Figure 2.4). As late as 1337 Winchelsea provided more ships and more mariners than any other port town in England: the following year only (Great) Yarmouth supplied a greater number. During the 1320s the town's ships effectively ruled the Channel, a point well illustrated in 1321 when, on 30 September 'the men of Winchelsea appeared off the port of Southampton in strength. Their thirty ships were more than a match for Southampton. They landed to burn 15 ships drawn up on the strand, contemptuously rejecting the burgesses' offer of two good ships, fully equipped, to help them in the policing of the Channel. The next day, two more ships were destroyed and the marauders sailed off leaving damage estimated, six years later, at over £8,000'.[5] Given that the shippers of Southampton were serious rivals to those of Winchelsea, especially with regard to the wine trade, the motive for this attack is perhaps obvious - 'take out the opposition!'

That the barons of Winchelsea were able to maintain their trade successfully whilst undergoing the upheaval of moving to a new site is a testament to the town's economic strength and the level of wealth available to its more important residents. To many towns such an ordeal would have been a serious setback, if not the cause of their destruction. Yet, as far as can be told, there was hardly any decrease in the town's economic activities, and construction work on the new town moved forward at a rapid pace. Already by 1297, when the king visited during an assembly of the fleet, parts of the defensive walls and gates (on the northern side of the town at least) were in place. Work on the defences along the western flank was moving ahead in 1321, and by 1330 the town dyke and New Gate, at the extreme southern end of the town, about a mile distant from the port, were already built. No expense was spared on the main church, the remaining part of which Pevsner has described as 'on the proudest scale' and adds that it is 'grand architecturally, rich decoratively. The scale is almost that of a cathedral'.[6] The number of stone-built houses present within the town in the 14th century is further indication of the wealth of its barons. As discussed in Chapter 10, stone houses must always have represented a tiny minority of the total building stock, yet there were more of them here than in other southeastern towns and (except in areas where stone was the principal available building material) more than in most large provincial English towns of the period. And in this respect the many costly stone-vaulted cellars should not be overlooked.

The question remains, how was Winchelsea able to play such a prominent role in the maritime activities of the crown and the southeast region? It is tempting to suggest that Winchelsea was in fact a much more significant settlement than has been assumed. The town's plan reveals an overall area (*c*.150 acres) and allotment of properties (690 owners holding 802 plots) comparable to those of several of the first- and second-rank port towns of the period – for example Boston, Hull, (King's) Lynn, Sandwich, Scarborough, Southampton, and (Great) Yarmouth (*see* Figure 14.1). But as no detailed analysis of Winchelsea's land-use, plot distribution and household densities is possible for the period following the town's

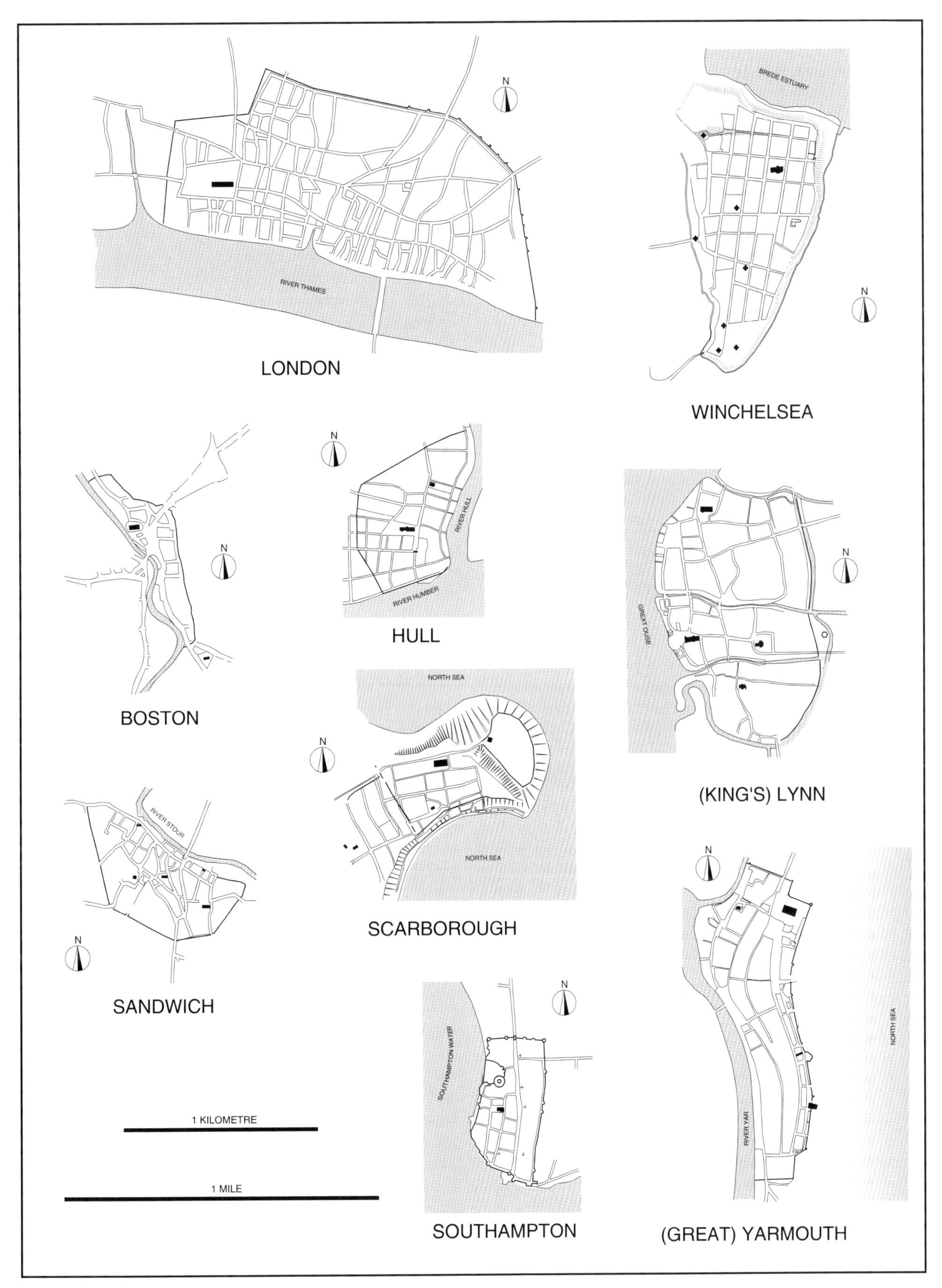

Fig. 14.1.
The layouts of selected medieval port towns reproduced to a consistent scale

refoundation, it would be inappropriate on the evidence currently available to suggest that it ranks among these recognized maritime communities.[7] The hinterland of the port town, which acted as a barrier to inland communication and exchange, undoubtedly forced the residents of Winchelsea to pursue their fortunes at sea. This distinctive maritime orientation, in many ways similar to that of Dartmouth in Devon, may explain the surprising shipping capacity of the town and the role its residents played in the economic and naval affairs of the realm. Nevertheless, much remains to be revealed about Winchelsea in its heyday.

As must inevitably be the case, published overviews of history and archaeology are strongly influenced by two factors: the survival of evidence, and the degree to which that evidence has been analyzed and published. It is inevitable, therefore, that all studies will be affected by the pattern of research, and this can, on occasions, seriously distort our views and result in major oversights. With this in mind, Winchelsea may have been considerably larger and more influential during the 13th and early 14th centuries than is usually considered to have been the case. Owing to an unfortunate combination of factors – the exemption from key taxes,[8] the loss of its early Corporation records, the nature of its post-medieval history and its current very rural appearance coupled with the absence until now of any detailed published research, it has not attracted the attention it deserves. It is noteworthy as a prime archaeological site of immense potential. In how many other towns of this calibre do deposits survive, uncontaminated by both earlier settlement and later disturbance? In particular, the harbour area with its riverside plots must have enormous potential, yet currently it is hardly afforded any protection and has been subjected to no archaeological investigations.

It is surely no coincidence that the one element of the town which has been published - its planned grid of streets - is the most often quoted. It is to be hoped that the points discussed within this present volume will help redress this situation and encourage those who research English medieval towns to give greater consideration to this potentially underrated town.

THE LATE 14th AND 15th CENTURIES

If the importance of Winchelsea as a port of national significance remains open to debate, what is beyond dispute is that its period of prosperity was relatively short-lived. By the second half of the 14th century Winchelsea was in serious trouble. However, in this respect too the evidence presented within this volume does not support the commonly held notion that Winchelsea's collapse was meteoric. It is not true that it descended from being a significant port to little more than a village over a short period during the middle decades of the 14th century. Rather the evidence points to a two-stage decline with a far more important late 14th- and 15th-century role in the southeast of England than is generally realized.

There are few signs during the 1340s of the problems which were to befall the town during the late 14th century. It is often noted that already by the early 1340s (before both the Black Death and the serious French raids) the bailiff's accounts include a list of 94 tenements within the town lying uninhabited and decayed. But as has been demonstrated in Chapter 8, these decayed rents were limited to a number of harbour plots (which may in any case never have been developed for topographical reasons) and to peripheral plots on the southern and western fringe of the town. They should not be seen as indicators of serious decline. Indeed, the extent of the decayed rents at Winchelsea pale into insignificance when compared to the situation at Hull in the opening decades of the 14th century.[9] However, it cannot be ignored that by 1358 a further 90 properties were described as 'in ruins' and an inquiry held early in 1359 reported that there were then within the town many inhabitable houses which were at that time unlet and uninhabited. Similarly, by 1357 when the Black Friars acquired Quarter 4 consolidation of plots had reduced the number of holdings upon the quarter to just five - half the total originally laid out.

The causes of the town's decline are not hard to find and some are general to all the eastern ports, rather than being site-specific. The changed political and economic climate following the outbreak of the Hundred Years' War not only resulted in more difficult trading conditions with threats and interruptions to shipping, but in a marked rise in the importance of the western ports and a general decline in trade at the eastern ports - London excepted. Furthermore, from the mid-14th century onwards the western ports supplanted those of the south and east coasts as the dominant suppliers of ships for naval duties. To these factors must be added the more general effects of the Black Death and subsequent outbreaks of plague. A major decline in the Yarmouth fishery had a specific impact on the Cinque Ports because of the special privileges they held at Yarmouth, and this served to weaken Winchelsea's economy further. As has been emphasized on a number of occasions within this volume, Winchelsea's weak hinterland should never be ignored. Unlike Southampton, which serviced Winchester, and Sandwich, which serviced Canterbury, Winchelsea never had a major inland urban centre within its catchment. It was surrounded by a relatively poor, heavily wooded and quite sparsely populated area which lacked major industries and had very limited agricultural potential. It shared this impoverished hinterland with two other ports: Rye two miles to the northeast, and Hastings six miles to the southwest, although admittedly at this date neither were as important as Winchelsea. Given these factors, it is hardly surprising that the town was almost entirely dependant upon the wealth generated by its harbour and its ships. As pointed out in Chapter 2, there can be few English ports of Winchelsea's size which were so

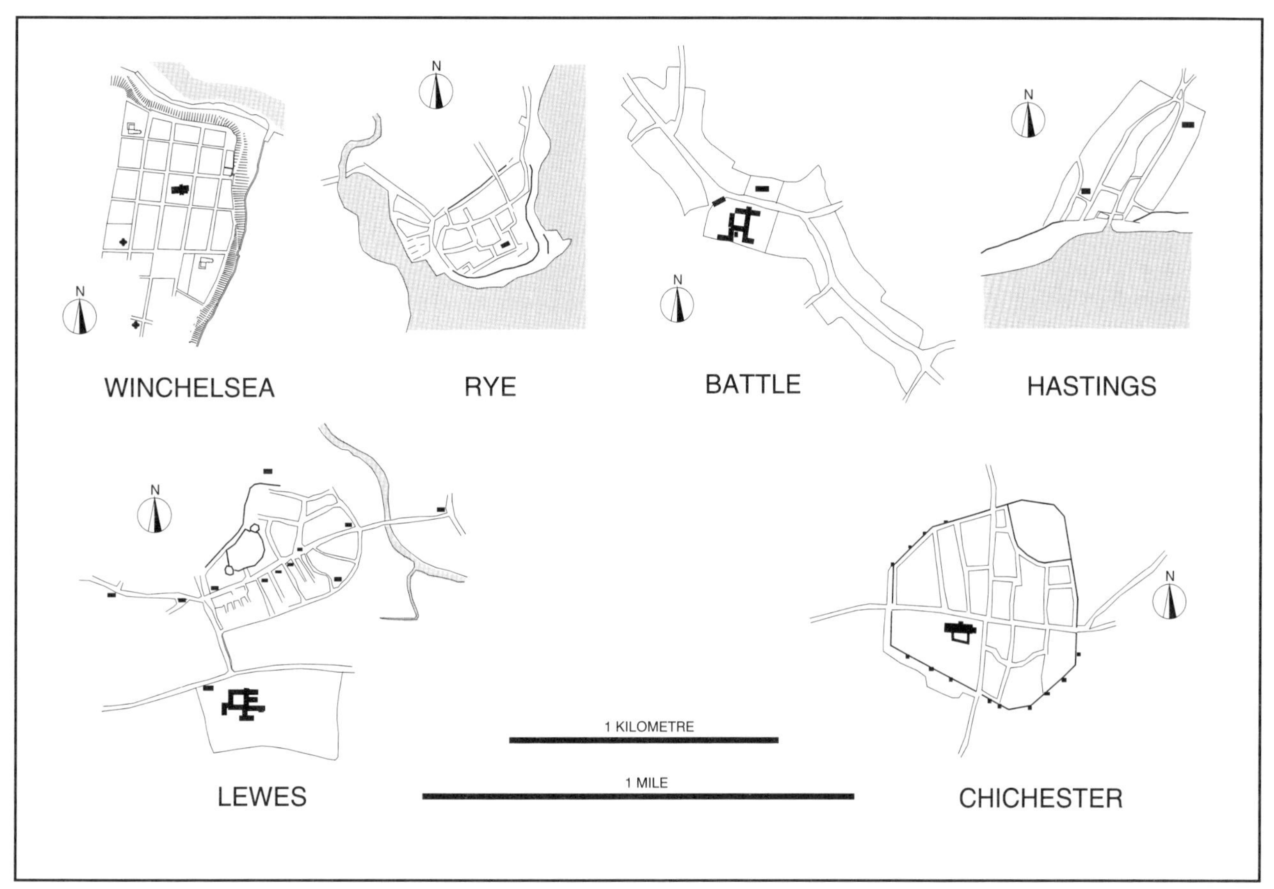

Fig. 14.2
The 15th-century layouts of selected Sussex towns reproduced to a consistent scale

dependant upon the sea. If the opportunities available to its ships reduced, this inevitably had a major impact upon the whole town. Situated on a river which was never a deep-water channel, Winchelsea was not able to accommodate ships of much over 200 tons. This was not a problem during the late 13th and early 14th centuries, when ships over that size were exceptional, but during the late 14th and 15th century there was an increasing tendency to use larger ships. This was a factor which, in an increasingly competitive climate, inevitably made the port less attractive. This latter point probably had more effect on Winchelsea than the level of silting, for although the port was undoubtedly becoming increasingly choked, in 1433 it was still able to receive vessels of up to 200 tons, suggesting little serious deterioration at this period.

It is against this weakened economic background that the French and Spanish raids of the second half of the 14th century need to be considered. In 1360 the town suffered a catastrophic raid by the French. The tide had turned, for until this date Winchelsea had largely escaped such attacks, despite its ships being at the forefront of English attacks on French towns. Six years after the raid the bailiff's returns record no fewer than 385 tenements (a little under half of the total) as 'wasted, burnt and uninhabited'. In contrast to the previous pattern of decay the abandoned plots were scattered throughout the town. A further French raid in 1377 was successfully repelled, though only with the aid of assistance from a force mustered by the Abbot of Battle. Just two years later, in 1380, the Spanish surprised the town and sacked it. A Letter Patent dated 3 March 1384 records that Winchelsea was 'once well inhabited, but by being burnt by the King's enemies and much more by the withdrawal of its burgesses is now so desolate and almost destroyed that the proprietorship of vacant plots and tenements can scarce be known'. It is worth noting that the withdrawal of the burgesses was given as a more serious cause of desertion than the raids: what is not known is whether this was caused primarily through fear of further attacks, or because there was insufficient trade to sustain the previous high number of residents.

The case presented above appears to support the notion of Winchelsea's sudden collapse. But to judge from the town's accounts, by 1388 the commercial core of the town had largely been reoccupied. Furthermore, comparison of the town's expenditure records for 1388/1389 and 1399/1400 indicates that the commercial recovery continued throughout the remainder of the century. There are references in the latter accounts to the acquisition and custody of a town clock - not an acquisition which suggests a failed town! In the years around 1400 income was sufficient for the Pipewell Gate (allegedly destroyed in 1380) to be rebuilt.

Although the fortunes of the town were clearly much recovered, it became consolidated within the northeastern corner of its original site. The western and southern parts were largely abandoned. That the town's officials accepted the reduced size as a permanent feature is indicated by their petitioning of the King in 1414 to reduce the defended area of the town, enclosing 21 of the original 39 quarters. The intended line still gave a surprisingly large defended area - larger in area than most other local towns (*see* Figure 14.2) - implying a not insignificant resident population. The planned line was a very logical one. It placed the parish church of St Giles near the southwestern corner of the new circuit, the precinct of the Grey Friars would occupy the site in the extreme southeastern corner, and that of the Black Friars the extreme northwestern corner. St Thomas's church stood almost centrally within the contracted site. It should be remembered that the inquiry held in 1415 found that only five dwellings would be destroyed by the work, a clear indication of how few houses then stood in these outlying areas of the town, away from the contracted commercial centre. Many of these by now peripheral plots had been amalgamated into larger holdings. But surely if the population of the town was by this date insignificant in number, a smaller area would have been encompassed in order not to stretch the defenders beyond their capabilities. That Winchelsea was at this date still considered of some importance is indicated by the King's grant of 600 marks towards the cost of the works. Evidently work was not restricted to the sections of new wall alignment. During this general period a considerable sum appears to have been expended on other sections of the defences too (*see* Chapter 5), though it is significant that no attempt was made at rebuilding the existing gates on a grander scale. Indeed, in the event even the reduced circuit of town walls were nothing like completed. It is also relevant to note that there is a general lack of identifiable alterations to the town's other principal monuments during this period, presumably indicating that the calibre of building undertaken during the late 13th and early 14th centuries was superior to any alterations and improvements which could be afforded subsequently. Nevertheless, the general impression suggested by the documentary sources of modest recovery and consolidation during the closing years of the 14th century and throughout the 15th century is fully supported by the archaeological investigations. These give no indications of serious long-term desertion within the town centre prior to the late 15th or 16th centuries. Similarly, the town's surviving domestic architecture does not imply poverty at this time. On the contrary, a number of the surviving houses were rebuilt during the last three decades of the 15th century, whilst others were modified and extended. The designs tend to be urban in form. One of the new houses was the three-storeyed, fully-jettied Periteau House. Internally the boarded ceilings speak of the quality of the original construction work. And it is not the only example of a boarded ceiling within the town.

If further proof were needed that Winchelsea did not totally collapse, but maintained itself as a viable port of local importance throughout the 15th century, it is graphically supplied by the local customs records. Even as late as 1490/91 the customs revenues from Winchelsea accounted for 60 per cent of the total revenues raised from Chichester's catchment of ports, covering the 110 miles of coast between Folkestone in the east and Chichester in the west. It was easily the most active port within the group. Yet over the next 40 years all this changed. By 1513/14 Winchelsea's share had reduced to 41 per cent - on a par with Rye - and by 1528/29 it represented a mere 13 per cent of the total. After this date the figures plummet still further as the harbour silted and vessels could no longer reach the town. Having been so reliant upon the port, most residents deserted the town (*see* Chapter 3).

In comparison to its size and importance during the late 13th and early 14th centuries, it may be true that Winchelsea collapsed during the late 14th century. But set against the background of other local towns and ports, it undoubtedly remained a town of local importance. As late as the 1490s the only towns in Sussex which are likely to have been larger were the county towns of Chichester and Lewes, and there were few of comparable size in Kent either. Winchelsea may at this period have been small in comparison to many English towns, but, set against the generally small size of the towns in Kent and Sussex, until the early 16th century it was still a port that was not to be ignored.

NOTES AND REFERENCES

ABBREVIATIONS

AC	Archaeologia Cantiana
Archaeol.J.	Archaeological Journal
BL	British Library, London
CCR	Calendar of Close Rolls
CChR	Calender of Charter Rolls
CMR	Calendar of Memoranda Rolls (Exchequer)
CPR	Calendar of Patent Rolls
EcHR	Economic History Review
ESRO	East Sussex Record Office
HEH	Henry E Huntington Library, San Marino, California, USA
HMC	Historical Manuscripts Commission
OD	Ordnance Datum
OS	Ordnance Survey
PRO	Public Record Office
SAC	Sussex Archaeological Collection
SNQ	Sussex Notes and Queries
SRS	Sussex Record Society
UCLFAU	University College London Field Archaeology Unit
VCH	The Victoria History of the Counties of England
WSRO	West Sussex Record Office

Most other publications referred to in the following notes are cited by author/editor and date only; full publication details are supplied in the bibliography.

NOTES AND REFERENCES

1 THE ORIGINS OF WINCHELSEA

1 Eddison 1998, Fig 5.6.
2 Mayhew 1987, 233-237; Martin 2003, 179-190.
3 Eddison 2000, 30 *et seq.*
4 Long *et al.* 1998, 45-63.
5 CPR 1272-81, 414; 11 November 1280.
6 Gardiner 2000, 76.
7 Martin 1993, 73-78; Gardiner 2000, 89.
8 Eddison 1998, 82.
9 *VCH Sussex*, **9**, 49. The evolving importance of the association of the Cinque Ports is discussed in detail by Murray, 1935.
10 Pipe Roll of 6 John, (*Pipe Roll 50)*; Stenton, 1940, 218.
11 *VCH Sussex*, **2**, 130; **9**, 49.
12 Britton 1937, 90-125.
13 Eddison 2000, 65-73.
14 Luard 1872-83, **v**, 175-6, 272, Rolls Series 87.
15 CPR 1261; Eddison 1998.
16 Eddison 2000 and unpublished information.
17 *VCH Sussex*, **9**, 49.
18 PRO MPF 212, reproduced in Mayhew 1987, book cover; and partially in Eddison 2000, Fig. 65.
19 Cal. Charter Rolls, 177, 6 Nov. 1271.
20 CPR 1272-81, 414, 11 November 1280.
21 Homan 1949.
22 *VCH Sussex*, **9**, 62-75; Homan 1942, 6.
23 Britton 1937, 124.
24 *Gervase Opera* **2**, 292, Rolls Series 73; see also ESRO RYE 57/4 fo. 131.
25 BL Add. Ch. 20169.

2 THE DEVELOPMENT OF WINCHELSEA AND ITS MARITIME ECONOMY

1 Murray 1935, 1.
2 '*Nobiliora Membra Quinque Portuum*'; *CChR 1226-57*, 321.
3 For a discussion of the refounding, Sylvester 1999, 153-60.
4 Brandon and Short 1990, 4.
5 For the most recent monograph on the archaeology of medieval London *see* Milne 2003.
6 Luard 1872-83, **v**, 272.
7 *See* Thomas 1924, 21; Sharpe 1885, 80-1, 88, 100; Thomas 1926, 171; and *London Plea and Memoranda Rolls, Roll Aib*, 33, 34, 37, 47, 48, 55. Tension between London and Cinque Port retailers was inevitable and metropolitan vintners took steps to limit Winchelsea merchants from selling wine in the capital at the close of the 13th century. In a 1298 appeal for assistance from their townsman, Robert de Winchelsey (then Archbishop of Canterbury), the barons complained that the Mayor of London was interfering with their customary right to transport wine to the capital for sale to whomever they pleased. Dated 16 December, 1298; Sharpe 1901, 31.
8 Campbell *et al.* 1993, 61. Queenhithe, near London, was designated in 1224-5 as the depot for grain shipped to the

capital from the Cinque Ports; Britnell 1996, 87.

9 *CCR 1234-37*, 402; *CCR 1247-51*, 54, 430; *CCR 1251-53*, 68; *CCR 1256-59*, 153; *See* also Cutting 1956, 118.

10 Searle and Ross 1967, 63.

11 *CPR 1272-81*, 344.

12 Pelham 1951, 262.

13 The local customs accounts of Winchelsea regularly record the visits of alien shippers and merchants during the 13th and 14th centuries; *See* PRO SC6/1031/19-26; PRO SC6/1032/1-13; and PRO E122/124/17-18. For a discussion of the early 14th-century contact between the Cinque Ports and Norman port towns, see Pelham 1930a, 129-33, 136-7; Mollat 1952, 37, 98-100, 101, note 46, 146-7, 166, 173, 35, note 183; and Mollat 1947, 144, 148.

14 Mayhew 1984, 121-3.

15 Orton 2004, 115-137; *see* also this volume, Chapter 13.

16 Cooper 1850, 71, 98; Childs 1977, 14, 21, 29, 32.

17 Stenton 1940, 218. The 1204 assessment is not without its problems as it omits ports, or may include them under the totals of other ports. For example, Hastings is not on the list and may have been included under Winchelsea's total. Also, the tax is not a reflection of all exports and focuses principally on wool and hide exports. For a discussion of this record *see* Lloyd 1977, 11-13.

18 Childs 1996, 125, 134.

19 PRO SC6/1031/19. The Winchelsea local customs accounts predate the national customs which were instituted in three stages: in 1275 the Ancient Custom began to tax aliens and denizens exporting wool, wool fells, and hides; in 1303 the New Custom increased the taxes described above on aliens and added a levy on aliens importing wine, and importing or exporting cloth, wax and other goods; in 1347 the Cloth Custom increased export taxes and extended these to denizens; *see* Gras 1918, 66, 72.

20 PRO SC6/1031/23; PRO E122/124/16. Bulk goods continued to dominate the trade with shipments of grains constituting 30 per cent, salt 16 per cent, iron 16 per cent, cloth 13 per cent, and wine 7 per cent of the total shipments recorded. Approximately 30 per cent of home ports are unidentified, the majority of these were non-English.

21 Pelham 1930a, 129-33, 136-7, examined the existing accounts for the Cinque Ports, namely PRO E122/124/17-18.

22 Much of this came from Battle Abbey properties. In 1278/79, 30 cartloads of wood and 11,000 faggots were delivered to Winchelsea; Searle and Ross 1967, 45.

23 Pelham 1930a, 143.

24 The types of imported goods recorded in the 1266/67 accounts are not all that different from those coming to the port in the 1320s. The absence in the earlier accounts of smaller items such as cups, bowls, and wax is explained by the fact that these items were not taxed until the introduction of the New Custom in 1303.

25 Cooper 1871, 23; *VCH Sussex* **9**, 70.

26 Sharpe 1901, 31; PRO E122/124/13, E122/124/14; Kowaleski 1993, 51, 116, 146, 193. For the unwarranted arrest of Winchelsea ships at Bordeaux, see *CPR 1258-66*, 477.

27 The *prise* or *prisage* of wine dates from the 12th century and was a royal exaction in kind. For a discussion of the evolution of the *prise*, *see* Gras 1918, 37-48; Sargeant 1918, 282. Citizens of London received exemption in 1327, while York freemen had to wait until 1376.

28 Naval service itself stimulated the Cinque Ports' role in the shipment of wine, especially when its harbours were designated as points of assembly. For wine shipments into Sandwich while the fleet prepared to sail to the continent, see *CCR 1339-41*, 504.

29 Searle and Ross 1967, 17, 19.

30 James 1971, 96, 98-109.

31 Behind London, Southampton, Boston, Bristol, Sandwich, Exeter, Ipswich, and Yarmouth; Gras 1918, 399 based on PRO E122/78/3a.

32 Along with Sandwich and Bristol; *CCR 1341-43*, 646-7. In 1346, the appropriately-named Benedict Taverner of Sandwich was appointed the head gauger of wines in England; *CPR 1345-48*, 163. For 15th-century purchases at Winchelsea, *see* James 1971, 65.

33 The 300 tuns of 'good wine' were purchased from a variety of ports, including nearby Hull (120 tuns), London (100 tuns), Bristol (30 tuns), Winchelsea and Sandwich (20 each), and Boston (10 tuns); *CCR 1333-37*, 602. Winchelsea and Sandwich also provided 100 tuns each to royal purveyors in 1341; *CPR 1340-43*, 252-3.

34 In addition to the Butlerage accounts, wine imports into Winchelsea are listed in PRO E122/147/12, 13, 14. Wine imports are also taxed in the 13th-century Winchelsea bailiff's accounts (PRO SC6/1031/19-26), but there is no easy way to determine the scale of the trade since many importers were custom-exempt.

35 PRO E101/158/10; PRO E101/160/3; PRO E101/161/3; PRO E101/162/1; PRO E101/162/5. I am grateful to Maryanne Kowaleski for permission to use her transcriptions of these Bordeaux wine accounts.

36 PRO E122/78/3a.

37 Cooper 1871, 23-4. In the latter 14th century, alien merchants were recorded importing wine into Winchelsea in 1361/62, 1366/67 and 1367/68; *See* Beardwood 1931, 179-80.

38 Cooper 1871, 23.

39 *CCR 1259-61*, 413. Unfortunately, Peregoz was arrested for heresy in Bordeaux and the king seized his wine upon arrival. The Winchelsea mariners were paid cash for freightage; Cooper 1871, 25-6. Winchelsea ships imported Rochelle and St Jean wines into Winchelsea and Rye in 1265; *CPR 1258-66*, 402-3.

40 Cooper 1871, 23.

41 *London Plea and Memoranda*, Roll A5, 165.

42 James 1971, 74-5. The case of for Gascon vintners in Sandwich was appealed by the crown, but the Sandwich barons won the right to enfranchise the aliens.

43 James 1971, 98-116.

44 Kowaleski, (Kowaleski 2000, 478-83, 485-7, 481, especially Table 19.3) traces the general decline of the eastern ports and the rise of the western ports.

45 A practice common throughout England. Hythe shippers, for example, imported wine into Southampton and then distributed it to other regional destinations; *See* James 1971, 185.

46 *See* Gras 1918, 49, n 1. Even though many of the Winchelsea ships calling at Exeter were importing from overseas it is possible that they left Devon either to carry their goods to another English port, or they may have taken on a new cargo; Kowaleski 1993, 15, 26, 127, 136, 149, 176, 194; and Gras 1918, 191. Butcher 1974, 16-22 has demonstrated a remarkable amount of inter-urban trade and communication among the Cinque Ports of Kent during the 15th century. Examples of coastwise freight charges for shipping wine between British ports (including Winchelsea) are recorded in the Butleredge accounts; *See* James 1971, 154-5.

47 PRO SC6/1031/19, 23; and PRO E122/124/16.
48 Kowaleski 1995, 227-9, especially 229, note 24 and Table 6.1, 227,
49 *CPR 1225-32*, 370.
50 *See* Rodger 1997 69; Clowes 1897-1903, 194-8 and Oppenheim 1907, 130.
51 PRO E372/78/16; *CLR*, VII, 2254; *CCR* 1256-9, 155-6, 231, 242-3, *CLR* IV, 399-400, 418, 465; *CPR* 1334-8, 12, 117, 203, 212, 221.
52 Oppenheim 1907, 130.
53 *Foedera*, vol. I, 809; Oppenheim 1907, 132.
54 PRO E101/5/28 and 5/30; Prestwich (*Edward I*, 384-5) describes the mission in detail and gives 25,000 infantry recruited, ships assembled at Winchelsea and Plymouth. The departure was delayed until late January 1296 because Edmund was sick. It eventually sailed up the Gironde to Bourg and Blaye. Edmund died on the trip (5 June 1296).
55 Clowes 1897-1903, 211-12.
56 *CCR 1323-7*, 608-12.
57 *CCR 1323-27*, 608-13, 641-2. The average number of crew members aboard ship was 30, while Winchelsea ships carried an average of 37 mariners.
58 PRO E101/19/22. The size of ships is reflected in the number of tons per crew member, with Winchelsea's ships averaging 1.7 tons per individual, the highest figure for the Cinque Ports.
59 Great Yarmouth‘s relative proximity to Orwell accounts, at least in part, for its tremendous contribution of ships. The full record of ships in the Antwerp campaign is printed in Lyon 1983, 363-86.
60 The Cinque Ports as a whole supplied 229 ships, approximately 14 per cent of all shipping, though they made up less than 1 per cent of all port towns supplying ships.
61 Runyan 1986, 94-5; Runyan compiled a list of ships in naval pay-lists during the period and Winchelsea vessels comprised 44 per cent of Cinque Port vessels identified, though the confederacy provided less than 1 per cent of all ships in service.
62 Kowaleski 2000, 488.
63 Rodger 1996, 648-51.
64 Mayhew 1984, 119-123.
65 Mayhew 1984, 113.
66 Murray 1935, 207.
67 *VCH Sussex* **2**, 264.
68 *Calendar of French Documents*, 43.
69 Mollat 1983, 42, 40.
70 Haskins 1918, 343-4; *VCH Sussex* **9**, 34.
71 *Calendar of French Documents*, 43.
72 The only complete record of the share system in the South East is the post-medieval custumal regulating the Brighton fishery; *see* Turner 1849, 38-52; and Webb and Wilson 1952. The many similarities included in the 12th-century Rye agreement with Fécamp suggest the practice was in existence early in the medieval period and much of the discussion here is guided by the premise that the share system was in place long before 1580; Dulley 1969, 36-64 accepts this argument. *See* also Statham 1902, 78, 82; Mayhew 1987, 285; Centre for Kentish Studies, *New Romney Assessment Book,* vols. 1-2; and Salisbury 1887, 12-33.
73 Morant 1872, 232-3; and Millican 1945, 83-6. Fishers at other northern towns like Scarborough rendered tithes and twentieths on their catch beginning in the mid-13th century; Heath 1968, 54-6.
74 Bailey 1990, 105; A system of shares was also practised in Normandy where customary law allowed coastal overlords most of the bounty along tidal waters.
75 The bailiff's accounts of Winchelsea defining the town's share as, 'the custom on all fishing boats of ten oars' are similar to the Brighton custom regulating the local Drawnett, Harbour, Cokfare, and Tucknett fares. In all but the Drawnett fare, a fisher received one full share. Shares are defined in this way in the enrolled receipts of the Winchelsea minister's accounts in PRO E372/150/35, 154/47, and 207/46.
76 *CPR 1272-81*, 203-4. The 1403 document *Adventus Baronum* (printed in Boys, *Antiquities of Sandwich*, 575-8 attached incorrectly to the Sandwich custumal) is a practical application of the 1277 directives. It was analyzed by Felix Hull and compared to a later Tudor description of the barons' behaviour at the fair; See Hull, 'Coming of the Barons,' 1-8.
77 The barons' right to 4d. from every boat trading at the fair was turned over to Yarmouth at this time in exchange for a £6 grant. The amount suggests that at least 360 ships other were visiting the fair; Holloway 1847, 97.
78 PRO SC6/1031/19-24; PRO SC6/1028/10, 14. Based on the approximate number of 15 ships sent each year in the late 13th century and the Brighton Custumal's stipulation of 12 men per ship.
79 Rye successfully petitioned the crown in 1305 to change the date of their local fair to accommodate the fishery; PRO *SC8/487; Rotuli Parliamentorum*, vol. 1, 477, no. 98. When the Faversham fleet was away, its residents were not obliged to answer at the abbot's court; Murray 1936, 99. At Sandwich the keeping of the assize of bread and the regular Monday hundred court was suspended only during special events, namely, at Easter, Christmas, and during the Great Yarmouth fair, because for [as the custumal states] 'that ys a fyshyng tyme of heryng.'; Gardiner 1954, 61. Evidence from the 14th and 15th centuries indicate that the hundred courts of Dover, Faversham, Fordwich and Sandwich were suspended during the fair; Murray 1935, 19, 146.
80 These meetings usually took place in July and December; Murray 1935, 152-4.
81 From a Battle Abbey charter; cited in Cooper 1850, 16, note 3.
82 'Saltfare' is so defined by Kowaleski (forthcoming) 'Commercialization of the Sea Fisheries' 10.
83 The fishery shares are recorded in PRO SC6/1031/19-24. The calculations are based upon the actual shares collected in the medieval town from the local and North Sea fisheries and the custom regulating the Elizabethan Sussex fisheries. The problems of using a 16th-century custumal to derive figures for the medieval fishery are not insignificant, but the similarities between the share system at medieval Rye and Winchelsea and the 'ancient' customs of neighbouring Brighton are consistent. For full discussion and calculations, *see* Sylvester 1999a, 233-42.
84 More likely, the combined fisheries would be worth double these figures, using the ¼ share described in the Brighton customal. *See* Sylvester 1999a 232.
85 Calculated on a full share for the town, based upon the share in the Brighton custumal. If the town received only a ¼ share from the local fishery, the amount would have been even higher (in excess of £1000 per year).
86 This figure does not included the loss of an additional £50 that the barons usually earned from privileges at the fair; Murray 1935, 148; *VCH Sussex* **2**, 267.
87 PRO E372/123/7. Five times greater than Rye's shares in 1272/73; PRO E372/123/21; PRO SC6/1031/21; and PRO SC6/1028/8.

88 See PRO *SC6 1031/25* (1292-95) and the incomplete accounts of Thomas Alard, *see* PRO SC 1031/26 (1296-1306). The summary, enrolled version of Alard's accounts are printed in PRO E372/150 m.32 d and a Latin copy can be found in BL *Add. Ch. 8813*. Cooper 1850, 119-20. Historians make little of the absence of the fishery by that name and there is no indication of who may have collected the Yarmouth and Saltfare shares if they were transferred. Dulley (1969, 38) assumes throughout his analysis of the Rye and Winchelsea fishery that the bailiff's accounts reflect the towns' total fishery.

89 *See*, for example, PRO SC6/1031/19-24; and PRO E122/187/12.

90 PRO SC6/1031/19-24; PRO SC6/1032/11; *See* also Pelham, 1930b, 185.

91 Sandwich maintained a similar relationship with the cellarer of St Augustine's Priory; Gardiner 1954, 42. The local market in the town of Battle specialized in meat because of its proximity to the cattle-producing region of the Weald and sheep.

92 The 'fishman' at Hastings (and possibly Winchelsea) was Gilbert Roger in 1306/07 and at Winchelsea and Hastings John Fyssher in 1409/10 and 1412/13, and in 1420/21 Richard Stapelet, *Fyssher*.; Searle and Ross 1967, 47, 101, 102, 105-6, 110. The fishbuyers at Rye were known as '*osts*' (hosts) during the 16th century; Dulley 1969, 51.

93 Searle and Ross 1967, 19, 56. Though porpoises (along with whales and sturgeons) were royal fish reserved to the king, Battle held special rights from the Conqueror to at least the tongue and two-thirds of every porpoise (sometimes described as a sea pig, *porcus maris*) which washed ashore in the region; *VCH Sussex* **2**, 264, 266.

94 Searle and Ross 1967, 29.

95 The Abbey's expenditures are very conservative for only those records in which Winchelsea and Hastings are specifically named have been included. The number of years in which purchases took place at the Winchelsea and Hastings markets and the amounts for the fiscal years given were without a doubt much greater. The calculations are low for two reasons: 1) the manuscript is illegible in many places and 2) the location of purchase is frequently omitted. In both cases, it was deemed unwise to assume the location of purchase, even in those cases where Winchelsea or Hastings preceded the entry.

96 Searle and Ross 1967, 52. Alard served as the Abbey's attorney in a land transaction that took place the following year; Cooper 1850, 157.

97 Searle and Ross 1967, 52.

98 For the rippiers at Winchelsea, see PRO E372/200/34.

99 Winchelsea and Rye provided plaice and whiting to the royal court in 1237; Cutting 1956, 118.

100 *VCH Sussex* **2**, 266.

101 In 1369/70, the Abbey paid the master of a Rye vessel 14s. 4d. to transport foodstuffs from London to Battle; Searle and Ross 1967, 63. For shipping costs from East Sussex to London *c*.1300, *see* Campbell *et al.* 1993, 61. The attendance of the barons at London is confirmed by a complaint in 1327 that they had been mistakenly levied a toll on fish brought to Southwark; *London Plea and Memoranda*, Roll AIb, 38.

102 PRO E101/684/54.

103 *See*, for example, PRO E101/5/28; CCR 1323-27, 608-12; and PRO E101/19/22.

104 PRO E101/6/23.

105 *CCR 1339-41*, 59, 263. For a description of the Battle of Winchelsea (a.k.a. the Battle of Les Espagnols sur Mer), *see* Froissart's account; Geoffrey Brereton, ed. *Froissart Chronicles*. (London 1968; repr. 1978), 113-9; Oppenheim 1907, 139. Upon landing at Winchelsea, Edward set out on horseback to 'le manoir' two leagues outside the town; Blaauw 1851, 120-1; Burrows 1888, 114-15; Cooper 1850, 54-5.

106 Cooper 1850, 80-2, 88-92; *VCH Sussex* **9**, 66-7.

107 *CCR 1360-64*, 98, 101; Cooper 1850, 80-2; Riley 1859, 340; The accounts agree that a large French force landed at Winchelsea (*c*.3,000 attackers) and burned many buildings before entering the church where many townspeople were hiding. They killed several of its occupants and gang raped one young woman until she died, then raped nine other 'illustrious women' of the town. Before leaving the town, the French killed 40 townsmen and drowned in the harbour another 400 locals who had come to the assistance of the Winchelsea residents. They sailed away with 13 English ships laden with wine and other goods, leaving two of their own because they were stuck in the mud. According to Cooper, the St Giles graveyard was enlarged to accommodate the burials and the nearby street was renamed 'Dead Man's Lane' (but *see* this volume, Chapter 7). In 1380 the French burned the town and allegedly severely damaged its walls; Cooper 1850, 91-2.

108 *CCR 1377-81*, 23.

109 Complaints against ballast dumping were made in 1336 and 1357; *CPR 1334-38*, 259; and *CCR 1354-60*, 315. Oppenheim 1907, 137.

110 Rye was the exception to this trend and its harbour flourished during the 16th century; Mayhew 1987, 17-22.

111 Kowaleski 2000, 478-83, 485-7, 481,

112 Dunwich suffered a similar fate when the inundations of the late 13th century eroded the harbour's protective shingle spit and merchants discovered Southwold and Walberswick to be more favourable ports of call; Bailey 1991, 196-7.

113 Murray 1935, 208-10.

114 Saul 1968, 78-80. For example, the murage accounts record that the number of Flemish ships arriving declined dramatically beginning in the mid-1360s (99 in 1370, 61 in 1373, and only 11 in 1385).

115 Heath 1968, 65-6; and Saul 1975, 259-61.

116 Saul 1981, 41.

117 Saul 1979, 83; Saul 1975, 35-9, 162, 202; Bailey 1991, 198. 205; and Unger 1978, 350, note 24.

118 The estimated cost of the project was £1,000; Saul 1979, 83.

119 Saul 1981, 37-41.

120 Records from the coastal Suffolk villages of Sizwell and Thorpe record an increase in the number of vessels engaged in the fishery at this time; Bailey 1990, 109.

121 Dulley 1969, 41.

122 An *inquisition ad damnum* and a subsequent inquisition with names of jury inquiring into ramifications; Dell 1962, 272; *See* Cooper 1850, 96; *VCH Sussex* **9**, 64 for further detail.

123 Murray 1935, 225.

124 *See* PRO E101/158/10; PRO E101/160/3; PRO E101/161/3; PRO E101/162/1; PRO E101/162/5.

3 A FIGHT FOR SURVIVAL: THE SIXTEENTH CENTURY AND BEYOND

1 Cooper 1850, 96-8.

2 Homan 1942, 198, 202.

3. Homan 1942, 218, 232.

4. Pelham 1930a, 144-5; *VCH Sussex* **9**, 69.
5. Mayhew 1987, 235-6.
6. SRS **56**, 164-66. The 32 foreigners in Rye exclude eight men who could not be found and a further three listed as dead. Most of the Rye foreigners were French (two being recorded as Norman and one as Burgundian) though the list also includes one Italian. Of those in Winchelsea twelve were French, four Scottish and one Flemish.
7. PRO E179/190/200.
8. ESRO WIN 55, fo. 1; WIN 51, f. 43.
9. ESRO WIN 52 fos. 158, 160; and ESRO WIN generally.
10. Brent 1975, 36.
11. Cooper 1850, 106-7.
12. ESRO WIN 53 fos. 73-75.
13. Brent 1975, 36.
14. ESRO WIN 52, fo. 146.
15. *VCH Sussex* **9**, 69.
16. ESRO WIN 53 fo. 152; ESRO RYE 146/8.
17. ESRO WIN 53 fos. 59, 216, 223; WIN 54 fos. 44-45.
18. ESRO WIN 55 fos. 245-247.
19. Homan 1942, 252; Brent 1975, 36.
20. Stevenson 1991, 183-193.
21. ESRO AMS 5788/1. The block of five occupy the northwestern corner of Quarter 2 and are today called 'The Five Houses'; the block of fifteen are on the northeastern corner of Quarter 7 and have now been partly demolished. That part which remains, 1-10 Barrack Square, bears Nesbitt's initials and the date 1763.
22. The total of inhabited houses is that within the town and at the Strand. It excludes houses within the detached part of Winchelsea on the eastern side of the River Rother.
23. Lovegrove 1964, 103.

4 THE TOWN'S HISTORIC INFRASTRUCTURE

1 BL Add. Ch. 18623.
2 Homan 1949, 40-41; Lovegrove 1956, 162-65.
3 PRO SC11/656.
4 ESRO AMS 5806/3; AMS 6606/9/3; Martin and Martin 2002, 87-92.
5 ESRO WIN 2315.
6 ESRO WIN 51 fos. 34, 62-70; WIN 53, fos. 98, 184, 244.
7 Beresford 1967, 17; Homan 1949. The principal modifications to Homan's plan relate to the location of Monday Market, Quarter 23, Quarters 36-38 and his assumed line of the town defences. Minor revisions have also been necessary to the layout of the individual tenements within some of the quarters, particularly with regard to Quarters 1, 4, 11, 22, 23, 27, 32, 34, 36. For the detailed evidence upon which the revisions are based *see* Martin and Martin 2002.
8 Homan 1949, 36. In general terms Homan's observations regarding the original width of the streets have been confirmed, though his opinion that the section of north-south street between Quarters 23/24 and 28/29 was widened to 5½ *virgae* in order to give sufficient room for the market is now known to be incorrect - it is now known that the town was planned with a fully developed and spacious market square rather than a street market as he thought.
9 Homan 1949, 24.
10 HEH BA 39/1229; Homan 1949, 25.
11 PRO C145/293 (18).
12 ESRO WIN 53, fo. 210.
13 ESRO AMS 5806/3.
14 Information gleaned from a detailed rental of 1543, combined with abutments given in 16th-century property deeds. For full details *see* Martin and Martin 2002.
15 ESRO RYE 146/7; ESRO WIN/52, fo. 143; WIN 53, fos. 132, 150, 201; WIN 54, fos. 3, 167; WIN 55, fos. 105, 181, 206; WIN 58, fos. 18, 94, 98, 125, 157, 213, 214, 252, 258, 266. See also Martin and Martin 2002.
16 PRO C 145/293 (18); ESRO RYE 146/2.
17 ESRO WIN 51 fos. 206, 215; WIN 53 fos. 13, 150; WIN 55 fo. 262; WIN 56 fo. 234; WIN 58 fos. 237-238; WSRO Ep II/5/2 fo. 28; ESRO T475/2. For a discussion *see* also Martin and Martin 2002, 45-49. This location for the Butchery is contrary to the location given for it by Homan, who for some unclear reason placed it along the southern side of Quarter 19, immediately outside the houses of some of the leading tradesmen.
18 The only area of street where a deep deposit has been noted is at the junction of Back Lane and Rookery Lane where the ground has been deliberately raised by up to 750 millimetres (2ft.6ins.) in order to overcome a dip in the road surface. Formerly the eastern end of Back Lane sloped down very gently so as to take into account the natural gradient of the hill as the street extended eastwards between Quarters 12 and 17, across what is now Rookery Field. When both the eastern end of Back Land and the southern end of Rookery Lane fell out of use, a thick layer of redeposited clay was laid so as to level the surface of the two streets. This deposit was observed in September 2003 when Southern Water dug a large pit to make modifications to their existing water main.
19 Homan 1949, 36 and 1940, 58.
20 See note 18. Buried below made ground was an earlier road 'surface' on average 400 millimetres (1ft.4ins.) thick, sloped gently down towards the east and overlying what appeared to be undisturbed natural clay. The deposit was inspected from the side of the contractor's trench only. It formed a very distinct layer of dark grey, almost black organic-looking soil which contained a very dense admixture of debris: small pebbles, oyster shell, stone fragments, West Country slate, tile and bone were all noted. In places distinct horizontal lenses of material were visible including, at one point roughly half way up, a thin, discontinuous band of stone slabs which appeared to have been tipped in, perhaps to fill a shallow pothole. Except for its extensive area and consistent thickness, the nature of the deposit had much the appearance of a midden, yet it was located near the middle of a cross roads.
21 ESRO WIN 53 fo. 173; WIN 54 fo. 51.
22 Homan 1940, 9-10; PRO C145/293 (18).
23 ESRO WIN 52, fo. 149. *See* also Martin and Martin 2002, 87-92 and Sylvester 1999, 71.
24 PRO C145/293 (18); ESRO WIN 53 fo. 202; WIN 55, fo. 134; AMS 5806/3; WIN 51 fo. 45; *See* also Martin and Martin 2002.
25 ESRO WIN 53 fos. 29, 223, 245.
26 *VCH Sussex*, **9**, 70.
27 PRO SC 11/674; Cooper 1850, 53.
28 Homan 1940, 8-12.
29 PRO SC 12/15/78.
30 PRO E101/6/23; BL Add. Ch. 20173; Eddison 2000, 96.
31 Homan 1940, 188.
32 ESRO WIN 51, fo. 54; WIN. 52, fo. 149; WIN 53, fos. 50, 99, 166, 180, 236; WIN 54, fo. 9. For shops on the Strand at Rye *see* Mayhew 1987 and for shops on the Strade at Hastings *see* ESRO HBR 1/1234.

33 ESRO WIN 51, fo. 54; WIN 53, fos. 107, 167, 200, 223; WIN 54, fos. 18, 20, 116; WIN 55, fo. 67.
34 ESRO WIN 51, fo. 52; WIN 53, fo. 51, 162, 179.
35 ESRO AMS 5806/3; WIN 2315. *See* also Martin and Martin 2002, 87-92.
36 The Black Friars later moved to the northern marshes and subsequently to Quarter 4 - see this volume, Chapter 7. For an account of the development of Kings Green *see* Martin and Martin 2002, 105-106.
37 ESRO WIN 52, fos. 149, 159; WIN 53, fos. 150, 191, 192; WIN 55, fos. 5, 176, 192, 200, 210, 212.
38 BL Add. Ch. 18623.
39 Cooper 1850, 38.
40 ESRO WIN 52, fos. 155, 162; WIN 54, fo. 44; WIN 55, fo. 31; WIN 58, fos. 100, 123, 130, 147, 152; WIN 354.
41 ESRO WIN 58, fo. 92; WIN 55, fo. 110; Pratt 1998, 59-66.
42 PRO PROB 11/73. The two probable wells identified by excavation are at Rectory Lane, Quarter 15, Plot 21 (excavated 1976-89) and Winchelsea C. of E. School, Quarter 18 (excavated 2003). The possible example was at Truncheons, Quarter 20 (excavated 1990). That in Rectory Lane was excavated to a depth of a little in excess of six metres without reaching the bottom: on the other sites the tops only were examined.
43 ESRO AMS 5788/1.
44 ESRO WIN 54, fo. 66; WIN 55, fo. 83; WIN 58, fo. 306.

5 THE DEFENCES

1 Cooper 1850, 36; Homan 1940, 78-79; Homan 1949, 22-41.
2 PRO C145/293 (18); 16th-century copy in ESRO RYE 146/ 2.
3 CPR 1292-1301, 147 (15th September 1295).
4 Thomas Hog (ed) 'F Nicholai Triveti . . . Annales' (English Historical Society, 1845), 359-60. Trivet's passage was copied by William Rishanger in the early 14th century, which was in turn copied by Thomas Walsingham late in the same century. Walsingham's chronicle alone was used by Cooper (1850, 35) and Homan (1940, 58). The incident is discussed in Michael Prestwich 'Edward I' (Yale English Monarchs. Yale University Press, new edition 1997), 111.
5. Trivet's editor reads this *'moeniorum'* which he glosses *'i.e. moenium'* [of defensive walls], but states that earlier editors have read the word *'nemorum'* [of groves]; the latter reading was followed by both Rishanger and Walsingham (or their editors). The problem phrase was omitted by Cooper and embroidered with conjecture by Homan.
6 Peers 1933, 15.
7 CPR 1321-1324, 14 (21st August 1321), augmented by Homan 1940, 61-66, 76-77; Rot. Parl. 15 Edw II; PRO C145/ 88 no. 3 (formerly no. 15).
8 BL Add. Ch. 18623 - Transcript of *c.*1580.
9 CCR 1343-1346, 446.
10 Homan 1942, 77, 92.
11 CPR 1358-1361, 350 (15 March 1360), 411 (18 March 1360). In his chronicle, Henry Knighton gave the date of the attack as the Feast of St. Matthew the Apostle, in Lent [24 February 1360]. According to him 'the French landed to the number of 20,000 men-at-arms and killed thirty-five of the townsmen . . . and they took away with them nine beautiful women from the town and violated them in a manner horrible to relate' (Martin 1995, 174-75).
12 *VCH* Sussex, **9**, 66-7; Cooper 1850, 91-92.
13 CPR 1377-81, 500 (5th July 1380); Rot. Parl. **3**, 201a.
14 Martin 1995, 348-49.
15 ESRO WIN 53 fo. 110.
16 ESRO WIN 53 fos. 211, 225-226.
17 BL Add. Ch. 18623, survey of 1330.
18 ESRO WIN 52 fo. 162; WIN 55, fos. 183, 206; WIN 58, fo. 89.
19 ESRO ACC 3738; WIN 55, fo. 211.
20 PRO C145/293 (18).
21 ESRO RYE 146/5; PRO MPF 212; Bodleian Library, KeS/ 15.
22 PRO MPF 212; Bodleian Library, KeS/15; ESRO RYE 146/ 5; WIN 51, fo. 231; WIN 53, fo. 179.
23 PRO C145/293 (18).
24 Homan 1942, 174-5.
25 ESRO WIN 53, fo. 96.
26 PRO MPF 212; Bodleian Library, KeS/15.
27 ESRO WIN 54, fo. 101.
28 ESRO WIN 53 fo. 237.
29 Cooper 1850, 36.
30 Homan 1949, 27.
31 PRO SC11/649. Later rentals prove this to be on the hill at Winchelsea - *see* ESRO Acc 7024, Brede rental of 1716. For the Queen's grant of 1586 *see* ESRO WIN 2359/1/1. By 1586 Castle Field was privately owned, but was one of a number of former church properties included within the grant at the request of their owners in order to strengthen their titles to them.
32 ESRO WIN 53, fo. 253.
33 *VCH* Sussex, **9**, 185; Biddle *et al* 2001, 21.
34 ESRO RYE 146/7.
35 Cooper 1850, 175-180; Biddle *et al* 2001, 41-2.
36 ESRO WIN 51, fo. 43.
37 PRO C145/293 (18); ESRO RYE 146/2.
38 As an example of such a reference *see* ESRO WIN 53, fo. 179.
39 ESRO AMS 5806/3.
40 *VCH Sussex*, **9**, 63.
41 *VCH Sussex*, **9**, 63. For evidence of Helde's mayoralty in 1399 *see* PRO E368/174-5, cited in J. S. Roskell, Linda Clark and Carole Rawcliffe (eds), *The History of Parliament - The Commons 1386-1422*, **3**, 342. John Helde was specifically referred to as the mayor of Winchelsea when he witnessed a conveyance dated 26th January 1405 - *see* HEH BA 50/988.
42 BL Add. Ch. 18623 - transcript of *c.*1580.

6 GOVERNMENT AND THE MUNICIPAL BUILDINGS

1 *VCH Sussex*, **9**, 67.
2 Homan 1940, 8-11.
3 PRO SC11/674.
4 BL Add. Ch. 20168; PRO SC 6/1031/26.
5 PRO SC 6/1031/25-26; SC 6/1032/6-13; *VCH Sussex*, **9**, 67-69.
6 ESRO WIN 55 fo. 176.
7 Cooper 1850, 192-199, 218-227; *VCH Sussex*, **9**, 67-69.
8 Dell 1963, viii-x.
9 Cooper 1850, 218-227; *see* also ESRO WIN 54 fo. 72.
10 Homan 1940, 31-38.
11 PRO SC 6/1032/10.
12 PRO SC 6/1031/25.

13 Parker 1971.
14 HEH BA 47/1393.
15 ESRO WIN 51 fo. 39; WIN 52 fo. 150.
16 ESRO WIN53 fo. 54.
17 ESRO WIN 55 fo. 231; WIN 55 fo. 284; WIN 58 fo. 50.
18 ESRO WIN 58 fo. 176.
19 ESRO WIN 58 fos. 314-315.
20 Martin and Martin 2002, 22-24; ESRO HBR 1/1362.
21 ESRO WIN 58 fos. 57, 174.
22 PRO Add. Rolls 16431 and 16432; Cooper 1850, 202-3.

7 ECCLESIASTICAL BUILDINGS AND HOSPITALS

1 ESRO WIN 2359/1. See also ESRO RYE 146/5 & 7.
2 *VCH Sussex*, **9**, 75.
3 PRO SP 46/36 1 MPF3; PRO SP 12/254 (751) MPF 212.
4 Nairn and Pevsner 1965, 633-635. For a full description *see* *VCH Sussex*, **9**, 71-75.
5 ESRO WIN 58 fo. 213.
6 Cooper 1850, 122; *VCH Sussex*, **9**, 72.
7 Dell 1963, Plate III.
8 Cooper 1850, 129; Bodleian Library, KeS/15.
9 ESRO AMS 2490 Bk.4. p.18.
10 Bodleian Library, KeS/15.
11 ESRO WIN 58 fos. 52, 69, 72, 74, 96.
12 Cooper 1850, 122-143.
13 Blair *et al*. 2000, 5-30.
14 PRO E164/29 fo. 171; PRO E326/3935.
15 HEH BA 53/1065; PRO C143/454 no. 12.
16 Blair *et a*l. 2000, 19.
17 *VCH Sussex*, **9**, 75.
18 BL Add. Ch. 20182; ESRO WIN 51, fos. 213, 226; WIN 56, fos. 369, 384, 430, 448; WIN 58, fo. 336.
19 Cooper 1850, 143; Rot. Pat. 33 Edw III pt. 1 m.4 and Cal. Rot. Orig. p.255.
20 Martin 1995, 174-175; Cooper 1850, 80; Homan 1942, 132-33.
21 PRO C145/293 (18); ESRO RYE 146/2. The total area of Quarter 21 as originally laid out was 4 acres 0 rods 23 perches which, after subtracting the 1 acre 3 rods 12¼ perches occupied by the fifteen plots listed in 1292, gives an acreage of 2 acres 1 rod 10¾ perches for the churchyard at the time of the town's foundation. These figures suggest that any increase in size must have been minimal.
22 ESRO WIN 2315.
23 PRO C143/334 no.14.
24 ESRO RYE 146/7.
25 For full details of the excavations upon the site see Martin and Rudling 2004, 75-93.
26 *VCH Sussex*, **9**, 75; Homan 1939, 5.
27 *VCH Sussex*, **9**, 75; ESRO WIN 55 fo.1.
28 Homan 1942, 233; Mayhew 1984, 113.
29 ESRO WIN 54 fo. 20; ESRO PAR 511/1.
30 Cooper 1850, 143.
31 *VCH Sussex*, **9**, 75.
32 PRO C145/293.
33 *VCH Sussex*, **9**, 75.
34 WSRO Ep II/5/5 fo.317-20; ESRO WIN 55 fo. 167; WIN 58 fo. 3.
35 BL King's Library K. Top - XLII-26-D.
36 *VCH Sussex*, **2**, 96.
37 Homan 1949, 25.
38 Monumenta Franciscana 2/60-62.
39 ESRO WIN 2043.
40 PRO PROB 11/12; 11/22.
41 Colvin 1982, 423.
42 Cooper 1850, 146-148; VCH Sussex, **2**, 96.
43 BL Add. Mss. 5670 fos. 21 (2 drawings) and 25.
44 Nairn and Pevsner 1965, 635-636.
45 ESRO HBR 1/1168.
46 Martin and Martin 2002, 10-13, 105-106.
47 PRO C145/293 (18); ESRO RYE 146/2.
48 Liber Studiorum, cxviii M.
49 Cooper 1850, 36.
50 Colvin 1982, 423.
51 PRO SC11/674.
52 Martin and Martin 2002, 75-77.
53 *VCH Sussex*, **2**, 107.
54 Martin and Martin 2002, 75-77.
55 ESRO W/A3.126, W/A5.166, WIN 51 fo. 70.
56 ESRO WIN 54 fo. 10.
57 ESRO WIN 56 fo. 209.
58 Martin and Martin 2002, 84-86.
59 *VCH Sussex*, **2**, 107.
60 ESRO WIN 2054.
61 *VCH Sussex*, **2**, 107.
62 ESRO WIN 51 fo. 70; WIN 52 fo. 162.
63 ESRO RYE 146/7; ESRO WIN 52 fo. 113.
64 ESRO WIN 2359/1/1.
65 BL Add. Ch. 16209-16210, 20187; Martin and Martin 2002, 84-86.
66 *VCH Sussex*, **9**, 70; BL Add. Ch. 18623; Bodleian Library, KeS/15.

8 THE BURGAGE PLOTS

1 PRO SC11/674.
2 For a detailed published discussion and interpretation of the rental readers are directed to W. M. Homan's pioneering article published in the *Sussex Archaeological Collections* (Homan 1949, 22-41). As noted in Chapter 4, some later documents of considerable significance were not available to Homan and these, together with the results of recent earthwork surveys, show that a few important details in his plan are incorrect (*see* Chapter 4, Note 7).
3 Saul 1986, 178.
4 Homan 1949, 30-31, 36-37. Beresford 1967, 24-25, gives a very different interpretation of the rents per acre. However, by calculating the rent per acre directly from the original 1292 rental (PRO SC 11/674), it can be shown that his comments were either based upon corrupted data or upon grossly inaccurate calculations. Beresford's conclusions relating to the rental value of the individual quarters and regarding the their significance must be totally ignored.
5 Martin and Rudling 2004, 1-9; also King 1975.
6 BL Add. Ch. 20166.
7 BL Add. Ch. 20173.
8 HEH BA 47/1393.
9 Martin and Rudling 2004, 1-9; also King 1975.
10 PRO C 145/293(18); Martin and Martin 2002, 27-28.
11 Martin and Martin 2002, 33-35.
12 Martin and Martin 2002, 33-35.
13 ESRO T475/2.
14 For a description and interpretation of the excavations *see* Martin and Rudling 2004, 41-57.

15 Martin and Martin 2002, 17-18.
16 PRO SC 12/15/55. For a discussion of the evidence *see* Martin and Rudling 2004, 54-57.
17 PRO SC12/15/78.
18 *VCH* Sussex, **2**, 95.
19 PRO C143/326 no.10.
20 PRO C143/334 no. 14.
21 PRO SC 6/1032/11 (included is a writ to discharge the bailiff. He says he cannot levy rents because of plague, burning of the town by enemies and the flooding of [marshland in the manor of Iham called] *Spadelond* by the sea). *see* also PRO SC 12/15/55.
22 Homan 1942, 158.
23 PRO C145/293 (18).
24 ESRO RYE 146/5.
25 ESRO RYE 146/5, Quarters 7, 12 and 13.
26 Martin and Martin 2002, 1-106.
27 ESRO RYE 146/7.
28 ESRO AMS 5806/3; WIN 2315.
29 For a plan dated 1738 of the farm called The Friars *see* ESRO Acc 3738.

9 THE WINCHELSEA CELLARS

1 Faulkner 1966, 120. For the cellars of Chester *see* Brown 1999, 15-18, 33-38; for Southampton *see* Faulkner 1975, 78-124. The most comprehensive recent account of 13th- and early 14th-century cellars and undercrofts in English towns is that included within Roland Harris's 1994 D.Phil thesis (Harris 1994).
2 For examples of Winchelsea cellars destroyed or filled in during the 16th century *see* ESRO WIN 52 fos. 149, 152; WIN 54 fo. 52
3 Smith and Carter 1983; Robert Smith pers. comm. 2002. By far the greatest known concentration of vaulted cellars in any English town is in Norwich, which boasts no fewer than 101 known examples, of which 68 still survive. However, these are somewhat different to those in other towns in that they are thought to date from a later period - probably from the 15th century - and most are entered either from the interior of the building only, or from a private rear yard. The principal purpose of the Norwich examples is thought to have been the formation of a level, fireproof building platform.
4 Cooper 1850, Plate 1.
5 McCann and Mackie 1997, 10-13.
6 These excavations were carried out by UCLFAU, under the site direction of Richard James, in advance of building works (report forthcoming).
7 For further details *see* Martin and Rudling 2004, 41-57 and 1-9 respectively.
8 Cooper 1850, Plate 1.
9 *See* note 6 above.
10 A number of the survey reports indicate the existence of straight-jointed end walls, but others do not mention whether the walls are bonded or straight-jointed, or, indeed, whether the evidence was visible. For this reason, the extent to which this method was utilized is not currently known.
11 For a report on the excavations at Blackfriars Barn *see* Martin and Rudling 2004, 11-40, and for North Street *see* Martin and Rudling 2004, 41-57. Regarding the excavations on Quarter 18 *see* note 6 above.
12 Homan's theoretical medieval ground levels are followed by Roland Harris in his 1994 appraisal of the Winchelsea cellars.
13 ESRO WIN 53 fo. 191.
14 Homan 1940, 49.
15 Cupboard recesses with square heads exist within Cellar 10, Quarter 3; Cellar 11, Quarter 5; Cellar 15, Quarter 7; Cellar 17, Quarter 7; Cellar 20, Quarter 8; Cellar 24, Quarter 12; Cellar 25, Quarter 13; Cellar 30, Quarter 15; and Cellar 33. Quarter 12. Cupboard recesses with arched heads are to be seen in Cellars 3, 4 and 5, all on Quarter 2; Cellar 14, Quarter 7; Cellar 18, Quarter 8; and Cellar 29, Quarter 14. Cellar 3 has a total of four recesses and Cellars 10, 20, 25 and 30 each have two recesses. All the other cellars listed above possess one each.
16 Faulkner 1975, 111-14.
17 Faulkner 1975, 118.
18 For Chester *see* Brown 1999, 44-54, and for Winchester *see* Keene 1985, 166-167. We are grateful to Sarah Pearson for informing us of her recent discoveries at Faversham (as yet unpublished).
19 ESRO HBR 1/1362.
20 For further details *see* Martin and Rudling 2004, 1-9 and 99-104.
21 For further details of the possible medieval examples *see* ESRO HBR 1/1127, 1325, 288 and 603. For the two likely post-medieval examples *see* ESRO HBR 1/585 and 1378.
22 Homan 1940, 39-49; PRO E101/6/23. *See* also Sylvester 1999, 72, note 48.
23 Faulkner 1975, 122-130.
24 Dominic Leahy, pers. comm.
25 Sylvester 1999, 200; CPR 1292-1301, 18, 21.
26 James 1971, 76.
27 Sharpe 1901, 111-12.
28 James 1971, 76, 138-139, 184.
29 James 1971, 73-75.
30 David Sylvester, pers. comm.
31 Sylvester 1999, 32, note 9.
32 James 1971, 135.
33 James 1971, 65, 96, 99-101.
34 PRO E 143/10/2/13.
35 PRO E122/78/3a.
36 CCR 1333-37, 62.
37 CCR 1341-43, 646-7.
38 James 1971, 98.
39 James 1971, 65, 99-101.
40 Sylvester 1999, 94-6 and David Sylvester, pers. comm.
41 Harris 1994, 245.
42 James 1971, 76, 164-5.
43 James 1971, 176, 190-3.
44 Keene 1985, 166-167. For Canterbury *see* Urry 1967, 192-194.
45 Harris 1994, 230-231, citing Keene and Harding 1987.
46 Keene 1993, 187-190.
47 Harris 1994, 288.
48 Harris 1994, 230-247.
49 James 1971, 190.
50 ESRO AMS 4617.
51 Cooper 1850, Plate 1.
52 Brown 1999, 62.
53 Harris 1994, 125.
54 Although the undercrofts and cellars at Chester differ from those usually found, an informative account of the varied uses to which they were being put in the 16th century is to be found in Brown 1999, 87.
55 PRO SP12/75/70.
56 ESRO WIN 52 fos. 149, 152, WIN 54, fo. 52.

10 DOMESTIC BUILDINGS: LAYOUT AND DESIGN

1. For full reports on all of these buildings *see* ESRO HBR 1/ 0237, 1/1362, 1/0260, 1/0223, 1/217, 1/1442, 1/582
2. For full details of the excavated remains *see* Martin and Rudling 2004, 1-111.
3. Pantin 1962-3, 202-239.
4. Brown 1999, 25-27.
5. HEH BA 47/1383.
6. Quiney 1990, 148.
7. For full details of the excavation at Mill Road *see* Martin and Rudling 2004, 63-73.
8. For full details of the excavation at North Street, *see* Martin and Rudling 2004, 41-57.
9. Leach 2000, 1-10.
10. ESRO HBR 1/857.
11. For reports on all of these buildings *see* ESRO HBR 1/1375, 1/0222, 1/220, 1/837, 1/288, 1/1378, 1/834, 1/1127, 1/1389, 1/585, 1/922.
12. For a discussion of quasi-aisled halls using base crucks, sling braces and hammer beams within their open trusses *see* Mason 1964, 20-24; Barnwell and Adams 1994, 32-35.
13. Faulkner 1966, 124-125.
14. Martin and Martin 2002, Quarter 13. 33-35.
15. Bridge, 2004.
16. ESRO RYE 146/5; WIN 51, fo. 206.
17. ESRO RYE 146/5. An attempt at tree-ring dating proved unsuccessful.
18 For full details of the excavation in German Street, Quarter 19 *see* King 1975, 124-145, and Martin and Rudling 2004, 1-9.
19. For full details of the excavation on Quarter 15, Plot 21 in Rectory Lane *see* Martin and Rudling 2004, 11-40.
20. PRO SP 12/38 fo. 28.
21. PRO E 101/5/28.
22. PRO E 143/10/2/13. In total 29 Winchelsea ships were arrested at Winchelsea (a thirtieth ship at Winchelsea was from Folkestone) and a further two ships were arrested at ports in North Wales. The total tonnage was 3505[t]. In the early 14th century a ratio of approximately one man per four tons of ship was usual to crew vessels of more than 100 tons (Ian Friel, *The Good Ship*, 1995, 33).
23. Homan 1942, 35-36, 117.
24. PRO E 101/19/22.
25. ESRO WIN 52, fos. 150-51, 161.
26. ESRO WIN 52 fo. 158.
27. ESRO WIN 52, fo. 162; WIN 53, fos. 59, 276; WIN 54, fos. 20, 29 (2 refs.), 79 (3 licences), 108, 113, 145; WIN 55, fos. 12, 56, 61, 62 (2 licences), 105 (2 licences), 121, 161, 163, 176.
28. HEH BA 50/1484.
29. Late-medieval and transitional 'houses' which show no obvious signs of having contained a hearth or chimney when first built are known from a number of towns in England, including neighbouring Rye. Some students argue that the occupants of these buildings used some form of charcoal brazier for heating and either cooked within a detached building or purchased their hot food from cook shops. Others suggest that these buildings were not initially used as houses, but fulfilled a specialist function. The evidence from Winchelsea does not progress the debate, which remains unresolved.
30. The high number of gentlemen and esquires resident within the town during the 16th century becomes apparent when the rank and occupations of Winchelsea residents mentioned in the enrolled deeds (ESRO WIN 51-53) are added to the names of inhabitants assessed in 1532/3 (ESRO RYE 146/6) and those included on the town rental of 1543 (ESRO RYE 146/7).
31. ESRO AMS 2445-2449 and ESRO AMS 2487-2490. Book 5, pages 131 and 144.
32. ESRO WIN 53 fos. 200, 237.
33. For these houses compare the 1758 and 1763 town maps (ESRO AMS 5806/3; ESRO WIN 2315) with the Nesbitt survey dated 1767 (ESRO AMS 5788/1). For further details regarding Arnold Nesbitt esq. and the English Linen Company *see* Stevenson 1991, 183-193 and *VCH Sussex* **2**, 258.

11 MEDIEVAL AND 'TRANSITIONAL DOMESTIC BUILDINGS: MATERIALS AND CONSTRUCTION

1. As a sample of available references *see* ESRO WIN 52 fo. 162; WIN 53 fo. 276; WIN 54 fos. 20, 29, 52, 79, 81.
2 R. W. Gallois, *British Regional Geology: The Wealden District* (4th Edition 1965) 25, 26, 28.
3. For a discussion of the geological material recovered from the excavations *see* C. Cartwright, 'Geological Material' in Martin and Rudling, 2004, 163-166. As normally only the unusual material was sampled for examination, the report underplays the extensive use of Tilgate stone.
4. Martin and Rudling 2004, 1-111. For a general discussion of Flemish-type bricks *see* Ryan 1996, 44-45.
5. Martin 1989, 116-117; ESRO HBR 1/828, 1/381.
6. Pelham 1929, 105-111; Dell 1965, 59, 60, 89, 95, 96, 102, 107, 125, 126, 141.
7 Ryan 1996, 44-45.
8. King 1975, Figure 5, No.5.
9. Martin and Martin 1989, 52-55, 61-62, 69-75. The earliest use of close-studding known in East Sussex is at Bridge Cottage, Uckfield, which has been tree-ring dated to 1436, although here, the studs were of non-local 'thick' type exposed within both faces of the walls (ESRO HBR 1/1274; M. C. Bridge, 'Dendrochronological investigation of samples from Bridge Cottage, Uckfield, East Sussex', (Unpublished, Sept. 2001)). Close-studding is also used within the main range at The Pilgrims Rest, Battle, known from the Battle Almoner's accounts to have been built in 1445/6 (ESRO HBR 1/207) and within the parlour crosswing at The Chantry, Warbleton, thought to have been built in 1443, when a chantry was set up in Warbleton Church by the executor of William Prestwyk, 'late clerk of the King's parliament' (ESRO HBR 1/514; *VCH Sussex* **9**, 209). All three buildings are of high status.
10. ESRO HBR 1/356; HBR 1/25.
11. For further details regarding the roofing materials *see* Martin and Rudling 2004, 155-158. For the use of West-Country slate in Sussex generally *see* Holden 1965, Murray 1965, and Holden 1989. For the use of roof louvres *see* Dunning 1959 and Wood 1965.
12. For further details of the hearths *see* Martin and Rudling 2004, 24-36, 44-46, and 65-67.
13. The argument sometimes put forward that the number of fireplaces is merely a reflection of the number of stone buildings in the town, and that within a stone-built house one

might as well have a fireplace as an open hearth is not a valid one. Two of the fireplaces within the house on Quarter 15 are associated with timber framing, whilst many medieval stone buildings lack fireplaces.

14 Martin and Rudling 2004, 24-26.

15. Martin and Rudling 2004, 33-35; ESRO HBR 1/217.

16. ESRO HBR 1/806.

17. For medieval fireplaces and chimneys in general *see* Wood 1965, 261-291. As Wood points out (p.265), the form of fireplace adopted after the abandonment of the hooded/canopied type has much in common with 12th-century Norman examples, and therefore occasional examples of this type are likely to have persisted throughout the 13th and 14th centuries.

18. Martin and Rudling 2004, 100-104 and 108-109

19. Martin and Rudling 2004, 41-57.

12 WASTE DISPOSAL

1 ESRO HBR 1/589.

2 Martin and Rudling 2004, 63-73, 95-97 and 24-36 respectively.

3 It is unlikely that all the cesspits in Winchelsea were circular: in other towns most are rectangular or square in plan. An apparently unlined pit of this type discovered during excavations in 2003, within the grounds of the C. of E. primary school on Quarter 18, could have been dug as a cesspit, but this is still to be confirmed. Post-excavation analysis has still to be carried out. Similarly, a stone-lined rectangular feature seen during evaluation work undertaken at Truncheons, Quarter 19, may represent a cesspit, but is perhaps more likely to be a cellar (Martin and Rudling 2004, 102) as is an apparently unlined pit at New Inn, Quarter 14 (Martin and Rudling 2004, 107-108).

4 The conditions upon the hill at Winchelsea are not conducive to the preservation of timber remains. A similar pit upon the former site of Phoenix Brewery, Bourne Street, Hastings, still retained its timber barrel lining but only because of the waterlogged conditions; *see* Rudling and Barber 1993, 86-88.

5 Schofield and Vince 1994, 68.

6 Salzman 1952, 283-285.

7 ESRO HBR 1/300, 1/1190, 1/1202.

8 Martin and Rudling 2004, 68-73.

9 The exceptions could be features seen in plan during the evaluation of the New Inn and Truncheons sites on Quarters 14 and 19. Because these excavations were intended only as evaluations, the features were not fully excavated and thus their forms remain unknown. Some larger pits were also discovered in 2003 during excavation on the site of the C. of E. primary school on Quarter 18, but the results of this excavation are still to be analyzed.

10 Schofield and Vince 1994, 119. A good Sussex example of the opportunist use of features for the disposal of rubbish was noted during excavation at St Nicholas' Hospital, Lewes, Sussex, where disused quarry pits were used for this purpose; *see* Barber and Sibun, 'Excavations at the Medieval Hospital of St Nicholas, Lewes', (forthcoming).

11 ESRO WIN 52, fos. 149, 152.

12 For a review of the development of waterfront areas in medieval towns *see* Schofield and Vince 1994, 54-59.

13 TRADE AND STATUS: AN ARCHAEOLOGICAL PERSPECTIVE

1 For detailed and illustrated reports by specialists on all the finds from the 1976 to 1982 excavations at Winchelsea, the reader is referred to Martin and Rudling 2004 115-176.

2 For a full report *see* Orton, Streeten and Barber in Martin and Rudling 2004, 115-138, and details by Luke Barber of pottery sherds, including some wasters, found during a landscape survey in 1993 (Martin and Rudling 2004, 137-138).

3 For Dover *see* Dunning 1956; for Seaford *see* Machling 1995, 204, and for Southampton *see* Brown 1997, 91.

4 Vidler 1933, 1936; Barton 1979; Wetherill 2001.

5 Barton 1979, 118-121.

6 Orton, Streeten and Barber in Martin and Rudling 2004, 138.

7. Barton 1979, 182-84.

8. Allan 1983, 193, 196.

9. Hurst 1980, 123.

10. Orton 1982a, 94; Watkins 1983, 246.

11 Chapelot 1983, 51.

12. Watkins 1983, 249.

13 Watkins 1983, 246; Brooks and Hodges 1983, 235.

14 Allan 1983, 202-3.

15 Streeten 1985, 117 fig. 34, no. 58; Streeten 1983, 103 fig. 43, no. 52.

16 Streeten 1983, 99.

17 Freke 1979.

18 Whittingham 2001.

19 A full report on the glass by John Shepherd is included in Martin and Rudling 2004, 139-143.

20 Child n.d.

21 Cropper 2001, 283.

22 Charleston 1975, 210.

23 Maxwell-Stewart in Child n.d. 8-9.

24 Cropper 2001.

25 Charleston 1984, 50; Sim 1997, 58; Cropper 2001, 292.

26 Child n/d, 2 and page 4 of the illustrations.

27 A full report on the coins and jetons by David Rudling is included in Martin and Rudling 2004, 145-146.

28 Child n.d., 2.

29 Biddle *et al.* 2001, 300.

30 For a full report *see* Alison Goodall in Martin and Rudling 2004, 147-150.

31 For full reports *see* Ian Goodall, Nicky Moyle and David Rudling in Martin and Rudling 2004, 151-154.

32 King 1975, 140.

33 Thomson 1970, 210; Caldwell 1975, 219-221.

34 For a full report *see* Rod Clough in Martin and Rudling 2004, 150.

35 For a full report *see* Elizabeth Eames in Martin and Rudling 2004, 159-161.

36 For a full report *see* Caroline Cartwright in Martin and Rudling 2004, 163-166.

37 For a full report *see* Sue Browne in Martin and Rudling 2004, 86-93.

38 For full reports *see* Myrtle Kyllo, Caroline Cartwright and Pat Hinton in Martin and Rudling 2004, 169-176.

39 Connell and Davis 2001, 311.

14 CONCLUSIONS

1. I am very grateful to David Sylvester for his considerable help with this chapter and for sharing with me his detailed knowledge of the early history of Winchelsea. I wish also to thank Rosemary Horrox for making available to me her published data relating to the morphology of the port town of Hull, which highlighted the lack of definition contained within the surviving documents relating to Winchelsea's individual tenements (Horrox 1982, 1-26). While the research reported in this volume may very well suggest that the importance of Winchelsea as a port town during the late 13th and early 14th centuries has so far been underrated and possibly misunderstood, the work of both Sylvester and Horrox has demonstrated that it would be premature to conclude too much from the currently available data.
2. *See* the discussion in Chapter 2 on King John's 1204 assessment.
3. For a discussion of medieval town migration, *see* Palliser *et al* 2000, 154-6.
4. Beresford 1967, *passim.*
5. Platt 1973, 107.
6. Nairn and Pevsner 1965, 633-635.
7. For studies assessing the various factors in determining borough status, see Kermode 2000, 441-65, and Keene 2000, 545-82.
8. As a member of the Cinque Ports Confederation Winchelsea's native residents were exempted many taxes and the town had the right to make its own terms regarding others (Hudson 1909, xv). This means that Winchelsea and the other Cinque Ports are excluded from an important source of data used by economic historians. Of course, this does not mean that if Winchelsea had been included it would necessarily have been high in the list
9. Horrox 1982, 5-6.

BIBLIOGRAPHY

ABBREVIATIONS

Archaeol.J.	Archaeological Journal
EcHR	Economic History Review
SAC	Sussex Archaeological Collection
SNQ	Sussex Notes and Queries
SRS	Sussex Record Society

Allan, J. 1983. The Importance of Pottery to Southern England *c.*1200-1500, in P. J. Davey and R. Hodges (eds.), *Ceramics and Trade*, 193-208.

Bailey, M. 1990. Coastal Fishing off South East Suffolk in the century after the Black Death, *Proceedings of the Suffolk Institute of Archaeology and History* **37**, 102-14.

— 1991. *Per Impetum Maris:* Natural Disaster and Economic Decline in Eastern England, 1275-1350, in Bruce M. S. Campbell (ed.), *Before the Black Death: Studies in the 'Crisis' of the Early Fourteenth Century.* Manchester: Manchester University Press, 184-208.

Barnwell, P. & Adams, A. 1994. *The House Within: Interpreting Medieval Houses in Kent.* London: HMSO.

Barton, J.K. 1979. *Medieval Sussex Pottery.* Chichester: Phillimore.

Beardwood, A. 1931. *Alien Merchants in England 1350-1377.* Cambridge, Mass: Medieval Academy of America.

Beresford, M. 1967. *New Towns of the Middle Ages: Town Plantation in England, Wales and Gascony.* London: Lutterworth Press. 2nd edn. 1988: Gloucester: Alan Sutton.

Biddle, M., Hiller, J., Scott, I. & Streeten, A. 2001. *Henry VIII's Coastal Artillery Fort at Camber Castle, Rye, East Sussex.* Oxford: Oxford Archaeological Unit.

Blaauw, W.H. 1851. The vessels of the Cinque Ports and their employment, *SAC* **4**, 101-126.

Blair, C., Goodall, J. & Lankester, P. 2000. The Winchelsea Tombs Reconsidered, *Church Monuments* **15**, 5-30.

Brandon, P. & Short, B. 1990. *The Southeast from AD 1000.* London and New York: Longman.

Bridge, M.C. 2004. *Tree-Ring Analysis of Timbers from Six Buildings in Winchelsea, East Sussex.* Report 15/2004, English Heritage Centre for Archaeology. Fort Cumberland, Portsmouth.

Britnell, R. 1996. *The Commercialisation of English Society, 1000-1500.* (2nd edn.), Manchester: Manchester University Press.

Britton, C.E. 1937. *A meteorological chronology to AD 1485.* London: HMSO.

Brooks, C. & Hodges, R. 1983. Imported pottery in eastern Britain *c.*1200-1500, in P. J. Davey and R. Hodges (eds.), *Ceramics and Trade*, 231-43.

Brown, D.H. 1997. Pots from Houses**,** *Medieval Ceramics* **21**, 83-94.

Brown, A. (ed.) 1999. *The Rows of Chester.* London: English Heritage.

Burrows, M. 1888. *The Cinque Ports.* Reprinted 1903, London: Longmans, Green and Co.

Butcher, A.F. 1974. The Origins of the Romney Freemen, 1433-1523, *EcHR*, 2nd series, **27**, 16-22.

Caldwell, D.H. 1975. Fragments of a brigandine from Coldingham Priory, Berwickshire, *Proceedings of the Society of Antiquaries of Scotland* **106**, 219-221.

Campbell, B.M.S., Galloway, J.A., Keene, D, & Murphy, M. 1993. A Medieval Capital and its Grain Supply: Agrarian Production and Distribution in the London Region, *c.*1300, *Historical Geography Research Series* **30**.

Chambers, G. 1937. The French Bastides and the Town Plan of Winchelsea, *Archaeol. J.* **94 (2)**, 177-206.

Chapelot, J. 1983. The Saintonge pottery industry in the later Middle Ages, in P. J. Davey and R. Hodges (eds.), *Ceramics and Trade*, 49-54.

Charleston, R.J. 1975. The Glass, in C. Platt and R. Coleman-Smith, *Excavations in medieval Southampton 1953-1969,* vol. *2: The Finds*. 204-226. Leicester: Leicester University Press.

— 1984. English glass and the glass used in England, *circa* 400-1940. London: Allen and Unwin.

Child, I.B. (Dick) n/d. *The excavation of a stone-lined pit in the garden of Richmond House, Cooks Green, Winchelsea, 1988-1989.* St Leonards-on-Sea: Hastings Area Archaeological Research Group.

Childs, W. 1977. *Anglo-Castilian Trade in the Later Middle Ages.* Manchester: Manchester University Press.

— 1996. The English Export Trade in Cloth in the Fourteenth Century, in R.Britnell and J. Hatcher (eds.), *Progress and Problems in Medieval England: Essays in Honour of Edward Miller.* Cambridge: Cambridge University Press, 127-47.

Clowes, W.L. 1897-1903. *The Royal Navy: A History from the Earliest Times to the Present*, 5 volumes. London: S. Low, Marston and Co.

Colvin, H.M. (ed.) 1982. *The History of the King's Works,* vol. **4**: 1485-1660 (Part II). London: HMSO.

Connell, B. & Davis, S. 2001. Chapter 8: The Animal Bones, in

M. Biddle, J. Hiller, I. Scott and A. Streeten, *Henry VIII's Coastal Artillery Fort at Camber Castle, Rye, East Sussex,* 301-332.

Cooper, W.D. 1850. *The History of Winchelsea, one of the Ancient Towns added to the Cinque Ports.* Republished (1986) Lewes: East Sussex County Council.

— 1871. Further Notes on Winchelsea, *SAC* **23**, 25-26.

Cropper, C. 2001. Vessel Glass, in M. Biddle, J. Hiller, I. Scott and A. Streeten, *Henry VIII's Coastal Artillery Fort at Camber Castle, Rye, East Sussex,* 283-292.

Cutting, C. 1956. *Fish Saving: A History of Fish Processing from Ancient to Modern Times.* New York: Philosophical Library.

Davey, P.J. & Hodges, R. (eds.) 1983. *Ceramics and Trade.* Sheffield: Department of Prehistory and Archaeology, University of Sheffield.

Dell, R.F. (ed.) 1962. *The Records of Rye Corporation: a catalogue.* Lewes: East Sussex County Council.

— (ed.) 1963. *Winchelsea Corporation Records: a catalogue.* Lewes: East Sussex County Council.

— (ed.) 1965. Rye Shipping Records, 1566-1590, *SRS* **64.**

Dulley, A.J.F. 1969. The Early History of the Rye Fishery, *SAC* **107**, 36-64.

Dunning, G.C. 1956. Pottery and other finds from a medieval garderobe in Snargate Street, Dover, *Archaeologia Cantiana* **69,** 138-156.

— 1959. Roof Structures, *Archaeol. J.* **116**, 174-9.

Eddison, J. 1998. Catastrophic Changes: A Multidisciplinary Study of the Evolution of the Barrier Beaches of Rye Bay, in J. Eddison, M. Gardiner and A. Long (eds.) *Romney Marsh: Environmental Change and Human Occupation in a Coastal Lowland, Oxford University Committee for Archaeology,* Monograph **46**, 65-87.

— 2000. *Romney Marsh, Survival on a Frontier.* Stroud: Tempus.

Faulkner, P.A. 1966. Medieval Undercrofts and Town Houses, *Archaeol. J.* **123**, 120-35 [Reprinted in full in *Studies in Medieval Domestic Architecture.* (1975) 118-133].

— 1975. Part 1 - The Surviving Medieval Buildings, in Platt, C. *et al., Excavations in Medieval Southampton, 1953-1969*, vol.**1**: *The excavation reports.* Leicester: Leicester University Press, 56-124.

Freke, D.J. 1979. The excavation of an early sixteenth-century pottery kiln at Lower Parrock, Hartfield, East Sussex, 1977, *Post-medieval Archaeology* **13**, 79-125.

Gardiner, D. 1954. *Historic Haven: The Story of Sandwich.* Derby: Pilgrim Press.

Gardiner, M. 2000. Shipping and trade between England and the Continent during the eleventh century, *Anglo-Norman Studies* **22**, 71-93.

Gras, N.S.B. (ed.) 1918. *The Early English Customs Systems.* Cambridge, Mass: Harvaed University Press.

Harris, R.B. 1994. The origins and development of English medieval townhouses operating commercially on two storeys. Unpublished PhD thesis, Hertford College.

Haskins, C.H. 1918. A Charter for Cnut for Fécamp, *Economic History Review* **33**, 343-4.

Heath, P. 1968. North Sea Fishing in the Fifteenth Century: The Scarborough Fleet, *Northern History* **3**, 53-69.

Holden, E.W. 1965. Slate Roofing in medieval Sussex, *SAC* **103**, 67-78.

— 1989. Slate Roofing in Medieval Sussex: A Reappraisal, *SAC* **127**, 73-88.

Holloway, W. 1847. *History and Antiquities of the Ancient Town of Rye in the County of Sussex with Incidental Notices of the Cinque Ports.* Reprinted from local newspaper articles in 1863. London: John Russell Smith.

Homan, W.M. 1939. The Churches of Winchelsea. Unpublished: a copy has been deposited at ESRO.

— 1940. The Founding of a 13th Century Town. Unpublished: catalogued at ESRO as AMS 2497.

— 1942. The History of Winchelsea. Unpublished: catalogued at ESRO as AMS 2497.

— 1949. The Founding of New Winchelsea, *SAC* **88**, 22-41

— n/d. The Hill of Iham and the Laying Out of New Winchelsea. Unpublished: catalogued at ESRO as AMS 2497.

Horrox, R. (ed.) 1982. Selected Rentals and Accounts of Medieval Hull, 1293-1528, *The Yorkshire Archaeological Society Record Series*, **141**.

Hudson, Rev. W. 1909. The Three Earliest Subsidies for the County of Sussex in the Years 1296, 1327, 1332, SRS **10**, xv.

Hurst, J.G. 1980. Medieval Pottery Imports in Sussex, *SAC* **118**, 119-124.

Inderwick, F.A. 1892. *The story of King Edward and New Winchelsea.* London: Sampson, Low, Marston and Company.

James, M.K. 1971. *Studies in the Medieval Wine Trade.* Oxford: Clarendon Press.

Johnson, C. 2000. Archaeological Recording (Phase 1) of the Medieval Town Wall in Rookery Field, Winchelsea, East Sussex. Unpublished Archaeology South-East report on Project **1294**. A copy of this report has been deposited with the East Sussex County Council Sites and Monuments Record.

Keene, D. 1985. Survey of Medieval Winchester, *Winchester Studies* **I**.

— 1993. *The Character and Development of the Cheapside Area: an overview*, in J. Schofield, P. Allen, and C. Taylor, Medieval Buildings and Property Development in the area of Cheapside, *Transactions of the London and Middlesex Archaeological Society* **41** (for 1990, but published 1993) 179-94.

— 2000. The South-East of England, in D.M. Palliser (ed.), *Cambridge Urban History of Britain*, vol. **I**: 600-1540. Cambridge: Cambridge University Press.

Keene, D. & Harding, V. 1987. *Historical Gazetteer of London before the Great Fire*, part **1**: Cheapside. Cambridge: London Record Society.

Kermode, J. 2000. The greater towns 1300-1540, in D.M. Palliser, (ed.), *Cambridge Urban History of Britain* **I,** 600-1540, Cambridge: Cambridge University Press.

King, A. 1975. A Medieval Town House in German Street, Winchelsea, *SAC* **113**, 124-145.

Kowaleski, M. (ed.) 1993. Local Customs Accounts of the Port of Exeter, 1266-1321, *Devon and Cornwall Record Society* **36**. Exeter: Devon and Cornwall Record Society.

— (ed.) 1995. *Local Markets and Regional trade in Medieval Exeter.* Cambridge: Cambridge University Press.

— 2000. Port Towns in England and Wales 1300-1540, in D. M. Palliser (ed), *The Cambridge Urban History of Britain,* vol. **1**, 600-1540. Cambridge: Cambridge University Press.

— forthcoming. The Commercialization of the Sea Fisheries in Medieval England and Wales, *International Journal of Maritime History.* St John's, Newfoundland: International Commission on Maritime History.

Leach, R.H. 2000. The Symbolic Hall: Historical Context and Merchant Culture in the Early Modern Town, *Vernacular Architecture* **31**, 1-10.

Lloyd, T.H. 1977. *The English Wool Trade in the Middle Ages.* Cambridge: Cambridge University Press.

Long, A., Waller, M., Hughes, P. & Spencer, C. 1998. The Holocene Depositional History of Romney Marsh Proper, in J. Eddison, M. Gardiner and A. Long (eds.), *Romney Marsh: Environmental Change and Human Occupation in a Coastal*

Lowland, Oxford University Committee for Archaeology, Monograph **46**, 45-63

Lovegrove, H. 1956. Three old roads to Winchelsea Peninsula, *SNQ* **14**, 162-165.

— 1964. The Local Government Status of Winchelsea in the Nineteenth Century, *SNQ* **16**, 102-104.

Luard, H.R. (ed.) 1872-83. *Mathew Paris's* Chronica Majora (7 volumes).

Lyon, M., Lyon, B. & Lucas, H.S. (eds.) 1983. *The Wardrobe Book of William De Norwell, 12 July 1338 to 27 May 1340.* Brussels: Commission Royale d'Histoire de Belgique.

Machling, T. 1995. Pottery report, in M. Gardiner, Aspects of the history and archaeology of medieval Seaford, *SAC* **133**, 189-212.

Martin, D. 1989. Three Moated Sites in North-East Sussex, Part 1: Glottenham, *SAC* **127**, 89-122.

— 1993. The Development of Old Hastings, in D. Rudling *et al.*, Excavations at the Phoenix Brewery site, Hastings, 1988, *SAC* **131**, 73-113.

— 2003. Winchelsea - A Royal New Town, in D. Rudling (ed.), *The Archaeology of Sussex to AD 2000.* King's Lynn: Heritage Marketing and Publications.

Martin, D. & Martin, B.J. 2002. A Quarter-by-Quarter Analysis of the Town of Winchelsea, East Sussex. Unpublished: a copy has been deposited at East Sussex Record Office.

Martin, D. & Rudling, D. 2004. *Excavations in Winchelsea, Sussex, 1974-2000.* King's Lynn: Heritage Marketing and Publications.

Martin, G.H. 1995. *Knighton's Chronicle 1337-1396.* Oxford: Clarendon Press.

Mason, R.T. 1964. *Framed Buildings of the Weald.* Horsham: Coach Publishing House.

Mayhew, G. 1984. Rye and the Defences of the Narrow Seas: a Sixteenth-Century Town at War, *SAC* **122**, 107-26.

— 1987. *Tudor Rye.* Falmer: Centre for Continuing Education, University of Sussex.

McCann, W.A. & Mackie, P.C. 1997. Greyfriars, Winchelsea, East Sussex, A Geophysical Survey: Final Report. Unpublished report by The Clark Laboratory, Museum of London Archaeology Service.

Millican, P. 1945. Christ's Dole, *Norfolk Archaeology* **28**, 83-86.

Milne, G. 2003. *The Port of Medieval London.* Stroud: Tempus.

Mollat, M. 1947. Anglo-Norman Trade in the Fifteenth Century, *Economic History Review* **17,** 144-148.

— 1952. *Le Commerce maritime Normand à la fin du moyen âge: étude d'histoire, économique, et sociale.* Paris: Plon.

— 1983. *La vie quotidienne des gens de mer en Atlantique (IXᵉ - XVIᵉ siècle).* Paris: Hachette.

Morant, A.W. 1872. Notices of the Church of St. Nicholas, Great Yarmouth, *Norfolk Archaeology* **7**.

Murray, K.M.E. 1935. *The Constitutional History of the Cinque Ports,* Manchester: Manchester University Press.

— 1936. The Common-Place Book of Faversham, *Archaeologia Cantiana* **48**, 98-99.

Murray, J.W. 1965. The Origin of some Medieval Roofing Slates from Sussex, *SAC* **103**, 79-82.

Nairn, I. & Pevsner, N. 1965. *The Buildings of England: Sussex.* Harmondsworth: Penguin Books.

Oppenheim, M. 1907. Maritime history of Sussex, in *VCH Sussex,* **2**, 125-168.

Orton, C.R. 1982. Pottery evidence for the dating of the revetments, in G. Milne and C. Milne, Medieval Waterfront Development at Trig Lane, London, *London Middlesex Archaeol. Soc.* Special Paper **5**, 92-9.

— 2004. Pottery from the 1976-1982 excavations, in D. Martin and D. Rudling (eds.) *Excavations in Winchelsea, 1974-2000,* 115-137.

Palliser, D.M., Slater, T.R. & Dennison, E.P. 2000. The topography of towns 600-1300, in D. M. Palliser (ed.), *The Cambridge Urban History of Britain,* vol.**1**: 600-1540. Cambridge: Cambridge University Press.

Pantin, W.A. 1962-3. Medieval English Town-House Plans, *Medieval Archaeology,* **6-7,** 202-239.

Parker, V. 1971. *The Making of Kings Lynn.* Chichester: Phillimore.

Peers, C. 1933. Pevensey Castle, *SAC* **74**, 1-15.

Pelham, R.A. 1929. The Foreign Trade of Sussex: 1300-1350, *SAC* **70**, 93-118.

— 1930a. The Foreign Trade of the Cinque Ports, 1307-8, in Iowerth C. Peate (ed.), *Studies in Regional Consciousness and Environment.* New York: Freeport.

— 1930b. Some further aspects of Sussex trade during the fourteenth century, *SAC* **71**, 171-204.

— 1951. Fourteenth-Century England, in H. C. Darby (ed.), *An Historical Geography of England Before AD 1800.* Cambridge: Cambridge University Press.

Platt, C. 1973. *Medieval Southampton, The port and trading community, A.D. 1000-1600.* London: Routledge & Kegan Paul.

Pratt, M. 1998. *Winchelsea, A port of stranded pride.* Bexhill-on-Sea: Privately published.

Riley, H.T. (ed.) 1859. Thomae Walsingham, Quondam Monachi Ancti Albani, *Historia Anglicana*, **1**,

Rodger, N.A.M. 1996. The Naval Service of the Cinque Ports, *English Historical Review* **111:442**.

— 1997. *The safeguard of the Sea: A Naval History of Britain,* vol. **1**: 660-1640. London: Harper Collins.

Rudling, D. & Barber, L. 1993. Excavations at the Phoenix Brewery Site, Hastings, 1988, *SAC* **131**, 73-113.

Runyan, T. 1986. Ships and Fleets in Anglo-French Warfare, 1337-1360, *American Neptune* **46:1**.

Ryan, P. 1996. *Brick in Essex from the Roman Conquest to the Reformation.* Chelmsford: Privately published.

Quiney, A. 1990. *The Traditional Buildings of England.* London: Thames and Hudson.

Salisbury, E. (ed.) 1887. Report on the Records of New Romney, *Archaeologia Cantiana* **17**, 12-33.

Salzman, L.F. 1907. Sussex Industries, in *VCH Sussex,* **2,** 229-272.

— 1952. *Buildings in England down to 1540: A Documentary History.* Oxford: Clarendon Press.

Sargeant, 1918. The Wine trade with Gascony, in George Unwin (ed.), *Finance and Trade under Edward III.* Reprinted 1962, Manchester: Manchester University Press; reprinted London: F. Cass, 1962.

Saul, A. 1975. Great Yarmouth in the Fourteenth Century: A Study in Trade, Society and Politics. Unpublished PhD thesis. Oxford.

— 1979. Great Yarmouth and the Hundred Years' War in the Fourteenth Century, in *Bulletin of the Institute of Historical Research* **52:126**, 105-15.

— 1981. The Herring Fishery at Great Yarmouth, *c.*1280-1300, in *Norfolk Archaeology* **38:1**, 33-43.

Saul, N. 1986. *Scenes from Provincial Life. Knightly Families in Sussex 1280-1400.* Oxford: Clarendon Press.

Schofield, J. & Vince, A. 1994. *Medieval Towns.* London: Leicester University Press.

Searle, E & Ross, B. (eds.) 1967. Accounts of the Cellarers of Battle Abbey, 1275-1513, *SRS* **65**.

Sharpe, R.R. (ed.) 1899. *Calendar of Letter-Books preserved*

among the archives of the Corporation of the City of London at the Guildhall, Letter Book A, c.1275-1298. London: John Edward Francis.

— (ed.) 1901. *Calendar of Letter-Books preserved among the archives of the Corporation of the City of London: Letter Book C, c.1291-1309.* London: John Edward Francis.

Sim, A. 1997. *Food and Feast in Tudor England.* Stroud: Alan Sutton.

Smith, R. & Carter, A. 1983. Function and Site: Aspects of Norwich Buildings before 1700, *Vernacular Architecture* **14**, 5-18.

Statham, S.P.H. 1902. Dover Chamberlain's Accounts, 1365-67, *Archaeologia Cantiana* **25**, 75-87.

Stenton, D.M. (ed.) 1940. The Great Roll of the Pipe, the Sixth Year of the Reign of King John, Michaelmas 1204 (Pipe Roll 50), *Pipe Roll Society* **18.**

Stevenson, J.H. 1991. Arnold Nesbitt and the Borough of Winchelsea, *SAC* **129** 183-193.

Streeten, A.D.F. 1983. Pottery, in A. D. F. Streeten, *Bayham Abbey,* Sussex Archaeological Society Monograph **2**, 91-105.

— 1985. Pottery, in J. N. Hare, *Battle Abbey, The Eastern Range and the Excavations of 1978-80.* London: HBMC(E) Archaeological Report no. **2**, 103-126.

Sylvester, D.G. 1999a. *Maritime Communities in Pre-Plague England: Winchelsea and the Cinque Ports.* PhD dissertation, Department of History, Fordham University, New York, U.S.A. A copy has been deposited at ESRO.

— 1999b. Shaping the Urban Landscape of Maritime England: the Role of the King and the Barons in the 1292 Founding of New Winchelsea, in Jan Bill (ed.) *Maritime Topography and the Medieval Town; Proceedings of the Third International Waterfront Conference.* Copenhagen: Centre for Maritime Archaeology, 153-60

Thomas, A.H. (ed.) 1924. *Calendar of Early Mayor's Court Rolls Preserved Among the Archives of the Corporation of the City of London at the Guildhall, 1298-1307.* London: Cambridge University Press.

— (ed.) 1926. *Calendar of Plea and Memoranda Rolls Preserved Among the Archives of the Corporation of the City of London at the Guildhall, 1323-1364.* Cambridge: Cambridge University Press.

Thompson, T.D. 1970. Coldingham Priory Excavations-III, *History of the Berwickshire Naturalists' Club* **38**, 209-213.

Turner, E. 1849. The Early History of Brighton, as illustrated by the 'Customs of the Ancient Fishermen of the Town', *SAC* **2**, 38-52.

Unger, R.W. 1978. The Netherlands Herring Fishery in the Late Middle Ages: The False Legend of Willem Beukels of Biervliet, *Viator* **9**.

Urry, W. 1967. *Canterbury under the Angevin Kings.* London: The Athlone Press, University of London.

Vidler, L.A. 1933. Medieval pottery and kilns found at Rye, *SAC* **74**, 44-64.

Watkins, G. 1983. Northern European pottery imported into Hull 1200-1500, in P. J. Davey and R. Hodges, (eds.) *Ceramics and Trade,* 244-53.

Webb, C. & Wilson, A.E. (eds.) 1952. *Elizabethan Brighton: the Ancient Customs of Brighthelstone 1580.* Brighton: John Beal.

Wetherill, E.C. 2001. *A Medieval Kiln-Waste Tip On Rye Hill.* St Leonards-on-Sea: Hastings Area Archaeological Research Group.

Whittingham, L. 2001. The ceramic assemblage, in M. Biddle, J. Hiller, I. Scott and A. Streeten, *Henry VIII's Coastal Artillery Fort at Camber Castle, Rye, East Sussex,* 213-256.

Wood, M. 1965. *The English Medieval House.* London: J.M. Dent & Sons, reprinted (1981) London: Ferndale Editions.

INDEX

The following index excludes endnotes. Illustrations are listed under the page number upon which they occur and are not separately identified.